Human Resources Administration
Personnel Issues and Needs in Education

SECOND EDITION

L. Dean Webb
Arizona State University

Paul A. Montello
Georgia State University

M. Scott Norton
Arizona State University

Merrill, an imprint of
Macmillan College Publishing Company
New York

Maxwell Macmillan Canada
Toronto

Maxwell Macmillan International
New York   Oxford   Singapore   Sydney

Editor: Linda A. Sullivan
Production Editor: Jonathan Lawrence
Art Coordinator: Ruth A. Kimpel
Text Designer: Anne Flanagan
Cover Designer: Robert Vega
Production Buyer: Patricia A. Tonneman
Electronic Text Management: Ben Ko, Marilyn Wilson Phelps
Illustrations: Steve Botts

This book was set in Zapf International and Swiss by Macmillan College Publishing Company and was printed and bound by R.R. Donnelley & Sons Company. The cover was printed by Phoenix Color Corp.

Macmillan College Publishing Company
866 Third Avenue
New York, NY 10022

Macmillan College Publishing Company is part of the
Maxwell Communication Group of Companies.

Maxwell Macmillan Canada, Inc.
1200 Eglinton Avenue East, Suite 200
Don Mills, Ontario M3C 3N1

Library of Congress Cataloging-in Publication Data
Webb, L. Dean.
    Human resources administration : personnel issues and needs in
    education / L. Dean Webb, Paul A. Montello, M. Scott Norton. —2nd
    ed.
        p.   cm.
    Rev. ed. of: Personnel administration in education.
    Includes bibliographical references (p.) and index.
    ISBN 0-02-424973-4
    1. School personnel management—United States.   I. Montello, Paul
A.   II. Norton, M. Scott.   III. Title.   IV. Title: Personnel
administration in education.
LB2831.58.P445   1994
371.2'01'0973—dc20   93-20450
                                                                        CIP

Printing: 1 2 3 4 5 6 7 8 9   Year: 4 5 6 7 8

This textbook is dedicated to the following individuals who have made lifelong contributions to education as teachers, administrators, and mentors.

Miss Hazel G. Scott, former teacher and administrator in the Lincoln Public Schools, Lincoln, Nebraska

Mrs. Kathryn G. Hurst, former teacher and administrator in the Lincoln Public Schools, Lincoln, Nebraska

Dr. Dale K. Hayes, former teacher and administrator, and professor emeritus, University of Nebraska, Lincoln

and to

Madeline Knight McDaniel, who not only taught others in the classroom but taught her daughters life's most important lessons

Preface

*P*ublic education in the United States is a labor-intensive enterprise. Personnel costs make up 75 to 85 percent of the typical school district budget. Because personnel are so important to the achievement of the goals and objectives of an educational system, human resources administration is of central importance. How individuals are recruited, selected, evaluated, motivated, compensated, and aided in their development are factors in determining their personal and professional satisfaction and performance. Human resources administrators can be successful if they have not only gained an adequate knowledge of specifics—such as relevant laws and policies, the application of computer technology, or successful collective negotiation strategies—but have developed and integrated planning processes and communication systems and, perhaps most important, fostered a relationship of mutual respect and cooperation among the staff, the administration, and the school board.

In recent years, what was traditionally referred to as *personnel administration* has become known by the more inclusive concept, *human resources administration.* Human resources administration expands the view of personnel administration to consider the environment as well as the utilization and development of human resources. This concept emphasizes the human element as central to the progress of an organization.

This second edition of *Human Resources Administration* differs from the first edition in both substance and pedagogy. It provides important new chapters on performance appraisal and policy and regulation development, as well as substantive expansion and revision of all material included in the previous edition. Three case studies have been added in each chapter to illustrate the application of chapter concepts to realistic situations in the workplace and to provide the stimulus for discussion of complex and controversial issues. In addition, new tables and figures serve as visual organizers for chapter content and add to the text's visual appeal.

The text consists of fourteen chapters that address all the traditional topics in human resources administration along with the most current concerns in the field. The initial chapters describe the development of human resources administration and explore its present functioning in the organizational context of the school system. Subsequent chapters discuss the human resources administrator's major areas of responsibility. In addition, the pivotal role of the human resources office in strategic planning is discussed, as is the use of computer technology in human resources administration and the future direction of human resources administration.

Human Resources Administration is intended for students, human resources administrators, educational administrators, professional educators, policymakers, social scientists, and the interested public. The material in each chapter reflects the most accepted concepts found in the research and literature on that chapter's topic. In addition to establishing a strong research base, consideration has been given to presenting principles that are relevant across all school systems and all states. Where appropriate, illustrations and examples are included.

We wish to express appreciation to the many people who contributed to the publication of this book. We would like to thank our reviewers for their helpful suggestions: R. E. Anderson, Wichita State University; Charles H. Ashley, University of New Hampshire; T. J. Betenbough, Western New Mexico University; Dorothy J. Gurley, Alabama A&M University; and Saundra J. Tracy, Lehigh University. Special thanks goes to Donna Larson of Arizona State University for typing. Finally, we wish to acknowledge Linda Sullivan and Jonathan Lawrence of Macmillan for their support and assistance in the completion of the project.

L. Dean Webb
Paul A. Montello
M. Scott Norton

Contents in Brief

1   Human Resources Administration—Past to Present   1

2   Contemporary Issues and Related Problems in Human Resources Administration   27

3   The Human Resources Function—Organization and Processes   49

4   Strategic Human Resources Planning   81

5   Policies and Regulations in the Human Resources Function   111

6   Screening and Selection of Professional Personnel   151

7   Performance Appraisal   185

8   Maximizing Human Resources   215

9   Legal Aspects of Public School Human Resources Administration   251

10   Collective Negotiations in Education   277

11   The Compensation Process   313

12   The Support Personnel Program   351

13   Technology and Its Utilization in Human Resources Administration   379

14   Future Trends in Human Resources Administration   403

Contents

1

Human Resources Administration—Past to Present 1

Human Resources Administration Prior to 1900   1
The Influence of the County Superintendent 2
Personnel Administration After 1900—Personnel Duties Become
More Centralized   3
Scientific Management and Human Resources Administration   4
Human Resources Administration and the Human
Relations Movement   11
Personnel Administration and the Behavioral Science Movement   14
Contemporary Views of Behavioral Science and New Schools
of Thought   19
Summary   22
Discussion Questions   23
■ *Case Studies*   23
References   25

2

Contemporary Issues and Related Problems in Human Resources Administration 27

Human Resources Issue 1: School Governance and Leadership   28
Human Resources Issue 2: Human Resources Relationships and
Cooperation in Education   30
Human Resources Issue 3: Effective Human Performance   32

Human Resources Issue 4: Compensation of Educational Personnel and Cost of Benefits   33

Human Resources Issue 5: The Demands Upon Professional Personnel in Education   36

Human Resources Issue 6: External Mandates and Legal Impacts   38

Human Resources Issue 7: Teacher and Administrator Supply and Demand—Alternative Certification Programs   39

Human Resources Issue 8: Developments in Automation and Technology   40

Summary   43

Discussion Questions   44

■ *Case Studies*   44

References   46

3

The Human Resources Function—Organization and Processes   49

What Is Human Resources Administration?   50

The Human Resources Processes   51

Processes of Human Resources Utilization   53 ■ *Processes of Human Resources Development   58* ■ *Processes of the Human Resources Environment   59*

The Central Human Resources Unit   60

Organization of the Central Unit   61 ■ *Site-based Governance Structures   62*

Competency–Performance Concepts   64

Tasks, Competencies, and Indicators for Human Resources Administration   66

Position Analysis and Position Description for the Central Human Resources Administrator   68

Common Problems and Satisfactions Encountered in Human Resources Administration and Ethics and Standards of Personnel Administration   68

Kinds of Problems Encountered   68 ■ *Impact of Problems and Concerns on Human Resources Administrators   71* ■ *Ethics for School Administrators   72*

Summary   73

Discussion Questions　76

■ *Case Studies*　77

References　79

4

Strategic Human Resources Planning 　　　*81*

Definition and Background of Strategic Human Resources
Planning　81

Characteristics of Strategic Human Resources Planning　84

Evolutionary Stage of a School Organization　85

Professional Staff Mix　85

Integrating Human Resources Planning into the Strategic Plan　86
　　Environmental Scanning (1.0)　*88*　■　*Strategic and Operational
　　Planning (2.0)*　*91*　■　*Implementation (3.0)*　*96*

Correlation with the System Plan　96

Information Needs and Forecasting　97
　　Forecasting Personnel Needs　*98*　■　*Forecasting Student
　　Enrollments*　*100*

Policy, Regulation, Processes, and Personnel Changes　101

Personnel Recruitment　102
　　Analysis and Development　*102*　■　*Need*　*103*　■　*Recruitment
　　Program*　*103*

Summary　105

Discussion Questions　106

■ *Case Studies*　106

References　109

5

*Policies and Regulations in the Human
Resources Function* 　　　*111*

The Development of Personnel Policies and Regulations　111
　　Goals, Policies, and Regulations　*111*　■　*The Benefits of Personnel
　　Policies and Regulations*　*112*　■　*Criteria That Identify Policies,
　　Regulations, and Bylaws*　*114*　■　*Topical Headings for Personnel
　　Policies and Regulations*　*115*　■　*The Codification of Personnel Policies*

and Regulations 118 ■ How Personnel Policies and Regulations Are Developed 125

Model for Policy and Regulation Development   127

Characteristics of Effective Policies and Regulations in Human Resources Administration   129

Appraisal of Performance   130

Selected Examples of Personnel Policies and Regulations   131

Staff Health and Safety—Communicable Diseases 131 ■ Rights, Responsibilities, and Duties—Academic Freedom 132 ■ Policies Relating to Staff Protection—Sexual Harassment 136 ■ Employee Dismissal Policies 136

Summary   140

Discussion Questions   146

■ *Case Studies*   147

References   149

6

Screening and Selection of Professional Personnel   *151*

Preemployment Testing   152

Position Analysis   152

I. Strategic Nature of the Position 154 ■ II. Changing Aspects of the Position 156 ■ III. Behaviors 157 ■ IV. Screening and Selection Criteria 157

Job Description   157

Advertising Position and Establishing Applicant Pool   162

Paper Screening of Applicants   162

Background Checks   163

Reference Checks 163 ■ Credentials Checks 164 ■ Criminal Background Checks 164

The Interview as a Screening Tool   164

The Preliminary Interview 165 ■ The Behavioral Interview 165

Selection, Offer of Position, and Acceptance   178

Notification of Unsuccessful Candidates   179

Summary   180

Discussion Questions   180

■ *Case Studies*   180

References   182

7

Performance Appraisal *185*

Evaluation as a District Priority   185

Determining the Purposes of the Evaluation System   186

Types of Evaluation   187 ■ *Matching the Purposes of Evaluation
With the Types of Evaluation   187*

The Evaluation Plan   188

Criteria   190 ■ *Standards   193* ■ *Data Collection
Procedures   194* ■ *Program Appraisal and Review   207*

Standards for the Development and Operation of a Sound Evaluation
System   207

Technical Standards   207 ■ *Legal Standards   208*

Summary   209

Discussion Questions   210

■ *Case Studies*   210

References   212

8

Maximizing Human Resources *215*

The School as a Social System   215

Human Motivation Theories   216

Staff Orientation   220

Operational Procedures for Staff Orientation   220 ■ *Orientation for
the Beginning Teacher and Other New Teaching Personnel   224*

Staff Assignment   225

Position Assignment   225 ■ *Teacher Work Load   227*

The Troubled Staff Member   232

Staff Development   234

Operational Procedures for Staff Development   235 ■ *Staff
Development Methods and Strategies   238*

Adults as Learners   243

Summary   244

Discussion Questions   245

■ *Case Studies*   246

References   249

9

Legal Aspects of Public School Human Resources Administration

Terms and Conditions of Employment   251
*Certification   252 ■ Citizenship and Residency Requirements   253
■ Health and Physical Requirements   254 ■ Competency
Testing   255 ■ The Employment Contract   257 ■ Tenure   259
■ Mandatory Retirement   261*
Due Process   261
Procedural Due Process   262 ■ Substantive Due Process   263
Discrimination   264
Adverse Employment Decisions   265
*Dismissal   266 ■ Suspension   268 ■ Involuntary Transfers,
Reassignments, and Demotions   269 ■ Reduction in Force (RIF)   270*
Summary   271
Discussion Questions   272
■ *Case Studies*   272
References   274

10

Collective Negotiations in Education

Collective Negotiations Defined   278
Collective Bargaining Rights   278
Historical Perspectives: Bargaining by Employee Groups   279
The Growth of Negotiations in Education   279
Negotiations and the Central Human Resources Unit   284
The Collective Negotiations Process   286
Planning and Preparation for Collective Negotiations   286
*Gathering Related Information for Decision Making and Cost
Analysis   286 ■ Determining Goals and Objectives for
Negotiations   288 ■ Establishing Ground Rules for Conducting
Negotiations   289 ■ Determining the Scope of Negotiations   290 ■
Clarifying Procedures in Case of Impasse   291*
Determination and Recognition of the Bargaining Unit   294
The Bargaining Agent   295
Determination of the Composition of the Negotiations Team, Including
the Chief Spokesperson   296

Initial Negotiations Procedures and Appropriate Table Strategies 300
    The Nature of Integrative Bargaining—Win-Win Approaches 301 ■
    Proposals and Counterproposals in Collective Negotiations 302

Implementation of the Contract Agreement 304
    Basic Content of the Written Agreement 305 ■ *Grievances 305*

Summary 306

Discussion Questions 308

■ *Case Studies* 309

References 310

11

The Compensation Process   *313*

Compensation Policies 313

Determinants of Compensation 314
    Supply and Demand 314 ■ *Ability to Pay 316* ■ *Cost of
Living 316* ■ *Prevailing Wage Rate 317* ■ *Unionization 317*
■ *Government Regulations 318*

Direct Compensation: Teacher and Administrator Salaries 318
    The Single Salary Schedule for Teachers 319 ■ *Incentive Pay
Plans 322* ■ *Compensation for Extracurricular Activities 326* ■
Administrator Salaries 328

Indirect Compensation: Employee Benefits and Services 334
    Legally Required Benefits 335 ■ *State Retirement Plans 336* ■
Private Welfare and Security Programs 337 ■ *Pay for Time Not
Worked 340* ■ *Income Equivalent Payments 341* ■ *Flexible
Benefits Plans 344*

Summary 346

Discussion Questions 346

■ *Case Studies* 347

References 348

12

The Support Personnel Program   *351*

Development of a Classification System 352
    Job Analysis 352 ■ *Job Classification 355* ■ *Job
Descriptions 356*

Salary Determination 357

Salary Studies 357 ■ *Establishing the Salary Schedule 358*

Recruitment   359

Advertisements 360 ■ *Employment Agencies 360* ■ *Educational Institutions 360* ■ *Professional Organizations and Unions 361* ■ *Employee Referrals 361*

Selection   362

Application Form 362 ■ *Preliminary Interview 362* ■ *Employment Tests 363* ■ *Background Check 363* ■ *Employment Interview 365* ■ *Medical Examination 365* ■ *Final Selection and Assignment 366*

Staff Development for Support Personnel   366

Orientation 367 ■ *Employee Training 368*

Performance Appraisal   370

Summary   374

Discussion Questions   374

■ *Case Studies*   375

References   376

13

Technology and Its Utilization in Human Resources Administration   *379*

Emergence of Technology in Education   380

Components of a Computer System   381

Computer Hardware 381 ■ *Computer Software 382*

Local Area Networks   385

The Evolution of Electronic Data Processing in an HRIS   388

Data and Decision Making   391

Management Information System (MIS)   393

Human Resources Information System (HRIS)   396

Advantages and Disadvantages of an HRIS 396 ■ *Cost-Benefit Study of Instituting an HRIS 397*

Future Technological Developments for Human Resources Administrators   398

Summary   399

Discussion Questions   399

■ *Case Studies*   399

References   401

14

Future Trends in Human Resources Administration 403

General Trends   404
Demographic Trends   406
Economic Trends   409
Social Trends   412
Political Trends   414
Long Wave Theory   417
Implications for Human Resources Administration   420
A Final Word   423
Summary   424
Discussion Questions   424
■ *Case Studies*   425
References   426

Author Index   *429*

Subject Index   *439*

1

Human Resources Administration— Past to Present

Education is inextricably related to the social, political, and economic influences of its time; its human resources function is no exception. The progress realized in the development of human resources administration is in part a history of education. Chapter 1 presents a historical perspective of the human resources function and discusses some of the concepts and people that have influenced contemporary personnel practices.

HUMAN RESOURCES ADMINISTRATION PRIOR TO 1900

Prior to 1900 employers assumed responsibility for personnel matters in the business and industrial sectors, in most cases delegating some of this function to front-line supervisors or foremen. The "line boss" generally took charge of such personnel activities as hiring, rating, on-the-job training, and firing. Even as late as 1886, no group existed that was concerned with the practice of management. It was not until 1886 that Henry R. Towne created an

> "Economic Section" to act as a clearinghouse and forum for "shop management" and "shop accounting." Shop management would deal with the subjects of organization, responsibility, reports, and the "executive management" of works, mills and factories. Shop accounting would treat the questions of time and wage systems, determination and allocation of costs, bookkeeping methods, and manufacturing accounts. (Hellriegel & Slocum, 1989, p. 36)

Select lay committees assumed personnel duties in the area of education. Parents and religious groups were reluctant to trust the "proper education" of their children to persons outside the home or church. The title **selectmen** was commonly bestowed upon these early control groups that consisted largely of local influentials and religious officers (Lucio & McNeil, 1969). Selectmen exercised tight control over the policies of the school, the supervision of the subjects taught, and the personal habits of the teacher. Although they knew little about education, these select committees were not reticent to criticize, to make suggestions, or to recommend the dismissal of an "incompetent" teacher.

The slow development of professional leadership in education before the turn of the nineteenth century contributed to the administrative authority of select committees. Records indicate that New York appointed the first state superintendent of common schools in 1812. The appointment lasted for 9 years before these duties were placed in the office of state secretary. It was not until 1853, more than 40 years later, that New York reestablished the state superintendent's position (Cubberly, 1927). Michigan is credited with having the first state-level administrative position that has been in continuous operation since it was first established in 1829. "By 1850 all northern and some southern states had actual or ex officio chief state school officers" (American Association of School Administrators [AASA], 1952, p. 41).

Administration at the local school level also developed slowly during the 1800s. In 1837 Cleveland established a board of managers to operate the public school system. This attempt to establish one of the first "boards of education" lasted only 4 years. The board's responsibilities were delegated after its demise to one member of the city council, who was paid $100 per year for services rendered. Later the individual was given the title of acting school manager and performed business duties for the city's schools (Reller, 1935).

The school board of managers of Baltimore made an official request to the city council for a school superintendent in 1848, but the request was denied. As a result, the school board of managers appointed a superintendent of its own. The appointee, the Reverend J. N. McJilton, soon found the duties of the position too burdensome. The city council and mayor of Baltimore then created the position of superintendent of schools in 1866 (Reller, 1935).

The common practice of using lay "standing committees" to perform many of the personnel administration duties of the school waned under the pressures of a growing national population, its increased demands for more schools and teachers, and the complexities of a growing educational enterprise. The need for full-time administrators to meet these demands became apparent. By 1870, 29 superintendents of schools served school districts across the nation (Lucio & McNeil, 1969).

The National Association of School Superintendents was established in 1866. In 1870 this superintendents' association merged with the National Teachers' Association and the American Normal School Association to form the National Education Association (NEA) (Fenner, 1945). The practice of educational administration was still in its infancy, and the question that was of concern professionally, What do administrators do? continued as a central topic of discussion.

The Influence of the County Superintendent

The county superintendency had much influence on personnel activities, both before 1900 and for some time afterward. This office reigned nationally in most states from 1850 to 1925. Delaware is credited with having the first recorded county superintendent, as early as 1829 (AASA, 1952). By 1879, 34 of the 38 states plus 4 territories had created the office of county superintendent (Newsom, 1932).

Teaching staffs in the nineteenth century, and for some years after, were marginally prepared for their tasks. Many elementary school teachers had only a high school education, with no formal teacher training. Although the 2-year normal school reached prominence by 1870, much of the teacher training was accomplished through other means. Part of the importance of the county superintendency comes from the county institutes operated by that office. The county institute became a landmark for in-service training for teachers.

As early as 1839, Henry B. Barnard (1811–1900) had suggested that the State Legislature of Connecticut allocate $5,000 for "various" objects, especially a teachers' institute. When refused Barnard reportedly utilized personal funds to hold a meeting of teachers of Hartford County. For several days he and other "competent men" gave lessons in the teaching of reading, arithmetic, use of globes, and "school keeping." The record indicates that 25 teachers attended. The event marked the date of one of the very first regular teachers' in-service institutes (Jenkins & Warner, 1937).

The county institute flourished for many years. As noted by Indiana's superintendent of public instruction in his annual report,

> no one familiar with the educational progress of this state can fail to recognize the influence of the County Institute in improving the work of teachers in city, town, and county schools. It affords an opportunity of meeting each other, and of comparing methods of discipline and instruction. The able and well qualified gain confidence by comparing their methods with those of recognized professional ability; the inexperienced observe the work of others and profit by it, and all measure themselves with their professional brethren. This alone is an important factor in a teacher's education. (Bloss, 1882, p. 61)

Bloss's report stated further that

> it is believed that while the County Institute has done much to raise the educational standards in the State, it has by no means reached the limit of its usefulness. . . . The chief object of an Institute is to impart a knowledge of principles and methods of teaching and school management. Its great aim is professional training. (pp. 61-63)

The report listed a total of 2,724 institutes held during the 1880 to 1881 school year in Indiana that included 7,744 teachers at a cost of $9,606.10.

As urban populations increased and public high schools evolved in greater numbers toward the end of the nineteenth century, the work of the county superintendent was gradually assumed by local supervisors, and teacher training programs became available in higher education institutions. However, the county superintendent continued to serve many of the smaller school districts and had more limited responsibilities for larger districts for several years after 1900.

PERSONNEL ADMINISTRATION AFTER 1900—
PERSONNEL DUTIES BECOME MORE CENTRALIZED

During the later part of the nineteenth century, various forms of personnel departments began to emerge in business and industry. Such duties as record keeping, preparing salary schedules and rating reports, and other clerical tasks were assigned to one individual (McCoy, Gips, & Evans, 1983). Later one person became responsible for other, more specialized personnel tasks such as selecting and assigning the needed personnel.

Prior to 1900 there was little evidence of an organized central personnel office in school systems; however, educational institutions began to initiate personnel practices similar to those in business and industry. One common practice was to delegate certain activities, such as compensation and personnel matters, to the business administrator. With the emergence of assistant superintendent positions, more personnel activities related to the professional teaching staff were assumed by these administrators. Building principals did perform personnel duties, but many were only part-time administrators and had teaching responsibilities as well.

After 1900 and during much of the first half of the twentieth century, professional administration began to emerge. Moore (1966) points out that "personnel administration as the term is commonly understood, began with World War I. The recruiting, training, and paying of masses of workers in war production forced assignment of such responsibilities to specialized personnel" (p. 5). Moore notes further that "school surveys conducted by management consultants . . . and by research and field agencies in universities, particularly Teachers College, Columbia University, especially in the 1940s and later, recommended the establishment of positions charged with the management of personnel" (pp. 5–6). The establishment of central offices to coordinate the personnel function increased significantly during the 1950s. In 1966 Moore noted that "it can be safely estimated that there are about 250 such positions in public school systems" (p. 6).

In 1983 the American Association of School Personnel Administrators had 1,018 members practicing in schools (McCoy et al., 1983). By March of 1993, the association had 1,542 members. A further discussion of the nature of the central human resources unit is included in a later section of this chapter.

Administration and personnel practices historically have been influenced significantly by many individuals and administrative concepts, such as the movements in scientific management or classical organization, human relations, and the behavioral sciences. Each of these developments and their contributions to human resource administration are discussed in the following sections of this chapter. Although each of the "movements" to be discussed flourished during various time periods, it is not possible to state the specific dates when each movement started or ended. Seeds of each movement were planted far in advance of its domination of thought. Also, concepts of each are witnessed in current practices.

SCIENTIFIC MANAGEMENT AND HUMAN RESOURCES ADMINISTRATION

Scientific management principles had a major impact on the human resources function in business, industry, and education. This movement, which became extremely popular in the early 1900s, was exemplified in large part by the work of Frederick W. Taylor (1856–1915) and other strong advocates of scientific management methods.

As chief engineer of a Pennsylvania steel company, Taylor had an opportunity to implement his management concepts in industry. His critical attention to worker efficiency and productivity earned him the title Father of Scientific Management. Today

Taylor's methods are considered by most as insensitive and authoritarian. Yet his work, along with that of others who contributed to the scientific management concept, did much to focus attention on the important relationships between task achievement and human activity. Many of the concepts that evolved from this era continue to be "foundational" to many contemporary practices in human resources administration.

Taylor's concepts of management, set forth in *Scientific Management* (1911), were published only 4 years before his death. He was highly critical of the practice of "soldiering," whereby employees make a pretense of working while really loafing. His management methods required managers to plan in advance the daily tasks of each worker and detail the specific procedures for completing them. The manager also was to enforce the standards for completing the task and arrange the necessary relationships and cooperation for accomplishing each task *efficiently*. The art of management, according to Taylor (1911), was "knowing exactly what you want men to do, and then seeing they do it in the best and cheapest way" (p. 21). Although Taylor often is accused of treating workers like "machines," his thorough studies of work and work performance did include attention to the human element. This attention is evidenced by his work with Simonds Rolling Machine Company where he made noted improvements in production and employee morale through the implementation of worker rest breaks, incentive pay, and job restructuring.

Taylor's management approaches gained both national and international attention for two reasons. First, management was in dire need of definition. The question, What do managers do to assure efficient employee productivity? was foremost at the time. Management methods in general in the early 1900s were largely pragmatic and in need of "professional bearing." Second, the methods of scientific management proved extraordinarily effective relative to production outcomes.

Taylor's (1911) management concepts, which he identified as **the task system**, claimed that efficiency and production were conditioned primarily by the following methods:

1. *The identification of tasks*   Scientific methods should be used by managers to discover the most efficient ways to perform minute aspects of every task.
2. *The setting of controlled conditions and specified equipment for completing each task*   The procedures for doing the task and the time specifications for completion must be stated and enforced.
3. *An incentive system that awards efficiency and high production*   A piecework pay system rewards the worker for high productivity. Merit pay and job incentives are essential in the compensation process; "punishment" or personal loss in case of failure also is to be considered.
4. *Management's responsibility to plan work and control its accomplishment*   Workers are to be hired and trained to carry out the plans under close supervision.

Thus, scientific management served to replace the more arbitrary management procedures with a "scientific" approach for each job task. Workers were then selected and assigned based on the specific job requirements and personal qualifications. Foremen and/or line managers supervised workers by the implementation of the scientific procedures determined for each task. Finally, the method made clear the division of labor between management and the workers. Management was to plan and organize the work to be done; workers were to complete each task according to these predetermined procedures.

Taylor is credited by some writers as the person most responsible for planting the seeds for the first industrial personnel department in the United States. His in-depth studies and implementation of such personnel practices as selection, training, and compensation served as a forerunner for specialized personnel activities within organizations.

Many other individuals made special contributions to scientific management. Henry L. Gantt (1861–1919), Lillian Gilbreth (1878–1972), and Frank Gilbreth (1868–1924) contributed ideas that have remained in contemporary practice. Gantt was an industrial engineer who became acquainted with Frederick Taylor at the Midvale Steel Works in Pennsylvania. Gantt's ideas on scientific management included the consideration of such topics as motion and time study, record keeping, cost accounting, planning and control, task and bonus, and task setting. In regard to task and bonus, Gantt (1961) stated that "the ideal industrial community would be one in which every member should have his proper daily task and receive a corresponding reward" (p. 77). Gantt devised charts that remain in use in the industrial sector, charts for recording a wide variety of worker behaviors, including progress charts, order charts, machine record charts, idleness expense charts, production charts, and others. In regard to the use of a production and progress chart used by a military ordnance department, Gantt (1961) noted that

> each production section has production and progress chart systems. . . . Even without rigid standardization, the charts give a picture of the progress of the whole ordnance program, including lags and the causes therefor . . . they show the requirements as to workers, as well as materials, transportation, accessory machinery, and all other factors which make or break the program. (pp. 141–142)

Gantt's contributions to scientific management, and to industry in general, were recognized in 1961 by the American Management Association and the American Society of Mechanical Engineers when they combined in establishing the Gantt Medal to be awarded from time to time to an individual who has made an outstanding contribution in the world for industrial statesmanship (Gantt, 1961).

Frank and Lillian Gilbreth often are remembered because their work and concern for efficiency were portrayed in the popular movie *Cheaper by the Dozen*. As industrial engineers, they worked as a husband-and-wife team to improve worker efficiency through such techniques as time and motion studies and were much concerned with job simplification. Both were fascinated with the development of various approaches for eliminating inefficiency. In one instance, Frank Gilbreth observed bricklayers on the job and devised standards and techniques for assigning workers, designing work materials and equipment, and positioning the bricks and bricklayers so that physical movements were optimally efficient. Reportedly, he reduced the number of physical movements of the workers from 18 to 5 and increased work productivity by an estimated 200% (Griffin, 1987).

The concepts of scientific management were accepted enthusiastically by practitioners in educational administration as well as in business and industry. In the early 1900s, educational administration, like business and industry, was in need of professional direction and improvement. As noted by Callahan (1962),

> in the academic year of 1899–1900, Teachers College offered only two courses in administration.... But from 1914 on, the growing response to the pressures [i.e., business efficiency] is clearly discernible. Teachers College began to give more attention to business methods, finance, and the adaptation of efficiency methods to schools in its standard courses in administration. (pp. 196, 197)

Taylorism in education was evident in both administrative practices and terminology in the early 1900s. ***Educational engineering***, ***scientific education***, the ***chief executive***, and ***administrative management***, became part of the new vocabulary in education. Schools, in order to be efficient, had to exemplify the principles of scientific management and emulate practices of a successful business. Accountability, merit pay, personnel evaluation, cost accounting, efficiency, and worker qualifications were among the practices that received major attention in education during these years. The full impact of Taylorism on education was far-reaching. The twelfth yearbook of the National Society for the Study of Education (Bobbitt, 1913) emphasized the implications of the business efficiency concept for the educational administrator.

> In any organization, the directive and supervisory members must clearly define the ends toward which the organization strives. They must coordinate the labors of all so as to attain the end. They must find the best methods of work, and they must enforce the use of these methods on the part of the workers. They must determine the qualifications necessary for the workers and see that each rises to the standard qualifications, if it is possible; and when impossible, so that he is separated from the organization. This requires direct or indirect responsibility for the primary training of the workers before service and for keeping them up to standard qualifications during service. Directors and supervisors must keep the workers supplied with detailed instructions as to the work to be done, the standards to be reached, the methods to be employed, and the materials to be used. They must supply the workers with the necessary materials and appliances. They must place incentives before the worker in order to stimulate desirable effort. Whatever the nature or purpose of the organization, if it is an effective one, these are always the directive and supervisory tasks. (p. 80)

Others in education echoed Bobbitt's call for "efficiency" in the schools. In 1918 James L. McConaughy of Dartmouth University stated that "this is an age of efficiency. In the eyes of the public no indictment of a school can be more severe than to say it is inefficient" (1918, pp. 191–192). Elwood P. Cubberly, a school superintendent and later university professor, wrote in 1916 that

> our schools are, in a sense, factories in which raw products (children) are to be shaped and fashioned into products to meet the various demands of life. The specifications for manufacturing come from the demands of life. The specifications for manufacturing come from the demands of twentieth century civilization, and it is the business of the school to build its pupils according to the specifications laid down. (p. 325)

Personnel development in education also was influenced by the work of other scientific management proponents such as Henri Fayol, Luther Gulick, Lyndall Urwick, and Max Weber. Fayol (1841–1925) set forth five basic elements for all administrative activities: to plan, to organize, to command, to coordinate, and to control. The implications of these principles for personnel management were clear. Administrative personnel, according to Fayol (1916/1949), were responsible for

1. determining those activities necessary to meet the needs of the future;
2. organizing the required physical and human resources;
3. overseeing the work of employees through leadership and direction;
4. coordinating the efforts in the organization through relating harmonious activities and units;
5. controlling all of the procedures and methods that have been determined and outlined by the principles and rules of the organization.

Fayol set forth 14 principles for managerial effectiveness that continue to be reflected in contemporary practice. Although Fayol was not the only contributor to these concepts, he was a major proponent of these guidelines for management.

Many of Fayol's (1916/1949) management concepts remain in practice today. These include such principles as **division of labor**, the more people specialize the more efficiently they can perform their work; **unity of command**, each employee must receive instructions about a particular operation from only one person to avoid conflicting instructions and resulting confusion; **unity of direction**, the efforts of employees working on a particular project should be coordinated and directed by only one manager; and **scalar chain**, a single uninterrupted line of authority should run in order by rank from top management to the lowest level position in the company.

Gulick (1892–) extended Fayol's five elements for personnel management previously mentioned to include reporting and budgeting responsibilities and extended the personnel consideration under the responsibility of staffing (Urwick & Gulick, 1937). Thus Gulick's now renowned POSDCoRB paradigm (*P*lanning, *O*rganizing, *S*taffing, *D*irecting, *Co*ordinating, *R*eporting, and *B*udgeting) gave new emphasis to the process of staffing by considering it a separate entity rather than a subsidiary of organizing. Gulick's management concept of specialization proved to be of particular importance to administrative organization. This concept stipulated that workers are more effective when tasks are divided into specific parts. The task parts included both the content and methods for completing the work. According to the specialization concept, all tasks are to be considered as jobs, and all jobs are to be assigned appropriately to departments. Not only did the concept tend to reinforce the idea of departmentalization, it emphasized the need for such personnel activities as the development of job descriptions and the completion of "scientific," in-depth job analyses. Specialization supported the hierarchical supervisory structure commonly utilized in organizational administration today. Gulick argued that his POSDCoRB formula was equally applicable to all executives, even to presidents such as Franklin D. Roosevelt. Gulick's seven functions for managers were devised when he was participating as a member of President Roosevelt's Committee on Government Administration (Urwick & Gulick, 1937).

Urwick's (1891–1983) management views were published in *Papers on the Science of Administration* (Urwick & Gulick, 1937). He set forth seven universal principles of organization that held significant implications for the human resources function. The principles of assignment of duties, of definition, and of organization are especially noteworthy. Urwick's ***principle of assignment*** of duties stated that the duties of every person in an organization should be confined as far as possible to performing a single function. This idea of specialization ultimately permeated educational practice at both the management and professional teaching levels. The ***principle of definition*** stipulated that the duties, authority, responsibilities, and relations of everyone in the organizational structure should be clearly and completely defined in writing. Thus, as noted previously, job analyses and job descriptions became essential parts of the personnel activity. According to Urwick's ***principle of organization effectiveness***, the final test of an industrial organization is the smoothness in its operation. Such a test was considered more in terms of the ways departments were grouped and related than to the human relationships in the organization, as viewed in contemporary practice.

Sociologist Max Weber's (1864–1920) early work in social and economic organizational theory provided a foundation for the study of a bureaucracy that he viewed as the ideal organizational structure (Weber, 1910/1947). His work proved instrumental in the implementation of many later investigations by behavioral scientists. Weber conceived the ideal organization as having the special elements illustrated in Figure 1.1: (1) a hierarchical structure with a well-defined hierarchy of authority; (2) a functional specialization exemplified by a division of labor based on the ability to perform a certain task; (3) rules of behavior that prevent the unpredictability of the individual employee; (4) impersonal relationships that are free of strong personal and emotional relationships that tend to result in irrational decisions; and (5) career orientation based on prescribed competence that focuses on certification of abilities. Promotion must be related to job-related performance. Security for the worker through protection from unfair dismissal, voluntary resignation, and provisions for retirement contributes to loyalty and career orientation. Weber contended that such ideal bureaucracies were more impartial, more predictable, and more rational than the norm. In Weber's view, these factors allow workers to function with a minimum of friction and confusion.

FIGURE 1.1

Weber's Ideal Organizational Structure

Source: From Max Weber, *The Theory of Social and Economic Organizations,* Translated and Edited by Talcott Parsons and A. M. Henderson. Copyright © 1947, renewed 1975 by Talcott Parsons. Reprinted with the permission of The Free Press, a Division of Macmillan, Inc.

Hierarchical Structure	Division of Labor	Control by Rules	Impersonal Relationships	Career Orientation
A BUREAUCRACY Ideal Organizational Structure Legal Authority				

Weber's concept of rationality in organizations was further illustrated in his taxonomy of domination (1910/1947). The taxonomy describes the three types of authority in organizations as *charismatic, traditional,* and *legal.* **Charismatic authority** is power based on the charismatic attraction of the leader that results in an emotional form of follower/leader relationship. **Traditional power** is based on dominance inherent to a position or role. That is, the position itself legitimizes certain authority and accompanying privileges exercised by the position holder. **Legal authority** is based on a body of principles, rules, and laws that provide the authority for the position. Weber considered legal authority to be best for forming the foundation of an ideal bureaucratic organization.

Weber's concepts have had much influence on practices in educational administration and, in turn, on the human resources function. His ideas of hierarchical authority, division of labor, files and records, rules for behavior, and his concepts of authority can be identified with many contemporary practices in human resources administration.

Hoy and Miskel (1991) have summarized the basic features of the scientific management or traditional approaches to organization as follows:

1. Time and motion studies
2. Division of labor and specialization
3. Standardization of tasks
4. Span of control
5. Unity of command
6. Uniqueness of function
7. Formal organization (pp. 11–12)

New emphasis on accountability, teacher evaluation, merit pay, teacher selection, scientific supervision, on-the-job training, and job analyses were among the personnel outcomes of the scientific management era. In education, teaching personnel learned goals and how to accomplish them. The personnel performance evaluation practices that had been introduced into business and industry soon were incorporated into the personnel process in education as well. Merit pay and incentive plans were advocated in the early 1900s by both supporters and critics of education. Only the initiation of the single salary schedule concepts, credited to the NEA in 1923, thwarted the implementation of merit salary plans in many schools throughout the nation. The single salary system guided personnel compensation practices for the next 70 years and still remains a common compensation practice in education today.

Hanson (1979) illustrated how the aforementioned traditional approaches have been adapted to education. For example, in relation to division of labor and specialization, school boards represent the legislative dimension of school governance and the professional administrative staff serves as the executive dimension. Specialization is represented by English teachers, coaches, teacher aides, guidance counselors, maintenance personnel, and so forth. Span of control is reflected in pupil and teacher ratios, assistant principals and principal ratios, and assistant superintendents and superintendent ratios in today's schools. The fact that individual teachers generally report to one principal, principals report to one assistant superintendent or superintendent, and the superintendent is directly responsible to the school board illustrates the adaptation of unity of command.

Traditional management features influenced practices in educational administration, not without question, for many years. As emphasized throughout this discussion, many of the "principles" remain in both thought and practice in human resources administration today.

HUMAN RESOURCES ADMINISTRATION AND THE HUMAN RELATIONS MOVEMENT

As early as 1920, the scientific management approach was being brought into question. In *Personnel Administration*, one of the first personnel textbooks written for industry, Tead and Metcalf (1920) stated that

> the new focus in administration is to be the human element. The new center of attention and solicitude is the individual person, the worker. And this change comes about fundamentally for no sentimental reasons, but because the enlistment of human cooperation, of the interest and goodwill of the workers, has become the crux of the production problem.
>
> . . . the human approach to effective production administration is through a specialized administrative agency—through the operation of a separate staff department in management. Present development is in the direction of a new science and a newly appreciated art—the science and art of personnel administration. (p. 1)

The scientific management philosophy, which tended to view workers as machines, was by now considered inhumane by most standards and evoked the concern of a number of writers. Mary Parker Follett (1868–1933) was among the first to recognize the importance of human factors in an organization. She based her concepts on studies of managers at work. Follett set forth a philosophy opposing scientific management and said that "organizations are people." In a series of papers and in her book, *Creative Experience* (1924), she emphasized the need to consider the human element and social ethic in administration.

Follett's fundamental premise was that the primary concern of any organization is the building and maintenance of dynamic, yet harmonious, human relations. Certainly, she was one of the primary founders of the human relations movement in educational administration. She stressed that one of management's primary responsibilities was to establish positive working relationships with workers. She believed that her concepts of coordination were instrumental in refocusing methods of supervisory and personnel practices toward the goal of organizational harmony. In brief, Follett (1940) stipulated the following views of coordination in organizations:

1. *Coordination by direct contact*   The persons responsible for work must be in direct contact regardless of their position in the organization. Horizontal communication is just as necessary as vertical communication in the organizational hierarchy to achieve coordination.
2. *Coordination in the early stages*   The persons responsible must be involved in the policy decisions as these considerations are being formulated, not merely informed about the decisions after the fact. As a result, motivation and morale will increase.
3. *Coordination as the "reciprocal" relationship of all factors in a situation*   All factors surrounding a situation must be related to one another, and these existing relationships must be carefully weighed and considered.

4. *Coordination as a continuing process*   Participative involvement, ongoing relationships, internal communication, and other such factors of coordination must be viewed as continuing responsibilities of the administrator.

Follett believed that cooperative responsibility must be established to assure an organizational unity, where each person accepts responsibility for a unique role played in the enterprise and, in turn, is given full recognition for the contributions realized. She stated in her writing that "an executive decision is only a moment in the process. The growth of a decision, the accumulation of responsibility, not the final step, is what we need most to study" (1940, p. 146).

Follett's views concerning the resolution of conflict through "integration" were revolutionary. Rather than attempting to resolve conflicts through use of authoritative measures or by compromise, which often leads to a less than ideal result, Follett suggested that an integration approach was best for all parties. In brief, integration elicits the talents of the parties in conflict, and through discussion, leads both parties toward a solution that serves the best interests of all concerned.

Elton Mayo (1880–1949), Fritz Roethlisberger (1898–1974), and others were motivated by the concepts of Follett. Mayo came to the United States in 1922 as an industrial researcher. As a member of the faculty at Harvard University, Mayo and his associates studied such personnel problems as turnover, working conditions, work incentives, employee motivation, and employee production (Mayo, 1933). As early as 1923, he and other researchers investigated the working conditions of a textile plant in Philadelphia. Descriptions of the working atmosphere revealed high levels of monotonous work that led to boredom and low production. Through an experimental plan of incentives and periodic rest times, employee turnover was virtually eliminated in the plant (Mayo, 1933; Monahan, 1975).

The now classic Hawthorne studies, conducted primarily by Mayo and Roethlisberger over a 5-year period from 1927 to 1932, were to gain national attention in the fields of business, industry, and education. These studies were conducted at the Hawthorne plant of the Western Electric Company near Chicago. Through the introduction of such variables as illumination into the work setting, these investigators observed the effects on workers and productivity. The principal finding was that the physical condition of room lighting was not a significant factor on worker efficiency and work production. This led the researchers to conclude that what goes on inside the worker is more important to productivity than the conditions of the job or workplace. This extraordinary fact has become known as the ***Hawthorne effect***. The studies gave support to the concept that factors other than salary were important in motivating employee output. The Hawthorne studies not only served to refute many of the "principles" set forth by Taylor and other scientific management proponents, but set the stage for new inquiry into the dimensions of organizations as human entities.

Hoy and Miskel (1991) summarized the conclusions of the Hawthorne studies in the following list. Each conclusion has had significant influence on the human resources function.

1. Economic incentive is not the only significant motivator. In fact, noneconomic social sanctions limit the effectiveness of economic incentives.

2. Workers respond to management as members of an informal group, not as individuals.
3. Production levels are limited more by social norms of the informal organization than by physiological capacities.
4. Specialization does not necessarily create the most efficient organization of the work group.
5. Workers use informal organizations to protect themselves against arbitrary decisions of management.
6. Informal social organizations will interact with management.
7. A narrow span of control is not prerequisite to effective supervision.
8. Informal leaders are often as important as formal supervisors.
9. Individuals are active human beings, not passive cogs in a machine. (p. 15)

Mayo's work gave strong support to the concepts of Follett and gave considerable thrust to the human relations movement in organizations generally. The implications for human resources administration were clear: Human motivation, morale, employee satisfaction, and social relationships were factors of paramount importance. The physical makeup and structure of an organization were secondary to the need for attention to the human element.

Fritz Roethlisberger, William Dickson, Ralph White, Kurt Lewin, and Ronald Lippitt were among other individuals who contributed to human relations theory. Roethlisberger and Dickson (1939) coauthored *Management and the Worker*. Among the research reported in the book are the experiments conducted in the Bank Wiring Observation Room. Through the placement of an observer in the room and the use of interviewing techniques, the social relationships of several workers were recorded. One major finding was that "informal group" influences shaped an individual worker's behavior, including the completion of too little or too much work. Social pressure and sanctions applied by the informal group had a major impact on worker productivity.

Lewin, Lippitt, and White (1939) conducted research that provided new insights toward leadership approaches and resulting human behavior. Their studies described leadership as *democratic, authoritarian,* or *laissez-faire.* **Democratic leadership** is characterized by a structured but cooperative approach to decision making. It focuses on group relationships and sensitivity to the people in the organization. **Authoritarian leadership** utilizes autocratic methods in arriving at decisions and is structured so that authority is vested in the upper hierarchy of the organization. Employee behavior is closely controlled through such means as punishment, reward, arbitrary rules, and task orientation. **Laissez-faire leadership** is characterized by a free-rein approach. Having little structure, this passive style provides great latitude for personal worker initiative. Few restrictions are placed on the employee concerning choices and procedures for accomplishing job tasks.

The 1938 study by Lewin (1890–1947) and his colleagues examined the responses of young children to these various leadership styles. Without using value judgments as to the "rightness" or "wrongness" of the leadership style, the investigators concluded that different leadership styles do indeed produce different behaviors (White & Lippitt, 1960). For example, the children supervised under the democratic style tended to exhibit superior morale, cooperation, work quality, unity, and self-direction. Whereas authoritarian leadership resulted in a higher level of production, it also was associated with a higher level of frustration and lower levels of morale, cooperation, and self-direction. The laissez-faire style resulted in inferior work quality, less productivity, and higher degrees of dissatisfaction. These results had far-reaching effects on the human relations approach in working with personnel in organizations. The study's findings soon were interpreted in terms of "good" administration and the words *democratic administration*, *democratic supervision*, *democratic teaching*, and *democratic personnel practices* became a part of the terminology of the human relations movement.

The human relations movement had a strong impact on personnel practices in education. During the 1930s and 1940s it embraced the concept that teachers were people with attitudes, emotions, and needs that had to be considered for positive motivation. Although administrative strategies often were manipulative and based on preconceived goals, the humane processes of cooperation in planning, work completion, and decision making became common procedures during this era. Administrative titles such as *supervisor* frequently gave way to less threatening ones such as *coordinator*, *consultant*, and *resource teacher*. In addition, staff development as a human resources process was approached through democratic supervision as opposed to a critical focus on the individual teacher. Staff improvement was considered to be a system goal, whereby each unit was viewed as having influence on the success of other units and on the system as a whole.

The foregoing developments that placed a new emphasis on the human element in organizations served to support the growth of human resources services in school districts. Centralization of personnel services, which began as early as 1919, continued at an increasing rate during the 1930s and 1940s. The organization of personnel administrators was evidenced as well. Gibson and Hunt (1965) noted that the organization of personnel administrators evolved from a conference of teacher examiners that took place in 1935. In 1951 the group became the American Association of Examiners and Administrators of Educational Personnel and remained such until 1959, when the present title of American Association of School Personnel Administrators was adopted.

PERSONNEL ADMINISTRATION AND THE BEHAVIORAL SCIENCE MOVEMENT

The behavioral science movement also affected the development of human resources practices in education. According to the behavioral science viewpoint, an organization has a structural, or institutional, element and a human element that are always interacting. How these two elements relate to influence the human behavior needed to achieve organizational goals is of major interest to the behavioral scientist.

Chester Barnard (1866–1961) is generally recognized as the first individual to relate administration to behavioral sciences. His work, *The Functions of the Executive* (1938), is a classic in educational administration literature, and many educators view it as the most important book ever published in the field of administration. Although Barnard's work was concerned with administration generally, its implications for personnel practices were inescapable. His concepts influenced human resources administration throughout the 1940s and continue to have an impact on contemporary practices.

Barnard was president of the Bell Telephone Company and director of the New Jersey Relief Administration. During World War II, he organized and administered the United Service Organization (USO). He believed that cooperation was essential for individuals in an organization (1938). Because individuals have limited powers of choice due to circumstances and biological restrictions, cooperation is the most effective way of offsetting these limitations. Cooperation, then, necessitates a commitment to a group goal and requires personal interaction. In this way, individual behavior becomes subordinate to a nonpersonal goal and its accomplishment. An individual's degree of cooperation is dependent upon the level of satisfaction realized, which is based on subjective personal judgments.

Barnard (1938) maintained that the mere existence of an organizational purpose does not assure cooperation. Acceptance of the organizational purpose by members is essential. Therefore, Barnard believed that an essential function of every executive is to instill acceptance of a common purpose in the minds of all organizational members.

Another essential function, as defined by Barnard (1938), is communication: the linking of common purpose with members who are willing to cooperate. Such communication must consider both the formal and informal organizational structures that influence members' attitudes and commitment. In brief, three principal tasks are required of each executive: (1) maintenance of communication in the organization, (2) obtainment of necessary performances from organizational members, and (3) formulation of organizational purpose and objectives.

Barnard's concepts of *effectiveness* and *efficiency* continue to influence human resources practices. **Effectiveness** is the extent to which organizational goals are met and realized. **Efficiency**, then, is the extent to which a cooperative system remains viable through its satisfaction of individual desires and interests. Barnard termed this phenomenon the organization's **capacity of equilibrium**. This new concept directly considered the human element and its relationship to the achievement of organizational goals. Figure 1.2 illustrates several contemporary human resources practices in education that are implemented toward the goal of realizing organizational equilibrium in school systems. Barnard's analysis put into proper perspective the scientific management concepts expounded by Taylor and others and the human relations views of Follett, Mayo, and others.

Numerous other investigators supported the behavioral science movement initiated by Barnard, including Herbert Simon, Jacob Getzels, Chris Argyris, Douglas McGregor, Andrew Halpin, Rensis Likert, Frederick Herzberg, Henry Mintzberg, James March, and Abraham Maslow. As a result of the research and writing of these individuals and others, the democratic/human relations approach was replaced gradually by the concepts of behavioral science methods. As noted by Hoy and Miskel (1982):

> In the 1950's . . . the behavioral science approach started to make inroads, and by the 1960's a full-scale theory movement emerged to guide the study and teaching of educational administration. Democratic prescription was replaced by analysis, a field orientation by a discipline orientation, raw observation by theoretical research. (p. 11)

Work satisfaction and human motivation were primary topics of research and inquiry by behavioral scientists during the 1950s and 1960s. During this period, Frederick Herzberg and Douglas McGregor set forth their now well-known theories

Satisfaction of Organizational Goals

Effectiveness

organizational goals, position descriptions, in-service programs, performance evaluation, recruitment/selection practices, orientation programs, supervision strategies, compensation, promotion

Organizational

Equilibrium

participative decision making, tenure, position assignment on basis of personal talents/interests, EAPs, benefit programs, in-service programs, compensation

Efficiency

Satisfaction of Individual Needs and Interests

Employee Observed Behavior

FIGURE 1.2
Barnard's Concepts of Effectiveness and Efficiency

of human behavior in organizations. Both theories held significant implications for human resources administration. Herzberg (1923–) and his associates set forth a major hypothesis that the factors leading to positive attitudes toward work and those leading to negative attitudes are different. His two-factor theory of motivation, published in *The Motivation to Work* in 1959, questioned whether different kinds of factors were responsible for bringing about job satisfaction and dissatisfaction.

Herzberg (Herzberg, Manser, & Snyderman, 1959) utilized in-depth interviews of engineers and accountants to determine what factors actually were associated with job satisfaction and dissatisfaction. Factors that appeared in the positive attitudes, those associated with job satisfaction, appear in Figure 1.3. Herzberg maintained that the first five factors were the most important in increasing job satisfaction. These five factors also were closely related in that, in contrast with the other factors, they focused on the *job itself*: achievement on the job, recognition in the job, the work itself, the job responsibilities, and job advancement. Therefore, Herzberg called these factors **motivators**.

The factors identified with negative attitudes and job dissatisfaction also are listed in Figure 1.3. Each factor is related to the environment in which the job takes place: those factors surrounding the job itself. Thus these factors were termed **hygienes**.

Figure 1.3 illustrates Herzberg's theory. Theoretically, if a worker had neither a positive nor a negative attitude toward the job, the positive presence of achievement, recognition, work itself, responsibility, and advancement would increase job satisfaction. However, according to the theory, the absence of the same factors does not, in

FIGURE 1.3
Herzberg's Two-Factor Theory
of Motivation

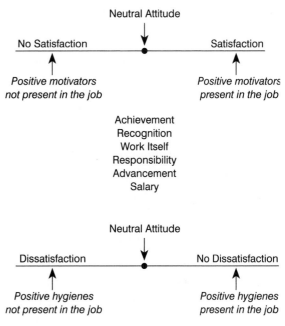

itself, result in negative attitudes and dissatisfaction. Rather, such absence would result in a return to a neutral position. In a similar manner, if a worker were neither positive nor negative about the job, dissatisfaction would result if such factors as company policy and administration or the technical aspects of supervision were negatively altered. Thus the administrator must focus on the positive existence of hygiene factors in order to resolve worker dissatisfaction, then address the factors that serve to promote worker satisfaction and personal motivation.

Investigators have conducted empirical studies in education using Herzberg's theory to discover whether it was applicable to teachers and administrators. The results of such studies vary. Sergiovanni (1967) found, for example, that the factors of advancement and work itself were not significant motivators for teachers. Wickstrom (1971), on the other hand, found that the four top-ranking satisfactions for teachers were the work itself, a sense of achievement, good personal relations with subordinates, and responsibility. Achievement was not among the top-ranked sources of satisfaction in Wickstrom's research. Friesen, Holaday, and Rice, in a 1983 investigation of administrators, found that school principals rated interpersonal relationships, sense of accomplishment, responsibility, and autonomy as significantly satisfying. Major dissatisfactions were administration and policy, amount of work, and constraints on the job.

Considerable disagreement exists as to the viability of Herzberg's theory. Nevertheless, it has had significant impact on approaches to motivation in human resources practices. Certainly, Herzberg's work has emphasized the importance of employee motivation and has provided a basis for new inquiry into morale and organizational climate.

As discussed previously, traditional concepts, illustrated by Taylor's scientific management approach, tended to view the worker as an individual with no ambition, initiative, or intelligence, and one opposed to change. Douglas McGregor (1906–1964) refuted these views in his *theory Y*, explained in *The Human Side of Enterprise* in 1960. McGregor called Taylor's views of the worker *theory X* beliefs.

In introducing his now classical theory Y concepts, McGregor (1960) asks,

Have we not made major modifications in the management of human resources during the past quarter century? Have we not recognized the importance of people and made vitally significant changes in managerial strategy as a consequence? Do the developments since the twenties in personnel administration and labor relations add up to nothing? (p. 45)

McGregor's (1960) concepts of theory Y behavior are summarized as follows:

- The expenditure of physical and mental effort in work is as natural as play or rest.
- External control and the threat of punishment are not the only means for bringing about effort toward organizational objectives. People will exercise self-direction and self-control in the service of objectives to which they are committed.
- Commitment to objectives is a function of the rewards associated with their achievement.
- The average human being learns, under proper conditions, not only to accept but to seek responsibility.
- The capacity to exercise a relatively high degree of imagination, ingenuity, and creativity in the solution of organizational problems is widely, not narrowly, distributed in the population.
- Under the conditions of modern industrial life, the intellectual potentials of the average human being are only partially utilized. (pp. 47–48)

McGregor's theory Y was revolutionary because it placed emphasis on fostering individual self-direction and full potential, exceeding the mere satisfaction of personal needs. Although it has received criticism as being an oversimplification of reality, McGregor's concepts have encouraged several human resources activities. Perhaps the principal strategy deriving from this theory is a "decentralization of activities and a delegation of authority by giving subordinates a larger measure of control, participation, and responsibility in organizational events" (Hanson, 1979, pp. 85–86). Generally, human resources administration was influenced by McGregor's theory Y to

1. place new emphasis on the importance of the human dimension in organizations and give a new meaning to the utilization of human resources;
2. emphasize the positiveness of employees' potential to contribute in intellectual and meaningful ways to organizational effectiveness;
3. underline the fallacy of total centralization of administrative actions and emphasize the values of employee participation on a broad scale throughout the organization;

4. present a new view of expectancy motivation and human behavior in that, when management concepts allow for high-level performance expectations, employees tend to respond.

CONTEMPORARY VIEWS OF BEHAVIORAL SCIENCE AND NEW SCHOOLS OF THOUGHT

The complexity of organizations and the wide diversity of personalities within them have led to close scrutiny of the various behavioral science approaches to administration and management. Because organizations are not static entities but continuously changing, all-encompassing principles for guiding administrative behavior are evasive. Nevertheless, scholars and practitioners continue their interest and inquiry in search for better answers to the understanding of human behavior in organizational settings. *Systems theory* and *contingency approaches* represent two contemporary extensions of behavioral science.

Haimann and Scott (1970) state that "they [systems] are sets of interrelated, interdependent parts in which the function of any one part fully depends on the other parts which, in turn, rely on the part initially singled out" (p. 3). In educational administration and its human resources function, administration is concerned with the elements or units of the school system, and how they interact with one another effectively to accomplish school goals. An open-systems approach to problem solving includes a thorough analysis of the interrelationships of a system's inputs, transformation process, and outputs, as illustrated in Figure 1.4. In brief, *environmental inputs* are represented by the available human, physical, financial, and information resources. Inputs in a school system are represented by financial resources, students, teachers, school objectives, material resources, and communication technology. The *transformation process* is exemplified by the tools and technologies that are applied to inputs to gain the desired outputs. Transformation processes in the school system include such tools and technologies as the organizational administrative, teaching, and support personnel systems, instructional technologies, reward systems, supervisory strategies, and many other tools and processes. *Outputs* represent the results of the transformation process on the inputs originally introduced into the system. Output in a school system is represented by competent students who possess desired scholarly and behavioral qualities (Saxe, 1980). *Feedback* represents various reports, analyses, diagnoses, and "learnings" concerning the system's effectiveness. In a school setting, feedback is exemplified by such information as graduation rate data, program evaluation reports, student dropout statistics, student promotion/retention data, student attendance data, financial reports, and reports of the numbers of students entering college or realizing gainful employment upon graduation.

Systems concepts hold several benefits for human resources administration:

1. The systems approach can be beneficial in establishing interpersonal and interdepartmental work patterns that enhance organizational communication and understanding.
2. The systems approach can be beneficial for gaining insight into system functions that can lead to the identification of organizational strengths and weaknesses.

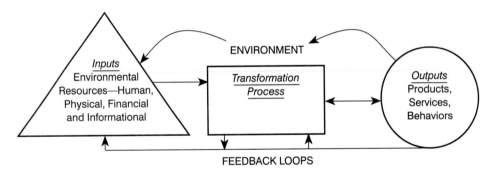

FIGURE 1.4
Systems Model

3. The systems approach can be beneficial in helping the entire organization to focus on its primary goals and objectives.
4. The systems approach can be beneficial in helping human resources personnel to utilize human resources in ways that enhance the possibility of more productive outputs in relation to the related costs of inputs and transformation process expenditures.

Extensions of systems theory have been developed that go far beyond the scope of this chapter. Although the aforementioned benefits of systems approaches to the human resources function are worthy, the concept has its critics and limitations as well. For example, some authorities argue that systems approaches and quantitative techniques can be used primarily for technical planning and operations related to decision making. According to Hellriegel and Slocum (1989),

> these techniques have not reached the stage where they can be used effectively to deal with human aspects of management. Variables representing behavioral considerations and human values are difficult—if not impossible—to build into a mathematical model. Since these subjective variables must be considered, managerial judgment will continue to be indispensable in decision making. (pp. 64–65)

As Hellriegel and Slocum (1989) point out, "the organization's external environment, technology, and people are its ***contingency variables***. The relative importance of each variable depends on the type of managerial problem under consideration" (p. 65). Thus contingency approaches in the areas of leadership, goal setting, motivation, planning, and control are among those that have received considerable attention in recent years. As early as 1965, Fiedler set forth a contingency leadership theory contending that the job should be "engineered" to fit the manager. His theory states that the specific leadership style utilized in a specific situation, to be effective, must consider the nature of the task to be performed, the power position of the leader in the situation, and the existing relationships between the leader and individuals involved in the situation (Fiedler & Chemers, 1974). In brief, Fiedler's contingency leadership theory contends that in some situations, a "task-motivated" leadership style is most effective but in other situations a "relationship-motivated" leadership style serves best. Task-motivated leaders emphasize structure and tend to gain satisfaction through the efficient accomplishment of tasks. Relationship-motivated leaders, on the other hand, place an emphasis on positive interpersonal relationships that are exemplified by subordinate or staff support and approval.

Table 1.1 shows the eight-celled model of Fiedler's contingency theory. The three situational factors of leader-member relations, task structure, and leader position power reflect the variables within each situation. ***Leader-member relations***, assessed as being either good or poor, focus on the status of existing interpersonal relations between the leader and other group members. Task structure is either structured or unstructured. A ***structured task*** has identifiable steps or procedures. Each step, for example, can be completed and evaluated before moving to the next. The task of improving the organizational climate of a school is ***unstructured*** in that there are no set procedures for accomplishing the task; at best the task is only vaguely defined. ***Leader position power*** represents the extent to which the leader holds authority or control over the group members. A school superintendent, for example, has certain authority over a group of the system's school principals. In this instance, the positional power of the superintendent would be strong rather than weak. On the other hand, a school principal, who is chairing a committee of other principals in the system, holds no specific position power or power to "reward or punish" members of the committee; position power in this case most likely is weak.

Fiedler (Fiedler & Chemers, 1974) summarized his research findings by noting that task-motivated leaders generally perform best in situations that are clearly favorable or unfavorable (see Table 1.1). Relationship-oriented leaders tend to be most effective in situations that are moderately favorable, situations in which the leader holds only moderate power, control, and influence. Thus, Fiedler's views place

TABLE 1.1
Fiedler's Contingency Model of Leadership

The Situational Favorableness	Leader-Member Relations	Task Structure	Leader Position Power
	Good	Structured	Strong
Favorable	Good		Weak
	Good	Unstructured	Strong
	Good		Weak
Moderate	Poor	Structured	Strong
	Poor		Weak
	Poor	Unstructured	Strong
Unfavorable	Poor		Weak

Source: From *Leadership and Effective Management* (p. 14) by F. E. Fiedler and Martin M. Chemers, 1974, Glenview, IL: Scott Foresman and Company. Copyright © 1974 by Fred E. Fiedler. Reprinted by permission.

the leadership emphasis on assigning the right leader in the specific situation and/or altering the situation itself, as opposed to the more popular view that individuals change their leadership style to meet the situation.

As is the case with most theories, the Fiedler contingency theory has its share of critics. Nevertheless, Lunenburg and Ornstein (1991) note the major contributions of Fiedler's leadership model as follows:

1. The contingency model was one of the first approaches to leadership to examine the situation—the people, the task, and the organization.
2. The theory implies that leadership should not be thought of as either good or bad. . . . A more realistic approach is to view an administrator's leadership style as effective in one set of circumstances but ineffective in another.
3. Leadership is a function of the interaction of leadership style and situational dimensions within the organization. (p. 142)

SUMMARY

Throughout America's history, education has been influenced significantly by evolving social and economic developments. Education and human resources practices have reflected the needs, demands, and pressures of America's social influences.

Education in America in the early 1800s was placed under the close scrutiny of selectmen, whose responsibilities were to make certain that the instruction provided did not depart from that desired by the local community. These early committees performed the personnel responsibilities of hiring, advising, dismissing, and controlling. As the population increased and the work required became too burdensome for lay personnel, part-time workers were selected to perform certain duties, mainly related to business affairs. Later, states appointed individuals to head the educational program, county superintendents became prominent, and local school administration personnel emerged in increasing numbers.

The scientific management movement led primarily by Frederick Taylor revolutionized personnel practices in business and industry and influenced educational personnel practice in the early 1900s. Workers were considered to be "machines" to carry out the work planned and controlled by management. Nevertheless, scientific management made many contributions to the human resources function. Such concepts as division of labor, span of control, unity of command, standardization of tasks, and incentive pay are found in contemporary personnel practice.

Mary Parker Follett and others refuted the scientific management concepts and argued that interpersonal relationships were essential in the world of work. Follett inspired others such as Elton Mayo to study human relations in-depth in organizations. Democratic administration practices were a result of much research during the 1920s and 1930s.

During the early part of the twentieth century, the central personnel office began to emerge, both in industry and in educational practice. Such centralization increased at a rapid rate during the 1930s and 1940s. The national spread of employee groups, governmental involvement in education, influence of the social sciences, and the effects of World War II all had an impact upon human resources administration.

Chester Barnard's writings in the area of behavioral science in administration influenced human resources administration by emphasizing the importance of communicating, formulating organizational purposes, and gaining the necessary performances from members in the organization. Other writers supplemented the behavioral science concepts and gave added strength to the democratic administration principles initiated by Follett and others. Concepts of behavioral science most recently have included inquiry in the area of systems and contingency theory.

During the 1950s and through the 1980s, human resources administration came into its own. Although it shares the responsibility with many other functions in the school system, human resources administration has direct relationships with virtually every individual in the school system. Almost every problem and program development has implications for the human element in the organization.

DISCUSSION QUESTIONS

1. Chapter 1 illustrates that education is closely tied to the social, political, and economic influences of its time. Discuss the various impacts of social, political, and economic events upon education and human resources practices within the last 10 years.
2. Scientific management of the early 1900s had a major impact on human resources practices. Discuss its influence as reflected in various contemporary personnel practices.
3. Discuss Barnard's concept of capacity of equilibrium. What specific implications does the concept hold for human resources administrators in relation to the effectiveness and efficiency dimensions?
4. Assume that your leadership style is task motivated. You are confronted by a situation where your relationship with the group members is good, the task is unstructured, and your leader position power is weak. What does this situation indicate to you about your chances of leading successfully in this instance? Suggest several ways you might alter the situation to make it more favorable for your leadership style.
5. A major premise of Chapter 1 is that all administrators in a school system are human resources administrators. Present several facts for evidence that this premise indeed holds true in practice.

CASE 1.1
Aren't You Working Too Hard, Scott?

Randall Scott was enthusiastic about his new teaching position at Union High School. It had been a difficult task completing his BS degree in mathematics while working part-time and raising two young sons. He was assigned to teach four classes of 11th grade algebra and one class of geometry. Although first-year teachers often were excused from extra duty assignments at Union, Randall asked if he might serve as sponsor of a math club and also serve as an "unpaid" junior varsity basketball coach. These assignments were granted.

Nora Belle, district curriculum coordinator, sent a memorandum to all math teachers regarding the initiation of a curriculum committee to work on the revision of the math curriculum during the ensuing semester. After conferring with his principal, Emory Ross, Randall decided to volunteer for the committee and was named as a member.

Randall thoroughly enjoyed the math curriculum work. He took the leadership in completing two special committee projects and also served to chair the textbook selection committee for 11th-grade algebra.

Randall was beginning to think this was his best year ever. His performance ratings as a teacher were excellent, and this added to his satisfaction.

At the monthly faculty meeting, Principal Ross made some brief remarks about special activities of several staff members, including the several contributions of Randall. At one point, the principal asked if anyone might be interested in working with a representative parent group on student discipline. One faculty member commented softly so only those at his table could hear, "Let Randall Scott do it, he's got all the ideas." On the way out of the meeting, one faculty member said to Randall, "Say, Scott, aren't you working too hard?"

Questions

1. Comment on the foregoing case generally. Do you find the situation realistic?
2. What do informal groups in school settings do to "control" the work setting?
3. How do the findings of Mayo and Roethlisberger relate to this case?

☐ **CASE 1.2**
Job Rotation

Union High School is one of seven high schools in the Hallmark School District. You have served as Union High School principal for 8 years and the average time of service for the district's other principals is 8 years. Only one principal, George Schroeder, is nearing retirement.

Considerable discussion has taken place in the district relative to rotating principals in the various schools every 5 years. The school board, school superintendent, and principals tend to favor the concept. Teachers are somewhat passive about job rotation for principals and only the general public has tended to question the implementation of such a program.

Superintendent Jones has asked you to chair the principals' group that will examine the job rotation concept in-depth and recommend specific plans for its possible implementation. Such matters as the rotational timetable, selection of school assignments, articulation considerations, and communication needs are to be addressed by the principals' group.

Superintendent Jones informed you that you were selected as group chair because she and others perceive you as having good relationships with the other principals. Various assessments of your leadership behavior indicate that you are task oriented.

Questions

1. In the foregoing scenario, what can be said about the task structure relative to the group's assignment?
2. Would you expect your position power to be high or low in this situation? (Evidence suggests that your leader-member relations in this case are good.)
3. In view of the available information, what can be said about your leadership "fit" in this instance?
4. What might be done to change the situation in order that your leadership behavior might be more effective?

☐ **CASE 1.3**
Amelia, What Would You Do?

Principal Stephen Craig scheduled an appointment with his assistant principal, Amelia Wilson.

"I'm getting more and more concerned about the negative attitudes of the faculty," commented Principal Craig. "I've never seen such overall apathy on the part of our teachers. I talked to Sharon Crutchfield recently. She's one of our most positive teachers, yet she inferred that faculty satisfaction in general was as low as she had ever seen it. We have to find a solution, but I'm just not sure where to begin."

"Amelia, what would you do?" Craig asked.

Questions

1. Assume the role of Assistant Principal Amelia Wilson and set forth your response to Principal Craig.
2. How might Herzberg's two-factor theory of motivation be useful in determining a solution to the situation of faculty dissatisfaction?

REFERENCES

American Association of School Administrators. (1952). *The American school superintendency* (thirteenth yearbook). Washington, DC: Author.

Barnard, C. I. (1938). *The functions of the executive.* Cambridge, MA: Harvard University Press.

Bloss, J. M. (1882). *Thirtieth report of the superintendent of public instruction of the state of Indiana to the governor.* Indianapolis: State of Indiana.

Bobbitt, J. F. (1913). *The supervision of city schools: Part I. Some general principles of management applied to problems of city school systems* (pp. 7–8). Twelfth yearbook of the National Society for the Study of Education. Chicago: University of Chicago Press.

Callahan, R. E. (1962). *The cult of efficiency.* Chicago: University of Chicago Press.

Cubberly, E. P. (1916). *Public school administration.* Boston: Houghton-Mifflin Company.

Cubberly, E. P. (1927). *State school administration.* Boston: Houghton-Mifflin.

Fayol, H. (1949). *General and industrial management.* London: Sir Isaac Pitman and Sons. (Original work published 1916)

Fenner, M. S. (1945). *NEA history.* Washington, DC: National Education Association.

Fiedler, F. E., & Chemers, M. M. (1974). *Leadership and effective management.* Glenview, IL: Scott Foresman.

Follett, M. P. (1924). *Creative experience.* New York: Longmans, Green.

Follett, M. P. (1940). The meaning of responsibility in business management. In H. C. Metcalf & L. Urwick (Eds.), *Dynamic administration: The collected papers of Mary Parker Follett* (pp. 146–166). New York: Harper and Brothers.

Friesen, D., Holaday, E. A., & Rice, A. W. (1983). Satisfaction of school principals with their work. *Educational Administration Quarterly, 19*(3), 35–38.

Gantt, H. L. (1961). *Gantt on management.* New York: American Management Association and the American Society of Mechanical Engineers.

Gibson, R. O., & Hunt, H. C. (1965). *The school personnel administrator.* Boston: Houghton-Mifflin.

Griffin, R. W. (1987). *Management.* Boston: Houghton-Mifflin.

Haimann, T., & Scott, W. G. (1970). *Management in the modern organization.* Boston: Houghton-Mifflin.

Hanson, E. M. (1979). *Educational administration and organizational behavior.* Boston: Allyn & Bacon.

Hellriegel, D., & Slocum, J. W. (1989). *Management* (5th ed.). Reading, MA: Addison-Wesley.

Herzberg, F., Manser, B., & Snyderman, B. (1959). *The motivation to work.* New York: Wiley.

Hoy, W. K., & Miskel, C. G. (1982). *Educational administration—Theory, research and practice* (2nd ed.). New York: Random House.

Hoy, W. K., & Miskel, C. G. (1991). *Educational administration theory* (4th ed.). New York: McGraw-Hill.

Jenkins, R. C., & Warner, G. C. (1937). *Henry Barnard—An introduction.* Hartford: The Connecticut State Teachers Association, Finaly Press.

Lewin, K., Lippitt, R., & White, R. (1939). Patterns of aggressive behavior in experimentally created "social climates." *Journal of Social Psychology, 10,* 271–299.

Lucio, W. H., & McNeil, O. (1969). *Supervision* (2nd ed.). New York: McGraw-Hill.

Lunenburg, F. C., & Ornstein, A. C. (1991). *Educational administration—concepts and practices*. Belmont, CA: Wadsworth.

Mayo, E. (1933). *The human problems of an industrial civilization*. New York: Macmillan.

McConaughy, J. L. (1918). The worship of the yardstick. *Educational Review*, 55, 191–192.

McCoy, M. W., Gips, C. J., & Evans, M. W. (1983). *The American school personnel administrator: An analysis of characteristics and role*. Unpublished manuscript, American Association of School Personnel Administrators, Seven Hills, OH.

McGregor, D. (1960). *The human side of enterprise*. New York: McGraw-Hill.

Monahan, W. G. (1975). *Theoretical dimensions of educational administration*. New York: Macmillan.

Moore, H. E. (1966). *The administration of public school personnel*. New York: The Library of Education, The Center for Applied Research in Education, Inc.

Newsom, N. W. (1932). *The legal status of the county superintendents* (Bulletin No. 7). Washington, DC: U.S. Department of the Interior, Office of Education.

Reller, T. L. (1935). *The development of the city superintendency of schools in the United States*. Philadelphia: Author.

Roethlisberger, F. J., & Dickson, W. J. (1939). *Management and the worker*. Cambridge, MA: Harvard University Press.

Saxe, R. W. (1980). *Educational administration today: An introduction*. Berkeley, CA: McCutchan.

Sergiovanni, T. J. (1967). Factors which affect satisfaction and dissatisfaction of teachers. *Journal of Educational Administration*, 5(1), 66–82.

Taylor, F. W. (1911). *Scientific management*. New York: Harper & Row.

Tead, O., & Metcalf, H. C. (1920). *Personnel administration*. New York: McGraw-Hill.

Urwick, L., & Gulick, L. (Eds.). (1937). *Papers on the science of administration*. New York: Columbia University, Institute of Public Administration.

Weber, M. (1947). *The theory of social and economic organization* (T. Parsons, Ed., A. M. Henderson & T. Parsons, Trans.). New York: Free Press.

White, R., & Lippitt, R. (1960). *Autocracy and democracy: An experimental inquiry*. New York: Harper & Row.

Wickstrom, R. A. (1971). An investigation into job satisfaction among teachers (Doctoral dissertation, University of Oregon, 1971). *Dissertation Abstracts International*, 32, 1249A.

2

Contemporary Issues and Related Problems in Human Resources Administration

■

The increase of the activities and earnestness of teacher organizations, the growing influence of legal mandates and requirements, including civil rights and due process considerations, and the introduction of collective negotiations have had notable impacts on the school administrator. In addition, the public concern for accountability and increased quality in education, along with the growth of professionalism within personnel administration itself, have brought about added importance to the human resources function. More recently, such developments as restructuring and calls for educational reform, changes in school governance systems exemplified by site-based management, and trends in the area of alternative certification for teaching have raised new questions. Each new development, issue, or problem in education has resulted in new demands and new directions for the human resources function.

By the 1980s human resources administration had become soundly entrenched as an integral function in school districts. During the years of 1980 to 1990, the human resources function faced numerous disparities. The exodus from cities resulted in enrollment decline in some districts and often caused student growth problems in nearby suburban areas. While some school districts were busy establishing personnel policies to deal with reduction in force (RIF), others were experiencing teacher shortages in certain areas of specialization. Although 1980 was characterized by an oversupply of teachers, by 1983 severe teacher shortages were witnessed in several areas. Demands for more high school courses in many subject areas, including foreign language, mathematics, and science, caused a surplus of teachers in some specialties and teacher shortages in others.

Other conditions also affected human resources administration during the 1980s. Various publics were demanding improved instruction in schools while, at the same time, alternative certification programs for teachers were being proposed, including the hiring of persons with no preparation in instructional methodology. Attention to student performance and teacher competency was prominent during this period, yet funding to attract and retain quality instructional personnel continued to be a major problem. Such matters as class size and teacher load, both factors in instructional quality, were given little serious attention. And although much discussion focused on the growing proportions of minorities in the general population and in the schools, such minority representation was not reflected among teaching or administrative staffs.

In the early 1990s emerging movements held far-reaching implications for human resources administration. As mentioned previously, educational reform, including new approaches to school governance and organizational structure, gained general support and program changes were witnessed in many school districts nationally. In 1992 some districts were giving serious thought to dissolving the central human resources unit in the district and delegating this function to individual local schools.

This chapter presents several issues and problems that face human resources administration in the 1990s and are likely to continue as important issues in the years ahead. Later in the text many of these issues and problems are addressed further.

HUMAN RESOURCES ISSUE 1: SCHOOL GOVERNANCE AND LEADERSHIP

Cetron and Gayle (1991), both representatives of forecasting agencies, set forth several trends in school governance and leadership as education enters the twenty-first century. Their several predictions for education included the following contentions:

1. Educational bureaucracies, local school boards, and other regulatory agencies will lose their power as the second wave of reform takes hold during the 1990s.
2. Exploration of research topics on school governance will be undertaken that go beyond centralization and decentralization to, for instance, distribution of authority among government, teaching professionals, and families.
3. All community stakeholders (parents, students, teachers, business leaders, and others) will continue to demand more involvement in the decisions governing education, but they will have little knowledge about what should be done to restructure; much is done with little research basis.
4. The educational system will become more fragmented. . . . Implementation of numerous schooling alternatives will erode the traditional schooling pattern.
5. The current shortage of qualified candidates for school administration positions will continue well into the twenty-first century. Three-quarters of American school superintendents, and as many as half of all principals, will retire by 1994. (p. 229)[1]

These forecasts are indicative of several developments and problems related to the issue of school governance. Teacher empowerment, site-based management, and organizational restructuring are issues faced by most every school community. Their implications for human resources administration are far-reaching. Every human

---

[1] Adapted from the book *Educational Renaissance* by Marvin Cetron and Margaret Gayle. Copyright © 1991. Reprinted with permission from St. Martin's Press, Inc., New York, NY.

resources process is affected by these developments. One major issue is the deployment of human resources responsibilities. Although a limited movement to date, central human resources units in some school districts are being displaced; local schools are assuming the duties formerly performed by central office human resources personnel. Site-based management has become a major force in the restructuring movement.

The support for changes in school governance comes from many sources, including business, government, professional, and private groups. As Elam, Rose, and Gallup (1991) point out,

> the general public seems to share this view. In the current poll, 76% of the respondents favor giving principals and teachers more say in how their local schools are run; 14% oppose the idea. Moreover, the public favors giving policy-making powers to councils composed of local principals and teachers . . . rather than leaving it with boards and top administrators. (p. 52)

Most authorities believe that accountability will continue to be a major issue during the 1990s. Where accountability will be placed in cases of decentralization of authority is a major question. If indeed policy-making councils are formed to "replace" certain powers of local school boards, and if local schools within school districts assume major administrative responsibilities, the question of accountability becomes an issue of paramount importance.

A summary of pro and con arguments on the matter of school restructuring was stated by Lunenburg and Ornstein (1991). This summary, set forth in Table 2.1, illustrates some of the specific issues and problems related to this development.

The arguments favoring restructuring of school governance emphasize its potential for professionalizing the teaching profession. Yet related demands on the teacher's time are self-evident. The matters of position assignments, staff utilization, staff development, compensation, and other processes are human resources considerations of primary importance in the restructuring issue.

An issue related to school organization that has implications for school governance and leadership is *choice*. Choice constitutes a new organizational structure that results in an indirect control of the schools through parental choice of school attendance. "The 23rd Annual Gallup Poll of the Public's Attitudes Toward the Public Schools" (Elam et al., 1991) found that 61% of the male respondents and 62% of the female respondents favored allowing students and parents to choose which public schools to attend in the community regardless of where they live (p. 23). As the Gallup Poll report points out, "If parental choice ever becomes a reality in more than a few experimental situations in America, parents will face more problems" (p. 23). There is little question that such a change would present a host of new changes for the human resources function in education as well.

The issue of school governance and leadership holds important implications for practices in human resources administration. The processes of planning, recruitment and selection, staff utilization, performance evaluation, staff development, compensation, and others are subject to major changes as a result of alterations in school governance.

TABLE 2.1
Arguments For and Against School Restructuring

Pro	Con
1. Bureaucratic restraints impede teachers. . . . They cannot make decisions about curriculum or resource personnel allocation quickly and easily.	1. The educational bureaucracy protects teachers. Administrators assume the burden of making decisions . . . so that teachers are free to concentrate their energies on teaching and learning in the classroom.
2. Teachers must be held more accountable for outcomes. . . . They must have the authority to change whatever needs to be changed in order to improve the outcome.	2. Teachers don't want to participate in school decision making; their expertise is teaching and learning.
3. Serious problems require drastic solutions. If we don't restructure schools, another generation of . . . children will be lost.	3. Drastic restructuring is too risky. We should proceed with caution, engage in research, and carefully plan the future.
4. The bureaucratic model is obsolete. . . . Business is abandoning it because it no longer works.	4. Schools are highly complex organizations. Efficiency demands a clear division of labor. . . . To ensure that everyone is treated equally, we need administrators who are impartial judges.
5. The notion of bureaucracy is less and less relevant in postindustrial society.	5. Teachers are attempting to gain control of schools. School restructuring is the union's strategy to eliminate school administrators.

Source: From *Educational Administration—Concepts and Practices* (p. 31) by F. C. Lunenburg
and A. C. Ornstein, 1991, Belmont, CA: Wadsworth.

HUMAN RESOURCES ISSUE 2: HUMAN RESOURCES RELATIONSHIPS AND COOPERATION IN EDUCATION

A national study of school superintendents, sponsored by the American Association of School Administrators (AASA) (Glass, 1992), found that 44.6% of superintendents in the smallest school districts had left their prior positions due to conflicts with the school board. Data including all school districts indicated that approximately 22% of the superintendents moved from their previous school districts due to board conflicts. In the same study, internal board conflicts and employee relations were named by superintendents as two of the most difficult problems their board members faced, and administrator/board relations was the sixth highest ranked issue and challenge facing school superintendents nationally.

Frustration with the school board was one of the top 10 issues listed as most likely to cause superintendents to leave their position. Norton's study (1989) of Arizona personnel directors identified serious problems facing them. School board/staff relations was named as one of the 10 most serious problems.

A report in *Education Week* stated that more than half of the 50,000 members of the Washington Education Association voted to authorize a strike if the state legislature did not adequately address teachers' concerns in its current session (Bradley, 1991, p. 5). Diegmueller (1991) reported that "the number of strikes, by district, . . . began to drop each year until 1986, when there were 55. By 1988, strikes had risen to 87, only to fall again the following year to 59" (p. 14). But according to Diegmueller (1991, p. 14), there were 73 strikes in 1990 and 61 strikes already had been recorded in the nation as of January 1991. Writing on the topic of the costs of reform and the nation's economic recession, Sokoloff and Lazerson (1990) noted that

> already, the tension between forces is revealing (once again) how vulnerable school improvements are to financial strain. If the storm clouds burst, there will be conflict between schools and their communities, reduced funds for education, strife between teachers and school districts, and incalculable losses to our children. (p. 26)

Current practice often has the human resources director serving as the school board's chief negotiator, which tends to place this position in an adversarial relationship with teaching and support personnel. Such an arrangement often poses problems in fostering amicable working relationships between the human resources director and other employees. For example, the responsibilities of the director in such areas as personal counseling and personnel protection are viewed by many as incongruent with the responsibilities of the director for developing a positive organizational climate and trustworthy interpersonal relationships. Thus, the use of the personnel director as chief negotiator for the school board is controversial, even though the role appears to be an obvious one from certain perspectives.

Some movement has been made toward viewing collective negotiations as a cooperative problem-solving procedure as opposed to an adversarial relationship. Such relational "improvements" are credited in part to the maturation of both teacher and management groups in the negotiation process. Other observers point out that school boards are losing control of the financial function of school systems and therefore distributive bargaining approaches are becoming less effective. A detailed discussion of the integrative, or "win-win," approach in collective bargaining is included in Chapter 10.

In view of the many problems associated with the issue of human relationships and cooperation in education, the concept of shared school governance, previously discussed as Issue 1, certainly will alter unilateral policy adoption by school boards without ratification by local teacher groups and other publics. As discussed in the prior section, if governance changes are generally implemented, human resources practices will be altered immeasurably. Approaches to teacher evaluation, teacher load, staff utilization, compensation, and other human resources activities will depend on the deliberate involvement of all concerned.

HUMAN RESOURCES ISSUE 3:
EFFECTIVE HUMAN PERFORMANCE

Staff quality has been an ongoing issue in education. In his 1882 report, Bloss of Indiana noted that

> our children must be taught by competent teachers. . . . If it be the good teacher who makes the good school, and this is undoubtedly true, it must follow that if we are to have better schools in Indiana we must have better teachers. (p. 150)

Concern for the quality of human performance was expressed by Gibson and Hunt in 1965 as follows:

> With the rising enrollments in educational institutions, the number of school personnel can be expected to increase throughout and beyond the present century. At the same time, the quality of school personnel should certainly be improved. . . . Since the demand for professional personnel is expanding, the competition is becoming keener . . . dual pressures pose problems for the maintenance of quality in school personnel. (p. 38, 41)

The concern for quality staffing in schools continued in the 1980s. Albert Shanker, president of the American Federation of Teachers (AFT), stated before the AFT's 68th Annual Convention that "teachers must 'take control' of their profession, including responsibility for removing people who should not be teaching." He further commented that "there is recognition that some teachers are excellent, some are very good and some are terrible" (Currence, 1984).

The 1991 Gallup Poll on public education provided evidence of citizen concern for human quality in education. When asked what factors might be considered in choosing a public school for a child, 85% of the public named the quality of the teaching staff (Elam et al., 1991, p. 48). This was the highest percentage for any of the factors listed. In addition, poll results revealed that difficulty in getting good teachers was named as the biggest problem facing public schools in 1991, and nearly 70% favored the idea of extra pay for those teaching "particularly effectively" (p. 30).

Table 2.2 shows the results of public opinion concerning teacher, principal, and school board quality. Although the poll resulted in 40% of the public giving local schools an A or B and 18% giving national schools an A or B, marks for schools overall were marginal. Fifty percent of the public graded schools in their communities as C or below. Grades of C or below were given to schools nationally by 70% of the public. Ratings for the schools that the oldest child attended were considerably higher, with 64% giving grades of A or B. In any case, the poll results indicated that, in the opinion of the citizenry, improvements in education are needed. Additionally, citizens listed "difficulty in getting good teachers" as the seventh biggest problem with which the public schools must deal (Elam et al., 1992).

When asked to identify specific problems encountered presently, school personnel directors in one state listed staff quality, securing quality administrative personnel, and dismissing incompetent staff among the 20 leading problems facing them (Norton, 1989).

Current developments in the areas of reform in teacher and administrator preparation programs; certification standards, including alternative certification approaches, merit pay, and testing of teacher competency; and others serve to emphasize the importance of the crucial issue of effective human performance in education.

TABLE 2.2

Americans' Ratings of Local Public Schools, Public Schools Nationally, and School Oldest Child Attends

Source: Data from "The 24th Annual Gallup/Phi Delta Kappa Poll of the Public's Attitudes Toward the Public Schools" by S. M. Elam, L. C. Rose, and A. M. Gallup, September 1992, *Phi Delta Kappan*, p. 41. Copyright © 1992 by Phi Delta Kappa. Reprinted by permission.

Rating	Local Public Schools	Public Schools Nationally	School Oldest Child Attends
A	9%	2%	22%
B	31%	16%	42%
C	33%	48%	24%
D	12%	18%	6%
F	5%	4%	4%
Don't know	10%	12%	2%

HUMAN RESOURCES ISSUE 4: COMPENSATION OF EDUCATIONAL PERSONNEL AND COST OF BENEFITS

Historically, school finance has been a leading problem in education. Bloss, in 1882, lamented several reasons why the inexperienced and ill-prepared teachers find positions in schools. He wrote in his annual report to the governor of Indiana that "first, the compensation offered is too small to induce teachers to remain in their profession" (p. 156). More than 100 years later, the problem of adequate compensation remains. In a national study by Glass (1992), school superintendents ranked "lack of financing" as the number one cause for their leaving the superintendency. In a statewide study in Arizona (Norton, 1991), adequate financing was named as the most serious problem facing school superintendents; nearly three-fourths of these administrators shared this opinion. In a similar study of personnel directors, once again adequate financing was listed as the most serious problem facing them now and in the years ahead (Norton, 1989).

Teachers' salaries have not compared favorably with those in other professions. Increases in salaries for teachers have been consistently lower than increases in other career fields, including construction workers, librarians, city bus drivers, sanitation workers, and personnel directors in industry (U.S. Department of Labor, 1984). Comparisons of salaries for graduates in education to graduates in other fields show similar results. Table 2.3 shows the average beginning salary from Arizona schools' salary schedules for teachers in relation to the offers made to June 1991 graduates in other career fields. Average beginning salaries for teachers with BA and MA degrees were below offers made to graduates in the fields of accounting, business administration, chemistry, computers, economics/finance, engineering, liberal arts, mathematics/statistics, sales/marketing, and other fields.

The average salaries of teachers continue to vary considerably among the states. In 1991–1992, the average teacher salaries in the United States ranged from $47,300 in Connecticut to $22,376 in South Dakota ("School Spending Slows," 1992, p. CL11).

Not only does the compensation level for educators continue to be a major issue, but also the methods of deciding salary payments. Merit pay, whereby one employee receives more dollars than another for better performance or more productivity as measured by quantifiable standards, is an example of such an issue. During the past

TABLE 2.3

Entry-Level Teaching Salaries
for the 1991–1992 School Year
in Arizona Compared to Entry-
Level Salaries for Other Career
Fields

Source: From *Endicott Report:
Placement Center of Northwestern
University* by Victor R. Lindquist,
December 1991, Evanston, IL:
Northwestern University.
Copyright © 1991 by Victor R.
Lindquist. Reprinted by permission.
(The *Endicott Report* is based on
surveys of approximately 250 well-
known businesses and industrial
concerns, 1991–92.)

Career Field	Average Entry-level Salary 1991–1992
BA Degree Minimum	
Teaching	$21,225
Accounting	27,408
Business administration	26,496
Chemistry	29,088
Computer	29,100
Economics/finance	26,712
Engineering	32,304
Liberal arts	26,364
Math statistics	28,944
Sales/marketing	27,728
Other fields	28,728
MA Degree Minimum	
Teaching	$23,219
Accounting	33,444
Engineering	36,924
MBA with nontechnical BA	41,784
MBA with technical BS	39,552
Other, nontechnical	34,860
Other, technical	35,208

several years, a variety of merit pay programs for personnel and schools has been witnessed. Career ladders, master teacher plans, merit school programs, mentor pay systems, forgivable loans, and other incentive pay programs are among those in place in school systems. Although the NEA believes that performance pay schedules, such as merit pay, are inappropriate (NEA, 1991b), the public overwhelmingly favors the concept (Elam et al., 1991). Of the national sample, 69% favored extra pay for teaching particularly effectively and only 24% opposed it (Elam et al., 1991, p. 26). In previous Gallup polls, people who said that teachers' salaries were too low generally have outnumbered those who believed them to be too high or about right. In 1991, 54% of the public favored raising teachers' salaries immediately and 32% opposed it; 14% didn't know or had no opinion (Elam et al., 1991, p. 26). People listed low teacher pay among the 15 biggest problems that the public schools in their communities must deal with (Elam et al., 1992, p. 43).

It is apparent that the matter of teacher, administrator, and support staff compensation will continue as an issue during the 1990s. The human resources function must provide leadership in such activities as researching relationships between monetary incentives and staff performance as well as between such matters as compensation and teacher recruitment and retention.

Cost of benefits (COB) is a major issue facing schools and the human resources function presently. Not only are the costs of benefits historically provided to personnel escalating, but many additional employee benefits are being introduced that make increasing demands on limited available dollars. The NEA's 1991–92 Resolutions (1991b) state, "The Association believes that education employees should be provided with benefits including, but not limited to

a. Comprehensive health insurance
b. Sick leave, with unlimited accumulation
c. Personal leave
d. Bereavement leave
e. Maternity/paternity leave, including adoption
f. Dependent day care
g. Sabbatical leave
h. Paid professional leave
i. Paid association leave
j. Workers' compensation
k. Life insurance
l. Severance pay
m. Tuition reimbursement
n. Personal assault protection
o. Long-term physical and mental disability insurance
p. Benefit extension for laid-off employees
q. Religious leave
r. Retirement compensation
s. Employee assistance program
t. Unemployment insurance
u. Vision insurance
v. Dental insurance
w. Legal insurance
x. Reimbursement for damage to or loss of personal property
y. Child care centers (p. 22)

In addition, the NEA believes that education employees should have access to comprehensive health, dental, and vision insurance, and employee assistance programs for their spouses, domestic partners, and/or dependents (NEA, 1991b).

Medical costs are one of the largest expense items for employing agencies and these costs continue to escalate. Luthans and Davis (1990) state,

> Rising health care costs have reached crisis proportions. We are currently spending 11.4% of our gross national product (GNP) on health care. This means that, on the average, more than 11 cents of each dollar spent is used for physicians and hospital charges, prescription drugs, and other health needs. . . . Health care is our third-largest business. Employers bear much of these staggering costs because approximately 85% to 90% of all health insurance is purchased through group plans, and the HR department is asked to manage these plans. (p. 24)

There is evidence that health care costs are being assumed increasingly by the employee. According to Kovach and Pearce (1990), in 1980 50% of employee-sponsored health care plans required employee contributions. In 1988 the figure rose to 62%, and by the year 2000 it is predicted that 80% of such programs will require some monetary payment by the employee. For the foregoing reasons, many predict that some form of national health plan in the United States is imminent in the near future. A recent U.S. Chamber of Commerce report (1991) indicated that employee benefits make up nearly 40% of the compensation of employees and in some cases such benefits comprise as much as two-thirds of the total payroll costs.

The International Foundation of Employee Benefits Plans (1991) has noted the increasing number of employers offering employee benefit plans. For example, the foundation found that 91% of businesses in a national survey already provide tuition reimbursement for employees and 97% plan to do so by the year 2000. Additionally, 29% presently provide child care benefits and 74% said they would do so by the year 2000. Flextime work arrangements were offered as benefits by 52% of the businesses in 1990, and by the year 2000 the figure is expected to reach 86%. The present 49% benefit level for family leave is projected to rise to 84% by the year 2000. The survey included a cross section of 463 businesses and included those with fewer than 500 employees to those with more than 5,000.

The issue of compensation and cost of benefits is complex; related problems in many cases seemingly have no solutions. Nevertheless, the human resources function must provide leadership to reach more workable solutions to problems in this area.

HUMAN RESOURCES ISSUE 5: THE DEMANDS UPON PROFESSIONAL PERSONNEL IN EDUCATION

The demands upon personnel within the various roles in educational administration pose serious difficulties for education and for the effectiveness of the human resources function. Responses of school superintendents in the 1992 AASA national study provide insight into the demands upon professional personnel in education. The study (Glass, 1992) revealed the following:

1. 84% of the superintendents said they feel "considerable" or "moderate" stress in the role.
2. The increase in pressure from special interest groups was a particular concern of school superintendents.
3. Compliance with external mandates, accountability, new teaching demands, administrator/board relations and changing priorities in curriculum were among the leading ten issues and challenges facing school superintendents nationally.
4. Nearly 35% of the superintendents were realizing only a "moderate" degree of self-fulfillment in their roles.
5. Nearly one-third of the superintendents, if doing it all over again, would choose a position other than school superintendent.
6. Relations and support of the local power structure, board conflicts, and community support were named issues most likely to cause superintendents to leave their positions if not corrected.

Demands on administrators weigh heavily upon the human resources function as well. A study of personnel directors in one state (Norton, 1989) revealed that 82.8% perceived job stress as "very high" or "high." Lack of time, demands upon the personnel office, job expectations that are too great, and too small a staff were named as negative job influences by the directors. Work load, inadequate resources, and external mandates and requirements were listed among the leading factors inhibiting job effectiveness.

Accountability demands have placed increasing pressures upon administrators and staff personnel. Calls for quality in all educational programs have placed new demands in the areas of performance evaluation, assessment of student achievement, program equity, and a variety of pay-for-performance plans. In Rochester, New York, teachers voted against a ground-breaking "accountability" contract that would have based teachers' pay on their job performance (Bradley, 1990a, p. 4). The contract was unique in that it was based on a new evaluation system, largely controlled by teachers, that classified them into three categories: those teachers meeting or exceeding high standards, those found in need of improvement, and those judged unsatisfactory. Of special interest was the fact that both the school board and the officers of the teachers' union backed the accountability contract. Factors surrounding the accountability movement often result in increased tensions between school boards and teachers, school boards and administrators, administrators and teachers, teachers and the community, and other individuals and groups.

The work load of educational personnel is an increasing problem. Human resources directors in one state named work load as the second leading problem facing them (Norton, 1989). Only the problem of external mandates and requirements ranked higher.

Increasing demands on the time and energy of human resources administrators are reflected in both the growing complexity of problems faced and the increase of new tasks within the personnel function. Employee background checks, cases of litigation, employment assistance programs, the administration of benefit programs, grievance counseling, fair employment practices, harassment cases, site-based management, and AIDS cases are a few of the new and growing demands being made on human resources personnel.

The push toward higher achievement expectations for students has resulted in commensurate higher work load expectations for teachers. Yet, the concern for teacher work load has been limited primarily to class size. Although class size is one element of work load, such factors as the number of subjects taught, preparation requirements, number and length of periods taught, and assigned extra duties have received limited attention. Human resource administrators have responsibilities for maximizing human effectiveness. Attention to such matters as work load equity and work load balance constitutes part of such responsibility.

Teacher turnover continues to be a problem in education. Haggart (1990) noted that one of every two teachers in California leaves the profession in the first 5 years. He states further that "today only one in four teachers entering the profession will continue beyond their fifteenth year. Teachers suffer twice the dropout rate of students they are being asked to save" (p. 43). Haggart (1990) summarizes the reasons teachers leave the profession as follows:

1. They did not enjoy teaching—the stress, isolation and powerlessness.
2. They felt unsuccessful, unappreciated and saw few opportunities for advancement.
3. They found jobs that paid more and offered more opportunity for success. (p. 43)

The foregoing considerations emphasize the issues and problems related to the demands upon professional personnel in education. Each consideration has important implications for the human resources function in education.

HUMAN RESOURCES ISSUE 6: EXTERNAL
MANDATES AND LEGAL IMPACTS

The courts and governmental legislation have had a major impact upon the human resources function during the past several years. As noted by McCarthy and Cambron-McCabe (1992), "The authority for the establishment and control of American public education is grounded in law. State and federal constitutional and statutory provisions provide the framework within which school operational decisions are made" (p. 1). Such personnel matters as terms and conditions of employment, freedom of expression, discrimination in employment, termination of employment, collective bargaining, and personal liability are only a few examples in which legal activity has had significant influence on procedures and practices in human resources administration.

Special federal and state legislation has had significant impact in the human resources arena as well. Legislation and/or state board of education mandates in such areas as teacher/administrator certification, contracts, desegregation, equal employment opportunity, strikes, personnel evaluation, retirement, personal appearance, lifestyle choices, sexual harassment, due process, and reduction in force are only a few of the areas in which legislation has set direction and influenced procedures in human resources administration. In regard to employee certification, there are proposals in some states to establish certification programs/standards for support personnel such as clerical, maintenance, and cafeteria workers. McCarthy and Cambron-McCabe (1992) note that "since the mid-twentieth century, legislation relating to schools has increased significantly in both volume and complexity, and courts have played an important role in interpreting statutory and constitutional provisions" (p. 20). This fact continues to have a major influence upon the administration of human resources in America's schools. A national study of school superintendents (Glass, 1992) placed "complying with mandates" and "the federal legislation for special education, 94.142," among the 10 greatest issues and challenges facing them. Superintendents in another statewide study named external mandates/requirements and the political climate/attitudes of the state legislature toward education as two of the leading three most serious problems facing them (Norton, 1991). In addition, 20% of the superintendents named legal impacts on school operations as a "serious" problem for them, and 50% viewed it as among the 10 leading problems in their administrative position. Human resources directors express similar views. Of the many problems being encountered in their work, external mandates/requirements and legal impacts on education were named as the number one and number two problems in their roles, respectively.

The significance of such external involvements for human resources administration is at least two-fold: (1) Such involvements clearly influence and often establish policy in personnel matters and, in turn, involve the courts and legislative bodies in the administration of schools; and (2) human resources personnel administrators and other school employees need to be well versed in matters of school law.

Problems relating to external involvement in education are varied and complex. Interference in "local control" is a major concern of many persons. Historically, education has been viewed as a national *concern*, a state *responsibility*, but a local *function*. When state legislatures and the federal government assume responsibilities of policy development and procedural specifications, thought by most to be the role of local school boards, problems of governance and control are inevitable. What state agencies might view as necessary and important educationally, local school districts often consider as interfering and disrupting. Also, approved legislation, which most often is a result of compromise, is often viewed as weakening education rather than improving it.

HUMAN RESOURCES ISSUE 7: TEACHER AND ADMINISTRATOR SUPPLY AND DEMAND— ALTERNATIVE CERTIFICATION PROGRAMS

Cetron and Gayle (1990) projected supply and demand data for teachers. These writers made the following forecasts:

1. The United States will need 2 million new teachers in the public school system between 1990 and 1995, but historical projections indicate that only a little over 1 million will materialize.
2. The expected attrition of the aging teaching force, class-size policies, and school enrollment projections will be major factors determining the numbers of new teachers required to staff U.S. schools.
3. The supply of newly graduated teaching candidates is expected to satisfy only about 60% of the "new hire" demand over the next 10 years.
4. Most states will implement alternative routes to certification by 1995 as a solution to teacher shortages, especially in the sciences. (p. 236)

The U.S. Department of Education (1989) has projected the annual demand for "new hire" teachers to the year 2000 (1989). The department's data indicate that from 1994 to the year 2000, an estimated 1,375,000 new teachers will be needed. The National Center for Education Statistics projects that the supply of new teachers will fall short of demand by approximately 40% in the year 2000. The issue of teacher supply and demand is complicated further by contentions that even in the teaching areas where teachers are more plentiful, the supply of "quality" personnel remains limited. The quality argument is presented for administrative personnel as well. The National Commission on Excellence in Education Administration (Griffiths, Stout, & Forsyth, 1988) reported that

> there are 505 institutions offering courses in school administration in the United States, but less than 200 have the resources and commitment to provide the excellence called for by the Commission. . . . Because it is concerned about the great number of individuals being prepared and licensed in programs with inadequate resources and little commitment to quality, the Commission recommends that the campuses prepare fewer—better (p. 36).

Due to both the demand for teachers in many subject matter areas and the demands for quality personnel in the classroom, the issue of alternative certification has gained momentum and has been implemented in various ways in the states. Wise and Darling-Hammond (1991) note that alternative routes to teacher certification have spread across the country like dandelions in a suburban yard. The idea is popular at both the federal and state levels . . . more than thirty states already have introduced initiatives under the rubric, although these initiatives are as different from one another as they are from any state's "regular certification route." (p. 56)

Bradley (1990b) reported that from 1985 to 1990, 33 states had certified an estimated 12,000 to teach through alternative certification programs that did not require prospective teachers to have graduated from approved teacher education programs. The crux of the pro and con arguments regarding alternative certification is that of quality personnel. Some of the arguments set forth by the proponents and opponents of the practice are presented in Table 2.4.

Issues in the area of teacher and administrator supply and demand and alternative certification programs pose critical problems for the human resources function. Further complications are revealed in such disparities as teacher shortages in some districts and reduction in force a phenomenon in others. In June 1991 lawmakers in New York approved early retirement incentives for some teachers in an effort to save the jobs of other teachers who were facing layoffs. California reported a shortage of 14,000 bilingual teachers with no indication that the situation would improve in the near future (Schmidt, 1991). Such incongruous situations add greatly to the difficulties and complexities facing personnel in human resources administration.

HUMAN RESOURCES ISSUE 8: DEVELOPMENTS IN AUTOMATION AND TECHNOLOGY

Automation and technological advancement have had a dramatic impact on industry. Technologies such as robots, laser scanners, ultrasonic probes, supersonic welding, and other innovations in computer utilization are revolutionizing practices in many fields. Robots are completing various repetitive tasks, and some jobs become obsolete as new technology comes into place. Some people forecast that robots ultimately will complete all routine tasks and that computer technology will replace jobs such as bookkeeping, drafting, and welding. In teleconferencing, software technologies and other computer systems have altered approaches to the traditional means of conferring with employees. As a result of these advancements and other automation and technology, several personnel problems have evolved. The implications for administering the human resources function are many. According to Knapp (1990),

We are seeing tremendous changes in the evolution of technology that will enable companies to deliver a broad array of benefits to employees. . . . From the end-user's point of view, the industry has evolved to deliver a growing spectrum of desk top applications. . . . Relational technology and advances in application functionability provide for dramatic increases in our ability to access and manage information. (pp. 56–57)

A new computer software program gaining favor among Fortune 500 companies such as AT&T and Apple Computer is one that scans thousands of application resumes, compares their contents with the qualifications needed for available jobs, and produces the best matches. Human resources specialists enter the picture when it is time for interviews. The system considers all resumes submitted, keeps them for as long as 2 years, and reconsiders all of them whenever job openings occur, even if candidates are not aware of the openings ("Resume Software," 1992, p. E3).

TABLE 2.4

Arguments For and Against Alternative Certification

Pro	Con
1. Traditional teacher education preparation programs are not producing quality personnel; alternatives are needed.	1. Proposed alternative routes to certification are attempts to circumvent standards that are essential for teaching quality.
2. Alternative certification helps solve the teacher shortage problem by allowing bright college graduates in other disciplines to teach.	2. Alternative certification programs are based on highly questionable standards; programs leading to various degree programs for the alternative certificate vary widely in credit requirements.
3. Existing certification criteria and processes impede the certification of qualified individuals.	3. Research supports the fact that teacher training results in better teaching performance and better student learning than when individuals do not possess such preparation.
4. Allowing individuals from areas such as business, industry, and other liberal arts specialties to teach serves to bring needed "relevance" to the currently outdated school curriculum.	4. Alternative certification is just an attempt to provide "temporary" work for graduates in the liberal arts and other fields until the time more lucrative job opportunities open for them in their specialty areas.
5. Local school districts are in a much better position to determine who should teach in their communities. Traditional certification procedures are outmoded; such decisions should be placed in the hands of local employers.	5. All teachers need to acquire an understanding of the students whom they teach as well as knowledge concerning how students learn and effective strategies for meeting all learners' needs. Alternative training programs unsuccessfully teach these skills in abbreviated "crash" courses. Education for the learner will not be improved by lessening standards for entry into the teaching profession.
6. The present results of student achievement testing are evidence enough that education must attract more capable individuals to the teaching profession. Alternative certification programs serve the specific purpose of increasing quality in teaching and improving learners' outcomes. The best teachers should have the opportunity to enter the marketplace.	6. Those individuals who are licensed through alternative certification programs and have no teaching experience are often assigned to teach the students who need the most experienced teachers.
7. Student performance in the areas of science, mathematics, foreign language, and others indicates that the present teaching of these subject areas is inferior. Persons who know science, mathematics, and foreign language are what is needed, not people who are trained in teaching methodology.	

Employees are concerned about the effects of automation and technological changes, specifically as they relate to job loss and reassignment to an automated job. Automated jobs tend to be low skilled, poorly compensated, monotonous, and socially isolated. Mental stress and health problems related to such work environments are paramount problems for human resources administration. *Cyberphobia*, fear of new technology, is a potential source of stress for some employees. New technology makes new demands upon the employee. Individuals often must prepare for new jobs, develop new skills, and work in ever-changing environments. In some cases social isolation becomes quite possible. Social contacts and relationships with supervisors and other employees often are altered drastically. Because information is most often available through computer technology, there is a decreasing need for traditional supervisor/employee meetings and one-to-one communication. In some instances, arrangements for employees to work at home reduce the face-to-face relationships of workers. Flextime job arrangements allow employees to begin and complete tasks as they wish as long as the jobs are satisfactorily finished within the time specified. As a result, employees may lose many of the more rewarding social interactions of work.

Because of these problems and concerns, human resources administration must be actively engaged in **sociotechnology**, the matching of mechanical and technical aspects with human aspects of the work environment. Sociotechnology focuses on the interrelationships of the social and technological systems of the organization and the relationship of the total organization to the environment in which it operates. Its purpose is to maximize both the social and the technological systems toward the needs of the whole organization and its subsystems. Thus human resources administration faces the challenge of making relationships between the social and technical subsystem compatible and productive. Because developing technologies in education affect employee relationships and create changes in structure within the school system, the human resources unit must be able to create unique program activities. As stated by Davis (1986), "The future is never what it is expected to be. Technological innovation abruptly destroys the present while creating the future" (p. 1).

Developing technologies in education, similar to changes required in industry, will necessitate role changes for many personnel. Human resources administrators must prepare to work effectively with such human factors as fear of change, reluctance toward retraining, and human motivation for continued productivity. More than merely providing training in new skill areas, human resources administrators must place additional emphasis on the human element to help employees adjust to required changes and to develop an understanding of new relationships in changing settings with changing co-workers. Such needs require changes in the roles of human resources administrators and other supervisory personnel at all levels in the organization. They must be prepared to deal with the possibility of anxiety, hostility, and resistance that often accompanies technological changes. Human resources personnel must function more closely with the technological aspects of the educational program. Finally, human resources administrators must understand clearly the cultural characteristics that the school system desires to promote. Shared values, beliefs, and stated incentives are forceful factors in helping the school achieve its purposes.

Only a few of the implications for human resources administration in relation to automation and technology have been mentioned. Many others, such as employee assistance programs, employee benefits, new job requirements, new definitions of authority and supervisor/employee relationships, employee participation in technological changes, and related sociotechnological considerations, have implications for effective human resources practices. Many of the considerations underlined by the issue of automation and technology in education are discussed in various chapters of this text. Chapter 13 focuses specifically on the use of technology in human resources administration.

Certainly not all of the issues and problems relating to human resources administration have been delineated here. Such matters as troubled staff, job sharing, preemployment testing, dismissal of incompetent staff, negotiations, staff morale, teacher apathy, absenteeism, problems of noncertificated personnel, employee performance evaluation, substitute teaching, image of education, multiculturalism, and others have not been fully explored. Nor have all the social and economic factors been presented that have influenced the school as a social system. The issues and problems presented in this chapter represent the major challenges and opportunities for leadership in the area of human resources administration. They underline the significance of human resources administration in education. Many of these issues serve as major topics in the remaining chapters.

SUMMARY

Because of education's inextricable tie to societal development, issues of society bear directly upon education and human resources practices. The issues facing the human resources function pose difficult challenges for school administrators.

The issue of school governance and leadership holds important implications for the human resources processes of planning, selection, staff assignment, and others. Human relationships and cooperation in education focus attention on the need for improved relations between school boards and staff members as well as renewed attention to the specific responsibilities of school boards, administrators, and staff personnel. Effective human performance in education continues to be an ongoing issue in education. There is little doubt that the matter of compensation will continue to be a primary issue in education during the 1990s. Although the problems related to compensation and benefits are difficult and complex, school administrators must assume a leadership role in the determination of better solutions to problems in this area. Demands upon school administrators and staff personnel in the name of accountability weigh heavily upon the human resources function as well. Work load, turnover, and stress undermine the need for quality performance in education. Problems relating to external requirements and mandates for education have had major impacts on all areas of education. Virtually every process of the human resources function has been influenced by the legal world of education. The projections for "new hire" teachers to the year 2000 indicate that the supply will fall far short of the need. Issues in the area of teacher and administrator supply and demand pose new problems in licensure of professional staff personnel and for quality education. Finally, the impact of automation and technological advancement on education generally will continue. Concerns about job loss, retraining, reassignment, and human relationships in work are ones that the human resources function must face and ultimately resolve.

DISCUSSION QUESTIONS

1. Several important issues facing human resources administration were identified in the chapter. Select a specific problem relating to one of the issues. Does the problem have a solution? What specific personnel actions would be helpful or necessary to find a solution?

2. Cetron and Gayle (1990) forecast that new systems of school governance and leadership will be explored in the 1990s that go beyond centralization and decentralization to, for instance, distribution of authority among government, teaching professionals, and families. Focus on the implications of "authority of families." What forms might such authority assume?

3. Assume that you have been asked to present a brief recommendation to the school board on the topic of effective human performance. Outline the major recommendations that you will present. Specifically, what three or four primary actions are needed to make a positive difference in human effectiveness in education?

CASE 2.1
Let's Ask George to Do It!

George Nelson had been a science teacher at Union High School for 4 years. He was approved for tenure status after his third year of teaching. George's performance evaluations ranged from good to excellent, and his work in the areas of professional and extracurricular activities was noteworthy. His evaluations during the first 3 years emphasized George's "cooperative attitude" and willingness to assume extra assignments. Among his extra duties were sponsor of the science club, member of the science curriculum committee, assistant basketball coach for the junior varsity team, and director of the science fair.

Principal Edwards and Assistant Principal Gomez were discussing the establishment of the new parental advisement committee. One

high school teacher was to be selected as a liaison with the committee. Even though a request for volunteers had been extended to the faculty, no one had offered to serve.

"We need a person who will take on this assignment without complaining," stated Mrs. Edwards.

"Let's ask George Nelson to do it," offered Assistant Principal Gomez.

Questions

1. First, discuss the implications of Case 2.1 relative to human resources practice. For example, what long-range problems might develop in relation to George Nelson's work performance?

2. How might objective data relating to teacher load be useful in the assignment of duties such as in the foregoing case?

☐ **CASE 2.2**
What's the Alternative?

The College View School District is located in a rural community that draws its students from five small towns. The district has been faced with shortages of teachers in such areas as mathematics, high school science, special education, and foreign language for several years. College View tends to lose its "best" teachers to the larger city school districts in the state. This year, courses and programs in Spanish, science, and special education had to be eliminated due to the district's inability to attract teachers in these areas.

The state department of education was to hold statewide hearings on alternative certification for teachers. The proposal under consideration would allow the certification of "teachers" through programs that did not require graduation from approved teacher-education programs. In brief, persons holding a bachelor's degree in an area such as mathematics could begin teaching in a regular classroom, but would be required to complete 12 semester hours of education courses or an approved equivalent within a period of 3 years.

The College View School Board favors the alternative plan.

Questions

1. Assume the role of Superintendent Valdez of the College View School District. The school board has asked for your opinions on the pending alternative certification for teachers. In view of the information stated in Case 2.2, what will be your recommendations?
2. Discuss the matter of teacher supply and demand in your region or state. What are the major disparities in teacher supply and demand (i.e., special areas of need, oversupply of teachers in teaching areas, quality vs. quantity, etc.)?

☐ **CASE 2.3**
The Big Bucks

Patrick Joseph had served as school principal at Lincoln High School for 6 years. His work on the salary committee was instrumental in the development of a proposal that, if approved, would give both teachers and administrators their largest salary increase in 6 years.

Principal Joseph's neighbor, Walter Crockett, was in the front yard as Patrick arrived home at 5:30 p.m. on Friday.

"Hi, Patrick," shouted Walter. "What are you guys going to do with all that money? I see in the paper that taxes will be going up again if those new salaries are approved for the school."

"I certainly hope our proposals are approved," answered Patrick. "Salaries for teachers and others in education are considerably lower than comparable fields."

"Yeah, but an average salary of $37,413 a year for teachers ain't bad," responded Walter, "and for only 9 months work. I wish I could make that in my print shop."

"In comparison to other professions, teachers and administrative personnel are below most all fields," said Patrick. "For example, what do you think the highest paid physician in the city might earn annually? Or, what do you think is the top salary of the highest paid lawyer in town?"

"I don't know," answered Walter. "The *highest* paid physician might earn $350,000 a year and the top lawyer, I'd guess, might be getting $250,000."

"Well, what do you think the highest paid educator in the city earns, the school superintendent?" asked Patrick.

"Gee, I don't know," responded Walter.

"He earns $97,402 a year and runs the biggest business in the entire city," said Patrick.

"$97,402 a year! Wow! I had no idea he earned that kind of money," said Walter. "And what's his raise going to be next year? No wonder our taxes are skyrocketing."

Questions

1. Give your reactions to the case. Is Walter Crockett's reaction to salaries for educators typical?

2. Why do you believe that most polls reveal that the general public views teachers' salaries as adequate or "about right"?

REFERENCES

Bloss, J. M. (1882). *Thirtieth report of the superintendent of public instruction of the state of Indiana to the governor*. Indianapolis: State of Indiana.

Bradley, A. (1991, March 27). Washington state teachers support 'multilocal' strike. *Education Week*, p. 5.

Bradley, A. (1990a, October 3). Rochester teachers reject 'accountability' contract. *Education Week*, p. 4.

Bradley, A. (1990b, September 19). Even as gaps in data are filled, teacher supply debate lingers. *Education Week*, p. 14.

Cetron, M. J., & Gayle, M. E. (1991). Seventy-five trends in education. *Educational Renaissance* (pp. 221–238). New York: St. Martin's Press.

Currence, C. (1984, August 29). Shanker urges A.F.T. to move against incompetent teachers. *Education Week*, p. 1.

Davis, D. D. (1986). Technological innovation and organizational change. In D. D. Davis & Associates, *Managing Technological Innovation* (pp. 1–22). San Francisco: Jossey-Bass.

Diegmueller, K. (1991, April 17). Tight budgets escalate school labor tensions. *Education Week*, p. 14.

Elam, S. M., Rose, L. C., & Gallup, A. M. (1991). The 23rd annual Gallup Poll of the public's attitudes toward the public schools. *Phi Delta Kappan*, 73(1), 41–56.

Elam, S. M., Rose, L. C., & Gallup, A. M. (1992). The 24th annual Gallup/Phi Delta Kappa Poll of the public's attitudes toward the public schools. *Phi Delta Kappan*, 74, 41–53.

Gibson, R. O., & Hunt, H. C. (1965). *The school personnel administrator*. Boston: Houghton-Mifflin.

Glass, T. E. (1992). *The study of the American school superintendency*. Arlington, VA: American Association of School Administrators.

Griffiths, D. E., Stout, R. T., & Forsyth, P. B. (Eds.). (1988). *Leaders for America's schools: The report and papers of the National Commission on Excellence in Educational Administration*. Berkeley, CA: McCutchan.

Haggart, B. (1990). Who is at risk—students or teachers? *Thrust*, 19(5), 42–44.

International Foundation of Employee Benefit Plans. (1991, September 11). Employee-benefit plans. *Education Week*, p. 3.

Knapp, J. (1990). Trends in HR management. *Personnel*, 67(4), 56–57.

Kovach, K. A., & Pearce, J. A., III. (1990). HR strategic mandates for the 1990s. *Personnel*, 67(4), 52.

Lunenburg, F. C., & Ornstein, A. C. (1991). *Educational administration—Concepts and practices*. Belmont, CA: Wadsworth.

Luthans, F., & Davis, E. (1990). The health care cost crisis: Causes and containment. *Personnel*, 67(2), 24–31.

McCarthy, M. M., & Cambron-McCabe, N. H. (1992). *Public school law—Teachers' and students' rights* (3rd ed.). Needham Heights, MA: Allyn & Bacon.

National Education Association. (1991, September). The 1991–92 resolutions of the National Education Association. *NEA Today*, 10(1), 15–25.

Norton, M. S. (1989). *The personnel administrator in Arizona—A research study*. Tempe: Arizona State University, Division of Educational Leadership and Policy Studies.

Norton, M. S. (1991). *The school superintendency in Arizona—A research study*. Tempe: Arizona State University, Division of Educational Leadership and Policy Studies.

Resume software offers high-tech way to get job. (1992, March 10). *The Arizona Republic*, p. E3.

Schmidt, P. (1991, June 19). California is short 14,000 bilingual teachers, panel finds. *Education Week*, p. 14.

School spending slows. (1992, April 9). *The Arizona Republic*, p. CL11.

Sokoloff, H. J., & Lazerson, M. (1990, October 3). When reform meets recession. *Education Week*, p. 26.

U.S. Chamber of Commerce. (1991). *Employee benefits 1990*. Washington, DC: Author.

U.S. Department of Education. Office of Educational Research and Improvement. National Center for Education Statistics. (1989). *Projections of education statistics to 2000*. Washington, DC: GPO.

Wise, A. E., & Darling-Hammond, L. (1991, September 4). Alternative certification is an oxymoron. *Education Week*, p. 56.

3

The Human Resources Function—Organization and Processes

Chapter 2 presented various contemporary issues that have a direct impact upon the human resources function. These issues and related problems have specific implications for the work of the human resources unit and school administrators throughout the school system. Some require establishing new procedures; others demand that administrators assume new responsibilities and develop additional competencies to remain effective in their role. Each issue serves to underline the paramount importance of the human resources function in education—the realization that its effectiveness is essential to the achievement of school purposes.

This chapter examines the human resources function in education from several perspectives. First, what is the nature of the human resources function? What are its primary purposes? What are the major processes that comprise the human resources function and who implements these processes in the school setting? The next section focuses on the organization and specific tasks of the central human resources unit and answers these questions. What is the work of the central human resources unit? What is its relationship with the total system?

One section examines the concept of competency as it relates to effective performance of human resources administrators. What is the difference between the administrator who is performing effectively from a competency point of view and one who is not? Next the position analysis and position description for the central unit human resources director are discussed. Finally, the specific nature of the problems encountered by human resources administrators and the opportunities of human resources administrators to make positive differences in the school system are discussed. In this section the ethics and standards that guide professional practices in this field also are examined.

WHAT IS HUMAN RESOURCES ADMINISTRATION?

Based upon the realization that successful, effective schools depend directly upon the success and effectiveness of those who work in them, we believe that human resources administration is the most important function in education. The quality of education programs in large part depends upon (1) the quality of the human resources within the system; (2) the extent to which productive human relationships are realized; and (3) the development, motivation, and utilization of existing human qualities. Whereas a positive organizational climate depends upon a variety of factors, the human resources function assumes a major responsibility for providing a high quality of work life in the school system by focusing upon the goals of the system in relation to its human resources.

One of the earliest definitions of personnel administration was presented by Tead and Metcalf (1920). These writers defined personnel administration as "the direction and coordination of the human relations of any organization with a view to getting the maximum necessary production with a minimum of effort and friction, and with proper regard for the genuine well being of the workers" (p. 2). Tead and Metcalf's text, *Personnel Administration, Its Principles and Practices*, was one of the first works devoted exclusively to personnel. Its publication in 1920 came at the time scientific management was waning. The authors' (1920) following statement exemplifies early attitudes related to the new movement in human relations:

> The new focus in administration is to be the human element. The new center of attention and solicitude is the individual person, the worker. And this change comes about fundamentally for no sentimental reasons, but because the enlistment of human cooperation, of the interest and goodwill of the workers, has become the crux of the production problem. (p. 1)

Stahl's (1962) succinct definition stated that "personnel administration is the totality of concern with the human resources of the organization" (p. 15). In 1964 Van Zwoll stated that

> personnel administration is the complex of specific activities distinctly engaged in by the employing agency (school district, other unit of government, or business enterprise) to make a pointed effort to secure the greatest possible worker effectiveness consistent with the agency's objectives. (p. 3)

The complex of activities is that aspect of Gulick's POSDCoRB paradigm concerned with staffing activities. Thus, according to Van Zwoll, the staffing considerations related to the administration tasks of planning, organizing, staffing, directing, coordinating, reporting, and budgeting are concerns of the human resources function.

More contemporary definitions of the human resources function are those set forth by Rebore (1991) and Castetter (1992), although their definitions are stipulated in terms of goals. Rebore (1991) stated that

> the goals of the personnel function are basically the same in all school systems—to hire, retain, develop, and motivate personnel in order to achieve the objectives of the school district, to assist individual members of the staff to reach the highest possible levels of achievement, and to maximize the career development of personnel. (p. 11)

Castetter's definition closely resembles that of Rebore. According to Castetter (1992),

> The goals of the personnel function in any educational system are to attract, develop, retain, and motivate personnel in order to (a) achieve the system's purposes; (b) assist members in satisfying position and group performance standards; (c) maximize personnel career development; and (d) reconcile individual and organizational objectives. (p. 5)

All of the foregoing definitions express the comprehensiveness of the human resources function in education as well as the basic concept that "schools are people." People, therefore, are a primary concern of human resources administration.

For the purposes of this text, **human resources administration** is defined as those processes that are planned and implemented in the organization to establish an effective system of human resources and to foster an organizational climate that enhances the accomplishment of educational goals. This view emphasizes human resources administration as a foundational function for an effective educational program. The primary elements of the human resources processes, implied in the definition, are recruiting, selecting, and developing staff, as well as the need for establishing a harmonious working relationship among personnel. Although this definition emphasizes the significance of the human element, it also states that the purpose of human resources administration is focused on achieving the goals and objectives of the system. This focus includes a major concern for developing a healthy organizational climate that serves toward the accomplishment of school goals and the meeting of the personal needs of the school's employees.

THE HUMAN RESOURCES PROCESSES

The several processes of the human resources function and their relationships are illustrated in Figure 3.1. These 12 processes within the human resources function are shown as subsets of three major components. **Human resources utilization**, for example, is a comprehensive component that encompasses the processes of planning, recruitment, selection, orientation, assignment, collective negotiations, compensation and welfare, and stability. **Human resources development** includes the processes of staff development and evaluation. The **human resources environment** component includes the processes of organizational culture and protection. Each of the processes is interrelated in that its effectiveness depends directly or indirectly upon the effectiveness of the others. Human resources planning ties closely to recruitment, selection, assignment, compensation, and other processes. As part of planning, forecasts of human needs provide the focus for the implementation of the recruitment process, the selection of specific personnel, directions for personnel assignments, and the monetary considerations of budget and compensation. Effective human resources and the successful achievement of school goals, as illustrated in Figure 3.1, are founded on the concept of personal competency of the system's personnel.

Each of the processes of the human resources function is described briefly in the following sections and in detail later in the text.

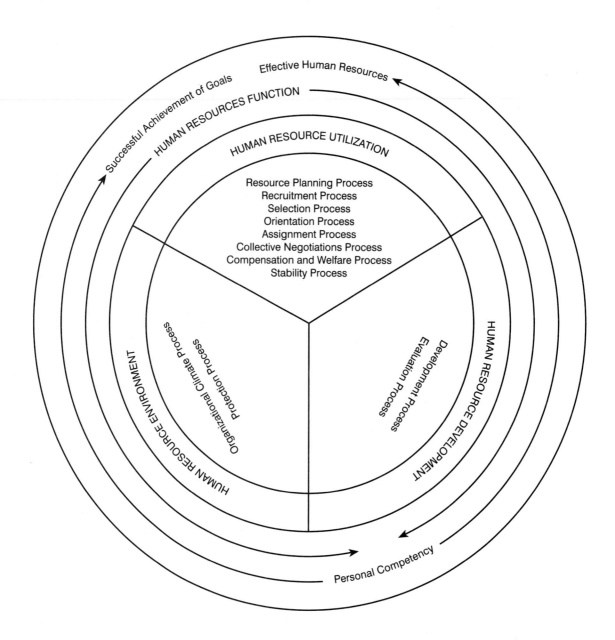

FIGURE 3.1

The Personnel Processes and Human Resources Relationships

Processes of Human Resources Utilization

Resources Planning.   How does the school system determine its direction and priorities? What kinds of data and information are essential for the successful completion of the human resources tasks and responsibilities? The resources planning process serves in answering these questions. The purposes of resources planning are (1) to clarify the objectives and mission of the organization; (2) to determine in advance what the organization and its parts are to do; and (3) to ascertain the assets on hand and the required resources for accomplishing the desired results. Effective resources planning is essential in helping the school system determine what it wants to be and provides a blueprint for guiding action. Such a process is essential to avoid guesswork and happenstance, to offset uncertainty, and to ensure efficient accomplishment of goals. Planning constitutes a purposeful set of activities that focuses available resources upon the achievement of school goals.

Planning is not synonymous with the plan. A plan is a product of the planning process. Planning, on the other hand, is a continuous, ongoing process characterized by flexibility and subject to change. Effective planning forms a foundation for decision making. It encourages responsive administration and capitalizes on employee talents by establishing goals that elicit the most effective performance from individuals in the organization. Planning is a comprehensive, continuous process that must remain flexible and responsive to changing conditions. Activities within the human resources planning process include developing planning assumptions, determining organizational relationships and structures, completing inventories of need, making assessments of labor markets, developing forecasts of resource needs, completing projections of student populations, participating in policy development, completing position analyses and position descriptions, and evaluation of the process's effectiveness. The human resources planning process is developed in detail in Chapter 4.

Recruitment of Personnel.   How can highly qualified individuals be attracted to the school system for consideration of possible employment? The purpose of the recruitment process is to establish a "pool" of qualified candidates to meet the needs of the school system. It focuses on strategies for attracting the best qualified persons for the specific positions available. The amount of recruitment necessary depends on such factors as enrollment growth and decline, staff turnover, and program design. Recruitment is not only a primary responsibility of the human resources function but, when coupled with the selection process, is considered by many practitioners as the most time-consuming responsibility. Human resources directors in one state named recruitment and selection processes as using up the greatest amount of their time (Norton, 1989); 70% of the directors so responded.

In view of the forecasts of teacher shortages through the 1990s, the recruitment of talented personnel assumes an ever increasing role of importance. Shortages increase the competition for quality personnel and make an effective recruitment program even more necessary. New talent resources must be identified and tapped. The recruitment process begins by establishing policy guidelines during the planning process that direct such specific activities as developing recruitment resources, implementing application procedures, establishing formal interview and evaluation procedures, and designing appropriate staff involvement strategies for each of these activities.

Although the process of recruitment is one shared by the central human resources unit and personnel in other units of the system, it is administered primarily by the central unit. A major question facing the human resources function presently is related to the reform/restructuring issue discussed in Chapter 2. As site-based management is implemented within local school districts, the responsibility for recruitment likely will be shifted more to local schools. Chapters 6 and 12 consider the recruitment process in detail, as related to both professional and support staff personnel.

Selection of Personnel.   How does the school system determine the best person for a specific position? Does selection depend primarily on individual perceptions of an applicant's qualifications or are there "tools" that lead to staff selection on a more scientific basis? Selecting the right person for the right job is a basic responsibility of effective human resources administration. Many potential administrative and staff problems of a school system can be avoided through an effective selection process. In addition, effective personnel selection serves to reduce the major costs related to the retraining of inadequately prepared employees. When asked to cite their most important task, human resources administrators most often mention "the selection of personnel." Selection necessitates attention to matters other than merely filling vacancies. Although placing the right person in the right job is a primary objective, such considerations as staff load, staff balance, and staff diversity are significant. Background checks and investigations are important activities of the screening process. Fingerprinting and searches of applicants for prior criminal convictions or other unethical practices are commonplace.

Selection often is carried out under complex and confusing conditions. For example, reduction in force and hiring of personnel in special areas might be necessary in the same school district. A reduction in force (RIF) in spring followed by rehiring in the following summer is not an unusual procedure for many school districts. The hiring of individuals in alternative certification programs seems necessary in shortage areas, but is nevertheless a controversial practice.

Interviewing, legal compliance, screening, evaluation, and selection decisions are important activities of the human resources selection process. The selection process is discussed in detail in Chapters 6 and 12.

Orientation of Personnel.   How are personnel introduced into the school setting and how important are such orientation activities to the system and the individual employee? Orientation often is given such labels as ***induction***, ***introduction of employees***, ***preservice programs***, or ***staff development***. We define ***orientation*** as the complex of activities designed to gain congruence between institutional objectives and employee needs. It begins with the job application and continues on an ongoing basis for as long as the employee or the organization views it as necessary. Thus, the orientation process assumes a comprehensive perspective as opposed to the traditional practice of scheduling one or two days of informational sessions for employees at the outset of a school year.

Orientation activities have gained added attention and importance in view of research results. Studies have underlined the importance of planned orientation activities during the early years of service because beginning teachers and other employees need help with special problems. Orientation activities are the important links between recruitment, selection, and staff development. Chapter 8 includes a comprehensive consideration of orientation and its relationships with other human resources processes.

Assignment of Personnel. How are personnel assigned so that their personal talents and interests optimally serve the system and their own self-development? Traditionally, assignment of personnel has centered on the match between personnel and positions, or placing the right person in the right job. Effective employee assignment, of course, is instrumental in assuring the effectiveness of individuals to achieve the organization's goals. The placement of individuals in positions that best suit their individual competencies and interests remains a primary consideration of staff assignment. Today a more comprehensive view of assignment regards it as the complex of activities related to the talents and interest of the employee and the environment in which the work takes place. Thus, deployment of talent in the best interests of the system, the employee, and the student; conditions of work including work load; effective staff supervision; staff improvement practices; organizational climate; and evaluation methods all relate to the effective utilization of personnel.

Proper assignment includes more than matching position and qualifications. Other significant factors such as the teacher's work load must be considered. With the exception of class size, teacher assignments have given little attention to teacher load factors. Other important factors in the teacher's work load include the number of subjects and levels taught, length of class periods, the number of class preparations required, and related cooperative or extracurricular assignments. Although teacher load is only one consideration within the assignment process, it illustrates the need for cooperative efforts among administrative personnel in the school system. Chapter 8 provides a more detailed discussion of the assignment process and other important activities related to the utilization of human resources.

Collective Negotiations. How do employee groups and employers in school systems decide on matters of salary, working conditions, and other contractual matters? How are negotiation teams formed and how are negotiations carried out? The negotiations process has become the primary procedure whereby boards of education and representatives of employee groups decide such matters. In the opinion of many, no other development in education has had more impact upon the human resources function than the advent of collective negotiations. Although the methods for collective negotiations differ among the various states and their actual impact varies widely, the process has penetrated virtually every human resources activity. Negotiations consume a significant part of the human resources director's time. In addition, negotiations often is named as one of the leading problems facing personnel directors. Research studies reveal that the human resources director serves frequently as the chief spokesperson for the school board's negotiation team and is also involved in a major way in such activities as negotiation planning and proposal development, strategy sessions, and implementation of the agreement.

The matter of scope of negotiations and what is negotiable is changing. In 1991, "the Oregon Court of Appeals ruled that proposals on class size must be negotiated between a school district and a teachers' union" ("Class Size," p. 2). Under state law, the court ruled, class size is pertinent to "conditions of employment" and thus is included on the list of items to be negotiated during contract talks." The court went on to say that "substantial evidence supports the finding that the [class size] proposal significantly affects workload . . . it determines the number of parent-teacher conferences, the number of papers to be graded, and the hours spent on assistance to individual students" (p. 2). Heretofore class size was considered a matter within the jurisdiction of the governing board.

For various reasons, including difficult economic times, more problem-solving approaches to collective negotiations have been implemented. Often termed **win-win bargaining**, these integrative approaches are designed to achieve agreement between the two parties and at the same time make both parties "feel good" about the agreement and one another. Chapter 10 is devoted to the collective negotiations process. It examines both win-win and distributive negotiation approaches.

Compensation and Welfare of Personnel.   What factors determine the levels of compensation for professional and support personnel in the school system? What are the various kinds of compensation and benefits received by employees? The compensation of personnel constitutes by far the largest general fund expenditure of any school system; compensation comprises approximately 90% of most general fund budgets. The compensation and welfare process encompasses the considerations of contract salary agreements, fringe benefits, and other rewards and incentives, sometimes termed *psychic income*. The human resources unit in most school districts assumes major responsibility for administering these activities, and their impact upon related personnel processes is significant. As was indicated in Chapter 2, the issue of adequate compensation for personnel in education historically has been a leading concern. Its importance to the human resources function is self-evident; compensation plays a primary role in attracting highly qualified personnel to positions in education and retaining their services.

During the first half of the 1980s, there was significant activity in the area of personnel compensation. Local, state, and federal officials, concerned with educational quality, proclaimed that the status of professional staff salaries in education was unacceptable and ineffective in attracting and retaining high-quality personnel. In addition, quality performance was a major concern. As a result, new approaches to personnel compensation emerged and many were adopted by school districts. The concept of incentive pay, for example, included such pay programs as career ladders, master teacher pay, mentoring, effective schools, forgivable loans, merit school financing, and others. Legislation was enacted by the U.S. House of Representatives to provide additional financial incentives to lure top students into teaching, and many states enacted a higher level of financial support for education. In some instances, states approved special funding for scholarships in areas of teacher shortages. In the late 1980s and early 1990s, generally due to economics, the external "push" for higher salaries in education waned. And, as noted in the previous chapter, average entry salaries of classroom teachers continued to fall below those of graduates in other fields who entered the world of work.

An increasing demand upon the human resources unit is that of administration of the employee benefits program. This responsibility was named fifth among all listings for consuming the greatest amount of time by human resource directors in one statewide study (Norton, 1989). Additionally, the directors named adequate financing, budget/finances, compensation, and employee benefits in the list of the 10 most serious problems facing them. Compensation and welfare are considered in Chapter 11 and Chapter 12. Chapter 12 discusses compensation for support personnel.

Stability of Personnel Services.   How does the school system maintain a viable work force over a long period of time? What conditions and programs serve toward the stability of the school system and what conditions militate against the continuation of high-level service? Once the human resources function secures the personnel for the system, the responsibility for maintaining an effective work force to ensure continuous, high-level service becomes vitally important. Although stability encompasses a wide variety of program provisions, Castetter (1992) points out that such personnel considerations include two clusters of activities: "One group is concerned with the health, safety, and mobility of continuing personnel; the second is focused on members who are voluntarily or involuntarily leaving the system" (p. 473). These clusters include teacher and staff absences, substitutes to replace them, health and safety services, personal counseling, record maintenance, separation of employees from the system, and provisions that keep the system viably staffed. Thus the process of maintaining a stable work force has gained increased attention in the last decade. Teacher absences and scarcity of qualified substitutes are common problems in many school districts. The problems of quality and quantity continue to face the substitute teaching program in schools. In addition, an estimated 10–20% of the labor force utilizes mental and other health service counseling annually (Holoviak & Holoviak, 1984). In a national study, Norton (1988) found that 46 of 91 school districts had implemented some form of an employee assistance program to work with troubled employees. Thus personal counseling has become an essential activity of the stability process. In fact, a study in one state revealed that personal problem counseling of employees concerning family problems, grievances, personal crises, and others was second only to recruitment and selection in the amount of time devoted to it (Norton, 1989).

The array of activities that comprise the stability process is comprehensive and complex indeed. Technological advances have eased the burden of activities such as record keeping, which at one time was the most time-consuming activity of the human resources function. Computer technology has not only reduced the need for completing and filing most records by hand, it also has improved immeasurably the utilization and information value of these records. The growing concern for employee health has led to a new emphasis on wellness programs. Too, extended programs such as child care are predicated in part on the realization that employees' concerns for their children during working hours can serve as an inhibitor to effective work production.

Processes of Human Resources Development

Development of Human Resources.   What do organizations do to motivate employees to improve personal competency? What personal growth programs tend to be most productive for the system and for the individual? The fact that schools will progress as their personnel are motivated to achieve personal and professional growth has direct implications for human resources administration. Clearly, effective school programs are dependent upon the extent to which employees continue to grow and develop. Professional development activities are the primary means for helping personnel to reach their potential. As noted by Tyler in the early 1970s, "In-service education of the future will not be seen as 'shaping' teachers but rather will be viewed as aiding, supporting, and encouraging each teacher's development of teaching capabilities that he values and seeks to enhance" (1971, p. 15). Some writers, however, have attempted to differentiate terms such as *development*, *training*, and *education* (Nadler, 1974). The terms **staff development**, **in-service training**, **professional growth**, **continuing education**, **self-renewal**, and others often are utilized interchangeably in education. Differentiation between such terms can be useful. Harris (1989) makes such a useful distinction in his definition of the term **staff development**. He notes that "one aspect of staff development is . . . referred to as 'staffing' because it involves an array of endeavors that determines who serves, where, and when" (p. 21). The other side of staff development, according to Harris, includes in-service education and advanced preparation. **In-service education** involves any planned program offered staff members for purposes of improving the personal performances of individuals in the system. **Advanced preparation** differs from in-service in that it focuses on future needs. Reassignment, promotion, and the need for new skills resulting from organizational expansion programs are examples of the focus for advanced preparation approaches.

Staff development is often a shared responsibility by several units in an educational system; however, human resources directors are involved specifically in in-service training, internship programs, student-teacher programs, mentoring, and external training support programs. The human resources development process, and the responsibilities of all administrators who supervise personnel, have expanded significantly. Performance assessment centers, administrator academies and cadre programs, special mentoring programs, clinical supervision, peer-assisted leadership programs, local school district internship programs in teaching and administration, cooperative training programs between local school districts and institutions of higher education, and fifth-year teacher certification programs represent a few examples of such recent expansions.

The establishment of staff development policies, the determination of growth needs, and the implementation of special development programs are activities that concern all school administrators. Staff development and the concern for the maximization of human resources in the school system are presented in Chapter 8.

Appraisal of Personnel.   What purposes are served through personnel performance appraisal programs? Who benefits? What constitutes an effective personnel appraisal process? Although the instructional unit of the school system continues to assume the primary responsibility for the formal appraisal of the professional teaching staff, the human resources unit has assumed a major role in developing appraisal policy, monitoring the general process of appraisal, and maintaining the appraisal records completed by other units. Thus formal personnel appraisal is a shared responsibility—one that has assumed increasing importance in education. The level of involvement of human resources directors in appraisal activities ranges from complete responsibility to little or none at all.

Without question, the appraisal of personnel is a major concern in education. In 1984 a study entitled "Teacher Evaluation: A Study of Effective Practices" was conducted by the Rand Corporation and supported by the National Institute of Education. The study asserted that "teacher evaluation presently is an underconceptualized and underdeveloped activity" (Toch, 1984, p. 7). The report concluded that most schools lacked evaluation systems effective enough for introducing innovative personnel practices, and the researchers agreed that too often school principals lacked the qualifications to evaluate teachers effectively. As a result of these conditions, most states mandated programs for the purpose of certifying "qualified evaluators" in school systems. In brief, such state mandates directed school systems to present evidence that viable personnel evaluation programs were in place and that provisions for certifying evaluators for these programs had been implemented. Yet, in the early 1990s, litigation of cases in the area of personnel evaluation led the court cases under consideration in many states. Thus the quality of employee evaluation procedures holds legal implications for schools as well.

The need for improvement of appraisal policy and procedures, the continued push for personnel accountability and effective schooling, and competency-based performance concepts forecast the continued importance of the evaluation process. Chapter 7 considers this human resources process in detail.

Processes of the Human Resources Environment

Development of the Organizational Climate. What do school systems do to foster a healthy working environment for employees? How can the school become a better place to work? What affect does organizational climate have on employee performance? The complex of personal and organizational relationships within the schools necessarily is a concern of the human resources function. **Organizational climate** is defined as the collective personality of a school or school system. It is the atmosphere that prevails in an organization and is characterized by the social and professional interactions of the people.

The concept of **organizational culture** has become a significant force in educational thought. As stated by Bates (1984), "Organizations are cultures rather than structures and it is the maintenance and contestation of what is to constitute the culture of organizational life that provides the dynamic of rationality, legitimation, and motivation in organizations" (p. 262). Although the concept of organizational culture differs among authorities, most agree that schools and school systems, like other organizations, develop personalities of their own. As a person has a personality, a group is said to have a **syntality** that reflects its traditions, beliefs, values, and visions. School administrators need to understand the organization's culture in order to help it become what it can become. The school administrator must be knowledgeable about the beliefs and patterns of the organization; communication, influence, motivation, and other factors depend on such understanding. Additionally, the administrator must have the competencies needed to assess existing climates and understand the theories and practices associated with fostering positive environments to develop harmonious and productive working relationships among employees in the system. Chapter 8 discusses employee motivation concepts.

Protection of Personnel.   How are school employees protected from unfair treatment and physical harm? What are the **liberty rights** and **property rights** of school personnel? The human resources protection process has been receiving increasing attention because of such issues as employee rights and security. These issues have brought about major changes in school districts' policies and procedures in such matters as tenure, employee grievances, due process, academic freedom, and capricious treatment. Lessening personal employee anxiety and forecasting a more positive work climate have always been objectives of effective human resources administration. These concerns associated with personnel protection, however, have broadened in scope and are now reflected in virtually every process of the human resources function. Protection concerns include grievance procedures, transfers, dismissals, separation, liability protection, RIF, promotions, employee discipline, and tenure decisions.

A growing area of the protection process is that of security from bodily harm. Incidences of attacks on teachers, administrators, and other school personnel are growing problems for school districts nationally. The responsibility for maintaining a safe, healthy, and secure school environment is basic to the human resources protection process. Legal considerations are discussed in Chapter 9.

These 12 major human resources processes constitute the central focus of the human resources function in education. The central human resources unit, discussed in the following section, has assumed a significant leadership role in most school districts. Evolving governance structures, exemplified by site-based management, potentially could alter substantially the organization and operation of the central unit. We believe that the centralized administration of the human resources function will continue in the 1990s, although the sharing of the activities related to various human resources processes will be extended; greater authority in such matters as teacher selection, assignment, evaluation, development, and organizational climate will be found at the local school level under the leadership of the school principal.

THE CENTRAL HUMAN RESOURCES UNIT

Each of the major human resources processes relates directly or indirectly to virtually every other function in the educational enterprise, making the human resources function a shared responsibility. The responsibility for a personnel task or activity frequently is assumed in part by units other than the central human resources unit. For example, the central human resources unit often assumes responsibility for supervising such activities as position analysis and position descriptions, but the responsibility for hiring generally is shared with the instructional unit, local school administrators and staff, and other system personnel.

It has been noted throughout the discussions in Chapter 1 and this chapter that new governance movements portend considerations for change in the operations of the central human resources unit. And although we view the central human resources unit in school systems as the keystone to an effective personnel program, we fully support the contention that every school administrator and/or supervisor is a "director" of human resources. Neglect of the human resources processes at any level in the organization ultimately militates against the successful completion of the school system's mission. In the following section, the organization, responsibilities, and guiding ethics and standards of the central resources unit are discussed.

The American Association of School Personnel Administrators (AASPA) was first established in 1959, although it evolved from the Conference of Teacher Examiners that organized in 1940 to improve the qualifications and selection of teachers for America's schools (AASPA, 1988). It can be safely estimated that there are presently 2,250 directors of personnel serving in school districts nationally. Although **personnel director** is the most common title for the central unit's human resources administrator, less than one-half of these administrators hold that title. Other position titles for central unit administrators are **assistant superintendent for personnel, personnel specialist, supervisor of personnel**, and **personnel administrative assistant**, with the title of **director of human resources** becoming increasingly popular.

A study of personnel directors in one state (Norton, 1989) found that

1. their average age was 47 years;
2. 80% were caucasian;
3. nearly one-third held the doctoral degree;
4. the mean time of service in the present position was 5.5 years; nearly 50% had served in their present position for 3 years or less;
5. 60% were male;
6. nearly 89% viewed their position as "increasing in importance and influence";
7. job stress was "high" or "very high" in the role;
8. directors enjoyed the role "most all of the time";
9. 20 different position titles were held by the directors;
10. personnel records, recruitment, policy and regulation development, substitute teacher coordination, collective bargaining, and personnel benefits were their leading responsibilities;
11. 80% served on the board's negotiating team;
12. directors were spending 46.5 hours on the job weekly;
13. work load and the lack of understanding of others of the role of the personnel office were the two leading inhibitors of their personal effectiveness. (pp. 40–45)

Organization of the Central Unit

Organizational arrangements for administering human resources vary widely. In some instances, school districts delegate various personnel responsibilities among administrators throughout the system; place the responsibilities under the jurisdiction of the superintendent and/or an assistant superintendent; perform them using an administrative team headed by a general administrative officer of the school district;

or place the major human resources function within the office of a line administrator, such as an assistant superintendent, or a staff administrator, such as a personnel director or specialist.

Figure 3.2 illustrates a traditional line and staff organizational arrangement for a school district. The term **line administrator** refers to school officers in the hierarchical line of authority. A **staff administrator** is one who is not in the direct line of authority and whose position is created expressly to serve the major line functions of the organization. Thus staff positions are considered to be advisory and supportive. On a national scale, human resources administrators most often view themselves as staff administrators, although exceptions are numerous. The solid lines in Figure 3.2 indicate authority relationships. For example, the assistant superintendent for instruction, the assistant superintendent for business affairs, and the human resources director are subordinate to and supervised by the deputy superintendent. Dashed lines indicate informal working relationships.

Organizational charts illustrate the relationships of the human resources unit within a school system. Variations in practices and arrangements make it impossible to construct an organizational plan that is applicable to all schools. Most studies reveal that practicing human resources directors hold major professional responsibilities in addition to personnel administration. Such areas of responsibility include building/grounds/custodial services, business/purchasing/payroll services, pupil personnel services, curriculum/instruction, general administration services, transportation, and federal/state grants and programs. School district size, educational philosophy, financial ability, and other such factors influence structural arrangements of the school system as well. Data are not available for determining a correlation between the size of a school district's enrollment or staff and the existence of a central human resources administrator; there is no cutoff for such a position relative to school district size. Some schools with fewer than 1,000 students have a central human resources administrator; other much larger districts distribute personnel responsibilities among various units within the system.

Site-based Governance Structures

Such developments as restructuring, site-based management, and reform have been mentioned in previous discussions. The movement of responsibilities of many of the human resources processes to local schools is a reality in many school districts. Such developments are surrounded with much controversy; little data are available regarding the success of such restructuring. One view of the popularity of restructuring is given by Carnoy (1990): "For a public demanding educational improvement, any reform that looks promising is immediately attractive" (p. 32). He states further that

> restructuring is highly consistent with American values of decentralization, individual initiative, and individual responsibility, where "individual" in this case is the principal, the teacher, or the school team. It is a properly anti-bureaucratic idea that meets today's feeling about bigness and bureaucracy. (p. 32)

Carnoy underlines a major problem relating to restructuring: It places severe demands on an already precious resource—teacher time. "It is not surprising that most teachers and principals are leery of . . . reform, and many of those who have

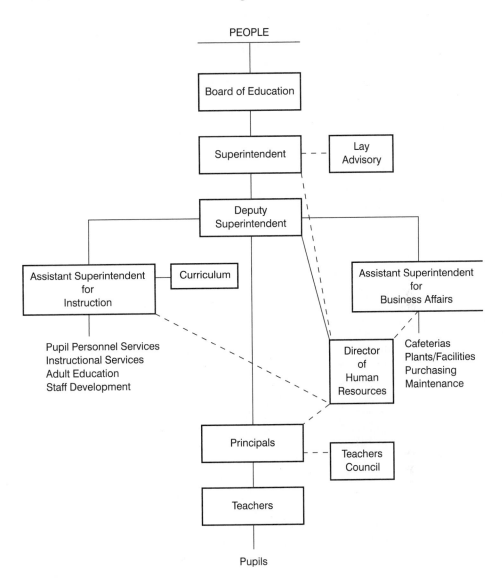

FIGURE 3.2
Line and Staff Organization for a School District

bought in are verging on burning out" (p. 24). Other pro and con arguments concerning decentralization are presented in a later section.

Figure 3.3 illustrates the interrelationship of units and resource groups within the traditional school structure to the central human resources unit. Each individual unit or group has an effect upon the ability of the others to reach their objectives. The success of the human resources unit in realizing its mission also depends upon the support of others. Similarly, the success of each unit or group depends in part on the effectiveness of the central unit. In this sense, the human resources unit is a part of the school district's systems management.

FIGURE 3.3
The Central Human Resources
Unit and Interrelated Units
and Agencies

New organizational structures for administering the human resources function
in schools are still evolving. The optimal model regarding the decentralizing of the
human resources processes has yet to be established. Figure 3.4 conceptualizes one
possible organizational arrangement that emphasizes decentralization of the human
resources function. Similar to traditional organization, schools in the decentralized
organizational arrangement still report to a deputy/assistant superintendent or
superintendent. The traditional human resources unit, however, moves to the central
advisory services unit that also is responsible to the deputy/assistant superintendent
or superintendent. The central advisory services unit holds a staff relationship with
local schools and provides consultative services in such areas as human resources
development, instructional services, and business/facility services. In such a decentralized arrangement, the central advisory unit services personnel work cooperatively
with individual schools in the determination of specific tasks that will be performed by
each: the assignment of responsibility for the various kinds of decisions encountered;
the identification of authority for various procedural/action approvals; and the establishment of appropriate communication channels for information dissemination.

It must be remembered that neither decentralization nor centralization is good
or bad within itself. And, as has been noted by Fayol (1984), "Everything which goes
to increase the importance of the subordinate's role is decentralization; everything
that serves to reduce it is centralization" (p. 74).

COMPETENCY-PERFORMANCE CONCEPTS

A **task** is a specific responsibility, obligation, or requirement associated with a professional position or function. Each of the human resources processes discussed earlier includes numerous tasks that require specific competencies. **Competency** refers
to the ability to accomplish a task at a satisfactory level of performance. To be com-

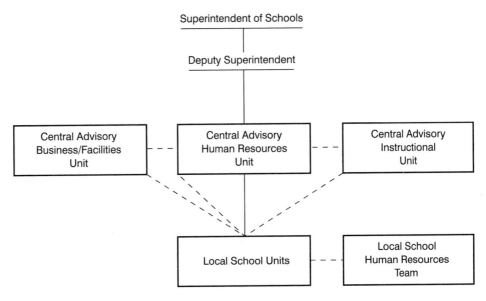

FIGURE 3.4
Decentralization of the Human Resources Unit

petent is to possess sufficient skills to meet a stated purpose or to have the capacity equal to the requirements of the task. Products or behaviors that illustrate one's capacity to perform competently are known as ***indicators of competency*** or performance specifications.

Gibson and King (1977) state that "a primary competency is reflected in administrative action that uses critical consciousness for purposes of error-reduction" (p. 24). They present the model in Figure 3.5 to illustrate administrative acts. The model suggests that competent administrative behavior is viewed as the ability to analyze a specific problem or condition and relate in a purposeful way the specific behaviors/actions needed to resolve the problem or to meet the condition. Thus "behaviors in unique administrative situations are seen as logically related indicators of degree of administrative competence" (Gibson & King, 1977, p. 22). Although an intuitive administrative act might be effective or successful, it is not considered a competent action as discussed here. Unless the behavior is related consciously to situational conditions and meanings through logical analysis and human interpretations, Gibson and King would not consider the behavior to be competent.

The competent administrator realizes that a competency focus does not always ensure successful results; it is important to be able to account for gaps in intention and reality outcomes. A competency focus requires a critical examination of the total process with a conscious effort to discover errors in original assumptions and/or methods utilized. Such critical thinking supports the administrator's ability to learn from experience. Thus the administrator is able to reduce future errors and improve personal administrative performance.

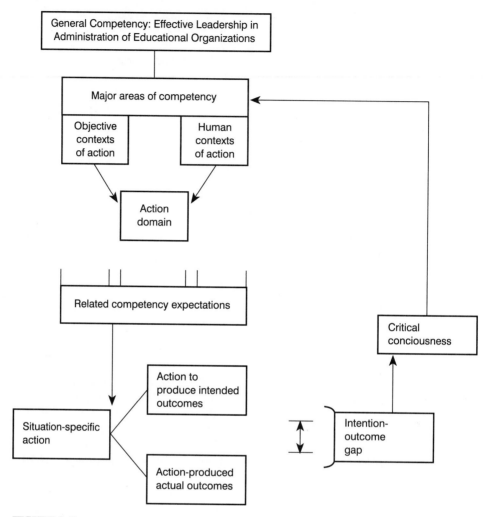

FIGURE 3.5

Conceptualization of an Approach to Competency Preparation in Educational Administration

Source: From "An Approach to Conceptualizing Competency of Performance in Educational Administration" by R. O. Gibson and R. A. King, 1977, *Educational Administration Quarterly*, *13*, p. 23. Reprinted by permission of the University Council for Educational Administration.

Tasks, Competencies, and Indicators for Human Resources Administration

Identifying the competencies that are needed by human resources administrators and the indicators of those competencies serves two primary purposes. First, identifying competencies provides insight into the nature of the role of the human resources administrator and the human resources function in education. Second, such knowledge points to the personal development required for successful performance.

1.1 Ability to communicate with others in the district in regard to current and future staffing needs.

1.2 Ability to evaluate data gathered on staffing needs.

1.3 Ability to identify primary sources of qualified applicants.

1.4 Ability to develop an appropriate screening process.

1.5 Ability to identify the knowledge, competencies, and abilities required for a given position.

1.6 Ability to determine the kinds of information needed by new and continuing personnel.

1.7 Ability to develop programs that enhance employee opportunities for self-improvement and advancement.

1.8 Ability to support and encourage the continuous use of self-evaluation/goal setting as a productive technique for change.

1.9 Ability to utilize effective counseling techniques with personnel.

1.10 Ability to develop and administer a program of employee compensation and benefits.

1.11 Ability to make all necessary preparations for negotiations.

1.12 Ability to develop specific records necessary to meet the needs of the human resources operation.

1.13 Ability to recognize competencies and talents of associates and utilize them effectively.

1.14 Ability to identify the unit's objectives and relate them to budget needs and limitations.

1.15 Ability to understand and interpret statutes, legal opinions, and court decisions relating to contractual relationships and employment conditions.

1.16 Ability to write viable policies and/or regulations; understand systems of codification.

1.17 Ability to assume a leadership role in developing a climate of mutual respect and trust which contributes to a high morale within the district.

1.18 Ability to articulate the human resources unit's objectives, practices, and accomplishments.

FIGURE 3.6

Selected Competencies for Administering the Central Human Resources Unit

Source: From *Competency-Based Preparation of Educational Administrators: Tasks, Competencies, and Indicators of Competencies* by M. S. Norton and R. D. Farrar, 1987, Tempe: Arizona State University, College of Education, Division of Educational Leadership and Policy Studies.

It is beyond the scope of this chapter to delineate a complete statement of needed competencies in relation to all the tasks of the human resources function. Figure 3.6 presents a statement of selected competencies and indicators of competency for the major tasks related to the work of the central human resources unit.

Another way of gaining insight into the nature of the work of the human resources unit is by examining the position description. Both the position analysis and position description for the position of human resources director are discussed next.

POSITION ANALYSIS AND POSITION DESCRIPTION
FOR THE CENTRAL HUMAN RESOURCES ADMINISTRATOR

A position analysis examines in depth the nature of a specific assignment and the complex environment in which the assignment takes place. The position analysis includes such considerations as the nature of the assignment itself, the primary work required, the conditions under which the work is performed, the competencies necessary for completing the work at the required level, the physical and mental requirements of the position, the educational preparation needed to perform successfully, the kinds of internal/external contacts required, specific problems encountered in the role, and other related information (see Figure 3.7).

Good personnel practice requires that a position analysis be completed periodically. The position of human resources director should not be an exception. Due to the time involved in conducting a thorough position analysis, as well as the need for objectivity in its completion, outside consultants and human resource specialists often are utilized to complete this task.

The position analysis serves as the source for developing the position description of the human resources administrator. As noted throughout this chapter, the central unit's human resources position is not characterized by a single description. Figure 3.7 is an example of a position description for the human resources director that contains many common elements from a general perspective. Note that the position description includes basic information relative to the director's position title, contract time, general responsibilities, position qualifications, immediate supervisor, supervisory jurisdiction, and major duties.

COMMON PROBLEMS AND SATISFACTIONS
ENCOUNTERED IN HUMAN RESOURCES
ADMINISTRATION AND ETHICS AND STANDARDS
OF PERSONNEL ADMINISTRATION

An examination of the kinds of problems encountered by human resources administrators provides additional insights into the human resources function. The following discussion views the human resources function from three perspectives: (1) the kinds of problems and concerns encountered by human resources administrators, (2) the impact of these problems on personal attitudes, and (3) the positive nature of the human resources function and the related satisfactions in roles of personnel administration.

Kinds of Problems Encountered

A study of human resources directors in one state (Norton, 1989) asked respondents to assess 41 specific personnel problems or conditions in relation to their own school districts. Table 3.1 indicates the specific problem and the percentage of the directors who reported the problem in their districts.

```
┌─────────────────────────────────────────────────────────────────────────┐
│                      Union High School District                          │
│                         Position Description                             │
│                                                                          │
│  Postion Title:      Assistant Superintendent of Human Resources         │
│  Department/Unit:  District Administration                                │
│  Contract:           12 months, 23 days vacation                         │
│                                                                          │
│  General Statement of Responsibilities                                   │
│  To plan, coordinate, and supervise the operation of the department of   │
│  human resources in such a way as to enhance the morale of school        │
│  district personnel, promote the overall efficiency of the school        │
│  system, and maximize the educational opportunities and benefits         │
│  available to the individual student.                                    │
│                                                                          │
│  Major Duties                                                            │
│  1. Supervises/directs:                                                  │
│      a. The planning and anticipation of human resources needs of the    │
│         school district;                                                 │
│      b. The recruitment program for certificated and classified          │
│         personnel;                                                       │
│      c. The screening and processing of all personnel recommendations    │
│         for submission to the Board of Education;                        │
│      d. Those phases of the human resources program that include:        │
│         1) Reports,                                                       │
│         2) Budgeting of personnel needs,                                  │
│         3) Placement on the salary schedule,                             │
│         4) Contracts,                                                     │
│         5) Payroll department,                                           │
│         6) Employee benefits program,                                    │
│         7) Certification,                                                 │
│         8) Unemployment compensation,                                     │
│         9) The Affirmative Action Program for the District (as the        │
│            officer).                                                      │
│  2. Evaluates:                                                           │
│      a. All prospective teacher and administrative applicants;           │
│      b. All prospective classified applicants;                           │
│      c. Substitute teacher applicants;                                   │
│      d. All employment practices and procedures;                         │
│      e. Current human resources policies;                                │
│      f. Personnel within the division.                                   │
│  3. Coordinates/assists:                                                 │
│      a. In the selection of qualified certificated and classified        │
│         candidates;                                                      │
│      b. In the review of requests for transfer or promotions of          │
│         personnel;                                                       │
│      c. As an administrative representative in the Meet and Confer        │
│         process;                                                         │
│      d. In the counseling of all personnel on matters relating to        │
│         difficult or sensitive matters;                                  │
│                                                                          │
└─────────────────────────────────────────────────────────────────────────┘
```

FIGURE 3.7

Position Description for Central Unit Human Resources Director (pp. 69–70)

    e. In research pertaining to human resources management:
       1) Salary and benefits research,
       2) Studies of staff characteristics,
       3) Professional standards,
       4) Other pertinent projects;
    f. In the budgeting process for personnel and employee benefits programs;
    g. As a member of the District Executive Council.
4. Develops/maintains:
    a. A system for personnel records for current and former employees;
    b. An up-to-date application file of prospective candidates for all positions;
    c. Salary schedules for Administrative-Supervisory personnel, Certificated personnel, and Classified personnel;
    d. Position descriptions for all existing and all new staff positions;
    e. Human resources and procedures;
    f. Human resources for employees.
5. Demonstrates:
    a. Knowledge of current administrative procedures and practices;
    b. Ability to provide adequate and timely reports;
    c. The skills to carry through on identified needs;
    d. Written and verbal communication skills with students, staff, and community;
    e. The skills for effective interpersonnel relations;
    f. Knowledge and commitment to district policies and procedures.
6. Other assignments:
    a. Special responsibilities (list);
    b. Developmental responsibilities (list).

Qualifications
1. Experience in school administration;
2. Experience in teaching;
3. Knowledge of personnel management and administration;
4. Knowledge of salary and benefit trends in education and industry;
5. Knowledge of theory and practice in discussing salaries and working conditions with various categories of employees;
6. Knowledge of problems of the classroom teacher;
7. Knowledge of office management;
8. Knowledge of school law.

Supervision Received
From the Superintendent.

Supervision Given
The employees assigned to the Human Resources Department.

FIGURE 3.7
continued

TABLE 3.1

Problems Encountered by
Human Resources Administrators
and Their Reports of Each
Problem in Their Own Districts

Problems Facing Human Resources Administrators	Percentage of Human Resources Administrators Reporting Problem
1. External mandates, requirements	65.7
2. Legal impacts on education	62.9
3. Director's work load	62.9
4. Job pressures/stress	60.0
5. Legal issues (litigation)	60.0
6. Dismissing incompetent staff	57.1
7. Substitute teaching program	57.1
8. Keeping up-to-date professionally	57.1
9. Benefits program	57.1
10. Negotiations	54.3
11. Compensation program	54.3
12. Teacher apathy	51.4
13. Staff morale	48.6
14. Teacher absenteeism	42.9
15. Record keeping requirements	42.9
16. Problems of non-certificated personnel	42.9
17. Quality staff	42.9
18. Public confidence in education	40.0
19. Securing quality administrative personnel	40.0
20. Impact of societal problems on education	40.0
21. Reassignments	40.0

The problems listed in Table 3.1 reveal a wide variety of areas in the work of the human resources administrator. A close examination of the problems indicates that nearly half relate directly to teachers and staff matters, whereas others focus more directly on the work requirements of the human resources director and external influences on the position.

Impact of Problems and Concerns on Human Resources Administrators

In spite of the many and varied problems challenging human resources administrators, evidence reveals that most find the position to be one that is increasing in importance and influence, one that provides self-fulfillment and personal satisfaction, and one they consider as vital to their school district and the accomplishment of its mission. Little research attention has been given to ascertaining the effects of personnel work on administrators. Although available data tend to be descriptive in nature, such information aids in the assessment of attitudes and conditions that surround the role. Data generated from studies on the topic reveal the following facts:

1. Human resources administrators, in general, indicate that they almost always enjoy their work. In addition, nearly all studies find that human resources administrators do find "considerable" or at least "moderate" self-fulfillment in their work.

2. A majority of human resources directors plans to remain in the role until normal retirement and considers the position as their final occupational goal, although some look ahead to different positions in administration.

3. Nearly all human resources administrators view their positions as being entrenched in the school system and increasing in importance and influence. Most all are of the opinion that they have "much influence" on personnel policy decisions.

4. If starting over again, nearly all human resources administrators state that they would become directors again.

5. The quality of relationships between the human resources administrators and teachers, in general, is viewed by directors as "good" or "very good."

Identifying the problems and concerns of human resources administrators, as well as their contributions and challenges, illuminates the nature of the assignment as well as the personal competencies needed for successful performance in the role. In addition, the study of related problems provides insight into the increasing complexity of the human resources function in education.

The nature of human resources problems and the expectation of position responsibilities demonstrate the importance of the training and preparation required for an effective human resources administrator, the need for a better research base for the human resources function, and the need for professional guidelines that direct and support personnel programs and resources. Another means of examining the work of the human resources function is through a study of the ethics and standards on which it is founded. The following section focuses on the ethics for school administrators and on the human resources standards developed at the national level.

Ethics for School Administrators

Chapter 1 discussed the historical development of the AASPA, which assumed its current name in 1959. The AASPA has been instrumental in advancing personnel administration research and practice since its establishment and set forth a statement of ethics (AASPA, 1988) to guide administrators generally. These guidelines are shown in Figure 3.8.

Another significant contribution of AASPA was the development of standards for school personnel administrators (1988) for the ethical administration of the human resources function. These standards have been updated and revised three times since 1960. The listing of selected standards in Figure 3.9 was completed in 1988 and defines and further clarifies the purposes, processes, responsibilities, and significance of the human resources function. These standards emphasize the importance of establishing a district philosophy to direct the total organization toward accomplishing its goals and objectives. Such a philosophical statement guides the school system in developing specific human resources policy and administrative regulations.

1. Makes the well-being of students the fundamental value of all decision making and actions.
2. Fulfills professional responsibilities with honesty and integrity.
3. Supports the principle of due process and protects the civil and human rights of all individuals.
4. Obeys local, state, and national laws and does not knowingly join or support organizations that advocate, directly or indirectly, the overthrow of the government.
5. Implements the governing board of education's policies and administrative rules and regulations.
6. Pursues appropriate measures to correct those laws, policies, and regulations that are not consistent with sound educational goals.
7. Avoids using positions for personal gain through political, social, religious, economic, or other influences.
8. Accepts academic degrees or professional certification only from duly accredited institutions.
9. Maintains the standards and seeks to improve the effectiveness of the profession through research and continuing professional development.
10. Honors all contracts with fulfillment or release.

FIGURE 3.8

Statement of Ethics for School Personnel Administrators

Source: From *Statement of Ethics for School Personnel Administrators* (p. 1) by the American Association of School Personnel Administrators, 1988, Sacramento, CA: Author. Copyright © 1988 by the AASPA. Reprinted by permission.

SUMMARY

This chapter discussed the human resources function by examining the major processes that it encompasses, by viewing the organization and relationships of the central human resources unit, by considering alternatives to the centralization of the human resources function, by presenting the concept of competent performance by human resources administrators, by examining the nature of the problems as well as the challenges and opportunities of human resources practitioners, and by presenting the ethics and standards to guide the professional practices of human resources administration.

The human resources function is composed of several major processes, each of which is comprehensive and complex. Human resources administration was defined in terms of a planned and distinct function that serves the goals of the district through establishing an effective system of human resources and an environment that fosters high levels of accomplishment.

Human resources administration was viewed as a function with a long history, but one that is still in transition. Traditional processes and activities are encompassing new methods and professional approaches. Other new processes have been added to the responsibilities of human resources administrators, requiring new competencies for effective performance.

1. The basic function of the board of education is policy-making and review of the total educational program of the school district.
2. The superintendent of the school district provides the professional leadership necessary for the continuous development of the personnel program to meet the objectives of the school district.
3. The personnel administrator has a clear understanding of the goals, objectives, and processes of the school system and the role which the personnel administration function has in accomplishing those ends.
4. Written personnel policies furnish guidelines for administrative procedures relating to personnel matters.
5. The personnel department is that specific section of the administrative structure established to carry out the personnel activities of the school system.
6. Personnel operations are conducted in a manner that provides for effective and friendly employee relationships and contributes to individual motivation and morale.
7. A well-developed system of personnel accounting and research helps predict staff needs and enables the administration to make sound projections for current and future employment needs.
8. The application form requests information necessary to facilitate screening; contributes to sound decision making on recommendations for appointment, and is in conformity with local, state, and federal laws and regulations.
9. Decisions involving staff selection are based upon a carefully planned program of investigation, screening, appointment, and follow-up support.
10. Placement, assignment, and transfer of personnel is a basic administrative responsibility through which attempts are made to meet the needs of the educational program, implement affirmative action plans, provide balanced staffing, and meet the desires of individual employees.
11. Orientation of teachers is a continuing process based upon a planned program designed to acquaint the teacher with his/her responsibilities toward the student, school, and community, and to acquaint the teacher with the resources in the school system and the community.

FIGURE 3.9
Standards for Ethical Administration
Source: From *Standards for School Personnel Administration* (pp. 5–6) by the American Association of School Personnel Administration, 1988, Sacramento, CA: Author. Copyright © 1988 by the AASPA. Reprinted by permission.

The central human resources unit has become a common organizational arrangement in education. Yet movements in restructuring school organization have led to more decentralization of responsibilities and further sharing of human resources activities by all units within the school system. The successful school administrator is aware that an effective educational program depends greatly upon maintaining a high quality of human resources. In this context, human resources administration becomes the most important function of all educational functions.

Viable unit relationships, both horizontal and vertical, within the organizational structure, have paramount importance in realizing the full potential of people within the system. Basic to the success of all human resources activities are the mission of

12. Appraisal of teaching performance is a cooperative process designed primarily to improve the quality of teaching.
13. The personnel evaluation and supervision system, while directed toward helping employees improve the quality of their performance, provides information which enables evaluators to make objective and fair decisions concerning termination, retention, or discipline when the employee's performance or conduct is marginal or clearly unsatisfactory, and rewards excellent performance.
14. In the interests of promoting high morale and leadership effectiveness, the personnel department will use its influence to assure that individuals on the professional staff are recognized for excellence and promoted on the basis of competency, performance, qualifications, fitness for the job, and probability of future growth and development regardless of age, sex, religion, and natural origin, ethnic heritage, marital status, or handicap.
15. Collective bargaining, as a personnel function, will conclude in an equitable agreement which preserves the board's responsibility to make policy and the administrator's right to manage the school district for the citizens and children and at the same time provide adequate wages, hours, and working conditions for its employees.
16. Compensation plans that place the school board in a favorable, competitive position and salary policies that encourage professional growth and personal improvement in service are essential elements of personnel administration.
17. Job descriptions and classifications include the duties to be performed, the immediate supervisor, educational preparation required, and personal qualifications needed for the position.
18. Regulations governing resignations should provide an orderly termination of service with a minimum of disruption to the school system and inconvenience to the employees.
19. The school district has written and publicized policies for the reduction of staff when needed.

FIGURE 3.9
continued

the central unit to serve all employees who contribute to the system, the need for understanding the purposes of the human resources function by all personnel, and the involvement of all administrative personnel in the achievement of the function's objectives regardless of the organizational structure. These considerations, if positively realized, will reduce the problems that human resources administrators encounter as well as the factors inhibiting accomplishment of personnel goals. The basic significance of the human resources function is revealed in its primary concern for the human element in the system. Accomplishment of system goals is inextricably related to the accomplishment of the goals and objectives of the human resources function.

AASPA's guiding standards provide both a foundation and a direction for setting policy and guiding the work of human resources administration. As implied by one of the AASPA standards, effective human resources administration is based on a strong commitment by the school board and the administrative staff to a planned and comprehensive program of developing human talent within the organization to achieve the goals cooperatively determined for the school district.

DISCUSSION QUESTIONS

1. The chapter discussion notes that effective human resources planning serves as the foundation for decision making. Consider the specific process of recruitment. Use several examples and/or illustrations to demonstrate the importance of planning as it relates to the recruitment process. What specific planning is required? What specific kinds of data/information are needed?

2. Examine the definitions and purposes of recruitment, selection, orientation, and assignment discussed in the chapter. Illustrate specific ways in which one process is related to another. For example, how does the orientation process relate to the assignment process?

3. Examine the list of specific problems encountered by human resources administrators today. Which of these problems are important ones in school districts in your area presently? Discuss these problems relative to their implications for the work performances of persons in your school district.

4. (Class exercise) Each student should list several specific problems encountered by *teaching* personnel today. Compare individual listings for the identification of common problems. Discuss the implications of these common problems for the work of the human resources administrator at the central level and for building level administrators.

5. Examine closely the position description and the selected competencies of the central unit human resources administrator. Discuss the type of preparation and experience necessary for effectiveness in such a position, as implied by the requirements of the role. What specific course work and field experiences appear essential?

6. Assume that a decision was made to decentralize the human resources function in your school system or one with which you are familiar. What kinds of administrative arrangements appear most likely? Discuss briefly these arrangements and identify the allocation of responsibility as related to human resources for implementing the human resources function.

CASE 3.1
Position Descriptions: Fact or Fiction?

Georgia Stephan had served as director of human resources in the Union School District for 1 year. The position description for director had been written 4 years ago and listed a comprehensive set of duties and responsibilities. As was the case with other central office administrative roles, however, Georgia was involved in several program activities not included in the position description. Some of the responsibilities listed in Georgia's position description, and in those of other administrators, actually were being carried out by persons in other units.

In Georgia's case, the position description stipulated that she was responsible for coordinating the teacher performance evaluation program for the district, yet she admitted that she spent less than 5% of her time in this area. The institutional unit in the district and local building principals were the ones who performed the evaluation activities. Georgia's part was to keep a general file of evaluation reports.

Even though the school board policies did call for a position description for every position, and such descriptions did exist, there was a general feeling at the administrative cabinet level that position descriptions were somewhat restraining. As was stated by the school superintendent on one occasion, "One way to inhibit individual creativity and incentive is to freeze them in a written position description."

Thus the position descriptions in the Union School District were not adhered to in a rigid fashion, and employees often were given responsibilities outside those stated in their specific position descriptions. No one was particularly concerned about this practice; in fact, it never was raised as being a major concern on the part of school employees.

Questions

1. What are the pros and cons of having position descriptions but not using them as typically intended?
2. Identify two or three specific problems that could develop from practices described in Case 3.1.
3. As the human resources director, Georgia Stephan, what actions, if any, might you take in this situation?

CASE 3.2
Qualifications: I'd Like to Be Considered

The Columbus School District has 15,220 students and 502 teachers. Personnel responsibilities are divided between the school superintendent, who handles the secondary school personnel, and the assistant superintendent, who is responsible for personnel activities at the elementary school level. Columbus's student growth has been phenomenal during the last 5 years; student enrollment has increased from 10,400 to its current figure of 15,220 during that time period. Forecasts for growth indicate that this suburban area will continue to grow at about the same rate for at least the next 10 years.

The central administrative officials and the school board are convinced that responsibilities for the personnel function are such that some new arrangements for administering the function are necessary. Both the school superintendent and assistant superintendent agree that the responsibility for personnel needs to be placed elsewhere, especially in view of their increasing work loads over the last few years.

Hobart Stout, a retiring school board member, has expressed a personal interest in the position of personnel director for the system. He will leave the board position in June and could assume the role on a full-time basis. Stout has a BS degree in business management and ran a small business for more than 20 years. Although he has never served as an educator, he has served on the school board for 12 years and was board president for 3 years. All of Stout's children are graduates of the Columbus School District.

"I've done most every job a small business requires," stated Stout. "I've kept books, hired sales personnel, trained employees on-the-job, and have evaluated personal performance. If the board does decide to advertise the position, I'd hope to be a leading candidate."

Questions

1. What are the implications in Case 3.2 regarding personnel competency and position qualifications?
2. Assume that you are Columbus's school superintendent. What recommendations/actions would you set forth on this matter?
3. Consider the matter of qualifications for the central office human resources director. What minimal qualifications do you believe are needed in the position? What specific preparation is important in your opinion?

☐ **CASE 3.3**
The Policy on Policy

Andrew Patrick had served in the Papillion School District as human resources director for 3 years. During that time, the school district evidenced a loss of population growth that resulted in an enrollment decrease of 1,200 students. Thus the school district had to reduce its professional staff by 40 teachers in the last 3 years.

Patrick had been delegated the primary responsibility for determining those teachers who were to be released. In brief, Patrick examined school needs using both enrollment data and program information. Although not widely "advertised," he took the opportunity to release

several teachers who were not performing at the level building principals viewed as satisfactory.

It became apparent once again that Papillion would need to RIF six teachers. Using the same general criteria for deciding who was to be given their pink slips, Patrick sent notices of release to six teachers at six different schools in the district.

Within 3 days after the notices were sent, Patrick received a telephone call from Bob Johnson, a social studies teacher at McClintock Junior High School.

"Why me?" asked Johnson. "I've been here longer than several teachers at McClintock. Furthermore, I have been in the district longer than many teachers that I know."

"Our decision is based on need," replied Patrick. "Our policy has been to release on the basis of program need."

"I've never seen a policy relative to teacher release," responded Johnson. "Is there something available in writing?"

"We've been consistent on the matter," answered Patrick, "but there is no written policy on the matter."

"I think it's unfair," said Johnson. "I plan to file a complaint."

Patrick met with Superintendent Elizabeth Watkins the next morning and informed her of the conversation with Johnson.

"Don't worry about it," counseled Superintendent Watkins, "I'll have our attorney look into the matter."

Questions

1. What kinds of questions/reactions do you think the superintendent will receive from the school attorney?
2. What would be the value of a board approved policy in this case with specific regulations outlining the procedures to be used for reduction in force?
3. Assume that you are to develop a guiding policy for the school board in this case. What specific provisions will you include?
4. What is the overall value of viable school board policies and regulations?

REFERENCES

American Association of School Personnel Administrators. (1988). *Standards for school personnel administration*. Foster City, CA: Author.

Bates, R. J. (1984). Toward a critical practice of educational administration. In T. J. Sergiovanni & J. E. Corbally (Eds.), *Leadership and organizational culture* (Chapter 14). Urbana: University of Chicago Press.

Carnoy, M. (1990, November 7). Restructuring has a downside, too. *Education Week*, p. 32.

Castetter, W. B. (1992). *The personnel function in education* (5th ed.). New York: Macmillan.

Class size must be negotiated with teachers, Oregon court rules. (1991, April 10). *Education Week*, p. 2.

Fayol, H. (1984). *General and industrial management* (revised by Irwin Gray). New York: The Institute of Electrical and Electronics Engineers.

Gibson, R. O., & King, R. A. (1977). An approach to conceptualizing competency of performance in educational administration. *Educational Administration Quarterly, 13*(3), 17–30.

Harris, B. M. (1989). *In-service education for staff development*. Boston: Allyn & Bacon.

Holoviak, S. J., & Holoviak, S. B. (1984). The benefits of in-house counseling. *Personnel, 61*(4), 53–59.

Nadler, N. (1974, May). Implications of the HRD concept. *Training and Development Journal, 28*, 3–13.

Norton, M. S. (1988). Employee assistance programs—A need in education. *Contemporary Education, 60*, 23-26.

Norton, M. S (1989). *The school personnel administrator in Arizona*. Tempe: Arizona State University, Division of Educational Leadership and Policy Studies.

Norton, M. S., & Farrar, R. D. (1987). *Competency-based preparation of educational administrators: Tasks, competencies, and indicators of competencies*. Tempe: Arizona State University, College of Education, Division of Educational Leadership and Policy Studies.

Rebore, R. W. (1991). *Personnel administration in education—A management approach* (3rd ed.). Englewood Cliffs, NJ: Prentice Hall.

Stahl, O. G. (1962). *Public personnel administration* (5th ed.). New York: Harper & Row.

Tead, O., & Metcalf, H. C. (1920). *Personnel administration*. New York: McGraw-Hill.

Toch, T. (1984, August 22). Schools' methods of evaluating teachers assailed in Rand study. *Education Week*, p. 7.

Tyler, R. W. (1971). In-service education of teachers: A look at the past and future. In L. J. Rubin (Ed.), *Improving in-service eduction: Proposals and procedures for change* (pp. 5–17). Boston: Allyn & Bacon.

Van Zwoll, J. A. (1964). *School personnel administration*. New York: Appleton-Century Crofts.

4

Strategic Human Resources Planning

This chapter discusses strategic planning from the human resources administrator's perspective. The discussion begins with a definition of strategic human resources planning along with background developments of the concept in order to show its emergence from strategic business planning to its current level of development. Then the six characteristics of human resources planning are described, followed by a discussion of the life cycle of school organizations and an overview of a school system's professional staff mix. This discussion provides the background for a general strategic planning model that highlights the integration of human resources planning into the strategic plan of a school system.

A graphic illustration is used to show the strategic planning model. The accompanying discussion reviews the model's three main elements: environmental scanning, strategic and operational planning, and implementation.

Methods of forecasting personnel needs and technological approaches to projecting enrollments are presented in the next section of the chapter. This discussion incorporates a Markovian analysis of personnel attrition and emerging computerized systems for projecting future student enrollments. Finally, recruitment of personnel from a strategic planning perspective is addressed in the last section of the chapter.

DEFINITION AND BACKGROUND OF STRATEGIC HUMAN RESOURCES PLANNING

Strategy, as the term is used by organizations, involves developing general objectives and using the organization's resources in the most effective way to attain these objectives (Baird, Meshoulam, & DeGive, 1983). A strategy determines what an organization's decision makers want to accomplish and how they plan to do it (Dyer, 1983). *Planning*, on the other hand, connotes a process pertaining to future events, where a set of decisions is prepared for future action and is directed at achieving specific objectives (Dror, 1970). What, then, is strategic planning? Pfeiffer, Goodstein, and Nolan (1986a) defined strategic planning in the following way:

> Strategic planning is the process by which an organization envisions its future and develops the necessary procedures and operations to achieve that future. This vision of the future state of the organization provides both the direction in which the organization should move and the energy to begin that move. (p. 2)

Strategic planning is a dynamic process for helping a school system shape its future. And through techniques of strategic management, school systems can effectively adjust to the unpredictable demands brought on by environmental changes. Thus strategic planning is a process that was developed to guide an organization in an environment of rapid and continuous change.

> Organizations need strategic planning because the world changes constantly. It is foolhardy and unrealistic to assume that economic conditions, consumer needs and expectations, competition, . . . or a host of other factors will be the same two, three, or five years from now as they are today. A strategic planning process is a systematic effort by an organization to deal with the inevitability of change and an attempt to envision its own future. The importance of this process is that it enables an organization to help *shape* its own future rather than simply *prepare* for the future. (Pfeiffer et al., 1986a, p. 24)

Therefore, any effort by a school system to respond effectively to change must include a careful analysis of information about its environment. The results of this analysis will have an important impact on the system's strategic plan and will be critical to effective human resources planning.

As with strategic planning, ***strategic human resources planning*** is a process of preparing an organization for future activities in which decisions related to the use of personnel must show evidence of contributing to the achievement of the organization's strategic objectives (Nkomo, 1980). Strategic human resources planning is not necessarily the making of future decisions; it is focused upon current decisions and their future implications. Strategic human resources planning produces current decisions about what should be done now to realize desired outcomes in the future. Accordingly, the purpose of human resources planning is to ensure the most effective use of personnel resources to move an organization toward its mission and achieve its strategic objectives.

Most strategic plans have human resources implications. Many of these implications can be anticipated, and if critically important, can support changes in the planning process (Dyer, 1983). In most instances planning involves the identification, analysis, and scheduling of events that will affect the management of personnel in the future (Sibson, 1983). Strategic human resources planning is based on information that justifies conclusions about existing trends, which in turn form a rationale for predicting future events. "Planning is making today's decisions with tomorrow in mind. It involves the objectives of the future and the actions that will lead to them" (Alpander, 1980, p. 24). Moreover, strategic human resources planning is a centralized function, integral to a school system's strategic plan (Alpander, 1980). Through the gathering and analyzing of information, the strategic human resources planning process influences the organization's strategic plan. This information is systematically collected and takes into account (1) the external supply of personnel, (2) audits of existing leadership talent, (3) forecasts of future professional and technical talent, and (4) succession planning for top leadership positions (Devanna, Fombrun, Tichy, & Warren, 1982).

Strategic human resources planning evolved from strategic business planning in the early 1970s. The concept of strategic business planning was an important tool for relating management decisions to organizational objectives. The process was developed to bring about an improved allocation of financial and other material resources for maximizing planned organizational outcomes. It provided ultimate accountability on the effectiveness of management decisions. The changes in net product-line profits measured in dollars gained or lost have been regarded as evidence of management's performance.

The concept served the private sector well until recent years. A number of changes and national trends have emphasized the importance of the human element in strategic business planning. Concurrently, the federal government became increasingly involved in regulating many aspects of personnel and human resources management (Nkomo, 1980). "The impact of this legislation has fallen mainly on the personnel function, where training programs, selection and recruitment methods, compensation systems, and promotion policies have had to be revamped in response to government pressure" (Nkomo, 1980, p. 72). Laws, court decisions, and executive orders of the last several national administrations have made the elimination of job discrimination a national priority. Also, societal changes prompted by the emerging trends in the family structure and the shifting age distribution of the population are a few among many considerations that have focused attention on improving human resources planning. Such considerations have had a profound effect on the operations of many organizations. Moreover, the social conscience of a growing number of organizational decision makers has been raised to include such factors in the framing of strategic objectives that are characterized by a sense of social responsibility (e.g., protecting the environment). All of these considerations, combined with the competitive challenges of foreign firms (Miles & Snow, 1984), have ushered in a growing awareness of the need to integrate strategic human resources planning into other organizational plans. Thus data about factors of human resources have become an important part of the overall planning process. Unfortunately, organizations are only beginning to value accurate, comprehensive human resources information in their planning (Devanna et al., 1982).

The implementation of human resource plans is far more difficult than planning the acquisition and allocation of material resources. Financial and other material resources, unlike human resources, are typically measured in dollars and cents. Systems for assessing and administering human resources are not as well developed as systems related to markets and finance. The expectations, values, and skills of personnel are important and must be respected. People cannot be transferred, changed, or modified as expeditiously as a financial or market plan in response to an organization's exigency (Baird et al., 1983).

The large body of literature dealing with strategic human resources planning attests to business executives' wishes to integrate human resources planning into business strategies. Unlike the well-developed concepts, techniques, and models for strategic business planning, strategic human resources planning and management are relatively new fields in management theory and are still in the conceptual stages of development (Wright & McMahan, 1992). Models for implementing such plans are emerging in many large corporations (Alpander, 1980; Devanna et al., 1982), such as IBM (Dyer & Heyer, 1984), American Hospital Supply, Corning Glass Works, and Merck (Dyer, 1984). Human resources planning was widely adopted in the 1980s, and it is expected to increase during the 1990s (Greer, Jackson, & Fiorito, 1989). In addition, important progress is being made toward the development and implementation of models for service agencies in the public sector, including education.

The educational institution is a personnel-intense industry. In most instances, school systems establish mission statements to guide their commitments of time, energy, and material resources. Within this context, strategic objectives are defined for the numerous subunits of the organization as a focus for operational plans. The factors that affect sound human resources planning are as important to strategic planning in education as they are in business. Strategic human resources planning must be integral to the strategic educational planning process and must possess certain characteristics to ensure its effectiveness.

Service agencies such as the public school system have a vital interest in the development of workable models of strategic human resources planning. Such models will provide school systems with the benefits of a focused program, targets for improvement, and a knowledge of the makeup and expectations of its constituencies. School systems will also have the advantage of becoming proactive rather than reactive.

CHARACTERISTICS OF STRATEGIC HUMAN RESOURCES PLANNING

Several of a list of characteristics specific to strategic planning (Williamsport Area Community College, 1982) have direct application to the processes of planning human resources strategically. The human resources planning process should be *comprehensive*. It must include the many subunits of the organization, for example, schools, departments, and divisions. All planning is done so that changes in one unit can be anticipated from planned or observed changes elsewhere in the organization.

Human resources planning is a process that is *integrative*. All parts should interrelate to form a whole. It is not simply a collection of plans from the several subunits of the organization, but rather a single plan reflecting personnel recruitment, selection, allocation, compensation, and development for all units.

The process is *continuous* and usually conforms to the organization's planning cycle. Data are continuously updated so that decisions can be made with the highest degree of currency and accuracy.

A *multiyear planning format* is essential to the continuous process of planning and should reflect activities and developments over a period of 1–5 years. This plan usually becomes less specific as it projects into the latter part of the 5-year cycle. On an annual basis, the plan is updated for each successive year of the planning cycle, and a new year is added annually to maintain the 5-year planning perspective.

The many constituencies affected by the plan should have input in the formulation process. Thus the plan must be *participatory* to gain individual commitment to implementation. Involvement in the planning process is a good investment that yields important dividends in commitment.

Finally, *flexibility* must be integral to the planning process. The plan should provide for modification and change as required by changes in the school system's internal and external environments and the specific needs of its constituencies. This flexibility should also be evidenced in the plan's sensitivity to the evolutionary stage of the school system and changes required in the professional staff mix, which is described next.

EVOLUTIONARY STAGE OF A SCHOOL ORGANIZATION

The process of strategic human resources planning must consider the evolutionary stage of a school organization just as a business considers the life cycle of a consumer product it markets (Baird et al., 1983). This approach will help to clarify the predictions for future human resources needs so that processes can be developed and implemented to fulfill these needs. How can such needs be derived from the consideration of a school district's life cycle?

A school system on the fringe of a major metropolitan area that is struggling with continuous enrollment increases, will be at a different evolutionary stage than a well-established central city district that is trying to retain a quality program in an environment of declining enrollments. The expanding system may need leadership personnel who are flexible, innovative, and committed to program development. On the other hand, the city system may desire educational leaders who can work with communities in the closing of schools and yet maintain high-quality programs through such transitions. Thus a strategic consideration is to match personnel with the requirements dictated by the evolutionary stage of the organization.

PROFESSIONAL STAFF MIX

Baird et al. (1983) explained a portfolio mix of human resources as one in which personnel with specific skills, abilities, and expertise can be moved among units of the organization to achieve the organization's strategic objectives. Specifically, procedures are established so that personnel can be transferred among units of the organization to optimize the use of their talents.

Developing the mix involves balancing the best human resources talents with program needs to achieve the strategic objectives of the school system. Similar to the example discussed earlier, several attendance areas of a school system may be growing rapidly while several others are struggling with enrollment declines. An analysis of the professional staff mix would take into consideration the strategic objectives of both the school system and the individual schools involved to determine the optimum mix of professional staff. This analysis may suggest changes in staffing to help achieve strategic objectives.

There are special considerations that are frequently given to the professional staff mix. One special consideration relates to those school districts that are under a court order to provide a particular racial blend of professional staff members in all schools. Another district may be required to balance the professional experiences of faculty members among the schools of the district. Apart from court orders, it is often worthwhile educationally to balance staff on the basis of age, ethnicity, gender, and teaching load.

Despite the need for improving the professional staff mix in a school system, the reality faced by many school organizations may mitigate against such efforts. School board policies, contract agreements, past practices, and traditions can make it difficult to optimize the professional staff composition. Although policies on transfer and assignment can be hard to modify, traditions and past practices will certainly be more difficult if not nearly impossible to change. Thus the human resources administrator must exhibit careful planning, expert leadership, and sensitivity to realize such changes.

INTEGRATING HUMAN RESOURCES PLANNING INTO THE STRATEGIC PLAN

The professional literature is replete with models for applying techniques of strategic planning to education. The model presented in Figure 4.1 was formulated to represent a synthesis of key elements of the strategic planning process rather than an elaboration on the many models found in practice. Figure 4.1 graphically represents the relationship among the various elements of a general strategic planning model for a school system with emphasis on integrated strategic human resources planning (operational planning). The major elements of the model include *1.0 Environmental Scanning* with its subelements *1.1 External Scanning* and *1.2 Internal Scanning*, and *2.0 Strategic and Operational Planning* with subelements *2.1 Strategic Plan* and *2.2 Operational Plans*. Elements *2.1* and *2.2* in turn contain several subelements, including *2.11, 2.12, 2.13,* and *2.14,* and *2.21* and *2.22,* respectively. The last major element of the model is *3.0 Implementation*. The following discussion will elaborate on the model presented in Figure 4.1.

Strategic human resources planning must be done within a context, and it is this context that forms a basis for establishing a school system's mission and developing its strategic and operational plans. The context is gained from an environmental scan. Moreover, it is the interpretation of the environmental scan that will influence a school system's mission and all aspects of the planning process. Information gained from environmental scanning must be analyzed carefully to support the development of a comprehensive plan for administering human resources strategically (Kydd & Oppenheim, 1990). Specifically, the planning process entails the development of human resources operational plans that are consistent with the overall strategic plan (Anthony & Norton, 1991). These operational plans are dynamic because they interact with those of other organizational units. In addition, operational plans are monitored continuously and can be modified to reflect changing conditions in the school system's environment.

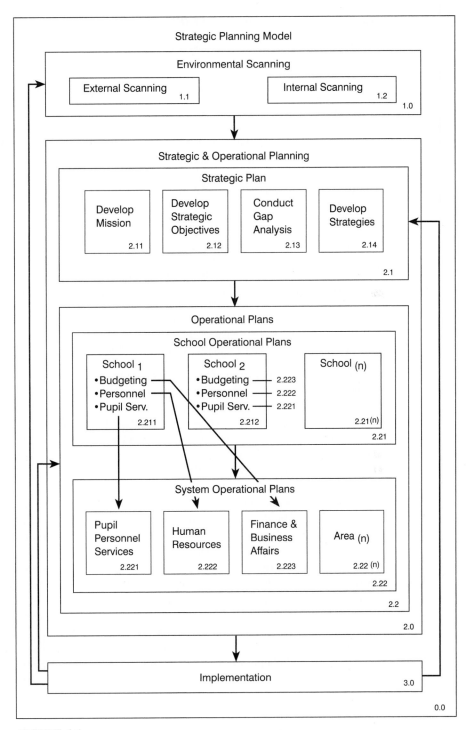

FIGURE 4.1
Strategic Planning Model

Environmental Scanning (1.0)

A school district's environment is viewed from two perspectives that are best illustrated by the acronym SWOT. *S*trengths and *W*eaknesses are regarded as internal environmental factors, whereas *O*pportunities and *T*hreats are the key factors of the external environmental scan. Based upon an interpretation of the environmental scan, assumptions can be developed to guide all planning efforts. A careful analysis of scanning information provides a school system with information that supports the development of a rationale for operating assumptions. These assumptions are used to assess the viability of the strategic plan. The assumptions relate to the external socio-cultural, economic, technological, political-legal areas, and to selected factors of the internal scan, such as human and financial resources.

From a strategic perspective, a school organization must be attuned to its environment.

> Seen from a global viewpoint, the organization exists only as a part of a larger reality, supported and nurtured by the larger system on which it depends: the nation, its culture, and many interest groups, the world economy and political system, and the physical and biological planet itself. To the extent that an organization acts in ignorance of the connections that link it to other parts, and to the whole system of the global environment, it will tend to experience surprise and shock at unanticipated events originating in the larger system. It will experience such events as deficient in meaning, and hence as a threat to its sense of reality and its own identity. (Harrison, 1983, p. 217)

Also, a description of a school system's educational environment includes many considerations that can be viewed simultaneously as constraints and opportunities. In each instance, strategic plans must be developed to minimize the negative effect of constraints and maximize the positive impact of opportunities.

Some of the obvious environmental factors include state board policies and regulations, the state aid funding model for education and other state legislation, relationships with teacher training institutions, services of intermediate service agencies, competition from surrounding school systems that draw from the same teacher pool, the school tax digest, and federal program regulations. Other environmental factors would relate to the demographic features of the constituencies that the school system serves, including, among others, racial and ethnic composition of the community, age distribution of residents, and socioeconomic status.

The processes of external and internal environmental scanning are continuous and fixed to the school district's planning cycle. Typically, the planning cycle is 5 years. Like the multiyear planning format, this plan is updated for each successive year of the planning cycle. A new year is added annually to maintain the 5-year strategic planning perspective. In each iteration of the planning cycle all elements of the strategic plan are updated to reflect changing conditions, new directions, and emerging basic beliefs about the educational processes. Environmental scanning is included as an integral part of the strategic planning model, and it impacts all elements of the planning process (see Figure 4.1).

External Scanning (1.1).

External scanning is the monitoring, evaluating, and disseminating of information from the external environment to key people within the organization. It is a tool used to avoid strategic surprises and to ensure the long-term health of the school district. Typically, the external scan focuses on emerging trends that present **opportunities** for the school district and potential **threats** to its continued effectiveness. Central to the process of the external scan are four focal points of investigation: sociocultural, economic, technological, and political-legal. Also, Milkovich and Boudreau (1991) identified two other important scanning areas: role of government and changing demographics (e.g., age distribution of population, number of immigrants, distribution of work force by gender, and availability of workers). The scanning of these areas may be done by staff members of the school district or external organizations such as research groups or universities.

Internal Scanning (1.2).   The internal scan is usually done by the staff of the district, but it can be done by outside groups or organizations. It addresses the questions of **strengths** that support strategies and **weaknesses** in the organization that constrain strategies. Specifically, this scan investigates the structure of the organization to determine the extent to which it facilitates the implementation of the organization's developed strategies. A second area to scan is the organization's culture. An analysis of the culture determines if organizational behaviors are consistent with planned strategies (Koys, Armacost, & Charalambides, 1990). "Management must constantly be aware of culture in strategic planning. If the culture is antagonistic to a strategic change, plans should include ways to change the culture as well" (Reichrath, 1990, p. 52). To be comprehensive, the internal scan must include an analysis of the district's financial, human, and facility resources.

Every school organization has a unique culture, and the several schools of a school system often develop subcultures within the system's organization. Moreover, the system's culture is represented by the values, ideology, and goals shared by the members of the organization, including the patterns of behaviors for getting work done.

Ernest (1985) suggested an examination of certain organizational artifacts to gain insight into an organization's culture. This evidence cannot only be uncovered in an organization's policies, but also by employee greetings, dress, language, ceremonies, gossip, and jokes. He also indicated that the best understanding of culture can be found in the practices of administrators. The beliefs, values, and philosophies of top administrators influence the practices of upper- and middle-level administrators, who in turn affect the behavior of subordinates (Harris & Harris, 1982). For example, *how* decisions are made is an indication of culture. Some school organizations value collegiality, working together in groups, and opportunities for participatory decision making. However, others might be characterized by a number of individuals working independently within some formalized decision-making process.

The rituals of the organization can be a part of the culture and vary greatly from system to system. Some may provide public commendations for exemplary accomplishments or promotions. Others might arrange extraordinary programs of special recognition for retiring personnel (Carlson, 1991). School systems give greater or lesser emphasis to such events by publicizing their importance in both external and internal communications.

Another aspect of the culture is the control of information in the school system. Some control information very tightly; others are more open. Additionally, patterns of communication among members of the system characterize a cultural value. Some exhibit a top-down pattern of communication; a top-down and bottom-up prevails in others. In a similar vein, some school systems tend to operate democratically, whereas others are more autocratic.

Many of these aspects of an organization's culture can be classified into Ernest's (1985) four-cell matrix depicting the two dimensions of people and action (see Figure 4.2). The people dimension spans the continuum of participative to nonparticipative; the action dimension ranges from reactive to proactive. School systems that respond to the external environment are classified as reactive, whereas those that attempt to affect it are proactive. Similarly, systems that encourage interaction and communication are regarded as high in participation.

The quadrants of Figure 4.2 identify four major cultural types. The **interactive** culture provides good services and focuses on employee and community needs. The **integrated** culture has a strong people orientation, and the system commits its energies and resources to innovative and creative activities. A **systematized** culture tends to be rule bound, with low participation of employees and other constituencies. Finally, the **entrepreneurial** culture tends to be change oriented, with little participation by employees.

Although influenced by the system's overall culture, an individual school often develops its own subculture. Different elements of the system's culture can exist in a similar form at the individual school level. For example, if a school system places great value on the accomplishments of staff members, an individual school may give great recognition to the achievements of students. This system value is transmitted to its organizational members and is evidenced through the emphasis placed on recognizing student accomplishments.

A study of teacher perceptions offered a different perspective of the impact of organizational cultures. Page (1985) conducted an ethnographic study of teachers' perceptions of students and a link among classrooms, school cultures, and the social order. She stated that "teachers translate the norms of an institutional ethos" (p. 7). Moreover, this ethos is a result of teachers' perceptions of the environment outside the school. Her analysis of two socioeconomically similar schools showed radically different role perceptions and behaviors of teachers. She concluded that teachers'

FIGURE 4.2

The Four Main Corporate Culture Types
Source: From "Corporate Cultures and Effective Planning" by Robert C. Ernest, 1985, *Personnel Administrator, 30*, p. 52. Reprinted by permission.

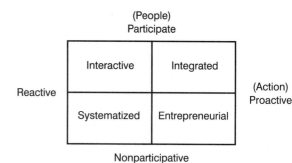

perceptions of students are circumscribed by the school's culture. Thus the subculture of individual schools can be quite different and can have a profound effect on several aspects of human resources management.

Strategic and Operational Planning (2.0)

Strategic and operational planning are key components of the strategic planning process. The strategic plan is consistent with the assumptions derived from an analysis of the environment, and it forms the bases for relating all operational plans.

Strategic Plan (2.1). The four elements of the strategic plan, as illustrated in Figure 4.1, are *2.11 Develop Mission*, *2.12 Develop Strategic Objectives*, *2.13 Conduct Gap Analysis*, and *2.14 Develop Strategies*. The actual strategic plan is published in a relatively brief document (usually 25 pages or less) that gives direction to all operational planning activities. Each operational plan relates to the strategic objectives and strategies in the strategic plan.

Mission Statement (2.11). A critically important factor in the development of a school system's strategic plan is its educational mission. The mission statement provides direction based on a perception of the environment. Specifically, it is a reflection of the top leaders' interpretation of the educational environment. By virtue of their position, leaders influence the system's culture and can respond to their perception of the environment in ways that manifest their beliefs and values about the nature of educating young people, the task of education, and its processes. Consequently, the identified mission directly influences the major direction of a school system. For example, one system may state its primary mission as vocational education, whereas others may concentrate on basic skills, college preparation, special education, or community education.

Over a period of time, all school systems experience changing environmental factors. These environmental shifts can create a need to redefine the general mission of the school system. For example, a school system that has moved beyond the period of expansion in its life cycle may begin to see population shifts away from the central city to suburban areas with expanding pockets of non-English-speaking populations. This important environmental change should bring about an examination of the system's mission. If a new mission statement results, the system needs to make changes in its strategic plan. On the other hand, if the leaders of the school system misinterpret or ignore the changing environment and do not refocus the system's mission, obvious conflicts will invariably arise between the system and its constituencies.

Tethered to the realities of the external environment, a mission statement for a particular school system is developed. A written mission statement helps the system define its vision for the future; it provides a clear focus for the system's personnel; and it identifies a rallying point for committing the human and material resources of the district. Establishing a mission and implementing it through planned strategies permits a school system to shape the organization that it wants to become. It provides a perspective for the future of the system and a purpose for the continued existence of the system. The mission statement addresses three important questions: *What* is the function of the school system (i.e., what client needs will it attempt to fulfill)? *Whom* does the system serve? and *How* will the system provide its services, (i.e., what methods will be used or technologies applied) (Pfeiffer, Goodstein, & Nolan, 1986b)?

Deciding what function the school system serves within its environment is the first step in deriving a mission. This function focuses upon the current and emerging educational needs of the community. A school organization should not only ask what its purpose is, but why the organization exists and what unique contributions it can make (King & Cleland, 1978). Answers to these questions help the school system to carefully identify its vision for the future. With a vision in mind, the question of whom it serves becomes germane. Environmental changes require a school system to reevaluate its mission statement periodically. Usually, the mission statement should be reviewed every 5 years to ensure that it meets the needs of the communities it serves. One essential ingredient of the mission statement is an identification of the segment of the population served. No school system can be everything to everyone. Market segmentation requires a review of the actual population the school system serves as well as whom it might potentially serve. In addition to geographical boundaries, the school system must know the ages of the people it serves; it must know the ethnic makeup of the community; it should have a good sense of the community's financial resources; and it should fully understand the values of the people. The school system completes its mission statement by determining how it will perform its function. The "how" response in the mission statement is expressed in general terms and gives guidance to material and personnel resource allocations, for example, *The district will use the latest technologies whose effectiveness is supported by research findings and will employ the most qualified teachers who demonstrate a readiness to use the technologies.*

The mission statement is carefully studied by the school system in relation to the realities of the external environment. A careful examination of the mission statement should be conducted to determine if it satisfies the following 10 criteria set forth by Pfeiffer et al. (1986b):

1. The mission statement is clear and understandable to all personnel, including rank-and-file employees.
2. The mission statement is brief enough for most people to keep in mind.
3. The mission statement clearly specifies what business the organization is in. This includes a clear statement about:
   a. "What" customer or client needs the organization is attempting to fill, not what products or services are offered;
   b. "Who" the organization's primary customers or clients are; and
   c. "How" the organization plans to go about its business, that is, what its primary technologies are.
4. The mission statement should have a primary focus on a single strategic thrust.
5. The mission statement should reflect the distinctive competence of the organization.
6. The mission statement should be broad enough to allow flexibility in implementation but not so broad as to permit a lack of focus.
7. The mission statement should serve as a template and be the means by which managers and others in the organization can make decisions.

8. The mission statement must reflect the values, beliefs, and philosophy of operations of the organization and reflect the organization's culture.
9. The mission statement should reflect attainable goals.
10. The mission statement should be worded so as to serve as an energy source and rallying point for the organization. (p. 82)

Develop Strategic Objectives (2.12).   A school system's strategic objectives should focus upon critical success indicators. As the system conceptualizes its future, it must identify specific factors for measuring both success or failure in achieving that future and the progress toward its mission (Pfeiffer et al., 1986b). These indicators are translated into specific objectives that provide directions for the use of the school system's resources (time, energy, and money). Achievement of these strategic objectives demonstrates the system's success in achieving its mission.

Objectives are usually focused on outcomes and are client centered and positively stated. Moreover, the strategic objectives should be related to those indicators against which the school system's constituencies evaluate its success (e.g., improved test scores, low dropout rate, scholarships and awards, employment after graduation, college entrance, etc.).

Conduct Gap Analysis (2.13).   The gap analysis applies reality to the strategic planning process. It involves a review of each strategic objective by comparing the desired outcomes to current outcomes in light of internal scanning information. In other words, the analysis reveals the gap between the outcomes desired and current outcomes in relation to available human and material resources, technologies, and instructional processes. One question frequently raised is whether the objectives provide sufficient challenge to stretch the creative thinking of the organization's members during the development of strategies. A response to this question may suggest that the outcomes sought by the strategic objectives be increased to press for greater challenges or, perhaps, lowered to reflect certain realities.

Develop Strategies (2.14).   Strategies are statements about how the proposed strategic objectives will be achieved. If the objective of increasing the reading scores of middle-grade students by a specified amount in a given period of time is established, one strategy might be to evaluate the middle grade's reading curriculum; another may stipulate the creation of an intensive staff development program in reading for middle-grades teachers; and a third might create a new screening and selection program for processing applicants to teach in the middle grades. Certainly, there could be others. Strategy selection is dependent upon the expertise of the system's strategic planners, the creativity and competencies of its staff, and their interpretations of both external and internal data from environmental scans.

Strategies are the administrators most important tools for coping with change, and they provide important bases for mitigating extraneous demands on the school system. Therefore, school administrators must learn to manage strategically; that is, their day-to-day decisions must relate consistently to the strategies adopted for the system's strategic objectives, and their decisions should move the organization in the direction of its mission.

The function of human resources must be integral to the school system's strategic plan by providing direction for future developments of human resources in conjunction with the system's identified mission, strategic objectives, and strategies. Human resources should never be overlooked in developing strategic objectives or strategies (Smith, 1982).

Human resources planning cannot stand alone; it must be part of the organization's strategic plan. The human resources operational plan is just as important as a curriculum or a financial plan and should be developed in ways that are consistent with objectives of the system's strategic plan. Additionally, system strategic objectives and strategies provide specific direction for the development of individual school operational plans, which also reflect the need for human resource considerations.

Operational Plans (2.2).   Operational plans are developed for all functional areas of the school system. These include central office departments or units as well as individual schools. To develop operational plans for the several subunits of the school system (e.g., departments, program divisions, and schools), each subunit engages in crafting plans to achieve the integrating function of the overall strategic plan.

Operational plans are specific to one or more of the established strategic objectives and strategies. The aggregate impact of all operational plans particular to the same strategic objective will contribute to achieving that objective. This concentration of effort is the appeal of strategic planning. It brings important systemwide priorities into focus through operational plans that impact in different ways the achievement of mutually agreed upon objectives. For example, if some area of student achievement is a priority, then the human resources department can develop an operational plan to direct its staffing practices for improving the personnel mix serving this area of the curriculum; the staff development unit could frame operational plans to improve instructional strategies or the knowledge base of teachers in the area; the curriculum unit might map this area of the curriculum to find possible incongruencies; the administration may establish an operational plan to increase public awareness; and the finance unit may work with another unit of the school system to seek external project funding. Each of these approaches can take the form of operational plans for individual functional units of the system or represent plans of cross-functional areas. This example is presented to show how many parts of the organization develop operational plans that target a single strategic objective, but use several strategies.

Included in the operational plans are goals to give direction to the overall effort, objectives to establish targets or outcomes sought by the plan, procedures for implementation, policy considerations, time schedules, implementation constraints, and monitoring procedures for control and evaluation. All plans are reviewed so that a coordinated effort can be used to minimize program overlap.

School Operational Plans (2.21).   The school is the primary unit for delivering services in a school system. Each school will have its own operational plan, which reflects strategic objectives that are consistent with the system's strategic objectives. An individual school's plan will focus upon the unique needs of its students and will be in harmony with its immediate environment.

Obviously, as operational plans vary from school to school, people with different skills and abilities will be required to achieve the school's strategic objectives. The requirements for a professional staff mix for two elementary schools might be quite different. For example, suppose a primary component of a system's mission is basic skills, and the system has the strategic objective of raising reading scores on a standardized achievement test to the national mean in 5 years. One school might identify reading as a strategic priority. Another school that has maintained a mean achievement score in reading that is well above the national norm may focus its energy and resources on another strategic priority. Accordingly, each school may require a different professional staff mix. Such considerations have important implications for staff development, recruitment, and selection. Thus these considerations should be reflected in the strategic human resources plan. In practice, the balancing of the professional staff mix has not been widely implemented, despite its importance to strategic planning. Strong school board policies that reflect the importance of professional staff mix to strategic planning may help to promote a more balanced mix in the future.

This situation can serve as another example for understanding a school's operational plan. Certainly, the strategic objective of increasing scores on basic skills tests has implications for site-based budgeting, possible curricular or organizational changes, and of course personnel. Figure 4.1 shows how these considerations become inputs into the operational plans of the system's functional areas.

System Operational Plans (2.22). Each functional area at the system level must have an operational plan for integrating all of the school unit strategies. The need for a different professional staff mix, as mentioned in the previous example, is again used for purposes of illustration. If shifts in staff are required to optimize the mix, the personnel function would incorporate in its operational plan changes that accommodate all school units at an optimal level. Similar changes in the areas of curriculum or budgeting could affect any number of functional areas. Consequently, the specific strategies of each of these functional areas may have implications for an integrated human resources strategy.

The **human resources (2.222) operational plan** reflects an integration of the various school unit plans and the system functional plans. The model does not represent a linear flow of information; on the contrary, there is neither a beginning nor an end. It is a continuous process of integration that supports the school system's strategic plan. Each unit and functional area of the system provides input to the human resources operational plan and has a role to play in its formulation and subsequent implementation.

Harvey (1983) identified eight principles involved in formulating a strategic human resources plan:

1. The individual unit plans (school plans and plans of other units) must be tied to the organization's plan. Each unit must plan with the aim of accomplishing the organization's strategic objectives.
2. Planning must be conducted systematically and routinely. Each plan should conform to a timetable and planning cycle. This is usually tied to the organization's budget year.

3. Long-range and short-range considerations should be reflected in the plan. Planning implies preparation for the future. Operational plans are usually done on a 6- to 12-month basis, whereas long-range planning is for 5 years or more.
4. The plan must be reviewed and modified. The plan must be flexible so that it can be modified to reflect unexpected changes in the environment (e.g., financial or legal).
5. Planning must be related to the budget if it is to be implemented. It should be completed before the budget so that the budget can reflect its requirements. It would be very unlikely that a plan would be implemented if it were not considered in the budget process.
6. The plan must be based on data. Certainly the decision process in human resources includes professional and expert judgment. If reliable, valid data are used to support decisions, the results will produce higher quality decisions. Fortunately, the emergence of new technology in recent years has brought data-based decision making to the smallest school systems.
7. The plan must be tied to administrative activities. It should lead to specific responsibilities and assignments. Objectives should be established to ensure a measure of accountability, and a timetable should be developed. The linkage of the plan to such action should be reviewed periodically.
8. Individuals with relevant data and keen perspectives should be involved in the planning. Although the top administrators still have to make final decisions, the involvement of those with special insights or information will produce decisions that can be more effectively implemented.

The human resources operational plan should accomplish three objectives. First, it should correlate with the strategic plan of the system. Second, it should enumerate required changes in personnel, school board personnel policies, and administrative regulations and processes so that the system's strategic objectives can be achieved. Finally, it should provide a master plan for recruiting, selecting, training, promoting, compensating, and developing human resources for the system (Galosy, 1983).

Implementation (3.0)

The results of implementing operational plans provides both product and process data that become feedback to other elements of the model. This feedback gives evidence to support a need for the refinement, modification, or reformulation of other aspects of the plan. In some instances objectives will be changed. On occasion the mission statement will be rewritten, or new strategies will be developed.

CORRELATION WITH THE SYSTEM PLAN

School systems generally have not extensively involved their human resources units in the development of strategic plans. Despite the obvious and important advantages of integrating strategic planning and human resources planning, the educational literature does not suggest that such planning is taking place. Historically, human resources administrators have not been involved in strategic decisions. Most decisions of a strategic nature have usually involved the superintendent and a small group of others, such as those responsible for finance or curriculum. If the human resources plan is to be integrated with the system's strategic plan, human resources administrators must give attention to four basic tasks (Dyer, 1984).

The first task is to discover how the school system's educational strategies are determined. Many decisions are based on formal planning procedures that are presented to the superintendent and board of education for approval. By contrast, many strategic decisions result from a response to a crisis or an ad hoc effort of a temporary task force. Thus the human resources administrator must be aware of both the formal and informal decision-making processes.

A second task is to determine how much consideration is given to human resources in the strategic planning process. Do the plans include factors of professional staffing, development, recruitment, and selection? Are appropriate data collected and correctly analyzed? Are these data used to forecast future human resources needs and supply of personnel? Are the results of such analyses used in decision making?

Another task is to decide the amount of consideration that should be given to human resources. Although education is a personnel-intense industry, different strategies will dictate different levels of involvement. A strategic plan to close several low-enrollment schools may dictate different human resources requirements than a plan for a bond election to renovate school facilities. Both would require human resources consideration. Yet the former may be more critical when considering human resources than the latter.

The fourth task is to work toward closing the gap between the amount of consideration that should be given and that actually given to human resources in strategic educational planning. This gap can be closed by continuously giving attention to the credibility of the human resources organization. The professional staff must be regarded as competent. They must be knowledgeable about education and educational issues as well as most other aspects of the educational processes in the school system, including curriculum design and development.

Finally, in order to integrate the human resources plan with the system's strategic plan, three excesses should be avoided: possessiveness, parochialism, and negativism. Possessiveness relates to those who feel that human resources issues belong to them alone. Parochialism stems from seeing everything from a personnel perspective rather than an educational one. Negativism is indicated by an automatic negative response rather than an attempt to formulate constructive approaches to critical personnel issues (Dyer, 1984).

INFORMATION NEEDS AND FORECASTING

Collecting and analyzing valid and current human resources information relative to the school system's strategic objectives can provide a basis for ensuring that the human resources development efforts correlate with strategic educational plans. Human resources information must be collected from the different units of the organization, compared, and reported in a form that supports strategic decisions. Specific data about compensation, professional staff mix, and performance appraisals are important factors around which data are collected.

Forecasting Personnel Needs

Personnel forecasts are needed to provide a basis of maintaining productivity levels, identifying future professional staff mix, preventing staff shortages, minimizing the costs of overstaffing, and complying with equal employment opportunity goals (Rothwell & Kazanas, 1988). Another factor includes forecasting the attrition of personnel. Attrition results from personnel who move to new positions within the organization, leave the organization for positions elsewhere, or retire. An investigation of such changes requires the human resources organization to develop expertise in forecasting.

A forecast of changes in personnel provides human resources administrators with information that can be used to guide action to achieve the strategic objectives of the system. Such changes are often studied through the use of cohort analyses, census analyses, or more complex procedures related to Markov chains. The reader is referred to Feuer, Niehaus, & Sheridan (1984) for a comprehensive review of current forecasting practices. Also, Bell (1974) provides an expanded discussion of many widely used forecasting methodologies. For a more technically oriented discussion, the reader should see Bartholomew and Forbes (1979). The following discussion is a simple example of a Markovian analysis for forecasting personnel changes.

Table 4.1 illustrates the movement of six classifications of personnel in a school system. In this example, the hypothetical system has 1,460 professional employees including 300 primary teachers, 250 intermediate-level teachers, 230 upper-level teachers, 500 secondary teachers, 80 supervisors, and 100 administrators. These employee classifications and current employment levels are listed in columns a and b. Data in columns c through h are probability factors for each of the classifications. The factors are based on the mean percentage of personnel changes for the past 5 years, and it is assumed that these transition probabilities remain stable over time. Column c shows a probability of .60 (60%) for primary teachers to remain on the job during the year, .15 (15%) for primary teachers to move to an intermediate-level teaching position, .05 (5%) to move to an upper-level teaching responsibility, .01 (1%) to become supervisors, and .19 (19%) to leave the system. In a similar manner, the intermediate-level teachers (column d) have a probability of .10 for moving to primary teaching, .70 to stay on the job, .10 to move to upper-level teaching; and .10 to leave the organization.

Projections by classifications for the following year are presented in column i. The projection for each classification is based upon the sum of the products of the probability factors and their corresponding employment level for the current year. For example, a projection of the number of primary teachers available the next year is $(.60 \times 300) + (.10 \times 250) = 180 + 25 = 205$. Similarly, a projection of upper-level teachers is $(.05 \times 300) + (.10 \times 250) + (.70 \times 230) + (.05 \times 500) + (.01 \times 80) = 15 + 25 + 161 + 25 + 1 = 227$. Using this procedure for the other classifications, the projection for intermediate-level teachers is 243; secondary teachers, 389; supervisors, 80; and administrators, 96.

If one wishes to conduct a Markovian analysis involving more classifications of personnel, an electronic spreadsheet such as Lotus 1-2-3 would render the analysis an easy task. The use of a spreadsheet would also allow the human resources planner to ask "what if" questions where different assumptions about attrition could be investigated.

TABLE 4.1
Markovian Analysis of Personnel Attrition

Classification a	Current Employment Level b	Primary c	Intermediate d	Upper e	Secondary f	Supervisors g	Administrators h	Projection i
Primary	300	0.60	0.10					205
Intermediate	250	0.15	0.70	0.10				243
Upper	230	0.05	0.10	0.70	0.05	0.01		227
Secondary	500			0.06	0.75			389
Supervisors	80	0.01			0.01	0.90		80
Administrators	100			0.01	0.01	0.05	0.85	96
Exit		0.19	0.01	0.13	0.18	0.04	0.15	

Forecasting Student Enrollments

One cannot dispute the importance of making reliable enrollment projections because they are related to strategic decisions about staffing, curriculum, facilities, and financing. Most projections are made from extensive data sets incorporating 10 years or more of data that may include past school enrollments, current enrollments, parochial and private school enrollments, nonresident enrollments, children per dwelling unit, resident live births, socioeconomic indicators, shifts of population, mobility of families, in/out migration, housing starts, transfer rates, home resales, and student retention rates. Additionally, selected factors such as building patterns, types of dwellings, community patterns, transportation changes, integration, and national trends are frequently used to temper the statistical treatment of the historical data for localizing projections.

Some of the early forecasting methods were discussed by Strevell (1952) and included the use of data related to class projections, retention ratio projections, housing projections, and total population forecasts. About the same time, Linn's (1956) approach for making enrollment projections included school enrollment trends over a 20-year period, current enrollments, parochial and private school enrollments, nonresident enrollments, birth rate trends, residential construction, children per dwelling unit, and the number of preschool children. About 2 decades later, Leggett (1973) and Engelhardt (1973) asserted that accurate forecasts could be made by using birth rate trends and cohort survival ratios. Strong and Schultz (1975) demonstrated the effectiveness of a regression model that used previous years' enrollments, increases in population of children by age, students not promoted, and students entering the labor force.

The cohort survival method has been a popular forecasting technique for much of the past 20 years. As enrollments began to decline in the late 1970s, "school administrators and boards of education face[ed] a major new public relations job: explaining the cost of decline" (Neill, 1979, p. 6), and a compelling interest emerged in forecasting enrollment declines. In a study of the cohort survival method, Shaw (1980) found that it functioned slightly better for school districts experiencing enrollment declines as compared to those with increasing enrollments.

Many methods of projecting student enrollments have been chronicled during the past 4 decades as being reliable, and each required the analysis of large data sets representing many factors with data for periods of 10 or more years. Such analyses were laborious and time consuming. Now with the emergence of powerful microcomputers, such analyses and data management problems can be handled with ease and speed.

There is no statistical model that can embody all important factors in projecting student enrollments. Fortunately, recent developments in formulating complex computer algorithms for forecasting student enrollments have increased the reliability of such projections through the inclusion of many more factors than was previously possible. One such software package has been developed by Ecotran Systems, Inc., of Beachwood, Ohio.

Ecotran's MAPNET system is a basic transportation package that has an enrollment projection module for forecasting population trends and future school district enrollments. The system uses advanced statistical methods and historical data to make projections by grade, school, and geographical area. The module incorporates cohort survival and advanced econometric modeling techniques and uses up to 10 years of historical data. The system has the capability of calculating future populations from birth to grade 12 as well as ethnicity of population. Also, the projection model generated can be displayed on the school district map for further analysis.

Another system with similar capabilities is the ONPASS planning system that was developed by Educational Data Systems of San Jose, California. It is an online, computer-aided, student demographic system that is designed to free educational planners from the time-consuming manual procedures of analyzing alternatives in the educational decision-making process. The system is capable of making 5-year projections for the number of students attending schools of the district, percentage utilization of schools, the number of students in each grade level, the number of students in each ethnic group, and the average walk/ride distance of students from each school and from each planning area. Additionally, the system can make projections for the planning area from which students attend school, the number and demographics of students from each planning area, and the number of classrooms that will be required at each school and grade level in relation to an established minimum and maximum class size, including combination classes where necessary. All of these projections are based on aging of the student population, in/out migration, new housing construction, cohort survival statistics, and entry-level enrollment projections.

EDULOG is a another enrollment projection model that was developed by Education Logistics, Inc., of Missoula, Montana. Like the two mentioned previously, this system projects enrollments by grade for the system, individual schools, planning zones, racial/ethnic categories, new attendance boundaries, user-defined student attributes, and other meaningful geographically defined planning areas. The system is based on a modified cohort survival technique that separately identifies the various factors determining enrollment patterns within a district. The model is capable of making enrollment forecasts out to 15 years.

Because of the improved reliability and ease of using such forecasting systems, the work of the educational planner can be greatly facilitated through their application in making strategic decisions. Certainly, there are other similar systems available and there will be more and improved systems in the future. It is most important for all school administrators to be aware of such developments and their potential for facilitating administrative decision making.

POLICY, REGULATION, PROCESSES, AND PERSONNEL CHANGES

"Almost all policies—whether called 'personnel policies' or not—affect staff members in some way" (National School Boards Association, 1982, p. 45). Therefore, the strategic plan of a school system will invariably require that certain school board policies and administrative regulations be changed or new ones developed so that strategic objectives can be accomplished. As a part of the strategic plan, the section of the document related to human resources should enumerate the need for these changes with specific recommendations.

For instance, the human resources plan may include the objective to raise the minimum level of certification or formal preparation for instructional personnel. This objective is to be fully implemented within a specified period of time. Also, an analysis of school board policies may suggest that there are inadequate policies and corresponding regulations for guiding the implementation of the objective. The human resources operational plan would include recommended additions or changes to policies and administrative regulations. Obviously, other functional areas, such as finance, may be affected by such changes.

A school system that is experiencing serious retrenchment problems due to declining enrollments provides another example. If the school district's objective is to close a number of schools, then specific human resources objectives that relate to the reduction of professional personnel must be developed. In this regard, a human resources objective might be to establish a program to eliminate a specific number of positions within a time period consistent with the staggered closing of schools. Of course, the plan would require investigations of personnel turnover trends, age distribution of personnel, professional staff mix for the total system, and other relevant considerations, such as personnel contract agreements and legal implications. If, for example, the analysis of all important data suggest offering early retirement incentives, the plan would have to be approved by the board of education. Certain policy areas and regulations would have to be examined to provide for the plan's implementation. In addition, the plan would require the consideration of system procedures and personnel changes.

PERSONNEL RECRUITMENT

An important aspect of a human resources plan is consideration of recruiting personnel. Glueck (1978) defined recruiting as a "set of activities an enterprise uses to attract job candidates who have the abilities and attitudes needed to help the enterprise achieve its objectives" (p. 150). From a strategic human resources perspective, the goal of recruiting is to identify a pool of qualified people from which to secure the services of those most qualified, who in turn would help the organization achieve its objectives. This goal sets the direction for discussing a four-element model. The elements include (1) analysis and development, (2) need, (3) a recruitment program, and (4) evaluation.

Analysis and Development

The focus of the beginning stages of the plan should center on an analysis of the system's objectives and of their implications for recruiting human resources. Such an analysis should provide a basis for developing strategic recruitment objectives. The system objective of raising the mean achievement score for students to the national mean might have as a consistent recruitment objective an increase in both the number and qualifications of persons in the pool of qualified teachers. The recruiting objective could specify seeking candidates with higher qualifications in mathematics at critical levels of need. For example, the objective might be stated as follows: "The recruitment of intermediate-level teachers of mathematics will be intensified so that the pool of qualified persons is increased by 20% with a mean increase of 30% in formal academic training or experience." Notice that this objective provides very specific directions for the recruitment of intermediate-level teachers of mathematics. Also, the specifications of the objective will produce a measure of accountability for the personnel in charge of recruiting.

A second level of analysis relates to school board policies and administrative regulations. The previously stated objective may have implications for existing policies or regulations. Current school board policies may not provide the latitude to implement the objective. Moreover, administrative regulations may be too restrictive for out-of-state applicants and may require modifications. If a board policy prohibits out-of-state travel to recruit personnel and the pool of intermediate-level mathematics teachers graduating from state colleges is too small, the plan would have to address possible modifications to the policy statement. Of course, this assumes the pool from other sources is also limited. Once the objective has been determined and a policy analysis conducted, need can be established.

Need

Generally, need is the gap between the number of qualified personnel required to staff a program and the number in existing positions. The assessment of need involves an analysis of information and data about several important areas. The areas include the staffing or destaffing needs of all schools and other units of the school system, the system's strategic objectives, forecast trends by classification, professional staff mix, and supply-demand studies. Supply-demand studies are often conducted by the Department of Labor, universities, and state departments of education. The Georgia Department of Education's Teacher Recruitment Office maintains data for school districts relative to teacher and administrator supply and demand.

A need analysis will provide a basis for determining the number of personnel to be recruited into each classification pool. It will help to determine where the greatest emphasis must be placed in recruitment according to classification area. It will also help to define individual roles and methods in the recruitment program.

Recruitment Program

The recruitment program identifies the involvement of specific individuals. It also identifies the most appropriate methods and the best recruitment sources for achieving the objectives of the recruitment plan.

Based upon a previous analysis of school board policies, the board of education may be required to develop and adopt new recruitment policies. Policies not only provide a legal basis for the action of recruiters, they also give specific direction about the board's commitment to the human resources recruitment process. The following examples are only a few of many policy areas that may be considered in a human resources plan:

- ☐ Recruitment from within or outside the system
- ☐ Employment of persons from other systems
- ☐ Travel expenses of candidates
- ☐ Moving expenses of candidates
- ☐ Involvement of building-level staff in recruiting
- ☐ Affirmative action

By examining this short list, it is apparent that a board of education can have a profound impact on the recruiting program of the system.

A board's commitment to affirmative action is but one example of its impact. An important consideration of a recruitment program is that its processes reflect practices of equal employment opportunities for all minorities (Kohl & Stephens, 1989; Laabs, 1991). Certain human resources strategies may mandate that the board demonstrate a strong commitment to the employment of women and minorities. Such a commitment can be demonstrated through a board policy and the establishment of an affirmative action plan on file with the Equal Employment Opportunity Commission (EEOC). Normally, affirmative action plans enumerate the following considerations provided for in the EEOC affirmative action guidelines. The first four items are paraphrased from "Affirmative Action Guidelines" (1979) and the last three from Harris, McIntyre, Littleton, and Long (1979).

1. A policy statement communicates the board's commitment to affirmative action.
2. The plan provides for public information, both internal and external, to explain it.
3. A school official has the responsibility and commensurate authority to administer the plan.
4. The plan includes a work-force utilization self-analysis to determine if current employment practices operate as restrictions to equal employment opportunities.
5. The plan provides for modifications of present practices to eliminate discriminatory practices.
6. When underutilized minority group members and women have been identified, the plan includes goals for improving their conditions and a timetable for implementing the goals.
7. The plan includes a system for monitoring, evaluating, and reporting to respond to the effectiveness of the plan's implementation processes.

The recruitment plan can also involve others in its implementation, including the superintendent of schools, the human resources administrator and staff, other administrators, and teachers, depending on their ability to assist in meeting the objectives for the recruitment plan.

The recruitment plan should include a description of the different methods to be employed in reaching the important recruitment sources. If it is determined that several colleges in the region consistently graduate high-quality students in an area of identified need, specific plans should be established to reach this source. Holzer (1989) identified the following areas for recruiting college graduates: referrals from on-campus interviews, listing jobs with college placement offices, and referrals from college faculty and staff.

The National School Boards Association (1982) listed other potential recruitment sources that included the following:

- [ ] Referrals from current employees
- [ ] Lateral transfers of current employees
- [ ] Promotions of effective personnel
- [ ] College and university placement offices
- [ ] Placement offices of professional organizations
- [ ] Letters to colleagues in other systems, especially in systems that are reducing their work force

A recent development that will help improve the recruitment process is the use of the electronic bulletin board. A number of organizations now maintain electronic listings of positions available. Some permit those seeking positions to place short summaries of their qualifications on the bulletin board for use by potential employers. This new tool should prove to be a valuable means of bringing employer and potential employee together, especially in rural areas where recruiting tends to present special challenges to human resources administrators.

Finally, the plan should present an outcome or product evaluation design to consider the effects of the recruitment directed toward the strategic activities of the program. In addition, the plan should identify procedures to determine the effectiveness of the processes involved in implementing the plan.

SUMMARY

Strategic human resources planning is a process of preparing a school system for activities in the future, and its decisions related to the use of personnel must show evidence of contributing to the system's objectives. Generally, its purpose is to ensure that the human resources of the school system are employed efficiently and effectively in pursuit of identified outcomes.

The effective planning of human resources requires a system for maintaining relevant systemwide data and information. This information is used to forecast trends on which to base decision making; provide for an optimal professional staff mix; and support other functions, such as recruitment, compensation, and affirmative action.

The implementation of strategic human resources planning must be based upon an analysis of the environment. It should be sensitive to the culture of the school system. In addition, the human resources objectives must be consistent with the system's mission and its strategic objectives.

The planning process should be comprehensive and include all subunits of the school system. The plans for each subunit should be integrated to form an overall plan for the total organization. The process is continuous and should conform to the planning cycle of the system, with a multiyear emphasis of 5 years. Finally, the process should be flexible and participatory to accommodate change and expert staff involvement.

DISCUSSION QUESTIONS

1. Either individually or in small discussion groups, identify two different school systems in your immediate area and describe the evolutionary stages that each school system has experienced. Share these descriptions with the class. Discuss how they are alike and how they are different. Can you predict the emerging evolutionary stage of each school system?

2. Based on the descriptions in question 1, what are some of the most important human resources needs for each system during the next 2–5 years? What priorities should be given to optimizing the professional staff mix? What will be the most important human resources needs in 10–15 years?

3. In discussion groups, make a list of cultural elements that exist in your school or school system. Discuss the differences found on each list and how the several elements affect the behaviors of personnel.

CASE 4.1
Mixed Expectations

Frank Hennessy was filled with excitement as he hung up the telephone. Dr. Brad Richardson, the superintendent, had just asked him to chair the newly created planning committee for strategic planning. As the director of human resources for the Cherryhill School District, he felt that he would now be able to play an important part in shaping the future of the district.

As Frank reflected on the challenges facing the committee, he felt that strategic planning would help the district to become proactive by carefully considering its primary thrust. In the past, Frank had argued to narrow the focus of the district. He felt there were so many demands being made on the limited resources of Cherryhill that every program ended up with only limited financial or personnel support. Now, he hoped that strategic planning would help the school district to narrow its focus by deciding what was important and making a serious commitment to the goals of highest priority.

The community has high expectations for the school district and has been willing to support requests for funds to improve nearly all academic programs. Parents have been very pleased with the apparent rigorous demands made of students. The district has always had a very strong college preparatory program, with 78% of its graduates entering college upon graduation, and a sizable number of the district's seniors have been successful in getting admitted to some of the more prestigious colleges.

Despite the fact that the curriculum has always been geared to the college-bound students, a number of pressure groups have been successful in getting the board of education to install a vocational program that has been a drain on the district's financial resources and according to some citizens is "taking money away from the more important challenge of preparing students for college." On the other hand, an emerging group of young parents has been working with the coaches to get more emphasis placed on athletics. Some board policies make it difficult for students to fully participate in interscholastic competition. Recently, two star football players were not allowed to participate due to poor grades in academic courses.

The first meeting of the committee was held in a retreat setting at a country lodge, where Superintendent Richardson welcomed the committee. He also talked about the importance of the committee's work and requested their total commitment to the strategic planning process. Frank knew that the superintendent's strong statement showing a commitment to and belief in strategic planning nearly ensured a good kickoff meeting.

After the superintendent spoke, Frank led the group in a discussion of strategic planning by presenting an applied model for school district planning. This model was the one recommended by the State Department of Education in a workshop that Frank attended last year. This was followed by several group exercises that involved the members in a discussion of values related to educational issues. All the exercises were focused on consensus decision making that precipitated much more discussion and heated debate than Frank anticipated.

Later, Frank administered a strategic planning readiness instrument and wrote the group's results on the chalkboard. At this point, Frank led a discussion of the results. He was surprised that the scores showed such a high degree of readiness for the team to plan strategically. This was the last activity of the day and the meeting was adjourned.

During the morning session on the next day, Frank explained environmental scanning by using the acronym SWOT. He talked about the importance of knowing both the external and internal environments of the school district. This led to a lengthy discussion of many aspects of the district's environment.

Following lunch, Frank introduced the concept of a mission statement and its relationship to strategic planning. He emphasized the importance of addressing the questions of What? Who? and How? He asked the planning team members to each develop a written response to the What question. Frank told the committee to write their statements on the chalkboard, and they would discuss their responses after the coffee break.

As Frank scanned the statements posted, he was surprised to find statements that were

very diverse. This concerned him because he feared that a discussion of these statements would deteriorate into serious arguments. Thus he decided to ask the committee members to read only their responses, and he told them that he would make copies of these statements for the next meeting. Frank wanted to give some careful thought to how he might handle the obvious conflicts that would emerge.

Charles Winters read his statement first. He said, "Cherryhill is committed to providing programs that meet the needs of students by developing excellence in both physical and academic abilities through challenge and competition."

Jeannie Crawford followed with, "It is the purpose of Cherryhill to provide quality education with an emphasis on the basics."

Board member Fredericks followed by very forcefully stating, "Cherryhill School District is committed to providing quality educational programs that will support gainful employment of its graduates."

The Teacher-of-the-Year, Cecilia Cousins, followed with, "It is our purpose to provide a comprehensive educational program that will satisfy the social, psychological, physical, and educational needs of our children."

Sandy Christian read, "The Cherryhill School System is committed to helping students to develop a strong self-concept and a sense of self-esteem."

Principal Joe Tensley offered, "We are committed to providing programs of quality basic education in an environment that supports trust and mutual respect."

Nelson Thomas showed his strong interest in vocational education when he read his statement. "Cherryhill School District will provide a program to support the development of job-related skills that are augmented by skills in basic education."

Terri Moore then read her statement, "Our school system commits itself to providing quality programs that support the educational development and personal interests of all citizens of the community."

Finally, Dr. Richardson stated, "We at Cherryhill commit ourselves to providing the highest quality of education for our students that is focused on student interests and academics."

Frank then thanked the group and told them that he would have the statements reproduced for the next meeting in 6 weeks. At this point he was glad that no discussion followed because he didn't want to end the meeting in controversy. As he drove home, he wondered if any of the statements really reflected what the Cherryhill community wanted. For the next several days, he was preoccupied with thoughts of what to do next.

Questions

1. What problem(s) will Frank have to deal with at the next meeting?
2. What are some symptoms of the problem(s)?
3. What are all of the possible actions that Frank might take to solve the problem(s)?
4. What consequences should Frank anticipate from implementing each of the actions?
5. What action should Frank attempt?

CASE 4.2
The State Mandate

Joan Ellis, a seasoned human resources administrator, attended several workshops on strategic human resources planning that the State Department of Education offered. She tried for several years to convince the superintendent to consider strategic planning in the district because she strongly valued the process and felt that it would greatly help her district. Also, she had reliable information from a friend at the State Department of Education suggesting that it was only a matter of time before the State Board of Education would mandate that all school districts develop annual strategic plans.

Joan knew that the superintendent did not value any type of serious planning. She fre-

quently recalled one of the superintendent's rebuttals to her planning suggestions, "We tried that comprehensive planning once, and it was a waste of time. The governor even had a conference on it. Then we had to submit that huge report that was probably never read."

As expected, the State Board adopted a regulation that required all school districts in the state to plan strategically and submit their plans to the Department of Education for approval.

When the superintendent received notification of the requirement from the State Superintendent of Public Instruction, he asked the assistant superintendent for administrative services, the assistant superintendent for business affairs, and the director of finance to write the plan. Joan was not asked to be involved.

Questions

1. Did the superintendent make a good decision?
2. What problems can be anticipated from the superintendent's decision?
3. What are the possible actions that Joan might take?
4. What consequences can be anticipated from each action?
5. What should Joan do?

CASE 4.3
Sara's New Assignment

At the last meeting of the board of education, Sara Brock was appointed as the new assistant superintendent for human resources. The board's approval was another vote of confidence for Dr. Jerry Nixon who was appointed superintendent only 1 year ago.

Superintendent Nixon's decision to recommend Sara was based on her strong background in strategic planning and previous experiences as the director of personnel in a neighboring school system. Previously she directed the strategic planning effort of a large school system in another state.

During her first day on the job, Sara was arranging her personal belongings in a beautifully redecorated office when Dr. Nixon stopped by to give her the old "Welcome aboard" greeting. After a few minutes of casual conversation, he said, "Oh, by the way, I need your help. The board is eager to support my suggestions on strategic planning for the district. They asked me to give them a set of recommended board policies that they can consider for getting this effort underway. This is going to be one of the most important things that this school system has ever done, and the community will be watching it closely. You'll have to be a key player in this effort. So, what I'd like you to do is set up whatever committees you need for developing the policies and get back to me as soon as possible."

Questions

1. What considerations should Sara give to forming the committee? Who should be involved?
2. What should be the committee agenda at the beginning of the committee's work?
3. What policy areas should be reviewed in preparation for making policy recommendations to the board?

REFERENCES

Affirmative action guidelines. (1979, January 19). *Federal Register, 44,* 4422–4430.

Alpander, G. (1980). Human resource planning in U.S. corporations. *California Management Review, 22*(2), 24–32.

Anthony, P., & Norton, A. N. (1991). Link HR to corporate strategy. *Personnel Journal, 70,* 75–82.

Baird, L., Meshoulam, I., & DeGive, G. (1983). Meshing human resources planning with strategic business planning: A model approach. *Personnel, 60*(5), 14–25.

Bartholomew, D. J., & Forbes, A. F. (1979). *Statistical techniques for manpower planning.* Chichester, UK: Wiley.

Bell, D. J. (1974). *Planning corporate manpower.* London: Longman Group.

Carlson, R. V. (1991). Culture and organizational planning. In R. V. Carlson & G. Awkerman (Eds.), *Educational planning: Concepts, strategies, and practices* (pp. 49–63). New York: Longman.

Devanna, M. A., Fombrun, C., Tichy, N., & Warren, L. (1982). Strategic planning and human resource management. *Human Resource Management, 21,* 11–17.

Dror, Y. (1970). The planning process: A facet design. In F. J. Lyden & E. G. Miller (Eds.), *Planning, programming, budgeting: A systems approach to management* (pp. 93–116). Chicago: Markham.

Dyer, L. (1983). Bringing human resources into the strategy formulation process. *Human Resource Management, 22,* 257–273.

Dyer, L. (1984). Linking human resource and business strategies. *Human Resource Planning, 7*(2), 79–84.

Dyer, L., & Heyer, N. O. (1984). Human resource planning at IBM. *Human Resource Planning, 7,* 111–125.

Engelhardt, N. L. (1973, June/July). How to estimate your future enrollment. *School Management,* pp. 38–41.

Ernest, R. C. (1985). Corporate cultures and effective planning. *Personnel Administrator, 30*(3), 49–60.

Feuer, M. J., Niehaus, R. J., & Sheridan, J. A. (1984). Human resource forecasting: A survey of practice and potential. *Human Resource Planning, 7*(2), 85–97.

Galosy, J. R. (1983). Meshing human resources planning with strategic business planning: One company's experience. *Personnel, 60*(5), 26–35.

Glueck, W. F. (1978). *Personnel: A diagnostic approach.* Dallas: Business Publications.

Greer, C. R., Jackson, D. L., & Fiorito, J. (1989). Adapting human resource planning in a changing business environment. *Human Resource Management, 28,* 105–123.

Harris, B. M., McIntyre, K. E., Littleton, V. C., & Long, D. F. (1979). *Personnel administration in educa-*

tion: *Leadership for instructional improvement*. Boston: Allyn & Bacon.

Harris, P. R., & Harris, D. L. (1982). Human resources management. Part 1: Charting a new course in a new organization, a new society. *Personnel*, *59*(5), 11–17.

Harrison, R. (1983). Strategies for a new age. *Human Resource Management*, *22*, 217–223.

Harvey, L. J. (1983). Effective planning for human resource development. *Personnel Administrator*, *28*(10), 45–52, 112.

Holzer, H. J. (1989). *Utilization of public and private job search mechanisms: The experiences of employers and employees*. (ERIC Document Reproduction Service No. ED 317 685)

King, W. R., & Cleland, D. I. (1978). *Strategic planning and policy*. Atlanta: Van Nostrand Reinhold.

Kohl, J. P., & Stephens, D. B. (1989). Wanted: Recruitment advertising that doesn't discriminate. *Personnel*, *66*(2), 18–26.

Koys, R. L., Armacost, R. L., & Charalambides, L. C. (1990). Organizational resizing and human resource management. *SAM Advanced Management Journal*, *55*(3), 30–36.

Kydd, C. T., & Oppenheim, L. (1990). Using human resource management to enhance competitiveness: Lessons from four excellent companies. *Human Resource Management*, *29*, 145–166.

Laabs, J. J. (1991). Affirmative outreach. *Personnel Journal*, *70*(5), 86–89.

Leggett, S. (1973, January). How to forecast school enrollments accurately—and years ahead. *American School Board Journal*, pp. 25–31.

Linn, H. E. (1956). *School business administration*. New York: Ronald Press.

Miles, R. E., & Snow, C. C. (1984). Designing strategic human resources systems. *Organizational Dynamics*, *13*, 36–52.

Milkovich, G. T., & Boudreau, J. W. (1991). *Human resource management*. Boston: Irwin.

National School Boards Association. (1982). *The school personnel management system*. Washington, DC: Author.

Neill, S. B. (1979, January–February). The demographers' message to education. *American Education*, 6–11.

Nkomo, S. M. (1980). Stage three in personnel administration: Strategic human resources management. *Personnel*, *57*(4), 69–77.

Page, R. N. (1985, April). *Teachers' perceptions of students: A link between classrooms, school cultures, and the social order*. Paper presented at the meeting of the American Educational Research Association, Chicago, IL.

Pfeiffer, J. W., Goodstein, L. D., & Nolan, T. M. (1986a). Applied strategic planning: A new model for organizational growth and vitality. In J. W. Pfeiffer (Ed.), *Strategic planning: Selected readings* (pp. 1–25). San Diego: University Associates.

Pfeiffer, J. W., Goodstein, L. D., & Nolan, T. M. (1986b). *Applied strategic planning: A how to do it guide*. San Diego: University Associates.

Reichrath, M. R. (1990). *A study of strategic planning readiness in Georgia public school systems*. Unpublished doctoral dissertation, Georgia State University, Atlanta.

Rothwell, W. J., & Kazanas, H. C. (1988). *Strategic human resources planning and management*. Englewood Cliffs, NJ: Prentice-Hall.

Shaw, R. C. (1980). Forecasting enrollment during periods of enrollment decline. *North Central Association Quarterly*, *55*(1), 19–24.

Sibson, R. E. (1983). Strategic personnel planning. *Personnel Administrator*, *28*(11), 39-42.

Smith, E. C. (1982). Strategic business planning and human resources: Part II. *Personnel Journal*, *61*, 680–682.

Strevell, W. H. (1952, March). Techniques of estimating future enrollment. *School Board Journal*, pp. 35–38.

Strong, W. B., & Schultz, R. R. (1975). Models for projecting school enrollments. *Educational Evaluation and Policy Analysis*, *3*, 75–81.

Williamsport Area Community College. (1982, September). *A strategic planning model*. Williamsport, PA: Author.

Wright, P. M., & McMahan, G. C. (1992, June). Theoretical perspectives for strategic human resource management. *Journal of Management*, *18*(2), 295–320.

5

Policies and Regulations in the Human Resources Function

THE DEVELOPMENT OF PERSONNEL POLICIES AND REGULATIONS

Many persons express the belief that a school district's personnel policies and regulations are a direct reflection of how it values its human resources. Governing board policies directly effect the work and life of the school employees and the school district's clients. One premise of this text is that schools are people; the school's human resources determine in large part the extent to which the school system will achieve its purposes. For this reason and others discussed in this chapter, the development of personnel policies and regulations is of paramount importance.

This chapter will focus on the development of policies and regulations that guide and facilitate the human resources function. Primary consideration is given to important differences between governing board policies and administrative regulations; the purposes served by a viable set of policies and regulations; the responsibilities of the school board, the human resources director, and other professional staff and lay persons in the development of policies and regulations; and ways in which personnel policies and regulations are developed. In addition, the characteristics of effective policies and regulations are discussed and examples of policies and regulations in selected personnel areas are presented.

Goals, Policies, and Regulations

The terms *goals*, *policies*, and *regulations* are defined in various ways in the literature. We find it important to differentiate among these terms and to clarify others often used in relation to them.

Goals are those statements that set forth the purposes of the school system. Goals serve to clarify the aims of the school system; they provide a focus for the organization and give it a meaningful direction. Goals express what is important to the school system overall and are undergirded by the beliefs, values, traditions, and culture of the school system's community. School goals are developed through cultural sanctions embedded in the school-community, through lay judgments expressed through such bodies as the district's school board, and through the professional judgments of professional and support staffs of the school district.

Governing board policies are comprehensive statements of decisions, principles, or courses of action that serve toward the achievement of stated goals for a local school system. Governing board policies answer the question of *what* the school system is to do; essentially they serve as guidelines for the administration of the school district. Policies are local adaptations of stated goals; they are developed through the actions of the school board with the leadership of the professional staff.

An *administrative regulation or rule* is a precise statement that answers the question of *how* a policy is to be applied or implemented. Although administrative regulations most often are approved by the governing board, they are developed primarily through the judgments of the professional staff with representative community input and ultimately through administrative decision. For our purposes, the terms *regulation, rule,* and *procedure* are used interchangeably.

Bylaws are those procedures by which the school board governs itself. They are regulations that apply to the internal operations of the school board. Such matters as the election of board officers, voting procedures, agenda development, parliamentary procedure, and the order of business are examples of topics included in the bylaws of the governing board.

Governing board policies, regulations, and bylaws are subject to state and national laws. A *law* is a rule recognized by the nation or state as binding on its members. Law emanates from actions by governing bodies such as state legislatures or from rulings by courts of law. It is not unusual for state laws and/or court actions to mandate school policy; that is, state statutes and court rulings often specify what school systems must do relative to a specific matter. Seldom is the specific law written verbatim in the school district's policy manual. Rather, a policy statement based on the requirements of the law is written as a school policy, followed by specific statute references or citations. There are exceptions to this provision. In many states, for example, policies and regulations concerning personnel dismissal are written verbatim from state statutes. This is due to the fact that dismissal cases frequently are litigated in court. As a result, school districts take all precautions to ensure that their policies and regulations follow state laws to the letter. Specific criteria for identifying policies and regulations are presented in a later section of this chapter.

The Benefits of Personnel Policies and Regulations

A viable set of personnel policies and regulations benefits the school system and the human resources function in numerous ways. First, viable policies and regulations help to establish the division of labor between the school board and the professional staff. The school board, as the legislative body of the school system, has the responsibility of adopting policies that serve to guide the school program. In this sense, the board of education "controls" the direction of the system through adopting policies that focus on *what* the school system is to do and what it wants to accomplish. The development and adoption of appropriate school policy, then, are the primary responsibilities of the school board.

On the other hand, the school superintendent and the professional staff represent the executive body of school governance. Viable school policies allow for discretionary actions by the professional staff. The implementation of board policy is administered through the development of specific regulations primarily through the leadership of the professional staff. Thus good policies and regulations serve to help the school board focus on its major legislative role and the professional staff to focus on its executive responsibilities. Policy provides the control that the school board must have to guide the school system and gives the professional staff the discretion it needs to operate the school program effectively.

Another benefit of school policies and regulations is that they serve to establish the basis for intelligent decision making and help to direct decision making at proper levels within the system. Without the direction that effective policies and regulations can provide, various units in the system invariably must seek a decision from a higher level unit before actions can be implemented. As a result, administrative effectiveness often is inhibited and organization efficiency and initiative are lessened.

A comprehensive set of school policies and regulations is the most important source of information about the goals and objectives of the school system. Policy statements and accompanying regulations serve to inform the public and the professional staff of the goals and objectives of the school system and serve as a foundation for effective system communication.

Viable policies and regulations help to avoid costly trial and error and serve to bring a sense of continuity to the organization. Board policies and regulations support the system's decision-making capability by providing a focus of what is to be accomplished and how to proceed administratively. Thus viable policies release the strength and creativity of the school administrators and other employees. Employees understand the priorities set forth by the governing board and are able to implement their professional judgment with some degree of assurance and personal security.

Lastly, in view of the fact that school boards are viewed as extensions of other legislative bodies, viable policies and regulations serve an important legal function for the board and the school district. In relation to governance practices and litigation stemming from personnel law suits, school policies and their dissemination serve as key evidence to document school board decisions and administrative practices.

As summarized by Clemmer (1991),

> Virtually all aspects of school district operation are benefitted by the consistent administration of appropriate policies. Generally speaking, policies enable organizations to get results with people rather than through them. Cooperative policy development fosters two-way communication and induces sound working relationships. Workers in all organizations benefit from the clarification of their employer's goals and objectives. (p. 28)

Clemmer (1991) further states that policies pay off by providing for

1. Greater efficiency—written policies and regulations save time and effort for board members and superintendents.
2. More unity in action—good policies presume the discretionary aspects of work as well as mutuality of interest among all school district employees.

3. Higher administrator morale—administrators are able to exercise professional judgment more effectively in behalf of established goals when they know they have support.
4. Better transitions—effective policies foster stability and continuity.
5. Permanent records—board minutes serve as the official repository of the record of board action that produces the policy manual that guides administrative behavior that directs staff that gets the job done with kids day after day after day.
6. Improved public relations—participation enhances the likelihood that decisions will be more valid and builds confidence in decision-makers. (pp. 28–30)

Criteria That Identify Policies, Regulations, and Bylaws

A school policy was defined as a comprehensive statement of decisions, principles, or courses of action that serve toward the achievement of stated goals. A ***policy*** is:

1. an assertion of intent/goals of the school system;
2. related to a general area of major importance to the school system and citizenry;
3. equivalent to legislation;
4. a broad statement that allows for freedom of interpretation and execution;
5. applicable over long periods of time;
6. mainly the concern of the school board, that is, only the school board can adopt policy;
7. an action undertaken to resolve or to give direction in ameliorating a problem of importance;
8. related to the question, What to do?

An ***administrative regulation*** is:

1. related to a specific area or problem; it is a procedure to carry out or implement a policy;
2. mainly the concern of the professional staff; it is executive in nature;
3. a precise statement calling for specific interpretation and execution;
4. able to be altered without formal board action;
5. related to the question, How to do?

A ***bylaw*** is a rule governing the school board's internal operations. It is a method by which the school board governs itself. A bylaw is:

1. a combination of parliamentary procedures and state laws that apply to school boards;
2. like any other rule in that it sets forth specific procedures, leaving little room for personal discretion;
3. a rule that applies to the internal operations of the school board only;
4. related to the question, How will the school board govern itself?

Consider the following policy statement:

The school superintendent and persons delegated by the superintendent are given the responsibility to determine the personnel needs of the school district and to recruit qualified candidates to recommend for employment to the board. The school board will employ and retain the best qualified personnel available. Concerted efforts shall be made to maintain a variation in staff relative to educational preparation, personal background, and previous experience. There shall be no discrimination against any candidate by reason of race, national origin, creed, marital status, age, or sex.

It is the responsibility of the school superintendent to certify that persons nominated for employment shall meet all qualifications established by law and by the school board for the position for which the nomination is made.

The employment of any individual is not official until the contract is signed by the candidate and approved by the governing school board.

The foregoing policy specifies *what* the board desires concerning practices for employment and sets forth what is to be done relative to employee qualifications. The policy represents a broad statement that allows the professional staff to use its judgment concerning specific recruiting and selection procedures. The policy is legislative in substance and is directly related to the question of what to do relative to the important matter of hiring school district personnel. Finally, although specific procedures regarding recruitment and selection might change, the policy could remain as stated for a substantial time period even though regulations for its implementation might be changed.

Next, consider the procedure illustrated in Figure 5.1 that sets forth steps for position application. This regulation relates specifically to the policy for personnel recruitment and selection; it is executive in nature, calling for specific procedures to be followed; it is possible to revise these procedures without having to change board policy; and it serves to answer the question of *how* selection of personnel is to be implemented.

Other examples of personnel policy and regulation statements will be examined later in this chapter. The foregoing statements serve to emphasize differences between policies and regulations and illustrate the various criteria that help to define them.

Topical Headings for Personnel Policies and Regulations

Policy and regulation development in human resources administration is an ongoing, continuous process. Due to the ever-changing nature of the human resources function, new policies and regulations become necessary, current ones need revision, and some become obsolete and must be deleted. The most viable topical headings for policies and regulations evolve from the vision and needs of the local school district. Because policies are comprehensive statements of decisions, principles, or courses of action that serve toward the achievement of stated goals, ideally they evolve from local school and community initiatives.

The Educational Policy System of the National School Boards Association (EPS/NSBA) and the Davies-Brickell System (DBS) are examples of educational policy systems that have been implemented in numerous school systems nationally. Both systems provide a comprehensive classification system to guide policy development in school systems. The EPS/NSBA is based on an "alpha" system; letters of the alphabet are used for coding policies and regulations (i.e., each major topical heading has a

Personnel: Certificated   **Code: 4111**
Recruitment and Selection

To aid in obtaining the best available personnel for school positions, the following criteria and procedures will be utilized:

Concerted efforts will be made to maintain a variation in staff relative to educational preparation, background, and previous experience through recruiting on a broad basis. All available sources of personnel supply, including college and university career placement offices, career information-day programs, student teacher information, advertisements in appropriate publications, and others that serve to identify a pool of qualified personnel for position openings will be used.

Written applications, official transcripts of college work, student teaching and teaching reports and recommendations, and personal interviews provide the primary data for personnel selection. The procedures for screening and selecting personnel for teaching positions are as follows:

1. Notices of position openings in teaching will be disseminated internally through the offices of school principals and externally through selected college and university teacher placement offices.
2. The central human resources office will collect and process applications; the official application form of the school district and other application materials, as required by the human resources office, must be completed and received before an applicant can be considered for a position.
3. The central human resources office will gather all evidence for purposes of screening applicants including the application form, evidence of certification or licensure for the position in question, teacher placement records of the applicant, official college transcripts, at least three professional references from former employers and/or supervisors, and other information of importance. In addition, the district's prescreening background-check form is to be completed and returned by the applicant.
4. Preliminary interviews of applicants who are best qualified will be conducted by the central human resources office, although other representatives may participate as interviewers as the case requires.
5. Finalists for the position, as determined by the human resources office, will be scheduled for interviews with appropriate building principals and/or supervisors. The human resources office, together with the appropriate building principal and/or supervisor, will decide if the position should be offered to a specific applicant.

FIGURE 5.1
Procedure for Position Application

6. When a position is offered tentatively and accepted pending school board approval, the human resources office will send its recommendation to the school superintendent. Upon the superintendent's approval, the nomination will be made to the school board for final approval.

7. All final applicants for a position shall be notified of the decision reached by the school board.

FIGURE 5.1
continued

letter). *G* is used for policies related to personnel. Thus, GCBC in the system refers to series G (personnel), the third subseries C (professional staff), the second division B (professional staff contracts and compensation plans), and the third subdivision C (professional staff fringe benefits). The Davies-Brickell System, which originated in 1957 and was revised in 1988, uses Arabic numbers for purposes of codification. Specific procedures for codifying policies and regulations are presented later in this chapter.

To illustrate topical headings for policies and regulations in the area of human resources administration, Article 4 (Series 4000) of the Davies-Brickell System is presented in Figure 5.2. Not all topical headings of the DBS would necessarily be included in the policy manuals of every school district, nor is the listing all-inclusive. The DBS does include numerous topics of importance in human resources policy development. Note that asterisks have been entered to denote selected additions to the DBS topical headings. Since policy and regulation development is a continuous process, new entries are made as needed by the local school district.

The Codification of Personnel Policies and Regulations

The comprehensiveness of policies and regulations in human resources administration necessitates some method of classifying or recording them. Without such a codification system, policy manuals become disorganized and difficult to use. Two codification systems were mentioned previously, the Educational Policy System of the National School Board Association and the Davies-Brickell System. An explanation of the Davies-Brickell Codification System (1988) follows.

The Davies-Brickell System uses nine major series (or sections) in its classification system:

Series	*Topical Heading*
Series 1000	Community relations
Series 2000	Administration
Series 3000	Business and noninstructional operations
Series 4000	Personnel
Series 5000	Students
Series 6000	Instruction
Series 7000	New construction
Series 8000	Internal board policies
Series 9000	Bylaws of the Board

Each major series is divided into subseries, divisions, subdivisions, items, and subitems. Series 4000 encompasses the content area of personnel. Consider the policy entry numbered 4123. Each number refers to a specific topical entry. For example, the number 4 indicates that the entry deals with the major series of personnel. The number 1 indicates that the entry is in the first subseries, certificated personnel. The number 2 notes that the entry is the second division under certificated personnel or

Article 4   **Personnel**   **Series 4000**

page

0. Concept and Roles in Personnel 4000
   A. Goals and Objectives 4010
1. Certificated Personnel 4100
   A. Permanent Personnel 4110
      1. Recruitment and Selection 4111
         a. Equal Employment Opportunity 4111.1
         b. Vacancies 4111.2
      2. Appointment and Conditions of Employment 4112
         a. Contract 4112.1
         b. Certification 4112.2
         c. Oaths..4112.3
         d. Health Examinations 4112.4
         e. Security/Credit Check..4112.5
         f. Personnel Records 4112.6
         g. Orientation..4112.7
         h. Nepotism; Husband/Wife Employment.................................. 4112.8
        *i. Staff Health and Safety 4112.9
            *(1)Communicable Diseases 4112.91
               *(a) HIV-AIDS 4112.911
      3. Assignment 4113
         a. Load/Scheduling/Hours of Employment...............................4113.1
         b. Promotion/Demotion 4113.2
         c. Work Year..4113.3
         d. Job-Sharing..4113.4
      4. Transfer/Reassignment..4114
      5. Evaluation/Supervision 4115
      6. Probationary/Tenure Status..4116
         a. Seniority 4116.1
      7. Separation/Disciplinary Action 4117
         a. Retirement 4117.1
         b. Resignation 4117.2
         c. Personnel Reduction 4117.3
         d. Dismissal/Suspension 4117.4
            (1)Just Cause 4117.41
            (2)Notice; Hearing 4117.42
            (3)Right of Appeal 4117.43
      8. Rights, Responsibilities and Duties 4118
         a. Civil and Legal Rights 4118.1

FIGURE 5.2

The Davies-Brickell System of School Board Policy-Making and Administration (pp. 119–124)
Source: From the Davies-Brickell System. Copyright © 1958, 1988 by Davies-Brickell Associates, Ltd.,
Naco, AZ. Reprinted by permission.

     (1) Nondiscrimination 4118.11
        (a) Grievance Procedure — Title IX 4118.111
     (2) Freedom of Speech 4118.12
     (3) Conflict of Interest 4118.13
    *(4) Harassment 4118.14
   b. Professional Responsibilities 4118.2
     (1) Academic Freedom 4118.21
     (2) Code of Ethics 4118.22
     (3) Conduct and Dress 4118.23
        (a) Smoking, Drinking, Use of Drugs on School Premises 4118.231
     (4) Staff/Student Relations 4118.24
   c. Duties 4118.3
B. Temporary and Part-Time Personnel 4120
  1. Substitute Teachers 4121
  2. Student Teachers/Internships 4122
  3. Home Teachers 4123
  4. Summer School Teachers 4124
  5. Adult Education Teachers 4125
  6. Consultants 4126
C. Activities 4130
  1. Staff Development 4131
   a. Exchange Teaching 4131.1
   b. Contributions to Fields of Knowledge 4131.2
   c. In-Service Education/Independent Study 4131.3
     (1) Tuition Reimbursement 4131.31
   d. Visitations; Conferences 4131.4
  2. Publication or Creation of Materials 4132
   a. Copyrights and Patents 4132.1
  3. Travel; Reimbursement 4133
  4. Tutoring 4134
  5. Organizations/Units 4135
   a. Agreement 4135.1
     (1) Recognition 4135.11
     (2) Personnel Covered 4135.12
     (3) Board/School System Rights 4135.13
     (4) Association Rights 4135.14
     (5) Savings Clause 4135.15
     (6) Work Stoppages 4135.16
   b. Communications/Contacts 4135.2
   c. Negotiations/Consultation 4135.3

FIGURE 5.2

continued

        d. Grievances/Complaints/Hearings 4135.4
    6. Meetings 4136
    7. Soliciting and Selling 4137
    8. Non-School Employment 4138
        a. Consulting 4138.1
D. Compensation and Related Benefits 4140
    1. Salary Guides 4141
    2. Salary Checks and Deductions 4142
      *a. Social Security Deductions 4142.1
    3. Extra Pay for Extra Work 4143
    4. Insurance/Health & Welfare Benefits 4144
    5. Retirement Compensation 4145
        a. Tax-Sheltered Annuities 4145.1
    6. Employment-Related Accommodations 4146
        a. Credit Union 4146.1
        b. Gifts/Awards from Board of Education 4146.2
        c. Employee Amenities 4146.3
        d. Protective Clothing/Devices 4146.4
        e. Professional Library 4146.5
    7. Employee Safety 4147
    8. Employee Protection 4148
E. Leaves and Vacations 4150
    1. Short-Term Leaves 4151
        a. Personal Illness and Injury 4151.1
            (1) Industrial Accident/Illness 4151.11
        b. Family Illness/Quarantine 4151.2
        c. Bereavement 4151.3
        d. Professional Purposes 4151.4
        e. Legal and Civic Duties 4151.5
        f.   Religious Observance 4151.6
        g. Emergency/Personal 4151.7
        h. Association 4151.8
        i.   Military 4151.9
    2. Long-Term Leaves 4152
        a. Sabbatical 4152.1
        b. Professional 4152.2
        c. Childbearing/Childrearing 4152.3
        d. Military 4152.4
        e. Health and Hardship 4152.5
        f.   Personal 4152.6

FIGURE 5.2
continued

       g. Political 4152.7
       h. Association 4152.8
     3. Vacations/Holidays 4153
 2. Non-Certificated Personnel 4200
   A. Permanent Personnel 4210
     1. Recruitment and Selection 4211
       a. Equal Employment Opportunity 4211.1
       b. Vacancies...4211.2
     2. Appointment and Conditions of Employment............................4212
       a. Contract 4212.1
       b. Certification or Licensing 4212.2
       c. Oaths...4212.3
       d. Health Examinations 4212.4
       e. Security/Credit Check..4212.5
       f. Personnel Records 4212.6
       g. Orientation...4212.7
       h. Nepotism; Husband/Wife Employment 4212.8
     3. Assignment 4213
       a. Load/Scheduling/Hours of Employment 4213.1
       b. Promotion/Demotion 4213.2
       c. Work Year...4213.3
     4. Transfer/Reassignment...4214
     5. Evaluation/Supervision 4215
     6. Probationary/Continuing Contract Status 4216
       a. Seniority 4216.1
     7. Separation/Disciplinary Action 4217
       a. Retirement 4217.1
       b. Resignation 4217.2
       c. Layoff/Rehire 4217.3
       d. Dismissal/Suspension 4217.4
         (1) Just Cause 4217.41
         (2) Notice; Hearing 4217.42
         (3) Right of Appeal 4217.43
     8. Rights, Responsibilities and Duties 4218
       a. Civil and Legal Rights 4218.1
         (1) Nondiscrimination 4218.11
           (a) Grievance Procedure—Title IX 4218.111
         (2) Freedom of Speech 4218.12
         (3) Conflict of Interest 4218.13
       b. Employment Responsibilities 4218.2

FIGURE 5.2
continued

    (1) Code of Ethics..4218.21
    (2) Conduct and Dress...4218.22
      (a) Smoking, Drinking, Use of Drugs on School Premises 4218.221
   c. Duties 4218.3
    (1) Librarians 4218.31
 B. Temporary and Part-Time Personnel 4220
  1. Substitutes 4221
  2. Teacher Aides/Paraprofessionals.................................4222
 C. Activities...4230
  1. Growth in Job Skills 4231
   a. Visitations; Conferences 4231.1
  2. Publication or Creation of Materials 4232
   a. Copyrights and Patents 4232.1
  3. Travel; Reimbursement..4233
  4. Organizations/Units 4234
   a. Agreement..4234.1
    (1) Recognition 4234.11
    (2) Personnel Covered 4234.12
    (3) Board/School System Rights................................4234.13
    (4) Association Rights...4234.14
    (5) Savings Clause 4234.15
    (6) Work Stoppages 4234.16
   b. Communications/Contacts 4234.2
   c. Negotiations/Consultation 4234.3
   d. Grievances/Complaints/Hearings..............................4234.4
  5. Meetings 4235
  6. Soliciting and Selling 4236
  7. Non-School Employment 4237
 D. Compensation and Related Benefits....................................4240
  1. Salary Guides...4241
  2. Salary Checks and Deductions 4242
  3. Overtime Pay 4243
  4. Insurance/Health & Welfare Benefits............................4244
  5. Retirement Compensation...4245
   a. Tax-Sheltered Annuities...4245.1
  6. Employment-Related Accommodations..........................4246
   a. Credit Union 4246.1
   b. Gifts/Awards from Board of Education 4246.2
   c. Employee Amenities 4246.3
   d. Uniforms, Protective Clothing/Devices.......................4246.4

FIGURE 5.2

continued

    7. Employee Safety..4247
    8. Employee Protection 4248
 E. Leaves and Vacations...4250
    1. Short-Term Leaves..4251
       a. Personal Illness and Injury...4251.1
         (1) Industrial Accident/Illness 4251.11
       b. Family Illness/Quarantine 4251.2
       c. Bereavement...4251.3
       d. Occupational Purposes 4251.4
       e. Legal and Civil Duties 4251.5
       f. Religious Observance 4251.6
       g. Emergency/Personal 4251.7
       h. Association...4251.8
       i. Military 4251.9
    2. Long-Term Leaves 4252
       a. Sabbatical 4252.1
       b. Professional 4252.2
       c. Childbearing/Childrearing...4252.3
       d. Military 4252.4
       e. Health and Hardship...4252.5
       f. Personal 4252.6
       g. Political...4252.7
       h. Association...4252.8
    3. Vacations/Holidays 4253

FIGURE 5.2
continued

temporary and part-time personnel. Finally, the number 3 indicates that the entry is the third subdivision under temporary and part-time personnel or home teachers. Similarly, the code number 4151.1 reveals that the entry is personnel (4), certificated personnel (1), leaves and vacations (5), short-term leaves (1), and personal illness and injury (.1). New subseries, divisions, subdivisions, items, and subitems can be added to the policies by using appropriate numbers. As a final explanation of this codification system, examine the following example. Using the Davies-Brickell System, a new item, social security deductions, would be classified under retirement compensation as follows:

Article 4	*Personnel*		*Series 4000*
(Series or section)	Personnel		4000
(Subseries)	1. Certificated Personnel		4100
(Division)		A.	
		B.	
		C.	
		D. Compensation & Related Benefits	4140
(Subdivision)	1. (Salary Guides)		
	2. Salary Checks & Deductions		4142
(New entry)		a. Social Security Deductions	4142.1

The use of Arabic numerals for coding systems provides the advantage of easy reading and referencing. One disadvantage of using numerals is that it limits the number of entries in any one subseries, division, subdivision, item, or subitem to nine. Once nine entries under any one of these classifications has been reached, some structural revision becomes necessary. For this reason, some individuals prefer the alpha system used by the NSBA and others. Because there are 26 letters in the alphabet, numerous divisions, items, and subitems can be utilized without the need to restructure. On the other hand, some persons find the use of letters for coding purposes to be less readable than numbers (e.g., 4146.2 vs. DADFB or in the EPS/NSBA Classification System, GCBCA). In any case a consistent codification system is of paramount importance. It enhances the development, readability, revision, and utilization of the school district's policy and regulation manual.

How Personnel Policies and Regulations Are Developed

Although quality varies considerably, most school districts have some form of a policy and regulation manual. Since policy development is a never-ending process, some school districts simplify completing this task by purchasing policies written by national organizations or policy consultants. Unless customized for the particular school district, such policy manuals tend to be no more than boilerplate products that do not reflect the real climate and educational needs of the system. Therefore, it is important that human resources administrators understand fully the process of policy development and be prepared to assume a major leadership role in that activity. In a national study of personnel directors in 1983 (McCoy, Gips, & Evans), 91.1% of the participants reported that personnel policy development was either their complete responsibility (43.1%) or was a shared responsibility (48.0%). Furthermore, 74.3% of these personnel directors indicated that they actually performed the task of personnel policy development and 18.7% stated that they supervised it. Policy development has remained as an important task area for personnel directors. In 1989, personnel directors in one state reported that they had "nearly complete" responsibility for personnel policy and regulation development in their school districts in 68.6% of the cases. Another 28.6% shared this responsibility (Norton, 1989).

Although most school districts have a nucleus of policy already established, the need to develop an entirely new set of policies is quite common. Even in those cases when school districts have a "complete" policy manual, it is not unusual to have one or more sections in need of complete revision. In those instances when major revisions are necessary, the question of who is to do the work arises. One approach is to have the school board appoint the school superintendent to do the policy work. The school superintendent is generally quite knowledgeable about the school district and its human resources purposes and needs. On the other hand, policy development is a monumental task and such an arrangement tends to take much time away from other work of the superintendent's office. Another approach is to set up a series of task force groups to do the policy work. Representative groups can benefit from personal involvement in policy development. Yet such an arrangement does not obviate the fact that policy development takes both time and skill. Professional staff members cannot always sacrifice the time necessary to do the work; nor are they always personally knowledgeable in the area of policy development.

Some school districts find it most expedient to use outside consultants to complete their policies. Policy consultants have special expertise for such work and are able to complete a quality product if it is founded on the district's culture and needs. Such an arrangement can be quite costly, however, because the time commitments for such consulting are lengthy. We caution against the procedure of buying the policy statements from external organizations. Although such statements can result in a policy manual for the school district, unless such services are customized for the district, its goals, values, problems, needs, and situation, policies tend to be of a generic nature that betrays the real meaning and value of localized policies.

Another arrangement is to allow the central personnel unit to take the primary leadership in the development of policies and regulations in the area of human resources. The human resources director is highly knowledgeable of the personnel objectives and needs in the school district. These administrators necessarily must be fully acquainted with the legal aspects of personnel administration important to policy and regulation development.

We support the arrangement whereby the human resources director is given the primary authority to develop viable personnel policy for the school district. Such an arrangement does not set aside the fact that the school board remains as the final authority on all policy recommendations and the only body that can adopt policy officially for the school district. Such an arrangement does not suggest that policy recommendations cannot evolve from any source or that participation in policy development should not include representatives from the school system's many publics. One model for policy development that has been utilized by numerous school districts is explained in brief in the following section.

MODEL FOR POLICY AND REGULATION DEVELOPMENT

The human resources director might utilize the following model for completing a comprehensive study and revision of the school district's personnel policies and regulations:

Step 1 Examine various school and community documents and resources for information relative to what "policies" and/or decisions already have been determined. Sources of policies and regulations include school board minutes, school board manuals, teachers' manuals, board correspondence, board committee reports, staff committee reports, school publications, citizen committee reports, newspaper files, interviews with past and present members of the school board and staff, legal documents related to the school district.

 Frequency of notations on certain personnel subjects may suggest the need for a definite district policy. Give special attention to specific goal statements set forth by the governing board.

Step 2 Check on established practices in the area of personnel administration. Operations of the school board and the district often reflect embedded practices that infer policy need areas. Unwritten policies often become formal statements of policy through such an analysis of practice.

Step 3 Investigate what other boards have done relative to personnel policy development. Such information is to serve as a guide to possible policy development rather than being directly applicable to the local district in question. Such information can be useful as a sounding board in revealing local policy needs.

Step 4 Consult the studies and writings of others in the area of school personnel administration. Guides and handbooks prepared by school board associations, state departments, and other organizations often are excellent sources of policy content. Once again, such information is used as a place to start rather than serving as a blueprint for meeting local needs.

Step 5 Enlist the aid of all concerned. It is good practice to solicit input from citizen groups, professional and support personnel in the school district, and other publics of the district. Such involvement is conducive to quality results and also to gaining the ultimate approval and effective implementation of the policies to be recommended.

Step 6   Organize study groups to examine policy needs and to recommend policy in various subsections and divisions of the personnel policy topical headings (i.e., the Davies-Brickell Series 4000 topical headings). Include such representative personnel as teachers, support staff, patrons, administrators, and at least one school board member in the study groups. The final approval and adoption are facilitated with the sanction of at least one board member serving on the committee.

Organize a steering committee of representatives most knowledgeable of policy development and the needs and purposes of human resources administration. These committee members serve as liaisons with study subgroups in checking for consistency in the policies developed.

Step 7   Have the school superintendent and the administrative cabinet review the policy work completed. The professional staff has an ongoing role as policies are being developed in the initial stages. Thus administrator, teacher, and support staff groups can participate by completing their own review of needed policies, by providing suggestions to study groups, and by acting as sounding boards for initial study group recommendations.

Step 8   Have the school board review the policy work completed. As is the case with the administrator, teacher, and support staff groups, the school board needs to participate in the initial stages of personnel policy development in ways similar to those recommended in Step 7. In addition, the school board as a whole should review the semifinal policy draft and make recommendations for revision.

Step 9   Have the draft of the policies tested for legality. The school board attorney serves to review the policy draft from a legal viewpoint. Legal clearance helps to build school board and district confidence and lends support to the final policy package.

Step 10 Use first and second readings of the personnel policy statements prior to official adoption by the school board. Policy is legally binding for all district personnel and in this sense is a legal contract between the school board and its personnel. Thus, due consideration necessitates attention to sunshine laws and other aspects of legal procedures.

Policy development, especially in the areas of compensation and conditions of work, has become increasingly an agenda item in the negotiation process. The line between policy authority of the board of education and the scope of negotiations tends to be less and less clear. For example, only recently a court in Washington declared the matter of class size a condition of work and, therefore, a matter for negotiation between the school board and the teachers' association ("Class Size," 1991). Thus under any circumstances today, policy *development* can no longer be a unilateral activity of the school board and the school administration. Nevertheless, policy *adoption* still remains as the official legislative responsibility of the governing board.

CHARACTERISTICS OF EFFECTIVE POLICIES AND REGULATIONS IN HUMAN RESOURCES ADMINISTRATION

In earlier sections of this chapter, policy and regulation definitions, criteria, topical headings, codification systems, and procedures for their development were presented. In the following sections, consideration is given to important characteristics of effective policies, including examples of several critical policy topics facing human resources administration today. These selected policy examples are ones that most every school district must consider.

Duke and Canady (1991) state that

> a good school policy is one that increases the likelihood that school goals will be achieved without adversely affecting any particular group. . . . Policies may not always please or benefit everyone, but at the very least they should not harm certain groups of young people served by the schools. (p. 7)

These writers note further that "the key to effective schools probably has less to do with the discovery of one best policy than with ensuring that all school policies are compatible, well coordinated, and consistently followed" (p. 7).

Clemmer (1991) set forth five characteristics of effective policies. Policies should be

1. *Complete.* A policy statement should tell its user what action should be taken, perhaps explaining why it should be taken, and occasionally who should take it. Policies also reveal who is affected by them.
2. *Concise.* Only the barest essentials need to be included in policy statements. Policies are intended essentially to set forth the expectations one group (the board) has for the behavior of another group (district employees).
3. *Clear.* Whatever is expected of whomever should be clearly stated. A flexible policy will allow various methods of implementation but it need not be ambiguous about the desired outcome.
4. *Changeable.* Policy statements should be reasonably easy to modify in accord with changing circumstances in society or in legal codes. This capability refers not only to policy content but also to the methods of codifying and preserving collections of policies. Replacement of outdated policies in district manuals should be simple and fast.
5. *Distinctive.* Policies should always be distinguishable from regulations promulgated by the board and administrators. (p. 107)[1]

We would add *consistent* to the policy characteristics set forth by Clemmer. School policies must serve to provide guidelines for consistently fair and equitable treatment for all employees. Although policies must provide for the use of discretionary judgments on the part of the professional staff, they must not be so stated as to permit capricious interpretations. In addition, consistency infers a compatibility between and among all district policies. The benefits of policies are negated if a specific policy can be nullified by another policy stated elsewhere in the manual. Finally, policies must be consistent with legal requirements of the nation and state.

---

[1]From Elwin F. Clemmer, *The School Policy Handbook: A Primer for Administrators and School Board Members.* Copyright © 1991 by Allyn and Bacon. Reprinted with permission.

Attention to the language of written policies can obviate many problems of interpretation and possible conflict. Since policies and regulations are utilized by a variety of publics, they must be readable and meaningful to all concerned. Poorly written, ambiguous policies tend to confuse rather than inform. Furthermore, since policies serve as legal extensions of the school board, precise language that is presented in a clear, straightforward manner is of paramount importance. In policy writing, the statement, "You get what you write," is a basic truth.

Consider the following personnel policy statement:

> In order to provide quality education to all students within the school district, a yearly evaluation of all certificated staff will be conducted. Evaluations should commend staff and provide avenues for staff improvement. Staff evaluations will be used to consider contract renewal.

This policy statement might appear to be clear and concise on the surface, but certain language questions must be raised. For instance,

1. Is only one performance evaluation annually permissible under this policy?
2. Is this yearly evaluation to constitute the totality of evidence for contract renewal consideration?
3. Is this evaluation to serve both formative and summative purposes?
4. How is the statement "Evaluations should *commend* staff and provide avenues for staff improvement" to be interpreted?
5. Are statements other than commendations permissible?
6. Does the policy suggest that the school district itself will provide the avenues for staff improvement?
7. Who will be responsible for planning and administering the evaluation program?

Appraisal of Performance

The following evaluation policy more clearly states the **intentions** of the school board relative to employee performance appraisals. It provides guidelines that allow for the development of specific administrative regulations and delegates the administration of the program to a specific office.

Certificated Personnel: Personnel Evaluation (4115)

The performance of all personnel in the Union School District will be appraised for the purposes of determining needs for individual personal/professional growth, to provide needed information for personnel compensation, and to help determine continuation of employment. Responsibility for administering appraisal programs is delegated to the superintendent of schools and those individuals designated by him or her. Appropriate performance appraisals will be administered for nontenured certificated employees that will provide sufficient evidence for the continuation of employment and will meet stipulations of law. Tenured personnel appraisals will be performed at least every third year. The school district will make every effort to disseminate to all employees the goals of the system, the position descriptions for individual roles, the standards of performance desired by the school system and the appraisal process(es) to be utilized, the criteria to be used in performance appraisals, and how appraisal results will be disseminated and discussed with them. Suggestions for improvement of performance based on appraisal results are to be part of all performance evaluations. Evaluation procedures must embody the fundamental aspects of due process, clearly articulated and properly followed. Evaluation processes are to be administered in a fair and equitable manner and with due regard for the respect and dignity of the individual.

Chapter 7 discusses the legal aspects of performance appraisal and Chapter 9 is devoted entirely to personnel law. As emphasized in these chapters, school administrators must be aware of state laws governing performance appraisal, and appraisal procedures must embody procedural due process. Additionally, appraisal criteria must be reasonably related to job requirements, must not have adverse effects on protected groups, must avoid subjectivity of the supervisor/evaluator, and must be void of any bias related to race or gender.

SELECTED EXAMPLES OF PERSONNEL POLICIES AND REGULATIONS

The remaining sections of this chapter include a discussion of selected policy areas in personnel of importance to all school districts. Specifically, the policy areas of communicable diseases, academic freedom, sexual harassment, and dismissal are considered.

Staff Health and Safety—Communicable Diseases

The U.S. Public Health Service estimated that 2,000 children under the age of 13 had been infected with the Human Immunodeficiency Virus (HIV) by 1988 and stated that by 1991 the number likely increased to between 10,000 and 20,000 students (Strouse, 1990). Strouse (1990) also reported that her national study revealed that 82% of the school boards in rural districts had not discussed the retention of personnel infected with Acquired Immune Deficiency Syndrome (AIDS) and that 89% of them did not have written policies (p. 83). Metropolitan districts were best prepared for dealing with AIDS infection, and suburban and city districts fell between metro and rural districts relative to written AIDS policies for students and personnel according to Strouse's study. "Some 53% of the personnel policies (AIDS) were categorized as medical, 31% as victim-oriented, 13% as communicable disease, and 3% as exclusion" (Strouse, 1990, p. 85).

Strouse (1990) states that effective AIDS policies:

1. Deal specifically with AIDS.
2. Take into account all that is known about how AIDS is transmitted.
3. Voice a commitment to the AIDS-infected individual to enable him or her to remain in the school setting if at all possible.
4. Contain procedures for protecting the privacy of the infected individual, for handling the publicity surrounding a diagnosis of AIDS, and for reassuring the public through education about AIDS. (p. 87).

Lastly, Strouse notes that all school districts must make the development of written policies for handling AIDS a priority. School boards should develop written policies for dealing with AIDS infection prior to the time it is actually diagnosed in their school population.

Hernandez and Bozeman (1990) point out that school districts that cannot answer yes to any of the following questions should review their policies.

1. Do the district's policies contain a general statement that AIDS is a handicap?
2. Do the policies require that all documents, current handbooks and policies be audited to ensure there is no discrimination based on AIDS?
3. Do the policies require training of all managers about AIDS, including procedures concerning medical records and examinations, employees with AIDS, systemwide approaches to employment practices, dealing with employees' refusal to work with actual or suspected AIDS-infected colleagues, and a system for answering questions about AIDS?
4. Do the policies provide a training program about AIDS for employees at all levels?
5. Do the policies require a review of pension and insurance plans to ensure there is no discussion of or discrimination based on AIDS?
6. Do the policies provide for an ongoing public information program about AIDS?
7. Do the policies include procedures for utilizing professional expertise (internal and external) in dealing with AIDS? (pp. 22–28)

The sample policy of the Union Unified School District shown in Figure 5.3 includes many of the foregoing criteria and characteristics of viable personnel health policy relating to AIDS and other communicable diseases. Note that the last section of the district's policy focuses on the intentions of the school system concerning HIV-AIDS education.

Rogers (1989) cautions that AIDS policies must be reviewed on a regular basis and kept up-to-date:

With so much new information being discovered, the medical and legal implications of HIV as it affects your schools are in constant flux. If your policies are more than a year old—or if they stop short of dealing with sanitation and privacy—it's time to review how you plan to ensure the health of your school community. (p. 26)

Rights, Responsibilities, and Duties—Academic Freedom

Policy heading 4118.21 of the Davies-Brickell System centers on rights, responsibilities, and duties, and specifically on professional responsibilities related to academic freedom. Academic freedom protection for teachers and the responsibility of teaching personnel for using good judgment in the classroom are included here. In one sense, academic freedom permits teachers to teach in a manner that they deem appropriate, yet the teacher must always be sensitive to the matter of indoctrination; teachers must be particularly careful about the students' freedom when teaching controversial issues and in cases when conflicting values are present. Administrators attempting to implement policies related to academic freedom need to proceed with judgment and caution. An example of a policy statement concerning academic freedom is given in Figure 5.4.

<table>
<tr><td>**Union Unified School District**
Governing Board Policy</td><td>**Topic:** Staff Health and Safety
District Code: 4112.911</td></tr>
</table>

Staff Health and Safety

Emergency Information

The Superintendent shall develop procedures to obtain and maintain emergency information for every employee.

Immunizations

The Superintendent shall develop guidelines for the immunization of employees in the event of an epidemic, in which this procedure can assist in controlling the epidemic. The Superintendent shall have the authority to require employees to be immunized except in cases immunization would be detrimental to health or violate religious beliefs.

Health Examinations

When deemed necessary by the Superintendent, employees may be required to undergo physical and/or psychiatric examination(s), by a doctor, to determine fitness for employment or retention. The costs shall be borne by the District.

Return to Work Evaluations

The suitability for any employee returning to work from a paid or unpaid leave of absence due to illness, injury, or any other health reasons, may require a written medical release, if requested by the Supervisor.

Communicable Diseases

The Governing Board recognizes that the health and safety risks and consequences associated with communicable diseases will vary depending on the specific disease an employee has and many other factors that must be assessed on a case-by-case basis. Therefore, any employee who is diagnosed as having a communicable disease shall be evaluated on an individualized basis to determine whether he/she may remain at work and, if so, the appropriate assignment for that employee. The District will also follow Department of Health Services rules and regulations.

FIGURE 5.3
Staff Health and Safety Policy Statement (pp. 133–134)

Acquired Immune Deficiency Syndrome (AIDS)

Cases of AIDS will be evaluated on a case-by-case basis, according to current medical information at the time of evaluation. Every effort will be made to ensure there is no discrimination against employees with AIDS. The Governing Board recognizes that education about AIDS can greatly assist efforts to provide the best care and treatment for infected individuals and help to minimize the risk of transmission to others. Therefore, the District shall endeavor to provide information to students, parents, and employees about current medical knowledge concerning AIDS. In addition, all school administrators will be trained concerning AIDS and proper procedures in dealing with AIDS cases.

Adopted: February 26, 19____

FIGURE 5.3
continued

Union School District
Sample Policy—Certificated   **Code: 4118.21**
Personnel Academic Freedom

This school district supports the teachers' freedom to think and to express ideas, to select appropriate instructional materials and methods of instruction, and to be free to take action within their professional domain. Such freedom carries with it the responsibility of using judgment and prudence to the end that it promotes the free exercise of intelligence and pupil learning. Through the use of good taste and professional judgment, teachers are free to conduct discussions of various issues that offer students experience in examining respective views of controversial questions.

Academic freedom must be exercised with the basic ethical responsibilities of the teaching profession and the level of student maturity in mind. These responsibilities are undergirded with a sincere concern for the welfare, growth, and development of students and the use of professional ethics and good judgment in selecting and employing materials and methods of instruction.

FIGURE 5.4
Academic Freedom Policy Statement

Policies Relating to Staff Protection—Sexual Harassment

In 1980 the Equal Employment Opportunity Commission (EEOC) set forth guidelines that have served to define sexual harassment and clarify the responsibility of organizations concerning such activities. In brief, these guidelines define sexual harassment as "sexual advances, requests, or demands for sexual favors and other verbal or physical conduct of a sexual nature" that explicitly or implicitly are suggested as a term or condition of an individual's employment, are used as the basis for employment decisions, have the purpose or result of unreasonably interfering with an individual's performance in the workplace, or result in an offensive working environment.

The human resources unit of the school district should assume the leadership for establishing specific policies and regulations relating to sexual harassment. At least two other responsibilities accompany this leadership role: (1) The human resources unit should lead in the development of effective education programs that focus on the nature of sexual harassment, the district's policies on harassment, and individual employees' responsibilities for totally eliminating sexual harassment in the school district; and (2) the human resources unit should make certain that employee assistance programs and services are available for employees who have experienced sexual harassment and need psychological counseling. Decker (1988) set forth several steps that school districts can take to prevent the occurrence of sexual harassment. Three of these steps are especially pertinent to the focus of this chapter. Decker recommends that school districts (1) develop a clear policy statement prohibiting sexual harassment, (2) create guidelines to implement the policy, and (3) publicize policy statements and grievance procedures (p. 28). An example of a sexual harassment policy statement is provided in Figure 5.5.

The policy discussion related to sexual harassment is a significant consideration for employee protection. Yet it is only one consideration under the basic personnel process. Policies relating to the stability and protection of employees include provisions for tenure, personal safety, academic freedom, a healthy work environment, and due process procedures. Such policies reveal much of what the school district believes about its employees. Academic freedom was discussed in some detail in this chapter. Other topics related to employee protection are discussed in several chapters in the text.

A matter of great concern, and often one of much frustration, is that of employee dismissal. This topic will be the focus of the final policy discussion in this chapter.

Employee Dismissal Policies

Dismissal has been a much-discussed topic in human resources administration. "To secure the best results in our schools, we must have able-bodied, energetic, active, industrious teachers—teachers who can control themselves under the most trying circumstances" (Bloss, 1882, p. 82). As indicated by the foregoing statement made more than 100 years ago, the significance of teacher quality historically has been recognized as critical to effective teaching and learning. Dismissal has been a matter of historical importance as well. In 1882 Bloss reported to the governor of Indiana that "the [county] superintendent may take every precaution, yet occasionally it happens that one is licensed who is unworthy to exercise the functions of a teacher" (p. 84). The 1882 School Law reference, Section 36 stated:

Human Resources   **Policy 4770**

Sexual Harassment

The Lincoln Board of Education is committed to providing an environment free from unwelcome sexual advances, requests for sexual favors and other verbal or physical conduct or communication constituting sexual harassment. Sexual harassment by and of Lincoln Public Schools employees and students is prohibited.

Date of Adoption (or Last Revision):   5-12-__

Related Policies and Regulations   Regulation
                                                                4770.1

Legal References: Section 703 of
                                                          Title VII of the
                                                          Civil Rights Act

It shall be a violation of school district policy to harass another employee sexually, to permit the sexual harassment of an employee by an employee or a non-employee, or to harass or permit the harassment of a student sexually. Sexual harassment may take many forms, including, but not limited to:

1. Verbal harassment or abuse including unwelcome sexually oriented communication;
2. Subtle pressure or requests for sexual activity;
3. Unnecessary touching of an individual, e.g., patting, pinching, hugging, repeated brushing against another person's body;
4. Requesting or demanding sexual favors accompanied by implied or overt threats concerning an individual's employment or student's status;
5. Requesting or demanding sexual favors accompanied by implied or overt promise of preferential treatment with regard to an individual's employment or student status; or
6. Sexual assault.

Any person who believes he or she has been subjected to sexual harassment should follow these procedures:

1. An aggrieved person should directly inform the person engaging in sexually harassing conduct or communication that such conduct or communication is offensive and must stop.

FIGURE 5.5

Sexual Harassment Policy Statement (pp. 137–138)

Source: Reprinted by permission of the Lincoln, Nebraska, Public Schools.

2. If an aggrieved employee does not wish to communicate directly with the person whose conduct or communication is offensive or if direct communication with the offending person has been ineffective, the employee should contact his or her principal or supervisor or the offending person's principal or supervisor or the Title IX Officer in the Human Resources Office. If an aggrieved student does not wish to communicate directly with the person whose conduct or communication is offensive or if direct communication with the offending person has been ineffective, the student should contact any teacher or other adult in the school whom he or she trusts. That person should then contact the principal or supervisor or the Title IX Officer in the Human Resources Office.

3. An aggrieved person alleging (1) sexual harassment by anyone with supervisory authority or (2) the failure of a supervisor to take immediate action on the complaint should communicate with the Title IX Officer in the Human Resources Office or the Office of the Superintendent of Schools or follow the grievance procedure outlined in the Personnel Handbook.

Allegation of sexual harassment shall be investigated and, if substantiated, corrective or disciplinary action taken, up to and including dismissal from employment if the offender is an employee, or suspension and/or expulsion, if the offender is a student.

Date Regulation Reviewed by the Board of Education: 5-12-__
Related Policies and Regulations:
Legal Reference:

FIGURE 5.5
continued

> The county superintendent shall have the power to revoke licenses, granted by him or his predecessor, for incompetency, immorality, cruelty, or general neglect of the business of the school, and the revocation of the license of any teacher shall terminate the school which the said teacher may have been employed to teach. (Bloss, 1882, p. 84)

Tead and Metcalf in 1920 underlined the momentous effects on the discharged worker as follows:

> So heavy a penalty as the dismissal of a workman (involving to him a serious dislocation of his life, the perils and demoralization attendant on looking for work, probably uprooting of his home and the interruption of his children's schooling, possibly many weeks of penury or semi-starvation for his family and himself) ought to be regarded as a very serious matter. (p. 245)

Today, employee dismissal continues to be a difficult and often traumatic personnel action. Norton (1989) found that personnel directors in one state viewed dismissing incompetent staff as the sixth leading problem facing them as administrators. Only external mandates and requirements, legal impacts, work load, job pressure and stress, and specific legal issues ranked higher as problems facing them.

The legal aspects of teacher dismissal are discussed in Chapter 9. The purpose here is to emphasize the need and significance of sound board policy and regulations in this area and to present an example of such a policy. As Grier (1984) has stated, before any dismissal hearing, "review school board policies, local laws, and state laws pertaining to the specific dismissal charges. Keep reviewing them and your responsibilities thoroughly" (p. 21). St. John (1983) underlines the importance of several questions for administrators to ask before a case gets to arbitration or court. Questions related to policy include the following:

1. Was the staff member adequately warned of the consequences of his or her conduct?
2. Was the school policy or procedure related to professional, efficient, or safe operations?
3. Were the rules, policies, and penalties applied even-handedly, without discrimination, and with equal treatment?
4. Were the school and district policies and procedures communicated carefully (e.g., handbooks, bulletin boards, orientation sessions, etc.)?
5. Did the school or district use recommended disciplinary procedures and follow due process provisions as applicable? (p. 106)

Grier and Turner (1990) emphasize other necessary actions as far as policies and rules are concerned, relating to occasions when dismissal procedures must be implemented.

> Often a dismissal hearing charges a teacher with violating school system policy or school regulations. It is not enough to cite the rule or policy the teacher allegedly violated—you will need to present a copy of the rule to the hearing officer or board. And you must be prepared to establish that the teacher in question also was furnished with a copy before the infraction took place or at least was well aware of the rule or policy.
>
> Proving awareness is difficult, so it's a good idea to make sure all teachers have copies of school regulations and let them know that board policy manuals are open to them. Sometimes school officials can prove a teacher was aware of rules and policies by referring to agendas of teachers' meetings or copies of teacher handbooks. . . . The teacher

contract should include a clause stating that teachers agree to abide by school system policy and their own school's regulations. (p. 21)[2]

In many states statutes set forth both policy and regulations for dismissals. In such cases, a brief board policy statement generally is set forth, followed by the specific statute as stated in law. Policy development guidelines usually recommend that statements from statutes *not* be rewritten verbatim as board policy. Rather, a policy based on the statute should be written. However, due to the sensitive nature of dismissals and the high potential for litigation in the courts, the use of specific state statutes as district policy is common. An example of a dismissal policy based strictly on a state statute is given in Figure 5.6.

It is clear that dismissal procedures and requirements will differ as laws of the various states differ. The consideration of dismissal as it applies to tenured and nontenured personnel is discussed in more detail in Chapter 12. The purpose of this section has been to discuss important guidelines for developing personnel policy and to present illustrations of policies and regulations in several selected areas of personnel practice.

As pointed out by Clemmer (1991), "Many of today's most conscientious educational administrators and dedicated board members enter their first policy-setting assignments with little or no understanding of the impact policies have on how school districts operate" (p. xx). This chapter has emphasized the benefits of having a viable set of school district policies and regulations in the area of human resources administration and has provided information as to how human resources administrators can assume a leadership role in their development and dissemination.

SUMMARY

Policy by its very nature is often surrounded by controversy. Since policy generally evolves from important issues, which are often in dispute, total consensus on specific policy is seldom the case. For this reason some persons take the position of letting well enough alone; after all, if one puts policy in writing it has to be followed. Such a view overlooks the reality that all organizations are governed by policy, and educational systems are no exception. Without policies and regulations the school district could scarcely be called a system. Policies and regulations serve to establish orderly operations within the school district and help to define the system's functions and organizational relationships.

Most people would agree that policy is designed to provide direction and purpose for the school system. One reason policy should be studied by human resources administrators is that it has significant effects on the lives of the personnel in the system. This chapter on policy and regulations in the human resources function represents an entirely new addition to this text. The challenges surrounding the human resources processes of selection, assignment, evaluation, collective negotiations, compensation and welfare, protection, and others demand the direction and guidance that personnel policies and procedures can provide. As pointed out by Davies and

---

[2]Reprinted, with permission, from *The Executive Educator*, *12*(2). Copyright © 1990, the National School Boards Association. All rights reserved.

Suspension and Dismissal of Certificated Staff Members
(Including Reprimand)

Suspension and Dismissal

Employees are expected to comply with the policies adopted by the Governing Board or as set forth in approved administrative regulations. Dismissal shall be in accordance with the laws of the state.

The procedures for suspension and dismissal of teachers shall be those prescribed by the State's Revised Statutes.

Legal Refs: A.R.S. 15-508; 15-521; 15-536; 15-550

Adopted: Date of Manual Adoption OC 2578
                 Tempe Elementary Schools, Tempe, Arizona

Log No. 166   **EPS File: GCPD-R1**

Rules and Procedures for
Disciplinary Action Involving a Teacher

1. *Purpose* These rules are prescribed pursuant to Arizona Revised Statutes, Section 15-341(A)(26) and are intended to be utilized as a disciplinary mechanism to deal with violations of statutory duties, School District regulations, Governing Board policies, and the duties of a teacher that do not constitute cause for dismissal or certificate revocation. The Governing Board reserves the right to initiate termination proceedings or to non-renew contract for serious or multiple violations of these rules or for any incident of insubordination, unprofessional conduct, or other reasons that it determines sufficient to constitute cause for severance of the employer-employee relationship. Dismissal procedures for teachers are governed by the contract of employment, District policy, and the statutory provisions contained in A.R.S. Title 15, Article 5, Chapter 3.

2. *General Provisions* These rules are intended to preserve the orderly and efficient administration of the school system and to serve as guidelines for the imposition of minor discipline not to exceed suspension without pay for a period of ten (10) days. Discipline may, but need not be imposed for violation of any of the following rules, that include statutory teaching duties, components of a teacher's job responsibility or any violation of Board policy, administrative rules or regulations, and any provision of the teacher or student handbooks.

FIGURE 5.6

Dismissal Policy Statement Based on State Statute (pp. 141–145)
Source: Reprinted by permission of the Tempe, Arizona, Elementary School District.

Each teacher employed by the Governing Board in this District shall:

Statutory duties—A.R.S. 15-521.A.:

1. Enforce the course of study for his or her assigned class or classes.
2. Enforce the use of the adopted textbooks for his or her assigned class or classes.
3. Enforce the rules and regulations governing the schools prescribed by the Governing Board, the Arizona Department of Education, and any other lawfully empowered authority.
4. Hold pupils to strict account for disorderly conduct.
5. Exercise supervision over pupils on the playgrounds and during recess if assigned to such duty.
6. Make the decision to promote or retain a pupil in grade in a common school or to pass or fail a pupil in a course in high school.
7. Present his or her certificate to the County School Superintendent before assuming charge of a school, except as provided in Arizona Revised Statutes 15-502, Subsection B.
8. Make such reports as may be reasonably required by the Superintendent of Public Instruction, County School Superintendent, Governing Board, or School Administration.

3. *Procedures*

   A. *Disciplinary action alternatives* Appropriate discipline is at the discretion of the Supervisor. The alternatives available include:

      1. Verbal warning;
      2. Verbal reprimand;
      3. Written reprimand;
      4. Suspension with pay;
      5. Suspension with pay and required remedial action, i.e., observation of other teacher, mandated in-service or educational program;
      6. Suspension without pay. A teacher may be given a suspension without pay for a period not to exceed ten (10) days;
      7. Termination. This remedy is reserved by law to the Governing Board, and procedures are described in applicable statutory provisions. The Governing Board may, if appropriate, determine that termination be imposed for serious or repeated violations of these rules. Notice of the Board's intent to dismiss and applicable procedures are not covered by these rules.

FIGURE 5.6
continued

B. *Notice of discipline*

1. An administrator, after a reasonable investigation, is authorized to impose minor discipline in any category described in Paragraph A.3 through A.6 above subject to notice, hearing, and appeal rights described below. A reasonable investigation shall include some discussion with the employee to ascertain if grounds exist to justify imposition of discipline.
2. When it is determined that grounds exist for disciplinary action, a written notice shall be sent to the teacher. The notice shall identify:
   a. The date the infraction occurred;
   b. The rule or duty violated;
   c. A summary of the factual information supporting the recommended discipline;
   d. The nature of the disciplinary action to be imposed.

C. *Request for hearing* A teacher who has received notice of discipline has the right to request a hearing in writing within five (5) school days after the date the teacher receives the notice. The request for a hearing shall be in writing and filed with the Personnel Office and shall contain the prior written notice of discipline.

D. *Hearing tribunal* The hearing will be held before the Superintendent or designee.

E. *Hearing procedure*

1. The hearing shall be scheduled within ten (10) school days after receipt of the teacher's request unless extended by mutual agreement of the parties.
2. Notice of the hearing shall be served on the teacher and Supervisor by the Hearing Officer and shall contain:
   a. The time and place of the hearing.
   b. A copy or summary of the written disciplinary notice previously served on the teacher.
   c. Notice that disciplinary action will be imposed if the teacher fails to appear.
   d. A statement to advise the parties that they may present oral or written evidence relevant to the alleged violation of rules or policies.
   e. State that the hearing will be conducted informally without adhering to the rules of evidence.
   f. State that within seven (7) school days after the hearing a written decision shall be served on the parties.

FIGURE 5.6
continued

  g. Advise the parties that they may, if they desire, be represented by another employee at the hearing.

 3. The hearing shall be held at the time and place stated in the notice. The designated person or persons shall conduct the hearing in an informal and orderly fashion recognizing the rights of all parties. A statement should be made by the Hearing Officer as to the purpose of the hearing. Parties shall be advised if a record shall be made by tape, stenographer, or the notes of the Hearing Officer. Any party may tape the hearing for his own use, but it will not be the official record.

 4. Subsequent to the hearing, the Hearing Officer shall prepare a written decision to be served on the parties within fifteen (15) calendar days.

F. *Decision* The decision shall contain a brief summary of the hearing and a finding of whether the teacher committed a violation and if the discipline was appropriate. If it is found that the teacher committed the violation, the teacher's right to appeal the written decision to the Governing Board for review of the record shall be provided as part of the decision.

G. *Appeal to governing board*

 1. Any appeal to the Governing Board via the Superintendent must be in writing, filed within five (5) school days after service of the hearing decision, list the issue or issues upon which review is requested, and specify the relief sought from the Governing Board.

 2. All evidence the teacher wishes to have the Governing Board review shall be attached to the appeal. No new information, other than that already submitted at the hearing, will be allowed.

 3. The supervisor shall be served with a copy of the appeal and have five (5) days after service to file material and information submitted at the hearing and which are deemed appropriate in support of the discipline imposed.

 4. When the Superintendent receives the appeal, it shall be transmitted to the Governing Board.

 5. The Governing Board has no obligation to conduct another hearing or to receive new evidence not previously presented to the Hearing Officer in a minor discipline matter.

 6. The Board shall schedule an executive session to review the appeal. No additional testimony or input shall be allowed unless expressly requested by the Board.

 7. Written notice of the Board's decision shall be served on the parties. The Board shall have a reasonable time, not to exceed thirty (30) school days to review the matter and render its decision.

FIGURE 5.6
continued

8. Discipline shall be held in abeyance during the hearing and appeal procedures under these rules.

Cross refs: KK-R
             GBCB
             GBCC
Legal References: A.R.S. 15-341

Issued: _____   Tempe Elementary Schools
                                                      Tempe, Arizona

FIGURE 5.6
continued

Brickell (n.d.), "the whole process of policy formulation is rich with opportunities for stimulating good thinking about school goals and their relation to policies by the many persons and groups concerned with the schools" (p. iv).

This chapter has presented information that not only underscores the vital importance of policy development for the human resources function, but has set forth the fundamentals for policy and regulation development in that area.

DISCUSSION QUESTIONS

1. You have been selected by your teacher colleagues to serve on a districtwide committee for the purpose of revising the school district's leave policy. All forms of absence from duty are concerns of the committee. Although the overriding concern is that of the development of a viable policy for all professional staff members, what are several specific provisions that you would want to have implemented as a teacher? For example, what stipulations would you see as important in the area of personal leave, sabbatical leave, and so forth?

2. Use the information provided in question 1 to set forth several specific provisions that you, as a member of the school board, would consider imperative to an effective policy on personnel leaves. Examine the differences, if any, between the stipulations arrived at for question 1 and question 2.

3. Information in the chapter indicated that the development of policies and regulations served to clarify the division of labor between the school board and the school superintendent. Discuss this contention in more detail. Why is such a division important in school operations? Isn't there some danger that such a division will result in board/superintendent conflicts?

4. Obtain a copy of your school district's policy manual or that of another school district. Rate the following characteristics from *low* (1) to *high* (5) as they pertain to the policy manual examined: completeness, conciseness, clarity, distinctiveness, and consistency. (Review the discussion of these characteristics included in the chapter for further term clarification.)

5. Use the Davies-Brickell System to determine each of the following topical headings. Write the topic of the series, subseries, division, subdivision, and so on, for each entry.
   a. 4117
   b. 4117.41
   c. 4143
   d. 4148
   e. 4251.11

CASE 5.1
Pay or No Play

Ce Ce Rose has taught instrumental music at East High School for 6 years. She holds a BS degree in music and will complete a master's degree at the end of the second term at State University.

Principal Hodson received a call from one of the school's patrons, Mrs. John Adams. Mrs. Adams, whose son is a sophomore at East, also is the mother of two daughters who both graduated from East and participated in the school's instrumental program.

"Miss Rose has informed my son, Mark, that he needs special help in order to retain his place in the school band," reported Mrs. Adams. "She implied to Mark that his trumpet playing was below the standard expected for the marching band," she remarked. "Miss Rose has made herself available for special lessons at $12.50 an hour. She'll work with Mark after school on Wednesdays and on two Saturday mornings a month."

Principal Hodson was silent for a moment. If this was true, this information was new to him.

"Aren't teachers supposed to give special help to students after school hours if needed?" asked Mrs. Adams. "I understand that she already is giving lessons to three other orchestra students."

"Well, many of our teachers do give help after regular classroom hours," said Principal Hodson, "and I do know that some of our teachers moonlight as tutors at night and on weekends."

"It seems to me that the charging for special lessons could lead to problems," commented Mrs. Adams.

"Mrs. Adams," said Principal Hodson, "let me search for more information on this matter. I'll get back to you at the earliest possible time. I appreciate your concern and thank you for contacting me on this matter."

Questions

1. Place yourself in Principal Hodson's role. What action plan would you implement in this situation?
2. Identify three or four issues of importance in this case.
3. Assuming that the school district has no written policy concerning the issues you identified in question 2, is a guiding policy needed to deal with such cases? Why or why not?

CASE 5.2
Teachers' Academic Freedom

On the opening day of school in September, Keefe, a tenured part-time English teacher, who is also head of a high school English department and Coordinator for grades 7 through 12, gave each member of his senior English class a copy of the prestigious *Atlantic Monthly* magazine . . . and asked the students to read the first article that night. . . . Keefe discussed the article with his class—especially a particular word that was used in it. He explained the word's origin and context, and the reasons the author had included it (the word, admittedly highly offensive, was a vulgar term for an incestuous son). Keefe said that any student who felt the assignment personally distasteful could have an alternate one.

The next evening Keefe was called to a meeting of the school committee and asked to defend his use of the offensive word. (Parents had complained.) Following his explanation, a majority of the members of the committee asked him informally if he would agree not to use it again in the classroom. Keefe replied that he could not, in good conscience, agree. No formal action was taken at the meeting, but Keefe was suspended shortly thereafter, and school administrators proposed the he be discharged.

Claiming a violation of his civil rights, Keefe sought a temporary injunction before a federal district court forbidding any action on the part of the school board prior to a hearing on the alleged violation. The court refused to grant the injunction, and Keefe appealed to the United States Court of Appeals, First Circuit.

His position was that, as a matter of law, his conduct did not warrant discipline and therefore there was no ground for any hearing. The position had two relevant parts:

1. His conduct was within his competence as a teacher, as a matter of academic freedom, whether the defendants (school board) approved or not.
2. He had no warning by any regulations then in force that his actions could bring about his discharge.

The school board denied Keefe's contentions and the following statement appeared in court records:

> They (the board) accept the existence of a principle of academic freedom to teach, but state that it is limited to proper classroom materials as reasonably determined by the school committee in the light of pertinent conditions, of which they cite in particular the age of the students. Asked by the court whether a teacher has a right to say to the school committee that it is wrong if, in fact, its decision was arbitrary, counsel candidly and commendably (and correctly) responded in the affirmative. This we consider to be the present issue.

Questions

1. What do you believe about the freedom of teachers to select and use materials of instruction despite the objections of some parents?
2. Discuss your views of the position set forth by Keefe. Do the same with the statement by the school board that appeared in the court records.

From "Teachers' Academic Freedom" by D. R. Davies and H. Watt, August 1970, *School Board Policies.* Copyright © 1970 by Daniel R. Davies. Reprinted by permission. Davies and Watt based this discussion on the case of Keefe v. Geanakos et al. (1st Cir. 1969).

☐ **CASE 5.3**
Miss North's Dilemma

Miss North has served in the Jefferson school system for 19 years as an elementary teacher. Her employment record in the Jefferson schools shows that she taught at Longfellow Elementary School for 5 years, Mark Twain Elementary School for 9 years, Whitman Elementary School for 3 years, and in her present position as grade five teacher at Emerson for 2 years. She has served under four different superintendents, including the present school head, Dr. Donnelly, who has been in Jefferson for 2 years.

During Miss North's 2 years at Emerson, one board member called Dr. Donnelly to inquire about Miss North. The board member stated that he had received many calls about Miss North in the last 2 days.

"I just wanted to let you know about the calls," said the board member. "You'll most likely be receiving some yourself soon. Better be on your guard."

Dr. Donnelly reviewed the permanent file of Miss North. Evaluation reports on Miss North pointed out that it was felt that she was a strict teacher and did not have the most friendly classroom atmosphere but most pupils performed better in her classroom than in one with more permissive surroundings.

One anecdotal notation in Miss North's file outlined a conversation between her and the assistant superintendent, Dr. Seward. Dr. Seward had telephoned Miss North to inform her that it would be necessary to transfer her from Mark Twain to Whitman. The reasons outlined for the action as recorded by Dr. Seward centered upon an apparent feeling of growing parental dissatisfaction and the fact that several parents had requested that their children not be placed in her room the next year. Thus the decision was reached to move Miss North to Whitman for a new start.

The record revealed that Miss North was greatly disturbed about the transfer decision. "I don't drive an automobile," Miss North had pointed out. "How do you expect me to get back and forth to school each day? Everyone knows what it means when you're placed at Whitman," Miss North had stated, according to Dr. Seward.

Mr. Smith, principal at Whitman Elementary School, was quoted by Dr. Seward as saying, "You never know how she will react from day to day. We've gotten along as well as can be expected. She doesn't have much patience for the slow learner, but her good kids can compete with most other grade five pupils."

At a special board meeting later that week, a second member of the board of education mentioned the concern centering upon Miss North. "Parents tell me that the pupils are afraid of her," one board member stated. "She apparently is 'cold' toward parents. In one instance, I was told that one of her pupils had written a note on the blackboard wishing her a happy birthday. Miss North insisted that the one who wrote it on the board erase it in front of the whole class. The parent of the child indicated that her embarrassed daughter didn't want to return to school."

Another board member stated, "This must be her thirtieth year of teaching in Jefferson. Doesn't she retire soon?"

The matter was referred by the board to Superintendent Donnelly for immediate study. After the meeting, Dr. Donnelly conferred with Mr. Malloy, principal at Emerson.

"She is a rather cold person, but I've received no official complaints from parents to date," said the principal. "However, my visit last week to her classroom revealed that some children are not responding. Her room was all business. The science lesson which I observed was well presented."

Dr. Seward apparently felt that it would be best to release Miss North. "She is starting one of her problems again. I think we've gone along with her long enough. Mr. Malloy would just as soon have her out of his building," Dr. Seward related to Dr. Donnelly. "She is a 'loner' in my opinion. She didn't even attend the faculty social last month."

Dr. Donnelly noted that the date was March 1 and school was to close on May 27. Obviously, the board was anticipating immediate action on the part of the administration.

Questions

1. Assume the role of Dr. Donnelly, school superintendent, and discuss/write your follow-up procedures and recommendations to the school board.
2. What policy and regulation matters are significant in this case? Why?
3. Explain how a viable set of policies and regulations might have proven of special value in this case.

REFERENCES

Bloss, J. M. (1882). *Thirtieth report of the superintendent of public instruction of the state of Indiana to the governor*. Indianapolis: State of Indiana.

Class size must be negotiated with teachers, Oregon court rules. (1991, April 10). *Education Week*, p. 2.

Clemmer, E. F. (1991). *The school policy handbook*. Allyn & Bacon: Boston.

Davies, D. R., & Brickell, H. M. (n.d.). *An instructional handbook on how to develop school board policies, by-laws, and administrative regulations*. Naco, AZ: Daniel R. Davies.

Davies, D. R., & Watt, H. (1970, August). Teachers' academic freedom. *School Board Policies*. Croft Consulting Services.

Decker, R. H. (1988). Eleven ways to stamp out the potential for sexual harassment. *The American School Board Journal*, 175(8), 28, 38.

Duke, D. L., & Canady, R. L. (1991). *School policy*. McGraw-Hill: New York.

Equal Employment Opportunity Commission. (1980). Guidelines concerning sexual harassment: Title VII legislation, § 703 of the Civil Rights Act. (P.L. 88-352)

Grier, T. B. (1984). Review these do's and don'ts for teacher hearings. *The Executive Educator, 6*(10), 21–22.

Grier, T. B., & Turner, M. J. (1990). Make your charges stick. *The Executive Educator, 12*(2), 20–21.

Hernandez, D. E., & Bozeman, W. C. (1990). AIDS policies and public school employees: A review of recent court decisions. *ERS Spectrum, 8*(2), 22–28.

McCoy, M. W., Gips, C. J., & Evans, M. W. (1983). *The American school personnel administrator: An analysis of characteristics and role.* Unpublished manuscript, American Association of School Personnel Administrators, Seven Hills, OH.

Norton, M. S. (1989). *The personnel administrator in Arizona: A research study.* Tempe, AZ: Arizona State University, College of Education.

Rogers, J. J. (1989). Regular review will keep your AIDS policies sound and up to date. *The American School Board Journal, 176*(1), 26–27.

St. John, W. (1983, October). Documenting your case for dismissal with acceptable evidence. *NASSP Bulletin*, pp. 104–106.

Strouse, J. H. (1990). School district AIDS policies. *Urban Education, 25*(1), 81–88.

Tead, O., & Metcalf, H. C. (1920). *Personnel administration.* New York: McGraw-Hill.

6

Screening and Selection of Professional Personnel

One of the quickest ways to make an important improvement in the services of a school organization is through its screening and selection processes. Every vacancy offers an opportunity to improve the quality and effectiveness of the organization's services. With each teaching vacancy, the principal has the freedom to improve significantly the quality of instruction. A well-planned and carefully executed screening procedure can potentially identify a person who will bring new life into the organization. The right teacher can infuse in students a new excitement for learning and can exhibit a set of professional behaviors that serve as a role model for fellow teachers. A poorly planned or hasty selection can precipitate a potentially endless flow of personnel problems. The employment of the wrong person can reduce the effectiveness of instruction, jeopardize existing working relationships among staff members, and require costly remedial support. In extreme instances, a poor decision can necessitate an unpleasant termination—for both the school and the individual being dismissed. Redeker (1989) audaciously stated, "You hire a problem and you will have to fire a problem" (p. 6). Moreover, staffing a position with an inappropriate or ill-prepared person can cause serious professional and personal problems for the individual.

The implications of selection decisions for professional personnel are manifold. Such implications mandate that screening and selection be conducted in ways that ensure the highest probability for success. This requires that appropriate and valid information about candidates be used in making employment decisions. The process discussed in this chapter was designed to improve the reliability of selection decisions through the use of valid screening criteria and pertinent personnel data and information.

The first section of the chapter briefly discusses preemployment testing. The next relates to the development of the position analysis that is the first step in the screening process. This is followed by a discussion of several subsequent steps: writing the job description, advertising the position and establishing an applicant pool, conducting a paper screening of applicants, and performing background checks. Because the interview is used so extensively in the screening and selection process, and because it is frequently misused, the next section includes an expanded discussion of developing and conducting interviews. Finally, the closing sections deal with making a selection, offering the position, the candidate's acceptance, and notifying the unsuccessful applicants.

PREEMPLOYMENT TESTING

Medical examinations, substance tests, skill appraisals, and psychological evaluations are the four general categories of preemployment tests. These types of tests have declined in use recently because of the expense and strain of liability litigation. To avoid such litigation in these four categories, the tests must have a relationship to the job and must be free of potential disparate impact on protected minorities. The results of such tests must be accessible only to those employees with a legitimate right to know.

Medical, substance, and psychological tests results must be regarded with the highest degree of confidentiality (Redeker, 1989). "Employers risk being sued for invasion of privacy if, without the employee's consent, they reveal information in a personnel file to people not legally entitled to it" (Bible & McWhirter, 1990, p. 185). Generally, when supervisory personnel discuss confidential information in good faith and for a legitimate business reason, they can act without fear of being liable. In view of possible liability consequences, however, prudent boards of education should adopt comprehensive policies that govern access and dissemination of employee records (Shepard, Duston, & Russell, 1989).

A complete discussion of the legal basis for workplace privacy is presented in Chapter 9. Also, the reader is encouraged to consult Shepard, Duston, and Russell (1989) for a state-by-state summary of the statutes and court decisions affecting employee privacy rights in the nation's 50 states, the District of Columbia, Puerto Rico, and Virgin Islands. This summary can be used to gain a general understanding of the legal basis of workplace privacy in each state. However, a knowledgeable attorney should be consulted when planning a personnel screening and selection process.

POSITION ANALYSIS

From a strategic human resource point of view, it is extremely important that the person responsible for making an employment decision be very familiar with the position to be filled. This individual should be knowledgeable about the organization's mission and culture and the environment of the subunit (school, central office department or division, etc.) where the vacancy exists. Moreover, this person must be aware of the strategic objectives of the organization and those of the subunit. The position analysis is a description of such important requirements, and a major part of its delineation includes a deductive process to produce a rationale for establishing the screening and selecting criteria (Cascio, 1989).

The position analysis includes a description of the position in relation to other aspects of the organization. This description outlines the relationship of the position to individuals and groups, both within and outside the organization. In addition, it is carefully developed to be consistent with and supportive of the organization's mission, its strategic objectives, and the objectives of the subunit where the vacancy exists. The outline of the position analysis employs a deductive procedure, beginning with a general description of the position and ending with the enumeration and definition of screening and selection criteria. "Decision makers need a set position description and a clear understanding of the criteria of teachers' job performance" (Bredeson, 1985, p. 14). The use of explicit criteria will provide some assurance that the person selected will possess the knowledge, experiences, skills, and abilities to work in a complementary manner with others toward the attainment of the unit's strategic objectives.

The position analysis for professional staff members was first used by Bolton (1970) in the area of teacher selection. Although the outline in Figure 6.1 was developed for all professional positions, it does include several elements that were adapted from Bolton's work on teacher selection.

FIGURE 6.1

Position Analysis Outline

*The term *subunit* is used as a broader concept to include schools and departments or functional areas of a school system (e.g., human resources department, elementary curriculum unit, transportation department, etc.).

I. Strategic Nature of the Position
   A. Mission of school system
      1. Strategic objectives of school system
   B. Strategic objectives of the subunit*
   C. Organizational structure of subunit
   D. Expectations
      1. At work site
      2. In relation to other system employees
      3. In relation to members of subunit
      4. In relation to outside groups, agencies, or individuals

II. Changing Aspects of the Position
   A. At the beginning of the assignment
   B. Anticipated changes
   C. Effects of others
   D. Description of important constituencies

III. Behaviors
   A. At work site
   B. In relation to other system employees
   C. In relation to outside groups, agencies, and individuals

IV. Screening and Selection Criteria
   (three to five criteria developed from position description in I–III above)

I. Strategic Nature of the Position

A description of the strategic nature of the position should enumerate the important direction statements for the organization and the subunit for which an employee is sought. Combining this with a description of the organizational structure of the subunit will provide a basis for understanding job expectations that are consistent with the strategic objectives of the subunit. As an example, a position analysis for a school vacancy would include the mission statement for the school system and its strategic objectives, the school's strategic objectives, and a description of the school's organizational structure. This will form a basis for enumerating general expectations for the position.

A. Mission of the School System.   The mission statement of the school system is a very precise elaboration of the system's reasons for existence. Usually, within 100 words or less, the school system addresses the questions of what, who, and how. Specifically, *what* client needs are met by the system's products and services? For *whom* are they provided? And *how* will it go about providing the products and services? The mission heralds what the school system wants to become in the future and is followed by strategic objectives.

Strategic objectives give attention to long-range targets that will provide a specific focus for the allocation of the system's time, energy, and material resources. Moreover, the strategic objectives provide a framework for the subunit's strategic objectives. Structurally, the subunit's strategic objectives must contribute to accomplishing the system's objectives.

B. Strategic Objectives of the Subunit.   The strategic objectives of the school system subunit seeking to fill a vacancy should be included in the position analysis. The subunit's objectives, written within the context of the system's mission statement and strategic objectives, give specific suggestions about attributes integral to the position being filled. For instance, a human resources department of a school system may have established a strategic objective for elementary school teachers that enumerates the increase of knowledge about instructional strategies in reading. Although this objective has implications for staff development, and perhaps other areas of human resources management, it offers specific strategic considerations for screening and selection of elementary school personnel. More specifically, the efforts of a school system in Atlanta, Georgia, provide a good example of the way a strategic focus was effectively used for improvement.

The Atlanta Public School System adopted two important strategic objectives in August 1980. At that time, 69% and 67% of the system's students tested below the national mean in mathematics and reading, respectively, on the California Achievement Test. Under the leadership of Superintendent Alonzo Crim, the board of education approved strategic objectives that mandated the system to raise the mean achievement level of its students in reading and mathematics to that of the national average within a period of 5 years. These objectives were widely publicized throughout all subunits of the school system. Strategies to achieve the objectives were developed by the many subunits of the school system; this included the personnel department as well as local school units. In this regard, personnel department resources were directed toward accomplishing related strategic objectives (e.g., by bolstering recruitment of teachers with strength in the two areas of focus). In addition, the achievement of specific strategic objectives in the many system subunits contributed to a realization of the strategic objectives for the school system by 1983. By the target year, 1985, 56% of the students tested above the national mean in mathematics and 63% did so in reading (Lewis, 1985).

C. *Organizational Structure of the Subunit.* The description of the organizational structure should include the general form of operation and type of supervision. If elementary school teacher candidates are being screened for a specific school, then the organizational structure of the school should be outlined to include the grade structure, such as K–8, K–4, 5–7, and so on. Other elements would include considerations of individual progress, self-contained classrooms, ungraded unit formation, lead teacher or unit coordinator involvement in supervision, available resource personnel, and any other items relating to organizational structure. A statement describing the organizational structure combined with the system's mission statement and system and unit strategic objectives can provide a central focus for determining a set of general expectations for the teacher being sought.

D. *Expectations.* General written expectations for the person filling a vacancy should apply to tasks at the work site as well as to interaction with other members of the subunit. The expectations should be established for relationships with both members of the school system and individuals, groups, and agencies outside the system.

In the immediate work setting, expectations relate to work load, involvement in decision making and planning, and other expectations specific to the tasks of the job. Expectations for an assistant human resources administrator, in the human resources subunit of a school system, might include coordinating applications for the position of paraprofessionals, reviewing applicants' personnel files, conducting preliminary screening, and planning paraprofessional work orientation workshops.

The expected relationship with members of the subunit should include responsibilities for working with peers, subordinates, and superiors. An outline of these relationships should address several important questions: Will the individual work on task forces or teams? What will the individual's relationship be to other team members? Will the involvement require leadership responsibilities? Is the position supervisory in nature? What type of supervision is required? What relationship is expected with the employee's immediate superior?

The interactions with external groups, agencies, and individuals usually relate to involvement in parent or civic groups, public relations, and professional organizations. Examples of such expectations for different positions might include serving as liaison with the curriculum division of the state department of education, serving on the school PTA advisory board as a unit-level representative, or representing the school to the local professional teacher's organization.

II. Changing Aspects of the Position

Educational institutions are certainly not immune to the influences of our changing society. During the past two decades, many widely held societal values have changed significantly. These changes have resulted from many important influences (i.e., demographic, technological, economic, and political). Among the changes that have had a profound impact on our nation's educational institutions and their staffs of professional educators are attitudes toward work; the information explosion and technological advancements; and the requirements of fair employment practices, equal employment opportunities, equal educational opportunities, and an expanding multicultural population.

The changing attitudes toward work have forced curricular changes in vocational education. Educators are now struggling with administrative and program changes brought about by the information explosion and the new technology of the microcomputer. Important changes in equal educational opportunity have been realized through court mandates to integrate schools.

However, some aspects of the educational processes do not change so rapidly, especially in attendance areas with homogeneous constituencies. School organizational structures and processes for decision making can be quite stable over an extended period of time.

Such dynamic and static considerations should be examined and, when relevant, included as important elements of the position analysis. The following topics should be considered in this analysis.

A. At the Beginning of the Assignment.   What important conditions might have immediate impact on the position? Using the previously mentioned example of the assistant human resources administrator, assume that a proposed change in the state educational funding model is being considered by the state's legislature. The legislative bill would increase state allocations to local educational agencies for the employment of additional paraprofessionals. This could be an important factor to consider in screening for the position of assistant human resources administrator. Certainly, the passage of such legislation would influence the position early in the assignment.

B. Anticipated Changes.   Certain changes will require different skills from the persons filling positions if they are to remain effective in the position after such changes. For example, a school considering the implementation of a new curriculum requiring a different organizational structure will want a newly employed teacher to possess the abilities and skills needed in the new organization. Another school expecting to experience a significant increase in the total percentage of students from a single ethnic minority will want to hire a teacher who will be able to work effectively in the school both before and after the transition. Awareness of such requirements may be important when considering two equally qualified candidates. Anticipated changes may suggest a need for unusual position requirements. Thus one applicant may have a higher probability of success in a position than another.

C. Effects of Others.   What effect will other people have on the position? If the position requires work on a task force or team, what are the competencies of the others? Are additional competencies needed to make the group more effective? Additionally, what resource personnel are available to lend assistance to the employee? What is the attitude of these persons toward providing help and support? The answers to these and similar questions may support the selection of candidates with special strength in interpersonal skills, organizational competencies, or exceptional creative abilities.

D. Description of Important Constituencies.   A position may require working with persons within or outside the organization, including school board members, administrators, students, parents, and other community members. A description of the nature of such working relationships may suggest the importance of employing a person with great strength in certain areas (e.g., negotiation, facilitation, etc.).

III. Behaviors

Based upon a review of the information about the strategic nature of a position and its changing aspects, the expected behaviors of an applicant should be considered. Evidence of behaviors must be supported by the applicant's past experiences to merit further consideration for the position.

Behaviors should be described relative to one or more of the following: (1) at the work site, (2) in relation to other system employees, and (3) in relation to outside groups, agencies, and individuals. For a teaching position, the description of behaviors might list interaction with students, fellow teachers, and resource personnel. It also could include communications with school system personnel and parent groups.

IV. Screening and Selection Criteria

The preceding section considered the identification of behaviors; this section describes criteria or dimensions that may be implied by such behaviors. Essentially, the behaviors are translated into screening and selection criteria including skills, abilities, knowledge, educational background, and experience. Once these criteria have been developed, they must be clearly defined. It is usually desirable to limit the number of criteria to four or five. Streitman (1975), Zubay (1976), and Draper (1979) showed that additional factors will not significantly improve the quality of the selection. Finally, each criterion or dimension can be weighted to emphasize required considerations or deemphasize those that are just desired. A representation of a completed position analysis for a second-grade teacher is shown in Figure 6.2.

JOB DESCRIPTION

A job description is derived from the position analysis. Some school districts develop position analyses for classes of jobs and then write job descriptions for each, (e.g., library/media specialist, high school classroom teachers, speech therapists, etc.). Once written, job descriptions are presented to the board of education for approval. Upon approval, they take the form of board policy.

I. *Strategic Nature of the Position*

A. *Mission of the School System*

The Pine Meadows School System is committed to excellence in elementary and secondary school education. We commit ourselves to working cooperatively with parents and the community to facilitate the growth of our students intellectually, emotionally, socially, and physically, and to create an awareness of our multicultural society. To accomplish this, we will employ the best qualified professional and auxiliary personnel available; use innovative materials and technologies; exploit creative methodologies, and enlist community resources.

1. *Strategic Objectives of School System*

The mean scores on the State Basic Skills Test (SBST) for elementary students in reading and mathematics will increase to 90 percent by 1998.

Computer labs will be installed in all elementary schools by 1998.

A middle-grades computer literacy and keyboarding curriculum will be developed and implemented by 1998.

By the end of the 2000 school year, 95 percent of all seventh grade students will demonstrate computer literacy and keyboarding skills on a systemwide test.

B. *Strategic Objectives of School*

1. All reading and mathematics teachers will be able to demonstrate computer literacy as measured by the System's Computer Literacy for Teachers Examination (CLTE) by 1997.

2. All teachers of reading and mathematics will be able to demonstrate through classroom instruction and the presentation of lesson guides methods for integrating the microcomputer into their teaching by 1997.

3. The mean test scores by grade level for each reading subtest of the State Basic Skills Test will increase to 90 percent by 1997.

4. The mean test scores by grade level for each mathematics subtest of the State Basic Skills Test will increase to 90 percent by 1998.

FIGURE 6.2
Position Analysis for Second-Grade Teacher (pp. 158–161)

C. *Organizational Structure of School*

The grade structure is K–7. Classes are self-contained and are set up heterogeneously. Students are taught material to achieve grade-level objectives. Instruction is supplemented with special remedial reading and mathematics instruction provided by specialists in each area. Leadership staff include the principal, an instructional lead teacher, and a lead teacher for student services. The school provides special classes for four categories of special education. Also, programs for gifted education and speech are provided.

D. *Expectations*

1. *At Work Site*

   The teacher is expected to engage in cooperative planning with other teachers by providing expertise and leadership in mathematics instruction and the integration of the microcomputer into classroom instruction in mathematics.

2. *In Relation to Other System Employees*

   The teacher is expected to work with the System's elementary school coordinator to develop methods for integrating the microcomputer into the teaching of elementary school mathematics.

3. *In Relation to Members of School*

   The teacher is expected to work cooperatively with all members of the staff on schoolwide committees. Specifically, the teacher will be expected to guide a self-study subcommittee in mathematics that will be convened next year.

4. *In Relation to Outside Groups, Agencies, and Individuals*

   The teacher is expected to work with the PTA and be a member of professional associations at the state and national levels.

II. *Changing Aspects of the Position*

A. *At the Beginning of the Assignment*

   Most teachers will be involved in computer literacy training and may call upon this teacher for assistance.

FIGURE 6.2
continued

B. *Anticipated Changes*

The Writing Express Program (WEP) will be implemented in the second-year classes. The teacher will be required to participate in an inservice program during the first semester of the school year to be prepared to implement WEP at the beginning of the second semester.

C. *Effects of Others*

All second-year teachers are exceptionally competent with strong leadership skills. Therefore, the teacher needs to show cooperation and a willingness to be supportive and flexible. Also, the teacher must be able to work in a collegial environment.

D. *Description of Important Constituencies*

Parents and community members are actively involved in the school. The teacher must be willing to engage these constituencies in a professional and cooperative manner.

III. *Behaviors*

A. *At Work Site*

Flexible, cooperative, tactful, helpful, sensitive, empathetic

B. *In Relation to Other System Employees*

Cooperative, willing to assume extra responsibilities, high energy

C. *In Relation to Outside Groups, Agencies, and Individuals*

Professionalism, strong verbal facility and oral communication, enthusiasm

IV. *Screening and Selection Criteria*

A. *Interpersonal Skills*

Shows caring for others; open to the ideas and feeling of others; earnestly seeks candor and openness; maintains a cool and rational approach on a constant basis throughout conflict situations.

Behavioral indicators: empathetic, caring, rational, poised, tactful, flexible, cooperative, helpful, sensitive.

FIGURE 6.2
continued

B. *Oral Communication Skills*

Ideas are well organized and clearly presented; effective eye contact; strong voice projection and articulation; easy to understand.

Behavioral indicators: clear enunciation, expressive, poised, self-confident, projects voice, correct grammar and usage, free of distracting mannerisms, effective nonverbal messages.

C. *Knowledge and Skills Base*

General knowledge of elementary curriculum and teaching with specialized knowledge in educational technology.

Behavioral indicators: diagnostic reading skills, knowledge of effective grouping methods, computer literacy including skill in using DOS and hard drive operations, installing application programs, operating application programs, effective use of manuals, basic computer maintenance.

FIGURE 6.2
continued

A job description usually includes the following categories of information: position title, objective that incorporates specific responsibilities, person to whom the individual reports, duties, and required knowledge, abilities, and skills. Periodically, job descriptions should be evaluated in conjunction with reviews of position analyses. This is necessary so that new persons being hired to fill vacancies can gain realistic expectations of a position's demands.

ADVERTISING POSITION AND ESTABLISHING APPLICANT POOL

Most school districts have policies that give direction to the screening and selection of personnel and, in many instances, adopt specific policies for advertising vacancies. Procedures stemming from such policies may require all vacancies to be advertised within the school district and in published materials external to the district. These announcements usually include position title, position objectives with responsibilities, required qualifications, application procedures, application deadline, and a description of the community and school district. Advertisements have for a long time been included in newspapers, professional and technical journals, and brochures sent to colleges. Now electronic bulletin boards of professional organizations also are used for advertising positions in the hope of attracting more applicants and expanding the applicant pool.

The creation of an applicant pool is the object of a well-developed recruitment program. To establish an applicant pool of qualified persons, the human resources administrator must give careful attention to the process of handling all applications. Moreover, it is extremely important to have a well-established procedure for keeping applicants informed. A good procedure will help to maintain the interest of qualified applicants and minimize the number of inquiries.

A microcomputer and a good data base software package can make this communication task an easy chore. A software package that is integrated with a word processor can routinely send letters to applicants advising them of receipt or need of materials, such as transcripts, recommendations, teaching certificates, and so on. Once all applications materials are received, dated, and filed, the process of "paper screening" can begin.

PAPER SCREENING OF APPLICANTS

Paper screening of applicants refers to the reviewing of all forms and materials submitted by the applicants to determine if they meet minimum qualifications for the job. These materials are usually reviewed by the human resources department's staff and include transcripts, letters of recommendation, application form, teaching or administrative certificates, test scores, and any other necessary documentation.

Based on this screening, a decision is made either to retain each applicant in the applicant pool or remove the applicant from further consideration. At this point, a background check is frequently conducted of those who are "screened in."

BACKGROUND CHECKS

A recent study found that about one out of every two candidates had lied at least once on a resume or application. The most commonly lied about things were job performance, compensation history, employment history, and educational background ("Recruiters Beware," 1992). Almost every school district has had at least one experience with counterfeited transcripts, falsified licenses, or distorted work histories (Jordan, McKeown, Salmon, & Webb, 1985). Even more seriously, a number of districts have too late found that they have in their employ persons with previous convictions for child molestations or substance abuse. For this reason it is important that the credentials, references, and employment history of candidates be checked and that a criminal background check be conducted. In so doing, the district must maintain the proper balance between the district's need to know and the applicant's right to privacy. The district must also comply with state and federal laws and the guidelines provided by court decisions in performing background checks. In performing background checks, the district is subject to the same restrictions that are applicable to all other aspects of the selection process. That is, information is not to be solicited or used unless valid and job related.

An important consideration for the district in performing background checks is the cost benefit of the process (Seidler, 1990).

> Background checking not only requires a fiscal outlay, but also extends the time it takes before an applicant can be hired. Some administrators would like a complete background on all candidates but then complain that it takes forever before an applicant can be hired. (p. 35)

Another major consideration in background checks is who will do the checking (the human resources department, the immediate supervisor, a member of the selection committee, or some other member of the staff) and how will negative information be handled. Background checks are usually performed in the following areas: references, credentials, and criminal background.

Reference Checks

Applicants should be informed on the application form that by supplying names of references or letters of reference, they are agreeing that these references may be contacted. The most commonly used methods of checking references are letters and telephone calls, with preference given to telephone calls because they save time and are more likely to produce more candid responses. At least three references should be contacted. "The most reliable information usually comes from supervisors, who are in the best position to report on an applicant's work habits and performance" (Sherman, Bohlander, & Chruden, 1988, p. 166). When contacting references be businesslike, maintain the focus on the job, and be sure to ask the reference if he or she would rehire the applicant. Most importantly, whatever information you obtain from references should not be disclosed to applicants.

Credentials Checks

An applicant's credentials include such items as high school or trade school diploma, college or university transcript, teacher or administrator credential, professional license, and health certificate. It is estimated that as many as 25% of all applicants have inflated their educational attainment (Seidler, 1990). Transcripts and health documentation should not be accepted if presented by the applicant, but must be mailed directly to the human resources office by the school, college, university, or physician. However, because administrator and teacher certificates, as well as various other professional certificates and licenses, are issued directly to the person, they may be accepted from the applicant. Nonetheless, a check should still be made to verify that they are valid, because when a license or certificate has been suspended or revoked, the actual document is not always returned to the issuing agency (Rebore, 1991).

Criminal Background Checks

The statutes of most states bar individuals who have been convicted of drug- or sex-related crimes from employment in the public schools. Laws are generally not so specific regarding conviction as a result of other felonies. It is permissible to ask on the application form if the applicant has been convicted of any crime and the nature of the offense. To conduct a criminal background check to verify the accuracy of these responses is both time-consuming and controversial. However, the heightened publicity given to cases of school employees involved in illegal conduct, as well as the heightened liability of school districts who have hired such persons without having conducted a background check that would have revealed similar behaviors, has led to an increase in criminal background checking. A number of states have enacted statues requiring that some background checking be done through fingerprint checks against state and federal files or with the Teacher Identification Clearinghouse (TIC). The TIC is operated by the National Association of State Directors of Teacher Education and Certification and maintains records of all teachers who have been denied certification or have had their certificates suspended or revoked for moral reasons in the last 15 years. The information is provided by the certification officer of each member state and can be accessed only by states, not individual school districts.

After all background checks are completed, the screening and selection process moves to the interview stage. Typically, several types of interviews are used prior to a selection decision.

THE INTERVIEW AS A SCREENING TOOL

The most widely used process of screening personnel for employment is the interview. Because the purpose of the interview is frequently misunderstood and its use in making a selection decision is often inappropriate, it is perhaps the most misused process of screening personnel. Many who use the interview in the screening process unfortunately make their decision to hire an applicant during the interview. One such method is the "survival approach" of selection. Each applicant is evaluated during the interview, and the applicant who remains as the best in the mind of the interviewer during a series of interviews with other applicants for the position is usually recommended for employment. No systematic record of applicant information is kept. This approach often produces undesirable outcomes for both the employer and the applicant. Many applicants are forgotten before all are interviewed. They often depart from the interview with the feeling that they were not really considered for the position.

Such experiences leave many with the opinion that the interview is too subjective and therefore ineffective for screening professional personnel. Objections such as these mandate certain requirements for the person conducting interviews. The process of developing and conducting an effective interview with a prospective professional employee requires extensive training to acquire a set of carefully honed interview skills.

When properly developed and conducted by a skilled person, the interview can be extremely worthwhile and act as an integral part of the overall precision screening and selection process. The interview is not the time to make a decision; it is for gathering and corroborating important information about an applicant's qualifications, and it allows the applicant to expand upon or provide additional details about related work experiences.

Generally, there are two types of interviews. Both the preliminary and behavioral interviews are data-gathering processes. The information collected in the preliminary interview is used to determine whether or not the applicant meets minimum qualifications.

The Preliminary Interview

The functions of the preliminary interview serve (1) to determine the correctness and completeness of the information obtained in the application file, (2) to eliminate from the applicant pool those who are obviously not qualified for the position, and (3) to provide information for the behavioral interview of applicants to be considered further (Fear, 1990).

The preliminary interview is usually conducted by personnel counselors of the human resources department. It is typically short and offers the applicant an opportunity to get answers to questions about the vacancy or school system. This is subsequently followed by the behavioral interview.

Information collected in the behavioral interview is used in conjunction with data and information from the personnel file to form the basis for making a comprehensive evaluation of an applicant relative to a set of selection and screening criteria. The evaluations of several candidates are later reviewed and analyzed to make a selection decision.

The Behavioral Interview

The behavioral interview is a process of gathering information about an applicant relative to predetermined dimensions or criteria. The criteria are strategically developed through a position analysis that focuses on the specific position and its relation to the objectives of the organization. During this process, the interviewer and the applicant engage in a developmental conversation that explores the applicant's qualifications, skills, and experiences relative to the criteria. Both positive and negative aspects of the applicant's background are discussed with equal importance.

Collecting information about applicants in relation to predetermined criteria requires that a systematic process be established for identifying appropriate criteria. Next, a procedure must be installed that will produce salient information about applicants in the most objective manner possible. Finally, the system used for processing the information and making a selection must ensure that all potential prejudices and biases (e.g., national origin, racial, religious, etc.) are eliminated. The information that is collected through the interview should be viewed with the same concern for validity and objectivity as any paper-and-pencil test used in other screening processes. Every possible effort should be made to develop a structured, behavioral interview that is valid for the position to be filled. The interview should be conducted in a manner that employs screening criteria and interview questions related to the job.

Patterned or structured interviews are characterized by a set of job-related questions uniquely developed for each applicant. The questions are usually ordered to support a developmental approach to the interview (e.g., chronological, career path, professional accomplishments, etc.). The patterned or structured behavioral interview is an information-gathering process for bringing objectivity into the screening procedure. When the interview is specifically developed for an applicant in relation to a position analysis, selection decisions can be made with the assurance that the best available applicant for the position has been selected.

Developing the Behavioral Interview.   The central focus in developing the behavioral interview is the set of screening and selection criteria identified and defined in the position analysis. Using these criteria, a content analysis is conducted of all pertinent data and information in an applicant's personnel file. Specifically, the person conducting the content analysis reviews the materials in the file relative to the criteria for items of exceptionality, (i.e., data and information that may be indications of exceptional strength or weakness relative to the screening and selection criteria). These items of exceptionality can be gleaned from written materials such as the application form, academic records, and letters of recommendation. This is followed by the development of nonleading questions (i.e., questions not suggesting an obvious response) around each selection criterion and related to the applicant's background information. Figure 6.3 illustrates a completed planning form. It shows how data and information are associated with the predetermined screening and selection criteria.

The first step in conducting a content analysis of an applicant's personnel file is to carefully read all materials contained in the file, and then write a general first impression of the applicant by giving special attention to areas of strength and areas of needed development. Then the reviewer looks for information related to the screening and selection criteria, and the information is recorded on the planning form.

In recording information, the reviewer condenses information and lists only relevant phrases, comments, and data under the corresponding selection criteria (see Figure 6.3). If the criterion *interpersonal skills* is one of several identified in the position analysis, for example, each item of information found in the written materials that shows strength or needed improvement in interpersonal skills is listed below the criterion and includes a reference to its source (i.e., application form, recommendation from academic supervisor, etc.).

```
┌─────────────────────────────────────────────────────────────────────────┐
│                    Behavioral Interview Planning Form                     │
│                                                                           │
│ Applicant's last name: Thomas      First name: Mildred                    │
│                                                                           │
│ Interviewer:  Carol McKenzie                                              │
│                                                                           │
│ After reading all application information, record your general            │
│ impressions of the candidate's strengths and areas of needed              │
│ development for the job being considered.                                 │
│                                                                           │
│ Strengths:                                                                │
│                                                                           │
│   Knowledge and Skills Base                                               │
│                                                                           │
│     Very strong preparation in reading, technology, and computers. Has    │
│     conducted many computer workshops for teachers.                       │
│                                                                           │
│   Oral Communication Skills                                               │
│                                                                           │
│     Appears to possess highly developed speaking skills.  Evidence        │
│     suggests much experience speaking to groups including both            │
│     teachers and parents.                                                 │
│                                                                           │
│   Interpersonal Skills                                                    │
│                                                                           │
│     Seems to understand and appreciate the importance of student          │
│     self-concept and need for success.  Can be a helpful and caring       │
│     person.                                                               │
│                                                                           │
│ Areas of Needed Development:                                              │
│                                                                           │
│   Oral Communication                                                      │
│                                                                           │
│     Shows some impatience with others and may need to develop better      │
│     listening skills.                                                     │
│                                                                           │
│   Interpersonal Skills                                                    │
│                                                                           │
│     May have difficulty working effectively with others who are less      │
│     able.                                                                 │
│                                                                           │
└─────────────────────────────────────────────────────────────────────────┘
```

FIGURE 6.3
Behavioral Interview Planning Form (pp. 167–171)

Applicant: <u>Mildred Thomas</u>

Screening Dimension Number 1

On the following lines provided, identify the first screening dimension that was derived from the Position Analysis. This is to be followed by a definition of the dimension. Add behaviors that would suggest evidence of strength in the dimension.

Screening Dimension: <u>Knowledge and Skills Base</u>
Definition: <u>General knowledge of elementary curriculum and teaching with specialized knowledge in educational technology</u>
Behaviors suggesting strength in dimension: <u>Diagnostic reading skills, knowledge of effective grouping methods, computer literacy including skills in using DOS and hard drive operations, installing applications programs, operating applications programs, ability to use technical manuals, basic computer maintenance</u>

In the spaces provided, carefully review all written application information and identify each item of information that relates to the screening dimension; develop nonleading interview questions; after the interview, record responses.

Background Information: (A—application form, T—college transcript, R—reference)

Conducted computer workshops for teachers on DOS, computer literacy, word processing, and data base. (A)

BS in elementary education, cum laude; MED—Reading (T)

State certification: elementary education, reading specialist (A)

College reading courses: Tch. Reading in Grades K–6, Psychology of Reading, Diagnosis of Reading Difficulties, Remedial Reading Difficulties (T)

18 credit hours beyond MED in educational technology and computers (T)

"Extremely knowledgeable of the microcomputer." (R)

"Very effective in assisting teachers with computer problems." (R)

Interview Questions:

Interview Responses:

FIGURE 6.3
continued

Applicant: Mildred Thomas

Screening Dimension Number 2

On the following lines provided, identify the second screening dimension that was derived from the Position Analysis. This is to be followed by a definition of the dimension. Add behaviors that would suggest evidence of strength in the dimension.

Screening Dimension: Oral Communication Skills
Definition: Ideas are well organized and clearly presented; effective eye contact; strong voice projection and articulation; easy to understand
Behaviors suggesting strength in dimension: Clear enunciation, expressive, poised, self-confident, projects voice, correct grammar and usage, free of distracting mannerisms, effective nonverbal messages

In the spaces provided, carefully review all written application information and identify each item of information that relates to the screening dimension; develop nonleading interview questions; after the interview, record responses.

Background Information: (A—application form, T—college transcript, R—reference)

Conducted microcomputer workshops for teachers (A)

"Tries to put parents at ease during conferences." (R)

"Working on ability to be a better listener." (R)

"Very poised and shows great professional maturity while talking to groups." (R)

College courses: Public Speaking 101, grade A; English 101, 102, grades A, B (T)

"Effective in speaking to parent groups." (R)

Interview Questions:

Interview Responses:

FIGURE 6.3
continued

Applicant: <u>Mildred Thomas</u>

Screening Dimension Number 3

On the following lines provided, identify the third screening dimension that was derived from the Position Analysis. This is to be followed by a definition of the dimension. Add behaviors that would suggest evidence of strength in the dimension.

Screening Dimension: <u>Interpersonal Skills</u>
Definition: <u>Shows caring for others; open to the ideas and feelings of others; earnestly seeks candor and openness; maintains a cool and rational approach on a constant basis throughout a conflict situation</u>

Behaviors suggesting strength in dimension: <u>Empathetic, caring, rational, poised, tactful, flexible, cooperative, helpful, sensitive</u>

In the spaces provided, carefully review all written application information and identify each item of information that relates to the screening dimension; develop nonleading interview questions; after the interview, record responses.

Background Information: (A—application form, T—college transcript, R—reference)

Developed unit on student self-concept (A)

"Children must experience success." (A)

"On occasion, shows some impatience with other teachers." (R)

"As a general rule, she is a helpful and sensitive person. She is extremely intelligent, but can be a little abrupt with others who are having some difficulty." (R)

"Working on ability to be a better listener." (R)

Interview Questions:

Interview Responses:

FIGURE 6.3
continued

Applicant: <u>Mildred Thomas</u>

Summary

After reviewing all application information and the responses to the interview questions listed above, develop a summary of the applicant's strengths and areas of needed development for the dimensions developed for the position.

Strengths:

Areas of Needed Development:

FIGURE 6.3
continued

171

The individual processing a personnel file must judge the statements and other information in the file relative to the screening and selection criteria. This is not difficult if the criteria or dimensions are clearly defined in the position analysis and the processor is very familiar with them.

One hazard for the beginning reviewer is the tendency to write evaluative statements about the applicant rather than facts from the file. For example, a letter of recommendation in a file being processed might include the statement, "Her single most important strength is relating effectively to the parents of handicapped children." If this statement is judged to be distinctive and related to interpersonal skills, the inexperienced reviewer might write a statement like "She has very good interpersonal skills," rather than actually quoting or paraphrasing the letter of recommendation. The evaluation of interpersonal skills is not made during the information-processing phase but only after all written information has been recorded and combined with new or corroborating information from the behavioral interview.

After all written materials in the personnel file have been processed and pertinent information recorded, each criterion must be analyzed further. An important question must be asked about the information included under each: Is the written information for the dimension sufficient to allow an evaluation of the applicant on this factor? If yes, the dimension need not be pursued in the behavioral interview. Conversely, if more information is needed to substantiate or corroborate existing information, then relevant interview questions must be developed, questions that relate to the applicant's previous experiences. These questions are developmentally ordered and used in the behavioral interview with the applicant. The types of interview questions and the development of the actual interview will be discussed under the next topic, "Conducting the Behavioral Interview."

The behavioral interview should always focus on its purpose, namely, to gather information about an applicant relative to predetermined dimensions or criteria. Notes taken during the interview are recorded in the Behavioral Interview Planning Form under the appropriate criteria.

With both the personnel file and the interview information on the screening and selection criteria recorded, the applicant can be evaluated. Usually a scale is designed with appropriate descriptors for evaluating each criteria. A 5- or 7-point scale, where 1 is *low* and 5 or 7 is *high*, works well.

The applicant is evaluated on each criterion based on all recorded personnel file and interview information. After the criteria have been evaluated, a narrative summary of the evaluation is written relative to each criterion, emphasizing the applicant's strengths and areas of needed development. The written statement should be developed objectively and include comments that reflect a synthesis of the information from the personnel file and the interview. Some interviewers include a graphic profile depicting the criteria on one axis and the numerical evaluation on the other. This provides a quick view of the applicant when reviewing the summaries of several applicants for a position. The graph and summary statement are particularly helpful if a decision is to be made several weeks after the evaluation is conducted. In the final analysis, a decision must be made to identify the one applicant profile that "best fits" the profile sought in the position analysis.

Conducting the Behavioral Interview.   Behavioral interviews are conducted with those applicants screened through the preliminary interview. As stated before, the purpose of the behavioral interview is to gather information about an applicant relative to predetermined criteria or dimensions. The interview is only a part of the total screening and selection process. Essentially the process is an attempt to predict the job performance of an applicant 1 year after hiring. How well will the applicant perform on the job in 1 year? A response to this question can be improved if it is based upon past work experiences: ***The best predictor of what an applicant will do in the future is what he or she has done in the past.*** Therefore the task of the interviewer is to explore past work experiences with the applicant and record information that provides insight into strengths and areas of needed development relative to the identified criteria. The quality of information obtained has a direct relationship to the following aspects of the interview process: physical setting for the interview, psychological atmosphere, interviewer's interpersonal modus operandi, interviewer's ability to listen, quality of note taking, and quality of interview questions.

The interview should be conducted in a private location, where the environment can be psychologically supportive and free of physical distractions. Meeting these requirements will promote feelings in the candidates that they are having a developmental conversation with an important representative of the organization. The interview should not be conducted at a hotel swimming pool, in a restaurant, lounge, or lobby. These places have too many distractions, do not offer privacy, and do not support a feeling of confidentiality in the applicant. The best location is a private office.

The interviewer should communicate the need for privacy to the secretary, so that all telephone calls and other interruptions can be avoided. An interruption during the interview can cause the applicant to lose a line of thought at a time when important information is being communicated. In addition, it is difficult for the interviewer to show interest in the applicant and to record all relevant information if other business is being transacted simultaneously. The interviewer and applicant should not sit across a desk from each other. The desk tends to symbolize authority and may formalize the atmosphere unnecessarily. Many experienced interviewers prefer to sit at a table at a right angle to the applicant. Some have conversation areas in their offices with comfortable straight chairs. Finally, furnishings that cause distractions should be removed from the office (e.g., clocks that chime, fish tanks with bubblers, etc.).

The psychological atmosphere must be considered with great care to promote the best conditions for the interview. For the interview to be developmental, the interviewer must minimize the applicant's stress by being friendly and supportive, genuine, open, attentive, and undemanding. Stress is particularly great at the beginning of the interview, and careful efforts should be made at that time to put the applicant at ease. This atmosphere should be maintained throughout the remainder of the interview.

At the end of the interview, the applicant should feel that the experience was pleasurable and nonthreatening. The applicant should also feel that both strengths and areas of needed development for the position were discussed with equal importance. These feelings can more readily occur when the interviewer's beliefs and assumptions about people are positive and supportive.

Another aspect of the interview process is the interviewer's interpersonal modus operandi, or manner of dealing with people. Generally interviewers should not try to use a set of behaviors different from those consistently employed in other settings. The interview is no place to experiment with behaviors. However, it is important for the interviewer to be aware of behaviors that can affect the quality of information gained in the interview.

Body language is one of these considerations. We all realize that our nonverbal behaviors communicate meaning to others. Likewise, the nonverbal behaviors of an interviewer can significantly affect the interview process. An authoritative and formal manner on the part of the interviewer will tell the applicant to respond to interview questions in a formal way. On the other hand, a more relaxed manner will tend to put the applicant at ease, and the applicant will respond accordingly. When the interviewer leans toward the applicant with eye contact, it shows that the interviewer is interested and is sincerely concerned about what the applicant is saying. When the interviewer leans back and gives a periodic "ah ha" or other similar utterance to show understanding and attentiveness, the applicant will know that ample time is available to explore background experiences and qualifications for the position. Conversely, an interviewer's glance at a wristwatch, gaze out the window, or shuffling of papers may tell the applicant that the interviewer is not interested, that a negative decision has been made, or that other, more important things need to be done.

One of the most difficult yet important interview skills to learn is listening. We not only listen to what is being said verbally but temper its meaning by the tone of voice, inflections, and nonverbal expressions of the speaker. If the applicant responds quickly to a question, pauses before responding, or avoids responding, the interviewer must interpret whether or not these behaviors have important meanings.

The task of listening is difficult because the interviewer is trying to record information as it is communicated while thinking about the next question and trying to maintain eye contact with the applicant. An interviewer is obviously not listening when an applicant begins the answer to a question with, "Well, as I mentioned a few minutes ago." These difficulties combined with certain pitfalls for conducting a quality behavioral interview present a formidable challenge to those wishing to become skilled in the process.

Lopez (1972) identified five pitfalls to good listening: anticipation, intolerance, impulsivity, indolence, and suggestibility. Some interviewers tend to anticipate what is going to be said by an interviewee after a few words or a sentence. Thoughts about what should be asked next can tend to obstruct quality listening. Mannerisms, appearance, and speech patterns often cause an intolerance that can get in the way of listening. Making a snap judgment about what is said occasionally causes the interviewer to interrupt with another question. This impulsivity can hamper opportunities to hear important facts. Many interviewers do become bored and let their attention wane. This form of indolence is another inhibitor to high-quality listening. Finally, suggestibility can be a problem. This occurs while interpreting emotionally loaded terms or phrases that are used by the applicant, for example, "My boss was super." In such instances, an interviewer who does not ask what is meant by the term *super* may incorrectly interpret the response.

Thus the interviewer must be able to listen well to be in control of the interview and accomplish its purpose. The only way that this can happen is through thorough preparation of a structured behavioral interview.

The recording of information obtained in the interview raises some important concerns. Many inexperienced interviewers feel that it is too difficult to record information during the interview. They say that it forces a sense of undesirable formality. Moreover, they question their ability to simultaneously take notes, maintain eye contact, and listen carefully. Although these concerns are all valid, one must not lose sight of the purpose of the interview—to obtain information about an applicant relative to predetermined dimensions or criteria. If the interviewer attempts to rely on memory alone, important information can be lost and the interview is of no value. It is difficult to conduct a 30-minute to 1-hour conversation with a person about experiences specific to him or her and remember all the significant information. In addition, applicants expect the person conducting interviews to take notes, for it signifies that what is said is important and will not be overlooked in the employment decision. It emphasizes the applicant's importance as a prospective employee of the organization. Any detriment to the interview process brought on by note taking is more than made up for by the information recorded. Many of the difficulties of taking notes can be overcome with practice. Interviewers find that they can develop their own shorthand or write down key words or phrases that can be expanded to a fuller meaning later.

Another consideration of note taking is the timing of writing notes. As a general rule, it is best to write notes at a time when it will not affect what is being said. If the applicant mentions something important, it is best for the interviewer to wait until the conversation moves to a subject where note taking is expected before the important information is recorded. For instance, an applicant may be talking about a very sensitive, job-related issue. To write a note at that moment may inhibit any further expansion on the issue. Note taking can also become a signal that whatever is being said is important, causing the applicant to direct inappropriate comments to that area. Finally, ease of note taking can be improved through experience in using patterned interview questions. Such questions are written down and sequenced in a way that builds rapport before more sensitive issues are addressed.

Skill in developing and asking questions is the most difficult yet most important quality for the interviewer to possess. To develop appropriate interview questions, one must be aware of the many considerations that detract from objectivity or contaminate information obtained through positive or negative bias. It is extremely important that all questions be totally job related. Bible and McWhirter (1990) stated that

> The oral interview is but an extension of the data-seeking process that begins with the application. Thus, questions asked during an interview can raise the same problems that inquiries on application forms do. In several respects, moreover, oral interviews have even more potential for creating difficulty. First, employers do not have the firm control over what goes on in an interview that they have over what appears on a written application form. What occurs will depend on the idiosyncrasies and biases of the individual hiring officer. There may also be problems in proving what was or was not said. Because of this, interviewing personnel should be carefully trained and receive written guidelines for conducting interviews according to existing legal requirements. (pp. 74–75)

Most interviewers are well aware that questions concerned with marital status and family, religion, life-style, political affiliation, and the like are inappropriate. To be job related, questions must be centered on previous work experiences, skills, and training in relation to the dimensions established in the position analysis. Figure 6.4 presents a list of areas to avoid when questioning applicants in an interview.

Two types of questions can be used in the interview. First, a direct question can be used to complete a description of the applicant's background. If the applicant omitted information in the application materials, a direct question can be used to complete the record (e.g., "How many years did you teach at Cherryhill Elementary School?"). Direct questions are informational in nature and do not provide much opportunity for the interviewer to gain understanding of the applicant's skills and qualifications for the position. To gain this kind of understanding, the interviewer should ask nonleading questions.

FIGURE 6.4

Inappropriate Topics for Interview Questions
*Some items can be questioned as bona fide occupational requirements, for example, asking about a car if one is required for the position.

Worked under another name
Birthplace, birthplace of parents, spouse, or relatives
Age
Date of birth
Religion
Name of church
Religious holidays observed
Arrests
Nationality
Naturalized citizen
How parents or spouse acquired citizenship
Mother tongue, national origin or ancestry
Foreign languages applicant reads, speaks, or writes
How applicant acquired ability to speak foreign language
Branch of military service
Type of discharge from military service
Spouse's employment
Wife's maiden name
Mother's maiden name
Names of brothers and sisters
Number of dependents or children
Ages of children
Child care arrangements
Renter or homeowner
Car ownership
Nearest relative
Plan to have children
Pregnancy
Use of contraceptives
Disability or handicap
Height
Weight
Membership in nonprofessional organizations

The nonleading question is open-ended and does not suggest a favored or preferred response. The question allows the applicant to structure an individual response. One technique of using nonleading questions involves asking two questions that are considered a polarized pair. If the interviewer wants the applicant to relate an ability to get along with the people in a previous position, the direct question, "Did you get along with the people you worked with at ———?" will yield an obvious response. A polarized pair of questions might include the following two questions: "What did you like the most working with the people at ———?" would be later followed by "What did you like the least in working with these people?" Both responses may require follow-up questions to gain a greater depth of understanding.

Occasionally, it is important to ask follow-up questions to understand more fully an applicant's work background. If an applicant tells you that she was excited about being appointed to the new school, do not assume that she was excited about working in a new situation with new challenges and opportunities to develop professionally. Ask her why. She may have been excited because she was getting out of a situation where she was not successful.

Some words can be quite threatening to the person being interviewed. In the question "What is your most serious weakness for the job?" the word *weakness* can be a threat to the applicant who may view it as a trick question. A less threatening question might be, "What one area do you feel is important for you to develop professionally?" Again, follow-up questions are usually needed to explore fully the applicant's response.

Softening the impact of a question is a useful interviewing technique. When a teacher applicant is being asked about classroom management, it is sometimes helpful for the interviewer to draw upon personal experiences to soften the impact of a question. "When I taught mathematics, I did many things that worked well with children. Yet most of us who have taught for a while know that certain situations or types of children give us great difficulty no matter how hard we try. Can you give me an example where you experienced this same feeling?" Usually when this question is asked, the interviewee will give an affirmative, nonverbal nod. If this indication is not given, it might be helpful to first ask, "Have you ever had this experience?" A negative response would raise some obvious concerns about the applicant's veracity. A polarized pair of questions also can work well in pursuing this area of interest.

Avoid hypothetical questions. Quite frequently the interviewer of a teacher applicant will ask, "What would you do if ———?" A question like this will only elicit a hypothetical or "textbook response." It is far better to ask about actual experiences and accomplishments. If the applicant does not have experience, then it would be better to ask about similar situations that he or she has witnessed rather than ask a hypothetical question. Questions about learning situations and instruction that the applicant observed or participated in as a student would yield far better information than that from a hypothetical question.

One of the most widely used questions with teacher applicants is "What is your philosophy of education?" This is the kind of question that will usually yield a textbook response. If knowing the applicant's philosophy is important, evidence can be found by asking questions about previous teaching strategies, assumptions held, curriculum, and methods of evaluation. An applicant's verbal statement about philosophy may have nothing to do with the ability to teach, manage a classroom, or relate to children. Again, past teaching experiences provide the best guide to what the interviewer can expect of the applicant on the job.

Silence is a very powerful way to ask a question without really saying it. Silence after an applicant's response to a previous question implies that the interviewer wants to hear more. Although this technique can be difficult to master, experience through repeated attempts will minimize the tendency to offer another question after a few seconds of deafening silence. Five or six seconds may seem like 10 minutes to the interviewer, and the temptation to talk increases in intensity with each succeeding second.

Several other pitfalls that can affect the interview also should be mentioned. For example, the interviewer should not give the applicant advice. It takes valuable time and is inappropriate in the interview. On occasion, an applicant will say something with which the interviewer will greatly disagree. When this occurs, the interviewer should not argue with the applicant or attempt to "set him straight." It should be remembered that the purpose is to accumulate information about the applicant and not offer another point of view or give evaluative feedback. The best response to negative comments by the applicant is "Ah ha, I see."

The halo effect is another common pitfall. If the interviewer learns that the applicant went to the same college as he or she did, this may positively skew the interviewer's interpretation of the applicant's qualifications. Other examples might include belonging to the same fraternity or church, being involved in high school or college athletics, and serving in the same military service group. A negative halo can also occur if the applicant speaks very positively about a mutual acquaintance that the interviewer does not hold in high esteem. All of these examples have the potential of inappropriately tempering the interviewer's understanding of an applicant's qualifications for a position. Every effort should be made to guard against such biases.

The total process of screening and selection should be evaluated on a continuous basis. The performance appraisals of candidates employed should be compared to the screening evaluations to determine their degree of agreement. Where differences exist, a careful analysis of both evaluation procedures should be made to determine ways of improving the screening process. If an applicant were employed for possessing strong organizational skills and the performance appraisal found the opposite to be true, then a careful analysis of the screening process should provide some insight into the screening problem. The administrator should try to learn from this experience and make the necessary changes to eliminate the recurrence of such an error. The following principles outlined by Redeker (1989) summarize the previous discussion of the interview process:

☐ Really know the job for which individual is needed.
☐ Understand what characteristics you are looking for.
☐ Plan the interview in order to obtain the information you need.
☐ Establish a comfortable conversational style to build rapport.
☐ Maintain objectivity about the applicant as the interview progresses.
☐ Remain flexible, and guide the conversation from general to specific and from harmless to sensitive areas.
☐ Pace the interview and apportion interview time approximately. Don't permit the applicant to spend too much time on one area, which results in your rushing to

complete the interview in a timely fashion, thus covering other important areas incompletely.

☐ Listen. Concentrate on what the applicant is saying and respond appropriately.

☐ Structure the interview so that you use a variety of questioning techniques. Use open-ended questions rather than questions that can be answered "yes" or "no."

☐ Don't ask questions that could be considered discriminatory.

☐ Use silence to obtain more information. If the applicant seems to run out of things to say, let the silence build up for a few minutes. The applicant probably will offer more information.

☐ If there are statements you'd like the applicant to expand on, repeat them in another way. This is called "echoing" and is an effective information-gathering technique.

☐ Watch for the "halo" effect! This is a situation where an interviewer permits an applicant's one or two favorable traits, such as a good appearance or ability to speak well, to influence the interviewer's overall impressions. The halo effect can work in reverse, biasing the interviewer unfavorably because of one or two bad impressions.

☐ Don't talk too much, but do show energy and enthusiasm. A stiff, formal interviewer will turn off most applicants.

☐ Follow up hunches and unusual statements. If the applicant says, "I don't get along with certain kinds of people," you will want to find out what those kinds of people are.

☐ Close the interview in a reasonable period of time. Close on a positive note, but don't lead an applicant on or promise anything you can't deliver.

☐ As soon as the interview is over, write down the facts and your impressions of the interview. (pp. 373–374)

SELECTION, OFFER OF POSITION, AND ACCEPTANCE

The selection of the person to whom the position will be offered depends on the type of position and particular procedures of the school district. Generally the decision about teaching positions is made by the principal of the school where the vacancy exists. The decision to hire, if accepted by the applicant, takes the form of a recommendation through the human resources department to the superintendent. At this point a contract is drafted for approval by the board of education upon the recommendation of the superintendent.

Employment decisions for other types of professional positions are often made by high-level system administrators as recommendations to the superintendent. And, of course, the superintendent frequently makes such decisions with only minimal input from other administrators.

NOTIFICATION OF UNSUCCESSFUL CANDIDATES

Only after a position has been filled should all candidates be notified to advise them that the position has been offered to and accepted by another. There are a couple of reasons for doing this soon after filling the vacancy. First, candidates may want to follow up on other job opportunities with different school districts as quickly as possible. A second consideration is to maintain good public relations with candidates who may want to remain in the pool of qualified persons for future consideration.

SUMMARY

This chapter presented a process for implementing a screening and selection procedure for professional personnel. The process included developing a position analysis and a job description, advertising the position to establish an applicant pool, initial screening of applicants, conducting background checks, developing and conducting preliminary and behavioral interviews, analyzing and evaluating the personnel file and behavioral interview information, writing summary profile statements, and making the selection decision. Finally, the chapter discussed the job offer and acceptance and the notification of unsuccessful candidates.

DISCUSSION QUESTIONS

1. Develop a position analysis for your present job or one you recently held. In small discussion groups, contrast the rationale for the screening criteria used for each position represented in the group. Do certain criteria consistently appear on all position analyses despite the different positions? Discuss the diverse criteria among position analyses and try to identify their relationship to the dynamic and static aspects of the position.
2. Form small discussion groups. Using the position analysis in Example 6.1 and a set of fictitious credentials appropriate for the position, analyze the credentials relative to the screening criteria of the position analysis (i.e., identify all information in the fictitious set of credentials that represents strength or needed development).
3. Develop a set of nonleading questions for each of the criteria included in Figure 6.3. Critique the questions in groups and attempt to improve each.

CASE 6.1
The CEO's Daughter

Sara Mobley leaned back in her chair and reflected on her first year as principal of Finley Elementary School. With a great sense of satisfaction, she thought about the progress that was made in the initial year of implementing a strategic plan for Finley. Two of the school's key strategic objectives related to reading, and Sara was pleased that the school had made great improvement in reorganizing the library media center with the hope of changing the trend in declining reading achievement scores. Sara felt that much of the credit could be attributed to Helen Monti, one of the finest library media specialists in the system. Helen was instrumental in working with the Library Media Committee to adopt new rules and regulations for library operations that were wholly supported by the entire faculty. She developed a curriculum map of the collection and established critical acquisition priorities for the basic book collection. In fact, the PTA executive council was so pleased with the apparent improvements that it approved a resolution praising the good work of Mrs. Monti and appropriated $3,000 for the acquisition of a CD-ROM system for placement in the media center. Sara thought about how lucky she was to have recruited Helen last summer.

As that thought passed through her mind, Helen appeared at Sara's door and asked to talk with her. After a short period of small talk, Helen told Sara that she would not be returning to Finley next year. Her husband was being transferred to the West Coast and they would be moving in late June. Sara expressed her deep regrets and told Helen that she could count on her for a strong recommendation when she sought employment for next year.

Within a week, Sara met with the Library Media Committee to ask for their assistance in finding a replacement for Helen. Sara told the members that it was important for the school to find a person of Helen's caliber so that the momentum of this year's efforts would not be lost. The selection of the right person for this position was not only critical to the school's program, but both the faculty and parents had high expectations for the library media program as well.

Sara and the committee worked for several weeks developing a position analysis for the media specialist. Several preliminary screening criteria were sent to the system's department of human resources, and within 2 weeks, the director of the department sent Sara the credentials of six highly qualified candidates. The committee met to conduct a content analysis of the candidates' files in preparation for the behavioral interviews. The committee assisted Sara in preparing the interviews, and during the next 3 weeks, all six candidates were interviewed by Sara. Also, the committee members met with each applicant to provide an orientation to the school's program and priorities as well as get to know the applicant. When Sara completed the interviews and subsequent evaluations of the candidates, she called a meeting of the committee to present the findings and decide on the person. The committee and Sara all agreed and were excited about offering the position to John Ashworth. All felt that they had made an excellent choice, and Sara told the members of the committee that she would call John this afternoon.

As Sara returned to the main office, her secretary told her that Superintendent Wilks was on the phone and was anxious to speak to her. Sara picked up the telephone to greet Dr. Wilks. The superintendent expressed his pleasure with the great progress that Sara was making at Finley and indicated his hopes and expectations for her long career in the system. He then men-

tioned that the Chamber of Commerce President, Fran Snell, had been working to assist Henry Mallory, CEO of Albion Manufacturing Corporation, with arrangements for the firm's move of its regional headquarters to the city. Ms. Snell felt that Mr. Mallory would prove to be a strong supporter of the school system and a civic-minded member of the community. Dr. Wilks told Sara that he had assured Ms. Snell that he would do everything he could to gain Mr. Mallory's support.

The superintendent also mentioned that Ms. Snell told Mr. Mallory that she was certain that the school system could find a job for his daughter, Emily, who was graduating from an upstate college as a media specialist this spring. Dr. Wilks then asked Sara to seriously consider Emily Mallory for the media specialist position. In fact, he told Sara that he had already asked the director of human resources to hand-deliver a copy of Emily's credentials to her, and the file should be in her hands before the end of the day.

Questions

1. What problem(s) must Sara solve?
2. What are all the possible approaches Sara can use to solve the problem(s)?
3. What are the likely consequences of using each of the approaches?
4. Which approach is the best one to implement?
5. What outcomes can Sara expect from such action?

☐ CASE 6.2
Inappropriate Questions

Dr. Anthony Banelli is the assistant superintendent for human resources management in the Pine Valley School District. He recently learned that Frank Honeycutt, a longtime high school principal in the system, was using interview questions related to applicants' age, family, and church membership. He also learned that Frank had been told by the superintendent on two previous occasions to avoid using such questions.

Due to a slowdown in the economy there was a large pool of well-qualified applicants for all teaching positions in the system. Most recently, Frank received 32 applications for a vacant social science position at his school, and he interviewed 14 candidates. After one of the interviewees was recommended by Frank and hired by the board, Dr. Banelli received a telephone message from the superintendent: "Tony, I just got a call from the EEOC office about Frank Honeycutt. There are three complaints against him. I need to see you right away."

Questions

1. Should Dr. Banelli do anything prior to seeing the superintendent? If so, what should he do?
2. What should Dr. Banelli expect as an outcome of his conference with the superintendent?
3. Is it possible that Dr. Banelli may share some responsibility for the alleged complaints against Frank Honeycutt?
4. What preparations should Dr. Banelli make to remove the possibility of such interview questions being used by other administrators?

☐ CASE 6.3
To Lead or Not to Lead?

Middle school principal Pat Kemp prides herself on her ability to interview applicants for teaching positions. She is known to use a lot of tough questions, typified by the following lead-ins:

"What would you do if ———?" "How would you go about doing ———?" and "What do you believe ———?"

Despite her confidence in her interview skills, she has an uncomfortable and growing concern that she has not made the best selection decisions. In fact, the last two teachers she hired are behaving differently than she expected. One teacher, Cheryl Hennessy, demonstrated a lot of knowledge about classroom management in her job interview, but now she is having serious behavioral problems with children. Another newly hired teacher, Kevin Smith, articulated many innovative ideas about classroom instruction in his interview, yet parents complain that he uses worksheets as his only method of instruction. Pat recollected that Mr. Smith does spend most of his time sitting at his desk.

One afternoon, Pat read an article in a personnel journal titled, "The Value of Nonleading, Behaviorally Focused Questions in the Employment Interview." She reflected on the content of the article and wondered how she could test such questioning techniques against her own.

Questions

1. Aside from leading questions, what other things could be causing Pat to make poor selection decisions?
2. What could Pat do to test the two approaches to interviewing teacher candidates?
3. What precautions should she make to ensure a fair test of the two approaches?

REFERENCES

Bible, J. D., & McWhirter, D. A. (1990). *Privacy in the workplace: A guide for human resource managers.* New York: Quorum Books.

Bolton, D. L. (1970). *Instructor's guide for use of simulation materials for teacher selection.* Columbus, OH: University Council for Educational Administration.

Bredeson, P. L. (1985). The teacher screening and selection process: A decision making model for school administrators. *Journal of Research and Development in Education, 18*, 8–15.

Cascio, W. F. (1989). *Managing human resources: Productivity, quality of work life, profits* (2nd ed.). New York: McGraw-Hill.

Draper, J. M. (1979). *A comparative study of elementary school principals' on-the-job rating and their ratings from an assessment center designed to identify developmental needs*. Unpublished doctoral dissertation, Georgia State University, Atlanta.

Fear, R. A. (1990). *The evaluation interview* (4th ed.). New York: McGraw-Hill.

Jordan, K. F., McKeown, M. P., Salmon, R. G., & Webb, L. D. (1985). *School business administration*. Beverly Hills, CA: Sage.

Lewis, D. (1985, May 16). Atlanta students raise test scores in math, reading. *The Atlanta Journal*, p. 1.

Lopez, F. M. (1972). The employment interview. In J. J. Famulo (Ed.), *Handbook of modern personnel administration* (pp. 13/1–13/12). New York: McGraw-Hill.

Rebore, R. W. (1991). *Personnel administration in education: A management approach* (3rd ed.). Englewood Cliffs, NJ: Prentice-Hall.

Recruiters beware: Lying is common among applicants. (1992). *HR Focus, 69*(10), 5.

Redeker, J. R. (1989). *Employee discipline: Policies and practices*. Washington, DC: The Bureau of National Affairs.

Seidler, E. H. (1990). Developing a policy on applicant background checks. *School Business Affairs, 56*(6), 35–37.

Shepard, I. M., Duston, R. L., & Russell, K. S. (1989). *Workplace privacy: Employee testing, surveillance, wrongful discharge, and other areas of vulnerability* (2nd ed.). Washington, DC: The Bureau of National Affairs.

Sherman, A. W., Jr., Bohlander, G. W., & Chruden, H. J. (1988). *Managing human resources* (8th ed.). Cincinnati, OH: Southwestern.

Streitman, H. W. (1975). *The use of simulation techniques to identify potential effective educational administrators*. Unpublished doctoral dissertation, Georgia State University, Atlanta.

Zubay, A. H. (1976). *The use of the assessment center to identify potentially effective educational administrators*. Unpublished doctoral dissertation, Georgia State University, Atlanta.

7

Performance Appraisal

One of the major focuses of the educational reform movement of the last decade was the improvement of the performance of educational personnel. More than half of the states added statutes aimed at improving the accountability and quality of teachers and administrators. And as performance expectations have increased, so has the need for every school district to have in place a sound evaluation system. A sound evaluation system can be characterized as one that has (1) established performance evaluation as a school district priority; (2) determined and disseminated clearly articulated evaluation purposes; and (3) adopted an evaluation plan that has a sound methodology, "provides an orderly sequence of implementation stages, and follows a natural progression from intended purposes through actual use" (Stronge, 1991, p. 78). In this chapter each of these elements is examined, followed by a discussion of the standards involved in developing and operating a sound evaluation system.

EVALUATION AS A DISTRICT PRIORITY

The establishment of performance appraisal as a school district priority is critical if the evaluation system is to make a meaningful contribution to the improvement of the district and individual employees. If the evaluation system does not have the strong support of the school board and the administration, evaluation will be superficial at best (Stronge, 1991). One of the ways the school district can demonstrate its commitment to the evaluation system is through the policies it adopts to govern and direct the evaluation system. A strong policy such as the example given in Figure 7.1 demonstrates both the board's philosophical position regarding evaluation and its importance to the organization and the board's commitment to the evaluation process. Additional policies that clearly articulate the purposes and procedures to be followed in the evaluation of all employees and that emphasize administrative responsibility and accountability for the effectiveness of the system further demonstrate the importance placed on evaluation.

In the Paradise Valley Unified School District the parents, Governing Board members, and staff are committed to the continued growth of the district's strong educational program designed to meet the individual needs of the student. While recognizing the integrity of the teacher's individual instructional style, an effective teacher evaluation system which focuses on the improvement of instruction is essential to this commitment.

While the primary focus of evaluation is to improve instruction, an effective system requires teachers to meet established performance expectations. Therefore, the process for teacher evaluation must clearly state performance expectations (classroom and outside the classroom), must contain criteria for measuring effective teacher performance, and must have an instrument for assessing the competencies relating to the criteria.

It is also vital that the teacher evaluation system allow for and encourage productive dialogue, appropriate commendation, and when required, specific recommendations for improvement including reference to human and material resources. The system must provide for both written and oral communications within designated time lines. The process must be continuous and constructive, taking place in an atmosphere of cooperation, mutual trust, and respect among evaluator, evaluatee, and observer.

FIGURE 7.1

School District Statement of Philosophy for a Teacher Evaluation System
Source: From *Paradise Valley Unified School District No. 69 Teacher Evaluation System*, Paradise Valley Unified School District, 1988, Paradise Valley, AZ: Author.

A school district should solicit the involvement and review of administrators, instructional staff, and school patrons when developing evaluation policies. The district should also ensure that policies are written in easily understandable language with clearly defined standards. The failure to do so leaves the district open to charges of arbitrary and capricious conduct (Rossow & Parkinson, 1992).

DETERMINING THE PURPOSES OF THE EVALUATION SYSTEM

Determining the purposes of the district's evaluation system before it is implemented and continuing to communicate these purposes to affected individuals is paramount to defining evaluation. Evaluation systems that lack clearly articulated purpose(s) are essentially meaningless and contribute little to the accomplishment of the district's goals (Stronge, 1991). One approach to clarifying the purposes of evaluation is to distinguish the types of evaluation and then match the most appropriate use of these various types to the purposes of evaluation. A discussion of the four basic types of evaluation—summative, formative, norm referenced, and criterion referenced—follows. The matching of these types with the most common purposes of evaluation is presented in the subsequent section.

Types of Evaluation

Summative evaluation is evaluation that is conducted at the end of an activity or period of time and is designed to assess terminal behaviors or overall performance. Summative evaluation is used to make personnel decisions regarding such matters as contract renewal, tenure, merit pay, assignment to levels of a career ladder, and termination. "Summative evaluation has as its primary function ... the determination of a teacher's competence—not the augmentation of that competence" (Popham, 1988, p. 269). Summative evaluation is formal, somewhat infrequent, and focuses only on the person being evaluated. The individual being evaluated is normally not as involved in the summative evaluation process as in the formative process, and in many cases may only be informed of the results or decision (Sperry, Pounder, & Drew, 1992).

Unlike summative evaluation, which is a terminal activity, **formative evaluation** is an ongoing evaluation designed to provide feedback to the person being evaluated for the purposes of self-improvement. "The decisions riding on formative ... evaluation involve a host of choices focused on 'How can I do it better?'" (Popham, 1988, p. 270). Formative evaluation is only quasi-formal, intimately involves the person being evaluated, and, because its purpose is the improvement of performance, it may have several foci relative to the employee's work in the context of the operation of the school district (Sperry et al., 1992).

In spite of the fact that summative and formative evaluations have different purposes, most school districts in the United States attempt to combine the two functions so they can be carried out simultaneously, which according to many experts is a mistake (Popham, 1988). Because nobody wants to get fired or not receive a promotion, merit pay, or other commendation, the weakest employees—in fact the ones most in need of improvement—are least likely to identify their own weaknesses. Even when the principal or other administrator sets out to make the appraisal focus on improvement, "the contaminating specter of summative ... appraisal serves to stultify that improvement mission" (Popham, 1988, p. 271). Thus many experts agree that given the limited impact of summative evaluation (i.e., that few individuals are actually terminated or not given a raise), the attention and limited resources allocated to evaluation should be focused on summative evaluation that will impact on a larger number of employees and have greater potential of bringing improvement districtwide.

Although not as commonly found, according to Sperry et al. (1992) two additional types of evaluation may be used in the evaluation of personnel in education. **Norm-referenced evaluation** is evaluation that compares the individual's performance with that of other employees or with the average of a larger group. In contrast, **criterion-referenced evaluation** compares the employee's performance, not to any other person(s), but to an established standard.

Matching the Purposes of Evaluation With the Types of Evaluation

Each type of evaluation is used for different evaluation purposes. The stated and actual purposes of evaluation meet a variety of evaluation ends. Consider, for example, the following purposes articulated by the Tolleson Elementary School District (n.d.) for the evaluation of professional staff:

☐ Evaluation shall determine how well the objectives held by the school are being carried out. The success of the educational program is dependent upon the quality of classroom instruction, supervision, and administration.

☐ Evaluation shall provide the basis for motivation and for self-improvement. Personnel must be aware of their strengths and weaknesses in order to improve.

☐ Evaluation shall provide the basis for in-service training and supervisory activities. Such activities can be most effective when they are based upon clear evidence of need as shown by evaluation studies.

☐ Evaluation shall provide the basis for administrative decisions. Such decisions may include the employment of personnel, their assignment, the granting of continuing status, promotion, demotion, or termination. (p. 2)

The purposes of teacher performance appraisal according to the National School Boards Association (NSBA) are:

☐ To ensure that students are provided high quality instruction.

☐ To meet statutory and contractual requirements.

☐ To recognize outstanding teacher performance.

☐ To provide opportunities for teachers to develop their professional skills.

☐ To provide an avenue for two-way communication about school system and individual staff member goals, objectives, and other performance-related concerns.

☐ To document, in a fair manner, the objective information the board and administrators need when making decisions relative to assignments, transfers, granting of tenure, promotions, or destaffing.

☐ To provide evidence to the community that proper care is taken to hire, develop, and retain good teachers. (p. 121)

And the *Encyclopedia of Educational Research* identified three purposes of principal evaluation: (1) to assist in annual evaluation decisions regarding district-level employment and professional improvement, (2) to provide data relevant to the assessment of administrative abilities or potential and principal selection, and (3) to satisfy legislative and/or state board requirements for administrator certification. (Ellett, 1992).

The multitude of reasons for evaluating personnel relate to four broad personnel purposes: (1) staff development, (2) rewarding performance, (3) promotion, and (4) retention, contract renewal, or termination. The match of each of these purposes with the types of evaluation that might best be used to achieve it is presented in Table 7.1.

THE EVALUATION PLAN

Having decided the purposes of the evaluation, the school district must design an evaluation plan to achieve these purposes. The evaluation plan has three major elements that, in effect, involve the answers to three questions: (1) What will be evaluated? (the criteria); (2) What level of performance is expected? (the standards); and (3) How will evidence be collected? (data collection).

TABLE 7.1

Matching Evaluation Purposes With Types of Evaluation

Staff Development

This purpose might best be evaluated using *formative evaluation* that is criterion referenced, particularly if one is pinpointing specific skill areas. *Norm-referenced assessment* might be helpful if the perspective is a competitive one, but the predominant and most useful approach would be *criterion-referenced formative assessment* because this combination addresses ongoing evaluation that focuses on specific skills.

Promotion

Evaluation used for promotion might employ the approaches noted for rewarding performance. Additionally, there may be a *summative assessment* component in cases in which promotion reflects a significant movement from one level to another.

Rewarding Performance

Norm-referenced evaluation would likely be used when rewarding someone for being more able than others (thereby comparing his or her performance with that of others, or some norm or average). By contrast, *criterion-referenced evaluation* might be employed when rewarding all persons who reach a certain level of skill. Lastly, if one is intending to reward improvement, then it is necessary to track the progressive development of performance using *formative evaluation* (assuming it is undesirable to wait an extended period of time to reinforce good performance).

Retention, Contract Renewal, or Termination

These personnel decisions typically rest on a *criterion-referenced assessment* to determine if an individual did or did not demonstrate the minimum job skills necessary to continue employment. The final decision is based on formal, *summative evaluation* and may have contractual and legal parameters such as due process. It is possible, however, that *norm-referenced evaluation* would be used in some termination decisions, such as reduction-in-force. The types of evaluation used for these personnel actions may also vary with the stage of the decision process. For instance, prior to a final employment decision there should be efforts to remediate substandard performance. This evaluation may become focused on skill areas needing improvement and therefore employ *formative evaluation*.

Source: From "Educator Evaluation and the Law: A Case Study of Common Statutory Problems" by D. J. Sperry, D. G. Pounder, and C. J. Drew, 1992, *West's Education Law Quarterly, 1*, pp. 415–429. Copyright © 1992 by West Publishing Company. Reprinted as abstracted with permission from 75 Ed. Law Rep. 965.

Criteria

The criteria are the job-related behaviors expected of the teacher, administrator, or other staff member (Valentine, 1992). The first place that must be looked to for guidance in determining what will be evaluated is state statutes. As previously stated, in the last decade more and more states have enacted legislation dealing with the evaluation of public school employees. As of the writing of this text, 35 states have passed legislation requiring that teachers be evaluated, and 5 of the remaining 15 have state department of education or board of education policies that require the evaluation of teachers (Valentine, 1992). Over one-half of the states also require the formal evaluation of principals.

State statutes requiring the evaluation of school personnel vary widely as to their level of specificity. Some states only require that the school board adopt some evaluation policy and leave the details to the board, whereas other states mandate all aspects of the evaluation and leave the local board no flexibility (Rossow & Parkinson, 1992). In 29 of the 40 states where teacher evaluation is required, criteria that define effective teaching are provided (Valentine, 1992). The criteria approved for use in one state are presented in Figure 7.2.

In addition to compliance with state statutes, local school district evaluation plans must comply with any agreements that may exist with the teachers' and administrators' bargaining representatives (Rossow & Parkinson, 1992). Although these agreements will not always address criteria, they normally will address the evaluation and appeal process.

Whether derived from state statute or negotiated agreement or developed by a team of the local school district, there are three types of criteria that may be included in the district's evaluation plan. The first type is *trait* or attribute criteria. The assumption in using these criteria is that there are definable traits or attributes that are necessary for good performance. That is, trait criteria describe what the employee is, rather than what the employee does. Although most school districts do not rely heavily on trait criteria today, some trait criteria, such as dependability and personal appearance, are still found in many evaluation systems (Ginsberg & Berry, 1990).

A second type of criteria is concerned with *results.* The rationale for this approach is that teachers and administrators should achieve certain objectives and that their performance can be meaningfully assessed by examining the extent to which those objectives have been accomplished. How the objectives are met is not considered to be as important as the results. Results criteria include such things as improved achievement test scores, lower drop-out rates, and more staff development (Ginsberg & Berry, 1990).

The third type of criteria, and by far the most commonly used in the evaluation of teachers, is *performance-based* criteria. When used, these criteria should be based on the research about effective teaching (or administration). They should "describe what effective teachers do when they are working with students in the teaching-learning process" (Valentine, 1992, p. 36) and be "center[ed] around the strategies to be used to assist students to reach the established goals" (Findley & Estabrook, 1991, p. 297). Other criteria that relate to the role of the teacher in the effective operation of the school should also be identified (Valentine, 1992). Some of

Uses Knowledge of Subject Matter
1. Demonstrates knowledge in subject area.
2. Demonstrates knowledge of curriculum development to include scope and sequence.

Displays Interpersonal Skills
1. Communicates effectively with students.
2. Promotes positive self-concepts in learners.
3. Maintains a positive and stimulating learning environment.
4. Communicates enthusiasm for learning.
5. Uses correct written and oral expression.

Plans for Instruction
1. Defines objectives and subobjectives in terms of the content to be learned and the intended behavior of the learners.
2. Assesses students' skill levels to determine the appropriate learning objectives.
3. Plans instruction to achieve selected objectives.
4. Chooses relevant academic activities to ensure appropriate student time on task.
5. Sequences learning activities to achieve specific goals and objectives.
6. Plans instruction at varying and appropriate levels of cognitive thinking.
7. Organizes instruction to meet individual differences and specific needs.
8. Organizes resources such as time, space, materials, and equipment to facilitate the achievement of goals and objectives.
9. Specifies procedures for monitoring and assessing student progress.

Provides Instruction
1. Provides instruction at students' skill levels.
2. Teaches to the learning objectives as specified in the lesson plan.
3. Teaches necessary objectives in a logical sequence.
4. Provides instruction at a variety of levels of thinking.
5. Uses strategies to maximize the amount of time students are engaged in relevant tasks.
6. Uses a variety of instructional techniques and methods related to the objectives.
7. Uses techniques to involve most of the learning time.
8. Models correct performance for students.

FIGURE 7.2
Criteria to Use in Evaluating Teaching Skills, Arizona Department of Education (pp. 161–162)
Source: From Arizona Department of Education, Phoenix, AZ.

9. Gives clear directions and explanations related to lesson(s).
10. Assesses student learning throughout the learning process.
11. Obtains responses for each objective to check student mastery before proceeding.
12. Adjusts instruction so that students attain mastery of the objectives.
13. Provides appropriate instruction and services to exceptional students.
14. Adjusts instruction to meet individual differences and specific needs.
15. Evaluates students according to consistent objective criteria.

Uses Learning Principles in Providing Instruction
1. Communicates to students the purpose and value of learning objectives.
2. Provides sufficient teacher directed and independent practice with monitoring to ensure that students are accurate and successful.
3. Communicates the importance of the learning by holding all students accountable for learning.
4. Provides specific and appropriate feedback in a variety of ways during instruction.
5. Uses motivation techniques to enhance student learning.
6. Provides an appropriate focus for students at the beginning of learning objectives.
7. Utilizes a variety of ways to summarize learnings.

Uses Classroom Management Strategies
1. Uses effective classroom management techniques.
2. Communicates expectations for appropriate classroom behavior.
3. Demonstrates ability to work with individuals, small groups or large groups as determined by instructional objectives.
4. Manages inappropriate classroom behavior.

Displays Professionalism
1. Engages in professional development.
2. Seeks and shares professional ideas.
3. Acts in accordance with defined teacher responsibilities, both legal and professional.
4. Identifies exceptional students and refers them to appropriate specialists.
5. Uses effective strategies for parent-teacher communication, including conferences.

FIGURE 7.2
continued

these criteria will apply to all teachers in the system, whereas others will apply to teachers at certain grade levels or with certain teaching assignments. Figure 7.3 provides examples of some performance criteria that might be used to assess teaching performance.

The use of these three types of criteria is not necessarily mutually exclusive. Many districts have an evaluation system that combines more than one type (Ginsberg & Berry, 1990). What is important is that whatever criteria are adopted must be objectively documented and be clearly communicated to the individuals being evaluated.

Standards

Whereas the criteria define the dimensions of performance to be evaluated, standards are the levels of performance required with respect to the criteria (Stiggens & Duke, 1988). One or more standards may be related to a specific criterion. The ultimate success of the evaluation system in assessing an employee's performance relative to a particular criterion lies not in how many standards are associated with it, however, but in

---

I. Instructional Process
    The teacher:
    A. Demonstrates evidence of lesson and unit planning and preparation.
    B. Demonstrates knowledge of curriculum and subject matter.
    C. Uses effective teaching techniques, strategies, and skills during lesson.
    D. Uses instructional time effectively.
    E. Evaluates student progress effectively.
    F. Provides for individual differences.
    G. Demonstrates ability to motivate students.
    H. Maintains a classroom climate conducive to learning.
    I. Manages student behavior in a constructive manner.

II. Interpersonal Relationships
    The teacher:
    A. Demonstrates positive interpersonal relationships with students.
    B. Demonstrates positive interpersonal relationships with educational staff.
    C. Demonstrates positive interpersonal relationships with parents and other members of the school community.

III. Professional Responsibilities
    The teacher:
    A. Follows the policies, regulations, and procedures of the school and district.
    B. Assumes responsibilities outside the classroom.
    C. Demonstrates a commitment to professional growth.

FIGURE 7.3
Performance-based Criteria for Evaluating Teaching
Source: From Jerry W. Valentine, *Principles and Practices for Effective Teacher Evaluation.* Copyright © 1992 by Allyn and Bacon. Reprinted with permission.

how clear and objective they are and how effectively they have been communicated to the employee. Vague and subjective standards will only result in disagreements in interpretations (NSBA, 1987). A failure to communicate what is expected of each employee will greatly reduce the validity of the evaluation (Ginsberg & Berry, 1990).

Standards may be calibrated to distinguish between levels of performance ranging from "unacceptable" to "superior." Or they may be stated so as to require a more definitive judgment, for example, "meets expectations" or "does not meet expectations" (NSBA, 1987). Figure 7.4 illustrates the type of performance standards that might be associated with one of the performance criteria presented in Figure 7.3, "Evaluates student progress effectively."

Data Collection Procedures

The data used in the evaluation process will vary depending on both their source and the way they are collected. For example, not only will the type of data generated from a classroom observation differ from that obtained from a survey of parents, but the classroom observation data may vary as a result of the degree of formality of the observation, the frequency of the observation, the duration of the observation, and whether it is announced or unannounced. Whatever process is used to collect data, it is imperative that the procedures be well defined and adhere to any state laws, employment contracts, and school board policies. It is also imperative that all evaluators receive the training necessary to competently perform the evaluation and that they adhere to all applicable laws, contracts, and policies.

A number of techniques may be used by the district, singularly or in combination, in order to gather the quantity and quality of data necessary to accomplish the purposes of the evaluation system. The more common of these data collection tech-

---

Criterion: Evaluates student progress effectively.
Standards: 1. Uses evaluation techniques that are consistent with school and district philosophy.
2. Uses evaluation techniques appropriate to curricular goals and objectives.
3. Uses a variety of evaluation techniques (e.g., pre- and posttesting, teacher-made tests, tests from other sources, oral and written activities, projects).
4. Constructs tests directly related to skills and concepts taught.
5. Provides evaluative feedback in a timely manner.
6. Uses a variety of techniques for communicating progress (e.g., immediate feedback, written and verbal comments, grades, scores, individual and group conferences).

FIGURE 7.4

Example of Performance Standards

Source: From Jerry W. Valentine, *Principles and Practices for Effective Teacher Evaluation.* Copyright © 1992 by Allyn and Bacon. Reprinted with permission.

niques are described in the following sections, along with some of the major considerations surrounding their use.

Rating Scales.   Rating scales are lists of criteria items that are presumed to constitute effective performance, be it in teaching or administering. Each item is given a range of possible evaluation ratings, typically on a scale of from 1 to 5. On some scales items are weighted and given a numerical value depending on their relative importance. A total score may then be derived to produce a summary judgment of performance (NSBA, 1987). Typically the ratings are made after observation of an individual's performance, for example, a classroom visit made for that purpose.

The most serious problem with the use of rating scales is that the judgment regarding any item is purely subjective. Another serious threat to the validity of ratings is the so-called **halo effect**—the tendency of an evaluator to form a strong general impression of the person being evaluated and to then give basically the same rating on every item on the scale (Medley, 1992).

There are several things that can be done to reduce the halo effect and to increase the overall validity of ratings. The first is to choose the rating scale to be used with care and make sure that those aspects of performance to be rated are the kind of performance the schools and the employees really want and that they are clearly stated and easily recognizable. Even with the large volume of literature on effective teachers and effective administrators, specifying exact behaviors is difficult. Second, evaluators should be trained and drilled until they can agree on their evaluations of the same performance. Ratings scales are not as easy to use as they appear. Distinguishing between relevant and irrelevant behaviors and discounting the halo effect requires training and practice. Third, make more visits; the more items to be rated, the more visits that should be made. If possible, each visit should be made by a different rater (Ginsberg & Berry, 1990; Medley, 1992).

Notwithstanding their possible shortcomings, rating scales are used extensively by school districts throughout the nation. The exclusive use of rating scales in many school districts appears to be an attempt to find an easy solution to a complex problem. If the scale has been cooperatively developed and the employee agrees that the items identified as needing improvement are indeed deficiencies, however, the rating scale can serve as a basis for providing help to improve performance. Overall, rating scales are probably most useful as self-evaluation instruments that are not expected to be objective, or for supplementing and summarizing other evaluation techniques (NSBA, 1987).

Observation.   Observation is perhaps the most commonly employed methodology in the assessment of teachers. The observation may focus on a narrow range of behaviors, or it may attempt to encompass all that is being observed. The duration of the observation may be for an entire lesson or period or for a few minutes. Observations may be spaced throughout the course of the year; in other situations it may be more desirable to conduct the observations several days in a row (Stiggens & Duke, 1988).

Observations may be classified as ***formal,*** scheduled and planned, observations or ***informal,*** unscheduled, observations. According to Murphy (1987) a well-conducted formal evaluation will include the following stages:

1. a preconference in which the substantive focus and procedural conditions for the evaluation are established;
2. an observation during which the supervisor objectively describes and records activities that are occurring in the classroom;
3. a period of analysis and interpretation of the data collected during the observation;
4. a postconference during which the supervisor and the teacher review the analysis of the lesson together for the purpose of planning further efforts at instructional improvement; and
5. a postconference analysis in which the supervisor and teacher analyze the usefulness of the first four phases of the observation cycle. (p. 168)

A variety of approaches have been used to gather and record observation data. A classification framework used in the *Handbook of Research on Teaching* to classify the plethora of approaches and instruments available to observers is presented in Table 7.2. Four classes of collection procedures were identified: categorical systems, descriptive systems, narrative systems, and technological records. Each system in turn is described in terms of four types of information about the system: (1) the general nature of the system (e.g., whether it is open or closed or whether it utilizes a set of preset categories to describe behaviors), (2) the type of system, (3) the methods of recording data, and (4) the general goals of the users of the system (Evertson & Green, 1986).

No one of these systems is necessarily better than another. The particular observation system that should be used in a school district is the one that is best suited for the specific purpose of the observation and the one that will provide the type of evidence needed for the kind of decisions that need to be made.

Informal observations can often yield more important data than formal observations. Even when observations are considered informal, they should be conducted with a specific purpose in mind (Stiggens & Duke, 1988) and should be followed by brief written feedback on what happened during the visit (Murphy, 1987). A dozen or more informal observations per class per year may be necessary to provide a complete picture of the teaching and learning that is taking place in the classroom. The time involved is worth the results. In combination with other sources of data, "informal observations allow administrators and other supervisors to make judgments about teacher performance with a good deal of surety" (Murphy, 1987, p. 169).

Critical to the success of the evaluation is that the person being observed be made aware of the purpose(s) of the observation and that good communication be maintained throughout the process. It is also important that the evaluation be conducted as unobtrusively as possible and that the time and length of the observation be appropriate to ensure that the behavior observed is a representative sample. Lastly, those conducting the observations must be trained in observation skills and the techniques and processes of the particular observation system (Evertson & Holley, 1981).

Self-evaluation.   Although self-assessment is rarely used as the sole source of information for an evaluation, it can serve as an important source of data and a valuable ingredient to any evaluation system. "The fields of psychology, psychotherapy, and philosophy are based, in part, on the belief that individuals possess important knowledge about themselves" (Stiggens & Duke, 1988, p. 139). Not only do employees

TABLE 7.2
Ways of Recording and Storing Observations: Broad Classifications

	Category Systems	Descriptive Systems	Narrative Systems	Technological Records
Nature of Systems	Closed system	Open system	Open system	Open system
	Always has preset categories.	May have preset categories.	No preset categories.	No preset categories.
	Samples of behaviors, events, processes that occur within a given time period. Boundaries of events are often ignored. Focus on behavior in general.	Meaning is viewed as context specific. Boundaries of events are considered during as well as prior to observations. Samples behaviors, events, processes that occur with naturally occurring boundaries.	Meaning is viewed as context specific. Boundaries of events are considered during as well as prior to observation for live recording. Samples behaviors that occur within naturally occurring boundaries.	Meaning is viewed as context specific. Samples behaviors, events, processes that occur within a given time period or a given event. No attempt to filter or mediate what is observed.
Types of Systems	Category, sign, checklist, rating scales	Structured descriptive analysis systems	Specimen record, diaries, anecdotal records	Still pictures, videotape, audiotape
Methods of Recording	Selected behaviors coded on form using tallies, numeric representations, ratings. Records one behavior at a time. Used live and on line. Behaviors coded on special form.	Selected behaviors recorded using verbal symbols and/or transcription. Records multiple aspects of behaviors. Also considers broad segment of event. Generally used with permanent record (e.g., audiotape, videotape).	Broad segments of events recorded orally or in written form. Observation recorded in everyday syntax.	Potentially the widest "lens." An unfiltered record of all behaviors and events that occur in front of the camera or within pickup of microphone. Depending on the focus of the researcher the lens can be wide or narrow.
Goals of Users	Study a wide range of classrooms to obtain normative data, identify laws of teaching, generalized across cases. Less interest in individual variation within cases.	Obtain detailed descriptions of observed phenomena, explain unfolding processes, identify generic principles from explorations of specific situations, and generalize within cases as well as compare findings across cases.	Obtain detailed descriptions of observed phenomena, explain unfolding processes, identify generic principles and patterns of behavior in specific situations. Goal is to understand specific case and to compare findings across cases.	Obtain a permanent record of event to be recorded. Decisions on what to record are related to goals of researcher and questions under consideration. The purpose is to freeze the event in time for analysis at a later point in time.

Source: From "Observations as Inquiry and Method" by C. M. Everton and J. L. Green in M. C. Wittrock (Ed.), *Handbook of Research on Teaching* (3rd ed., p. 169), 1986, New York: Macmillan. Copyright © 1986 by Macmillan Publishing Company. Reprinted by permission.

indicate a preference for self-assessment (Stiggens & Duke, 1988), but providing employees the opportunity to evaluate their own performance results in employee ownership of performance (Koehler, 1990). Self-evaluations can serve as the basis for individual goal setting and the development of self-improvement plans.

Self-evaluation may be accomplished by using self-rating forms that are similar to the evaluation forms used by other evaluators (see the example in Figure 7.5) or by using a report format that requires the employee to provide brief answers to a number of questions related to areas of expected performance. Whatever format is used, if a self-evaluation has been requested and subsequently conducted by the employee, it must be considered in the employee's overall evaluation. It cannot be ignored by the supervisor because it is perceived as being too self-serving. The self-evaluation may be incorporated into observation reports, combined with rating scales, or used in other ways, but it cannot be ignored.

In order to ensure that self-evaluations be of maximum value and continue to improve, the supervisor should discuss the self-evaluation with the employee without placing value judgments on it, but rather focusing on the basis for the employee's judgments. In areas where there appears to be a significant difference in the employee's perception of his or her performance and the evaluator's perception, the data that led to each conclusion should be discussed in a nonconfrontational manner.

Peer Review.   Peer review is the process by which an employee's performance is judged by his or her colleagues. The peer review may be conducted by visitation to the classroom or workplace or by an examination of documentary evidence. Although the process is not used extensively at the elementary and secondary level, it does provide a method of including "expert" judgment in the evaluation process. Administrators are the ones usually charged with conducting evaluations. Yet administrators cannot be experts in all areas. Who then is more singularly qualified to judge the subject matter or the situation than one's peers?

Peer review has some distinct benefits. Not only can it contribute to the improvement of performance, it is seen as a way to strengthen the education profession by having those involved in it set the standards for it and monitor it, as is done by other professions. Peer review also provides the means for exemplary practice to be recognized and shared.

A number of reservations do exist about the use of peer review, however. Perhaps the most significant is that research has shown serious problems with the validity and reliability of peer reviews, especially those involving classroom visitations. Peer review is also fairly expensive to conduct relative to other forms of evaluations, such as administrator reports or client surveys. The peers conducting the reviews must either be released from their duties and substitutes hired for the times when they are engaged in the review process, or they must have their full-time contract reflect a part-time assignment as a reviewer and a part-time assignment as a teacher, department head, or whatever. In either case, the cost of the peer evaluation system can be significant. Other problems associated with peer review stem from the very collegial culture of education that pressures individuals to get along with each other and works against judgments that might be viewed as negative or critical. And often there are not enough qualified reviewers, so it is quite likely that the employee and the reviewer will not only know each other but be friends (McCarthy & Peterson, 1988).

Name _____ School Year _____ Date _____

Directions: Your job description (performance responsibilities) is shown below. Please review each item and place a check in the appropriate column. "Area of Strength" means you believe your performance in that area is one of your strong points. "Satisfactory" means you are satisfied with your performance. If you are not satisfied with your performance, check "Target for Growth." You may also check "Target for Growth" for performance responsibilities where you also feel you are performing at a satisfactory level. Remember, this is a **SELF ASSESSMENT** and must reflect *your* judgment. We recommend you select or target at least 3 to 5 areas to become the basis for the goals you prepare for the Fall Conference with your evaluator.

Descriptor Applicable	In the left hand column check each of the descriptors which is applicable to your job responsibilities. **PERFORMANCE RESPONSIBILITY**	Area of Strength	Satisfactory	Target for Growth
	I. Planning for Classroom Activities: The teacher			
	A. Consistently plans lessons and activities which incorporate the district's scope and sequence (or other approved curriculum).			
	B. Develops a plan and method for evaluating the students' work.			
	II. Implementation of the Lesson (the teaching act): The teacher			
	A. Clearly communicates the objectives of the lesson (in large or small groups or, individually, or both).			
	B. Shares with the students the importance of what they are learning (in advance or by discovery, depending on the intent of the lesson).			
	C. Describes for the student how (methods, activities, etc.) the lesson is going to be taught.			
	D. Provides for discovery or acquisition of the information of the lesson.			
	E. Provides for appropriate activities and practice.			
	F. Monitors student progress.			
	G. Provides for summary of key points of the lesson.			
	H. Demonstrates command of the subject matter.			
	I. Uses effective questioning techniques.			
	J. Recognizes different learning styles and employs materials and techniques accordingly.			

FIGURE 7.5

Self-Evaluation Form for Teachers (pp. 199–200)

Source: From *Paradise Valley Unified School District No. 69 Teacher Evaluation System* (pp. 9–10), Paradise Valley Unified School District, 1988, Paradise Valley, AZ: Author.

K. Makes reference to and use of other disciplines in order to expand and enrich the learning process.			
L. Provides for enrichment of the curriculum through the use of a variety of appropriate materials and media.			
M. Other mutually identified responsibilities. 1. 2. 3.			
III. Classroom and Instructional Management Responsibilities: The teacher A. Uses effective classroom and instructional management techniques.			
B. Establishes effective student-teacher and student-student relationships.			
C. Arranges the physical environment to complement the learning atmosphere.			
D. Recognizes the value of time-on-task and demonstrates overall good use of the instructional period.			
IV. Other Duties and Responsibilities: The teacher A. Uses effective classroom and instructional management techniques.			
B. Maintains effective communication with parents.			
C. Upholds and enforces school rules, administrative regulations, and Governing Board policies.			
D. Participates in school related activities.			
E. Maintains a professional attitude in relations with other persons and programs.			
F. Keeps up-to-date in areas of specialization.			
G. Supports the goals and objectives of the district and school.			
H. Provides individual counseling and guidance to students.			
I. Other mutually identified responsibilities. 1. 2. 3.			

FIGURE 7.5
continued

To overcome these obstacles the peer review process must maintain a clear focus, the improvement of performance, and the rationale for the process must be clearly and carefully communicated. The process also must be planned carefully in cooperation with all those involved. It can include both voluntary and required phases. For example, a principal could mandate a schoolwide format, and decisions about which teachers will serve as reviewers can be a shared decision (Murphy, 1987).

Survey of Clients. Data generated from students, parents, and teachers can be useful information in the evaluation of administrators (Ginsberg & Berry, 1990). Student and parent data can also be important sources of information in the evaluation of teachers. In the case of parents, the results may really measure "the effectiveness of teachers' (or administrator's) public relations rather than actual classroom performance, but good communications with parents are important and worth evaluation" (NSBA, 1987, p. 128).

Unlike parents, students are in the position of observing the classroom performance of the teacher every school day. Student evaluations have historically been criticized as being nothing more than popularity contests, grade-dependent, and of little value because of the immaturity of students and their inexperience in both evaluation and distinguishing good teaching from good performing. But the extensive body of research on student evaluation of instruction, although the majority of it has been conducted at the collegiate level, does not support any of these criticisms if the instruments and the process have been carefully developed and are valid and reliable. Student assessment can provide valuable feedback to the teacher and often can be more effective in changing behavior than administrative evaluation (NSBA, 1987). Student assessment also provides an opportunity for communication between student and teacher that might not otherwise exist and provides students the opportunity to participate in decisions about their own education.

In developing and using student or parent surveys, or interviewing students or parents, care should be taken to ensure that questions are only asked about topics for which the student or parent can reasonably be expected to have answers and only asked about things that are of real importance. This means that questions should be directly related to the teaching-learning process or to school and teacher goals and objectives that the student or parent can reasonably be expected to know about (Murphy, 1987). Figure 7.6 provides an example of a student survey developed using these principles.

Portfolios. It is not uncommon in professions other than education for members of the profession to present their credentials for assessment by other members of the profession and the public by means of a portfolio. For example, an artist's, architect's, or designer's portfolio is a collection of samples of the individual's best work, intended to demonstrate professional knowledge and skill (Collins, 1991). In education a portfolio is viewed more broadly than a set of representative works. It embodies the concept that assessment is dynamic and that the richest representations of student, teacher, or administrator performance are based on multiple sources of data collected over time in authentic settings (Wolf, 1991). Portfolio assessment has gained favor in recent years as an "authentic" approach to student assessment. However, its use as a technique for personnel evaluation has not been as widespread.

KINDERGARTEN AND FIRST GRADE PUPIL RATING OF THE TEACHER – FORM A

Note to Teacher: Read items to students, asking them to mark column (face) that describes how they feel about the item. Explain "teacher." Explain any terms as needed.

	Dislike or Not Agree	Neutral or Don't Know	Like or Agree
EXAMPLE:			
A. My teacher lets me choose things.	☹	😐	🙂
1. My teacher treats me fairly.	☹	😐	🙂
2. My teacher uses words I know.	☹	😐	🙂
3. My teacher makes school seem fun.	☹	😐	🙂
4. My teacher lets students tell about things in class.	☹	😐	🙂
5. My teacher shows me what to do.	☹	😐	🙂
6. My teacher helps me learn new things.	☹	😐	🙂
7. My teacher has me do lots of things.	☹	😐	🙂
8. My teacher tells me how well I'm doing.	☹	😐	🙂
9. My teacher praises me for good work.	☹	😐	🙂
10. My teacher never gets mad.	☹	😐	🙂
11. My teacher listens to me.	☹	😐	🙂
12. My teacher expects me to do my work.	☹	😐	🙂

FIGURE 7.6
Sample Pupil Survey
Source: From *Certified Employee Appraisal System Teacher Guidelines* (p. D5), Kyrene Elementary School District, 1986, Kyrene, AZ: Author.

The documents that are included in a portfolio are not selected at random. They should not only represent best work but should reflect the important things that take place in the classrooms of effective teachers. Thus the first task in portfolio development, before any *entry* is made into the portfolio, is to identify the critical teaching tasks. Next, various artifacts representative of each teaching task (e.g., lesson plans, samples of student work, letters to parents or administrators, videotapes of teaching), as well as the teacher's own reflections on the meaning of these artifacts and the other events of classroom life, are selected for entry into the portfolio. To prevent the portfolio from becoming too cumbersome, limits must be set on the amount of evidence that can be submitted for each task. To facilitate review, brief captions should be written to identify and explain the purpose of each piece of evidence (Wolf, 1991).

Because each portfolio is unique, the evaluation of portfolios does not lend itself to the use of checklists or analytic scoring schemes. In most cases what is involved is the exercise of professional judgment in assessing the extent to which the portfolio documents the teacher's knowledge and skills in meeting rather broad-based criteria related to effective teaching. The five criteria/rating categories utilized by the Teacher Assessment Project at Stanford University, which investigated the use of portfolios as one of several approaches to teacher evaluation, are presented in Figure 7.7. The criteria were based on the standards adopted by the National Board for Professional Teacher Standards (1989) concerning what board certified teachers should know and be able to do. Teachers should (1) be committed to students and their learning, (2) know the subjects they teach and how to teach them to students, (3) be responsible for managing and monitoring student learning, (4) think systematically about practice and learn from experience, and (5) be a member of learning communities. The particular form in Figure 7.7 was used in the evaluation of the portfolios of biology teachers participating in the project.

Each of the criteria or categories is rated on four scales: *relevance* (the extent to which the portfolio entries were relevant to the criterion), *evidence* (the extent to which the quantity of evidence presented was sufficient to base judgments on), *difficulty* (the relative difficulty of the performance), and *goodness* (a judgment regarding the level of performance). The first three scales use a range of scores from 1 to 3. A default scale of 2 was placed in the rating box, and the evaluator had to change the rating to a 1 to indicate, for example, that the entry was irrelevant or change it to a 3 to indicate the entry was especially relevant. The last scale, the goodness scale, uses a range of from 1 ("unacceptable, even from a novice") to 5, with a default score of 3. At the bottom of the form is a space for the evaluator to write notes explaining the scores. The back of the form can be used by the evaluator to make notes while examining the portfolio entries (Collins, 1991).

Portfolios can be time-consuming to construct, awkward to store, difficult and costly to evaluate, and subject to misinterpretation. Yet they provide teachers the opportunity to document their teaching in an authentic setting in a way that no other assessment can. "Through portfolios, teaching and learning can be seen as they unfold and extend over time" (Wolf, 1991, p. 136).

RATING FORM   Candidate:

                                                          Rater:

  Exercise: Date:

DOMAIN:

```
┌─────────────────────────────────────────────────────────────────┐
│                                                                   │
│                                                                   │
│                                                                   │
│                                                                   │
│                                                                   │
│                                                                   │
└─────────────────────────────────────────────────────────────────┘
```

| RATING CATEGORY | SCALE | Relevance | Difficulty | |
		Evidence		Goodness
1. The candidate attended to students and their learning.	2	2	2	3
2. The candidate knew the subject matter and how to teach it.	2	2	2	3
3. The candidate attended to class management and monitoring.	2	2	2	3
4. The candidate thought about, learned from the activity.	2	2	2	3
5. The candidate participated in a learning community.	2	2	2	3
6. Overall Rating.	X	X	2	3

FRONT NOTES (justifications and qualifications):

BACK NOTES: enter aids to memory on the back of the form.   5/30/89 TB

FIGURE 7.7
Portfolio Rating Form
Source: From "Portfolios for Biology Teacher Assessment" by A. Collins, 1991, *Journal of Personnel Evaluation in Education*, 5, p. 162. Copyright © 1991 by Kluwer Academic Publishers. Reprinted by permission.

Portfolios may also be used in the assessment of administrators. Basically the same process is used in their development as in the development of teacher portfolios: establish clear instructions for the portfolio format, identify the critical tasks (performance criteria), and make sure all documentation is directly related to the performance tasks. Concerns similar to those related to teacher portfolios also exist, concerns regarding the time and expense involved and questions of validity and reliability. However, as was true for teacher portfolios, if properly constructed and evaluated, administrator portfolios can provide data valuable to the performance assessment process (Ginsberg & Berry, 1990).

Assessment Centers. An assessment center is a "location where candidates go to participate in a series of exercises or tasks that tap various abilities relative to the particular focus of the assessment" (Grover, 1991, p. 113). Assessment centers have their origins in World War II when they were used by both the United States and Germany for candidate selection. In the decade after the war, a number of large American industries, including AT&T, IBM, GE, and Sears set up assessment centers as a tool for screening prospective managers. In the 40 years since, the methodology has become institutionalized and widely used by a variety of institutions and organizations (Davey, 1991).

The first major use of the assessment center methodology in education came in the 1970s when the National Association of Secondary School Principals (NASSP) collaborated with the American Psychological Association to apply assessment center concepts and practices to the evaluation of candidates for principal. Since that time 63 NASSP assessment centers have been established in cooperation with universities, state departments of education, local school districts, and other organizations.

The NASSP model utilizes a series of simulated job exercises, such as case study analyses, in-baskets, leaderless groups, and interviews. Based on their observation and analysis of behaviors, a cadre of trained assessors rates candidates on 12 skill dimensions identified as being essential to the success of a school principal: problem analysis, judgment, organizational ability, leadership, decisiveness, sensitivity, range of interest, personal motivation, stress tolerance, written and oral communication, and educational values.

A number of other assessment center models are or have been in operation among school districts across the country. In large city districts that have numerous vacancies and many candidates, the assessment center may function more or less as an ongoing operation. In smaller districts where the need occurs less often, or in districts of any size where vacancies for positions like the superintendency occur with less frequency, the assessment center may be operated more on an "as needed" basis.

To be successful, the developers of any assessment center must first identify the job-related skills and behaviors that are important in the successful candidate. Second, exercises that elicit these skills and attributes must be designed. And, third, those persons serving as evaluators must be trained in the techniques of observing, recording, and assessing job-related behaviors. Two other principles for the operation of assessment centers set down by the International Congress on the Assessment Center should also be kept in mind in the development of an assessment center:

(1) In order to get a true measure of the candidates performance and abilities, use multiple exercises and pool information across exercises; and (2) to minimize the possibility of bias, use multiple assessors and diversify by age, gender, ethnicity, and functional work area (Davey, 1991).

In education up to this point, assessment centers have been used almost exclusively as a screening device for administrators. The use of assessment centers for other assessment purposes, such as in the required annual evaluation, or to inform decisions regarding professional development, has been limited. Yet the assessment center format as a method for evaluation of teachers and administrators offers several significant benefits (Grover, 1991):

1. It forces the articulation of the dimensions and standards for effective performance and makes them public.
2. By making the standards and criteria public the assessment center creates expectations for staff development programs and teacher and administrator training and certification programs to incorporate the standards into their curricula.
3. The tasks involved in the development, administration, and scoring of an assessment require thoughtful consideration and reflection by each individual involved in the process, as well as their collegial interaction to achieve consensus, which leads to a broadening of their knowledge base and perspective.

Despite these benefits, the extent to which they outweigh the costs associated with time and financial commitments will be the most important factor in determining their use as a tool in the performance assessment of education personnel. However, the continued use of the assessment center as a screening device in administrator selection appears assured.

Student Performance Data.   The last several years have seen increased interest is using student achievement data, primarily norm-referenced standardized achievement test scores, in the evaluation of both teachers and principals. However, the majority of professional opinion is against the use of such data in the summative evaluation of teachers (see, e.g., Findley & Estabrook, 1991; Stiggens, 1989). The major objections to their use center around the concerns that (1) it is virtually impossible for test instruments to determine the effect of a particular teacher, (2) assessment instruments do not effectively measure what is taught, (3) so much of what affects learning is beyond the control of the teacher, (4) variations among students and classes taught does not allow objective comparisons among teachers, and (5) there is no universal agreement as to what should be taught or measured.

It is at this point that education finds itself in a quandary. As Stiggens (1989) so aptly described it,

> On one hand, we believe that one legitimate source of evidence of the effectiveness of teacher performance should be whether students are learning. We feel certain that if teachers are held accountable for student achievement, then teacher and student performance will improve. Yet, on the other hand, the one index of achievement that we always thought we could count on—standardized achievement test scores—cannot and will not do the job. (p. 7)

How then can student performance data be used in the evaluation of teachers? The best answer to that seems to be to use classroom measurements of student progress for formative evaluation purposes. Teachers continuously measure student achievement in their classrooms. Teacher-developed and text-embodied classroom assessments, pre- and posttests, and tests designed to measure the specific objectives of instruction are all legitimate indicators of student performance. If teachers are properly trained in developing classroom assessment formats and instruments that generate valid, reliable data, their use will not only increase the validity and reliability of the results of the evaluation, but will provide data that can be used for instructional improvement (Stiggens, 1989; Stiggens & Duke, 1988).

Program Appraisal and Review

Once in operation the entire evaluation system should be subjected to ongoing review by the school board, the administration, and representatives of employees to ensure that the system is fulfilling its intended purposes. As a part of this review, the performance of evaluators and the utility of the various instruments and techniques in generating the desired data should be carefully examined (NSBA, 1987). The system should also be continually monitored to verify that it is meeting the technical and legal standards described in the following section.

STANDARDS FOR THE DEVELOPMENT AND OPERATION OF A SOUND EVALUATION SYSTEM

For an evaluation system to be considered sound, it must meet certain technical and legal standards. The technical standards—validity, reliability, and utility—are primarily concerned with the accuracy of the measurements. The legal standards are intended to ensure that the system meets substantive and procedural due process requirements and is free from discrimination.

Technical Standards

"*Validity* in personnel evaluation is deemed as the degree to which the evaluation process measures the performance that it purports to measure" (Stronge, 1991, p. 81). The clarity of the criteria and standards, the data collection methodology, and the competence of the evaluators all affect validity (Ginsberg & Berry, 1990). Furthermore, validity is not established in a vacuum; it has a contextual reference. A major source of invalidity is the attempt to use a process designed for one audience with a different audience. For example, an evaluation instrument that is intended for use in applicant screening for initial employment, where predictive validity is a major concern, would probably not be appropriate to use in making merit pay decisions where distinguishing between teachers' performances (discriminant validity) is important (Sperry et al., 1992). Nor would the use of a clinically oriented teacher evaluation model be valid to evaluate school counselors. As Stronge (1991) noted,

This type of endeavor produces futility rather than usable evaluative data. If evaluation **procedures** are inappropriate, one can guarantee that the evaluation **product** will be no better. Unless the evaluation system is designed and used for its intended purpose, all involved would be a step ahead not to evaluate! (p. 81)

"*Reliability* in evaluation refers to the consistency of measurements across evaluators and observations" (Ginsberg & Berry, 1990, p. 221). Evaluation is by its very nature judgmental. However, if different evaluators using the same criteria and standards assign substantially different results to an individual being evaluated on the same performance or to different individuals being evaluated on similar performances, the evaluation system is suspect (Stronge, 1991). The possibility for such subjectivity is one of the reasons it is important to use multiple sources of data, to train evaluators in the use of the various evaluation instruments and techniques used by the school or school district, and, when possible, to use multiple evaluators.

Utility relates to both reliability and validity and refers to the realistic considerations that must be addressed to ensure each. If the use of a complex evaluation process requires a great deal of training, with associated costs, before evaluators can use it reliably, the utility of the process is reduced. Likewise, even if a particular process or instrument has been judged extremely valid and reliable by measurement experts, if it is opposed by the teachers and administrators its utility is reduced.

The Joint Committee on Standards for Educational Evaluation (Stronge, 1991) has developed five utility standards for evaluation in education. If evaluations are to be "informative, timely, and influential," they should (1) be constructive, (2) have identified uses, (3) utilize credible evaluators, (4) yield reports that have practical utility, and (5) be followed up to guarantee understanding of the results and appropriate actions.

Legal Standards

The legal standards that must be followed in the development and operation of the school district evaluation system can be broadly categorized as substantive due process standards and procedural due process standards. Substantive due process standards are concerned with the objectivity of the criteria, the standards, the evidence, and the results. Procedural due process standards are concerned with the fundamental fairness of the evaluation process. (See Chapter 9 for a more detailed discussion of substantive and procedural due process.) The following lists of standards are summarized from the discussions of Beckham (1992), Frase and Downey (1990-91), and Rossow and Parkinson (1992).

Substantive Due Process Standards

1. The criteria on which the evaluation is based should be
    a. consistent with state statutes and state department of education regulations;
    b. job related and observable;
    c. clear and sufficiently specific to inform a reasonable person of performance expectations;
    d. attainable and ascertainable;

     e. communicated to all employees;

     f. uniformly applied;

     g. comprehensive; and

     h. developed in cooperation with employees.

2. The evaluation process should yield, and decisions be based on, evidence and documentation that is

     a. relevant to job behaviors;

     b. collected from multiple sources and, when possible, multiple evaluators;

     c. sufficient in quantity and depth to support the evaluation conclusions and recommendations; and

     d. credible and noncontradictory.

3. Any deficiencies noted must be consistent with the job-related evaluation criteria.

Procedural Due Process Standards

1. The process should

     a. be conducted in a uniform and consistent manner by trained personnel;

     b. follow state statutes, state department of education regulations, and school board policies;

     c. be communicated to all employees in advance of the process;

     d. require that the evaluation results be communicated both in writing and at a postevaluation conference;

     e. provide the opportunity for response to an unsatisfactory evaluation;

     f. provide a written statement of specific deficiencies and directions for corrective action;

     g. provide the opportunity to remediate deficiencies;

     h. provide a reasonable time to remediate; and

     i. provide the opportunity to appeal, including the right to a hearing.

2. The evaluation procedures must be free of any implication of an invidious discriminatory intent.

3. The evaluation process should not be used as a means of retaliating against the employee's exercise of free speech or other constitutional rights.

SUMMARY

One of the most important and sometimes difficult jobs of the school administrator is the evaluation of personnel. Although evaluation can provide the opportunity for professional growth and school improvement, unless properly conducted it can also become a source of controversy and low morale. It is imperative that the school district demonstrate its commitment to a sound evaluation system through clearly articulated and publicized board policies and by the adoption of an evaluation system that is technically sound and ensures substantive and procedural due process. And, even though such as system may employ multiple data collection techniques and serve a number of personnel purposes, the evaluation system should not attempt to combine the summative and formative evaluation functions.

DISCUSSION QUESTIONS

1. Does your district have written job descriptions for teachers and principals? Do you feel the job descriptions accurately reflect what teachers and principals do?
2. How may a school system combine formative and summative evaluations of its professional staff without damaging morale and effectiveness?
3. How well do you feel your colleagues would be able to evaluate your performance? How well would your students be able to evaluate your performance? Name three ways you use peer input and three ways you use student input to improve your performance. How is this information generated?
4. If you were asked to develop a portfolio of your job-related best works, what would be the six most significant entries?

CASE 7.1
Evaluation Choice

In the Taylor School District teachers have traditionally been evaluated annually by both the principal and department chair using classroom observation procedures. During the past year the representatives of the teachers' association met with the administration and expressed their concern that the current process was inadequate because it provided only a single source of data. Instead of the sole and uniform use of classroom observations, they recommended that each teacher should be able to choose from several techniques or combination of techniques to be used for their annual review. Specifically, they suggested that each teacher should be able to choose either portfolio assessment, client surveys, self-evaluation, or the existing classroom observation procedure as the principle method of appraisal.

Questions

1. What are the advantages and disadvantages of using differential appraisal techniques for education personnel?
2. Do you agree with the teachers' association that classroom observation provides too limited a data base for appraisal? Why is classroom observation the most commonly employed assessment technique used in elementary and secondary schools, whereas peer review and student evaluation

of instruction are the commonly used techniques in higher education?
3. If differential performance appraisal techniques were available to you, which of the ones discussed in this text would you choose to be evaluated by and why?

CASE 7.2
Evaluation Instrument

Figure 7.8 is an excerpt from the teacher evaluation instrument used by the Tempe School District No. 3. Review the instrument and answer the questions that follow.

Questions

1. Which of the following types of evaluation criteria are reflected in the instrument in Figure 7.8: (a) trait or attribute, (b) results, or (c) performance based?
2. Examine the levels of performance that are associated with each item: satisfactory, needs improvement, unsatisfactory, and no evidence. How adequate are these levels for judging the performance of the individual teacher (e.g., what is the difference between "needs improvement" and "unsatisfactory")? What changes would you propose to improve the rating scale?
3. What steps are necessary to ensure that the instrument meets the technical standards of validity and reliability?

Use of Materials (The teacher incorporates materials to reinforce instruction.)

S NI U

☐ ☐ ☐

1. Uses appropriate materials for lesson being taught including sequence and correct level of difficulty.
2. Engages student interest.
3. Provides variety.
4. Incorporates appropriate basic and supplemental materials.
5. Assures student access to relevant materials.
6. Other:

Effectiveness of Instruction (The teacher provides for student achievement.)

S NI U

☐ ☐ ☐

1. Analyzes student responses and adjusts instruction to lessen student errors.
2. Monitors student learning on a regular basis.
3. Evaluates periodically for retention of proper learning.
4. Maintains accurate and complete records.
5. Other: _____

S NI U NE

☐ ☐ ☐ ☐

Presentation (The teacher utilizes effective instructional practices.)

1. Directs student attention to objective being taught.
2. Teaches to one objective at a time using relevant information, activities, questions, and responses.
3. Generates active participation of most of the students most of the time.
4. Motivates students, i.e., by providing knowledge of results, success, interest, feeling, tone, and/or level of concern.
5. Provides specific responses to reinforce student learning.
6. Directs students to summarize after significant learning increments.
7. Facilitates retention by providing meaning, modeling, and correct practice.
8. Other: _____

FIGURE 7.8

Excerpt From a Teacher Evaluation Instrument

Source: From *Teacher Improvement and Evaluation Program* (p. 2), Tempe School District No. 3, Tempe, AZ.

CASE 7.3
Parent Survey

Recently the Mayflower Elementary School District has come under great pressure from the community because of the low achievement test scores of its students. Within the context of criticism of the quality of education provided by the schools, criticism has also been directed at the quality of the instructional staff. In an effort to become more sensitive to parental concerns, Superintendent Ralph Jones decided to survey parents and guardians regarding their perceptions of the effectiveness of instructional staff. He has notified all teachers that the results of the parent survey will become the principal feature of the teacher improvement and evaluation program. The parent survey asked parents to rate their child's teacher on the extent to which the teacher met the following criteria:

1. Monitors the student's progress and provides adequate and timely feedback
2. Introduces the goals and objectives for the lesson and how they will be obtained
3. Creates a safe environment conducive to learning
4. Gives clear directions for tasks
5. Uses appropriate teaching strategies
6. Checks regularly for comprehension and understanding
7. Provides for active student participation
8. Adapts the content to meet the varied needs of students

Questions

1. Which of the listed criteria are inappropriate for inclusion on a survey of parents and guardians? Why?
2. Choose three items from the survey and reword them so that they are more appropriate and useful for evaluating the quality of instruction.
3. In addition to including surveys of parents and guardians in the annual evaluation of teachers, what other methods might the school district employ to respond to community concerns regarding the quality of instruction?

REFERENCES

Beckham, J. C. (1992, November 19–21). *Evaluation.* Paper presented at the annual meeting of the National Organization on Legal Problems of Education, Scottsdale, AZ.

Collins, A. (1991). Portfolios for biology teacher assessment. *Journal of Personnel Evaluation in Education, 5,* 147–167.

Davey, B. (1991). Evaluating teacher competency through the use of performance assessment tasks: An overview. *Journal of Personnel Evaluation in Education, 5,* 121–132.

Ellett, C. D. (1992). Principal evaluation and assessment. In M. C. Alkin (Ed.), *Encyclopedia of educational research* (Vol. 3, pp. 1345–1351). New York: Macmillan.

Evertson, C. M., & Green, J. L. (1986). Observation as inquiry and method. In M. C. Wittrock (Ed.),

Handbook on research on teaching (3rd ed., pp. 162–213). New York: Macmillan.

Evertson, C. M., & Holley, F. M. (1981). Classroom observation. In J. Millman (Ed.), *Handbook of teacher evaluation* (pp. 90–109). Beverly Hills, CA: Sage.

Findley, D., & Estabrook, R. (1991). Teacher evaluation: Curriculum and instructional considerations. *Contemporary Education, 62,* 294–298.

Frase, L. E., & Downey, C. (1990–91). Teacher dismissal: Crucial substantive due process guidelines from court cases. *National Forum of Applied Educational Research Journal, 4,* 13–21.

Ginsberg, R., & Berry, B. (1990). The folklore of principal evaluation. *Journal of Personnel Evaluation in Education, 3,* 205–230.

Grover, B. W. (1991). The teacher assessment dilemma: What is versus what ought to be! *Journal of Personnel Evaluation in Education, 5,* 103–119.

Koehler, M. (1990). Self-assessment in the evaluation process. *NASSP Bulletin,* 74(527), 40–44.

McCarthy, S. J., & Peterson, K. D. (1988). Peer review of materials in public school teacher evaluation. *Journal of Personnel Evaluation in Education, 1,* 259–267.

Medley, D. M. (1992). Teacher evaluation. In M. C. Alkin (Ed.), *Encyclopedia of educational research* (Vol. 4, pp. 1345–1352). New York: Macmillan.

Murphy, J. (1987). Teacher evaluation: A comprehensive framework for supervisors. *Journal of Personnel Evaluation in Education, 1,* 157–180.

National Board for Professional Teacher Standards. (1989). *Toward high and rigorous standards for the teaching profession.* Washington, DC: Author.

National School Boards Association. (1987). *The school personnel management system.* Alexandria, VA: Author.

Popham, W. J. (1988). The dysfunctional marriage of formative and summative teacher evaluation. *Journal of Personnel Evaluation in Education, 1,* 269–273.

Rossow, L. F., & Parkinson, J. (1992). *The law of teacher evaluation.* Topeka, KS: National Organization on Legal Problems of Education.

Sperry, D. J., Pounder, D. G., & Drew, C. J. (1992). Educator evaluation and the law: A case study of common statutory problems. *Education Law Quarterly, 1,* 415–429.

Stiggens, R. J. (1989) A commentary on the role of student achievement data on the evaluation of teachers. *Journal of Personnel Evaluation in Education, 3,* 7–15.

Stiggens, R. J., & Duke, D. L. (1988). *The case for commitment to teacher growth: Research on teacher evaluation.* Albany, NY: State University of New York Press.

Stronge, J. H. (1991). The dynamics of effective performance evaluation systems in education: Conceptual, human relations, and technical domains. *Journal of Personnel Evaluation in Education, 5,* 77–83.

Tolleson Elementary School District. (n.d.). *Teacher evaluation handbook.* Tolleson, AZ: Author.

Valentine, J. W. (1992). *Principles and practices for effective teacher evaluation.* Boston: Allyn & Bacon.

Wolf, K. (1991). The schoolteacher's portfolio: Issues in design, implementation, and evaluation. *Phi Delta Kappan, 73,* 129–136.

8

Maximizing Human Resources

A major responsibility of the human resources function is maximizing the human resources of the school system. Earlier, human resources administration was defined as the administrative and staff processes planned and implemented for the distinct purposes of establishing an effective system of human resources and fostering an organizational climate that leads to achieving the educational goals directing the school system. This definition emphasizes the purposeful utilization of people through positive motivation to achieve the organization's goals and employee self-fulfillment. The growing emphasis on maximizing human resources emanates from the realization that organizations progress to the extent that they are able to motivate and develop people. It is essential, therefore, that human resources administrators understand the basic concepts of human motivation as they relate to maximizing human resources. For this reason, several motivation and human behavior concepts are discussed at the outset of this chapter. Following the discussion of human motivation, the human resources processes of staff orientation, staff assignment, and staff development are considered. Special attention is given to teacher work load, the troubled staff member, and other considerations that serve to maximize human potential.

THE SCHOOL AS A SOCIAL SYSTEM

Researchers note that human behavior in organizations is influenced by both institutional and personal factors. Getzels and Guba (1957) described this concept in their social systems model presented in Figure 8.1.

According to the Getzels-Guba social systems model, the actual behavior outcomes (*B*) within a social system are determined by the institutional role (*R*) and the individual's personality (*P*); $B = f(R \times P)$. The role represents position, office, or status within the institution (i.e., superintendent, principal, supervisor, teacher, etc.) and is defined by both role expectations and the nature of the institution. The institutional role and the unique individual need-disposition constitute the dimensions of the Get-

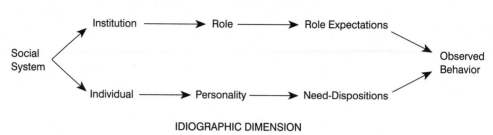

FIGURE 8.1

Social Systems and Social Behavior

Source: From "Social Behavior and the Administrative Process" by J. W. Getzels and E. G. Guba, 1957, *The School Review*, 65(4), p. 429. Copyright © 1957 by The University of Chicago Press. Reprinted by permission.

zels-Guba model. The role and role expectations of the institution are termed the **nomothetic dimension**. The individual personality and need-disposition is termed the **idiographic dimension** (Getzels & Guba, 1957).

The Getzels-Guba social systems model is a useful framework to explain what leadership is needed in human resources administration to maximize the human potential of a school system. According to these theorists, "The unique task of administration at least with respect to staff relations, is just this: to integrate the demands of the institution and the demands of the members in a way that is at once organizationally productive and individually fulfilling" (1957, p. 430). The implications of the social systems model for the human resources administrator are far-reaching. The administrator who considers only the institutional dimension without giving equal consideration to the individual aspects within the school system is likely to be insensitive to the environment and its elements and conditions. Such an individual not only will be indifferent to the various signals that indicate problems and needs within the school system, but will be unable to effect possible resolutions and improvements. Both the nomothetic and idiographic dimensions must be fully considered if equilibrium within the system is to be realized. As defined by Barnard (1938), **equilibrium** is the organization's capacity to be productive and at the same time satisfy individual employee motives.

HUMAN MOTIVATION THEORIES

School administrators who understand human behavior will be much more effective in making positive differences in the school climate and maximizing human potential. Chapter 1 included a brief discussion of human motivation as conceptualized by Herzberg, Mausner, and Snyderman (1959) and McGregor (1960).

Numerous other human motivation theories have been set forth in the literature. Some theories center on outcome behaviors that are influenced by individuals' perceptions of past events and/or how they perceive future outcomes relative to their personal needs and beliefs. Other theories view behavior as an action that can be changed through interventions that modify an individual's responses. The terms *behavior modification, drive-reinforcement theory, operant conditioning,* and **behaviorism** all relate generally to the concept that the behavior of an individual can be altered through reinforcement of desired actions. Several leading motivation theories are considered in the following discussion.

Probably more than any other single concept in personnel literature, Maslow's hierarchy has established a direct focus on the basic needs of human beings and their importance in human behavior. According to Maslow's hierarchy, a need is a potential motivator until it is realized or satisfied. As the need is satisfied, it becomes ineffective as a motivator and the next higher order need becomes the motivator for the individual (Maslow, 1954/1970). Figure 8.2 illustrates Maslow's hierarchy and the five basic needs from lower to higher order.

Alderfer's (1972) ERG theory (existence, relatedness, and growth) relates closely to the concepts set forth by Maslow. Existence needs include, in general, Maslow's physiological and physical safety needs (Figure 8.2); relatedness needs encompass the social needs, safety needs, and esteem needs, as they relate to relations with others; and growth needs are concerned with self-actualization needs and esteem needs, as they are reflected in positive self-concepts. ERG views motivation as being present within all of the three levels dependent upon the extent to which various needs have been satisfied or remain unsatisfied. In this view, individuals may seek needs at higher levels even though some needs at a lower level have not been met.

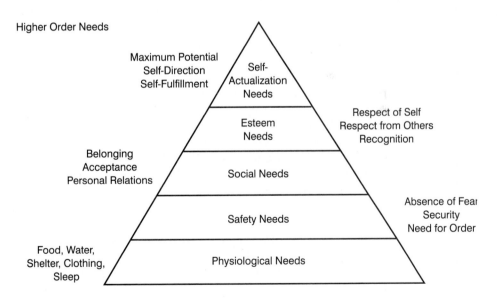

FIGURE 8.2

Maslow's Hierarchy of Basic Needs

Source: "Hierarchy of Needs" from *Motivation and Personality* by Abraham H. Maslow. Copyright 1954 by Harper & Row, Publishers, Inc. Copyright © 1970 by Abraham H. Maslow. Reprinted by permission of HarperCollins Publishers.

Vroom's expectancy theory of motivation was set forth in *Work and Motivation* (1964). Vroom stated that "we view the central problem of motivation as the explanation of choices made by organisms among different voluntary responses" (p. 9). He proposed several concepts to develop his motivation theory: (1) **valence**, a person's affective orientations toward particular outcomes; (2) **instrumentality**, the extent to which a person believes an object will lead to desired consequences or prevent undesired results; and (3) **expectancy**, a belief concerning the likelihood that a particular act will be followed by a particular outcome. The expectancy theory of motivation is based on the proposition that effort, performance, and rewards are inextricably related. This concept of motivation argues that effort and performance depend upon individuals' perceptions of their potential for meeting personal reward outcomes. Expectancy theory suggests that effort and performance in a particular activity (e.g., obtaining a degree or credential) depend upon the individual's perception of whether that activity will increase the realization of personal goals. For example, an individual who has a certain career goal is likely to be highly motivated toward obtaining the credentials needed for the desired position and will exert the required effort and performance. In brief, expectancy theory supports the belief that employees put forth more effort and are more productive when they perceive a relationship among effort, performance, and reward.

Brayfield and Crockett (1955), among others, believed that motivation depends upon the individual's pursuit of important goals. They stated that "we might expect high satisfaction and high productivity to occur together when productivity is perceived as a path to certain important goals and when these goals are achieved" (p. 416). This rather straightforward view supports the concepts of goal commitments that are important aspects of expectancy theory, theory Y, and needs theory. Such administrative approaches as management by objectives (MBO) are based on a path-goal theory. In *Managing by Objectives*, Raia (1974) contended that "whether or not the behavior is actually satisfying to the individual depends upon his latent motives and needs" (p. 97). Raia viewed MBO as being consistent with the path-goal theory of motivation, since MBO is based upon the establishment of clearly defined work objectives, progress assessments, a relationship between appraisal and development and compensation, as well as the element of participation in cooperative goal setting.

Theory Z organizations develop employee commitment to organizational goals and high productivity through the use of such incentives as lifetime job tenure, personal participation in decision making and problem solving by all employees, the use of team efforts to complete tasks, and a focus on the personal concerns of employees. Ouchi's (1981) theory Z has received much acclaim in business and industry and has provided an impetus for rethinking traditional approaches to management and employee relations. According to Ouchi, trust, subtlety, and intimacy exist in every theory Z organization. These components are exemplified by certain characteristics that provide for remarkable success of business and industry in Japan. He emphasized that positive human relations, not technology, make for increased production. The activities of participative management, consensus decision making, and reduced organizational "bureaucracy" promote job satisfaction and motivate the worker to make personal sacrifices that lead to extraordinary success for the organization.

B. F. Skinner's initial work, *The Behavior of Organisms* (1938), as well as his later works, advanced the proposition that an individual's behavior is modified through immediate rewards of favored responses and by no response to unfavorable behavior. Positive reinforcement, through personal reward, praise, recognition, or extended authority, is used to solidify the continuation of desired behavior. Undesirable behavior is dealt with by use of **extinction,** whereby the behavior is merely ignored. Skinner's concepts also suggest that desired responses can be learned through **shaping.** When favored responses are seldom or never demonstrated, initial rewards are given for behavior responses similar to the desired behavior. Finally, only the desired response is reinforced through appropriate rewards (Skinner, 1953, 1969).

Behavior modification suggests that providing careful feedback of positive job results to an employee would reinforce that behavior, that pay incentives or other rewards for exemplary attendance would reduce employee absence, and that rewards given an employee for reaching a desired skill level would lead to a continuation of positive personal development.

Behavior modification research provides several suggestions for administrative practice:

1. The kind of behavior desired should be determined as specifically as possible.
2. If the desired behavior is not currently present or is seldom demonstrated, shaping techniques should be utilized to bring about changes in behavior similar to the desired behavior. Similar behavior should be positively reinforced.
3. Desired behavior should be reinforced immediately. Material rewards and "psychic" or "social" rewards, such as benefits, commendations, carefully designed personal feedback, responsibility, and recognition should be scheduled as reinforcers.
4. Results should be measured and assessed and decisions reached concerning the appropriate schedule of reinforcements needed to ensure the continuation of the desired behavior.

The discussion of motivation reemphasizes the concept stated in Chapter 3 that schools are people. Effective human resources administration requires an understanding and concern for the individual needs of personnel. In this respect, the often-heard maxim Know Your Staff assumes a more comprehensive, purposeful meaning. The maximization of human resources within the school system requires a meaningful integration of the system's goals and the employees' need-dispositions. When these considerations are brought into relatively close congruence, achievement of goals and personal fulfillment are more likely to be realized. The variables of individual behavior and the realities of human organizations often defy simple analysis. Yet the realization of the full potential of human resources requires that the concepts and theories relating to human motivation and behavior be understood, applied, and evaluated in all human resources processes.

STAFF ORIENTATION

In Chapter 3 the orientation process was defined as that comprehensive complex of activities designed to gain congruence between institutional objectives and employee needs. Orientation begins with the job application, then continues through job candidacy and, on an ongoing basis, for as long as the employee or the organization views it as necessary. Orientation objectives focus upon facilitating the entry of employees into their new positions, minimizing the problems and distractions of the position, increasing employee efficiency and effectiveness, and promoting the highest level of personal satisfaction and confidence. Although the entry of new employees into the school system requires special orientation considerations, the process is not limited only to new employees; nor should it be viewed only as a first-year induction activity. Rather, the orientation needs of individual employees are ongoing and the orientation process is continuous. Orientation activities serve as important links to recruitment and selection as well as a complement to staff assignment and development.

If effectively planned and implemented, the staff orientation process serves several basic purposes:

1. Encourages individuals with qualifications congruent with district expectations to consider employment in the system.
2. Integrates effectively and efficiently new and experienced staff personnel into their respective roles in the school system.
3. Develops understanding and commitment to the stated goals and objectives of the school system.
4. Reduces and/or removes problems and conditions that tend to inhibit personal effectiveness and job satisfaction.
5. Identifies the specific talents of each employee and builds these abilities into the overall educational team.
6. Acquaints personnel with the important considerations of personal, professional, and community relationships within the school community.
7. Ascertains specific needs of school personnel and analyzes these needs in relation to the school system's expectations.
8. Identifies for each employee those human and physical resources that can enhance personal effectiveness.
9. Provides information and services that promote instruction and learning.

Thus orientation is a purposely planned process that is based upon the school system's stated goals and the roles of its human resources. The maximization of the system's human resources serves as the foundation and rationale for orientation activities and services.

Operational Procedures for Staff Orientation

As previously noted, the staff orientation process begins with the prospective employee's first contact with the school district and continues throughout employment, as needed. Properly planned and implemented, the process involves all members of the staff, appropriate community members, and employee associations. The general administrative procedures for planning, implementing, and evaluating the orientation process can be classified into four steps as follows:

Step 1   The governing board adopts policies that commit the school system to effective orientation practices and indicate *what* the school system desires from the process. Specific goals for the orientation process are developed cooperatively by the board of education, school employee personnel, and community representatives.

Step 2   All information that would assist in identifying the orientation program needs is determined. The clarification of specific position assignments and responsibilities for program implementation is completed. Individual problems and needs are identified through informal interviews or other means such as mentoring programs.

Step 3   Previously determined plans and procedures are implemented. Individualized programs for providing special services are determined and administered.

Step 4   Information that can be utilized to evaluate the program's results is collected. Objective assessments of feedback relative to accomplishment of program objectives and meeting individual needs are completed. These findings are utilized through debriefing sessions and other methods for improving future procedures.

Preemployment Activities.   Preemployment orientation activities generally are provided during the period between initial contact with the school district and the time the individual assumes a role in the school system. Upon initial contact with the school district, information is provided to a potential employee to build an understanding of the school district's nature, community makeup, and educational expectations; the general working environment; faculty-student information; and professional opportunities within the district, including compensation levels and benefits.

Preemployment orientation necessitates a variety of program provisions. Face-to-face communication, use of printed materials, group sessions, audio-visual technology, and other practices are common for both gaining and disseminating information. Various strategies are employed for carrying out preemployment orientation programs. The following procedures are examples of contemporary practices.

1.   Over a specified time period, school district employees are surveyed as to what information and personal assistance proved most beneficial to them as well as what communication and assistance should be added prior to employment. Results are analyzed and program activities designed to provide the most beneficial information and assistance.

2.   During the initial contact with the school district, a potential employee completes a brief questionnaire to ascertain the kinds of information and personal assistance that might prove most helpful (e.g., employment benefits, community information, school district policy and procedures, student evaluation procedures, etc.). Those individuals or offices assigned the responsibility for the requested information provide the information to groups and/or individual applicants.

3. Various offices and personnel gather information concerning the most frequently asked questions during preemployment, major problem areas regarding entry transition, and specific school district information of high priority. This feedback is synthesized, and appropriate orientation activities are planned to provide the necessary feedback to prospective employees.

4. Every effort is made to personalize preemployment orientation. Initial inquiries are expedited. To the fullest extent possible, internal personnel are assigned specific duties regarding preemployment orientation and communication. Briefing sessions are planned, one-on-one conferences are scheduled when feasible, and other special efforts are made to put the prospective employee at ease with the school system.

5. Orientation teams representative of both internal and external members of the school district are established. Each team serves as the primary information resource for a specific area of the preemployment orientation. In some instances, one particular resource member serves as the liaison person for one or more prospective employees.

Postemployment Orientation.   Following the district's decision to hire an individual, postemployment orientation must be implemented. Specific information relative to the employee's assignment, the environment in which the person will be working, professional resources available, formal staff relationships, policy and regulation resources, personal responsibilities, and provisions for personal assistance are among the orientation information and activities of importance at this time. Postemployment orientation focuses on facilitating an effective, efficient transition of personnel into their respective roles within the school system and community. Provisions and practices that add to the orientation program following employment include mentor programs, policy and regulation manuals, and personnel information handbooks.

Mentor Program.   Many school districts have a long history of providing a "helping-teacher" for new personnel, but the mentor program concept presents a more comprehensive approach to orientation and staff development. A ***mentor*** is an experienced professional who guides the personal development of a less experienced individual by serving as a role model. In a mentor program, each new employee is "teamed" with an experienced peer on the staff who serves as a sponsor, teacher, and advisor. Both the mentor and the new or inexperienced staff member benefit personally from this relationship. For example, the new or inexperienced staff member gains access to an experienced member of the staff for purposes of learning about the school system, its policies, and procedures. Additionally, mentoring provides help in building communication channels of importance to continued growth, allows for new knowledge relative to teaching approaches, develops a system of personal support and increased self-confidence, extends insight into district purposes, and provides a relationship with a master teacher who can serve as a role model for teaching. The mentor benefits through increased personal self-esteem and recognition as a successful teacher and contributor to the school's program. Mentoring requires keeping up-to-date on best practices in teaching and necessitates refinement and improvement of personal knowledge and skills. Overall, the school system benefits through increases in staff knowledge about the school district, increased confidence and morale of staff members, and improved staff member effectiveness. Successful mentor programs most often are based on the special needs and interests of the new or inexperienced staff member.

Policy and Regulation Manual.   A properly codified, comprehensive policy and regulation manual can serve as one of the primary orientation resources for school personnel. Policy and regulations are of special significance to the human resources function generally, but contribute to the orientation process by

1. informing school personnel as to what the school district wants to accomplish;
2. providing a common basis for understanding and a basic reference for effective communication;
3. clarifying the division of labor between the school board and professional administrative staff;
4. establishing a basis for action, effective school operations, and meaningful evaluation;
5. providing information concerning professional responsibilities and opportunities;
6. setting forth guidelines and procedures for completing specific practices and meeting personal responsibilities to the standards of the school system;
7. providing specific procedures for personnel in such areas as student evaluation, securing instructional resources, community participation, transfer, and professional development.

A comprehensive treatment of policy and regulation development relative to the human resources function is included in Chapter 5.

Personnel Information Handbook.   The importance of the personnel information handbook in the orientation process demands that its development and dissemination be given high priority by human resources administrators. The value of the personnel handbook extends beyond its contributions to the orientation process; its potential for orienting both new and continuing staff is far-reaching.

Although the personnel handbook often includes some information related to school district policy and administrative regulations, the handbook and the policies manual are different documents. The policies manual is the governance document for the district and sets forth the legislative (policy) and executive (regulations) guidelines under which the district is to operate. The personnel handbook is designed to provide information that answers questions relative to (1) the school district's goals, services, and facilities; (2) the community and its makeup; and (3) procedures relating to securing substitute teachers, obtaining curriculum materials, completion of grade reports, the school calendar, professional growth activities, insurance plans, and other information that the school district has determined to be of value to employees. A sample of one section of a personnel handbook is shown in Figure 8.3. The sample focuses on the employee assistance program in a school district.

Employee Assistance Program — Tempe School District No. 3 recognizes that unresolved personal problems may adversely impact the job performance of employees at all levels of responsibility. These problems may include, but are not limited to, chemical dependency, and marital, family, legal and/or financial concerns. To facilitate a timely resolution to these problems, the district provides employees and their dependents with the benefit of confidential counseling and assistance provided by the Employee Assistance Program. Employees are encouraged to take advantage of the services before any problem becomes overwhelming. Every person using the program is assured total confidentiality. For additional information call the Personnel Office, or for an appointment, call CONTACT, Inc., 820-2328.

Ref: Board Policy GCBC* and Regulation GCBC-R

FIGURE 8.3
Sample Section of Personnel Handbook
Source: From *Handbook, Certificated Personnel*, Tempe Elementary School District No. 3, 1991–1992, Tempe, AZ.

The human resources director, school principals, teaching staff, support personnel, and other supervisory staff members need to participate in the determination of content for the handbook, the dissemination of the information, and the evaluation of the handbook's effectiveness. The development of the handbook most often is coordinated by the central human resources unit that serves as the clearinghouse for needed additions, clarifications, and changes. Such practices as using brief questionnaires to gain feedback from new personnel, various school district units, and experienced personnel, are most useful in assessing the handbook's effectiveness.

Orientation for the Beginning Teacher and Other New Teaching Personnel

Special orientation activities must be provided for beginning teachers and other personnel new to the school district. Those activities that later become routine often pose considerable frustration for new personnel and detract attention from important position responsibilities. Procedures such as homework regulations, required records and reports, student tardiness, parental communication, ways of securing instructional materials, and reporting student absence are common administrative problems for beginning teachers. Policies and procedures for student grading, student promotion and retention, and parental conferences are other matters significant for orientation. Student discipline and governing regulations are of paramount importance as well. Orientation activities must be designed to provide personnel with the necessary guidelines for action, but also to ensure that personal assistance and support are available to staff members. The teaching environment, teacher work load, work schedule, position assignment, and other conditions of work also influence the effective transition of personnel into the school system. These considerations are discussed later in this chapter.

Relationships with other staff members and administrators often pose problems for beginning teachers. Orientation activities that establish attitudes of cooperation and team spirit are essential. The mentoring provision, previously discussed, can be instrumental in serving this need. Position descriptions, communication channels and resources, and an explanation of personnel and office relationships are invaluable.

New personnel also need community information such as educational support services, recreational and cultural opportunities, civic activities, demographic data, medical facilities, governance structure, and community/school support information. Faculty handbooks and planned community tours can be sources for such information.

Personal problems, such as financial need, can inhibit effectiveness on the job. During orientation, information should be provided about educational credit associations within the school system or community agencies. In addition, services provided through employee assistance programs (EAP) should be explained (see Figure 8.3).

STAFF ASSIGNMENT

Staff assignment is the human resources process that maximizes human resources through the (1) deployment of talent and competency in the best interests of the total staff and student population; (2) identification of staff talent and assignment of individual employees to facilitate an effective instructional program; (3) assessment of roles, including the identification of inhibitors and facilitators, to permit optimal utilization of resources; (4) recognition of individual staff differences and implementation of leadership styles that best fulfill the potential of all personnel; (5) utilization of available research, tools, and skills to provide the best possible working conditions, and (6) examination of staff work loads that facilitate rather that inhibit effective work performance. This activity includes the consideration of those environmental conditions that increase personal motivation, effort, and productivity: specific assignment, work load, and personal problem resolution.

Staff assignment is closely linked to other personnel processes. Selection, orientation, evaluation, development, and organizational climate especially complement the activities and purposes of staff assignment. Although staff assignment clearly reaches beyond the singular consideration of proper position assignment, because of its paramount importance position assignment will be discussed in detail.

Position Assignment

Human resources authorities agree that one of the most effective means by which human resources administrators can assist the organization to achieve its stated goals and maximize employee potential is through the determination of appropriate position assignments. As Coil (1984) concluded,

The most satisfied and productive employees are those who are carefully and appropriately matched to their jobs. An appropriate and productive job match means that the primary tasks of a job enable the employee to use his or her strongest and preferred skills. (p. 54)

Drucker (1974) agreed and held that "the final but perhaps the most important element in managing people is to place them where their strengths can become productive" (p. 308).

Position assignment requires several essential considerations: (1) the specific nature of the position, including role expectations, necessary knowledge and skills, and conditions under which the role is performed; (2) the professional preparation, competencies, and interests of the employee; (3) the relationship of the position and the employee's characteristics and competencies; (4) the extent to which the assignment provides for the personal motivation needed by the employee and the extent to which success can be realized in the position; and (5) consideration of the forces of organizational culture and informal group structure.

Effective assignments link closely with effective recruitment and selection. While securing personnel who possess the knowledge and skills needed in the assignment, recruitment and selection must also be aimed at providing an opportunity for the employee to use the knowledge and skills that are most personally rewarding. Individuals generally have developed personal competence in a large number of task areas. Most persons also have competencies that they most enjoy utilizing and that tend to bring both the highest level of productivity and highest level of personal satisfaction. Position assignment necessitates the careful examination of both the general qualifications of the individual and the specific competencies most rewarding to that person. When a match is found between the competencies required by the job and those most satisfying to the individual, both the school system and the employee are likely to benefit.

Information about the individual's specific qualifications for the position and his or her specific competencies is gathered through a variety of sources: placement credentials, job application forms, personal resumes, appropriately designed job questionnaires, structured interviews, examination of job references, and assessment methodology. Accurate information about job and employee competencies is necessary for proper position assignment. Proper position placement is a planned process that utilizes objective measurements and evaluations of position needs and individual competencies to match positions and individuals.

Owen (1984) recommended the use of a position and personal profile to enhance the scientific approach to position assignment. His technique is based on the development of a position profile to evaluate job candidates for respective positions. The development of the position profile begins with a thorough consideration of what the position is to accomplish and what primary knowledge and skills are required. Required knowledge and skill levels are quantified to the fullest extent possible and rated on a scale of 0 to 10, or some other appropriate scale. In a similar manner, all available information about the candidate is examined and rated according to the knowledge and skills required. Position and personal profile results are then plotted and evaluated to find the best fit for each candidate.

Several advantages are associated with the profile procedure. It enables the selection activities to concentrate on the requirements of the position as opposed to personality factors; it provides continuity to the processes of recruitment and selection; it can be automated to facilitate analyses. In view of the importance of proper position assignment, the technique appears to have significant implications for practice in position assignments. As the procedure develops within the school system, more objectivity can be established in the instruments used to evaluate individual competency. Although some judgments must be subjective in this profile development, its potential for job placement deserves consideration. As Cavanaugh (1984) pointed out,

> When a person's abilities (intelligence, creativity, energy, maturity) are reasonably consonant with the requirements of the job, this will act as a motivating force. When the employee's abilities are significantly higher or lower than those demanded by the job, this typically constitutes a contra-motivational factor. . . . High motivational levels in employees are the result of a good job, by the right person, working for a competent supervisor, under the banner of positive company philosophy. (pp. 77–82)

The goals, beliefs, traditions, and values of a particular school are important factors in the assignment of employees to that school. If an individual employee's personal characteristics and beliefs are significantly incongruent with the culture of the school, personnel problems most likely will develop. The leadership style of the local building administrator and the style of followership on the part of the employee also are important assessments in position assignment. The time taken to gather information concerning the matter of organizational culture, employee characteristics, and leadership/followership styles will produce positive dividends for the school district and the employee by enhancing job satisfaction and productivity.

Teacher Work Load

Staff assignment requires that careful attention be given to teacher load. Without such consideration, inequities in the work load are certain to persist and personnel who are most qualified to carry out an effective educational program in the school often are so overburdened that their efforts are forced to a level of mediocrity. Equity of assignment is not the only personnel consideration that undergirds the importance of teacher load. Load reductions are advisable in certain situations, including the case of individuals new to teaching. Maximization of human resources is inhibited seriously if inequitable distribution of load exists or if load is unwisely allocated. A comprehensive examination of the teacher's work load also serves to assess what teachers actually do in meeting the responsibilities of their assignment. Human resources administrators need this information to make intelligent and defensible decisions concerning the ways in which the talents of each staff member are utilized. In addition, teacher load information is useful concerning the assignment of extra duties, reveals imbalances between the teaching load and extra duty load of a teacher, and serves as evidence for the need for additional staff.

The actual load of the teacher includes more factors than class size and number of classes. Other load factors to be considered are the number of subject matter preparations, the length of class periods, the nature of the subject taught, the nature of the students taught, extracurricular or additional duty assignments, and, at the elementary school level, such factors as the number of grades taught. With the general exception of class size and number of classes taught, little attention has been given to these other important factors in considerations of teacher load and staff assignments. However, if staff assignment is to be considered in a more "scientific" and professional manner, objective measures must be utilized to assess these factors and must become a part of rational and justifiable decisions concerning work load assignments. The makeup of teacher load has certain commonalities that can be measured with reasonable objectivity. Two such measures are the Douglass teacher load formula and another is the Norton/Bria formula for elementary teacher load.

The Douglass Teacher Load Formula.   As early as 1928 Harl Douglass developed a formula to measure teaching load in high schools. Since that time the formula has been refined, validated, and tested through numerous empirical studies; it is the most carefully developed means available for measuring teacher load in grades 7–12. The result of the formula computation of load for each teacher is an ***index of load*** that may be directly compared among teachers, departments, schools, or with national norms. Several states have developed teacher load norms based on the Douglass formula for all major subject matter areas that can be utilized by individual schools to compare their school load with those of other state schools. The Douglass formula (1951) is

$$TL = SGC \left[CP - \frac{DUP}{10} + \frac{NP - 25\,CP}{100} \right] \left[\frac{PL + 50}{100} \right] + .6PC \left[\frac{PL + 50}{100} \right]$$

where TL = units of teaching load per week
  CP = class periods spent in the classroom per week
  DUP = number of class periods per week in the classroom teaching classes for which the preparation is very similar to that for some other classes
  NP = number of pupils in classes per week
  PC = number of periods per week in supervision of study hall, student activities, teachers' meetings, and other cooperations
  PL = gross length of class period in minutes
  SGC = subject grade coefficient [Appropriate SGCs for the various subjects have been calculated by Douglass (see Douglass, 1951; Jung, 1948).]

Application of the Douglass Load Formula. Determine the index of teacher load for a teacher who has the following duties:

☐ Teaches two classes of 12th grade English with 25 and 27 students. Each class meets five times per week. The teacher has only one preparation, because one class is a duplicate. Each class period is 60 minutes.

☐ Teaches three classes of 11th grade social studies with 30, 27, and 23 students. Each class meets five times a week. Two classes are duplicates. Each class period is 60 minutes.

☐ Spends an average of 360 minutes per week in nonteaching duties during the semester.

Determine the values for the variables:

SGC = 1.1 for 12th grade English and for 11th grade social studies

CP = 25 (The teacher instructs five periods each day and each period meets five times per week: $CP = 5 \times 5 = 25$.)

DUP = 15 (There are three duplicate classes per day, one English and two social studies. Thus there are 15 duplicates for the 5-day week: $3 \times 5 = 15$.)

NP = 660 (The teacher instructs $25 + 27 + 30 + 27 + 23 = 132$ students each day for the 5-day week. Thus the weekly total is 660 students: $132 \times 5 = 660$.)

PL = 60 minutes

PC = 6 (The teacher's 360 minutes of cooperative duties is the equivalent of six class periods where one class period is 60 minutes: $360 \div 60 = 6$.)

Substituting into the formula,

$$TL = 1.1 \left[25 \ - \ \frac{15}{10} \ + \ \frac{660 - 625}{100} \right] \left[\frac{60 + 50}{100} \right] +$$

$$(.6 \times 6) \left[\frac{60 + 50}{100} \right]$$

$$= 32.82 \text{ units}$$

As one gains experience using the Douglass formula, it takes only a few minutes to calculate the load of each teacher. With computerization, the time consideration is inconsequential. The computer readily can provide the administrator with subject area central tendency comparisons, school-to-school load comparisons, and when available, school load comparisons with other states. Because the Douglass formula does not apply to the elementary school grades, other tools such as the Norton/Bria formula are available.

The Norton/Bria Formula for Measuring Elementary School Teacher Load. The Norton/Bria Formula (Norton & Bria, 1992) considers the load factors of assigned hours of teaching, time spent in preparation for teaching, cooperative or extracurricular duties of a noninstructional nature, the number of students taught, and the load related to extra grades taught in a single classroom by one teacher. Unlike the Douglass formula, the following formula measures teacher load in hours of time spent per work in teaching rather than index load units. The Norton/Bria formula is written as

$$THL = {}^{3}\!/_{2}\,ATH + \frac{SL \times PH}{CM} + F'\text{ or }F''\,(OG \times PH) + .6\,(CH)$$

where TLH = total load hours of time per week

ATH = assigned teaching hours in the classroom per week

PH = preparation hours (one-half the actual time for assigned hours in the classroom per week: 1/2 ATH)

SL = actual number of students taught above or below the average class size for any given grade (Class sizes can be altered according to local or state class size norms.)

CM = standard class mean size

OG = other grades taught in a single classroom under the direction of one teacher (i.e., for a teacher who teaches grades 2 and 3 simultaneously in one room, $OG = 1$)

F' = 1/16 (Use for small and medium sized school districts.)

F'' = 1/13 (Use for larger school districts.)

CH = cooperative hours spent in noninstructional duties such as meetings, playground supervision, parental conferences, and other nonteaching assignments.

Application of the Norton/Bria Formula.   A third-grade teacher with an enrollment of 32 in a small school district begins teaching at 8:30 a.m. and ends at 2:45 p.m. The teacher has a 30-minute lunch break and has supervision duties for a 20-minute recess in the morning and again in the afternoon. Additional duties including faculty meetings, PTA, chairing a curriculum group, advising the science club, and district-level meetings require 675 minutes weekly.

Load calculation:

ATH = 25 hr 25 min [Assigned teaching hours per week are 5 days × 6 hours 15 minutes/day (8:30 a.m.–2:45 p.m.) less 5 days × 40 minutes/day for recess and 5 days × 30 minutes/day for lunch.] $PH = 1/2\,ATH = 1/2$ (25 hr 25 min) = 12 hr 43 min

SL = 7 [Student load is based on the actual number of students above or below the average class size for grade 3. It is calculated as a fractional measure of the time needed for preparation. The average class size for grade 3 is 25 (see below). Average class size data can be altered to reflect local norms].

$$\frac{7 \times 12 \text{ hr } 43 \text{ min}}{25} = 3 \text{ hr } 34 \text{ min}$$

Table for Average Class Size

Grade 1	24 students
2	25 "
3	25 "
4	27 "
5	28 "
6	28 "

CM = 25
OG = 0 (no extra grades taught)
F' = 1/16
CH = 6 hr 45 min (.6 × 675 min/week = 405 min/week = 6 hr 45 min)

Substituting into the formula and rounding any fractional minutes to the nearest whole minute,

$$THL = {}^3\!/_2 \,(25 \text{ hr } 25 \text{ min}) + \frac{7 \times 12 \text{ hr } 43 \text{ min}}{25} + {}^1\!/_{16}\,(0 \times 12 \text{ hr } 43 \text{ min}) +$$

$$.6 \,(6 \text{ hr } 45 \text{ min})$$

$$= 38 \text{ hr } 8 \text{ min} + 3 \text{ hr } 34 \text{ min} + 0 + 6 \text{ hr } 45 \text{ min}$$

$$= 48 \text{ hr } 27 \text{ min per week}$$

Consider the same teacher with the added dimension of extra grades. Assume that the teacher has 32 students in grade 3 and 16 in grade 4. The *OG* (other grades) factor is calculated as follows:

$$\frac{1 \times 12 \text{ hr } 43 \text{ min}}{16} = 47.7 \text{ min}$$

Add 48 min to the teacher load of 48 hr 27 min to get a *TLH* of 49 hr 15 min per week.

Tools such as the Douglass and Norton/Bria formulas have been neglected in human resources practices. In view of the time given to other utilization activities, the neglect of teacher load is indefensible. Teaching is demanding work. The work load of teachers and other personnel must be a primary consideration of any human resources program concerned with maximizing human potential.

THE TROUBLED STAFF MEMBER

A growing problem for human resources administrators at all levels is that of the *troubled staff member*. The interrelation between the work life and the personal life of the employee, and the effect of problems in each, is illustrated in Figure 8.4.

As Figure 8.4 illustrates, work-related problems have negative effects on the personal life. Personal life problems, in turn, contribute further to physical and emotional stress at work. Although the pattern between personal and work life is not exact, problems related to the employee's personal and work life are nonetheless interdependent and interrelated.

According to a report of the U.S. Department of Health and Human Services (1989), approximately 80% of all employees experience some degree of stress in their lives and wish to do something about it. A study of school employees in one state (Norton, 1987) revealed that job stress was the leading problem for teachers and administrators considered as troubled employees. In a national study of 91 school districts (Norton, 1988), human resources directors reported the leading problem areas for troubled workers, including teachers, administrators, and support staff, as shown in Table 8.1.

Fortunately, the number of employee counseling programs is increasing. In the national study of troubled workers previously mentioned, 46 of the 91 school districts had some form of EAP. EAP service arrangements include the provision of referral services to outside professionals, in-house service programs staffed by local district professionals, consortia that include cooperative funding for services within or outside the school districts, and the use of approved consultants who provide the necessary EAP services. Many school districts provide special fringe benefit programs in this area. Such personal assistance is integral to the maximization of human resources within the school district. Although the central human resources unit most often coordinates the EAP, local human resources administrators, such as the school principal, are instrumental in the program's success. Because the building principal works most closely with many troubled personnel, identification, referral, counseling, and mentoring all become part of the principal's human resources responsibilities.

Most authorities point out the problem of referrals as related to troubled employees. Rumsey (1992) notes that the professional is in a delicate position relative to gaining the employee's trust and then creating enough distance so that the employee

FIGURE 8.4
Work Life and Personal
Life Interact

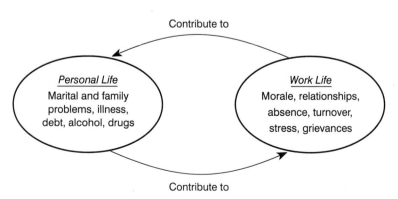

TABLE 8.1
Leading Problem Areas
for Troubled Workers in Education
Source: From "Employee Assistance Programs—A Need
in Education" by M. S. Norton,
1988, *Contemporary Education*,
60, p. 24. Reprinted by permission.

Problem Area	Number of School Districts Reporting
Medical health	52
Problem drinking/alcoholism	50
Mental/emotional problems	47
Marital/family problems	46
Employee/supervisor relationships	29
Personal crisis	21
Financial problems	17
Drug/chemical dependency	17
Work/peer relationships	11
Others	10

will accept the EAP referral without feeling unsupported. When the professional has enough information to understand the employee's problem, Rumsey recommends the following steps:

- ☐ Identify your concerns;
- ☐ Identify possible solutions;
- ☐ Develop strategy for the employee to look for and resolve in treatment;
- ☐ Match the employee with the provider(s) (case matching);
- ☐ Discuss providers;
- ☐ Explore resistance;
- ☐ Decide the next step; and
- ☐ Refer to the provider(s) (p. 42)

The following principles and personnel procedures aid the staff assignment process in serving the troubled staff members and providing positive leadership in this developing area:

1. Maintain a positive viewpoint regarding troubled staff personnel. The responsibility of the human resources function is to assist and develop human potential at all levels. The personal worth and dignity of troubled employees must be protected.
2. Establish procedures for ascertaining signs of personal problems demonstrated in the employee's behavior and effectiveness. Behavioral signals such as irritability, lack of motivation and interest, decreased physical energy, lack of commitment, loss of concentration, and self-deprecation serve as clues for needed action. Decreased effectiveness is revealed in such tendencies as setting low goals, inferior or deteriorating work, avoidance of difficult tasks, and increased human error.
3. Be fully aware of the assistance resources available for troubled personnel within the school system and through external agencies. Provide the necessary leadership for gaining personal counseling services. Work to promote a positive attitude toward the use of personal assistance counseling and services. The use of expert help when needed is the intelligent human consideration.

4. Utilize appropriate principles of effective human resources administration in working with troubled staff members. Proper position assignment, work load, and use of appropriate mentors are among the important considerations. Make certain that the employee knows about the support services available for counseling and guidance. Take special measures to establish open communication with the troubled worker. Utilize a sensitive approach that best fits the situation.

It was previously noted that staff assignment is closely related to the other processes of the human resources function. Staff assignment and staff development exemplify this interrelatedness. Staff development provides a variety of learning experiences for the employee that serve the goals of organization and personal self-fulfillment.

STAFF DEVELOPMENT

Staff development in education has many facets as evidenced by the numerous terms in the literature that name the process. Such terms include *professional growth, in-service education, continuing education, recurrent education, on-the-job staff training, human resources development, staff improvement, renewal,* and other combinations of these terms. Although various authorities have elaborated on differences among these terms, *staff development* and *human resources development* are used interchangeably in this text.

Historically, staff development has been a reactive program. The inadequacies in the preparation of teachers before 1900 and many years thereafter required major remediation programs. In fact, the need to provide the "missing education" for the ill-prepared teachers dominated in-service programs in most school districts during much of the first half of the twentieth century. Such motivation continues in many schools today. As a result, participants in such programs often approach in-service with little motivation and considerable passivity.

Staff development must be proactive rather than reactive; its effectiveness depends upon the extent to which it is personalized and based upon positive constructs. It is not that concern for deficiencies in staff preparation or the need to update skills are not appropriate concerns of staff development; rather, remediation is not to assume the *dominant* role. The human resources planning process must project and predict as accurately as possible the human skills and talents necessary to meet system needs in the immediate and long-range future. Armed with this information, along with important ongoing recommendations from building level personnel, staff development joins other personnel processes to build human resources necessary to keep the school system alive and vital. These program activities become cooperative endeavors that account for personal interest as well as for local building and organizational program needs. The position taken in this text is that staff development is self-development. The responsibility for personal growth must be assumed primarily by the individual.

This discussion of staff development, then, is based primarily on the following concepts:

1. Effective staff development primarily is a proactive consideration and is developmental in that its emphasis is upon an ever-developing individual. It focuses on projected needs and objectives that will help the school system remain creative and productive. Individual growth that meets these projected needs provides employees a personalized opportunity to reach higher levels of self-fulfillment and gratification. Staff development is an important investment in the school system's future.

2. Effective staff development places greater emphasis on the extension of personal strengths and creative talents than upon the remediation of personal weaknesses. The major focus of growth is upon what the individual can do and how this strength can be further developed and utilized.

3. Effective staff development is self-development. Growth is personal in the sense that what motivates each individual is an individual matter and in the sense that each person's self-image is instrumental in determining what incentives will encourage personal growth. Staff development is self-development in that growth begins with a personal need and individuals develop by taking responsibility for their own growth.

Staff development, from the foregoing perspectives, can be illustrated through the concepts of the Getzels-Guba (1957) social systems model. Each individual employee has unique need-dispositions based upon personality factors. The institution has certain expectations for the purposes of the organization and what it desires from each employee. The areas of agreement between personal needs and institutional expectations for the employee constitute areas of high potential for progress. As illustrated in Figure 8.5, as each person realizes new knowledge and skills, new and broadened aspirations of development become possible. Through the use of effective motivation and a system of rewards related to improved performance, personal development becomes an ongoing, continuous process.

The major purposes of staff development can be summarized as follows:

1. To provide planned staff development programs for the learning necessary to enable the employee to perform at the level of competency required in current and future position assignments.

2. To provide a climate that fosters opportunity for personal self-fulfillment and institutional effectiveness, a climate that facilitates human creativity and system renewal.

3. To serve the school system's primary goals: enhancing and achieving quality teaching and learning for students.

4. To establish viable and meaningful programs that enable system personnel to work cooperatively toward achieving the system's goals and their own personal goals in the areas of achievement, satisfaction, and self-fulfillment.

Operational Procedures for Staff Development

The operational procedures for the staff development process progress through five steps: (1) adopt a guiding philosophy; (2) develop goals and objectives; (3) plan pro-

FIGURE 8.5
Agreement Areas for Personal Growth

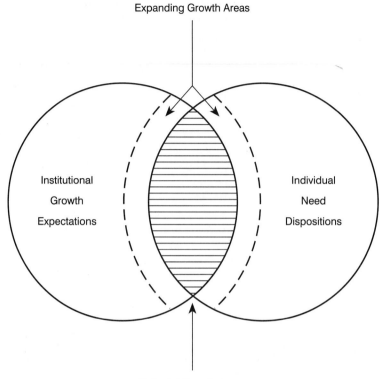

Expanding Growth Areas

Institutional
Growth
Expectations

Individual
Need
Dispositions

Potential Growth Areas

grams, activities, and delivery systems and determine responsibilities; (4) schedule and deliver plans and programs; and (5) evaluate the process.

Step 1, the guiding philosophy for staff development, is adopted as official board policy. Such policy is utilized by the school district staff to determine specific procedures through which to implement the program throughout the school system.

The following is an example of a board policy relative to staff development.

> The board of education supports the principle of continuous personal growth and development for all personnel employed in the school district. Such development programs and activities that serve to enhance the goals and objectives of the school district and to meet the immediate and future needs of district personnel should be made available through cooperative planning and implementation by members of the school district staff.
>
> The general responsibility for the administration of the staff development program belongs to the school superintendent who delegates program responsibilities among the staff as appropriate and who recommends, with proper input from employees, minimal requirements for development to meet changing certification requirements, to adjust to program changes, and to gain future knowledge and skills necessary to assure viability of human resources in the district.

This policy sets the guidelines for the administrative discretion necessary for its implementation. Such major administrative considerations as minimal requirements, needs assessments, program activities, implementation procedures, incentives, and resources are concerns primarily of the school district personnel. Staff development is a shared responsibility, with local school personnel assuming much of the responsibility for program design and implementation. The extent to which the central human resources unit assumes major responsibility for staff development is a function of the individual school district.

Step 2 of the operational procedure includes creating goals and objectives for staff development relative to identified system and employee needs. In-service programs that focus on realistic personal needs and local school problems are likely to be more effective than others. Further, those programs that consider both the needs of the organization's personnel and the needs of the organization provide an important organizational balance in staff development.

Step 3 links closely with Step 2. Programs, activities, and delivery systems must be planned and programmed. Both school and individual responsibilities must be determined. Ideally, school systems should have a unit/department whose prime responsibility is staff development. School district size, governance structure, and other factors, however, determine the extent to which this recommendation is possible. Sometimes the human resources unit or instructional unit serves the purpose of program coordination. In any case, the need for close cooperation and mutual sharing of program activities and responsibilities is important for program success.

Step 4 puts the plans and program options into place. The activities, experiences, and learning programs are scheduled and delivered. Staff development activities are both formal and informal. They include workshops, conferences, peer teaching, mentoring, independent study activities, assessment methodology, internships, job rotation, college courses, and other program pursuits. Selected program options are presented briefly in the next section of this chapter.

Step 5, evaluation of the staff development process, focuses on the assessments necessary to judge the extent to which the stated goals for the program are being met.

A comprehensive approach to the administration of staff development, the RPTIM model, has been conceptualized under five stages and 38 practices by Thompson (1982). This compliance model was utilized by Woods and others (Woods, Thompson, & Russell, 1981) in the National School Improvement Project (SIP) developed by the Institute for the Development of Educational Activities (IDEA). The 38 practices within each stage of the RPTIM model are research based, and the National Development Council and the Council of Professors of Instructional Supervision have endorsed these as practices that should serve as the basis for effective staff development in schools. The five stages of the RPTIM model are *r*eadiness, *p*lanning, *t*raining, *i*mplementation, and *m*aintenance. Each stage focuses on several practices. For example, readiness centers on the development of a positive climate before other staff development activities are attempted. Goals for school improvement are written collaboratively, goals for future program improvement are established, leadership and support are determined during the initial stage of development activities, and other appropriate preparation activities are completed. As previously noted the RPTIM model is generally accepted as the most comprehensive model developed to date.

Staff Development Methods and Strategies

The comprehensiveness of the staff development process and the variety of approaches utilized to achieve its purposes have been described in numerous publications. A brief description of several approaches to staff development including mentoring, quality circles, teacher centers, assessment centers, peer-assisted leadership, clinical supervision, and others is presented in this section. The following staff development approaches are among those that have been implemented successfully in many school systems.

Mentoring.   Mentoring was discussed previously as related to staff orientation. Mentoring also assumes a variety of forms in staff development. A mentor is selected to work with an individual staff member or small group of members for the purpose of personal growth. The mentor becomes the primary "coach" and counselor and (1) ascertains the special areas of interest and need regarding the mentee's personal development; (2) works with the mentee to design the most viable plan for individual growth; (3) assesses the most appropriate resources for meeting growth objectives; and (4) serves as a sounding board and constructive critic in evaluating progress and commitment. The need for a nonthreatening relationship and personal confidence is foremost. Since the mentor serves as a teacher, counselor, supporter, critic, and evaluator, the term *coaching* often is used as a synonym for mentoring.

Quality Circles.   Quality circles originated in Japan where small groups participate actively in planning, designing, and implementing work procedures in business and industry. The use of quality circles for staff development in education is a technique that places the primary responsibility for personal growth upon individuals linked together for the improvement of teaching and student learning. Members of a circle might include the teaching and support staff of one unit of a multi-unit elementary school, the teachers within a department of mathematics in a local school, a group of primary grade level teachers in a local school, foreign-language teachers from several schools within a district, or others whose common work interests or personal growth objectives can be enhanced through cooperative activities.

Quality circles generally are established and operated within the following guidelines:

1. The circle members focus upon an area or program of instruction that is determined to be important to the school's objectives and to their personal interests. The areas of special need, sources of knowledge, and skill development are identified. Individual members, or the group as a whole, determine responsibilities for personal learning. At times individuals serve as resource persons for all group members. Responsibilities for teaching subject area content are determined.

2. A variety of methods and procedures is utilized to provide practice of the skills and knowledge required to implement the desired program or teaching methodology. The use of modeling, simulation, observation, and video techniques provides opportunities to practice in classroom and nonclassroom settings.

3. Constructive feedback is provided through a systematic procedure of self-evaluation and group review.
4. Specific provision is made for implementing the behaviors or methods desired. Mentoring, peer counseling, or coaching is structured through a system that places primary responsibility for improvement upon the individual with full support of the circle members.

Quality circles can serve several important purposes and provide numerous benefits to the system and its human resources. Primary purposes and benefits include the following:

1. The development of new knowledge and skills to enhance present and future job performance, as viewed by staff members themselves
2. The establishment of the individual's responsibility for personal development through a process of "team mentoring" and individual leadership
3. The promotion of personal motivation and work satisfaction through opportunities for achievement, relevant growth, and appropriate rewards for improved performance
4. The improvement of personal performance and work quality to meet school goals and objectives that have been established by consensus
5. The general improvement of staff communication, human relationships, and trust through opportunities to be a member of the local school and school district teams and to be a significant member of the decision-making process

The Teacher Center. Another effort to place the primary responsibility for personal development on the individual teacher is through the teacher center, an enriched environment of resources, personal involvement, and peer communication. The teacher center concept makes the teacher an active participant in decisions and activities relating to personal growth. A teacher center need not be a permanent site or facility, but conceptually constitutes a teaching resource bank where teachers informally participate in activities that enhance their performance in the classroom. Teachers, alone or in groups with similar interests, examine instructional materials, design teaching aids, read materials related to teaching methods and strategies, develop new lesson plans, and communicate with other teachers and support personnel concerning creative ideas in an area of instructional interest. Based on the proposition that professional staff personnel are best qualified to determine the necessary training needed by their colleagues, the teacher center concept is governed primarily by teachers.

A teacher center might be a temporary site, such as a school district's reading center, that is used for a specified period of time for a specific instructional development purpose. It might be a self-contained room with a professional library, film and visual materials, a work design area for making instructional aids, and other resource banks available for examination and classroom use. In those school districts that have established extensive educational facilities for teaching/learning centers, facilities for examining instructional technology of various kinds, computer facilities, curriculum resource banks, research libraries, conference/workshop rooms, instructional design facilities, media resources, and support staff personnel are available for teacher and staff use. Not all activities in a teacher center are informal. Specific workshops, designed to develop new teaching concepts and skills, are generally given high ratings by teachers.

The positive aspects of teacher centers are numerous. The concept of teachers helping teachers is supported by research. Intrinsic motivation that leads to personal development activities is one important criterion for proactive growth. One concern, however, is the possible absence of research-based development programs. Conceptual frameworks founded upon tested theory, research, and empirical application are essential. If the delivery system for staff development depends exclusively upon individual opinions of "effective practice," the potential exists for misdirected effort and practice.

Assessment Center Methodology.   As noted in the previous chapter, assessment center techniques were first adopted by industry to select and promote management personnel. In education the first use of assessment centers was also in personnel selection, the selection of school administrators. As previously noted, beginning in the 1970s the National Association of Secondary School Principals (NASSP) assumed a major leadership role in the development of assessment techniques to select school principals. Since then, assessment center methodology has proven beneficial to assess performance in teacher and administrator preparation programs and in staff development.

According to Brown (1992),

> In a typical assessment center, participants work through tasks designed to elicit behavior considered important for the job involved. Assessors observe the process and take notes, using specially designed observation forms . . . assessors compare observations and make a final evaluation of each candidate for that exercise. At the end of the process, the assessors develop a summary report on each candidate. (p. 35)

Such a center is not viewed as a physical location; rather, assessment activities are conducted in various settings, whenever and wherever a qualified group of assessors meet together to assess the performance of an individual or group of individuals for a stated reason.

An assessment center is characterized by several activities:

1. Behaviors and skills, determined to be relevant to a specific job, are assessed through standard methods and activities.
2. Multiple assessment techniques are utilized to gain performance data (e.g., interviews, leaderless group activities, individual task exercises, in-basket simulation, pencil-and-paper tests, personality tests, and other simulation exercises).
3. A group of assessors is used in the evaluation procedures. Such individuals are specifically trained and certified in the methods being utilized and the procedures being followed.
4. Information and individual assessor results are pooled through a process of "jurying" that leads to a final consensus of performance results.
5. If the assessment is for staff development purposes, a system of thorough feedback is provided to the person assessed.

Mentoring, in particular, appears to have considerable potential as a growth model in conjunction with assessment methodology. One major advantage of such a relational approach is its potential for personalizing the growth process by the professional involvement of a specially selected mentor who works with a mentee on the strengths and needs as revealed in assessment results.

Wendel and Uerling (1989) contend that assessment center methodology can be used to prepare potential administrators during graduate school programs. They emphasize that assessment center methods can be used to "diagnose students developmental needs, broaden the scope of program activities, and measure the effectiveness of an institution's preparation program" (p. 74).

Clinical Supervision. Effective technical supervision significantly facilitates staff development and maximization of human resources. Clinical supervision places emphasis on systemwide instructional improvement through improved staff performance. Assessments provide information relative to the achievement of mutually determined teaching objectives. Clinical supervision is a cyclical procedure.

Step 1 The cooperative relationship between the teacher and supervisor essential to the procedure is fostered. During this phase they discuss the nature of clinical supervision, clarify follow-up procedures and responsibilities, specify purposes and focus on development objectives, and discuss uses of classroom observation information.

Step 2 The teacher plans an instructional unit with constructive input by the supervisor. Instructional objectives, teaching methods, instructional materials, monitoring strategies, and other teaching/learning considerations are determined. On the basis of this information, the supervisor and teacher determine the procedures relative to the actual classroom observation.

Step 3 The focus in this step is on planning the observation procedures. Collection of information on student learning needs or problems as well as the physical setting are determined.

Step 4 The supervisor makes the actual classroom observation. In this step the agreed upon methods for collecting information are implemented. Following the observation, both the supervisor and the teacher examine the recorded information individually to interpret the data relative to the teaching activities that took place and the objectives of the intended lesson.

Step 5 The supervisor incorporates the data collected into the most meaningful and reportable format, which the teacher can readily understand.

Step 6 The supervisor plans the postobservation conference with the teacher. The specifics to be discussed in the conference, the approach to be utilized, and the conference objectives are established in terms of the original planning agreements. Strengths and areas for improvement are analyzed for discussion purposes.

Step 7 The postobservation conference provides the opportunity for the teacher and supervisor to review the information collected and evaluate the results to predetermined objectives. The supervisor serves as an instructor, helping the teacher interpret the results of the classroom observation. Through a mutual discussion of actual classroom events, the teacher and supervisor focus on the kinds of changes needed in the follow-up classroom performance to achieve desired learning objectives.

Step 8   The teacher and supervisor plan the next teaching lesson and the behaviors and methods to be implemented in an effort to realize continually improved results. This final step leads to new directions in planning, the reestablishment of the relationship for the future, and the reimplementation of the steps in the clinical supervision cycle.

Career Development Planning.   Career development planning includes such activities as personal counseling, self-concept and assessment workshops, career opportunity seminars, and close coordination of the organization's human resources processes with employee career aspirations. The work experience and the employee's personal development program are planned to facilitate the individual's career goals in relation to the organization's future human resources needs.

Personnel Appraisal Methods.   The organization's appraisal process focuses primarily on gathering formative information that can direct the employee's growth and development. Rather than using summative ratings to determine job continuation, the appraisal process becomes a cooperative procedure that encompasses self-evaluation and mentoring feedback to motivate continuous employee development. A comprehensive discussion of performance appraisal is included in Chapter 7.

Task Force and Shadow Groups.   Service on task force groups that focus on the creation of better, more effective methods has viable personal development potential. Representatives from community, administrator, teacher, and student groups concentrate on an educational objective through cooperative problem-solving activity.

Industry especially has benefited from the use of "shadow groups," which generally involves the simulation of an activity by members of the organization. For instance, employees might assume the roles of the governing board members and conduct a board meeting using a proposed future agenda. The process helps management anticipate problems prior to the actual board meeting and gain insight on important employee perspectives on the issues and agenda items. Employee participants and other representatives are able to gain appreciation for the agenda issues, develop a better understanding of the organization's problems, and form new perspectives about their growth needs in relation to the goals of the organization.

Job Rotation.   Industry has experienced success in the practice of moving employees and managers to various positions to enhance organizational effectiveness and employee development. Education has not generally endorsed the practice; however, the idea has received some favorable acceptance as a positive growth practice for school administrators. After a certain time period, both the individual and the organization benefit when the employee can exercise personal talents and meet new challenges in a different assignment. Additionally, experience and knowledge of the different educational units and school programs are spread to more persons in the district. Arguments against job rotation in education center primarily on its possible "disrupting" effect on the local school community.

Peer-Assisted Leadership. PAL, peer-assisted leadership, is an acronym that describes the basic concept of this development process—participants helping other participants in the improvement of their personal skills. In 1983 the instructional management program at the Far West Laboratory in San Francisco established PAL in order to (1) help administrators develop skills that they can use to analyze their own and others' management behaviors, (2) give participants opportunities to learn how other administrators lead in their positions, (3) enable administrators to gain support from colleagues, and (4) provide a means for assisting administrators in the understanding of effective behavior in their specific setting. Since that time PAL activities have been proven effective with other professional staff personnel. Instruction relative to data collection through interviews, shadowing, reflective interviewing, and advanced reflective interviewing is provided. In early meetings participants are introduced to the model of the general framework for program leadership.

PAL differs from mentoring in that peer-assisted leadership is not a mentor-protégé arrangement. Rather, peers are placed in partnerships or triads and each participant helps others examine and reflect upon personal behaviors, skills, and activities in relation to the setting of the school environment, specific skills being implemented, and expected program outcomes.

PAL goals include helping participants to develop skills for analyzing personal behavior, enabling participants to gain support and insight from colleagues, and providing participants an opportunity to learn how others lead, teach, and create. Participants of PAL programs report that it serves to increase awareness of their own behavior, style, and intentions. It serves as an important self-evaluation tool and leads to the learning of new strategies and personal skills.

As previously noted, the field of education has numerous methods and strategies for implementing staff development. Although most of the discussion in this chapter has focused on teacher development, such programs as assessment centers, peer-assisted leadership, job rotation, internships, task force groups, career development planning, and mentoring apply equally well to administrative personnel. Perhaps the underlying importance of staff development in education is reflected in the basic concept that schools will improve as people progress.

ADULTS AS LEARNERS

Because school system personnel are adult learners, staff development activities must utilize the basic principles that facilitate optimal learning and growth for them. Adult learners need

1. to be involved in the determination of their learning activities; they must have a voice in setting learning goals, content, experiences, and evaluations.
2. to be considered as individual learners; each adult brings a varied background of experiences and knowledge to any learning situation.

3. to see the value of the learning experiences; they need to know that the activities and experiences will be applicable to their work and the resolution of problems in their work environment.
4. to see tangible outcomes from the learning activities and experiences; they need to receive some indication of their personal achievement toward learning goals.

The foregoing guidelines underline specific questions that staff development program personnel must answer: (1) To what extent have the participants been involved in establishing their own objectives and designing programs leading to their professional growth? (2) To what extent has the program evaluation built in appropriate assessments concerning program results and personal achievement? (3) To what extent has the program been individualized; is there an opportunity for self-direction based upon personal needs and learning interests? (4) To what extent is the program relevant to learner needs?

As emphasized by Seaman and Fellenz (1989),

> In learning situations, adults are definitely different from youth . . . the teacher must be aware not only of felt needs of the adult learner but must be able to use teaching strategies that will enable the adult to begin to meet those needs early in the instructional process. (pp. 2–3)

SUMMARY

The maximization of human resources in the school system is a primary responsibility of the human resources function. This concern emphasizes the purposeful development and utilization of people within the organization. It also underlines the perspective set forth throughout this text that the human resources function is a primary responsibility of all personnel in the school system. An organization's progress depends on the extent to which people are positively motivated and developed.

As a social system the behavior of individuals in the school system is influenced by the institution's expectations and the individual's personal need-dispositions. Staff utilization serves to establish a congruence between organizational roles and personal needs toward the goal of developing behaviors that harmonize with stated organizational purposes and personal self-fulfillment. Human motivation is an important consideration of the human resources function generally and of the processes of staff orientation, staff assignment, and staff development specifically.

Each of the human resources processes contributes uniquely to the maximization of human resources. Orientation is the comprehensive complex of activities designed to gain congruence between institutional objectives and employee needs. Orientation practices, when effectively implemented, enhance employee morale, development, and productivity. Mentor programs, policy and regulation manuals, personnel information handbooks, personal assistance programs, information sessions, one-to-one conferences, and socialization activities are some of the activities useful in orientation programs.

Staff assignment maximizes human resources when position assignments are closely related to the employee's talents and interests. Work load and provisions for troubled staff members are other important elements of effective staff utilization.

Approaches to staff development that emphasize remedial programs generally have proven ineffective. A focus on employee strengths and self-fulfillment fosters self-development from a positive perspective. Potential growth best occurs when the individual's dispositions agree with the organization's growth expectations.

The implementation of the staff development process consists of a planned sequence of procedures that begins with commitment by the board of education, continues through cooperative goal setting, program design and delivery, and culminates in opportunities to practice the knowledge and skills gained in a wide variety of learning activities. Evaluation leads to necessary program changes and ensures continuous program improvement. In all activities, basic principles of adult learning are utilized.

Staff development methods and strategies are virtually limitless and are provided through the local school district, institutions of higher learning, and employee associations. Such developments as mentoring, quality circles, teacher centers, assessment centers, peer-assisted leadership, and clinical supervision are among the viable approaches for meeting the purposes of the staff development process.

DISCUSSION QUESTIONS

1. Examine Maslow's hierarchy of basic needs (Figure 8.2). Discuss the hierarchy of needs as related to teacher personnel generally. For example, what specific provisions and/or activities are important in meeting the safety needs of teacher personnel?

2. Consider the Getzels-Guba social systems model and the matter of institutional expectations and the individual need-dispositions (Figure 8.1). Discuss several specific considerations that the school system might utilize to satisfy these dimensions. For example, what provisions can be implemented by the school system to help meet organizational goal expectations or the employee's needs relative to self-esteem?

3. Discuss a specific school district's orientation process in relation to its effectiveness. What factors tend to cause its ineffectiveness or foster its effectiveness? To what extent do the identified factors of effectiveness compare with the guiding principles for the orientation process presented in the chapter?

4. Staff development was discussed as a proactive experience rather than a reactive one. Discuss your personal staff development experiences. Have these experiences met the proactive criteria? Why or why not?

5. A high school teacher of social studies has two classes of grade 10 history with 26 and 32 students and three classes of government with 26, 31, and 33 students. The subject-grade coefficient for social studies is 1.1. Class periods are 55 minutes in length. On the average during the semester, the teacher spends 11 periods per week in cooperative duties. Use the Douglass load formula to calculate this teacher's units of teacher load. (Note: The answer is 35.40 units.)

CASE 8.1
A Question of Low Morale

Assume that the Union High School District is evidencing unusually high staff turnover. In addition, general morale throughout the district is low. Teacher absence has increased 20% over the last 3 years and general faculty and support staff complaints have increased substantially as well. Apply the Herzberg two-factor theory (Chapter 1) in the role of a school principal in the Union High School District.

Questions

1. What specific practices and relationships would you examine at the outset to ameliorate the problems indicated in Case 8.1?
2. What recommendations would you offer for obviating the problems described in the case?

CASE 8.2
Time to Teach

As assistant director of human resources, you receive the memorandum shown in Figure 8.6. Examine the memo and then present your ideas of follow-up in this case. Keep in mind the specific principles set forth in the chapter concerning effective in-service programs as well as the principles of adult learning.

Questions

1. What specific problems do you determine from the Case 8.2 scenario?
2. From the somewhat limited evidence provided, what necessary staff development practices appear to have been overlooked in this case in the past?
3. Discuss the alternatives for action at this time. As the school principal, outline a brief action plan that you would recommend in Ms. Petrov's case.

CASE 8.3
The Teacher Transfer

Melvin Schneider was in his third year of teaching at Union Elementary School when parental complaints about his student relationships started to increase weekly. Calls from parents to Principal Paul Andrews reported that Mr. Schneider was "cold"; children were afraid of him. Then, too, others complained that he couldn't work with the slower children; he lacked the patience necessary for working with slow learners.

Principal Andrews scheduled a meeting with Human Resources Director Brad Joseph and Superintendent Dorothy Rose. "I observed his classroom twice last week," offered Mr. Andrews. "His teaching methods seem satisfactory, but the class atmosphere doesn't come through as a happy one. Maybe we should transfer him next year."

"Well, you know that Mr. Schneider has been in the district for 11 years now," said Mr. Joseph. "He was transferred from Whittier after his first 4 years and then again after 4 years from Whittier to Phillips."

"How do his performance evaluations look?" asked Superintendent Rose.

"As I noted earlier," replied Mr. Andrews, "I've given him satisfactory ratings each of his years with me, but he doesn't come off well with parents and I have received more than the usual number of requests from the children themselves to move to Mrs. Martin's fifth-grade class."

Superintendent Rose called her secretary and asked for Mr. Schneider's personal file. The record did confirm that he had been transferred twice during his first 8 years in the district. Remarks in the record indicated that "parental complaints" and "lack of student rapport" were the primary reasons for these transfers.

"It looks like some specific action is needed again," said Ms. Rose. "This situation cannot continue."

MEMORANDUM

To: E. O. Herr, Assistant Director
From: Verna Petrov, Grade 3 Teacher, Union Elementary
Re: Program suggestion

I'd like to make a suggestion for you to consider in planning some of our inservice days. I know that you have run a survey of perceived needs in the district that gives you some general or overall ideas, but for some of us, surveys don't always fit our needs as individuals.

Here are a couple things I see as needs:

1. When we test with the battery of the Columbus Test of Basic Skills, and place so much emphasis on it, teachers tend to start teaching to the test, and I'm not sure that is good.
2. I don't want to sound negative, but when I have 27 children from residents in our district in my class and then get two or more who can hardly speak English, it is becoming impossible for me to take care of the class; the few non-English speaking students require all my time. Then, many of them will be gone again in a few weeks or months.

Please don't misunderstand me. I'm not saying we need inservice on working with these few children. I want help working with the whole class. Why not set up a training program for children with limited ability in English, and when they get up to grade level, place them in appropriate classes? It seems to me that the least restricted environment is one that would help these deserving students learn best.

Thanks!

Verna Petrov

FIGURE 8.6
Memo to Assistant Director of Human Resources

Questions

1. Assume that you are Superintendent Rose in this case. What specific recommendations would you offer at this time?
2. What are your assessments of the history of this case as you can best determine from the given information?
3. In view of the basic concepts of staff orientation, staff assignment, and staff development, what specific steps or programs apply in this case?

☐ **CASE 8.4**
How Am I Doing, Dr. George?

Mrs. Toms had taught at Columbus Junior High School for 39 years in the area of social studies. She was well respected by her colleagues and active in the overall school district activities. She gave an informal invitation to Dr. George, the new curriculum coordinator, to drop in and visit her class whenever he could. Dr. George was in his first year as coordinator and was selected for that position after 6 years as teacher of history in the same school district.

Dr. George had an appointment with the Columbus Junior High School principal, Merlin Scott, on Wednesday morning and after the appointment decided to accept Mrs. Toms invitation to visit her class.

Mrs. Toms was genuinely pleased to see Dr. George enter the classroom. After introducing Dr. George to the class, he took a chair near the rear of the room, and she continued her instruction.

After 55 minutes, the lesson ended. As Dr. George walked toward the classroom door, he turned, smiled, and waved to Mrs. Toms. However, Mrs. Toms asked him to wait, and as she approached Dr. George in the doorway asked, "Well, what did you think?"

Dr. George, believing that it really wasn't appropriate for him to give feedback of any formal nature merely indicated that the lesson was

enjoyable and he would like to return again sometime.

"Fine," said Mrs. Toms, "but what about today? Do you have any thoughts about the class?"

Dr. George wasn't certain what might be an appropriate response and was concerned that any remarks about his informal first visit might be out of order.

Mrs. Toms smiled and asked, "Any thoughts?"

In fact, Dr. George was of the opinion that he had just observed an outstanding teacher. After a brief pause, Dr. George commented, "It was an outstanding performance. If every teacher in the system was performing at the level I just witnessed, I'd be out of a job."

Mrs. Toms smiled. Tears formed in her eyes. Nothing more was said. Dr. George shook her hand and bid her good-bye.

Questions

1. What thoughts do you have concerning the case generally? What might you have done in Dr. George's place?
2. Discuss the implications of the case in regard to the maximization of human resources and personal motivation.

☐ **CASE 8.5**
A Matter of Load

"Hi, Greg, come on in," said Principal Owen, "Care for coffee?"

"Thanks," replied Greg, "What's on the agenda?"

"I want to explore the need for adding a class for beginners in band," replied Mrs. Owen. "Our one beginners' class is doing well, and the band and orchestra classes are exemplary in my opinion. The band's performance at last Friday's game made me proud to be at Union High School. However, I'm receiving numerous requests for band instruction by both students and parents."

"What are your thoughts, specifically?" asked Greg. "As you know, my teaching load is excessive already."

Principal Owen picked up a copy of the semester's teaching schedule and commented, "Well, as you know, Greg, our typical class load is five classes per day and presently you are teaching three."

"I know," responded Greg, "but band isn't typical. Our external commitments for public performances outweigh any consideration of one or two more instructional classes. In the last month I've had to prepare the band for three Friday night performances, we've performed for two civic clubs and marched in the Chamber parade, and the orchestra has performed for the state PTA Conference and our recent school assembly. Right now, I have four performance requests on my desk that need responses."

"External commitments are important to us," replied Principal Owen. "Give the additional class some further thought, and we'll visit again later. Thanks for coming in."

Questions

1. What thoughts do you have concerning Greg's work load situation? What other information or data does Principal Owen need in working to resolve this matter?

2. What does the case infer in general relative to problems and issues of teacher load in education?

REFERENCES

Alderfer, C. P. (1972). *Existence, relatedness, and growth: Human needs in organizational settings.* New York: Free Press.

Barnard, C. I. (1938). *The functions of the executive.* Cambridge, MA: Harvard University Press.

Brayfield, A. H., & Crockett, W. H. (1955). Employee attitudes and employee performance. *Psychological Bulletin, 55,* 416.

Brown, M. (1992). Only the best. *American School Board Journal, 179*(3), 35–36.

Cavanaugh, M. E. (1984). In search of motivation. *Personnel Journal, 63*(3), 76–82.

Coil, A. (1984). Job matching brings out the best in employees. *Personnel Journal, 63*(1), 54–60.

Douglass, H. R. (1928). Measuring teacher load in the high school. *The Nation's Schools, 2*(4), 22–24.

Douglass, H. R. (1951). The 1950 revision of the Douglass high school teaching load formula. *The Bulletin, 35*(179), 13–24.

Drucker, P. E. (1974). *Management, tasks, responsibilities, practices.* New York: Harper & Row.

Getzels, J. W., & Guba, E. G. (1957). Social behavior and the administrative process. *The School Review, 65*(4), 423–441.

Herzberg, F., Mausner, B., & Snyderman, B. (1959). *The motivation to work* (2nd ed.). New York: Wiley.

Jung, C. W. (1949). *The development of a proposed revision of the Douglass formula for measuring teacher load in the secondary school.* Unpublished doctoral dissertation, University of Colorado, Boulder.

Maslow, A. H. (1970). *Motivation and personality.* New York: HarperCollins. (Original work published 1954)

McGregor, D. (1960). *The human side of enterprise.* New York: McGraw-Hill.

Norton, M. S. (1987). *The status of employee assistance programs in education.* Unpublished manuscript, Arizona State University, Tempe.

Norton, M. S. (1988). Employee assistance programs—A need in education. *Contemporary Education, 60,* 23–26.

Norton, M. S., & Bria, R. (1992). Toward an equitable measure of elementary school teacher load. *Record in Educational Administration and Supervision, 13*(1), 62–66.

Ouchi, W. (1981). *Theory Z: How American business can meet the Japanese challenge.* Reading, MA: Addison-Wesley.

Owen, P. E. (1984). Profile analysis: Matching positions and personnel. *Supervisory Management, 29*(11), 14–20.

Raia, A. P. (1974). *Management by objectives*. Glenview, IL: Scott, Foresman.

Rumsey, M. J. (1992). Making EAP Referrals work. *EAP Digest, 12*(5), 42–43.

Seaman, D. F., & Fellenz, R. A. (1989). *Effective strategies for teaching adults*. New York: Merrill/Macmillan.

Skinner, B. F. (1938). *The behavior of organisms*. New York: Appleton-Century-Crofts.

Skinner, B. F. (1953). *Science and human behavior*. New York: Free Press.

Skinner, B. F. (1969). *Contingencies of reinforcement: A theoretical analysis*. Englewood Cliffs, N J: Prentice-Hall.

Thompson, S. R. (1982). *A survey and analysis of Pennsylvania public school personnel perceptions of staff development practices and beliefs with a view to identifying some critical problems or needs*. Unpublished doctoral dissertation, Pennsylvania State University, State College.

U.S. Department of Health and Human Services. (1989). *Health United States*. Washington, DC: GPO.

Vroom, V. H. (1964). *Work and motivation*. New York: Wiley.

Wendel, F. C., & Uerling, D. F. (1989). Assessment centers—Contributing to preparation programs for principals. *NASSP Bulletin, 73*(515), 74–79.

Woods, F. H., Thompson, S. R., & Russell, F. (1981). Designing effective staff development programs. In B. Dillon-Peterson (Ed.), *Staff development/ organizational development*. Alexandria, VA: Association for Supervision and Curriculum Development.

9

Legal Aspects of Public School Human Resources Administration

The public schools, like all other institutions in society, operate within the framework of laws—laws generated by the federal government, the state government, and the courts (case law). The operation of the schools is also subject to a multitude of ordinances, rules, and regulations promulgated by numerous federal, state, and local agencies and government entities.

All aspects of the employment relationship have been the subject of legislative and executive pronouncements and judicial interpretation. Whereas school administrators are not expected to be legal experts, they should be aware of the basic legal concepts in human resources administration and know when to seek legal counsel. It is imperative that school administrators understand their rights as well as their obligations under the law, and that these rights and obligations are translated into everyday personnel practices in their districts (Cascio, 1987).

The purpose of this chapter is to familiarize school administrators with the basic concepts of law as they relate to employment in the public schools. Although there is some variation in the application of these legal concepts from one state or locality to another, certain topics and issues are of sufficient similarity and concern to warrant consideration. These include (1) terms and conditions of employment, (2) due process, (3) discrimination, and (4) adverse employment decisions. Some of these topics also are discussed in other chapters of this text; here, attention is given to the legal considerations involved in each. The legal considerations related to collective bargaining are discussed in Chapter 10 and those related to evaluation in Chapter 7.

TERMS AND CONDITIONS OF EMPLOYMENT

Within the framework of state and federal constitutional and statutory protection provided for school district employees, the state has plenary power to conduct and regulate public education within the state. Accordingly, the state through its legislature, state board of education, state department of education, and local school boards has promulgated the rules and regulations for the operation of the schools. Among these rules and regulations are those that establish the terms and conditions of employment. These may vary considerably from state to state, but the areas most often affected by state statutory and regulatory provisions are discussed in this section and deal with certification, citizenship and residency requirements, health and physical requirements, teacher competency testing, the employment contract, tenure, and mandatory retirement.

Certification

To qualify for teaching, administrative, and many other positions in the public schools, an individual must acquire a valid certificate or license. The certification or licensure requirement is intended to ensure that the holder has met established state standards and is qualified for employment in the area for which the certificate or license is required. The courts have held that states not only have the right but the duty to ensure that school district employees meet certain minimum qualifications for employment. The certificate does not constitute a contract or guarantee employment; it only makes the holder eligible for employment.

Certification requirements may include a college degree with minimum credit hours in specific curricular areas, evidence of specific job experience, "good moral character," a specified age, United States citizenship, the signing of a loyalty oath, and more recently, a minimum score on a job-related exam. In determining whether candidates for certification meet state standards, the courts will generally interpret and enforce the standards quite literally and will intervene only if the denial of certification is clearly erroneous or unsupported by substantial evidence or if statutory or constitutional rights are violated (Beckham, 1983; McCarthy & Cambron-McCabe, 1992).

Not only is the state empowered to issue certificates, it is also authorized to revoke or suspend certificates. Revocation or suspension of a certificate is a more severe action than dismissal, because the former forecloses employment opportunities within the state in the area of certification. As a result of their severity, the evidentiary standards and conformity to due process in suspension or revocation actions are usually more rigorous (Beckham, 1983). The procedures to be followed in the revocation or suspension of a certificate and the grounds for the revocation or suspension are normally stipulated in statute. Immorality is the most commonly cited cause (31 states), followed by incompetence (24 states), contract violation (22 states), and neglect of duty (21 states) (Delon, 1977).

A lesser penalty, nonrenewal of certification, can also be imposed by the state when the individual seeking recertification fails to satisfy the requirements for recertification. In the past such requirements have usually been related to professional growth (e.g., completion of a specified number of credits during a certain period of time). More recently a few states have imposed a test requirement as a precondition for recertification. The courts have upheld requirements for recertification if they are shown to be reasonably related to maintenance of standards or improved performance. If the requirement is found not to be reasonably related, certification will be upheld. In a case involving a black elementary teacher in Alabama who was released on the basis of failure to pass a test required by the state for recertification, the court found the test to fall "so far below acceptable and reasonable standards that the test could not be reasonably understood to do what it purported to do" (*Richardson v. Lamar County Board of Education*, 1989, p. 825). Accordingly, the teacher was reinstated and granted back pay.

Where certification requirements exist, lack of certification can result in dismissal of the employee. For example, in a case in Texas a prospective teacher entered into a contract with a school district for a teaching position that required him to file his certificate with the personnel director no later than the issuance of the first payroll check (in this case September 20). The prospective teacher failed the state exam that was a requirement for certification twice before the school year began, but eventually passed it and so informed the district on October 20. In the meantime the district had hired another teacher and the prospective teacher was unsuccessful in his breach of contract suit against the district (*Grand Prairie Independent School District v. Vaughn*, 1990). If a school district knowingly employs a noncertificated individual, it may be subject to nonpayment of state aid. In fact, state laws usually provide that it is unlawful for a district to pay an uncertified teacher (*Flanary v. Barrett*, 1912). If an employee knowingly provides services without a certificate, some courts have viewed this service as voluntary and, as such, not demanding of compensation (see, e.g., *Floyd County Board of Education v. Slone*, 1957; *Sorenson v. School District No. 28*, 1966).

Citizenship and Residency Requirements

The courts have upheld both citizenship and residency requirements for certification and/or as a condition of employment. With regard to U.S. citizenship, the U.S. Supreme Court has held that education is one of those government functions that is "so bound up with the operation of the state as a governmental entity as to permit the exclusion from those functions of all persons who have not become part of the process of self-government" (*Ambach v. Norwick*, 1979, pp. 73–74). Further, the Court acknowledged a rational relationship between such a New York citizenship requirement and a legitimate state purpose. The Court found the requirement justified because of the critical part teachers play "in the developing students' attitudes toward government and understanding the role of citizens in our society" (p. 78).

Where state statute permits, more and more school districts are requiring employees to reside within the school district. Residency requirements have been upheld by the majority of state and federal courts when there is a rational basis for the requirements. For example, a residency requirement for all future district employees of the Pittsburgh school district withstood challenge by the Pittsburgh Federation of Teachers because the court agreed that the district's stated reasons for the requirement—namely that employees would have an increased personal knowledge of conditions in the district, would feel a greater personal stake in the district, would pay taxes in the district, and would have reduced absenteeism and tardiness—were all rational, legitimate, and justifiable (*Pittsburgh Federation of Teachers v. Aaron*, 1976).

In a more recent case, the Arkansas Supreme Court held that a school district's requirement that teachers reside within the district boundaries or within 10 miles of city limits did not violate equal protection even though it did not apply to noncertificated personnel. The court also determined that the policy was "rationally related to community involvement and district identity as it related to tax base in support of district tax levies, and [the] 10 mile limit was reasonable commuting distance and was not arbitrary" (*McClelland v. Paris Public Schools*, 1988, p. 908). It should be noted that although school district residency requirements have been upheld in several states and at the federal level, other states have statutory provisions against school districts imposing such requirements (McCarthy & Cambron-McCabe, 1992).

Health and Physical Requirements

Most states and school districts have adopted some health and physical requirements in an attempt to ensure that employees can meet their contractual obligations as well as to protect the welfare of students and other employees. For example, the U.S. First Circuit Court upheld a school district that required a psychiatric examination as a condition of the continued employment of a principal who had been involved in physical altercations with other administrators and a physical altercation with a child that resulted in criminal charges, and who admitted he was under stress and needed tranquilizers (*Daury v. Smith*, 1988). The courts have also upheld the release or reassignment of employees whose physical condition (e.g., failed eyesight or hearing) have made it impossible for them to meet their contractual duties.

In reviewing health and physical requirements, however, the courts have shown increasing concern that such requirements are not arbitrary and do not violate state and federal laws protecting the rights of the handicapped. For example, Section 504 of the Rehabilitation Act of 1973, which protects "otherwise qualified" handicapped individuals from discrimination, was used as the basis for the 1987 decision of the U.S. Supreme Court in a case involving a teacher with the contagious disease tuberculosis (*Arline v. School Board of Nassau County*, 1987). The court upheld a lower court decision that determined that the physical impairment associated with the disease justified the teacher being considered handicapped within the meaning of the Rehabilitation Act, and that discrimination based solely on the *fear of contamination* is discrimination against the handicapped. The lower court was instructed to determine if the risk of infection precluded the teacher from being otherwise qualified, and if her condition could be reasonably accommodated by the school district. The lower court ultimately found the teacher posed little threat of infection to others, was otherwise qualified, and ordered the teacher reinstated with back pay (*Arline v. School Board of Nassau County*, 1988).

The decision in *Arline* and Section 504 have been relied on by teachers with AIDS to fight alleged discrimination in employment. Although Section 504 does not specify that persons with AIDS are handicapped, several courts have interpreted the statute and related state statutes as protecting AIDS infected persons from employment discrimination (see, e.g., *Racine Unified School District v. LIRC*, 1991, which found persons with AIDS "handicapped" under the Wisconsin Fair Employment Act).

In the lead case, Vincent Chalk, a California teacher of hearing-impaired children, was excluded from the classroom and given an administrative assignment after being diagnosed as having AIDS. The Ninth Circuit Court ordered Chalk reinstated. Under the standard articulated by *Arline*, an otherwise qualified person will lose that status if they do pose a ***significant risk*** of communicating an infectious disease to others. In applying this standard to the Chalk case, the court determined that the overwhelming consensus of medical evidence regarding the nature and transmission of AIDS did not support the conclusion that Chalk posed a significant risk of transmitting the disease to children or others through casual social contact (*Chalk v. United States District Court*, 1988).

A more recent federal statute affecting the health and physical requirements for school employees is the Americans With Disabilities Act of 1990. This act, which went into effect for employers with 25 or more employees in 1992 and with 15 or more employees in 1994, prohibits employment discrimination against "qualified individuals with a disability." Such a person is defined as a person who "satisfies the requisite skill, experience, education, and other job-related requirements of the . . . position . . . and who, with or without reasonable accommodation, can perform the essential functions" of the position. This law, like Section 504, does not require that unqualified persons be hired or retained. But it does go further in prohibiting specific actions of the employer that adversely affect the employment opportunities of disabled persons (e.g., inquiry into disabilities before an offer is made, requiring a medical examination pre-offer, classifying jobs or writing job descriptions on the basis of nonessential functions), as well as requiring employers to make "reasonable accommodation" for a known mental or physical disability.

Competency Testing

Beginning in the early 1980s in response to the emphasis on educational reform and the public's concern about the quality of education and the quality of the teaching force, the number of states involved in teacher testing has increased dramatically. By 1990, 45 states required some form of competency assessment of teachers. Of these, 27 required testing for admission to teacher education programs, and 38 required testing for initial certification. Commercially available tests were used by the majority of states testing for either purpose. The most commonly used test for admissions was the Pre-Professional Skills Test (PPST), and the most commonly used test for certification was the National Teachers Exam (NTE) (Childs & Rudner, 1990).

The use of competency tests as either a prerequisite to initial certification or as a requirement for recertification of practicing educators has generated substantial controversy. The legal question is not whether tests can be used; the Civil Rights Act of 1964 specifically sanctions the use of "professionally developed" tests, as have the courts. Rather, the primary issues that continue to be litigated in regard to teacher testing involve allegations of discrimination in violation of Title VII of the Civil Rights Act of 1964 and unreasonableness in violation of the equal protection clause of the Fourteenth Amendment. In most instances where tests have been used in employment decisions, their use has disqualified proportionately more minorities than nonminorities. In these instances the courts have disallowed the use of tests if it can be shown that they are not significantly related to successful job performance (see, e.g., *Albemarles Paper Company v. Moody*, 1975; *Connecticut v. Teal*, 1982; *Griggs v. Duke Power Company*, 1971). The courts have disallowed testing in a number of school-related cases for this same reason. The state or district was not able to validate the job relatedness of the test being used and, therefore, it could not be shown to be reasonably related to a proper government function (see, e.g., *Chance v. Board of Examiners*, 1972; *Ensley Branch, NAACP v. Seibels*, 1980; *Richardson v. Lamar County Board of Education*, 1989; *United States v. North Carolina*, 1977; *Walston v. County School Board of Nansemond County*, 1974).

In the lead case involving the testing of employees in education, *United States v. South Carolina* (1978), the state conducted content validation studies, pilot tested the test (the NTE), and submitted test items to a panel of expert reviewers. Another review panel set the minimum score, which was then lowered further by the state department of education. When the test was administered, a disproportionate number of blacks, especially those educated in predominantly black institutions, fell short of the minimum score. Upon challenge, the federal district court ruled the validation procedure sufficient to support job relatedness and the test rationally related to a legitimate state purpose: ensuring that certified teachers possess the minimum level of knowledge necessary for effective teaching. The decision was upheld by the U.S. Supreme Court.

In these and other cases where the use of specific tests has been challenged, the courts have shown a concern for not only the Title VII issue of job relatedness but the ultimate use being made of the test scores—whether they are being arbitrarily used or are being used to create unreasonable or arbitrary classifications in violation of the equal protection clause. The Educational Testing Service, the developers of the NTE, the most widely used test of prospective teachers, specifically recommends against the use of arbitrary cutoff scores and the use of the NTE in determining a teacher's retention or tenure. Nevertheless, some states and school districts continue this practice. For example, the state of Georgia began to use a very high score (1225) on the NTE as a qualifier for 6-year teaching certificates that entitled the teacher to higher pay. A federal district court determined that such a high score was unreasonable and that because the state had not conducted any research to validate its use of such a score, the practice was arbitrary and in violation of the equal protection clause (*Georgia Association of Educators v. Nix*, 1976).

In several other cases the state or school district has been successful in articulating a legitimate governmental purpose for the use of test scores for salary purposes. In the South Carolina case previously discussed, the Supreme Court not only affirmed the use of the NTE for certification purposes, but for determination of placement on a salary scale. The Fourth Circuit also upheld a North Carolina school district's determination of salaries based on certification levels that were, in turn, based on NTE scores (*Newman v. Crews*, 1981). Although in both cases disproportionately more blacks were at lower salary levels than whites, the courts found that the practices served the legitimate state purpose of attracting and retaining the most qualified teachers and providing an incentive for teachers to improve their skills, both of which would, in turn, improve the quality of education in the district.

The most recent focus of litigation involving teacher testing, and one that will undoubtedly intensify as the practice increases, is the testing of practicing educators. The testing of practicing educators has been challenged in Arkansas and Texas, two of the first states to implement such programs. The Arkansas testing program, which went into effect in 1985, required that those teachers on the job in 1985 (and not those on leave or subsequently hired) must successfully pass a state-purchased test in order to renew their certificates. Because some individuals would not be up for renewal for 9 years whereas others would be up for renewal in 1 year, the statute was challenged as creating arbitrary classifications among employees (*Standfield v. Turnbow*, 1985). These allegations were rejected by the Chancery Court and the test requirement was upheld. Likewise, the Texas program, which required that both teachers and administrators pass an examination as condition of recertification, was upheld. In response to a suit by those who had failed the exam, the Texas Supreme Court ruled that (1) because the teaching certificate is a license, not a contract, the constitutional prohibition against impairment of contracts is not violated, (2) due process was not violated because teachers were given the right to take the test more than once and were given the right to appeal, and (3) teacher testing is a rational means of achieving the legitimate state purpose of maintaining competent teachers in the public schools (*State of Texas v. Project Principle*, 1987). Additionally, a lower Texas court found no breach of contract or violation of due process where teachers lost their certification for failure to pass the exam (*Swanson v. Houston Independent School District*, 1990), and a federal court, the Fifth Circuit Court of Appeals, found no discrimination against teachers who were dismissed after failing the test (*Fields v. Hallsville Independent School District*, 1991).

The Employment Contract

The general principles of contract law apply to the employment contract. That is, in order for the contract to be valid, it must contain the basic elements of (1) offer and acceptance, (2) legally competent parties, (3) consideration, (4) legal subject matter, and (5) proper form. In addition, the employment contract must meet the specific requirement of applicable state law.

Offer and Acceptance.　In order to be valid a contract must contain an offer by one party and an acceptance by another. Until the party to whom the offer is made accepts the offer (e.g., acceptance cannot be made by a spouse or other relative), the contract is not in force. For this reason it is good practice to require that acceptance be made in writing and within a specified period of time. And until acceptance has been received, unsuccessful candidates should not be notified that the position has been filled.

Legally Competent Parties.　The authority to contract lies exclusively with the school board. The superintendent or other authorized employee may recommend employment, but only the school board may enter into contracts. A school board can enter into contracts only when it is a legally constituted body. That is, contracts issued when a quorum of the board was not present or at an illegally called meeting of the board (e.g., adequate notice was not given) are not valid. In these instances the board is not considered a competent party because it lacks legal status. By the same token, a teacher or other employee who lacks the necessary certification or other requisite conditions is not considered to be a competent party for contractual purposes. Nor are individuals who are mentally ill, impaired by drugs or alcohol, or under duress at the time of entering into the contract.

Consideration.   Consideration is the "cause, motive, price, or impelling influence which induces a contracting party to enter into a contract" (Black, 1983, p. 161). Although school boards have considerable latitude in the matter of employee compensation, they must abide by any state statutes regarding minimum salary levels, and they must abide by the terms of any negotiated contracts. In the absence of any incentive pay program, salaries must be applied uniformly to individuals or groups of individuals who have the same preparation and experience and perform the same duties.

Legal Subject Matter.   In order to be enforceable a contract must pertain to legal subject matter. That is, a contract for the commission of a crime (e.g., the purchase of illegal substances or the performance of illegal services) is not enforceable.

Proper Form.   To be enforceable, the contract must be in the proper form required by law. Most states require that the employment contract be in writing. In the absence of statutory specification, however, an oral agreement that contains all the legal requirements can be legally binding on both parties (McCarthy & Cambron-McCabe, 1992).

The employee's rights and obligations of employment are derived from the contract. It is important, therefore, that the contract be specific and contain all the essential terms of the agreement (Greene, 1971), including rules and regulations of the school district applicable to employment conditions. Nonetheless, the courts have held that all valid rules and regulations of the school board as well as all applicable state statutes are part of the contract, even if not specifically included. However, the school board does have the responsibility to inform employees of its rules and regulations, including not only those in effect at the time of initial employment or at the time of awarding of tenure, but on an ongoing basis as they are revised. This point is especially important because the courts have held that even though a teacher has tenure, each yearly contract is considered a new contract and includes whatever rules and regulations are in effect at the time of the new contract.

Although it is desirable that the contract be specific in stating the terms and conditions of employment, the courts have held that employees may be required to perform certain tasks incidental to classroom activities regardless of whether the contract specifically calls for their performance. These have included such activities as field trips, playground and cafeteria duty, supervision of extracurricular activities, club sponsorship, and bus duty. Teachers cannot, however, be required to drive a bus, perform janitorial duties, or perform duties unrelated to the school program. If an employee refuses to perform extracurricular duties required as a condition of employment, regardless of whether the duties are specified under contract, the court may construe such refusal as an illegal strike or as insubordination justifying removal (Beckham, 1983). For example, in an Alabama case a guidance counselor was dismissed for refusing to perform his assigned rotational supervision duty before school. He maintained that counselors should be exempt from such supervision. The court upheld the dismissal (*Jones v. Alabama State Tenure Commission*, 1981).

Because of the importance of the employment contract, and because it is a legally binding document, it should be prepared and periodically reviewed by the school board attorney (Greene, 1971). If the district is a party to a negotiated labor agreement, the terms of the contract must be reviewed to ensure its compliance with the terms of the negotiated agreement.

Tenure

Tenure is "the status conferred upon teachers who have served a period . . . which then guarantees them continual employment, until retirement, subject to the requirements of good behavior and financial necessity" (Gee & Sperry, 1978, p. T-7). Tenure is a "creation of state statute designed to maintain adequate, permanent, and qualified teaching staffs (*1992 Deskbook Encyclopedia of American School Law*, 1992, p. 193). Because the tenure status (referred to in some states as "continuing" status) is created by state statute, specific provisions vary from state to state. Most statutes specify the requirements and procedures for both obtaining tenure and for dismissing a tenured teacher. (Dismissal of both tenured and nontenured teachers is treated in a later section.) Because tenure is created by the state, the terms of its acquisition and the requisites for dismissal cannot be altered by the local school board.

Tenure statutes normally require a probationary period before the awarding of tenure, usually 3 years. During the probationary period the probationary teacher is issued a term contract valid for a fixed period of time (e.g., 1, 2, or 3 years). Renewal of the contract at the end of the term is at the discretion of the school board. Legal issues surrounding the probationary period primarily have involved questions of what constitutes service during the probationary period and what protections are afforded probationary teachers. Most tenure statutes require "regular and continuous" teaching service during the probationary period. When teachers have spent a part of the probationary period as a guidance counselor, administrator, homebound teacher, social worker, or other position outside the classroom, questions have arisen as to their eligibility for tenure under the "regular" service requirement. Similar issues have arisen when service was as a substitute teacher, was for less than full time, was less than the full school year, or was interrupted by a leave. In deciding each of these cases, the courts have attempted to interpret the state tenure statutes to protect the teacher's rights while maintaining the discretion and flexibility of school officials in the administration of personnel matters. However, since the requirements of the probationary period have been strictly enforced by most courts, it is important that school administrators be aware that in asking or assigning individuals to "other" positions during the probationary period, they could, in fact, be jeopardizing those individuals' eligibility for tenure.

In the absence of a statute to the contrary, school boards may decide not to renew the contract of probationary teachers without giving cause or providing a hearing. However, most states require that the board give timely notice (usually no later than April 1) that the contract will not be renewed. And in no state can the contract be broken during the term of the contract without, at a minimum, a notice of dismissal and a hearing on the causes.

In some states tenure is automatically awarded at the end of the probationary period unless the school board notifies the teacher that he or she will not be rehired. In other states the school board is required to take some affirmative step to award tenure. When school officials fail to follow applicable state laws, the courts will attempt to balance the public policy interests of employing competent and qualified teachers against the rights of the individual. As a result, in a number of cases where the school board did not give timely notice of nonrenewal, the courts have ordered the teacher rehired, but still as a probationary teacher until the proper evaluation and notification takes place. In an equal number of other cases where the school board has failed to follow state tenure laws, the courts have said "it is the school district, not the teacher, that must bear the consequences," and the teacher has been granted tenure status (*Nixon v. Board of Cooperative Educational Services*, 1990, p. 905). However, *de minimis* (trifling, insignificant) violations of policy or state statutes have been decided in favor of school boards.

Another issue related to tenure that often becomes the subject of litigation is the application of tenure laws to permanent positions outside the classroom and to supplementary service appointments. A number of states do identify in statute the areas in which school personnel may acquire tenure. Unless provided by statute, the courts have generally interpreted administrative and supervisory positions to be outside the scope of tenure. On the other hand, the courts generally recognize such nonadministrative positions as guidance counselor, librarian, homebound teacher, or resource room teacher as within the scope of the tenure statutes. There has also been a question of whether teachers whose salaries are funded totally or in part by federal funds fall under teacher tenure statutes. The courts have generally held that they do unless specifically waived in the contract.

The supplementary service appointment most often the subject of efforts to acquire tenure is that of athletic coach. However, the courts have been almost unanimous in declaring supplementary service positions such as coaching as separate from teaching and not eligible for tenure status. In many cases the courts have noted that tenure rights accrue only to employment in certified areas, and thus the lack of a certification requirement of coaching negates the tenure claim (McCarthy & Cambron-McCabe, 1992). In other cases, even when state certification was required, the courts have noted the extracurricular nature of coaching, the awarding of supplementary pay, and the issuance of a separate contract for the coaching assignment as distinguishing it from the teaching assignment (see, e.g., *Lagos v. Modesto City School District*, 1988).

Employees with supplementary service appointments serve at the pleasure of the board and can be dismissed from these positions at any time without any procedural or substantive due process. By the same token, these employees may resign these positions and still maintain the primary teaching contract unless the offer of the teaching contract had been made contingent upon the individual performing specific supplemental duties (e.g., coaching). School administrators who consider offering contingency contracts should consult state statues to determine the status of such contracts in their state. They should also ensure that by combining teaching and coaching positions they are not eliminating the most qualified teachers and that they are not unlawfully discriminating against female applicants.

The awarding of tenure does not guarantee permanent employment. A tenured teacher may be dismissed for disciplinary reasons or as a result of declining enrollments or financial exigencies. Nor does the granting of tenure guarantee the right to teach in a particular school, grade, or subject area. Subject to due process requirements, teachers may be reassigned to any position for which they are certified. In addition, terms of employment (rules and regulations of the school district) different from those in effect at the time tenure was awarded may be imposed upon the teacher as circumstances, needs, and negotiated agreements dictate.

Mandatory Retirement

The federal Age Discrimination in Employment Act (ADEA) of 1967 prohibits mandatory retirement for most employees before age 70. The exception is where the employer can demonstrate that "age is a bona fide occupational qualification reasonably necessary to the normal operation of the particular business." Almost all states have enacted statutes similar to the ADEA, with a number setting no upper age limits. In practice, most school district policies either specify that retirement is mandatory at age 70 or that any continuing contract or tenure status of the teacher shall cease at age 70 and that, thereafter, employment shall be from year to year at the discretion of the school board. On challenge, school boards have been able to justify mandatory retirement as meeting legitimate state objectives. Among the legitimate reasons for early retirement requirements accepted by the courts are reduction in sick leave, reduction in student discipline problems, provision of employment opportunities for younger people and minority group members, employment of individuals with newer ideas and teaching methods, and the need for adequate planning for the future needs of both the district and the employees (see, e.g., *De Shon v. Bettendorf Community School District*, 1979; *King v. Board of Trustees*, 1977; *Palmer v. Ticcione*, 1978).

DUE PROCESS

The term **due process** is found in the Fourteenth Amendment of the U.S. Constitution, which provides that no state shall "deprive any person of life, liberty, or property without due process of law." The two aspects of due process are **procedural,** which guarantees fair procedures, and **substantive,** which protects a person's liberty or property from unfair government seizure or interference (Black, 1983). The essence of due process is to protect against arbitrary and unreasonable action.

Procedural Due Process

Procedural due process is not an absolute right. An individual is entitled to procedural due process only if he or she can show that the government's actions denied "life, liberty, or property." Presuming that life issues are not involved in school district personnel issues, the employee must show a property or liberty interest in order to be constitutionally entitled to procedural due process. In school district employment decisions, the courts have defined a property interest to be a "legitimate entitlement" to continued employment, not merely the desire to remain employed. The granting of tenure can vest a teacher with a property right to continued employment, as can an employment contract. A liberty interest can become a factor in education employment cases if government actions create such a stigma or cause such serious damage to the employee's reputation that it forecloses other employment opportunities. That is, simply because a person is demoted or even dismissed for reasons that are made public would not be enough to support a violation of a liberty interest. The courts have noted that almost any reason that is given for an adverse employment decision is going to cast negatively upon the affected employee. The two-part question is, first, did the employee actually suffer a loss of benefit, such as employment, and, second, did this happen as a result of publicly made charges by the board that resulted in the employee becoming the object of public ridicule or public scorn? (Charges made in a private meeting of the board cannot be said to hold the employee up to public scorn.) A liberty interest can also become involved if governmental actions violate the employee's constitutionally protected rights or if they infringe upon the employee's fundamental rights related to marriage, family, and personal privacy.

Once it has been established that an action requires procedural due process, the central issue becomes what process is due. In arriving at its decision, the court will look to standards of procedural due process embodied in state statutes, state agency or school board regulations, and employment contracts to determine both their propriety and the extent to which they were followed. In those states where state statutes specify due process requirements, the courts will insist upon strict compliance. And when the school district has adopted due process standards related to evaluation and employment decisions, the courts are equally adamant that they be followed. In an Oklahoma case, *Miller v. Independent School District* (1980), the school district had adopted a policy stating that teachers whose contracts would not be renewed would be notified in writing and the reasons for nonrenewal would be given. When a teacher received notice of nonrenewal with no reason given, the court ruled that the teacher was entitled to a statement of reasons if the board had adopted such a policy, even though this was not a requirement of state law.

In determining what due process should be provided in those cases not covered by statute, the courts have noted that no fixed set of procedures is applicable in all situations. Rather, due process entails balancing the individual and governmental interests involved in each situation (Cambron-McCabe, 1983). The Supreme Court (*Mathews v. Eldridge*, 1976) has said that the specific dictates of due process require consideration of three factors:

> (1) the private interest that will be affected by the official action; (2) the risk of an erroneous deprivation of such interest through the procedures used, the probable value, if any,

of additional procedural safeguards; and (3) the Government's interest, including the fiscal and administrative burdens that the additional or substitute procedural requirement would entail. (p. 321)

Applying this standard, it would appear that where limited interests are involved, only minimal procedures are required, whereas the deprivation of more serious interests requires a more extensive, formal process. Generally, the courts have held that an employee facing a severe loss, such as termination of employment, must be ensured the following procedural elements (McCarthy & Cambron-McCabe, 1992):

- ☐ Notification of charges
- ☐ Opportunity for a hearing
- ☐ Adequate time to prepare a rebuttal to the charges
- ☐ Access to evidence and names of witnesses
- ☐ Hearing before an impartial tribunal
- ☐ Representation by legal counsel
- ☐ Opportunity to present evidence and witnesses
- ☐ Opportunity to cross-examine adverse witnesses
- ☐ Decision based on the evidence and findings of the hearing
- ☐ Transcript or record of the hearing
- ☐ Opportunity to appeal an adverse decision. (pp. 381–382)

Notice must not merely be given; it must be timely (on or before an established date) and sufficiently specific to enable the employee to attempt to remediate or to prepare an adequate defense. Although a full evidentiary hearing conforming to all the rules of procedure and evidence is not required, the Supreme Court has ruled that if termination of an employee with property rights is a consideration, a hearing is required prior to termination where the employee is given oral and written notice of the charges, an explanation of the school board's evidence, and an opportunity to respond orally and in writing to the charges and evidence (*Cleveland Board of Education v. Loudermill*, 1985). The purpose of such a hearing is to determine if there are reasonable grounds to believe the charges against the employee are true and support dismissal (Fischer, Schimmel, & Kelly, 1991). Lastly, although the ability of the school board (the employer) to act as an unbiased hearing body when it is a party to the action has been frequently challenged, most courts have upheld this procedure (Alexander & Alexander, 1992).

Substantive Due Process

Substantive due process is somewhat more difficult to ensure than procedural due process. Substantive due process is meant to protect the employee from arbitrary, unreasonable, and discriminatory governmental action as well as vague and unclear policies and guidelines. Substantive due process is often equated with the concept of "just cause." Substantive due process also means that school officials cannot deprive an employee of "life, liberty, or property" unless to do so is necessary to accomplish a legitimate state objective. The provision of substantive due process requires a rational balance of individual and government interests. The Supreme Court has not articulated precise guidelines for properly balancing these interests; rather, the guidelines are constantly being refined by the courts and decisions are made on a case-by-case basis.

DISCRIMINATION

Discrimination on the basis of race, religion, national origin, sex, age, or handicapping condition is prohibited under both federal law and the laws of most states. Allegations of arbitrary and unreasonable actions, not overt discriminatory actions, form the basis of most discrimination suits in education. In order to bring a successful discrimination suit under the equal protection clause of the Fourteenth Amendment of the federal Constitution, claimants must prove that they have been the victims of purposeful discrimination. There must be proof that decision makers actually harbored a desire to discriminate rather than merely being aware that their actions might have discriminatory consequences (*Washington v. Davis*, 1976). Because of the difficulty in proving intentional discrimination, most cases involving allegations of discrimination are brought under Title VII of the Civil Rights Act of 1964 or under other federal laws modeled after Title VII, such as the Age Discrimination in Employment Act of 1967, Section 504 of the Rehabilitation Act of 1973, and, more recently, the Americans With Disabilities Act of 1990. Other statutory guarantees against discrimination in employment are found in the Equal Pay Act and, to a lesser extent, Title IX of the Education Amendments of 1972, both of which prohibit sex-based discrimination. Title VII, the most used statute, prohibits employers of 15 or more employees from discriminating against employees on the basis of race, color, religion, sex, or national origin. It covers many areas of human resources administration including hiring, promotion, compensation, sexual harassment, and conditions of employment. The Equal Employment Opportunity Commission is responsible for enforcing Title VII.

Two types of discrimination claims have traditionally been brought under Title VII. The first claim, **discriminatory treatment,** places the burden of proof squarely on the plaintiff. The plaintiff must first demonstrate a *prima facie* case of discrimination. This requires that the plaintiff show that he or she was a member of a group protected by Title VII and that he or she was treated less favorably than others by a facially neutral employment practice. If the claimant can establish the foregoing facts, the employer can still rebut the claim by articulating a nondiscriminatory reason for the action. This means the employer must show that the action was based on a legitimate business goal. If the employer meets this burden of proof, the burden of proof shifts to the plaintiff to show that the articulated reason is a mere pretext for discriminatory intent. Intent is very difficult to prove. In 1982 the Supreme Court said discriminatory intent can only be established by demonstrating actual motive and cannot be presumed from employment data that show something less than intent (*Pullman-Standard v. Swint*, 1982).

The other type of discrimination claim that may be brought under Title VII is based on employment practices that appear facially neutral but have a **disparate impact** on protected groups. Proof of intent is not necessary to prove discrimination based on disparate impact. A 1989 decision of the Supreme Court, *Wards Cove Packing Co. v. Atonio*, did increase the burden of proof requirement on the plaintiff, but the Civil Rights Act of 1991 restored the burden of proof requirement for disparate impact to those originally articulated under *Griggs v. Duke Power Company* (1971). According to *Griggs* and the Civil Rights Act of 1991, if the claimant can show that an employment practice or policy results in a disparate impact on a protected class, the burden shifts to the employer to demonstrate that the challenged practice or policy is job related and is consistent with business necessity. Although the Civil Rights Act of 1991 did restore the burden of proof to the employer to prove an employment practice is job related and consistent with business necessity, it did not specify exactly what was necessary for the employer to satisfy this requirement, only that it was codifying the business necessity and job related concepts articulated by Supreme Court in *Griggs* and other Court decisions prior to *Wards Cove*. However, since these decisions are not entirely consistent regarding the employer's burden of proof, the courts will undoubtedly formulate these requirements based on their own interpretations of the decisions prior to *Wards Cove*.

Even if the employer does demonstrate a business necessity for the discriminatory practice, it is still possible for the claimant to prevail by showing that the district could serve its interests by means that are not discriminatory. For example, a female applicant for a high school biology teaching position in Arizona filed a sex discrimination suit against the school district on the basis that its requirement that applicants for the teaching position also have the ability to coach varsity softball had a disparate impact on women (*Civil Rights Division v. Amphitheater Unified School District*, 1983). Although the board admitted the coupling of the two positions did have a disparate impact on women, it defended the practice by maintaining that it was a business necessity. In considering this defense, the court maintained that to be successful the district must show compelling business purposes and that there were no acceptable alternative practices or policies available that would better accomplish the business purpose advanced. Because the board was unable to demonstrate that less discriminatory alternatives had been attempted when, in fact, there was substantial evidence that alternatives were available, the appellate court held for the plaintiff and remanded the case to the lower court for a determination of damages.

If an employee is successful in a discrimination complaint, the court may order a stop to the discriminatory practice and order any "such affirmative action as may be appropriate, which may include, but is not limited to reinstatement or hiring of employees, with or without pay," as well as any other "equitable relief" the court may deem appropriate [42 U.S.C. 2000e-5(g)]. Attorneys' fees may also be awarded.

ADVERSE EMPLOYMENT DECISIONS

It is almost inevitable that school administrators will become involved in adverse employment decisions. These decisions include dismissals, suspensions, involuntary transfers and reassignments, demotions, and reduction in force. Not all cases involve disciplinary actions. Decisions may merely result from declining enrollments or other needs of the district that require the shifting of personnel. Whenever adverse employment decisions are contemplated, it is important that the employee be assured due process in the conduct of the action. In fact, the adequacy of the due process procedures provided by school officials is one of the major issues in the litigation involving adverse employment decisions (Cambron-McCabe, 1983).

Dismissal

Possibly the most undesirable task of a school administrator and/or school board is the dismissal of an employee. The impact on the employee's personal and professional life can be devastating. Lengthy proceedings may become costly both to the employee and the district. In controversial cases morale and the relationship between staff, administration, and school board may be negatively affected. Nonetheless, from time to time it seems in the best interest of the school district to dismiss an employee. All states have some statutory provisions regarding teacher dismissal. The reasons specified for dismissal vary from the very general (e.g., "good cause") to the very specific. The reasons most frequently cited in statute are immorality, incompetence, and insubordination. Other commonly cited reasons are neglect of duty, unprofessional conduct or conduct unbecoming a teacher, unfitness to teach, and, the catchall phrase, "other good and just cause." Although traditionally the courts have left the application and definition of each of these reasons to the discretion of the school board, a review of the three most frequently cited concepts will provide some insight into those conditions or behaviors that have sustained judicial scrutiny, as well as the judicial requirements to support a charge.

Immorality. In 38 states school boards are authorized to dismiss teachers on the basis of immorality and/or moral turpitude. Immorality may also be considered under the dismissal for "good and just cause" provided in the other 12 states. Immorality is the most cited ground for dismissal, but legislatures often have been reluctant to define the term ***immorality*** or to discuss its application to specific conduct. Consequently, these tasks have been left to the judiciary. And although the courts acknowledge that the concept of immorality "is subject to ranging interpretations based on shifting social attitudes [and therefore] must be resolved on the facts and circumstances of each case" (*Ficus v. Board of School Trustees of Central School District*, 1987, p. 1,140), a review of cases provides some guidance as to what is deemed to constitute immorality on the part of school employees. Dismissals related to immorality generally are based on one or more of the following categories of conduct: (1) sexual conduct with students; (2) sexual conduct with nonstudents; (3) homosexuality; (4) making sexually explicit remarks or talking about sex unrelated to the curriculum; (5) distribution of sexually explicit materials to classes; (6) use of obscene, profane, or abusive language; (7) possession and use of controlled substances; (8) other criminal misconduct; and (9) dishonesty.

Whereas this listing covers a wide range of behavior, certain standards have evolved from the cases in this area and are generally be applied to other cases involving a dismissal for immorality. First is the ***exemplar standard.*** Although this concept is not as universally accepted today as in the past, the courts do recognize that "a teacher serves as a role model for his student" (*Ambach v. Norwick*, 1979) and, thus, is required to have a higher standard of conduct than that of a noneducator. Second, the vast weight of contemporary judicial decisions in employee dismissal cases says that in order to justify a charge of dismissal there must be a "nexus" or link between the personal conduct of the employee and the teacher's ability to teach, or that the conduct must be shown to have an adverse effect on the school or be the subject of notoriety. About the only offenses not requiring the establishment of a nexus between the conduct and the fitness to teach are sexual misconduct with students and conviction of certain crimes (Delon, 1982). When the nexus is supported by sufficient evidence the dismissal will normally be upheld.

However, because this nexus may exist in one case involving a particular conduct but not in another, school administrators cannot expect to find definitive lists of impermissible or immoral behavior in case law. For example, the dismissal of a teacher in a small, rural town in Montana for living with a fellow teacher was upheld because his cohabitation had become a matter of public discussion in the community and at the school. (In fact, he had told his class that his girlfriend had to move from his home because of complaints by persons in the community.) In the judgment of the court this affected his teaching effectiveness and adversely affected the school and his relationship with students and other employees (*Yanzick v. School District No. 23*, 1982). On the other hand, the dismissal of a Florida teacher for living with her boyfriend was overturned by the courts. In this case the court found no evidence that her actions affected her ability to teach and that her relationship had not been commonly known until the school made the matter public (*Sherburne v. School Board of Swannee County*, 1984). Homosexuality is another area where the circumstances of the particular case very much dictate the ruling of the courts. With the exception of the 1977 Washington Supreme Court ruling in *Gaylord v. Tacoma School District No. 10*, most courts have agreed that homosexuality per se is not grounds for dismissal. However, in cases where public sexual conduct was involved or flaunting of sexual preference was involved, dismissal has been upheld (*Acanfora v. Board of Education*, 1973).

Employees in a number of cases have alleged that their dismissal for alleged immoral conduct infringed upon their constitutional right of privacy. Generally this defense has not been successful if the exercise of this freedom impacts on students. Most of the cases where such a defense has been successful have involved cohabitation, pregnant unwed employees, or when the school district's evidence consisted primarily of rumor and speculation. In cases involving alleged immoral conduct the courts will attempt to balance the employee's personal freedom against the interest of the school board in maintaining a proper educational environment.

Incompetency. Thirty-nine states cite incompetence and/or inefficiency as grounds for dismissal (Delon, 1977). Those conditions or behaviors that have been most successfully sustained as constituting incompetence fall into five general categories: (1) inadequate teaching methodology, (2) lack of knowledge of the subject matter, (3) failure to maintain classroom discipline, (4) physical or mental disability, and (5) willful neglect of duty. As previously stated, substantial evidence must be presented to justify the charge. And although testimony of students and parents is important, the courts pay closest attention to classroom observations by superiors (e.g., principals, curriculum supervisors, etc.) (Alexander & Alexander, 1992). In dismissals for incompetence the courts require that the standard against which the teacher is measured be one used for other teachers in a similar position, not the standard of the "ideal teacher," and that the dismissal be based on a pattern of behavior, not just a single incident. Additionally, a determination should be made as to whether or not the behavior in question is remediable, a notice of deficiency must be given, and a reasonable opportunity to correct the behavior must be provided. Greater discussion of the necessary evaluation, notice, and opportunity to correct is provided in Chapter 7.

Insubordination.   Insubordination is listed as a cause for dismissal in 21 states. A related cause, refusal to obey school board policy, is listed as a separate cause in 20 states (Delon, 1977). Regardless of whether or not it is specified in statute, insubordination is an acceptable cause for dismissal in all states. Among the meanings of insubordination that have been upheld by the courts are (1) refusal to follow established policies and procedures, (2) refusal to obey the direct and lawful orders of school administrators or school boards, (3) unwillingness to cooperate with superiors, (4) unauthorized absence from duty, (5) inappropriate use of corporal punishment, and (6) refusal to accept a school or class assignment. Unlike the charge of immorality, the school district is not required to show a relationship between the alleged insubordinate conduct and the teacher's fitness to teach.

In order to sustain a charge of insubordination the school district must demonstrate a persistent, willful, and deliberate violation of a lawful rule or order emanating from a school authority. If the violation involves an order that is not within the legal right of the school official or school board to issue, the dismissal for insubordination will not stand. In addition, the rule or order must be *reasonable*, clear, and unambiguous. Finally, school employees cannot be dismissed for insubordination for failing to follow rules that violate their constitutional rights (Fischer et al., 1991):

> For example, school rules prohibiting teachers from using certain materials in the classroom may interfere with a teacher's right to academic freedom. School rules limiting what teachers can say or write may also violate their First Amendment right to free speech. (p. 27)

Suspension

The power of the school board to suspend is inherent in the power to discipline employees. (See, e.g., the judgment of the court in *Board of Trustees of Hamilton Heights School Corporation v. Landry*, 1990, upholding the authority of the school board to suspend a teacher for 2 days without pay for removing the glossaries from 146 science textbooks). The types of conduct that can give rise to suspension are generally the same as those for dismissal, though less serious in nature. A few states have statutory provisions related to suspension, but more often they do not. For this reason it is more difficult to define what procedural due process must be provided. However, on the basis of case law, it would appear that professional employees can be suspended for a period of up to 5 days without a hearing. If the suspension is longer than 5 days, then the employee should be afforded a hearing with an opportunity to respond to charges.

Involuntary Transfers, Reassignments, and Demotions

The authority to transfer and reassign is an implied power of school boards. Employees have no common law rights to a specific location, grade assignment, or position and may be transferred to any assignment for which they are qualified by certificate. Whereas the school district has the power to transfer, this power may not be exercised arbitrarily, capriciously, or in violation of proper statutory or school board procedures. For example, when teachers in a Kentucky school district who supported for the school board a candidate opposed by the superintendent were transferred with the sole explanation that the transfers were for "the betterment of the schools," the court determined the transfers to be punitive in nature and ordered the teachers reinstated (*Calhoun v. Cassady*, 1976). Transfers related to a constitutionally or statutorily protected right are also subject to heightened judicial scrutiny.

A major legal issue in transfer and reassignment cases is whether the transfer constitutes a demotion. A transfer or reassignment may be considered a demotion if it (1) results in a reduction in salary or responsibility, (2) requires fewer skills than the previous assignment, or (3) requires a teacher to teach a grade of subject for which he or she is not certified or has not had significant experience in the last 5 years (*Singleton v. Jackson Municipal Separate School District*, 1970). Restrictions relative to transfer, reassignment, and demotion are often contained in statute. Generally, such laws require that proper notice and a hearing be provided. This does not mean that transfers or reassignments that are in fact demotions cannot be effected. Demotions may be lawfully accomplished for two purposes: efficient management of available resources (i.e., in the face of declining enrollments or other loss of revenue problems) and discipline of the employee (Valente, 1987). Disciplinary transfers that are not arbitrary, capricious, or in violation of the employee's statutory or constitutional rights will be upheld.

The transfer or reassignment of administrators is somewhat different from that of teachers. Since administrators generally serve at the will of the board, in most states their transfer can be made arbitrarily, with no notice, reason, or hearing afforded. Principals and other administrators who have challenged transfers from larger to smaller schools, from senior high schools to junior high schools, or from one administrative position to another (e.g., coordinator of an alternative school) or to the classroom have generally been unsuccessful. They might get a favorable judgment if (1) there has been a reduction in salary, (2) state statute provides for tenure as an administrator, (3) there are contractual provisions to the contrary, (4) state or locally mandated due process procedures were violated, or (5) there has been an abuse of discretion.

Reduction in Force (RIF)

Declining enrollments, school reorganizations or consolidations, financial exigency, curriculum changes, and other reasons often result in a reduction in the total number of employees needed by the district and the release of excess employees. Forty-two states have some form of statutory RIF provisions that address the proper reasons, the order of release, and the order of reinstatement. Some statutes also provide detail as to the procedures to be followed and the protections afforded teachers. These same issues are often addressed in school board policies and collective bargaining agreements.

The legal challenges to such actions usually involve two issues: whether the abolition of each position is bona fide and whether the release of the particular individual is justified. As a general rule, an employee has no right to a position no longer deemed necessary by the district. In fact, unless required by state statute, school board policies, or collective bargaining contract, the courts have most often held that employees released because of position abolition are not entitled to a hearing. The courts generally consider these dismissals to be impersonal, in no way impugning the teacher personally and, therefore, outside the scope of teacher termination statutes. However, the reasons articulated by the district must be reasonable and supported by substantial evidence (Valente, 1987). For example, when the position of a district business officer who had a longstanding dispute with the superintendent was "excessed" and the board showed no budgeting need for eliminating the position, the court determined that the excessing was being used to resolve a disciplinary problem and ordered the employee reinstated with back pay (*Green v. Board of Education*, 1980).

Unlike other terminations, the burden of proof for RIF is on the plaintiff to show the stated reason to be a subterfuge for an impermissible basis (e.g., discrimination, union activity, or exercise of constitutional rights). In the absence of evidence to the contrary, the courts presume that the board acted in good faith and with permissible motives (McCarthy & Cambron-McCabe, 1992; Zirkel, 1983). Neither does the board need to prove that it made the perfect decision in regard to a particular set of circumstances, only that the relevant evidence supports the board's decision as being rational, not arbitrary or capricious (*Palmer v. Board of Trustees*, 1990).

The abolition of the position must also be real. The abolition of the position, with the accompanying release of an employee, followed by filling the same position with a new employee under a new job title does not constitute a legally permissible release.

The RIF process may not be used as a means to circumvent state tenure laws. When a Massachusetts school board dismissed a tenured teacher, citing declining enrollments and budgetary constraints imposed by Proposition $2\frac{1}{2}$ and then rehired nontenured teachers for positions for which the tenured teacher was certified to teach, the court ruled that the district was using the statutory RIF authority granted it as a subterfuge to dismiss a tenured teacher without citing charges or providing a hearing (*Sherman v. School Committee of Whitman*, 1988).

The second issue, who should be released, involves questions of preference and has been the subject of the majority of litigation related to "RIFing." State statutes, school board policies, and employment contracts often specify the order of release in terms of tenure, seniority, or other criteria, as well as the procedures to be followed (notice, appeal, etc). When preference and due process requirements are articulated, the courts will require that they be followed. When statutes, policies, or agreements are silent or ambiguous about order of release, the courts almost unanimously have accorded qualified tenured teachers priority over nontenured teachers in similar positions. Certification has been the major, but not the exclusive, criterion considered by the courts in determining "qualifiedness." Between tenured teachers holding similar positions or between nontenured teachers holding similar positions, seniority has been the primary, but not the exclusive, factor in determining order of release. Absolute seniority preference may be qualified by other factors such as performance evaluations, affirmative action goals (see *Wygant v. Jackson Board of Education*, 1986), and collective bargaining agreements.

The order of recall of RIFed employees, should vacancies arise for which they are *qualified*, is roughly the inverse of the order of release. That is, qualified tenured teachers would be called back before qualified nontenured teachers, in the order of seniority rank within each group. The courts have been fairly unanimous in affirming that neither tenure nor seniority provides an absolute right to recall over certification or other evidence of qualifiedness.

SUMMARY

Perhaps no other aspect of public school administration is subject to the plethora of rules, regulations, and legal mandates that govern human resources administration. Every aspect of the employment relationship has been subjected to legislative pronouncements and judicial interpretation. The courts have upheld the right of state governments and local school districts to specify terms and conditions of employment. One of these conditions, the passing of a competency test, has generated substantial controversy as the practice has spread to almost every state. Whereas the testing of teachers has been upheld by the courts, in those situations where the tests have not been job related or where test scores have been used arbitrarily or used to create unreasonable or arbitrary classifications, the courts have disallowed their use.

The major issue litigated in adverse employment decisions is the extent to which adequate due process was provided. The more severe the action and the more serious the individual interests involved, the more extensive and more formal is the due process required. The procedures to be followed in the dismissal of a tenured employee are more extensive than those required for the dismissal of a nontenured employee. However, employees who are RIFed are generally not entitled to a hearing, because the courts consider their dismissals to be impersonal, in no way impugning the teacher personally and, therefore, outside the scope of teacher termination statutes.

Although the specific laws related to personnel administration vary somewhat from state to state, the basic legal concepts, especially those designed to protect individual rights and ensure fairness and reasonableness, are common to all jurisdictions. A failure by the school district to adhere to these concepts leaves it vulnerable to a charge of arbitrary and capricious conduct.

DISCUSSION QUESTIONS

1. List the terms and conditions of employment that are most often affected by state statutory and regulatory provisions. For each area, discuss the basis and/or the purpose for the requirement.

2. There are two elements of due process. Define each element and discuss what protection it affords school district employees.

3. All states have some statutory provisions regarding teacher dismissal or revocation of a certificate. What are the statutory provisions in your state? How do these compare with those most frequently cited in other states' statutes? What policies has your district adopted regarding RIFing of teachers and administrators?

CASE 9.1
I Prefer Whiterock, But . . .

The Whiterock School District has had a great deal of trouble securing a permanent, certified teacher of the severely mentally handicapped. They advertised in the major educational publications in circulation in the state and attended the recruitment "round-ups" at the six institutions in the state that prepare special educators. Nonetheless, only two people applied for the position. Of the two, by far the most attractive was Mark Thompson, a graduating senior at State University. His grades were excellent, as were his references. Mark had not passed the state certification exam, but was scheduled to take the exam in late May.

An invitation to interview was extended to both Mark and Susan Lewis, the other applicant. Susan interviewed on May 3 and Mark on May 16, the Monday after his graduation. Following his exit meeting with James McGee, the director of human resources, and Nancy Kirch, the principal of the school where the vacancy existed, they informed Mark that they would recommend at the next school board meeting that he be offered the position. They reminded him, however, that the offer would be contingent upon his passing the exam and becoming certified. Mark was excited by their announcement and assured them he would pass the exam and would be sending

them a copy of the test results and certificate as soon as they arrived. He said he wanted the position and would be looking forward to getting the board's offer. On June 3 the school board met and voted to extend an offer to Mark.

On June 6 Mark called Mr. McGee to say that he had not been able to take the exam because he had broken his foot two days before the exam while playing softball in a church-sponsored softball league. The exam would not be offered again until July 15, but Mark assured Mr. McGee that he had already made application to take the exam at that time. Mr. McGee asked Mark if he had received the board offer yet, and Mark said yes and that he would return it along with his test result. Mr. McGee told him he did not need to wait for the test results, that in fact he should notify the board of his acceptance within the next couple of weeks.

When Mr. McGee had not received the written acceptance by July 1, he called Mark and was assured by Mark that he would put it in the mail that very day. On July 6 Mark called Mr. McGee and told him that he had just received an offer from another district for $4,000 more than the Whiterock offer. Mark shared that he really prefers Whiterock, but that the additional $4,000 would make a big difference in his ability to pay off his student loans.

Questions

1. Balancing the district's need and Mark's actions thus far, what should Mr. McGee do? What options are there for making the Whiterock offer more competitive?
2. Is there a breach of contract if Mark accepts the second offer or if Whiterock withdraws its offer to Mark and makes one to Susan?
3. Suppose you offer the position to Susan. Would you be honest with her regarding the circumstances that have led to the belated offer? If Susan rejects the offer, how should the district proceed?
4. Is there an issue of professional ethics that should be reported to the state certification board or state board of education?
5. Some districts send a prospective teacher an "intent to hire" letter. How binding is this type of offer on a school district? on the prospective teacher?

CASE 9.2
Lot's Wife

Phil Harris, principal of Eastwater High School received the following anonymous note: "You should see what goes on in the coaches' showers after swim practice. Jim Murphy and Elaine Lorenzo are sinners. Fornicators and adulterers have no place in this district." Within the next 2 weeks several more notes arrived alleging the same thing. The last one added, "If you don't do something about this, you are as much a sinner as they are and I will see that the school board destroys you as surely as God destroyed Lot's wife for looking upon the evil of Sodom." The notes had all been delivered through school mail, so Mr. Harris assumes the sender is someone within the school system.

Before the matter goes any further, Mr. Harris feels compelled to meet with Jim and Elaine to share the essence of the letters with them. They both vehemently deny the allegations. However, they do admit that on three occasions they had both used the female coaches' showers after practice because of building repairs where the male coaches' showers are located.

Questions

1. Should Mr. Harris have confronted Jim and Elaine based on anonymous allegations? How else might he have responded? What type of investigation, if any, should take place now?
2. Based on the evidence thus far, what disciplinary action, if any, should be taken on Jim Murphy and Elaine Lorenzo?
3. If you were Jim or Elaine, how would you respond to the allegations? Would you hire an attorney? Have their rights to privacy been violated?

CASE 9.3
A Gun in Class

On January 25, 1988, Robert T., a sixth-grade student, brought a loaded revolver into the class of Mr. Chaddock, a language arts teacher. Mr. Chaddock asked Robert to give him the gun and Robert refused. He then opened a drawer and asked Robert to put the gun in the drawer, but Robert again refused to give up the gun. Mr. Chaddock then decided to go on with class. He felt he knew Robert well enough to know that Robert would not deliberately do anything to hurt his classmates and that violence would occur only if Robert felt threatened. Toward the end of the class, the principal, who had heard that Robert had a gun, sent for him to come to her office. When she demanded that he give her the gun, Robert aimed it at her and told her to get away from him, and then he ran from the school.

At a dismissal hearing stemming from the incident, Mr. Chaddock defended his actions by stating that because there was no school policy on handling such situations he had to rely on his instincts. West Virginia statute states that dismissal must be reasonable based on one of the just causes listed: immorality, incompetency, cruelty, insubordination, intemperance, or willful neglect of duty, none of which are defined.

Questions

1. How should Mr. Chaddock have acted? Should Mr. Chaddock be dismissed? Under which clause could he be dismissed?
2. What about the principal? To what extent did the action taken by the principal in calling the student from the class to come to her office endanger the safety of others? What, if anything, might she be

charged with? What disciplinary action, if any, should be taken in regard to her conduct?

3. Who is responsible for ensuring that the school district had a policy covering the now all-too-common situation of students bringing guns to school? Had someone been injured, what parties should be held responsible?

This case study is based on an actual court case, *Board of Education of County of Gilmer v. Chaddock*, 398 S.E.2d 120 (W. Va. 1990).

REFERENCES

Acanfora v. Board of Education, 359 F. Supp. 843 (D. Md. 1973).

Albemarles Paper Company v. Moody, 422 U.S. 405 (1975).

Alexander, K., & Alexander, M. D. (1992). *American public school law* (3rd ed.). St. Paul: West.

Ambach v. Norwick, 441 U.S. 68 (1979).

Arline v. School Board of Nassau County, 772 F.2d 759 (11th Cir. 1985), aff'd, 480 U.S. 273 (1987).

Arline v. School Board of Nassau County, 692 F. Supp. 1286 (M.D. Fla. 1988).

Beckham, J. (1983). Critical elements of the employment relationship. In J. Beckham & P. A. Zirkel (Eds.), *Legal issues in public school employment* (pp. 1–21). Bloomington, IN: Phi Delta Kappa.

Black, H. C. (1983). *Black's law dictionary*. St. Paul, MN: West.

Board of Trustees of Hamilton Heights School Corporation v. Landry, 560 N.E.2d 102 (Ill. App. Ct. 1990).

Calhoun v. Cassady, 534 S.W.2d 806 (Ky. 1976).

Cambron-McCabe, N. H. (1983). Procedural due process. In J. Beckham & P. A. Zirkel (Eds.), *Legal issues in public school employment* (pp. 78–97). Bloomington, IN: Phi Delta Kappa.

Cascio, W. F. (1987). *Applied psychology in personnel management* (3rd ed.). Reston, VA: Reston.

Chalk v. U.S. District Court Central District of California, 840 F.2d 701 (9th Cir. 1988).

Chance v. Board of Examiners, 458 F.2d 1167 (2d Cir. 1972).

Childs, R. A., & Rudner, L. M. (1990). *State testing of teachers: the 1990 report*. Washington, DC: American Institute for Research.

Civil Rights Division of the Arizona Department of Law v. Amphitheater Unified School District No. 10, 680 P.2d 517 (Ariz. 1983).

Cleveland Board of Education v. Loudermill, 470 U.S. 532 (1985).

Connecticut v. Teal, 457 U.S. 440 (1982).

Daury v. Smith, 842 F.2d 9 (1st Cir. 1988).

Delon, F. G. (1977). *Legal controls on teacher conduct: Teacher discipline*. Topeka, KS: National Organization on Legal Problems of Education.

Delon, F. G. (1982). *Legal issues in the dismissal of teachers for personal conduct*. Topeka, KS: National Organization on Legal Problems of Education.

De Shon v. Bettendorf Community School District and Board of Education of the Bettendorf Community School District, 284 N.W.2d 329 (Iowa 1979).

Ensley Branch, NAACP v. Seibels, 616 F.2d 812 (5th Cir. 1980), cert. denied, 449 U.S. 1061 (1980).

Ficus v. Board of School Trustees of Central School District of Green County, 509 N.E.2d 1137 (Ind. App. 1 Dist. 1987).

Fields v. Hallsville Independent School District, 906 F.2d 1017 (5th Cir. 1990), *cert. denied*, 111 S.Ct. 676 (1991).

Fischer, L., Schimmel, D., & Kelly, C. (1991). *Teachers and the law* (3rd ed.). New York: Longman.

Flanary v. Barrett, 143 S.W. 38 (Ky. 1912).

Floyd County Board of Education v. Slone, 307 S.W.2d 912 (Ky. 1957).

Gaylord v. Tacoma School District No. 10, 559 P.2d 1340 (Wash. 1077), *cert. denied*, 434 U.S. 879 (1977).

Gee, E. G., & Sperry, D. J. (1978). *Education law and the public schools: A compendium.* Boston: Allyn & Bacon.

Georgia Association of Educators, Inc., v. Nix, 407 F. Supp. 1102 (N.D. Ga. 1976).

Grand Prairie Independent School District v. Vaughn, 792 S.W.2d 944 (Tex. 1990).

Green v. Board of Education of the City School District of New York, 433 N.Y.S.2d 434 (App. Div. 1980).

Greene, J. E. (1971). *School personnel administration.* New York: Chilton.

Griggs v. Duke Power Company, 410 U.S. 924 (1971).

Jones v. Alabama State Tenure Commission, 408 So.2d 145 (Ala. Civ. App. 1981).

King v. Board of Trustees, Monahans-Wickett-Pyote Independent School District, 555 S.W.2d 925 (Texas 1977).

Lagos v. Modesto City Schools District, 843 F.2d 347 (9th Cir. 1988).

Mathews v. Eldridge, 424 U.S. 319 (1976).

McCarthy, M. M., & Cambron-McCabe, N. H. (1992). *Public school law: Teachers' and students' rights* (3rd ed.). Boston: Allyn & Bacon.

McClelland V. Paris Public Schools, 742 S.W.2d 907 (Ark. 1988).

Miller v. Independent School District No. 56, 609 P.2d 756 (Okla. 1980).

1992 Deskbook encyclopedia of American school law. (1992). Rosemount, MN: Data Research, Inc.

Newman v. Crews, 651 F.2d 222 (4th Cir. 1981).

Nixon v. Board of Cooperative Educational Services of Sole Supervisory District of Steuben-Allegheny Counties, 564 N.Y.S.2d 903 (App. Div. 1990).

Palmer v. Board of Trustees of Crook County School District No. 1, 785 P. 2d 1160 (Wyo. 1990).

Palmer v. Ticcione, 576 F.2d 459 (2d Cir. 1978).

Pittsburgh Federation of Teachers Local 400 v. Aaron, 417 F. Supp. 94 (Pa. 1976).

Pullman-Standard v. Swint, 456 U.S. 273 (1982).

Racine Unified School District v. Labor and Industry Review Commission, 476 N.W.2d 707 (Wis. App. 1991).

Richardson v. Lamar County Board of Education, 729 F. Supp. 806 (M.D. Ala. 1989).

Sherburne v. School Board of Swannee County, 455 So.2d 1057 (Fla. Dist. Ct. App. 1984).

Sherman v. School Committee of Whitman, 522 N.E.2d 433 (Mass. App. Ct. 1988).

Singleton v. Jackson Municipal Separate School District, 419 F.2d 1211 (5th Cir. 1970).

Sorenson v. School District No. 28, 418 P.2d 1004 (Wyo. 1966).

Standfield v. Turnbow, Chancery Court of Pulaski County, Arkansas, March 22, 1985.

State of Texas v. Project Principle, Inc., 724 S.W.2d 387 (Tex. 1987).

Swanson v. Houston Independent School District, 800 S.W.2d 630 (Tex. Ct. App. 1990).

United States v. North Carolina, 400 F. Supp. 343 (E.D.N.C. 1975), vacated 425 F. Supp. 789 (E.D.N.C. 1977).

United States v. South Carolina, 445 F. Supp. 1094 (D.S.C. 1977), aff'd 434 U.S. 1026 (1978).

Valente, W. D. (1987). *Law in the schools* (2nd ed.). New York: Merrill/Macmillan.

Walston v. County School Board of Nansemond County, 492 F.2d 919 (4th Cir. 1974).

Wards Cove Packing Company v. Atonio, 490 U.S. 642 (1989).

Washington v. Davis, 426 U.S. 229 (1976).

Wygant v. Jackson Board of Education, 106 S.Ct. 1842 (1986).

Yanzick v. School District No. 23, Lake County Montana, 641 P.2d 431 (Mont. 1982).

Zirkel, P. A. (1983). The law on reduction in force: An overview and update. In J. Beckham & P. A. Zirkel (Eds.), *Legal issues in public school employment* (pp. 171–195). Bloomington, IN: Phi Delta Kappa.

10

Collective Negotiations in Education

R ebore (1991) has commented that "collective negotiations has become a way of life in American education" (p. 292). Human resources administration has been influenced by collective negotiations in two distinct ways: The process of collective negotiations has impacted upon virtually every process and activity within the human resources function; and the human resources unit generally has assumed a major role in the administration of the collective negotiations process itself. Although collective negotiation approaches vary, the process is entrenched as a common practice in school systems today. Ways (1979) underlined the usefulness of negotiations in his statement that

> Despite its limitations, abuses, and hazards, negotiation has been an indispensable process in free societies. More effective than any alternative anybody has thought of so far, it enables us to realize common interests while we compromise conflicting interests. Since these are among the basic objectives of rational people, negotiation has to be counted among the greatest of human inventions. (p. 90)

As reported by Compton-Forbes (1984), since 1960 approximately 36 states and the District of Columbia have enacted some type of legislation regarding bargaining in the public sector. School superintendents and human resources directors consider collective bargaining among the most significant issues and challenges in education (Cunningham & Hentges, 1982; McCoy, Gips, & Evans, 1983; Norton, 1989).

Many factors have promoted increased activities in collective negotiations in education. The 1961 teachers' strike in New York City was a significant breakthrough. As a result of this strike, the American Federation of Teachers (AFT) was given the right to represent numerous bargaining units that previously had been negotiated individually. Other contributing factors that encouraged the growth of negotiations in education are discussed later in this chapter. This chapter also examines the evolution of negotiations in education, discusses the negotiation responsibilities of the human resources office, considers the impact of collective negotiations upon education, presents the legal aspects of negotiations, and discusses the collective negotiations process in detail.

COLLECTIVE NEGOTIATIONS DEFINED

In the early 1960s considerable effort was made to differentiate professional negotiations in education from collective bargaining in the private sector. The euphemism **professional negotiations** was viewed as the more appropriate term for practicing professional educators, whereas **collective bargaining** was more descriptive of the frequently bitter disputes between management and labor in business and industry. The original use of the term *professional negotiations* was intended to remove school boards and teachers from negotiations under the precedents provided by collective bargaining in the private sector.

In the late 1960s the term **collective negotiations** became popular in education. Specific legislation within the various states often defined what was meant by the terms *collective negotiations, collective bargaining, school board agreements, professional and employee relations, labor agreement discussion, meet and confer,* and others. For the purposes of this chapter, the terms **collective bargaining** and **collective negotiations** are synonymous. Other terms such as *distributive bargaining, integrative bargaining, win-win bargaining, win-lose bargaining,* and *lose-lose bargaining* are found in contemporary literature; each will be discussed later in the chapter.

Myron Lieberman and Michael Moskow (1966), early authorities in the area, defined *collective negotiations* as "a process whereby employees as a group and the employers make offers and counter offers in good faith on conditions of their employment relations for the purpose of reaching mutually acceptable agreement" (p.1). The American Association of School Administrators (Redfern, 1967) defined *collective bargaining* as

> the process by which teachers, through their designated representatives, negotiate with the board of education, or its designated representative(s), with reference to salary, working conditions and other matters of interest to negotiation practices. Collective bargaining and professional negotiations sometimes are used interchangeably. (p. 112)

Professional negotiations became the official policy of the National Education Association (NEA) at the 1962 Denver Convention. The NEA (1965) defined negotiations as

> a set of procedures, written and officially adopted by the local association and the school board, which provides an orderly method for the school board and the local association to negotiate, through professional channels, on matters of mutual concern, to reach agreement on these matters, and to establish educational channels for mediation and appeal in event of impasse. (p. 1)

Approximately 25 years later, the NEA passed the following resolution at its 1991 NEA Representative Assembly (NEA, 1991).

COLLECTIVE BARGAINING RIGHTS

> The National Education Association believes that the attainment and exercise of collective bargaining rights are essential to the promotion of school employee and student needs in society. The Association demands that these rights be advocated when they are now abridged or denied and strengthened where they are now secured. (p. 21)

The broadening scope of the negotiations process is reflected in the following definition by Van Fleet (1991): "Collective bargaining is negotiating a written contract covering all relevant aspects of the relationships among the organization and members of a union" (p. 636). Schoonmaker (1989) notes that "good negotiation produces two types of desirable results: Objective and psychological" (p. 6). That is, good objective results are when both parties realize their priorities while offering concessions to the other party. Schoonmaker's concept of good psychological results means that both parties are pleased about the results of negotiations and with the process used for reaching the agreement.

Regardless of the differences in phrasing of definitions, the process of collective negotiations most often is based upon the following concepts and procedures.

1. Employees have the right to form, join, and participate in the activities of organizations of their choosing for the purpose of representation on matters of employment relations.
2. An association has the right to request exclusive representation in negotiations when the majority of the employee membership so authorizes.
3. Representatives of the local association and the board of education meet to negotiate on matters relating to salaries, fringe benefits, and working conditions as set forth in cooperatively established ground rules or as set forth by law.
4. Recommendations (agreements) of the negotiation representatives, when ratified by the groups that they represent, result in the contractual agreements for the time period specified.
5. Failure to reach an agreement leads to impasse, in which case, established appeal procedures are implemented to reach a settlement.

For the purposes of this chapter, *collective negotiations* is considered to be the process whereby matters of employee relations are determined mutually by representatives of employee groups and their employer, within the limits of law or mutual agreement. Negotiations, under this definition, can occur under distributive or integrative approaches. These approaches are discussed in a later section of the chapter.

HISTORICAL PERSPECTIVES: BARGAINING BY EMPLOYEE GROUPS

The process of collective negotiations in education has evolved over several decades. Developments that have had an impact upon both the unity of employee groups and the legal pathways for negotiations in the public sector are outlined in Figure 10.1.

THE GROWTH OF NEGOTIATIONS IN EDUCATION

By 1857 there were 15 state teachers' associations including those in New York, Rhode Island, and Massachusetts, which had organized in 1845 (Wesley, 1957). In that year the National Teachers Association (NTA) was organized. In 1870 NTA merged with the Normal School Association and the National Association of School Superintendents to form the NEA. Later, in 1916, the AFT was established. The competition for membership between the NEA and AFT escalated efforts to serve the

1806	*Philadelphia Cordwainers Case:* Employee groups were found guilty of conspiracy to raise their wages. Any such organized action was declared illegal by the courts.
1842	*Commonwealth v. Hunt:* In a decision relating to the use of group action by employees, the Supreme Court of Massachusetts ruled that labor organizations did not constitute unlawful bodies by the mere fact that they represented a combination of individuals or bodies. This decision enhanced group action by employees.
1845	First state association of teachers and school officials was established in Massachusetts.
1857	National Teachers Association (NTA) is founded.
1870	National Education Association (NEA) is founded.
1886	American Federation of Labor (AFL) is founded.
1886	Federal regulation of interstate commerce is established. Federal legislation passed to regulate interstate commerce proved to provide important support to union activity. This legislation served as the legal rationale for federal government intervention in disputes between management groups and employees on an interstate basis.
1890	*Sherman Antitrust Act:* The act expanded to find labor unions guilty of conspiracy to restrain trade by striking.
1914	*Clayton Act:* The act removed unions from application of antitrust laws. However, the United States Supreme Court applied antitrust laws until much later.
1926	*Railroad Labor Act:* The act represented a major step in the support of collective bargaining through legislation. Its constitutionality was reinforced 4 years later in a ruling by the Supreme Court.
1932	*Norris-LaGuardia Act:* The act supported the right of employees to form unions and placed restrictions on the courts concerning the issuance of injunctions to restrict labor activities. Refusal by employers to bargain with representatives of employee groups was determined to be an unfair labor practice and subject to punishment by law.
1935	*National Labor Relations Act (Wagner Act):* Congress established the right of employees to bargain with their employers on matters pertaining to wages, job-related benefits, and conditions of employment. The act concerned employees in the private sector only and excluded public employees. Most agree, however, that this act has affected employer-employee contract relations more significantly than any legislation passed to date. Even though the Wagner Act applied only to interstate commerce, it confirmed certain employee rights in the area of collective bargaining.

FIGURE 10.1

Developments Impacting Employee Unity and Collective Negotiations (pp. 280–283)

1938   *Educational Policies Commission:* The commission stated that the entire
        staff should take part in the formulation of the educational process.

1947   *Labor Mangement Relations Act (Taft-Hartley Act):* This act provided further
        expansion and clarification of employee rights in the bargaining process.
        Although the act applied only to interstate commerce, its influence on
        legislation in the individual states and upon bargaining in the public sector
        was far-reaching. Employee-employer bargaining under the Taft-Hartley
        Act is summarized as follows:

   1. Collective bargaining is the performance of the mutual obligation of the
      employer and the representative of the employees to meet at reasonable
      times and confer in good faith with respect to wages, hours, and other
      terms and conditions of employment.
   2. Collective bargaining also includes negotiation of an agreement or any
      question arising there-under and the execution of a written contract
      incorporating any agreement reached if requested by either party.
   3. Such an obligation (to bargain) does not compel either party to agree to
      a proposal or to require the making of a concession (Labor Management
      Relations Act, 1947).

1955   Merger of American Federation of Labor (AFL) and Congress of Industrial
        Organizations (CIO): Unionization was a powerful movement and an
        effective influence for bargaining in the private sector.

1959   *Labor Management Reporting and Disclosure Act (Landrum-Griffin Act):* The
        act established more effective controls over the operations and funds of
        unions. Governance practices such as voting rights, participation in union
        affairs, and the right to sue in case of rights' violations were covered by the
        act. Financial reporting procedures, open or public expense accounting,
        election of union officers, and "democratic practices" were also included.
        Teacher organizations were excluded; however, the influence of the
        Landrum-Griffin Act upon public employee groups has been significant.

1959   Wisconsin became the first state to enact legislation pertaining to
        negotiations in the public sector. A state labor relations board was
        established to oversee the administration of the act and assist in the
        resolution of disputes.

1962   *American Federation of Teachers (AFT) Victory:* AFT Local No. 2 won the
        right to represent employees of the New York City public schools. This
        victory pushed the NEA to historical action at its Denver Convention in
        1962.

FIGURE 10.1
continued

1962   *Denver Convention of the NEA:* This convention marked the beginning of NEA's official position on professional negotiations for teachers. Resolution 18 modified a 1961 resolution that called for the right of professional education associations "to participate in the determination of policies of common concern and other conditions for professional service (NEA, 1961, pp. 216–217). Resolution 18, however, included NEA's first official reference to the term *professional negotiations.* The 1962 resolution set forth such strong wording as "the NEA insists on the right of professional associations through democratically selected representatives using professional channels to participate with boards of education in determination of policies of common concern including salary and other conditions for professional service" (NEA, 1962, p. 178).

1962   *Presidential Executive Order 10988:* The executive order by President John Kennedy opened the door for bargaining for federal employees. The order had significant effects on bargaining movements in the entire public sector. E.O. 10988 provided federal workers the right to join organizations of choice, provided for the recognition of organizations for purposes of negotiations, required the agency to meet and confer with recognized employee organizations with respect to personnel policies and conditions of work, and established advisory arbitration of grievances in relation to agreements reached. As a result, government employee unions flourished. The order encouraged similar actions by local and state government employees to win negotiation rights as well.

1965–
1968   *Professional negotiations agreements:* By 1965 an estimated 388 professional negotiations agreements in 35 states had been filed with the NEA. During 1967 and 1968 approximately 900,000 teachers were working under an estimated 2,200 agreements with at least some form of minimal formal acknowledgment of the existence of a teacher organization in the district (NEA, 1968). Professional negotiation legislation was passed in Oregon, Washington, Connecticut, California and Massachusetts.

1969   *Presidential Executive Order 11491:* President Richard Nixon's order was designed to bring labor relations in closer relationship to practices in the private sector. The order modified and expanded the earlier order by President Kennedy. E.O. 11491 established exclusive recognition in the bargaining process, required the inclusion of a grievance procedure, established the Federal Labor Relations Council to interpret the provisions of the order, and established the Federal Service Impasse Panel. The order tended to lend additional support for legislation concerning collective negotiations in the public sector, including teacher groups.

FIGURE 10.1
continued

1980–
1990   By 1980, 32 states had enacted collective bargaining laws that
        encompassed some or all categories of educational employees in the
        public sector. This count includes those states with "permissive legislation"
        whereby the employing agency could enter into contract discussions with
        employees, but such an action was not required. Peterson, Rossmiller, and
        Volz (1978) cite the case of the *Norwalk Teachers Association v. Board of
        Education* in noting that "in the absence of a statute either authorizing or
        prohibiting collective bargaining by teachers the prevailing view today
        seems to be that teachers have that right" (p. 432).

FIGURE 10.1
continued

welfare of teachers and resulted in the acceleration of negotiation activities in education. Walter (1975) described the ultimate results of the AFT and NEA competition as
follows:

> While the competition was at its strongest [for membership] and under the press of that
> competition, the NEA became a different organization. Its teachers clearly became the
> dominant power, and administration affiliates became much less influential. By the end of
> the sixties, fewer important differences remained between AFT and NEA. (p. 16)

According to a report of the U.S. Department of Labor, the membership of the
NEA in 1990 was 1.5 million, and that of the AFT numbered .5 million. Their combined membership represented over 80% of the nation's total number of teachers.

By 1947 NEA resolutions on negotiations reflected a growing concern for the
improvement of the economic conditions of teachers. Yet an NEA resolution in 1960,
suggesting that "representative negotiations are compatible with the ethics and dignity of the teaching profession," was soundly defeated (Carlton & Goodwin, 1969, p.
36). In the following year, however, the NEA enacted a policy stating specifically that
professional education associations "should be accorded the right ... to participate
(with school boards) in the determination of policies of common concern, including
salaries" (Carlton & Goodwin, 1969, p. 36). In 1962 at its Denver Convention, the
NEA set forth its policy on negotiations by stating that the NEA "insists" on the right
to negotiate with boards of education.

Negotiations in education developed rapidly following this official stand by the
NEA. Professional bargaining procedures in the private sector generally served as the
blueprint for negotiations in education. Even though the process of negotiations historically has been criticized and questioned by some as inappropriate for education,
by 1965 the die had been cast and by 1968 negotiations had become an acceptable
and expected practice in the field of education.

Other developments or conditions that served to foster and to support negotiations in education include the following:

1. A growing discontent with compensation levels on the part of teachers, whose salaries were viewed as losing pace with professionals in other fields.

2. The increased sophistication of teacher groups and individual teachers in the actual processes of negotiations. Although teachers' expertise in collective negotiating increased, administrators and members of boards of education were reluctant to give credibility to the negotiations process and, in the 1950s and 1960s, all too often tended to ignore its impact upon educational employee relations.

3. The increase of teacher strikes and threat of strikes. The NEA before 1966 avoided references to strikes in its negotiation policy. Yet since that date, associations with NEA affiliation have been involved in numerous such actions. In 1979–1980, 242 teacher walkouts were reported (Diegmueller, 1991, p. 14).

4. The mere growth in the number of negotiated agreements in education had a "spillover" effect on nonnegotiating districts and tended to cement the process as an expected right and practice. Once initiated, withdrawal from negotiations as a process was difficult.

5. Such developments as district reorganization, which resulted in larger school districts and more adequate financial resources; the changing composition of teacher groups, especially the increase in male teachers; the teacher supply and demand, with serious shortages of teachers in the 1960s; and the increased professional development of staffs, especially in the area of advanced preparation.

By 1984 the practice of collective negotiations was common in education and encompassed both professional personnel and support staff personnel. Even in those states with no legislative provision for bargaining, the "meet and confer" concept appeared to be well established. The process of negotiating has not been restricted to teacher groups. Principals, supervisors, middle management personnel, and staff in other classifications have negotiated agreements in a growing number of school districts.

NEGOTIATIONS AND THE CENTRAL HUMAN RESOURCES UNIT

A survey of 385 practicing human resources directors assessed three specific activities in the area of collective bargaining: proposal development, strategy development, and negotiations at the table. Of the directors responding, 48.7% reported that proposal development was a shared responsibility, 21% indicated that the task was their complete responsibility, and 11.4% held no responsibility for the negotiations activity. The development of negotiation strategy was a shared responsibility for 50.4% of the directors, whereas 18.4% had full responsibility for this activity. Negotiating at the table was a shared responsibility of 42.1% of the personnel administrators; nearly 25% assumed full responsibility for this task (McCoy et al., 1983). In a 1989 study personnel administrators reported that they had complete responsibility for the collective bargaining process in 45.7% of the cases. Another 37.1% shared this responsibility, and 11.4% had no responsibilities in this area (Norton, 1989). In the same study more than half the directors served as chief spokesperson for the school board's negotiations team.

The use of the human resources director as the chief negotiator or spokesperson for the board team varies among school districts. Smaller districts tend to use the school superintendent or a member of the school board more often than larger districts. The use of the school superintendent, board member, professional negotiator (from outside or inside the school district), or the human resources director are the four most common arrangements for chief negotiators nationally. It has also become common practice for the human resources director or the director of employment relations to coordinate the entire negotiations process for the school board.

Because the involvement of human resources directors nationally in collective negotiations is well established, it is important to identify specific responsibilities or tasks in which a director must be competent. These competencies have been identified and are summarized in Figure 10.2.

Figure 10.3 illustrates the influences and impacts of the negotiations process upon the human resources function. An understanding of these relationships is essential for the effective functioning of the human resources program. For example, not only are working conditions a major negotiations consideration, but the "definition" of working conditions is expanding. Class size, which previously had been determined as a school board matter only, was ruled within the scope of negotiations by an Oregon Court ("Class Size," 1991).

1.1 Ability to understand the nature of collective negotiations and the skills involved in the process.

1.2 Ability to make all necessary preparations for negotiations by gathering information, establishing priorities, and interpreting parameters.

1.3 Ability to contribute to the resolution of a collective negotiations agreement.

1.4 Ability to prepare news releases for the media.

1.5 Ability to interpret and communicate the negotiations agreement as it relates to the personnel function and employee contractual relations.

1.6 Ability to review and recommend revision of policies, regulations, and procedures as these relate to the "newly negotiated" agreement.

1.7 Ability to interpret, communicate, and evaluate the negotiated agreement as it relates to employer-employee relationships.

1.8 Ability to evaluate the negotiated agreements as these relate to future negotiations and school district policy development.

FIGURE 10.2

Negotiations Competencies of Human Resources Directors

Source: From *Competency-based Preparations of Educational Administrators—Tasks, Competencies and Indicators of Competency* (p. 109) by M. S. Norton and R. D. Farrar, 1987, Tempe, AZ: Arizona State University, College of Education.

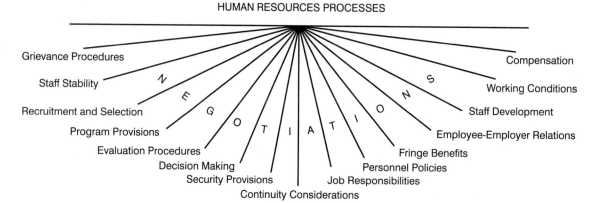

FIGURE 10.3
Negotiating and Related Human Resources Activities

THE COLLECTIVE NEGOTIATIONS PROCESS

The complex of activities included within the collective negotiations process may be classified into the following major areas:

1. Planning and preparation for collective negotiations
2. Determination and recognition of the bargaining unit
3. Determination of the composition of the negotiations team, including the chief spokesperson
4. Determination of the initial negotiation procedures and appropriate table strategies
5. Implementation of the contract agreement

Figure 10.4 illustrates the various activities related to each of these areas, which are discussed in the next section.

PLANNING AND PREPARATION FOR COLLECTIVE NEGOTIATIONS

Planning and preparation for collective negotiations include the following specific activities: (1) gathering the related information and data needed for decision making and cost analysis; (2) determining goals and objectives for negotiations; (3) establishing ground rules for conducting negotiations; (4) determining the scope of negotiations; and (5) clarifying procedures in case of impasse.

Gathering Related Information for Decision Making and Cost Analysis

At the outset of the planning and preparation activities, communication with local implementors of the current contract agreement must be established. The school board negotiations team must gather and analyze all information that identifies problems related to the current agreement and the issues that most likely will, or should, be given serious attention in future negotiations sessions.

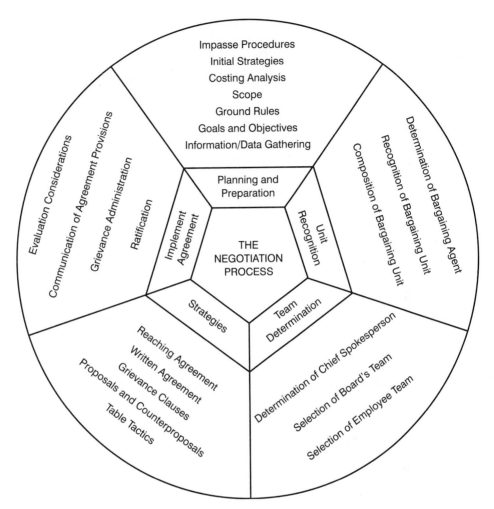

FIGURE 10.4
Negotiation Preparation Activities

The preparation and planning activity is a continuous procedure that focuses upon collecting, recording, and evaluating relevant information. Several information sources should be utilized in preparing for negotiations, including (1) information from the school district administrative staff about their concerns and needs; (2) troublesome areas in the present contract agreement; (3) publications, reports, press releases, and public statements by the respective professional groups; (4) information concerning the agendas for negotiations and troublesome areas in negotiations in other school districts; (5) data relating to budgets and the financial plans of the school district; (6) input from the school district's various constituencies concerning attitudes and opinions on employer-employee matters; and (7) information on the results of arbitration and/or court actions under present contracts in other school districts.

Once gathered, information must be analyzed in terms of related problems and their potential significance in the negotiations. Possible impact upon the school program, employer-employee relationships, budgets, and the school district's goals must be evaluated. Cost factors must include data relative to salaries, fringe benefits, program expenditures, human resource needs, administrative expenses, and other dimensions. Such information must not only be organized and properly recorded, but must be easily retrievable for use during the planning and preparation phases of negotiations as well as during table negotiations.

The importance of costing out contract agreements is emphasized in the following statement:

> The process of costing out the current labor agreement is one of the most important, albeit arduous, tasks that a school district entering negotiations must face. Prior to at-the-table negotiations, it is essential to examine each cost item as part of a total package and know what each item is worth to employees and how much it costs the board. This knowledge will enable management to make decisions at the table that are based on facts rather than "guesstimates." Once current anticipated costs are determined, union demands can be analyzed and costed to ensure that what is said at the bargaining table by management is accurate. (Wary, 1983, p. 1)

As stated by Rojot (1991), "It should be apparent that planning is essential to negotiations, but in practice it is very often neglected, generally with very unfortunate results . . . there is almost no doubt that a well-prepared negotiator has a definite edge over his opponents" (p. 176).

Determining Goals and Objectives for Negotiations

An essential activity in planning and preparing for negotiations is the establishment of goals and objectives that serve as the foundation for all negotiations activities and provide the necessary guidelines for the entire process. The school board team must understand the negotiation objectives of the school board and the level of importance of each item to be considered.

Anticipating the requests of employee groups is another important consideration. Once identified, the board team must determine the probable level of importance to the employee group. Although this determination is difficult, clues to the importance of employee requests often are provided in such information as employee grievances during the year, the substance of conferences and journals of state and national employee groups, and the negotiation requests by school districts that already are in the process of being settled or that have been settled for the ensuing year.

Consideration of the school board's objectives and a careful anticipation of the objectives of the employee group allow the board team to be proactive rather than merely reactive at the table. Such knowledge is essential in determining what the team wants to accomplish in the negotiations and what strategies best serve these purposes. Attempting to gather this information during table negotiations handicaps the team and severely inhibits its ability to react intelligently to requests or to question adequately the information provided by the other party.

Kennedy, Benson, and McMillan (1982) suggested that a team's objectives be ordered as follows: "(1) objectives you must achieve; (2) objectives you intend to achieve; and (3) objectives you would like to achieve" (p. 29). Such a ranking of objectives clarifies the expectations of the team and plays an important role in determining tactics and strategies during ongoing negotiations.

Establishing Ground Rules for Conducting Negotiations

Ground rules consist of the statements and agreements that govern the negotiations activities. Such rules encompass the establishment of the authority of the groups' representatives, time and place of meetings, length of table negotiation sessions, procedures for handling the agenda items, use of outside consultants, use of meeting minutes, use of open or closed meetings, quorum rules, use of a spokesperson, procedural rules, use of caucuses, use of press releases, ratification procedures, impasse provisions, a timeline for negotiation activities, and related guidelines.

Ground rules can be an unnecessary addendum to negotiations activities if they become dominant over primary issues of the negotiations and can inhibit later table negotiations if they cause major disputes. Because of their negative effects, the use of ground rules is decreasing. As team members become more sophisticated in the process of negotiations and if prior relationships have established mutual "trust," ground rules become less important to the process.

Nevertheless, when ground rules are used, the representative teams must agree upon answers to such questions as the following:

Authority of Team Representatives

1. Can representatives sign agreements?
2. Are spokespersons serving as authoritative representatives of the respective groups?
3. When a tentative agreement is reached, will representatives work diligently within their own group for its ratification?

Time and Place of Meetings

1. When and where will table negotiations be held? During school hours? Weekends? Holidays? After school hours?
2. What will be the length of each session? Can this time be extended by mutual agreement?
3. If teams agree to meet during school hours, who pays for substitutes, if needed?

The Agenda for Meetings

1. Is the agenda to be set in advance? Can new items be added? How is the agenda to be handled?
2. What if teams cannot agree on the agenda for the next meeting? Who determines the agenda?

Team Members

1. How many team members can represent a group? Must representatives be members of the school district? Can a professional negotiator from the outside be utilized?

2. What are the expected roles of team members? Will there be a chief spokesperson for each team?
3. Can parties bring in outside consultants to report or to testify? Can members of the employer and employee units attend the table sessions?
4. Can a consultant take over the spokesperson's role?

Meetings and Meeting Records

1. How are the meeting events to be recorded? Can either party use a stenographer? Can sessions be taped or videotaped? Who is to keep any records completed for the meetings?
2. Are meetings to be open or closed? If open, what kind of a group can teams bring to the meetings? Are the media to be invited? If the public is invited, what constitutes the public? Can an invited public person speak?
3. How are press releases to be handled?
4. What constitutes a quorum? Are Robert's Rules or a similar procedure to be utilized?

Procedural Considerations

1. During the table negotiations, can either party break at any time for a caucus?
2. What constitutes agreement on a specific item? On the total contract package?
3. How will the tentative agreement be ratified by both parties? How many days after the talks end must ratification be accomplished?
4. In case one or both parties fail to gain ratification, what are the time limits for renegotiations?
5. In case of impasse, who pays for mediation or fact finding?
6. When will an impasse be declared? What constitutes an impasse date?
7. What happens if the teams reach impasse during renegotiations? Are mediation procedures reinstated? Is arbitration to be utilized? Is a strike to be held if not prohibited by law?

Even though ground rules are determined before the primary issues to be considered at the table, the answers to these questions do not necessarily come easily. It is not the intent here to discuss strategy positions appropriate for each question posed; however, it is important that both parties study the implications of various answers that might be determined.

Determining the Scope of Negotiations

Inclusions and limitations concerning the scope of negotiations depend in large part upon state statutes and previous court rulings. State laws concerning the scope of negotiations vary widely. In the absence of legal guidelines, precedence is most likely to determine what is negotiable.

An examination of negotiation agreements in education makes it clear that the scope of issues continues to expand. The obvious position of representatives of employee groups is that no limits should be placed on the items that are negotiable; every matter has some influence on conditions of employment. Board of education representatives, on the other hand, argue that the public interest must be protected, and bargaining must not interfere with the board's right and responsibility to govern the school district. Consider such ground rule statements as the following: "Negotiations will encompass all educational matters of mutual concern"; "Negotiations shall encompass all matters pertaining to employment and the fulfillment of professional duties"; and "Negotiations will be determined by those matters presented to the board by the employee association." Clearly, these statements favor a broad scope for negotiations. Few matters in education, if any, would not be of some mutual concern or have some relation to employment, for example.

Preparation for collective negotiations, then, requires a careful examination of (1) existing statutes, court rulings, and legal opinions concerning the inclusions and limitations of bargaining items; (2) previously drafted preliminary statements of agreement; and (3) the role of various public groups in influencing the scope of negotiations and the procedures utilized for keeping such groups informed.

Clarifying Procedures in Case of Impasse

School boards and employee groups must determine well in advance of table discussions how an eventual impasse will be resolved. An ***impasse*** constitutes a difference or disagreement between the negotiating parties that has reached an unresolvable stage and brings a halt to table discussions.

Negotiation legislation, where enacted by the state, generally sets forth the specific means for resolving any impasse. With proper advanced planning and discussion, the parties involved are better able to design impasse procedures of a less disruptive, less traumatic nature than certain last resort alternatives.

Procedures for resolving impasse in collective negotiations include mediation, fact finding and advisory arbitration, voluntary binding arbitration, compulsory binding arbitration, last-best-offer arbitration, and strikes. Whereas some of these procedures are similar, certain important differences can be identified. Advantages and disadvantages are associated with each procedure.

Mediation. Mediation is the most commonly used procedure for resolving impasses. In mediation a jointly appointed, neutral third party serves as advisor and counselor for both parties. By conferring independently with representatives of the employer and employee groups, the mediator seeks to determine the reasons for the disagreement, the issues that surround it, and, to the extent possible, what constitutes acceptability on the part of each group. Through a process of interpretation and advisement, the mediator's objective is to bring the representatives back to the table to settle the issue at hand. Specific recommendations and alternatives most often are provided by the mediator but are not binding on either group.

Mediation almost always keeps both parties "talking," so it serves as a major strategy for successful negotiations. Perhaps a primary disadvantage of mediation is the extreme difficulty of the procedure itself. Because the impasse centers on complex issues and problems, mediation activities demand exemplary personal competence on the part of the mediator.

Fact Finding and Advisory Arbitration.   Fact finding and advisory arbitration are usually considered synonymous, because almost identical procedures are generally involved in each. However, fact finding is most often associated with impasses in table negotiations involving a future contract agreement, whereas advisory arbitration is generally associated with grievances and disputes under the present contract.

Fact finding involves the selection of a neutral third party, who serves as an investigator in studying all of the facts and circumstances that surround the impasse. As in mediation, fact finding can proceed as a relationship between the fact finder and the parties in dispute on an independent basis; however, arrangements often are made for a hearing in which both groups of negotiators present their cases.

In either the independent or formal hearing approach, the fact finder prepares a report of the facts and recommendations for action based upon the impartial findings. The representatives of each group study the findings and recommendations and respond with their acceptance or rejection. The fact finder's recommendations are advisory only.

Voluntary Binding and Compulsory Arbitration.   Voluntary binding and compulsory binding arbitration are procedures for resolving disagreements through the use of a neutral third party, whose decision is mandated for both parties. In the absence of state law specifying compulsory binding arbitration, voluntary binding arbitration may be agreed upon by the disputing parties. Specific procedures, including the arrangement for paying the costs of arbitration, most often are set forth in the master agreement. Empirical evidence suggests that, on the average, an arbitrator spends one day in preparation and two days in "hearings." Charges for arbitrator services vary greatly; a range of $250 to $1,000 per day is not unusual. Most commonly, costs are equally shared between the school district and the employee association. However, a procedure whereby the school district "pays" if it loses the grievance case and the grievant "pays" if the association loses the case also is utilized. The third party might be an individual, a group of individuals, or a panel board (e.g., board of industrial relations). Following an in-depth study of the issue and all relative information, the arbitrator or panel renders a decision that is final and binding.

The major advantage of compulsory arbitration is its potential to avoid more disruptive events, such as a strike. The fact that compulsory arbitration places the settlement outside the jurisdiction of the negotiating parties, especially the governing board of education, is considered a disadvantage by many persons. Yet the removal of the two parties from the personally traumatic experiences of face-to-face table disputes and further professional alienation is an advantage in the minds of others.

Last-Best-Offer Arbitration.   In last-best-offer arbitration, a neutral third party is called upon to study the last-best-offers stated by each of the two parties in the table negotiations. Rather than reach a decision based on a "down-the-middle" compromise, the arbitrator reviews each last offer in view of the facts (e.g., salary trends, agreements settled in competitive school districts, ability to pay, supply and demand, etc.). In the final analysis, *one* of the two last-best-offers is recommended and considered binding upon both parties.

An advantage of this procedure centers on the possible results of the competitive atmosphere it fosters. That is, because each party attempts to present a reasonable, well-intentioned best offer that might be most favorably viewed by an arbitrator, the result likely could be an agreement at the table itself. The need for arbitration is then obviated. Last-best-offer arbitration has been utilized extensively in baseball for resolving salary disputes. However, Standohar (1975) notes that the primary areas of application are to situations in which strikes cannot be tolerated by the public or those involving such problems as inordinate economic loss, danger to public health, or danger to personal safety.

Critics of the procedure point out that because only one group's offer can be recommended, the other group must live with an "unfair" decision. The effects on morale due to the use of last-best-offer arbitration could be negative.

Strikes. Strikes are actions that result in stoppage of work and services rendered by an employee group. As would be expected, the National School Boards Association (NSBA) supports state legislation that makes strikes against public schools illegal and provides for mandatory penalties (NSBA, 1991), whereas the NEA believes that the right to strike must be an integral part of any collective bargaining process (NEA, 1991). The American Association of School Administrators (AASA) historically has opposed strikes and has emphasized the basic responsibility for school administrators to keep the schools open with protective measures for both students and those persons who report to work should a strike occur. The American Association of School Personnel Administrators (AASPA) several years ago set forth its views concerning school strikes. First, the association proposed that if there was a strike, retroactive contract settlements should be prohibited. Second, a secret ballot of all members of the bargaining unit should be taken prior to any strike to accept or reject the school board's negotiations team's last offer on the various issues. If approved, the contract is considered binding; if rejected, alternatives of a strike or further negotiations are in order. Third, AASPA recommended the implementation of a procedure for governing strikes, including a cooling-off period. Before any strike, a fact finder would be selected to study all issues and attempt to alleviate the dispute (AASPA, 1978).

From the school board's point of view, preplanning for a possible strike must be part of the preparation for collective negotiations. Essential activities included in such preparation are the following:

1. Well in advance of table negotiations or any indication of a possible strike, a comprehensive plan must be developed to retain the services necessary to operate the schools and to resolve the strike issues as expeditiously as possible.
2. An effective means must be established for communicating important information to both internal and external groups. Alternative communication methods and means of contact must also be identified in anticipation of an interruption of the usual communication channels.
3. A central office or unit should be organized to serve as the coordination and control center for information gathering, decision making, and implementation procedures. Key personnel who will serve in the central office must be identified in advance and their roles clearly delineated.

4. Resource pools of personnel who can keep the schools open and operating should be identified. This consideration includes the identification of employees who likely would cross picket lines and others who would be employable on a temporary basis.

5. Information concerning the legality of strike activities must be gathered, studied, and distributed appropriately. Legal information concerning strike activities in the state, restrictions of law, penalties, legal implications, restraining orders, the job status of strikers, and so forth, must be clarified. Legal alternatives available for board action must be investigated.

6. Building administrators and supervisors should develop local plans for dealing with the strike situation. Responsibilities must be clarified and program alternatives that meet instructional goals should be identified. Guidelines for establishing the safety and welfare of students and other personnel must be stated and understood.

7. Local security personnel must be kept well informed as to the ongoing conditions and potential problems that might occur. A straightforward approach with the media concerning developments and issues has proven to be the best policy.

8. Procedures must be determined for establishing meaningful communication with the employee group representatives. Attempts of serious efforts to keep talking in relation to the issues in dispute must be implemented. A well-organized, creative means for fostering ongoing internal discussions of the issues must be established in advance. Such a plan must be positive and focus upon a sincere attitude of resolution and possible agreement.

Increasingly, teachers' groups nationally are using various means to protest salary, working conditions, and other issues. For example, besides lengthy strikes, teachers nationally have staged 3-day walkouts, have had 1-day "blueouts" in which all teachers call in sick, have stacked contracts without signatures, have sponsored television commercials that portray their views of the state of education, have had work slowdowns, and have used other strategies to gain public support, to prompt positive action from state legislators, and to put pressure on school boards. As is basically the case with teacher strikes, the foregoing actions are designed to achieve various purposes. However, as noted by Creswell and Murphy (1980), "The main function of strikes is to 'change a bargaining position of the other side'" (p. 348).

DETERMINATION AND RECOGNITION OF THE BARGAINING UNIT

Before collective negotiations at the table can be initiated, the employee groups to be included in the bargaining unit and their official memberships must be determined. A school district consists of several different employee groups and clusters of employees within those groups. For example, teachers, librarians, nurses, counselors, and psychologists are among the professional staff personnel. Support staff personnel such as clerks, secretaries, maintenance workers, transportation staff, custodians, and food service workers represent employee groups and clusters. To which bargaining unit each of these employee groups belong is of paramount importance for purpose of negotiations. A **bargaining unit** is a group of employees certified as the appropriate unit for collective negotiations. This unit is the one to which the negotiated contractual agreements will apply. It is not unusual for a school district to have several bargaining units, although a common practice is that one unit represents the combination of teaching and nonadministrative professional personnel. Negotiations indeed are "collective" in that various groups and clusters are being represented as one group in the process.

Procedures to determine the bargaining unit often are established by statute. In some states certain employees such as administrators are not permitted to be members of a unit that also represents teachers (Strahan, 1969). In the absence of statute, the procedures for deciding which employees to include in the bargaining unit are determined mutually by the school board and employee groups.

Two criteria serve important roles in determining which employees will belong to a particular unit: **community of interest** (Lieberman & Moskow, 1966) and **fragmentation** (Walter, 1975). Employees who share common employment interests and concerns, who desire to be in the same bargaining unit, and who receive similar compensation and have similar working conditions represent examples of a community of interest. It is obvious that the larger the unit, the more difficult it is to establish a community of interest. Yet small bargaining units present problems for both employees and employers. From the employees' viewpoint, very small units are far less likely to carry the bargaining strength of those units with larger representation. Nevertheless, if the units in smaller districts are composed of members with dissimilar interests, negotiations are further complicated. The task for employer groups, then, is to establish bargaining units based upon the community interest principle and, at the same time, to attempt to avoid "fragmentation of their work force into many separate bargaining units . . . since it requires the employer to bargain many times, generally over the same questions, but with different groups of employees" (Walter, 1975, p. 25).

In actual practice unit determination is decided generally by (1) state statutes and law, (2) agreements reached by the school board and the various employee groups, (3) an external agency such as a labor relations board or other outside authority, or (4) the unilateral decision of the school board.

The Bargaining Agent

The bargaining agent is the employee organization designated as the negotiations representative of all employees in the bargaining unit. Two types of recognition are generally found in education: exclusive representation and multiple representation.

Exclusive representation is the certification of one particular employee organization to represent all employees in the unit. The general procedures for determining exclusive recognition include (1) the request by an employee organization to be the bargaining agent for all employees in the bargaining unit, (2) an election or other means of determining majority preference, and (3) results of an election in which at least 51% vote yes and certification by the school board that the organization has exclusive bargaining rights.

One nonvoting method of determining the bargaining agent is that of recognizing the organization, which for the last 2 or 3 years, has enrolled a majority of the school employees as members.

According to Strahan (1969), multiple representation generally takes one of the following forms:

1. Completely separate negotiations with each organization represented.
2. Joint negotiating committee with proportional representation based upon size of membership in the organization.
3. Joint negotiating committee with equal representation of the recognized organizations in the school.

Exclusive recognition is most widely used in education for the following reasons: (1) It is supported by both the NEA and AFT, (2) it is mandated for the public sector in many states and is the form of recognition most generally accepted when statutes do not specify what form of recognition is to be given, and (3) private business and industry serve as examples that exclusive recognition is most effective (Rebore, 1991, p. 302).

DETERMINATION OF THE COMPOSITION OF THE NEGOTIATIONS TEAM, INCLUDING THE CHIEF SPOKESPERSON

The selection of the negotiations team is a critical decision for successful negotiations. Each party must have individuals at the table who can answer the questions that will arise and who can complete the process effectively. The size of the team will vary and depends considerably upon the size of the school system and the representations needed.

The following criteria help to determine the selection of individuals for the negotiations team:

1. *Time.*   Do the individual's schedule and responsibilities allow the time required to serve on the team?
2. *Temperament.*   Does the individual have the emotional stability and personal poise necessary for serving on the team?
3. *Tenacity.*   Will the individual "stay with it" and work through the complex and tenuous process?
4. *Technical know-how.*   Does the individual have the necessary understanding of the process of negotiations and knowledge of the content information required in the collective negotiations?
5. *Talent.*   Does the individual have the talent for participating in the art of negotiations?

The inclusion of school board members, the school superintendent, the human resources director, the board attorney, or an outside professional negotiator on the board of education's team will depend largely upon the unique characteristics within each school district. The advantages and disadvantages in using each of these persons are summarized in Table 10.1.

TABLE 10.1

Advantages and Disadvantages of Including Certain Individuals on the Board of Education's
Negotiations Team (pp. 297–299)

School Board Member(s)	Participation can gain the confidence of the total board that their real interests are being protected; could facilitate acceptance of "final package" Participation may help the board understand the nature of the process and its complexity Could provide a psychological advantage to the board's team May have more time than other school district personnel who might represent the board's team	Board members on the team are viewed as members of the board rather than as members of the negotiating team; may tend to speak for the board instead of participating in the negotiations May inhibit the effectiveness of the team's chief spokesperson; employee team tends to look to the board member as confirming the power of acceptance or nonacceptance May not be skilled in the art of negotiation Conditions surrounding the negotiations process may cause board members to lose objectivity; value of board member "as a board member" in evaluating end product may be jeopardized; board members have to decide ultimately on ratification of the agreement
Superintendent of Schools	Most knowledgeable of the entire school system; expertise is invaluable at the negotiations table School board generally views the superintendent as having the kinds of competence required for successful negotiations	Time commitment required may interfere with other major responsibilities Although generally accepted that superintendent represents management, involvement in negotiations can promote poor attitudes and adversary relationships with employees

Research has not determined if team size affects successful negotiations. Multiple representation usually requires larger team numbers. According to Lieberman (1969),

> There is no magic in any particular figure. An appropriate number will be a compromise between several factors (i.e., smaller team facilitates ease of agreement due to factors of time and informality; need for more than one member to avoid serious mistakes and misunderstandings). (p. 30)

Those size recommendations that do exist most often specify from three to five members. Some individuals view a five-member team as ideal because it is large enough to

TABLE 10.1
continued

Position	Advantages	Disadvantages
	Because of responsibilities, superintendent is in best position to view school system as a whole and to conceptualize both organizational objectives and human resource needs	Employee representatives tend to want responses of administrative authority rather than negotiation strategy responses
		Membership tends to place the superintendent in untenable position—equal at table on one day and chief administrator of the district the next
Human Resources Director	Likely to have best understanding of employee relations in school district	Role as an adversary at table conflicts with responsibilities of personal counselor and enhancer of positive human relationships in office
	Normally well trained and highly skilled in negotiations and school law	
	Has key information relative to primary agenda items in negotiations	Time commitments detract from other major responsibilities
	Possesses experience and knowledge of human resource needs and their importance in fulfilling mission of the school district	Although knowledgeable of employee relations and negotiations, might be utilized much more advantageously as primary resource and consultant to negotiation team
School Board Attorney	Can provide important advice and counsel relative to statutes and court decisions that relate to negotiations process	May not be knowledgeable of school system and its internal problems and needs
		Legal expertise does not automatically translate into expertise in negotiation

provide for representative resource personnel and meets the need for different types of individuals with various competencies, yet it is not so large as to be unwieldy. Those who suggest that team size be limited to three members stress that this number facilitates the process and enables the teams to progress under less formal conditions. In addition, three team members can concentrate on assigned roles as spokesperson, recorder, and observer.

The ***spokesperson*** is the chief negotiator for the team and serves as team captain. The focus of unity for the team, the spokesperson generally serves as the single "voice" of the team's position. The team ***observer*** listens and watches for clues and

TABLE 10.1
continued

Position	Advantages	Disadvantages
	Can help develop language of the contract agreement in order to obviate unclear statements and possible problems of legal interpretations due to poor contract language	May prove costly both in time and money
	Can provide legal advice in ongoing negotiations at time of deliberations rather than after the fact	
Outside Professional	Often can save time by understanding importance and/or unimportance of activities	Professional fees quite costly
	Generally brings high level of expertise in negotiations to table	Usually unfamiliar with school district
	Allows internal personnel to concentrate on other educational matters	Does not remain to help implement contract agreement or to face possible grievances
	Has strong incentive to be highly effective in order to serve again and to build the reputation needed for expanded employment contracts	Problems can arise concerning payment arrangements; hourly contract arrangement with outside negotiator carries certain disadvantages whereas set fee can pose problems of performance
		In lengthy negotiations that encounter impasse or work stoppage, district encounters problem of paying outside negotiator for other services or being without counsel and advice

behaviors communicated by members of the other party. Verbal statements and body language are monitored for clues as to priority of issues, major concerns, closing arguments, and possible closure. The ***recorder*** maintains written information concerning strategy and positions as well as facts, decisions, and events surrounding each negotiations session.

The need for a set of comprehensive minutes that are read and approved by both teams following or before each table session is not recommended. Teams can encounter many disagreements and waste valuable time in attempting to establish the accuracy of the minutes of the session. In fact, the only notes that are essential are the tentatively signed agreements on agenda items reached during the process of negotiations. These tentative agreements, of course, are important and must be officially recorded and signed by each team before other agenda items are considered. Tentative agreements are subject to final approval of the total contract agreement. In short, the agreement as signed by the two representative teams is the test of what the two parties said.

INITIAL NEGOTIATIONS PROCEDURES AND APPROPRIATE TABLE STRATEGIES

It must be remembered that the basic purpose of negotiations is to reach an agreement. Successful negotiations more often occur when (1) the process of negotiations is conducted on a professional basis (i.e., mutual respect with the absence of name calling, accusations, etc.), (2) the resulting agreement is within the limitations established by the board, (3) the agreement results in no increases in the number of grievances filed against the district, and (4) the agreement is reached without an impasse being declared (Tozer, 1980).

Table tactics depend in large part on the bargaining strategies in place. Strategies exemplified by a labor-management model are primarily adversarial and designed to realize maximum gain on short-term negotiations through use of authority, power, or withdrawal of services. Perry and Wildman (1970) called this approach **distributive strategy**. Pure distributive strategy generally results in crises bargaining. On the other hand, **quasi-distributive strategy** is based on the desire to avoid a test of power. Quasi-distributive strategy is the one discussed primarily in the foregoing sections and the strategy that education has adopted generally, although win-win approaches have become more popular in recent years. As Perry and Wildman (1970) point out, the "game playing" that results from quasi-distributive strategy is characterized by

1. a series of specific demands and offers on a package of bargaining issues.
2. deferral of formal commitments until they can be supported by reference to an impending test of power.
3. controlled, distorted private communication designed to disguise true costs and goals and permit favorable trade-offs of concessions for demands.
4. withholding of concessions on all major issues until the last possible moment when they can be used as the final "buy-out" to avoid the impending test of power. (p. 63)

Quasi-integrative and **integrative bargaining** are two other approaches to negotiations. Even though quasi-integrative bargaining involves a *quid pro quo*, give-and-take process of compromise, it often equates with a win-lose concept of negotiations. On the other hand, integrative bargaining centers more directly on what many consider the **win-win approach.** Perry and Wildman (1970) stated that integrative bargaining

is based on strong long-run mutual interests and important short-run problems.... A pure integrative bargaining strategy commonly leads to "problem-solving" ... problem-solving has been concentrated in mature bargaining relationships in which external political and/or economic conditions force the parties to perceive a threat to their mutual survival in either continued conflict or continued reliance on short-run power as the basis for decision making. (pp. 64–65)

The Nature of Integrative Bargaining— Win-Win Approaches

Integrative bargaining, win-win bargaining, creative bargaining, and **joint problem solving (JPS)** are all names for bargaining approaches designed to eliminate adversarial relationships and to serve both parties in achieving their negotiations objectives while feeling good about the results. In their work *The Win-Win Negotiator* (1987), Reck and Long comment that

> the result [of win-win negotiations] is a simple, straight-forward and easy-to-use method of negotiating which helps you achieve the agreement you want, and at the same time, assures that the person you're dealing with feels good about you, the agreement and himself as well. Thus, both parties win and are therefore committed to holding up their end of the agreement. (p. 3)

Schoonmaker (1989) suggests that the use of a distributive approach or integrative approach to bargaining depends on the situation at hand. He suggests that certain conditions warrant a bargaining approach, whereas a joint problem-solving approach should be emphasized when other conditions are present. For example,

Emphasize bargaining when:

☐   your interests clearly conflict
☐   you are much more powerful
☐   you do not need or want a long-term harmonious relationship
☐   you do not trust the other party
☐   the agreement is easy to implement
☐   the other party is pure bargaining

Emphasize joint problem solving when:

☐   you have common interests
☐   you are weaker or power is approximately the equal
☐   you need or want a continuing, harmonious relationship
☐   you trust the other party
☐   implementing the agreement may be difficult
☐   the other party is problem solving (pp. 12–13)

Reck and Long suggest the PRAM model for win-win negotiations (see Figure 10.5). The PRAM Model begins with establishing win-win plans. In this step, parties agree on their own goals; anticipate the goals of the other party; determine probable areas of agreement; and develop win-win solutions to reconcile areas of probable agreement. Step 2 focuses on developing win-win relationships. Activities are planned which allow a positive personal relationship to develop; a sense of mutual trust is cultivated; and the relationship is allowed to develop fully before business is discussed in earnest. In Step 3, the win-win agreement is formed. The other party's goals are confirmed; areas of agreement are confirmed; proposals are considered for win-win solutions to areas of disagreement; and remaining differences are jointly resolved. In the final Step 4, maintenance of the win-win agreement is performed. Meaningful feedback concerning agreement performance is provided and each party works toward keeping the agreement in force. Party contacts are maintained and mutual trust is reaffirmed (pp. 105-106).

FIGURE 10.5
PRAM Model
Source: From *The Win-Win
Negotiator* (p. 84) by R. R.
Reck and B. G. Long, 1987,
Kalamazoo, MI: Spartan.
Copyright © 1987 by Spartan
Publications. Reprinted by
permission.

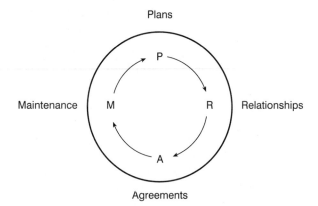

Of course, bargaining can be of a lose-lose nature as well. **Lose-lose bargaining** generally is the result of an excessive use of power by one party that evolves from a win-lose situation. In the end, neither party realizes its objectives. Due to its power base, one party is able to force its own wishes on the other party. The loser, due to lack of a power base, reluctantly accepts the solution proposed, and does so resentfully. The losing party adopts a "soldiering" posture, that is, goes along with the solution on the surface but does little if anything toward actual commitment. Thus a lose-lose result is faced by both parties.

Proposals and Counterproposals in Collective Negotiations

Once quasi-distributive negotiations have been initiated and negotiation items have been submitted by the employee group, good faith negotiations require that the board of education team respond. A first response on any one item might be *we agree*, *we will consider it*, *we cannot agree*, or *that item is not negotiable*, accompanied by appropriate reasons. From this point experienced negotiators concentrate on listening to the other team's responses to try to uncover key issues, major concerns, and position statements.

As previously noted, the goal of negotiations is not to win a debate, but rather to reach an agreement on the proposals. The tactics that serve best are the ones that include a possible response to a proposal or solution to differences between the two parties. A reasonable proposal or counterproposal has the potential for resolving the issue or settling the existing differences. Timing is critical. The art of negotiation requires a sense of when the best offer should be tendered and when the closing question should be posed.

Kennedy and colleagues (1982) discussed compromise toward the goal of reaching agreement in relation to team movement and "distance between the two parties." They illustrated the distance in terms of movement and suggested that each team has a limit and "break point." The range of settlement lies between a team's most favorable position (MFP) and that break point or limit (see Figure 10.6). The final position is defined by the relative strength of the parties and their negotiating skills. If the teams' limits do not overlap, reaching agreement is highly unlikely. If the first team's

FIGURE 10.6

Range of Settlement

Source: From *Managing Negotiations* by Gavin Kennedy, John Benson, and John McMillan, 1982, Englewood Cliffs, NJ: Prentice-Hall. Reprinted by permission of the publisher, Prentice-Hall/A division of Simon & Schuster, Englewood Cliffs, NJ.

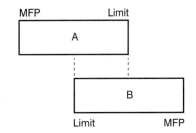

range overlaps the second team's MFP, the first team holds a decided advantage in the negotiations process.

Movement in negotiations infers flexibility; flexibility requires compromise. The Latin term *quid pro quo* means something for something or, in negotiation terminology, get for what you give. In negotiations each team moves closer to an agreement by giving something of value in return for receiving a desired goal. Thus both teams use the tactics involving submission of proposals and counterproposals in a give-and-take process to try and reach a tentative agreement.

Although there is no one best way to negotiate and negotiation is more art than science, empirical evidence suggests a number of guidelines for table negotiations that deserve consideration.

1. Always negotiate from the viewpoint of the total contract amount. Never agree on economic items separately.
2. Do not submit a proposal or counterproposal, then attempt to retract it. Do not "show your hand" before you need to do so.
3. Be cautious about stating that your team is anxious to settle early. When this becomes known, then the "ransom" often goes higher.
4. Remember that negotiation is a process of compromise. Generally, it is not good in the long run to "win it all." Seasoned negotiators try to build long-term relationships that include mutual trust and respect. Any agreement must have mutuality of benefit. Do not bluff. A team must be prepared to carry out threats. Try to develop a high degree of credibility through a positive relationship.
5. In negotiations say what you mean and mean what you say. Be certain that you write what you mean in any tentative or final agreement.
6. Do not present items for negotiations that are already within a group's jurisdiction (e.g., school board's legislative rights, administration's evaluation responsibilities, employees' academic freedom).
7. Team representatives negotiate with team representatives. The board of education, for example, should not take its case directly to the employee association.
8. Listen. A good negotiator spends the majority of time listening to the other team's responses, rationale, key issues, and major concerns. Responses such as "Tell me more," "I didn't know that," and "Why?" help the negotiator learn more of the other team's position statements and closing arguments.

9. Use closed-ended questions to bring issues into focus. Keep dialogue going. When teams stop talking, negotiations break down. The sophisticated negotiator wants to reach an agreement.

10. Develop signaling techniques, such as cue-cards, that serve your team (e.g., OBS, return to original bargaining statement; CQ, state the closing question; etc.). Verbal signaling, sending an intended message to the other team, is a necessary tactic as well. But be careful about body language. Hesitation in responding, for example, sends a message that you might accept the proposal.

11. Use reason rather than rhetoric to explain your stand. State your case and stay with the facts.

12. Realize that timing is a major aspect of negotiation. At the outset very little is agreed to. In the course of negotiations, teams tell each other their priorities and what they want.

13. Use the term *we* for the team's position and never the personal *I* at the table. Team representatives do not have a position; they represent the larger group.

14. Personal poise and behavior are of major importance. Self-control is essential. As presented previously, team members must be selected on the basis of their availability, temperament, tenacity, technical know-how, and talent.

IMPLEMENTATION OF THE CONTRACT AGREEMENT

The agreement, or master contract, is the ratified document that specifies the terms of the negotiated contract. Because the agreement is used by all parties to guide contractual employee relations, the contract language is of primary importance. Contract language represents the final product of the negotiations. It is what both parties must live with for the contract period. Carelessness in the use of words can lead to serious problems, including arbitration. The phrase **you get what you write** applies directly to the written agreement.

Consider each of the following contract statements.

Statement 1.   Elementary teachers will be granted ten 30-minute breaks per week.

Statement 2.   Regular teachers will be hired for summer school teaching on a first preference basis.

Statement 3.   This agreement becomes part of board policy and board policy becomes part of the contract.

Statement 4.   Employees have the right to file a grievance at any time, in case of violation of this agreement.

In Statement 1, the definition of teacher needs clarification. How does the agreement apply to a half-time kindergarten teacher or to art or music specialists who come in for only 20 minutes per week in various classrooms? Statement 2 tends to lock the school district into a summer school program. Also, how would the term *first prefer-ence* be applied? Is the contract agreement applicable to summer school as well? Board policy and contract agreements are two separate matters. Board policy can be changed unilaterally at any time. A contract agreement cannot be changed without mutual consent. Wording such as that in Statement 3 tends to bind the board of education to no policy development without the approval of the employee group. In Statement 4 a statute of limitations is needed. Such a limitation must stipulate the time period after the incident during which the grievance must be filed. With no such limitation, a grievance could be filed, withdrawn, and then refiled weeks, months, or even years later.

Research in Iowa public schools on teacher grievances that were pursued to the final step of binding arbitration has revealed that the language in benefits clauses in master contracts is so vague that it has resulted in losses by the school board at the arbitrator's table. Such losses have been extremely expensive for the school district (Colon, 1989).

Basic Content of the Written Agreement

Information included in the written agreement varies considerably in practice. However, most agreements include (1) a statement of recognition; (2) the nature of the agreement, its scope, time considerations, and communication channels; (3) the specific stipulations or articles of agreement; (4) mutual understandings concerning the agreement, including responsibilities of both parties; and (5) grievance and impasse procedures.

The statement of recognition stipulates the one specific organization or arrangement for the bargaining representation of the defined employee unit. The section centered on the nature of the agreement includes the curtailment of any further negotiations until the approved agreement has elapsed, and provisions for ongoing communication between the two parties. The specific agreement stipulations or articles include the agreements reached concerning compensation, employee benefits, and other conditions of employment. Included in the section concerned with mutual understandings and responsibilities are the obligations of both parties for implementation of the agreement, the responsibilities to administer professional working relationships and, thus, to provide high-quality education, and in some cases a statement concerning strikes. Grievance and impasse procedures are significant considerations of any written agreement as well.

Grievances

A **grievance** is a problem or complaint related to the contract agreement. It represents a violation, or purported violation, of the agreement that must be settled through the grievance procedures set forth in the contract agreement. A significant difference exists between a general complaint by an employee on a matter of school policy and a grievance based upon an alleged violation of the negotiation agreement. Whereas both kinds of employee problems are important for effective human resources practices, the grievances discussed here focus on arbitrable disagreements related specifically to the negotiated agreement. The grievance procedure is essentially a part of the ongoing collective negotiations process. Even though the written negotiated agreement should stipulate no further negotiations until the current contract expires (referred to as the **zipper clause**), the use of the grievance is one way in which the negotiations process continues. Thus designing grievance procedures that define time limitations, preliminary steps, and procedures is of crucial importance.

The grievance procedure has been described "as a means of allowing an employee to express a complaint to management without fear of reprisal and to have that complaint addressed by successively higher levels of management until an answer is provided that the grievant can or must accept" (McCollum & Norris, 1984, p. 106). In many cases procedures for grievances are stipulated in law. The following grievance procedures are generally applicable: (1) A written grievance is filed that includes a description of the basis for the grievance, a statement of any prior informal steps taken to attempt to resolve the issue, a statement of reasons as to why the alleged actions were unfair, arbitrary, or contrary to contract provisions, and actions that the aggrieved employee believes necessary to resolve the issue. (2) The immediate supervisor prepares a written statement concerning the grounds of the grievance and recommended solutions as appropriate to the case. (3) If not resolved, the next higher level of authority (e.g., human resources director, superintendent, or other appropriate staff member) conducts a further investigation and renders a decision with a recommended solution. (4) If not resolved in the foregoing investigation, a review board or the board of education considers the case. The recommendation by the review board is considered as final. If not accepted by the grievant, arbitration by a third party or litigation are possible alternatives (see Figure 10.7).

Contemporary grievance procedures tend to eliminate the board of education as a final review body. This is being done because the school board represents one of the contract parties and because this arrangement tends to place the board in the sensitive position of overruling the administration. The foregoing grievance model attempts to retain the solution of grievances within the internal jurisdiction of the school district. However, the use of advisory or binding arbitration by external individuals is also a common procedure for settling disputes. Such arbitration normally depends on existing law. In the absence of statute, arbitration procedures are subject to mutual agreement by both parties.

A grievance procedure should provide for due process and ensure that legitimate grievances and problems are heard, reviewed, and resolved. A properly designed procedure helps to place problems and complaints in the proper channels of supervisory relationships for possible solution at the most appropriate level of administration. Such procedures provide employees a fair consideration of grievances without reprisal and also safeguard the rights of supervisory personnel.

SUMMARY

Collective negotiations is a process whereby matters of employment relations are determined mutually by representatives of employee groups and their employer within the limits of law or mutual agreement. The development of collective negotiations in education has been influenced historically by collective bargaining in the private and public sectors.

The human resources unit in education is involved in collective negotiations in two specific ways. First, the human resources director assumes many of the responsibilities in the negotiations process itself. Second, the process of negotiations affects virtually every other facet of the human resources function. In order to be effective in the role, the human resources director must have a complete understanding of the

FIGURE 10.7
Operational Model for
Grievance Procedure

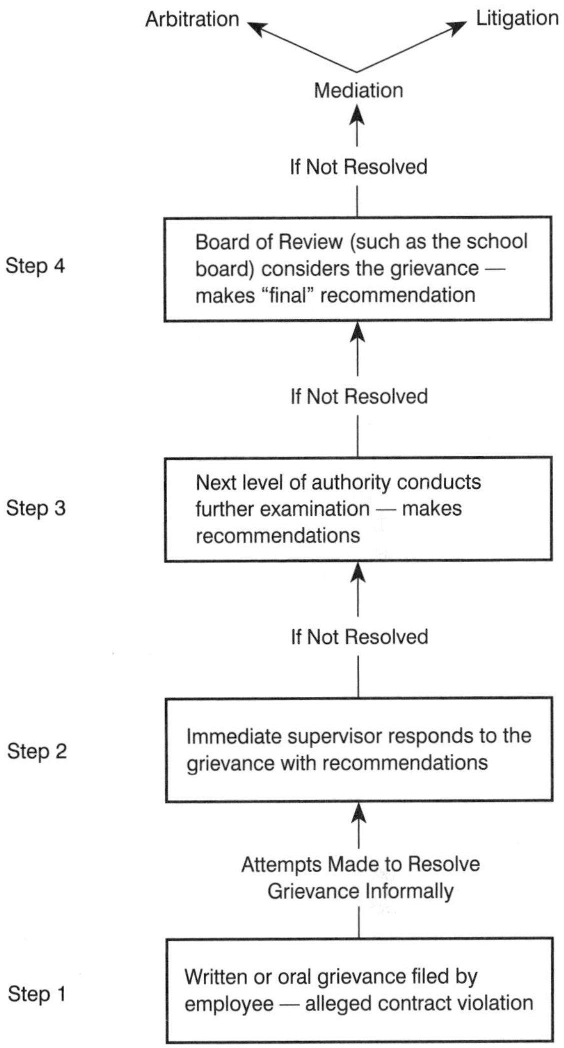

Arbitration ← → Litigation

Mediation

↑

If Not Resolved

Step 4 — Board of Review (such as the school board) considers the grievance — makes "final" recommendation

↑

If Not Resolved

Step 3 — Next level of authority conducts further examination — makes recommendations

↑

If Not Resolved

Step 2 — Immediate supervisor responds to the grievance with recommendations

↑

Attempts Made to Resolve Grievance Informally

Step 1 — Written or oral grievance filed by employee — alleged contract violation

tasks related to the negotiations process and possess specific personal competencies appropriate for these tasks.

The negotiations process includes (1) planning and preparation for collective negotiations; (2) determination and recognition of the bargaining unit; (3) determination of the negotiations team, including the chief spokesperson; (4) determination of the initial negotiation procedures and appropriate table strategies; and (5) implementation of the contract agreement.

Planning and preparation for collective negotiations include establishing goals and objectives for negotiations, establishing ground rules, determining the scope of negotiations, information gathering, costs analysis, determining initial strategies, and clarifying impasse procedures.

The membership of the bargaining unit must be verified and the bargaining agent certified. Team representation constitutes an important matter. Available time, personal temperament, individual tenacity, technical know-how, and talent are criteria that should guide the selection of individual team members.

Table tactics depend in large part on the bargaining strategies in place. In general, education has adopted the quasi-distributive strategy, in which both parties attempt to avoid a test of power and, through a procedure of proposals and counter-proposals, withhold concessions on all major issues until the last possible moment. Integrative bargaining has been initiated in school district negotiations increasingly for many reasons. This approach focuses on a win-win result through problem solving.

The tentative agreement reached by the negotiating parties must be ratified by the membership of each group. Once ratified, steps must be taken to communicate the provisions of the agreement. Grievance procedures, which have been identified in the master agreement, are implemented in case of a violation or grievance related to the contract.

DISCUSSION QUESTIONS

1. Rebore has commented that "collective negotiations has become a way of life in American education" (p. 292). What evidence supports this contention?
2. Consider the distributive bargaining strategy as compared to the integrative strategy. What evidence, if any, is available presently to suggest that the integrative approach is gaining ground in education?
3. In the chapter it was recommended that school board representatives negotiate directly with the teachers' group representatives. That is, the school board should not take its case directly to the teachers' organization; nor should the teachers' team take its case to the school board as a whole. Why does this recommendation make sense? What kinds of problems evolve from such actions?
4. Divide the class into appropriate triads that represent negotiations teams for the school board and for the teachers. Each of the teams has 30 minutes to consider the following situation.

> The teachers' organization bargaining team plans to request 3 personal-leave days as a negotiation item. Presently teachers have 10 days of sick leave available per year, accumulative to 180 days. Professional leave is available with administrative approval for 3 days per year and the teacher may take 3 days for deaths in the family.

   a. During the 30-minute time period, each of the teacher teams drafts its version of the personal-leave proposal as it will be presented at the table.
   b. Board teams are aware of the general nature of the teachers' request as presented here, but have not seen the specific proposal that ultimately will be presented. Thus, during the 30-minute time period, each school board team discusses the general proposal and considers its position relative to its provisions for compensation, approval authority, days such leave could be taken, limitation on the number of approvals, trade-offs, and so on.

c. After the 30-minute individual team sessions, the triads meet as board and teacher teams. Each teacher team presents its proposal and the board team reacts to it. Triads take another 30 minutes to "negotiate" a tentative agreement on this matter.

d. Each negotiation triad reports its results to the class as a whole.

CASE 10.1
A Win-Win End Run

Union School District had bargained with teachers on a meet-and-confer basis for 4 years. Because there were no state statutes to require collective bargaining between school boards and employee groups, negotiation practices varied widely throughout the state.

In the Union District, the human resources director had served as the school board's chief spokesperson for the last 4 years. Negotiations had gone well until last year when an impasse was declared and a mediator was called in to help resolve the matter relating to extra-duty assignments.

Budget restraints in the district were such that an override election was necessary last year to meet this year's operating expenses. The possibility of receiving a favorable vote on a second override appeared highly questionable in the eyes of the school board.

"I think we should move to a win-win, problem-solving approach in our negotiations with teachers this year," offered Merlin George, human resources director. "In view of the current economics, I can't see our past approaches to negotiations effective this year. I would be glad to serve as a resource person this year, but I recommend that someone else serve as chief spokesperson this year."

In the final analysis, the school board and superintendent agreed to George's recommendations. Leah Smith, the school business manager, was named as negotiations team leader for the school board. Overall, teachers were receptive to the proposal for win-win bargaining.

As negotiations for the year proceeded, Leah spent considerable time giving facts and figures relating to a tight budget and lack of needed legislative financial support. She underlined the fact that 90% of the operations budget already was directed to staff salaries and benefits. She informed the teachers' team that the district's publics would not stand for another override election. "Such an attempt would bring down the wrath of the community on the schools," Leah contended.

After several weeks of conversation between the school board and teachers' negotiations teams, Leah met with the school superintendent and Merlin George to brief them on progress to date.

"I've spelled out the budget situation for the teachers," stated Leah. "I think it's time to present the recommendation to the teachers that it would be the best win-win strategy for all of us to forego any salary increases for next year; only salary increments based on experience or degree-credits using the present salary schedule would be provided. I think that I've got the teachers' team convinced that we're in a dire situation. Timing is good; just last week the factory workers at Specialty Supply accepted a cut in hourly pay," she noted. "Are you both agreeable to my plan?"

Questions

1. Assume the position of Merlin George in this case. How would you respond to Leah Smith?

2. What evidence in the case justifies this situation as win-win bargaining?

3. Knowing the economic conditions prior to negotiations in this case, what approaches and recommendations for negotiations might you have suggested?

☐ **CASE 10.2**
Legislative Alert!

Prior to the passing of S.B. 1008 (Negotiations for Public Employees), no state legislation had ever reached the senate floor in the area of collective bargaining. As passed, S.B. 1008 allowed boards of education to negotiate with teachers' groups on a permissive basis. That is, boards could negotiate with teachers' groups if they chose to do so. If the choice was made to negotiate, the bill stipulated that representative parties "must negotiate in good faith on topics of salary, benefits and working conditions."

Teachers' groups were active during the discussion stages of the legislation and lobbied long and hard for its approval. Because the legislation was permissive, school boards took little active part in either supporting or opposing its passage. School administrators generally were passive about the bill and had no hand in its design.

During the time S.B. 1008 was in discussion stages, another bill, S.B. 1111, also was being considered. S.B. 1111 dealt with public employee benefits. On the day S.B. 1111 was passed, an amendment was approved on the floor. The amendment stipulated that "when the provisions of S.B. 1008 are exhausted, S.B.

1111 comes into force." In brief, the Board of Industrial Relations was authorized to intervene and authorized to decide ongoing negotiations issues between parties.

Early in the implementation stages of S.B. 1008, one local teachers' group approached its board of education and requested to negotiate salaries for the ensuing year. The school board, using S.B. 1008's permissive provision, refused the request. As a result, the court of appeals ruled that the provisions of S.B. 1008 had been exhausted and therefore S.B. 1111 would come into effect. The matter of teachers' salaries would be determined by the Board of Industrial Relations.

The school board appealed to a higher court, claiming that its legislative responsibilities had been usurped. The higher court ruled that the Board of Industrial Relations was created by the state legislature and indeed was an authoritative extension of the legislative branch of government. Thus the decision by the Board of Industrial Relations on the matter of salaries would stand.

Questions

1. Discuss the implications of the case generally. For example, what can be learned from the case concerning involvement in legislative proposals relating to education?
2. Why is it important for administrators, teachers, and school boards to be knowledgeable about the legislative process generally and pending educational legislation specifically?

REFERENCES

American Association of School Personnel Administrators. (1978). *Trends in collective bargaining in public education*. Seven Hills, OH: Author.

Carlton, P. W., & Goodwin, H. I. (1969). *The collective dilemma: Negotiations in education*. Worthington, OH: Charles A. Jones.

Class size must be negotiated with teachers, Oregon court rules. (1991, April 10). *Education Week*, p. 2.

Colon, R. J. (1989). Issues brought to grievance arbitration by Iowa Public School teachers: January 1982 through December 1986. *Journal of Collective Negotiations in the Public Sector*, *18*(3), 217–227.

Compton-Forbes, P. (1984). Interest arbitration hasn't worked in the public sector. *Personnel administrator*, *29*(2), 99–104.

Creswell, A. M., & Murphy, M. J. (1980). *Teachers, unions, and collective bargaining in public education*. Berkeley, CA: McCutchan.

Cunningham, L. L., & Hentges, J. T. (1982). *The American school superintendency—A summary report*. Arlington, VA: American Association of School Administrators.

Diegmueller, K. (1991, April 17). Tight budgets escalate school labor tensions. *Education Week*, p. 14.

Kennedy, G., Benson, J., & McMillan, J. (1982). *Managing negotiations*. Englewood Cliffs, NJ: Prentice-hall.

Labor Management Relations Act of 1947 (Taft-Hartley Act). 301 (a) 61 stat. 156.29 U.S.C. 185 (a) 1964.

Lieberman, M. (1969). Forming your negotiations team. *School Management*, *13*(12), 30.

Lieberman, M., & Moskow, M. H. (1966). *Collective negotiations for teachers*. Washington, DC: Office of Professional Development and Welfare.

McCollum, J. K., & Norris, D. R. (1984). Nonunion grievance machinery in southern industry. *Personnel administrator*, *29*(11), 106.

McCoy, M. W., Gips, C. J., & Evans, M. W. (1983). *The American school personnel administrator: An analysis of characteristics and role*. Seven Hills, OH: AASPA.

National Education Association. (1961). *Addresses and proceedings*. Washington, DC: Author.

National Education Association. (1962). *Addresses and proceedings*. Washington, DC: Author.

National Education Association. (1965). *Guidelines for professional negotiation*. Washington, DC: Office of Professional Development and Welfare.

National Education Association. (1968). Listing of 1967–68 agreements. *Negotiations Research Digest*, *1*(10), E-1–E-29.

National Education Association. (1991, September). The 1991–1992 resolutions of the National Education Association. *NEA Today*, pp. 15–25.

National School Boards Association. (1991, March 6). Resolutions: Proposed changes for 1991–92. *School Board News*, pp. 2–7.

Norton, M. S. (1989). *The school personnel administrator in Arizona*. Tempe, AZ: Arizona State University, Division of Educational Leadership and Policy Studies.

Norton, M. S., & Farrar, R. D. (1987). *Competency-based preparations of educational administrators—Tasks, competencies and indicators of competency*. Tempe, AZ: Arizona State University, College of Education.

Perry, C. R., & Wildman, A. W. (1970). *The impact of negotiations in public education*. Worthington, OH: Charles A. Jones.

Peterson, L. J., Rossmiller, R. A., & Volz, M. M. (1978). *The law and public school operation* (2nd ed.). New York: Harper & Row.

Rebore, R. W. (1991). *Personnel administration in education: A management approach* (3rd ed.). Englewood Cliffs, NJ: Prentice-Hall.

Reck, R. R., & Long, B. G. (1987). *Win Win negotiator*. Kalamazoo, MI: Spartan Publications.

Redfern, G. B. (1967). *Ways and means of PN: Professional negotiations and the school administrator*. Arlington, VA: American Association of School Administrators.

Rojot, J. (1991). *Negotiation from theory to practice*. London: Macmillan Academic and Professional.

Schoonmaker, A. N. (1989). *Negotiate to win*. Englewood Cliffs, NJ: Prentice-Hall.

Standohar, P. D. (1975). Results of final-offer arbitration of bargaining disputes. *California Management Review*, *18*(1), 57–61.

Strahan, R. D. (1969). Legal guidelines for the management of collective agreements in education. *Legal Briefs for School Administrators*. Houston, TX: Gulf School Research Development Association.

Tozer, J. E. (1980). *Components affecting successful negotiations in public schools in Arizona*. Unpublished doctoral dissertation, Arizona State University, Tempe.

Van Fleet, D. D. (1991). *Contemporary management*. Boston: Houghton Mifflin.

Walter, R. L. (1975). *The teacher and collective bargaining*. Lincoln, NE: Educators Publications.

Wary, C. (1983). *Costing out the labor agreement*. Trenton, NJ: New Jersey School Boards Association.

Ways, M. (1979, January). The virtues, dangers, and limits of negotiation, *Fortune*, p. 90.

Wesley, E. B. (1957). *NEA: The first hundred years*. New York: Harper.

11

The Compensation Process

One of the most difficult processes of the human resources function is compensation administration. Compensation decisions have significant consequences for both the school district and its employees. Between 80% and 90% of the current operating budget of a typical school district is allocated to personnel salaries, wages, and benefits. Compensation affects the district's ability to attract, motivate, and retain qualified employees. Compensation is a major factor in employee morale. The employees' status and recognition in society and in the school system, as well as their economic welfare, are linked to their compensation (Castetter, 1992).

The compensation program designed and adopted by the school district may be described in many ways. In this chapter the compensation program is described in terms of two broad components: direct compensation (wages and salaries) and indirect compensation (employee benefits and services). Before turning to a discussion of these components, however, the opening sections of the chapter deal with the development of school district compensation policies and the major determinants of school district salaries. The discussion of direct compensation in this chapter will focus on compensation of certificated personnel. Direct compensation (salaries) for classified personnel is discussed in Chapter 12.

COMPENSATION POLICIES

The development of school district compensation policies is central to the effective administration of the compensation program. The school district should stipulate in writing its intent with respect to the compensation of personnel (Castetter, 1992). Such stated policies, as pointed out by Johns, Morphet, and Alexander (1983),

> give assurance to the community that sound procedures will be observed in compensating employees, give assurance to the staff that recognized policies rather than haphazard procedures will be followed, and provide guidance to the personnel administration in devel-

oping satisfactory procedures for obtaining and retaining the services of competent personnel. (p. 312)

The following guidelines (Castetter, 1992; Foster, 1960; Foulkes & Livernash, 1983) should be considered by school districts in developing and implementing compensation policies.

1. All personnel in the district, certificated and noncertificated, should be included in the compensation policies.
2. The compensation system should be concerned with attracting, motivating, and retaining personnel at all levels.
3. The salary system should be equitable. This requires that each position be evaluated in terms of relative importance to other positions, a hierarchical arrangement established, and salary awarded accordingly.
4. The compensation program should be nondiscriminatory, defensible, and legal.
5. The compensation plan should be competitive with other school districts and, as much as possible, with other public agencies and the private sector.
6. Quality of performance should be recognized. Performance appraisal and accompanying differential reward structures should provide the basis for advancement in income and overcome the limitations of the single salary schedule.
7. Nondirect compensation should be a built-in feature of the compensation program. Employee benefits can constitute as much as one-third of the personnel budget. They are normally an important component of the negotiated agreement. School districts must recognize their obligation to provide competitive and attractive nondirect compensation.
8. The compensation program must be constantly monitored and reviewed to ensure its internal consistency and equity and its competitiveness with external agencies and organizations.
9. The compensation program and process should be openly derived and communicated to all employees and interested citizens.

DETERMINANTS OF COMPENSATION

A number of factors directly or indirectly determines the compensation program established by the school district, including (1) supply and demand, (2) ability to pay, (3) cost of living, (4) prevailing wage rates, (5) collective bargaining, and (6) government regulations. Although the effect of each factor may be difficult to determine precisely, each must be considered as a part of a collective force that is referred to as the wage mix (Sherman, Bohlander, & Chruden, 1988). Each of these factors is discussed in this section.

Supply and Demand

The economic concept of supply and demand states that the price (wages) paid for any good or service is a function of the supply of and demand for the good or service. The supply-and-demand concept applied to teacher salary determination is depicted in Figure 11.1. The demand curve D_t represents both the private (family or individual) demand for education and the spillover demand for education. Spillover, or social, demand for education results from the fact that everyone gains something from having a well-educated citizenry. The downward slope of the curve suggests that at very high salaries, everyone will buy less education and fewer teachers will be demanded. The supply curve, S_T, suggests that as teacher salaries rise, assuming other salaries remain the same, more people will enter the teaching profession. As the supply of teachers increases, salaries will decrease (Richardson & Williams, 1981).

The demand for teachers, although in large part determined by the number of students to be served, is also a function of nonmarket considerations. The state legislature, the state department of education, and local school boards can greatly influence both the supply and the demand for teachers and other education professionals through such actions as the establishment of certification and accreditation standards, the decision to offer certain types of programs, or the offering of retirement incentives.

The supply of teachers is composed of two groups: continuing teachers and new entrants. New entrants include not only new teacher graduates (20% of new hires), but those who secured teaching degrees who never entered teaching, those reentering teaching after some break in service (26% of new hires), and noneducation graduates entering the teaching profession through alternative certification routes (U.S. Department of Education, 1992).

The demand projections in Table 11.1 are based on the assumptions that the total K–12 enrollment will increase, that teacher-pupil ratios will continue in their gradual decline at the elementary level, and that the turnover rate of teachers will remain between 5% and 6%. The projected demand for hiring new teachers is expected to exceed 200,000 annually. Demand for both elementary and secondary teachers is expected to decline into the mid 1990s, before rising and ending the decade with an increase in demand of 10,000 per year.

Projecting the supply of teachers is far more difficult than projecting the demand. Although projections of the supply of new teacher graduates are available and indicate that this number would meet about one-half the demand (if they all entered teaching), it is more difficult to predict how many of the teacher education graduates

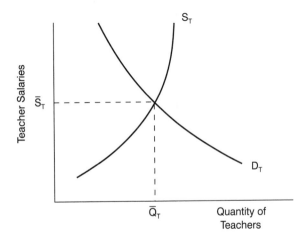

FIGURE 11.1
Supply and Demand for Teachers
Source: From "Determining an Appropriate Teacher Salary" by J. A. Richardson and J. T. Williams, 1981, *Journal of Education Finance*, 7, p. 193. Copyright © 1981 by the Institute for Educational Finance. Reprinted by permission.

TABLE 11.1

Projected Annual Demand for New Teachers, 1990–2000

Source: From *The Condition of Education 1990*, U.S. Department of Education, National Center for Education Statistics, 1990, Washington, DC: Author

Fall of Year	Total Number	Elementary	Secondary
1990	233,000	122,000	110,000
1991	205,000	109,000	95,000
1992	208,000	111,000	96,000
1993	226,000	120,000	106,000
1994	218,000	117,000	101,000
1995	219,000	117,000	102,000
1996	227,000	121,000	107,000
1997	234,000	124,000	110,000
1998	238,000	126,000	112,000
1999	239,000	126,000	113,000
2000	243,000	128,000	114,000

who never entered teaching or former teachers currently unemployed or in other positions are considering reentering teaching. It is also difficult to project how many persons in other professions are willing to enter teaching. Currently serious attention is being given to attempts to attract into teaching persons affected by the dramatic downsizing of the military and defense industry.

Ability to Pay

A fundamental determinant of school district compensation is the district's financial ability and willingness to pay. Differences in teachers' salaries among school districts can largely be explained by variations in local fiscal capacity (assessed valuation of property per pupil) and community willingness to tax and spend for education (effort), as King (1979) found in New York State and Kitchen (1983) in Texas. Adkison and McKenzie (1990) discovered the same held true for administrators' salaries.

Whereas a district has little control over its tax base, unless there are statutory tax or expenditure limitations to the contrary, it does have control over the effort it makes to support education. In fact, in the process of collective bargaining, unions have often justified their demands for increases in compensation or have been awarded increases by arbitrators because the district's tax rate was substantially below that of its neighbors or below the state average.

Cost of Living

The standard most often used for determining salary increases is the cost-of-living index (Beebe, 1983). The cost-of-living index is "a measure of the average changes in the cost of goods purchased by consumers against the cost during some base period" (Henderson, 1985, p. 746). Salary adjustments based on the cost-of-living index do not reflect judgments about the economic value of persons holding positions or their performance. Rather, they reflect the sentiment that unless personnel compensation keeps pace with the cost of living, the resulting decline in purchasing power has the same effect as a salary cut. As a result, a cost-of-living (COL) clause is commonly included in bargaining agreements. The three most common types of COL clauses are (1) the **escalator clause,** which provides for periodic adjustment during the contract year without additional negotiations if changes in the consumer price index (CPI) reach or exceed a certain limit; (2) the **reopener clause,** which provides for negotiations to begin immediately or at the end of the contract year if changes in the CPI reach or exceed a certain limit; and (3) the **end-of-year clause,** found only in multiyear contracts, which automatically, without further bargaining, translate changes in the CPI into salary adjustments (Educational Resource Service, 1987b).

The cost of living differs not only over time but among school districts in a state. Costs associated with energy services, construction, consumer goods, and personnel services vary among rural, suburban, and urban areas and among geographical regions in the state. For example, cost-of-living indexes for the largest cities in Florida ranged from 110 in Miami to 94 in Jacksonville (Nelson, 1990). In New York State the difference between Buffalo (100.5) and New York City (150.9) is greater than the difference between New York State and any other state (Nelson, 1991). If a school district is to maintain the purchasing power of its employees, it must consider these differences in making compensation determinations.

Prevailing Wage Rate

The second most important determinant of current wage increases is the comparability of current rates of pay with those of neighboring school districts (Beebe, 1983). It would be difficult for a school district to attract and retain competent personnel if its compensation levels were significantly below those paid by other school districts or other potential employers in the community. Data pertaining to prevailing wage rates may be obtained from state and national departments of labor, from surveys conducted by the school district personnel department, and from data supplied by employee organizations. It is common practice for employee groups to gather such data and, when supportive, to use it in collective negotiations. Although the veracity of data supplied by the union need not be doubted per se, because of the possibility of selectivity in collection (i.e., collecting data primarily from those districts and employers known to pay higher salaries), good practice dictates that the human resources office should assume some responsibility for the systematic collection of wage and salary data. The data collected should include not only direct compensation but, because of its impact on the attractiveness and value of the total compensation package, indirect compensation.

Unionization

If school district employees are unionized, wages and other conditions of employment may be greatly determined through the process of collective bargaining. In the negotiations process, both the union and the district will focus on those factors that support their bargaining positions (e.g., supply and demand, ability to pay, cost of living, and prevailing wage rates). As a result, wages and salaries are generally higher in areas where employee organizations are strong (Sherman et al., 1988).

Government Regulations

Like many other areas of human resources administration, compensation administration has become the subject of an increasing number of laws enacted by the state and federal governments. The majority of states have statutes providing minimum salaries for teachers. In a number of states, provision is also made for minimum salaries for administrators and other personnel. In addition, numerous state and federal laws address issues related to the compensation of support personnel.

The major piece of federal legislation dealing directly with compensation is the Fair Labor Standards Act (FLSA) passed in 1938 and amended many times. The major provisions of the FLSA are concerned with minimum pay, overtime pay, child labor, and equal pay. The Equal Pay Act of 1963 has become one of the most significant amendments to the FLSA:

> No employer having employees subject to any provisions of this section shall discriminate between . . . employees on the basis of sex by paying wages to employees . . . at a rate less than the rate at which he pays wages to employees of the opposite sex . . . for equal work on jobs the performance of which requires equal skill, effort, and responsibility, and which are performed under similar working conditions. (§206 (d)(1))

According to the provisions of the Equal Pay Act, any difference in pay because of sex must be rationally justified and be the result of a job evaluation study. The Equal Pay Act has been the basis for numerous suits in the field of education seeking to eliminate discriminatory compensation practices. However, wage differentials based on factors such as seniority, merit, or productivity are not prohibited by the Equal Pay Act. To sustain a claim under the Equal Pay Act, the employee must prove not only a disparity in wages between men and women, but also that the disparity exists in substantially equal jobs.

A number of other federal laws have a significant impact on the compensation practices of school districts. For example, the Social Security Act of 1935, the Health Maintenance Organization (HMO) Act of 1973, and several of the civil rights statutes are intended to protect the welfare and wages of employees. Title VII of the Civil Rights Act of 1964, which was discussed in Chapter 9 in relation to such human resources issues as hiring, promotion, testing, and termination, also protects against discrimination in compensation, as do the Equal Employment Opportunity Act of 1972, the Age Discrimination in Employment Act Amendments of 1978, and the Pregnancy Discrimination Act of 1978. In the last quarter century, legislatures and the courts have concerned themselves with questions of equity and discrimination in employment. Although these efforts declined somewhat during the Reagan and Bush administrations, they are expected to receive renewed attention during the Clinton administration.

DIRECT COMPENSATION: TEACHER AND ADMINISTRATOR SALARIES

The problems associated with the salaries of teachers have become more visible as a result of the publicity given both to employee activism and to the recommendations of the National Commission on Excellence in Education (1983) and later reform reports that recommended that salaries for the teaching profession "should be increased and should be professionally competitive, market sensitive, and performance based" (p. 30). Almost unanimously, these reform reports recognized that "teaching must offer salaries, benefits, and working conditions competitive with those of other professions" (Carnegie Forum on Education and the Economy, 1986, p. 99).

One of the more important trends that has emerged as a result of the school reform movement has been more active involvement of state legislatures in teacher compensation—a policy area that has historically been considered the domain of local school districts. Public officials wanting to improve teaching conditions came to recognize teacher pay as a critical policy variable. In an increasing number of states, now at least 30, state minimum salaries have been established (Darling-Hammond & Berry, 1988). In many states legislative willingness to improve funding for education and to increase teachers' salaries has been at least partially contingent upon a demonstration of increased teacher competence and improved student results. As a consequence various plans have been adopted by state and local governments to provide motivation and incentives for greater performance. In this section consideration will be given to the more popular of these plans. First, however, because the single salary schedule accounts for over 90% of teacher salary schedules across the nation (Educational Research Service [ERS], 1987b), attention will be given to the components and methods used with the single salary schedule, as well as compensation for extracurricular activities.

The Single Salary Schedule for Teachers

The single salary schedule pays equivalent salaries for equivalent preparation and experience. The single salary schedule is based on a set of assumptions that are the exact opposite of those underlying the position salary plan. Assumptions underlying the single salary schedule include the following (Greene, 1971):

1. Teaching of all grade levels and subjects is of equal importance and equally difficult.
2. The more professional preparation and training the teacher has, the more effective the teacher.
3. The more experience a teacher has, the more effective the teacher.
4. Salary variations are unnecessary and undesirable motivations for teachers.
5. The single salary schedule minimizes frictions and dissatisfaction among teachers.
6. The single salary schedule is the easiest to administer.

The single salary schedule has long been popular with boards of education because it is easy to understand and administer and allows for a rather simple budgeting process for salaries. Teacher organizations historically have also favored the single salary schedule but in recent years have given increased support to compensation plans that use this salary schedule as the base for programs that recognize greater performance or career progression.

The single salary schedule has two basic dimensions: a horizontal dimension made up of columns generally referred to as lanes, scales, or classes, which correspond to levels of academic preparation (e.g., bachelor's degree, master's degree, master's degree plus 30 hours, doctoral degree), and a vertical dimension of rows of "steps" that correspond to the years of teaching experience. A teacher's salary schedule does not have a standard number of columns or rows, although there are usually more rows than columns so that the schedule tends to form a vertical matrix.[1] (See Table 11.2.)

The Horizontal Dimension.   There are two basic ways to establish the professional preparation scales: (1) complete or full schedules and (2) additive schedules. The complete or full schedule, the more common of the two, normally recognizes at least two academic degrees, the bachelor's and the master's, as well as intermediate lanes that recognize a specified number of college credits beyond the academic degree (e.g., B.A. + 15 hours, M.A. + 30 hours, M.A. + 60 hours). Many such schedules also have columns for educational specialist degrees and doctorates. An example of a variation of this schedule is the Philadelphia "senior career teacher" program, which provides a bonus of $5,000 or more to teachers who are M.A. + 60 hours, have 10 years teaching experience, and have dual certification (Gursky, 1992b).

The additive schedule is not based on several academic degrees, but on the bachelor's degree and the number of college credit hours beyond it. Each salary scale represents a certain number of credit hours beyond the bachelor's. If an advanced degree is earned, however, a fixed amount or an amount related to a percentage of base is added beyond the salary figure represented on the schedule. The payment of the advanced degree additives creates, in effect, scales paralleling the established ones. A variation of the additive schedule establishes similar scales based on the master's degree. The major difference between the two schedules is that in the full or complete schedule, all possible salaries are represented, whereas in the additive schedule, salaries above those specified on the established schedule can be included.

The Vertical Dimension.   The vertical steps on the salary schedule provide salary increases based on the number of years of teaching experience. An upper limit generally is placed on the number of steps, usually around 15. A common practice is to offer more steps in the higher academic preparation scales than in the lower. This provides incentive for teachers to attain additional education.

Several factors determine the initial placement of a new teacher to a specific vertical step on a scale, but the most common factor is previous teaching experience. To receive credit for any previous year's teaching, the teacher usually must have taught 75% of the school year. Most school districts place a limit on the number of years of teaching experience that will be credited toward initial placement on the salary schedule. Whether the experience is in or out of the district or in or out of the state affects this decision.

Other considerations in making the initial placement are credit for related experience, credit for military service, and credit for other experience. Some districts recognize related experience such as public library experience for librarians or recreational

---

[1]The discussion of the single salary schedule is largely based on *Methods of Scheduling Salaries for Teachers* (pp. 1–4, 6), Educational Research Service, 1987, Arlington, VA: Author. Copyright © 1987 by the Educational Research Service. Adapted by permission.

TABLE 11.2
Mesa, Arizona, Teacher Salary Schedule, 1992–1993

	A BA	B BA+15	C BA+30	D BA+45 MA	E MA+15	F MA+30	G MA+30 EdS	H MA+60	I MA+75 EdD PhD
Line 3	23,466	24,221	24,976	25,731	26,486	27,241	27,996	28,751	29,506
Line 4	24,145	24,900	25,655	26,410	27,165	27,920	28,675	29,430	30,185
Line 5	25,050	25,805	26,560	27,315	28,070	28,825	29,580	30,335	31,090
Line 6	25,963	26,718	27,473	28,228	28,983	29,738	30,493	31,248	32,003
Line 7	26,417	27,653	28,408	29,163	29,918	30,673	31,428	32,183	32,938
Line 8		29,014	29,769	30,524	31,279	32,034	32,789	33,544	34,299
Line 9		29,522	31,130	31,885	32,640	33,395	34,150	34,905	35,660
Line 10			32,960	33,715	34,470	35,225	35,980	36,735	37,490
Line 11			33,537	35,545	36,300	37,055	37,810	38,565	39,320
Line 12				37,375	38,130	38,885	39,640	40,395	41,150
Line 13				38,029	40,254	41,009	41,764	42,519	43,274
Line 14					40,958	41,727	44,090	44,845	45,600
Line 15							44,862	45,630	46,398
Longevity A							45,759	46,543	47,326
Longevity B							46,656	47,455	48,254
Longevity C							47,553	48,368	49,182

Source: From Mesa Unified School District, Mesa, AZ.

experience for physical educators. Others grant full or partial credit for military service or for experience in the Peace Corps, VISTA, or the National Teachers Corps.

Vertical advancement from one step to the next within the scale is normally automatic after a stipulated period of time, usually 1 year, although longer periods may be required for advancement to the higher steps. Teachers' groups have continued to advocate automatic advancement, but in an increasing number of districts certain restrictions are being placed on vertical advancements. These include (1) advancement at specified points contingent on additional units of academic credit or completion of in-service training programs, (2) annual advancement contingent upon satisfactory performance, and (3) advancement based on merit.

To provide for teachers who have reached the maximum number of steps in a particular scale, some salary schedules also provide for supermaximum or long-term service increments beyond the highest step in the scale. Although in most instances the awarding of this increment is based solely on the attainment of a specific number of years of experience above the highest number recognized on the schedule, in some cases a performance or merit evaluation is required before the award is made.

Establishment of Salary Increments and Increases. An increment is the difference between two points on a salary schedule and may be either horizontal or vertical. The actual dollar difference between points on scales or points on steps can be established by:

1. a fixed dollar amount whereby each scale or step is the same dollar amount higher than the previous one;
2. a variable dollar amount between scales or steps;
3. a fixed ratio schedule whereby each step in all scales is determined by applying a ratio to some base amount (index), usually the B.A. minimum, and the specific ratio at each step varies from the ratio at the previous step by a fixed value (e.g., 1.03, 1.06, 1.09, etc.);
4. a variable ratio schedule that operates the same as a fixed ratio schedule, except the value of the ratio from one step to the next is not fixed but varies.

Both the actual dollar increments and the increases (raises) may be determined as a result of collective negotiations and may not follow any discernible pattern; however, most salary schedules are not haphazardly constructed but reflect some methodology. The most common salary schedule changes that provide for salary increases are (1) changes in the index or ratio base, (2) changes in the index structure, (3) across-the-board changes, and (4) variable changes. If a schedule is based on the indexing method, a change in the index or ratio base (e.g., B.A. minimum) on which all other salaries are based increases all salaries by the same percentage without altering the existing index structure. Alternatively, holding the base constant while modifying the index figures by fixed index points (e.g., 1.03 increased to 1.05, 1.06 increased to 1.08, 1.09 increased to 1.11, etc.) results in varying percentage increases at each step. Indexing is no longer the predominant method of scheduling salaries, however, so these two approaches for determining salary increases are not commonly used.

The most common method of providing salary increases is by fixed, across-the-board increases in either dollar amounts or percentages. Across-the-board dollar raises, although the more common of the two, are probably the most unfair because those at the lower end of the salary schedule receive the largest percentage increases. Those who have been with the district for a number of years or have sought additional education may feel penalized by a raise that percentage-wise is less than half that received by those at the lower levels of the schedules. Across-the-board percentage raises, on the other hand, maintain the established relationship between steps. An across-the-board percentage raise has the same effect as a percentage increase in the base or index of a ratio schedule.

The variable change approach to salary allows different dollar increases to be added to different salary levels. These variable increases, however, are not randomly assigned; they reflect district policy and philosophy. For example, faced with a teaching force characterized by higher levels of experience and education, some districts have felt financially constrained to refrain from hiring persons with advanced experience or education or to decrease the percentage or dollar awards to those beyond a certain number of years of experience or education. Yet other districts have adopted just the opposite policy and reward these individuals.

Incentive Pay Plans

The educational reform movement has brought school districts across the country under increased pressure to attract and retain good teachers, motivate them to greater performance, and reward them for outstanding performance. Teacher incentive plans are perceived as one strategy to achieve these goals. Some form of teacher incentive plan now exists in 25 states (Southern Regional Education Board, 1992). Although merit pay is often considered synonymous with incentive pay, the concepts are different. Merit pay is differential pay awarded to individuals with the same job description on the basis of higher levels of performance. The concept of incentive pay, on the other hand, includes not only merit pay but various other proposals that, in effect, pay teachers more for different work or additional work (e.g., master teacher plans or career ladder plans). In this section consideration will be given to the following incentive pay proposals: (1) merit pay, (2) educational productivity plans, (3) differentiated staffing and master teacher plans, (4) career ladders, and (5) market sensitive salaries.

Merit Pay.   Merit pay for teachers is not a new concept. Before the widespread adoption of the single salary schedule in the 1920s, many district salary plans were based on or had a "merit" component. Use of merit pay decreased throughout the 1930s and 1940s, received some revived interest in the 1950s and 1960s, but then continued to decline so that by the 1977–1978 school year, only 4% of the school systems reported using merit pay (ERS, 1979).

A major controversy surrounding merit pay is whether it can motivate teachers to improve teaching. The research seems to clearly indicate, and teachers consistently agree, that intrinsic psychological and symbolic rewards rather than extrinsic material rewards like money are the prime motivators of teachers (Dunwell, 1991; Kottkamp, Provenzo, & Cohn, 1986; Mitchell & Peters, 1988). Even if teachers were motivated by money, opponents of merit pay argue that paying a small percentage of teachers a merit supplement, and one that is usually small, provides a token, not an incentive.

In spite of past experiences or current controversy, beginning in the early 1980s a growing number of states and local school districts began experimenting with merit pay plans. Support for merit pay has increasingly come from outside the schools. Not only did various reform reports recommend performance-based teacher salaries, but according to the Gallup polls the public supports merit pay for teachers, as do a growing number of local, state, and national policymakers. Supporters of merit pay argue that if teachers are paid on the basis of performance, they will work harder and become more effective, and those not willing or able to do so will leave the profession (Mickler, 1987). They also believe that merit pay will encourage better teachers to remain in education and will attract higher quality individuals into teaching. It is also strongly argued that merit pay systems would tend to make schools operate more like businesses, would make them more productive and accountable, and would thereby make it easier for them to gain increased public support and services.

To be successful, any plan for merit pay must be based on careful planning, must have clearly articulated purposes, must have the support of teachers, and must ensure their involvement in its development and implementation. Major issues that must be resolved before any such plan can be implemented include the following: What criteria will be used to identify meritorious performance? How and by whom will teachers be evaluated? Will there be a quota on the number of teachers who will be rewarded, or will there be unlimited opportunity for reward? Will the additional pay be a one-time bonus, or will it become part of the teacher's salary base and thus increase the salary in all subsequent years?

If merit pay is based on classroom performance, evaluators must be trained in observation and evaluation techniques. Evaluation criteria must be job related, evaluation procedures must conform to due process standards, and evaluators must receive special training. Sufficient time must be given to the process. Financing must be adequate and secure. Merit raises must supplement, not supplant, the cost of living adjustments necessary for all teachers to keep pace with inflation. And, perhaps most important, there must be strong administrative commitment to the program and to ensuring that each of the "musts" is an actuality.

Educational Productivity Plans.   The educational productivity approach to incentive pay assesses and rewards teachers and other school personnel based on results and output measures of student progress as determined by the state or local school board. For example, Oklahoma City Public Schools pay a $300 bonus to teachers who accept positions in seven schools that have been identified as "academically troubled." An additional $400 is awarded if achievement improves and the school is declared to be no longer academically troubled. Other bonuses are given for improving achievement and attendance in special academic programs. Principals and assistant principals are also eligible to earn bonuses of more than $8,000 through incentives based on student progress, teacher attendance, and the school being removed from the academically troubled list (Southern Regional Education Board, 1992).

At the state level, South Carolina's *Campus Incentive Programs* is designed to reward principals, assistant principals, teachers, media specialists, guidance counselors, psychologists, school nurses, and others (as determined by a state advisory committee) in schools that demonstrate superior performance and productivity. Funding for the program in 1991 was about $30 per student (Southern Regional Education Board, 1992).

Master Teacher Plans.   The differentiated staffing concept differs significantly from the merit pay or educational productivity concepts. Instead of rewarding superior teaching, this approach awards higher salaries to individuals who have assumed additional responsibilities. The most popular forms of differentiated staffing currently being proposed include the designation of master teachers. Master teachers are those who have been identified for their teaching effectiveness and their ability to help other teachers improve their skills. A master teacher continues in the classroom but assumes additional responsibilities in working with other teachers.

One type of master teacher is the ***lead teacher.*** Lead teachers are intended to serve as instructional leaders, not as another layer of administration, and perform such functions as planning curricula, planning and organizing in-service training, coordinating schedules, and monitoring and analyzing student evaluations. The salary supplement given to lead teachers may be mandated by state statute, collective negotiations, or local practice. In some districts the supplement is a percentage (usually 5% to 15%) of current salary. In other districts a set amount is paid all lead teachers in the district. For example, as part of the highly publicized incentive pay programs in Granville County, North Carolina, lead teachers are selected by the entire staff, serve 2 years, and receive a $1,200 annual stipend (Gursky, 1992a).

Another form of master teacher is the **mentor teacher.** A mentor teacher is an experienced teacher with demonstrated competence in the classroom who has been formally designated to serve as a mentor to new teachers as they make the transition from the world of theory to the world of practice (Futrell, 1988). Mentor teachers normally are expected to observe the classroom instruction of the novice teacher and provide feedback, advise, and consult with the novice teacher in classroom management, lesson planning, and instructional strategies, and in various ways nurture and support the professional development of the beginning teacher. Compensation for these efforts may come in the form of a salary supplement during the year or in the form of supplemental contracts (Zimpher & Rieger, 1988). In California state law specifies that up to 5% of the teachers in a district can serve as mentors. In 1992 over 10,000 mentor teachers in California worked with 16,000 new teachers and received an average annual stipend of $4,300. In addition to California, in 1992 eight other states funded statewide mentor projects (Southern Regional Education Board, 1992).

Career Ladders. The career ladder plan differs from differentiated staffing in that it creates entirely new career steps and promotes teachers to more highly paid teaching levels. Teachers at higher levels may be responsible for teaching and evaluating other teachers, staff development, curriculum development, or supervision of student teachers. Some may teach more hours or more months. In all cases, however, the teacher remains in the classroom, at least in part, and assumes certain additional responsibilities. In effect, as noted by former Secretary of Education Terrel Bell (1988), career ladders "enable teachers to qualify for promotions without having to move out of the classroom" (p. 405).

The typical career ladder plan has three to five career levels, for example, (1) entry (or probationary or apprentice), (2) continuing (or regular or career), (3) senior, and (4) master. All new teachers begin at the entry level and are pretenure and on probation. Participation beyond level 2 is voluntary. Advancement to the next highest level is based on the number of years in the present level (normally at least 3 years) and on an evaluation that normally considers professional expertise, student performance, and professional growth and development. In addition, advancement to the master teacher level may require a demonstrated ability to work with other teachers. As teachers advance to higher levels, they are given not only higher pay but more responsibilities.

In recent years some 30 states have piloted or implemented career ladder programs (Ruhl, Johnson, & Steele, 1990). Most have failed or fallen victim to budgetary cutbacks. Nonetheless, in 1992 over $500 million will be paid to thousands of teachers involved in state and locally sponsored career ladder programs. In 1992 seven states (Arizona, Missouri, North Carolina, Tennessee, Ohio, Texas, and Utah) provided state funding for career ladder programs (Southern Regional Education Board, 1992).

According to administrators who have researched and administered career ladder programs, successful programs are distinguished from unsuccessful programs in five dimensions (Poston & Frase, 1991):

1. *No legislative involvement or restrictive outside funding.*   Successful programs most often are those that have decided to go it alone and have therefore been free of political ties and ill-considered mandates that result in unreasonable time restraints, lack of focus, unrealistic structures, discriminatory quotas, and inadequate funding.

2. *Teacher cooperation in planning.*   Those people who were going to make the system work were cooperatively and meaningfully involved in planning and developing the program in successful districts.

3. *Clear and attainable objectives.*   Successful programs have clearly stated, locally determined objectives designed to meet local needs, not obstruct objectives designed to address political goals.

4. *Freedom to determine the form of rewards.*   Successful programs not only provided increased pay but also used rewards that expanded teachers' intrinsic motivation to teach and improved their teaching skills. Examples include providing funds for professional travel, releasing them for professional activities, and providing equipment and materials otherwise unavailable.

5. *Sound and valid measures of teacher performance.*   Successful districts tended to utilize reliable evaluation systems that address those teaching behaviors that have been shown to be related to increasing student achievement.

Market Sensitive Salaries.   School districts often experience difficulty in recruiting and retaining teachers in certain subject areas. Currently many districts are finding it difficult to employ qualified special education, foreign language, and bilingual teachers. Other districts are finding it difficult to recruit psychologists and librarians. One approach to remedying this problem is to offer incentives to currently employed teachers to retrain in these areas of shortage. Another approach is to establish market sensitive salaries. This approach was recommended in the report of the National Commission on Excellence in Education (1983) and involves the establishment of differentiated beginning salaries and salary schedules for the shortage areas, which would reflect differentiated market rates. Salary distinctions would be based not on experience or degrees but on the forces of the market. The major weakness of the proposal lies in its impact on current salary arrangements and concepts of equity among teacher salaries (Cresap, McCormick, & Paget, 1984).

Compensation for Extracurricular Activities

At one time extracurricular activities were considered normal duties that teachers had to assume as part of their work. In the 1950s, however, as teacher salaries began to lose ground in a rising economy and as many teachers sought to supplement their incomes by working second jobs, teachers' organizations became more aggressive in seeking additional compensation for time spent in extracurricular activities (Greene, 1971). Today districts generally compensate teachers with supplemental pay for the guidance and supervision of students engaged in extracurricular activities. As indicated by the listing in Table 11.3, supplements are paid for a variety of extracurricular activities.

TABLE 11.3

Extracurricular Pay
Supplements, 1990–1991
(pp. 327–328)
Source: From *Extra Pay for Extra
Duties of Teachers* (5th ed., tables
5, 6, 16, 17), Educational Research
Service, 1991, Arlington, VA:
Author. Copyright © 1991 by the
Educational Research Service.

Activity	Mean of Maximum Supplements	Mean of Maximum Supplements as Percentage of Maximum Salaries Schedule for Classroom Teachers
Senior High Head		
Athletic Trainer	$ 3,911	9.30
Football Coach	3,608	8.76
Athletic Director	3,605	8.61
Basketball Coach	3,170	7.72
Hockey Coach (ice/field)	2,741	5.87
Wrestling Coach	2,708	6.36
Track Coach	2,497	6.03
Baseball Coach	2,458	5.88
Swimming Coach	2,426	5.60
Gymnastics Coach	2,423	5.46
Soccer Coach	2,287	5.23
Softball Coach	2,250	5.23
Volleyball Coach	2,235	5.41
Cheerleader Coach	1,870	4.39
Cross-Country Coach	1,870	4.40
Tennis Coach	1,828	4.31
Golf Coach	1,676	3.99
Intramural Coach	1,363	3.13
Band Director	3,205	7.87
Director of Music	2,236	5.37
Assistant Band Director	1,989	4.88
Chorus Director	1,807	4.42
Dramatics Director	1,712	4.00
Orchestra Director	1,637	3.93
Yearbook Advisor	1,564	3.64

The methods used by school districts in scheduling the supplements vary widely. A survey by the ERS (1991) found 67% of the districts compensated teachers for extra duties by paying a fixed amount unrelated to the teachers' salaries. The fixed amount could be a lump sum, multiple units of a specific amount, or a percentage of a fixed amount not on the teachers' salary schedule. The size of the fixed amount normally depends on some consideration of the activity involved.

Table 11.4 provides an example of the multiple units approach. In this example, the hours associated with each extracurricular assignment have been determined and a fixed amount per hour ($15) was applied to determine the amount of the supplement.

TABLE 11.3
continued

Activity	Mean of Maximum Supplements	Mean of Maximum Supplements as Percentage of Maximum Salaries Schedule for Classroom Teachers
Debate Advisor	1,443	3.69
Speech Advisor	1,456	3.57
Drill Team Director	1,446	3.50
Newspaper Advisor	1,328	3.07
Student Council Advisor	1,244	2.90
Dramatics Director (per play)	1,196	2.82
Class Sponsor	988	2.29
Literary Magazine Advisor	887	1.92
Professional Club Advisors	874	2.13
National Honor Society Advisor	690	1.61
Junior High Head		
Football Coach	1,706	4.30
Basketball Coach	1,539	3.81
Wrestling Coach	1,423	3.43
Track Coach	1,342	3.29
Volleyball Coach	1,269	3.15
Cheerleader Coach	966	2.31
Band Director	1,559	3.91
Orchestra Director	1,107	2.75
Chorus Director	1,045	2.59
Dramatics Director	1,021	2.29
Yearbook Advisor	893	2.03
Student Council Advisor	835	1.91
Newspaper Advisor	765	1.70

In 33% of the districts responding to the ERS (1989) study, the supplement is related to the teachers' salary schedule by the application of a ratio or percentage of a specific point on the schedule, commonly the B.A. minimum salary. Here, again, the size of the percentage is normally determined by some consideration of the activity involved. An example of one system used to rate activities is that utilized in Antioch, Illinois, and summarized in Figure 11.2.

Administrator Salaries

Historically, principals and other school administrators had to negotiate individually for their salaries (Greene, 1971). This practice is still common in the hiring of superintendents and other top administrators. However, for most administrative positions and in most districts, salary schedules for administrators have been adopted. Three types of salary schedules for school administrators are typical: (1) ratio or index schedules

TABLE 11.4
Multiple of Fixed Amount
Approach to Extracurricular
Pay, Galloway Township School
District, Absecon, New Jersey
Source: From *Extra Pay for Extra
Duties of Teachers* (5th ed., p. 75),
Educational Research Service, 1991,
Arlington, VA: Author. Copyright
© 1991 by the Educational Research
Service. Reprinted by permission.

Title	Hours	Salary
Athletic Director	240	$3,600
Basketball (boys' 7–8)	100	1,500
Basketball (girls' 7–8)	100	1,500
Cheerleading (7–8)	100	1,500
Flag Football (6–8)	25	375
Indoor Hockey (6–8)	50	750
Gymnastics (6–8)	90	1,350
Soccer (7–8)	100	1,500
Field Hockey (7–8)	100	1,500
Tournament of Champions Director	50	750
Track/Field (6–8)	50	750
Art Club (6–8)	25	375
Yearbook (6–8)	75	1,125
Drama (6–8)	60	900
Student Council (6–8)	150	2,250
Band (6–8)	150	2,250
Chorus (6–8)	150	2,250
Stokes Coordinator	60	900
Stokes Assistant Coordinator	40	600
Academic Coaching (7–8)	80	1,200
National Junior Honor Society	25	375
Builders Club (6–8)	80	1,200
Future Problem Solvers (6–8)	20	300
Activity Director	240	3,600
Unit Newsletter (7–8)	50	750
Environmental Awareness Club	40	600
Homework Club	50	750
Softball	25	375

related to teachers' salaries, (2) schedules based on additives to the teachers' schedules, and (3) schedules derived independently of teachers' schedules (ERS, 1987a).

Index or Ratio Approach. Indexing administrative salary schedules to teachers' schedules historically was the most common practice in determining administrative schedules. In this type of schedule the administrative salary is a ratio of some point on the teachers' schedule (e.g., lowest minimum salary, highest scheduled salary, or average salary). Each administrative position may be assigned a different ratio depending on school size, school level, number of staff supervised, or other variables that reflect the relative importance and complexity of the various administrative positions.

In the last two decades there has been a growing trend away from the practice of relating administrators', particularly principals', salaries to teachers' salaries by ratio or index. According to an ERS survey of methods of scheduling principals' salaries, only 9% of school districts used a salary approach that indexed principals' salaries to the teachers' salary schedule (ERS, 1987a).

1. *Student Contact Hours:* These are actual student contact hours and include practice time, dressing time, performance time, and travel time. (Limit of 2 $\frac{1}{2}$ hours per practice session.) 0–50 pts. 1 point/10 hours.

2. *Preparation and Planning:* This is time spent on the activity not involving the supervision of students. It would include designing formations, bookkeeping, scouting, keeping statistics, etc. 0–30 pts. 1 point/10 hours.

3. *Weekend and Holiday Involvement:* Certain activities require involvement on weekends and holidays and put an additional burden on that time as opposed to afterschool activities. 0–30 pts. 1.5 pts/Sat., Sun., or Nonschool day.

4. *Instructional and Organizational Skill:* This is a subjective category based on the preparation an individual must have to capably direct the activity and the skill necessary to instruct, organize, and conduct the activity. This category is divided into 4 sections worth a total of 25 pts as follows:

    a. Number of separate skills taught, 0–11 pts. 1 pt/skill.
    b. Success of program: 0–6 pts. Totally subjective based upon participation and holding power of the activity and reception by the public.
    c. Previous training required: 0–4 pts. 1 pt/year of participation in training at whatever level, high school, college, or teaching.
    d. Levels taught: 0–4 pts. 1 pt/level (Fr., Soph., JV, or Var.).

5. *Student–Advisor Ratio:* This is the number of student participants involved during the mid-point of the activity season. In the case of nonathletic activities that do not meet on a daily basis, only the officers are counted toward the student total. 0–20 pts. 1 pt/4 students.

6. *Equipment and Materials Management:* 0–20 pts. This determination is divided into 4 sections, 5 pts/section as follows:

    a. Budget:

    $$\begin{array}{rl} \$20,\!000+ &= 5 \text{ pts} \\ 8,\!000+ &= 4 \text{ pts} \\ 5,\!000+ &= 3 \text{ pts} \\ 3,\!000+ &= 2 \text{ pts} \\ 100+ &= 1 \text{ pt} \end{array}$$

FIGURE 11.2
Antioch, Illinois, Extracurricular Pay Factors and Point System
Source: From Antioch Community High School, Antioch, Illinois. Reprinted by permission.

Additive Approach.   Becoming less widely used according to the ERS study is the additive approach to determining administrative salaries, used by only 3.9% of the responding districts. Schedules that determine administrative salaries by making an addition to the teachers' schedule do so by adding either a specific dollar amount or a flat percentage to the point on the teachers' schedule where the administrator would be classified on the basis of his or her preparation and experience. This method is more commonly used in determining salaries in lower-level administrative positions than in upper-level positions. It is not uncommon for the salary of a department

b. Inventory:
            $80,000+ = 5 pts
            30,000+ = 4 pts
            5,000+ = 3 pts
            3,000+ = 2 pts
            100+ = 1 pt

c. Equipment volume (individual pieces of equipment issued)
            500+ = 5 pts
            100+ = 4 pts
            9+ = 3 pts
            5+ = 2 pts
            2+ = 1 pt

d. Handling repetitions (number of participants x pieces issued x times handled)
            500+ = 5 pts
            350+ = 4 pts
            250+ = 3 pts
            100+ = 2 pts
            25+ = 1 pt

7. *Exposure and Expectations:* This is a subjective item with points awarded by an estimate of the size of crowds and the public relations responsibility required. 0–15 pts.

   Exposure and expectations were determined by two categories:

   a. Spectator or service users per week of the season. Maximum 10 pts. 1 pt/100 users per week.
   b. Publicity contacts required. Maximum 5 pts. 1 pt/12 contacts.

8. *Travel Supervision:* This category makes provisions for the unique responsibility involved and responsibility for students while traveling in a school bus or other school vehicles above the time alone spent during the trip. 0–10 pts. 1 pt/trip.

9. *Other Adults Supervised:* This category recognizes that some positions require a supervisor of adults assigned to the activity. It does not include supervision of volunteer adults or student assistants. 0–5 pts. 1 pt/adult.

FIGURE 11.2
continued

chairperson or lower-level supervisor to be based on a bonus above the teacher's salary, but it would be rare to find a principal or superintendent whose salary is determined in this manner.

Independent Approaches. The vast majority of the salary schedules for administrators are established independent of teachers' salary schedules. They may be individually determined by a subjective decision made by the superintendent or school board based on negotiation or on performance evaluation. More often they are constructed to reflect a number of factors related to the administrative function as well as individual competence. Some of the factors that may be considered in constructing the schedule follow.

Instructional Level.   Most salary schedules for principals and assistant principals presume that greater responsibilities are inherent as grade levels increase. These schedules either provide a separate schedule for elementary, junior high, or senior high administrators or recognize instructional level as a factor in a single salary schedule.

Supervisory and Fiscal Responsibility.   Obviously administrative positions vary in responsibilities. Elements that influence the level of responsibility and consequently the points assigned each level include (1) number of adults supervised, (2) staff qualifications and experience, (3) number of students supervised, (4) number and types of special programs, (5) number and size of attendance centers, (6) size and number of budgets administered, (7) number and size of support programs (i.e., food services, transportation, etc.), and (8) student body and community characteristics.

Professional Experience.   The types of experience that are generally recognized under this factor include (1) number of years in present position, (2) number of years in a similar administrative position, (3) number of years of other administrative experience, (4) number of years of teaching experience, (5) number of years of other educational experience, and (6) number of years of service in the school district.

Education and Professional Development.   Most administrative positions require a certain minimum professional preparation. The administrative salary schedule may be constructed to recognize levels of academic preparation above the minimum or for specified professional development.

Performance.   There is growing interest in and use of performance appraisal as a factor in administrator compensation. As noted elsewhere in this text, however, when performance appraisal is used, care should be taken to ensure (1) that criteria are related to the position being evaluated, (2) that the appraisal is focused on improving the effectiveness of each administrator, and (3) that the appraisal is not used as a punitive measure or as a device for holding down administrative salaries (Castetter, 1992).

Number of Contract Days.   Another important variable that affects administrative salaries is the length of the contract year. Many administrators serve beyond the normal school term. Indeed, many administrative positions are year-round positions. Because the number of contract days does vary among positions, the salary schedule should reflect the longer work period.

The Point-Factor Method.   One approach to establishing administrative salaries that attempts to recognize the foregoing variables is the point-factor method. The point-factor method is based on an evaluation system that assigns a relative position value to each administrative and supervisory position in the district. Using a position evaluation rating form such as that shown in Table 11.5, the written position description of each position is evaluated on each factor.

TABLE 11.5
Point-Factor Method of Determining Administrator Salaries

Factors	Level and Points for Each Level									
	1	2	3	4	5	6	7	8	9	10
Education	10	20	30	40	50	60	70	80	90	100
Professional experience	15	30	45	60	75	90	105	120	135	150
Supervisory responsibility	20	40	60	80	100	120	140	160	180	200
Impact of decisions	10	20	30	40	50	60	70	80	90	100
Application of knowledge (The specific technical and professional knowledge required and the latitude in application of knowledge)	20	40	60	80	100	120	140	160	180	200
Contacts (The frequency and variety of internal and external human relationships involved in performing job duties)	5	10	15	20	25	30	35	40	45	50
Performance	20	50	60	80	100	120	140	160	185	200
Total scores	100	200	300	400	500	600	700	800	900	1,000

Each factor is broken down into levels and points are assigned to each level. For example, the levels and points for the education factor might be distributed as given in Table 11.6.

After the evaluation of each position, a total point value for the position is determined, and a pay scale is assigned commensurate with the position's total score and relationship to other positions on the organizational chart. If an organizational chart has not been developed previously, this evaluation process will force that necessary step to be taken.

Table 11.7 presents 1991–1992 salaries for a number of administrative positions. Ultimately, each school district must decide which level and type of administrative

TABLE 11.6
Levels and Points for the
Education Factor

	Level	Points
1	High school or equivalent	10
2	Postsecondary education—trade or business school	20
3	Two years college or specialized training equivalent to 2 years college	30
4	Bachelor's degree	40
5	Bachelor's degree plus a minimum of 15 hours of specialized training	50
6	Master's degree	60
7	Master's degree plus 30 hours of specialized training	70
8	Specialist's degree	80
9	Doctorate degree	90
10	Specialized postdoctoral training	100

salary structure it can best support. If a schedule is to be developed independent of teachers' salaries or other established bases, the district must decide what factors to include and the weight to be given to each.

INDIRECT COMPENSATION: EMPLOYEE BENEFITS AND SERVICES

Indirect compensation is the "in-kind payments employees receive in addition to payments in the form of money" (Henderson, 1985, p. 432). In the past benefits were supplemental to the paycheck and of minor value, so they were referred to as fringe benefits. Although the term is still used, it is misleading because these benefits are no longer a minor item (Sherman et al., 1988). The cost of indirect compensation in the United States increased from approximately 3% of wages and salaries in 1929 to 36% in 1992.

A major issue with respect to indirect compensation is the degree to which these dollars, as contrasted with wage and salary dollars, contribute to employee motivation (Foulkes & Livernash, 1983). Because these benefits and services are available to all employees and not related directly to performance, perhaps they should be considered maintenance factors rather than motivators (Rebore, 1991). Some evidence, however, indicates that a good quality, competitive indirect compensation program increases job satisfaction and morale, which in turn results in a reduction in turnover and absenteeism (Henderson, 1985). Regardless of whether it is a motivator or a maintainer, indirect compensation is an important part of an effective compensation program. Because these benefits and services are considered essential in our society, the quality of the program can have a significant effect on the ability of the district to attract and retain competent employees (Rebore, 1991).

Indirect compensation can be classified as either employee benefits or employee services. Employee benefits are those indirect compensation components that provide income security in case of health-related problems at some future date. Certain bene-

TABLE 11.7
Mean of Mean Salaries Paid
Personnel in Selected
Administrative Positions,
1991–1992
Source: From *Salaries Paid
Professional Personnel in Public
Schools, 1991–92* (table 1),
Educational Research Service,
1992, Arlington, VA: Author.
Copyright © 1992 by the Educational Research Service.
Reprinted by permission.

Position	Salary
Superintendents	$83,342
Deputy/Associate Superintendents	76,796
Assistant Superintendents	69,315
Directors, Managers, Coordinators and Supervisors for:	
Finance and Business	57,036
Instructional Services	62,102
Public Relations/Information	50,625
Staff Personnel Services	62,269
Other Areas (Pupil Personnel, Research, Food Services, Health, Transportation, Federal Programs, Media Services, Plant Operation, etc.)	51,854
Subject Area Supervisors	50,580
Principals	
Elementary School	53,856
Junior High/Middle School	57,504
Senior High School	61,768
Assistant Principals	
Elementary School	45,558
Junior High School	48,956
Senior High School	51,314

fits are required by law; others, including health and life insurance, sick leave, and disability protection, are voluntarily provided by the employer. Employee services are not required by law but "enable the employee to enjoy a better lifestyle or to meet social or personal obligations while minimizing employment-related cost" (Henderson, 1985, p. 434).

In this text indirect compensation for public school personnel is discussed in terms of the following components: (1) legally required benefits, (2) private welfare and security programs, (3) pay for time not worked, and (4) income equivalent payments. In addition an approach to compensation packaging, the flexible benefit plan, is presented, and Table 11.8 (p. 338) provides a profile of the nonrequired benefits currently available to public school teachers and administrators other than superintendents.

Legally Required Benefits

Both the federal and state governments have enacted laws to protect the welfare of employees. At the federal level the Social Security Act of 1935 established the Old-Age, Survivors, Disability and Health Insurance System. The system is financed by contributions by the employee (based on a percentage of the employee's salary) and a matching contribution by the employer. Under the social security system, totally and permanently disabled persons may be eligible for disability payments, and retirement income is provided to workers retiring at the age of 62 or insurance benefits to those working until age 65. The actual amount the employee receives is based on the number of years worked, average earnings, and number of dependents at the time benefits begin. The Social Security Act provides health care services (Medicare) to those 65 and older and benefits to eligible survivors of deceased workers. Only about 57% of school districts include teachers and administrators in the social security program (ERS, 1990a, 1990b) because they are usually included in the state retirement system. More often the social security program covers classified employees (Rebore, 1991).

The Social Security Act also requires states to provide unemployment compensation through state legislation. Unemployment benefits received are normally a function of the employee's previous wage and length of service. The costs of this program are paid by the employer.

In addition to the protections provided by the Social Security Act, all states require almost all employers to provide employees with workers' compensation in the event of occupational injury or disability. Each state has its own schedule of benefits that depend upon the wages of the disabled employee and the type of injury sustained. Workers' compensation insurance also provides burial expenses and income benefits for widows and children. Like unemployment compensation, the cost of the workers' compensation insurance is borne by the employer.

State Retirement Plans

All states also provide retirement benefit plans for public school professional employees. The vast majority of these employees (97%) are covered by state retirement systems, whereas only about 4% are covered by local retirement systems (some individuals are in both state and local systems). Of the statewide systems, approximately 72% are teachers' systems and the remainder are operated for teachers and other public employees (ERS, 1990a, 1990b).

State retirement systems vary regarding the service used to compute a member's retirement benefits (i.e., prior service credit, military service credit, in-state public employment other than teaching, out-of-state teaching credit, etc.). They also vary on other provisions such as vesting rights, age requirements, disability benefits (all states but Arizona and Iowa provide permanent disability benefits to members), provisions for borrowing, postretirement adjustments, work restrictions after retirement, and administration. Although administrators should be familiar with the provisions and restrictions of the state or local retirement plan, they must be cautious about rendering specific advice to employees. That task is more properly the job of personnel in the state or local retirement office (Greene, 1971).

In most states retirement benefits are financed jointly by employee and public contributions. In a few states, however, the retirement plan is financed entirely by the state. In an attempt to increase compensation for public school employees while maintaining the present level of state aid to education, several states have passed legislation requiring local school districts to pay not only the employer's share toward retirement but also the employee's share. This benefit has great appeal to employees because it has a significant impact on net income without increasing gross taxable income. Consequently, in an increasing number of school districts, this provision has become a popular item for negotiations.

Early retirement programs are also being adopted by many districts because of a need to reduce the number of employees or to lessen the financial strain resulting from the clustering of a large percentage of employees at or near the top of the salary matrix. If properly constructed, an early retirement program that offers special benefits to entice older employees to retire early can benefit both parties: The employee gets a larger pension and the school district can hire a younger, and presumably less expensive, replacement (Mackey & Uhler, 1990). A 1990 survey of practices by the ERS indicated that in over 48% of the responding districts some form of early retirement incentive program was in place for teachers, and in 46% for administrators (ERS, 1990a, 1990b). This represents a 20% increase in the participation rate of districts in 6 years.

Private Welfare and Security Programs

The provision of private welfare and security programs for school employees was limited before 1960. School districts did not consider the added incentives of these benefits until they began to experience the frustrations of teacher shortages and growing competition with other districts, business, and industry (Greene, 1971). The principal private welfare and security programs provided by school districts include health and hospitalization insurance, health maintenance organizations, life insurance, long-term disability insurance, severance pay, tax sheltered annuity plans, and professional liability insurance.

Health and Hospitalization Insurance. Although job-related accidents and injury are compensable under state workers' compensation laws, most illness experienced by school employees is not job related and, therefore, is a cause of financial strain on the employee. For this reason various forms of health and accident insurance are provided for school employees, some that are completely financed by the district and others whose costs are shared with the employee. The principal types of health and hospitalization insurance found in school district compensation programs are (1) group hospitalization, (2) medical/surgical, (3) major medical, (4) dental, (5) vision care, and (6) prescription drugs.

As the data from the ERS survey presented in Table 11.8 indicate, 98% of all responding districts provided group hospitalization insurance for teachers. Eighty-three percent of these paid the full premium for single coverage and 36% paid the full premium for family coverage. Medical/surgical insurance for teachers was provided by 96% of the responding districts and 96% provided major medical insurance. A very significant increase in the last few years has also occurred in the number of districts providing dental, vision, and prescription drug insurance: 84% provided dental insurance to teachers; 46% provided vision care insurance; and 75% provided prescription drug insurance. Data relative to the provision of these benefits to administrators are also found in Table 11.8.

TABLE 11.8
Benefits Available to Public School Teachers and Administrators, 1990

Type of Benefit	Percentage of Districts Providing Benefits to Teachers	Percentage of Districts Providing Benefits to Administrators
Group hospitalizations insurance	97.6	98.0
Medical/Surgical insurance	95.6	96.1
Major medical insurance	96.1	96.6
Dental insurance	84.2	85.2
Vision care	45.5	46.9
Prescription drugs	74.8	76.0
Group life insurance	75.8	79.5
Long-term disability insurance	35.4	41.7
Severance pay	38.0	37.7
Tax-sheltered annuity plans	72.4	73.6
Professional liability insurance	69.2	72.5
Sick leave	99.1	98.4
Personal/Emergency leave	96.4	90.6
Vacation leave	4.1	73.7
Sabbatical leave	72.2	59.4
Religious leave	70.8	N/A
Tuition reimbursements	37.7	35.3
Payment of meeting and convention expenses	N/A	81.2
Payment of organizational membership dues	.2	60.7
Transportation allowance	N/A	96.0
Payment of cost of physical exam	N/A	30.0

Source: From *Fringe Benefits for Administrators in Public Schools, 1989–90* (part 2) and *Fringe Benefits for Teachers in Public Schools, 1989–90* (part 3), Educational Research Service, 1990, Arlington, VA: Author.

Health Maintenance Organizations (HMOs).   The Health Maintenance Organization Act of 1973 requires employers covered by the Fair Labor Standard Act to offer an HMO as an alternative to health insurance if a federally qualified HMO is available in the community. HMOs provide comprehensive health care to members for a fixed monthly fee on a prepaid services basis. The growth of HMOs throughout the country has been nothing short of phenomenal. Their importance as a health care provider for school district personnel has grown concomitantly. This role is anticipated to increase as health care costs continue to rise.

Group Life Insurance.   Life insurance is the oldest form of employer-sponsored employee benefit (Flippo, 1980). The group plan permits the district and the employee to benefit from lower rates. Most group life insurance plans include all employees regardless of physical condition and provide for conversion to an identical policy without physical examination if the individual leaves the district. Two disadvantages of group life insurance plans are that they are term insurance policies, providing coverage during a contract period only, and that they have no cash loan or paid-up value. The ERS survey showed three-fourths of responding districts provided group life insurance coverage for teachers and 73% provided such coverage for administrators. Of these districts, 75% paid the full premium cost for teachers and 52% for administrators.

Long-Term Disability Insurance. Long-term disability insurance provides income continuation payments to employees unable to work because of health-related problems. Such insurance is a supplement to workers' compensation, which only covers occupational disabilities. Long-term disability plans may be provided in conjunction with a retirement plan or may be provided by separate coverage. Many group life insurance plans also have a total permanent disability feature. Approximately 35% of school districts included in the ERS survey provided long-term disability to teachers, and 42% provided this coverage to administrators. The mean percentage of salary coverage for teachers was 64% and for administrators was 65%.

Severance Pay. Severance pay normally is a one-time payment to an individual upon severing his or her employment with the district. This severance can occur at retirement or at an earlier point in the employee's career. The size of the payment is often based in part upon length of service before separation. Teachers' organizations have increasingly sought severance pay in addition to retirement benefits. When paid upon retirement, it is regarded as a bonus for long-term, loyal service and as an aid to bridging the gap between full service with pay and retirement on a reduced income (Greene, 1971). Very often severance pay is based on the number of unused sick days, with a set maximum number that will be reimbursed. Of those districts responding to the ERS survey, 38% provided severance pay for teachers and administrators. Of these, 40% paid this sum only for severance based on retirement from the district (ERS, 1990b).

Tax-Sheltered Annuity Plans. Tax-sheltered annuity plans allow school personnel to invest part of their salaries in annuities that are not taxed as current salary. The payment to the annuity is made before any computation of taxes owed. Thus income tax payments are reduced at the same time an investment is being accumulated. The annuity, or income from it, is paid to the employee upon retirement or at some future date. Income taxes are then paid on the amount received at a time when the employee's income presumably is lower. Almost three-fourths of the school districts in the ERS survey provided tax-sheltered annuity plans to which teachers and administrators could contribute.

Professional Liability Insurance. Lawsuits alleging misfeasance, malfeasance, nonfeasance, and malpractice are increasingly being filed against school districts and their employees. Because of their involvement with children, school teachers and administrators are particularly subject to increased liability. For this reason the major professional educational organizations provide professional liability coverage as a benefit of membership or at a nominal rate. School districts also often provide such coverage under a blanket provision in the board's policy. Professional liability coverage was provided to teachers by 69% of the districts included in the ERS study and to administrators in 73% of the districts.

Pay for Time Not Worked

For the employee, "possibly the most desired but frequently unrecognized benefit is time off with pay" (Henderson, 1985, p. 457). The most common time-off-with-pay provisions for public school personnel are sick leaves, personal/emergency leaves, vacation leaves, sabbatical leaves, religious leaves, family and bereavement leaves, civic and jury duty leaves, professional leaves, and military leaves.

Sick Leave.   Virtually all school districts provide employees paid sick leave. In fact, statutory provision for sick leave has been made in most states. Included under this category are leaves for family illness and death in the immediate family. In most instances a set number of days per year is provided, with 12 being the current mean number of days per year for teachers and 13 for administrators (ERS, 1990a, 1990b). In some systems the entire allotment of sick leave is made at the beginning of the school year, whereas in others the leave is earned monthly (e.g., 1 or 1½ days per month). Districts are about evenly split between set and unlimited in terms of the maximum number of days accumulation over the length of employment. The mean of the maximum accumulation is 145 days for teachers and 155 for administrators. Application of unused sick leave toward retirement service is allowed in one-third of the districts (ERS, 1990a, 1990b).

Personal/Emergency Leave.   School districts also recognize that employees will, from time to time, need to take leave for a variety of personal or emergency reasons. Almost all of the school districts responding to the ERS survey provided personal/emergency leaves for teachers (96%) and administrators (91%). The mean number of days allowed per year was 4. In about 40% of districts time taken as personal/emergency leave is charged against sick leave.

Vacation Leave.   Vacation leave is normally not provided for teachers; however, most districts (74%) provide vacation leave for administrators. The mean number of days allowed is 20. Most of these districts permit accumulation of leave from year to year, with a mean of 31 days accumulation (ERS, 1990a).

Sabbatical Leave.   Provisions for sabbatical leaves for teachers are found in 72% of the school districts (ERS, 1990b). Often the provision has come about as a result of collective negotiations. Professional study is the primary purpose for which sabbatical leave may be taken. The most common time periods granted, where leave is provided, are 6 months (30%) and 2 semesters (59%).

Six years of satisfactory service is the typical prerequisite for a sabbatical leave. Most districts also require some justification in terms of the value of the proposed professional study program to the district and an assurance that the employee will either return to employment in the district for a minimum period of time, usually 2 years, or repay any salary paid during the sabbatical. The district may also have a policy limiting the number of employees who may be on sabbatical leave at the same time.

The ERS study (1990b) found that about two-thirds of the districts offering this benefit provided salary during the sabbatical. Full salary was paid by only 4% of these districts; however, a percentage of salary was paid by 62% of the districts.

Sabbatical leaves for administrators are not quite as common as for teachers. Only 59% of the responding districts offered this benefit. When offered, the provisions for administrators are almost identical to those for teachers (1990a).

Religious Leave. Leave for religious holidays not observed in the school calendar is granted by most school systems. Most districts charge such days to the teacher's or administrator's personal leave bank.

Civic and Jury Duty Leaves. School districts have an interest in the involvement of their employees in various civic activities and functions. In an effort not to penalize such service, school districts often provide civic leave. Most often this leave is considered as personal leave or as leave without pay. Although in several states teachers are exempt from jury duty, leave for jury duty is granted by the majority of school systems. This leave is normally considered as a separate paid leave. In most jurisdictions any payment received for jury duty must be turned over to the school district if the employee is receiving full pay from the district. In other jurisdictions the jury pay is simply deducted from the employee's regular salary.

Professional Leave. Professional leave is granted to teachers and administrators in almost all school districts. Professional leave may be granted for a number of reasons, including (1) professional study, (2) attendance at professional meetings, (3) exchange teaching, (4) professional organization service, (5) visits to other schools, (6) teaching in a Department of Defense school, (7) research, (8) travel, and (9) work experience (Greene, 1971).

Military Leave. As with leaves for civic and jury service, school districts are particularly sensitive to the public duties and responsibilities of its employees. Consequently most districts provide military leave for their employees. Considered separate from personal leave, military leave lasts from 1 to 2 weeks. Because the employee receives military pay while on leave, districts are divided as to whether such leave is provided with or without pay.

Income Equivalent Payments

Income equivalent payments have been introduced into compensation programs in response to changes in the economic situation and to tax demands. They give the employee an opportunity for an improved, more enjoyable lifestyle. Income equivalent payments include in-kind benefits that, if purchased by the employee, would necessitate spending after-tax dollars. When provided by the district these benefits are normally not considered earned income (Henderson, 1985). Discussions of some of the more common income equivalent payments available to school district employees follow.

Credit Unions.   Credit unions have been established by employees in many large school districts and by a cooperative arrangement of employees of several smaller districts to serve the financial needs of the employees. In some districts if a credit union does not exist specifically for school district employees, they are eligible for membership in a credit union established by other public employees. Credit unions are operated by employees under federal and state legislation and supervision. Credit unions enable employees to make savings or loan payments through payroll deductions. This not only encourages thrift by the employee, but deposits normally earn a higher rate of interest or dividends than those paid at commercial banks or savings and loans. Loans are also made to employees at a lower interest rate than that charged by commercial enterprises. In addition, credit union members are often eligible for a variety of other benefits ranging from no-charge purchase of travelers' checks to dealer discounts on the purchase of automobiles.

Tuition Reimbursement.   More and more school districts are offering tuition reimbursements. This benefit provides employees with as many educational opportunities as possible while upgrading the knowledge and skills of the district work force. The 1990 ERS study found approximately 38% of responding districts offered tuition reimbursements to teachers and 35% to administrators. In about half of these districts, however, reimbursement was limited to graduate credits only.

Employee Assistance Programs.   Employee assistance programs (EAPs) represent one attempt by employers to lower the risk factors associated with mental and physical health problems of employees. In many instances employees may have access to psychological counseling through the district's health care policy or may be eligible to receive financial counseling from other sources. As noted in Chapter 8, however, a growing number of districts sponsor EAPs to provide "confidential evaluation, referral and outpatient counseling services for emotional and nervous disorders, marital and family distress, drug or alcohol problems, financial or legal concerns, stress related problems, and crisis intervention to employees and their families" (Martini, 1991, p. 10).

District-sponsored EAPs focus on job performance and restoring employees to full productivity, not on their problems. Through self-referral or supervisor referral employees consult with an EAP counselor who, depending on personal training, counsels with the employees or refers them to an outside agency or professional. Districts using EAPs have found them to have a positive effect on job performance and to provide a positive cost benefit to the district (Martini, 1991).

Payment of Meeting and Convention Expenses. Attendance at professional meetings and conventions is a means of professional renewal and development. In recognition of these benefits, many school districts reimburse some meeting and convention expenses. However, this benefit is most often provided to administrators (81%), not teachers. When such payment is provided, it almost always (96%) covers expenses associated with travel, registration, lodging, and meals (ERS, 1990a).

Payment of Organization Dues. A major function of professional organizations is educational and, as such, provides benefits both to the employee and the district. Like the payment of meeting and convention expenses, however, this benefit has been reserved almost exclusively for administrators (see Table 11.8).

Transportation Allowance. School district employees who use their own vehicles while performing school district business may receive a transportation allowance or a mileage reimbursement. Normally the only individuals affected by this benefit are administrators and supervisors. Almost all districts (96%) provide a transportation allowance. Of this group, 79% based the allowance on the number of miles driven (ERS, 1990a).

Wellness Programs. The health of its employees is of obvious concern to the district. Most districts require a preemployment physical. Some pay for periodic physical examinations. In addition, a number of districts have initiated wellness programs designed to improve the overall health of employees. Such programs include not only health education and fitness programs, but such affirmative steps as district-sponsored smoking cessation programs, early detection programs, fitness activities, attention to special diets in meal preparations, and ongoing health-related assessment. Such wellness programs pay off not only in terms of increased employee health, but in a reduction in sick leave and insurance claims. This in turn leads to reduced health insurance premiums for the district. As a result, a few districts have followed the lead of some businesses and offer employees a waiver of the employee deductible payment or actual cash payments for reduced claims or for maintaining positive health goals (e.g., reduced cholesterol, reduced weight, reduced blood pressure).

Subsidized Food Service. Most school districts operate a food service program that not only is nonprofit but is subsidized by both local and federal contributions. As a result, an adult meal purchased in the school cafeteria costs far less than a comparable meal purchased at a commercial establishment. In addition, vending machines are typically located in office areas, shops, and schools. The profits from these machines often go to some type of employee benefit or fund.

Child Care Services. The growing demand for child care has led many districts to add this service to their employee compensation program. Such services may be provided through a child care center operated by the district that enrolls children of both employees and students. A popular alternative is to include child care as one of the benefits in a flexible benefit plan such as those discussed in the following section.

Flexible Benefits Plans

Because each individual has different needs, no fixed compensation plan will satisfy everyone. Young married workers are interested in maternity or paternity benefits and tuition reimbursements, whereas older employees are more interested in retirement benefits. Families with two wage earners do not require duplicated benefits and services from each employer. Recognizing the differing needs and interests of employees, a number of businesses developed a flexible benefits program, called a cafeteria plan, that allows each employee to choose, within a fixed dollar allotment and legal requirements, the most attractive combination of benefits and services. Many businesses have also found that the cafeteria plan allows them to provide benefits to employees more cost-effectively. The popularity of this approach has led to its adoption by a wide range of both public and private organizations, school districts among them. The ERS studies (1990a, 1990b) reported that approximately 12% of districts provided some form of cafeteria plan.

Before involving the employee in the selection of benefits and services, the employer must identify which benefits and services will be made available, the cost of each benefit and service, and the total permissible cost for the entire program. Benefits required by the government must be included. The best way to determine which other benefits or services to offer is by an employee preference survey, which requires respondents to rank their benefit choices among a number of options (Henderson, 1985). It is incumbent upon the human resources office to provide adequate information and counseling about each option both at the time the preference survey is conducted and at the time employee selections are made, so that employees can make informed decisions in their own best interests. Informed decision making also reduces the desire or need to change selections. The administrative costs associated with a flexible compensation/benefit plan are high enough without employees changing benefits at will. Thus employers must establish time limits and schedules for stopping or exchanging benefits (Henderson, 1985).

The larger the school district, the more benefits that can be included in the cafeteria plan. Some employee benefits specialists maintain that cafeteria plans are most effective for school districts of 500 or more employees. This is true for the following reason:

> Since employees are free to elect whatever benefits they please, it's possible that a specific benefit would be chosen by only a small percentage of employees. And because the cost of those benefits is averaged over the number of employees likely to use them, the per person cost could be prohibitively high unless there is a large group of potential users. (Johnson, 1987, p. 30)

A second type of flexible benefit plan, one that can provide some of the benefits of cafeteria plans to school districts with fewer employees, is commonly referred to as ZEBRA (Zero Balance Reimbursement Account). This type of plan takes advantage of the Internal Revenue Service provision that allows an employee to place a portion of *before-tax* income into a special account, held by the employer, that can be used to pay for such allowable expenses as the employee's share of health, dental, or life insurance, deductible or coinsurance payments, and child or elder care. Employees must decide at the beginning of the tax year how much will be placed in the account. Then as expenses are incurred, employees submit claims and are reimbursed. Payment for other benefits can still be made by payroll deduction. In either case the allowable expenses are nontaxable (Johnson, 1987).

As the example in Table 11.9 illustrates, the benefits of this plan are not only the flexibility it provides employees, but the increased take-home pay. One drawback to the plan, at least from the employee's perspective, is that all funds in the account must be used by the end of the tax year or they are forfeited. The amount forfeited, however, may still be less than what the employee would have paid in taxes.

When the school district operates a flexible benefit plan, it is the responsibility of the human resources office to cost each benefit and determine the total value of benefits. It must also ensure compliance with Internal Revenue standards and establish schedules for enrollment and changes. Perhaps most importantly, the human resources office must assume a greater role in employee benefit counseling.

TABLE 11.9
Savings With a Zero Balance Reimbursements Account (ZEBRA)

	Without ZEBRA	With ZEBRA
Annual salary	$24,000	$24,000
ZEBRA account contribution (for health and dental insurance and child care)		2,500
Taxable income	24,000	21,500
Federal income tax (15%)	3,600	2,365
State income tax (5%)	1,200	1,075
Social security (7.65%)	1,836	1,645
Health and dental insurance	500	
Child care	2,000	
Net pay	$14,864	$16,415
Annual savings		$ 1,551

SUMMARY

The compensation of personnel is the largest item in the school district budget. Traditionally the direct compensation of teachers has been accomplished through the use of the simple salary schedule based solely on preparation and experience. However, with the renewed public interest in high-quality education, attention has focused on a number of incentive pay plans designed to attract and retain good teachers and motivate them to greater performance. Likewise, over the last two decades school districts have increasingly abandoned fixed salary schedules for administrators and adopted schedules that are based on factors such as responsibility of position, experience, professional preparation, length of contract year, and performance.

Indirect compensation represents the fastest growing area in the compensation of employees. The growth and strength of unions has contributed to this increase as has the realization by employers that they must provide increased benefits to remain competitive in the labor market. Flexible benefit plans are an approach to the provision of indirect compensation that has gained popularity in business and industry and is making some inroads in education. This approach allows employees to select, within a dollar limit, the mix of benefits best meeting their individual circumstances.

Through its compensation program the district aims to attract and retain competent personnel, motivate them toward optimum performance, create incentives for continued growth, and maintain control of budgetary expenditures. These goals can be accomplished only if the district, and the human resources administrator in particular, recognizes and implements a compensation program that is well planned, internally fair and equitable, and externally competitive.

DISCUSSION QUESTIONS

1. Discuss the factors that directly or indirectly determine the compensation program established by a school district. How has each factor affected the compensation program in your school district or a school district with which you are familiar?
2. How do merit pay and incentive pay differ? Describe any such programs in operation in your area or state. How successful are they? If none are operating in your area or state, describe those you have read or heard about.
3. Survey three districts and compare their indirect compensation programs. Also, determine which three elements have been the most recent additions to each program.
4. Compare the advantages and disadvantages of a flexible benefit plan with those of a fixed compensation program.

CASE 11.1
Comparable Worth

The Penzville High School Marching Band has won this year's regional band contest and has been asked to march in the Magnolia Bowl Parade on New Year's Day. Phil Smith has been the band director for 5 years and has given unlimited time and energy to transforming the band from a handful of stragglers to a full-size band and the pride of Penzville. Just before the Thanksgiving holiday Phil asks the principal to increase his extracurricular pay for serving as band director to equal that of the head football coach. He argues that he puts in as much or more time as Doug Jones, the football coach, and that his students have been more successful. From Phil's conversation and tone it is clear that he has given this matter a lot of thought and that he is not going to take no for an answer.

Questions

1. Does Phil Smith appear to have a legitimate comparable worth claim?
2. To what extent, if any, should student success be an issue in this case?
3. How would you respond to Phil? How would you respond to the sponsor of the debate team who made a similar request after the team won in a national competition?

CASE 11.2
ZEBRA Plan

The Rocky Point School Board has voted to implement a ZEBRA benefit plan. A survey of employees has shown that employees' preferences are distributed among an array of possible benefits and services. To include all of them would result in high per person costs.

Questions

1. What process should be used to decide what benefits and services will be included?

2. Should specific benefits (e.g., health, medical, and dental insurance) be required in order to lower per person costs for all employees, or should employees be allowed to choose whatever they please as long as they are willing to pay the cost from their ZEBRA?
3. Is it fair for the school district to keep the funds from unexpended ZEBRAs? How should these funds be used?

CASE 11.3
Incentives or Teachers?

Plainview School District No. 12 has adopted site-based management for its 15 schools. Authority for many curricular, instructional, budgetary, and personnel matters now resides with the administrator and a school council at each school. The school council is made up of parent representatives and representatives from the school staff.

Like most communities in the state, Plainview's economy has suffered during the current recession, and the school district is not anticipating any increase in funding for next year. Because of enrollment increases, however, Digrazzi Elementary School has been allotted two additional instructional positions for next year under the funding and staffing formula.

Digrazzi serves a lower socioeconomic neighborhood and in the last few years has experienced declining test scores and a high teacher turnover rate. During the last year the staff has been discussing a variety of measures to tackle these problems, including incentive pay plans that would reward teachers based on improvements in student achievement.

When the Digrazzi staff learns that funding has been authorized to hire two additional teachers, a formal proposal is made to the school council to forego the hires. The proposal suggests that the money allocated for the hires be used to fund an incentive pay program that would reward teachers for increased student achievement.

Questions

1. How would you respond to the proposal if you were a member of the school council?

2. What are the possible positive and negative implications for students?

3. What is the possible impact or reaction of students and staff in the other schools in the district?

4. What alternatives to hiring two additional teachers might you propose that would improve the working conditions or welfare of the teachers at Digrazzi?

REFERENCES

Adkison, J., & McKenzie, C. M. (1990). *Compensating school administrators. The impact of personal and organizational characteristics on administrator salaries*. Paper presented at the annual meeting of the American Educational Research Association, Boston.

Beebe, R. J. (1983). Determining the competitiveness of school district salaries. *NASSP Bulletin, 67*(461), 84–92.

Bell, T. H. (1988). Parting words of the 13th man. *Phi Delta Kappan, 69,* 42.

Carnegie Forum on Education and the Economy. (1986). *A nation prepared: Teachers for the 21st century*. New York: Author.

Castetter, W. B. (1992). *The personnel function in educational administration* (5th ed.). New York: Macmillan.

Cresap, McCormick and Paget. (1984). *Teacher incentives: A tool for effective management*. Reston, VA: National Association of Elementary School Principals, American Association of School Administrators, National Association of Secondary School Principals.

Darling-Hammond, L., & Berry, B. (1988). *The evolution of teacher policy*. Washington, DC: Rand Corporation.

Dunwell, R. R. (1991). Merit, motivation, and mythology. *Educational Considerations, 18*(2), 33–35.

Educational Research Service. (1979). *Merit pay for teachers*. Arlington, VA: Author.

Educational Research Service. (1987a). *Methods of scheduling salaries for principals*. Arlington, VA: Author.

Educational Research Service. (1987b). *Methods of scheduling salaries for teachers*. Arlington, VA: Author.

Educational Research Service. (1990a). Fringe benefits for administrators in public schools, 1989–90. *National survey of fringe benefits in public schools* (part 2). Arlington, VA: Author.

Educational Research Service. (1990b). Fringe benefits for teachers in public schools, 1989–90. *National survey of fringe benefits in public schools* (part 3). Arlington, VA: Author.

Educational Research Service. (1991). *Extra pay for extra duties of teachers* (5th ed.). Arlington, VA: Author.

Flippo, E. B. (1980). *Personnel management* (5th ed.). New York: McGraw-Hill.

Equal Pay Act of 1963 (P.L. 88-38), 29 U.S.C.A. § 206.

Foster, C. W. (1960). *Wage and salary administration: A handbook for school business officials*. Chicago: Research Corporation of the Association of School Business Officials.

Foulkes, F. K., & Livernash, E. R. (1983). *Human resources management: Text and cases*. Englewood Cliffs, NJ: Prentice-Hall.

Futrell, M. H. (1988). Selecting and compensating mentor teachers: A win-win scenario. *Theory into Practice, 3,* 223–225.

Greene, J. E. (1971). *School personnel administrator*. New York: Chilton.

Gursky, D. (1992a). Not without merit. *Teacher Magazine, 3*(7), 22–25.

Gursky, D. (1992b, April 22). Program that rewards senior teachers stirs flap in Philadelphia. *Education Week,* p. 8.

Henderson, R. I. (1985). *Compensation management: Rewarding performance* (4th ed.). Reston, VA: Reston.

Johns, R. L., Morphet, E. L., & Alexander, K. (1983). *The economics and financing of education.* Englewood Cliffs, NJ: Prentice-Hall.

Johnson, R. (1987). Flexible fringe benefit plans save you money and keep employees happy. *American School Board Journal, 174*(5), 30–31.

King, R. A. (1979). Toward a theory of wage determination for teachers: Factors which determine variation in salaries among districts. *Journal of Education Finance, 4,* 358–369.

Kitchen, W. E. (1983). *The relationship between local salary enrichment, local wealth, and selected socioeconomic variables in Texas.* Unpublished doctoral dissertation. Texas Tech University, Lubbock.

Kottkamp, R. B., Provenzo, E. F., Jr., & Cohn, M. M. (1986). Stability and change in a profession: Two decades of teacher attitudes, 1964–1984. *Phi Delta Kappan, 67,* 559–567.

Mackey, B. C., & Uhler, S. F. (1990). How to take an early out. *American School Board Journal, 177*(3), 27, 42.

Martini, G. R., Jr. (1991). Wellness programs: Preventive medicine to reduce health care costs. *School Business Affairs, 57*(6), 8–11.

Mickler, M. L. (1987). Merit pay: Boon or boondoggle? *The Clearing House, 61*(3), 137–141.

Mitchell, D. E., & Peters, M. J. (1988). A stronger profession through appropriate teacher incentives. *Educational Leadership, 46*(3) 74–78.

National Commission on Excellence in Education. (1983). *A nation at risk: The imperative for educational reform.* Washington, DC: GPO.

Nelson, F. H. (1990). *AFT local union teachers salary survey 1990.* Washington, DC: American Federation of Teachers, AFL-CIO.

Nelson, F. H. (1991). An interstate cost-of-living index. *Educational Evaluation, 13,* 103–111.

Poston, W. K., & Frase, L. E. (1991). Alternative compensation programs for teachers. *Phi Delta Kappan, 73,* 317–320.

Rebore, R. W. (1991). *Personnel administration in education: A management approach* (3rd ed.). Englewood Cliffs, NJ: Prentice-Hall.

Richardson, J. A., & Williams, J. T. (1981). Determining an appropriate teacher salary. *Journal of Education Finance, 7,* 189–204.

Ruhl, M., Johnson, B., & Steele, J. (1990). Career ladders: The Missouri model. *The Clearing House, 63,* 417–419.

Sherman, A. W., Jr., Bohlander, G. W., & Chruden, H. J. (1988). *Managing human resources* (8th ed.) . Cincinnati: South-Western.

Southern Regional Education Board. (1992). *The 1991 national survey of incentives and career ladders.* Atlanta, GA: Author.

Zimpher, N. L., & Rieger, S. R. (1988). Mentoring teachers: What are the issues? *Theory Into Practice, 3,* 175–182.

U.S. Department of Education, National Center for Education Statistics. (1992). *The condition of education.* Washington, DC: Author.

12

The Support Personnel Program

The major emphasis in any discussion of school human resources administration is on the certificated personnel, those individuals who are required to have some certificate of qualification from the state in order to teach, supervise, counsel, or administer. These individuals constitute the numerical majority of people in a school system and their salaries account for about two-thirds of the school district budget, so the attention given to them seems justified. Nevertheless, a very important group of employees cannot be overlooked in any consideration of the administration of human resources in education: the group of employees traditionally known as classified or noncertificated personnel, and more recently as support personnel. This group of employees makes up 31% of the full-time staff of the public schools and is composed of such employees as secretarial and clerical personnel, transportation staff, food services employees, plant operation and maintenance workers, and health and recreational staff (U.S. Department of Education, 1992).

The status of classified or support personnel varies widely among the states. Some states recognize certain groups of classified personnel for such purposes as tenure or retirement. State or local civil service arrangements cover all noncertificated personnel in some states. In yet other states local school districts are given complete authority and responsibility for the establishment and administration of the classified personnel system.

Within local school districts the responsibility for the administration of the classified personnel programs, like the certificated personnel program, is primarily a function of school district size. In small school districts the superintendent often assumes responsibility for the administration of the entire personnel program. As district size grows, the next central office administrator to be added is often an administrator in charge of business functions. This person often is given responsibility for the administration of all phases of the classified personnel program, from employment to retirement.

As a school district continues to grow, a human resources administrator is usually employed. It is not uncommon, however, for the business administrator to retain responsibility for the administration of the classified personnel program and for the human resources administrator to have responsibility for the certificated personnel. In large districts, however, the more common arrangement is for the business administrator to retain responsibility for some classified personnel functions (such as staff development, assignment, and schedules) and for the human resources office to handle such functions as recruitment and selection, employee testing, payroll, and record keeping.

Whatever plan is in operation for the administration of the classified personnel program, certain human resources functions and activities must be performed. Many of these functions are presented elsewhere in this text in regard to certified personnel. This chapter will discuss these functions as they differ from those in the certificated personnel system and will discuss other activities and problems specific to the classified personnel program. The first section presents the development of a classification system. Other sections include salary determination, recruitment, selection, staff development, and performance appraisal.

DEVELOPMENT OF A CLASSIFICATION SYSTEM

Unlike certificated personnel, who represent a more limited range of job categories (i.e., teachers, administrators, counselors, nurses, librarians), classified personnel represent a broad spectrum of employees with varying levels of skills and responsibilities. For this reason, in all but the smallest districts, it is necessary to differentiate among positions on the basis of duties and responsibilities. This can be done only after a job analysis. Following the job analysis, positions with similar duties and responsibilities can be grouped into common classes. This classification plan, as it is called, provides the foundation for the entire personnel program. The information about positions used to develop the classification plan and the classes subsequently established provide the basis for employee recruitment, selection, assignment, and evaluation, as well as salary determination.

Job Analysis

The development of the classification system begins with job analysis. **Job analysis** is the process of collecting, organizing, and evaluating information relating to the responsibilities and tasks associated with a specific job. The data collected serve a number of human resource functions such as recruitment and selection. The training objectives identified are used for orientation, and the training and performance criteria are used for competency or performance assessments (Denis & Austin, 1992). The importance of the job analysis has grown in recent years as the courts have increasingly looked to the job analysis when making judgments about various aspects of personnel selection, from content valid employment tests to the determination of the essential functions relevant for job-related medical screening.

The U.S. Department of Labor (1991) suggests the following four dimensions be included in a job analysis: (1) worker functions—what the worker does in relation to data, people, and things; (2) work fields—the methodologies and techniques utilized; (3) MPSMS—the *materials* being processed, the *products* being made, the *subject matter* being dealt with, and the *services* being rendered; (4) worker characteristics— the worker attributes that contribute to successful job performance (education, specific vocational preparation, aptitudes, temperaments, physical demands, and environmental conditions). The analysis of the physical demands and environmental conditions is particularly important in meeting the challenge of the Americans With Disabilities Act. An example of a data collection form used to made this analysis is provided in Figure 12.1.

The four most common approaches to collecting job analysis data are (1) questionnaires, (2) employee diaries, (3) observation, and (4) interviews. A **job analysis questionnaire** is designed to elicit the employee's own description and perception of the job, is usually standardized, and consists primarily of checklists or items to be rated. It seeks information relative to the type and number of tasks performed; the frequency with which the task is performed; the percentage of time spent on each task; the level of skill required; the title of the position(s) from which supervision is received and over which supervision is given; the equipment operated; the experience required; and any formal education, training, or license required.

A popular worker-oriented, as opposed to job-oriented, questionnaire that lends itself to quantitative statistical input is the Position Analysis Questionnaire (PAQ) (McCormick, Jeanneret, & Mecham, 1972). The PAQ consists of 194 job elements, which are categorized as (1) information input (where and how the employee gets the information used on the job); (2) mental processes (the reasoning, planning, decision making, etc., involved in the job); (3) work output (the physical activities performed and the tools or devices used); (4) relationships with other persons required on the job; (5) job context (the physical and social environment in which the work is performed), and (6) other characteristics. Although questionnaires are cheaper and quicker to administer than other job analysis techniques, they often suffer from inaccuracy and incompleteness. To be effective, questionnaires must provide for follow-up and clarification.

Employees may also be asked to record their work activities and time spent on them in a **diary.** Entries are made at specified times during the work shift (e.g., every hour or half-hour) and are normally kept for a period of 2 to 4 weeks (Sherman, Bohlander & Chruden, 1988). Although diaries may be very revealing, their wealth of detail may be more than many school districts can process, unless the analysis is limited to a relatively few positions (National School Boards Association [NSBA], 1987).

Observation as a method of job analysis is most appropriate for those jobs that require primarily manual, standardized, short-cycle activities (Cascio, 1987). Observation should include a representative sample of job activities. And it should be made clear to the employee being observed that it is the job that is being assessed, not the person. Observation may be done in person or the observation may be videotaped and reviewed at a later date by the job analyst or by the job analyst and the employee. The latter provides the opportunity for the analyst to ask the employee questions about various aspects of the job.

ID No. _____

Physical Demands

Comments

Strength

Position

Standing _____ %
Walking _____ %
Sitting _____ %

Weight/Force

	N	O	F	C
Lifting				
Carrying				
Pushing				
Pulling				

Controls: Hand-Arm _____ Foot-Leg _____

Strength Level: _____

Climbing
Balancing
Stooping
Kneeling
Crouching
Crawling
Reaching
Handling
Fingering
Feeling
Talking
Hearing
Tasting/Smelling
Near Acuity
Far Acuity
Depth Perception
Accommodation
Color Vision
Field of Vision

Environmental Conditions

Comments

1. Exposure to Weather
2. Extreme Cold
3. Extreme Heat
4. Wet and/or Humid
5. Noise Intensity Level
6. Vibration
7. Atmospheric Conditions
8. Moving Mechanical Parts
9. Electric Shock
10. High, Exposed Places
11. Radiation
12. Explosives
13. Toxic/Caustic Chemicals
14. Other Environmental Conditions

Protective Clothing or Personal Devices _____

Analyst _____ Date _____
Field Center Reviewer _____ Date _____
Additional Reviewer _____ Title _____

FIGURE 12.1

Data Collection Form For Physical Demands and Environmental Conditions

Source: From *The Revised Handbook for Analyzing Jobs,* U.S. Department of Labor, 1991, Washington, DC: GPO.

354

One observation technique, known as Function Job Analysis (FJA), attempts to identify *what* actions the employee performs (using an action verb), to whom or what (the object of the verb), *why* (the purpose of the action), and *how* it was done (in terms of equipment being used, nature and sources of instructions or supervision, and interactions with others). A section called *worker functions* attempts to get at the extent of interaction the employee has with ideas (data), with other workers or clients, and with equipment and machines (things) (Cascio, 1987).

The most common approach to job analysis is the **interview.** Either an individual interview, in which one or more job incumbents is interviewed extensively, or a group interview, where a number of job incumbents are interviewed simultaneously, can be used. In either case, under the interviewer's guidance and in response to a carefully prepared set of questions, the incumbents recall and discuss their work activities (Brademas, 1982). Because the employee acts as the observer during the interview, activities and behaviors that would often not be observed can be reported, as well as those that occur over long time periods. In addition, because of the incumbent's knowledge of the job, the analyst gains information about the job that might not otherwise be available (Cascio, 1987).

The actual analysis of the classified positions may be performed by a qualified district personnel specialist, or it may be necessary for the district to hire a personnel consultant specializing in job analyses. Regardless of who performs the analysis or the approach employed, the importance of the fundamental task cannot be overemphasized.

It is also important that the job analyses be periodically updated if they, and the products that emanate from them, are to remain valid. Jobs are dynamic. In some cases technological advances have reduced once difficult jobs requiring higher levels of education to jobs that can be performed by workers with only limited formal education but with specific technical training. Since the passage of the Civil Rights Act of 1964, numerous court decisions have emphasized a concern that job requirements be relevant and not be unrealistically high. Over time, job activities may also shift somewhat dramatically. These shifts should be reflected in changes in job descriptions and job specifications, as well as in job training programs (Cascio, 1987).

Job Classification

After all jobs have been analyzed, jobs with similar work requirements may be grouped into a common class. Positions within the class may differ in experience and skill requirements, or in degree of responsibility. For example, the custodial class might include a custodian I, custodian II, and head custodian. A good classification system will promote better employee understanding of how jobs are classified and belief in the equity of the pay system that is based on it (NSBA, 1987).

The final classification plan must be adopted by the school board. If classified personnel are covered by civil service arrangements, however, the classification plan may require approval by the civil service commission prior to presentation and adoption by the board. The preparation of job descriptions follows board adoption.

Job Descriptions

Job descriptions are the most immediate products of the job analysis process. A job description is a written, detailed outline of the duties and responsibilities of a specific job. The job description should describe the job, not the person who holds, or will hold, the position. Job descriptions not only assist human resources administrators, potential employees, and present employees in understanding existing positions and role expectations, but they also enhance employees' understanding of their roles by providing a concise statement of the duties and responsibilities expected, qualifications required, and relationships expected with other employees (Jordan, McKeown, Salmon, & Webb, 1985). Job descriptions provide the basis for recruiting and selecting candidates and evaluating job performance.

A job description will normally include the following items:

- ☐ Job title and classification
- ☐ Job summary
- ☐ Description of the essential and marginal job functions
- ☐ Description of the physical requirements of the job
- ☐ Description of tools and equipment used
- ☐ Required qualifications and skills, including education, experience, and license
- ☐ Working conditions and physical environment, including any biological or physical hazards
- ☐ Person(s) to whom responsible, and extent of supervision given or received
- ☐ Relationship with other jobs
- ☐ Conditions of employment (e.g., hours of work, wage scale, fringe benefits, and opportunities for promotion and transfer)

The descriptions of the essential and marginal job functions and physical requirements of the job are the most important sections in terms of compliance with the Americans With Disabilities Act and the determination of whether these can be accomplished with reasonable accommodation by the district. The essential functions of the job are those that, in the district's judgment, constitute business necessity. In determining the essential functions, the focus should be on the desired end rather than the means to accomplish it. In one case that was lost by the employer, the employer had required that each employee be able to use both arms when performing a particular task. One employee could not meet this requirement because his disability caused limited mobility in one arm. However, the court found that the essential function of the job was the ability to lift and carry a particular article, which he could do, not the ability to use both arms (Greenberg & Bello, 1992).

What happens to the job descriptions after they have been prepared by the personnel specialist depends upon the existence, if any, of any union agreements or civil service contracts. That is, in areas of high unionization, agreements may call for union agreement of initial job descriptions or any alteration of existing job descriptions (Candoli, Hack, & Ray, 1992). Ultimately, of course, it is the school board that must approve all job descriptions and classifications.

SALARY DETERMINATION

Once the classification plan has been established, the district is ready to develop the salary schedule for its classified employees. In some cases support personnel may be paid an hourly wage. The principles involved in the establishment and maintenance of hourly wages are the same as those involved in the establishment and maintenance of a salary schedule. The following basic rules should be followed in the development of the salary schedule:

1. School district salaries should reflect prevailing wages in the community.
2. Benchmark positions should be established for each class.
3. The salary schedule should be equitable: Placement of positions on the salary schedule should reflect accepted indications of difference.
4. The salary schedule should be internally consistent.
5. All classified positions should be on the schedule.
6. The salary schedule and all adjustments to it should be public and accessible.
7. Fringe benefits should be considered.
8. Provision should be made for periodic review.

Basic to the development of the classified employee salary schedule are the principles that school district salaries should be fair and competitive. A fair salary structure emphasizes unbiased decisions and justice. Competitive pay emphasizes sufficiency to attract and retain quality employees (Sibon, 1992). In the past school districts often assumed that the value of regular employment, vacations, and fringe benefits entitled them to pay somewhat less than business and industry. For most districts this is no longer a viable assumption. The security and protection offered by unions, combined with the expanded fringe benefit programs offered by many businesses, are equal or superior to that offered by most school districts. If the district is to attract and retain qualified, competent personnel, it must be competitive with both the private sector and other public agencies in its compensation program.

Salary Studies

The determination of prevailing wage rates in the community may be accomplished in several ways. In smaller communities the human resources administrator may contact the major employers in the district and solicit salary information. This may be supplemented with data from public and private employment offices and from state and federal departments of labor. In larger communities and districts a more formal **salary study** involving the solicitation of salary information from other districts, agencies, industries, and professional organizations may be conducted. Whatever data are being used for comparison should take into consideration indirect compensation (employee benefits and services), and ultimately this must be considered as a part of the total compensation program. In fact, a calculation of the cost of indirect compensation per employee should be made and shared with all employees.

It is important that classified employees be involved in the salary study. Agreement must be reached as to which districts, agencies, or industries will be contacted. Clearly, balance must be maintained between any attempt by administration to contact primarily those employers known to pay lower salaries or by employees to suggest only those employers known to pay higher salaries. It is also important that the results of the salary study be made available to employees for their response and reaction before any recommendations are made to the board.

Care should be taken in the collection of data from other employers to ensure that comparisons are indeed being made only between positions that are similar in duties and responsibilities. Once the salary data have been collected, an average salary for various positions may be determined. The average may be based on the data from all employers or, as is common, the top and bottom 10–25% may be eliminated.

It is generally not possible to determine the prevailing wage for each position in the district. It is necessary, therefore, to identify at least one position in each class as a benchmark position. A **benchmark position** is one whose duties and responsibilities are sufficiently common that it will be found in other districts and in most other businesses and industries. Once the prevailing wage has been determined for the benchmark position, it is possible to determine salaries for the other positions in the class.

Establishing the Salary Schedule

Before salaries can be set, the proper relationship between all the positions in a class must be established. Establishing this relationship is primarily a consideration of equity. Each position is assigned specific salary grades or ranges based on consideration of factors that reflect the varying levels of skills and responsibilities required. Among the factors to be considered are (1) education or training requirements, (2) license requirements, (3) experience requirements, (4) skills requirements, (5) number of employees supervised, and (6) number and range of responsibilities assigned.

The establishment of differentials between salary grades and steps in grades is a matter of internal consistency. The benchmark position for each salary grade should be within one step (on a five-step schedule) of the average. A common salary differential between steps in a grade is 2.5%. The differentials between grades should also be uniform. The 2.5% differential is also the common differential used between grades on school district salary schedules for classified personnel. A 5% differential would be the largest that could be justified, or afforded, by most districts.

The salary schedule should also recognize length of service. This can be accomplished by adopting a schedule that has five or more steps for each grade or range. The employee advances from one step to another after predetermined periods of service.

All classified positions should be included on the salary schedule. No position should be considered too high or too low, and no differential treatment should be given. Authority on final adoption of a salary schedule is given to the school board. The salary schedule adopted should not only be made public, as is required in most jurisdictions, but should be distributed and made easily available to employees and other interested parties.

Finally, provision should be made for periodic review of the salary schedule. Such review should consider not only data obtained from salary studies, but also data relative to the cost of living. In periods of inflation the cost of living can rise quite rapidly and unless consideration is given to periodic adjustments based on some indicator of price inflation, school district employees can fall behind their counterparts in other agencies and businesses. Whereas annual review of the master salary schedule would be most desirable, it is not uncommon for salary negotiations to fix salaries for periods of 2 years or more, making formal annual review unnecessary.

RECRUITMENT

The goal of any school district classified personnel recruitment program, as with any personnel recruitment program, is the identification of sufficient, qualified applicants to meet the personnel needs of the district. Since the classified service requires a staff with more varied skills and background than the certificated service, their recruitment is more varied and can often be more difficult. The importance of sound recruitment policies and practices cannot be overemphasized. Not only are they critical in maintaining employee morale and faith in the board's and administration's commitment to equity and fairness, but they are necessary cost saving measures given the costs associated with the high turnover rate that inevitably follows poor recruitment.

Prior to the actual solicitation of applications, an announcement of vacancy must be prepared. In preparing the announcement, the Equal Employment Opportunity Commission (EEOC) guidelines relative to the illegality of advertising job openings on the basis of sex and age must be followed. The announcement of vacancy should be as detailed as possible to allow potential applicants to determine if they are interested in the position or qualified for it. Sufficient copies of the announcement of vacancy should be prepared so that one is available to each applicant and so that some can be posted in each school or building and in other public locations in the district.

Recruitment for any classified position may involve both internal and external sources. For some openings qualified individuals, or individuals who can be made qualified, may already be employed in the district and may welcome the opportunity for transfer or promotion. Personnel records can be used to identify employees who have the qualifications for a specific vacancy. If current employees know that they will receive consideration for vacancies that are of higher salary and status, the effects will often be reflected in increased performance and morale (Jordan et al., 1985).

For some vacancies the district may lack the capacity to "grow their own" or may find it desirable to recruit from external sources. In these instances a variety of recruiting sources are available. They include advertisements, employment agencies, educational institutions, professional organizations and unions, and employee referrals. The specific source(s) utilized by the district will depend upon such factors as district size, district resources, the number of vacancies, and the type of position. That is, certain techniques, such as using private agencies, have proven to be more successful in recruiting administrative or technical personnel, whereas others, such as placing classified advertisements, have proven more successful in recruiting hourly employees (Levine, 1984).

Advertisements

Advertisements are often the only source used by school districts to fill classified vacancies. Advertising may be through radio, television, bulletins, professional journals, and newspapers. Advertising has the advantage of reaching the largest possible audience. At the same time, aside from its cost, this is its principal limitation. Advertising in any of the mass media results in unpredictable responses. Selectivity may be achieved by advertising in publications directed toward particular target audiences. Professional journals, trade or union publications, and newspapers or journals directed toward specific minority audiences are among the outlets used in targeted advertising (Sherman et al., 1988). At the same time, a well-written advertisement that effectively summarizes the job specifications, requirements, and prospects will not only improve the quality of applicants, but will improve the effectiveness and success of the recruitment process. Also, all advertisements should make it clear that the school district is an equal opportunity employer.

Employment Agencies

Sometimes it may be necessary or advantageous for the district to utilize the services of either public or private employment agencies. In addition to supplying job applicants, employment agencies often assist in the employment process by performing employment testing, evaluation, and counseling. Public employment agencies can be of most assistance for the unskilled, semiskilled, and skilled operative positions. Because unemployed individuals are required to register to work with the state employment service and must be willing to accept any suitable offer of employment before they can collect unemployment insurance benefits, these agencies have an identifiable pool of unemployed individuals available for immediate employment.

Private agencies can be of most assistance in filling technical and professional positions. Many private agencies specialize in certain fields. Private employment agencies can differ significantly in the services they provide and in the fee that is charged to the applicant or the employer. Thus if the school district finds it necessary or desirable to use an employment agency, it should, to the extent possible, use a public or other nonprofit employment agency. If this is not sufficient and the services of a private employment agency are needed, care should be taken to ensure that the agency will provide the services and applicants at a cost that either the district or the prospective applicant can afford. The school district should select an employment agency that is established, receives recruiter certification through the National Association of Personnel Consultants, and provides multiple services (temporary, full-time, and management-level recruitment). Perhaps the best gauge of the caliber of the firm is to ask three candidates two questions: What did the agency tell you about the school district and position? and How do you feel about your recruiter? (Falcone, 1992).

Educational Institutions

For some of the more advanced professional and vocational fields in the classified service (e.g., budget director, dietician, director of food services, director of transportation services, architect, and various engineers), it would be logical for the school district to recruit at colleges and universities. Almost all colleges and universities operate placement offices through which the school district can recruit and arrange interviews with applicants.

For a number of other classified positions, the district can recruit applicants from trade schools. The school district is also in the unique position to recruit the very best of the graduating seniors in the district. Personal references of students can be readily checked and school records can provide some indication of on-the-job performance (Jordan et al., 1985). Rather than letting its best graduates go elsewhere, the school district can hire them.

Professional Organizations and Unions

Many professional organizations provide placement services to their members. Placement activities often are conducted in connection with the organization's state, regional, and national conferences, and advertisements are carried in publications of the organization. For certain select positions, therefore, the district may want to place an advertisement in the trade journal. For others it might be more economical for the district to send a recruiter to a conference to interview a number of applicants rather than bring applicants to the district.

Labor unions, through their apprenticeship programs, are the primary source of applicants for certain types of jobs. In fact, in districts where some or all of the classified personnel are unionized, the district must rely on the union in their recruitment efforts.

Employee Referrals

Present employees are a very important recruitment source for any organization. Schwab's review (Rowland & Ferris, 1982) of numerous studies on recruitment sources concluded that, as measured by turnover rates, employee referrals were the most effective recruitment source. This may in part be because employees secured in this way have a greater initial understanding of job expectations, organizational policies, and working conditions. It may also be a function of the fact that in recommending someone, the employee is in effect putting his or her judgment on the line and will, therefore, be especially encouraged to help the recommended person to succeed. One note of warning: By relying on employee referrals, the district must be alert to the possibility of "inbreeding" and violation of EEOC regulations. Since employees and their referrals will likely be of similar backgrounds, districts who rely heavily on employee referrals may unintentionally screen out, and thereby discriminate against, protected classes (Sherman et al., 1988).

The human resources administrator should keep a record of the recruitment sources used and the quantity and quality of applicants received from each source. This information can be useful for future recruitment efforts and for any audit of equity or fair employment practices.

SELECTION

The selection process is essentially a series of activities designed to gain information about the job applicant that can be compared to the job description and, ultimately, result in the best match of person and position. Although no standard procedure for employee selection is practiced by all districts, the following stages are commonly found:

1. Application form
2. Preliminary interview
3. Employment tests
4. Background check
5. Employment interview
6. Medical examination
7. Final selection and assignment

The extent to which a particular district follows these steps will depend primarily upon the size of the district, the position(s) to be filled, and the policies and procedures in force in the district. The larger the district and the higher the level of the position being filled, the more comprehensive and formal the process is likely to become. It is important that all districts, regardless of size, develop systematic procedures for the selection of employees.

Application Form

Virtually every district requires all applicants to complete an application form as a part of the hiring process. Application forms provide the district with an easy and systematic method of obtaining a variety of factual information about the applicant. As a general rule, other than biographical data, information solicited on the application form should be limited to that pertinent to success on the job. The areas of impermissible inquiry for the interview noted in Chapter 6 are also impermissible on the application form.

In addition to these impermissible inquiries, questions that might be considered embarrassing or that might be easily misinterpreted should not be included on the application form. Lastly, EEOC guidelines prohibit asking questions about race, color, religion, national origin, age, or sex; however, because this information may be valuable to the school district or needed for inspection by state or federal officials, the school district is allowed to request it apart from the application on a separate form, which is voluntarily returned by the applicant.

Preliminary Interview

As noted in Chapter 6, the primary purpose of the preliminary interview is to screen out applicants who are obviously unqualified. For example, some applicants may not meet the size, legal age, or intelligence requirements for the position. In addition, whereas some basic data have been obtained on the application form, most application forms do not solicit the type of detailed information relative to knowledge and experience that can be determined in a personal interview. Nor can the application form generate data relative to attitude, appearance, and conduct. The preliminary interview also provides the applicant the opportunity to get answers to questions about the position and the school system. As was also noted in Chapter 6, the preliminary interview is usually conducted by human resources counselors in the human resources department and is usually short in duration.

Employment Tests

Following the initial interview, applicants may be required to take certain tests or submit validated scores from previous tests. The extent to which tests are used and the importance given them may vary from school district to school district. For a time in the last decade many employers limited their use of tests because of their concern about meeting EEOC requirements. More recently employment tests have come into greater use because the testing industry has made increased efforts to make tests more job related and employers have placed renewed confidence in the objectivity of tests as predictors and measurers of skills and knowledge.

Tests for classified personnel are normally either written general intelligence and aptitude tests or performance tests. The written test is often short and similar to a school achievement test for reading and math, with perhaps a few items common to those found on intelligence tests. If such tests are used, it is important that the school district recognizes that test results do not guarantee subsequent performance. And, as was discussed in Chapter 9, school districts must also be careful in developing and/or using employment tests to ensure that the tests are valid for the job in question and are nondiscriminatory.

The written general intelligence or aptitude test may be followed by a performance test. Applicants for secretarial and clerical positions may be asked to take a keyboarding test to determine speed and accuracy. A performance test for a bus driver may include starting, stopping, backing, turning, and parking the bus under specified conditions. The performance test gives applicants an opportunity to demonstrate their skills.

A growing trend in business and industry, which has been adopted by some districts, is testing designed to assess behavioral and attitudinal characteristics. Some of these psychometric tests are designed around such dimensions as "independence of thought," "team working," and "cooperativeness" (Storey, 1992), dimensions integral to the successful implementation of site-based management and the total quality management concept. As previously noted in this text, this concept has gained some acceptance in education.

Background Check

After the interview and employment test, the references, previous employment, and other information provided on the application form and in the interview by those applicants still under consideration may be checked. As noted in some detail in Chapter 6, the purposes of such checks are to gain additional information about the

Employer: _____

Supervisor: _____

Caller: _____

Date/Time: _____

_____

_____

Absenteeism/Punctuality:

Attitude:

Ability to work with others:

How long employed?

Would you rehire?

Additional comments:

FIGURE 12.2

Employer Reference Checklist

Source: From "School Bus Drivers Recruitment and Training" by D. Hammond and G. Blakey, April 1991, *School Business Affairs*, 57. Copyright © 1991 by *School Business Affairs*. Reprinted by permission.

applicant, to clarify questions or inconsistencies, and to verify the accuracy of information provided by the applicant. Figure 12.2 provides an example of a reference checklist, one used by the Branson, Missouri, R-4 School District in the screening of school bus drivers.

Employment Interview

Whereas the purpose of the preliminary interview was to screen out unqualified or overqualified applicants, the purpose of the employment interview is to obtain further information that will assist management in choosing from among qualified candidates and to predict success on the job. As discussed in detail in Chapter 6, employment interviews can be classified according to the methods or approaches that are used to elicit information, attitudes, and feelings from the applicant. Much of what was said in that discussion relative to interviewing certificated staff applies to interviewing classified staff. Perhaps the most important considerations are that the interview adhere to all EEOC guidelines, that the interview of each candidate be conducted using the same set of questions, and that each candidate be evaluated on the basis of the criteria enumerated on the job description.

The employment interview for classified staff will normally involve the head of the department where the vacancy exists, an employee with the same or a similar position as the one being filled, and a person selected at large. In some instances this person may be someone other than a district employee. For certain specialized positions, persons from business or industry may be asked to serve on the selection committee. In districts where site-based management has delegated personnel selection to the local site, the principal or other administrator may well be on the selection committee. Depending on the position, a teacher, counselor, librarian, other education professional, parent, or community representative may also be on the committee. Whomever serves on the committee, it is the responsibility of the administrator in charge of the selection process to provide interviewers with guidelines for conducting the interview and to ensure the effectiveness and fairness of the process.

Medical Examination

The preemployment medical examination is required by many school districts and, if required, should be paid for by the district. The Americans With Disabilities Act places limits on the use of medical exams in the employment process. A medical examination cannot be required before an offer of employment is made, and the school district can require the examination only if it is required of all entering employees in the same job category. Examinations must be job related and consistent with business necessity (Horwitz, 1992). Applicants cannot be screened out for a position unless the medical examination determines that, even with reasonable accommodation by the school district, they cannot perform the essential functions of the job (as detailed in the job description) safely and efficiently and without posing an unduly high risk to themselves, other employees, or the public.

Any information obtained from the medical examination must be kept in a separate form and in a separate medical file; it should not be placed in personnel files. Disclosure of information about the exam is permitted only to the following persons (Horwitz, 1992):

☐ Supervisors and managers regarding necessary restrictions on the employee's work and accommodations

☐ First-aid and safety personnel, when appropriate, if the disability might require emergency treatment

☐ Government officials investigating ADA compliance. (p. 7)

Final Selection and Assignment

In most government entities, including school districts, the final selection of individuals to fill job openings must come from lists of eligible candidates who have passed all the foregoing steps in the selection process. The use of eligibility lists is intended to increase the objectivity of the selection process. When a vacancy occurs, the names of three or more individuals are referred to the individual(s) authorized to make the final selection. Unless the requesting party can provide sufficient justification as to why none of these individuals should be selected, selection must be made from among those referred. Eligibility lists are normally declared invalid after a few months.

Before a new employee is assigned to a vacant position, consideration should be given to providing an existing employee the opportunity to make a lateral transfer to the vacancy. For example, if the vacancy is in what is considered the most desirable school in the district, policy might provide the opportunity for an employee in what is considered a less desirable school to transfer to the vacant position and assign the new employee to the opening created by the transfer. The opportunity for transfer is essential to staff motivation and morale. However, this consideration must be balanced against the district's interest in finding the right person for each job and in what best serves the needs of the district and its students. The human resources administrator should provide leadership in the development of policies that will govern transfers and assignments.

STAFF DEVELOPMENT FOR SUPPORT PERSONNEL

In 1992 organizations in the United States with 100 or more employees spent $42 billion providing 1.3 billion hours of formal training to 40.9 million employees, or an average of 32 hours and $1,024 per employee ("Industry Report," 1992). Unfortunately, development programs for support personnel in education have traditionally lagged behind those in other organizations. Only in recent years have school districts come to realize that the time and expense invested in development programs for support personnel are small compared to the dissatisfaction, inefficiency, ineffectiveness, and staff turnover resulting from the lack of such programs. All new employees, regardless of their previous education, training, or experience, need to be introduced to their new work environment and need to be taught how to perform specific tasks. All continuing employees need periodic retraining as new technology is introduced, as jobs change, and as employees are transferred or promoted.

Perhaps because of their job responsibilities, most development programs for support personnel are aimed more at training than education. There is a growing awareness, however, that support personnel—be they secretaries, maintenance engineers, bus drivers, or cafeteria managers—will perform more efficiently if they are provided the opportunity to participate in personal growth activities. Time management and human skills are important for all school district employees (Rebore, 1991). Thus in a growing number of districts, staff development activities of this nature as well as various other career development programs, such as those discussed under employee assistance programs in Chapter 11, are being made available to all employees, certificated as well as classified.

In most school districts development programs for classified personnel are concerned with informing employees of district policies and procedures and providing them with job skills. These activities are discussed under the major programs in which they fall: orientation and employee training.

Orientation

The aim of the orientation program is both to provide the new employee with information about the district and to help the new employee feel at home and positive about having accepted the position. Initial impressions and information are important to later attitudes toward the job, co-workers, and the district. Because over half of the voluntary resignations in an organization occur within the first 6 months, proper orientation can do much to reduce this problem and its accompanying expense (Flippo, 1980).

In certain respects the orientation needs of classified personnel are greater than those of certificated personnel. Most new certificated personnel have been oriented to various aspects of schools during their teacher or administrator preparation program. They also have some understanding of the role of the school and of education as a process. Many classified personnel, on the other hand, come to the job with certain skills or training but without a clear understanding of the role of the school, the educational process, or the workings of the educational system (Jordan et al., 1985).

Orientation is most effective when approached as a cooperative activity of the human resources department and supervisors. It consists of four phases. The human resources department is normally responsible for coordinating the orientation and for the first phase: the provision of information about the district and the particular school (if applicable), personnel policies, salaries and benefits, promotion opportunities, time recording and absences, holidays, grievance procedures, and other regulations. As much of this information as possible should be provided in an employees' handbook, which should also include an organizational chart clarifying lines of authority and communication. In presenting this information to new employees, it is best to be honest and to present a realistic preview of what is expected in working for the district. Research has shown that providing a realistic account, as compared to a "sales pitch," will reduce the number of voluntary resignations (Flippo, 1980).

The second phase of the induction program is conducted by the immediate supervisor. The supervisor introduces the new employee to other employees and describes the relationship of the new employee's position to other positions in the department, gives a tour of the department, and provides information about department rules and regulations, safety requirements, and the detailed duties and responsibilities of the job. The supervisor also provides information about such details as location of lockers, restrooms, and lunchrooms, parking, supply procedures, hours of work, and call-in procedures. Some school districts have borrowed from industry and developed checklists of items that are to be covered by the supervisor in the initial orientation of new employees. The use of the checklist ensures that no important item will be overlooked. It also compels the supervisor to pay particular attention to each new employee at a time when personal attention is most important (Sherman et al., 1988). The supervisor should also use this phase of the orientation program "to engage in a preliminary training needs assessment in order to determine any disparity between the basic knowledge and skills of the worker and those required of the job" (Pecora & Austin, 1987, p. 119).

A third phase of the orientation process is a form of on-the-job training. That is, the new employee will be assigned to a first-level supervisor or to an experienced employee, who will instruct and supervise the new employee for a period ranging from a few hours to a few days.

A follow-up interview several weeks after the new employee has been on the job constitutes the fourth phase of the orientation program. The interview may be conducted by either the supervisor or a representative of the district human resources office. The purposes of the interview are to determine employee satisfaction with the job, answer any questions the employee might have, review important information, and to apprise the employee of the perceptions of his or her performance thus far.

Employee Training

As employees continue on the job, various types of training may be needed. Educational program changes, the introduction of new technology into classrooms and offices, increased utilization of equipment in maintenance and operations, and new designs in school facilities have all contributed to job obsolescence and support the need for the continuing training of classified school personnel. Other training needs are created by employee transfers or promotions, changes in district requirements or procedures, and legal and government mandates. Employee training may be used to provide information to employees and to provide opportunities for the acquisition of new skills. As a result of training, it is anticipated that the employee will be more effective on the job and will qualify for higher level positions.

The specific content of employee training provided by the district will depend upon a number of factors, such as qualifications and skills of present employees, district employment needs, and changes in legal requirements. Reviewing school district records, such as accident reports and grievance reports as well as employee needs assessments, may also suggest training needs. The training formats and methods used will vary depending upon the objectives of the training, the availability of qualified trainers and training materials, the size of the district, and the size of the school district's training budget. To the greatest extent possible, employees should be involved in planning and conducting training activities.

On-the-job Training. The most commonly used training method for classified personnel development programs is on-the-job training. In addition to being the simplest to operate, it is the least expensive. As previously stated, on-the-job training is usually conducted by the supervisor or by an experienced or senior employee. This method has the advantage of providing hands-on experience under normal working conditions (Sherman et al., 1988). However, the success of the training depends in large part upon qualified trainers. More seniority or experience does not necessarily make a co-worker a good teacher. If the new employee is assigned to an employee who has neither the ability nor the inclination to teach the new employee properly, the results will be less effective. It is the responsibility of the human resources department to identify potential trainers and to provide them with instruction in how to train new employees.

Off-the-job Training. In addition to on-the-job training, most school districts find it necessary to provide some training of classified personnel away from their normal work location. Workshops lasting 1 day or more for all employees within a certain department are an off-the-job training technique common to school district personnel programs. This technique provides for the maximum number of trainees with the minimum number of trainers and lends itself to instruction in areas where information and instruction can be imparted by lectures, demonstrations, or the use of media (Sherman et al., 1988). If properly designed, instructional activities such as case studies or simulations that maximize trainee involvement may be employed. Increasingly school districts are also availing themselves of computer-based training that employs interactive video or computer-driven simulations. Although these technologies are perhaps the most expensive form of training, they have been shown to be not only highly effective, but to reduce learning time by 25–50% (Reynolds, 1990).

In addition to conducting their own training, school districts may also benefit from that conducted by the state department of education (or other government agencies) and various business concerns. State departments of education commonly conduct or sponsor training workshops on topics of general interest to school districts and for the benefit of those many small districts that do not have the personnel to develop viable training programs. These same functions may also be performed by two or more districts cooperating in the provision of training programs.

It is also common for manufacturing and business concerns to provide training in the use of their materials and equipment. School district personnel may be sent to a training facility operated by the business, or the provider may send trainers to the local school district. Companies also normally will provide materials that may be used by the district in its training efforts. Even when training related to the use of specific materials and equipment is not needed, companies often have persons available to give presentations on a variety of topics.

Evaluation.   The primary goal of employee training is to improve the on-the-job performance of employees. Certainly the school district will want to know if this goal has been met. It may also want to know if a training program, or certain parts of it, was worth the investment or if one program worked better than another or was more cost-effective. In order to answer these questions, some form of evaluation must take place. According to Patrick (1992), evaluation of training is "any attempt to obtain information concerning the effect or value of training in order to make decisions about any aspect of the training programme, the persons that have been trained, and the organizations . . . responsible for providing that training" (p. 515).

The evaluation of training can be anything from a simple pretest and posttest to determine gain in skill and knowledge, to an elaborate set of experiments with trainees randomly assigned to various treatments (training) and a control group. Four major approaches to evaluation of training have been identified: (1) the systems approach, which is concerned with the improvement of the training program; (2) the trainee-oriented approach, which focuses on the training effects that are valued by the trainees; (3) the cost-effective or statistical approach, which is concerned with measurement and the analysis of data in ways that support administrative decision making about training; and (4) the research approach, which is concerned with both carrying out research into training and systematically evaluating the effects of training programs (Patrick, 1992). Whether a school district uses one or all of these approaches at any point in time, the training program should be the subject of ongoing evaluation.

PERFORMANCE APPRAISAL

The guidelines and principles for a successful personnel appraisal system articulated in Chapter 7 apply equally to the appraisal of classified personnel. The objectives of the classified personnel appraisal system also closely parallel those of the certificated personnel appraisal system. Based on an extensive review of the literature, Swan, Holmes, Brown, Short, and DeWeese (1988) identified four objectives of appraisal systems for classified personnel: (1) to inform employees of their strengths and weaknesses and share expectations for improvement, (2) to provide data for merit pay recommendations, (3) to satisfy court requirements for cases involving alleged discrimination, and (4) to serve as the basis for disciplinary action.

Swan and colleagues (1988) have developed a Generic Performance Appraisal System for Classified Employees (GPASCE) that can be adapted by most school districts to meet their individual needs. According to its developers, the purposes of the GPASCE are to (1) encourage and facilitate improvement in the performance of employees, (2) provide a documented record of the employee's job performance, (3) provide an opportunity for communication between supervisor and employee on the subjects of job requirements and work expectations, (4) specify direction for work improvement, (5) assure employees that objective criteria are used in performance appraisal, (6) demonstrate that exceptional or unsatisfactory performance will be noted, and (7) exemplify the supervisor's and school's continuing interest in performance improvement.

The sequence of actions to be followed in GPASCE are as follows (Swan et al., 1988):

1. The supervisor and employee meet at the beginning of each year and discuss the employee's job in detail, including the criteria that will be used to appraise the employee's performance on each factor on the job description and any factors unique to the position (e.g., for bus drivers, maintaining discipline on the school bus).

2. The supervisor monitors the employee's performance throughout the appraisal period to obtain first-hand knowledge for the appraisal.

3. If any concerns develop during the appraisal period, the supervisor meets with the employee to provide encouragement, assistance, and direction for improvement. If necessary or appropriate, an improvement plan may be developed and negotiated with the employee and reviewed and approved by the supervisor's superior (the reviewer).

4. Within 2 weeks of the end of the appraisal period the supervisor completes the performance appraisal rating form (Figure 12.3). For any factor rated "1" or "5" the supervisor must provide narrative description. The supervisor must also provide a narrative justification for any overall performance rating of "outstanding" or "unsatisfactory." The average score across all factors is used as a guide for determining the overall rating: 5.0–4.3, outstanding; 4.2–3.4, superior; 3.3–1.9, satisfactory; 1.8–1.0, unsatisfactory.

5. The supervisor shares the completed appraisal form with the reviewer, who may provide recommendations for appropriate action for any "unsatisfactory" rating or provide supplementary information relative to any rating, but may not change the appraisal.

6. Within 2 weeks of the end of the appraisal period the supervisor meets with the employee to share and discuss the approved appraisal with the employee. At this meeting both the supervisor and the employee share perceptions, and the employee has the opportunity to present additional information of which the supervisor may be unaware.

7. Within 1 week of this meeting the supervisor completes and signs the finalized appraisal form and submits it to the reviewer for approval.

8. Within 4 weeks of the end of the appraisal period the employee receives the final performance appraisal. The employee acknowledges receipt of the appraisal by his or her signature and, if necessary and appropriate, may work with the supervisor to develop an improvement plan.

9. The final performance appraisal is filed in the employee's personnel file.

10. If the employee considers the final appraisal unfair or unreasonable, he or she may appeal directly to the reviewer for reconsideration. If reconsideration does not resolve the issue to the satisfaction of the employee, he or she may pursue the established grievance or appeal procedure of the school district.

Employee's Soc. Sec. #	Name (Last, First, Middle)	Position Title (&Series/Grade)

School	Rating Period From: To:	Check _Probationary One: _Mid-Year _Annual	Appraiser's Signature	Reviewer's Signature

I. Factor Appraisal System

Directions: Each employee is appraised on the common factors according to the contents of the job description (provide reference). An employee is rated on unique factors if contained in the job description. Provide narrative comments on separate page for all factors appraised as "5" or "1" and for unsatisfactory, outstanding, or postponed overall ratings.

Explanation of Appraisal Categories

5 = Exceeded requirements to exceptional degree
4 = Exceeded requirements, not to exceptional degree
3 = Met and sometimes exceeded requirements
2 = Usually met, but rarely exceeded minimum requirements
1 = Did not meet requirements
N = Irrelevant or no opportunity to observe employee's performance

A. *Common Factors — For All Employees*

	Job Description Reference	Appraised Category 5 4 3 2 1 N
1. *Demonstrates knowledge of job* (Includes technical, procedural, and regulatory knowledge)		|| || || || || ||
2. *Plans, organizes, and sets priorities* (Time scheduling, orderly arrangement of procedures, and systematic planning)		|| || || || || ||
3. *Produces expected quantity of work* (Amount of work produced/accomplished according to goals, objectives, and activities)		|| || || || || ||
4. *Meets schedules/timelines* (Accomplishes work on schedule/on time)		|| || || || || ||
5. *Communicates in written form* (Degree of completeness, clarity and conciseness, and organization of material)		|| || || || || ||

FIGURE 12.3

Performance Appraisal Form for Classified Employees

Source: From "A Generic Performance Appraisal Form for Classified Employees" by W. W. Swan, C. T. Holmes, C. L. Brown, M. L. Short, and L. DeWeese, 1988, *Journal of Personnel Evaluation in Education*, *1*, pp. 297–298. Copyright © 1988 by Kluwar Academic Publishers. Adapted by permission.

	Job Description Reference	Appraised Category 5 4 3 2 1 N
6. *Communicates in oral form* (Appropriateness of organization of material; clarity, conciseness, impact of presentation)		| | | | | | | | | | | |
7. *Informs/consults appropriately* (Provides information/seeks information when needed)		| | | | | | | | | | | |
8. *Makes judgments/decisions effectively* (Sees problems, chooses, and implements solutions)		| | | | | | | | | | | |
9. *Demonstrates positive interpersonal relationships* (Effective in working with others individually and in teams)		| | | | | | | | | | | |
B. *Unique Factors For Employees* 10.		| | | | | | | | | | | |
11.		| | | | | | | | | | | |
12.		| | | | | | | | | | | |
13.		| | | | | | | | | | | |
14.		| | | | | | | | | | | |

II. *Overall Performance Rating For Employee*
_____ Unsatisfactory _____ Satisfactory _____ Superior _____ Outstanding _____ Postponed

Acknowledgement of Receipt of Appraisal (Not Concurrence):_____

Employee's Signature   Date

_____

Narrative Comments

Factor #   Appraisal Category   Comment_____

Note:

_____
Appraiser's Signature   Date

FIGURE 12.3
continued

SUMMARY

Because of the number and importance of support staff, it is mandatory that sound personnel policies and practices relative to classified employees be in operation in all school districts. Districts need to conduct job analyses and prepare written job descriptions, after which they must develop a comprehensive classification plan. After the classification plan has been developed, the district is in a position to prepare salary schedules in which all classified positions are included. Because school district funds are public monies, information related to the schedule should be made public and accessible to employees and the public. The salary schedule should be subjected to periodic review, and indirect compensation should be considered in any discussion of the compensation program.

The goal of the school district recruitment program goes beyond merely recruiting the individuals needed to fill existing vacancies. Ideally, sufficient numbers should be recruited so that the district has the opportunity to select the very best employee from a number of qualified applicants. Given the investment made in recruiting, selecting, and training employees, it is incumbent that the district have an established systematic selection process that is not only equitable and nondiscriminatory but will generate the kind of data on which informed decisions can be based.

Following the lead of business and industry, in recent years school districts have placed new emphasis on the development and expansion of staff development programs for support personnel. There has also been an increased emphasis on the performance of education personnel, including classified personnel. The performance appraisal system for classified personnel, like that for certificated personnel, should be objective and based on job-related standards, effectively communicated to employees, and subjected to an ongoing analysis of results.

DISCUSSION QUESTIONS

1. As a newly appointed human resources director, you have been asked by the superintendent to revise the salary plan for classified personnel. What information will you require, and what activities must you perform to accomplish this task?

2. You are to hire a dietician, maintenance supervisor, and a secretary. How will you design your recruitment program for these positions? What is your rationale for selecting these various recruitment methods?

3. It has come to your attention that 30% of the classified employees leave the district prior to completing 1 year of service, and 60% of those who leave do so within 6 months. What programs might you consider implementing in order to reduce the turnover rate?

4. Describe the relationships among job descriptions, recruitment, selection, performance appraisal, and staff development.

CASE 12.1
Ruth or Roy?

The Maryvale School District has an opening for a Data Processor II. By advertising the position in the local newspapers and throughout the school system, the district has been successful in attracting 11 applicants. Of these, two candidates have emerged as having the best qualifications. The two candidates, Ruth Owens and Roy Evans, were equally ranked by the selection process. Ruth Owens was referred by Nancy Kraft, a valued and long-time employee in the same unit where the vacancy exists. The unit is currently all female. Roy Evans, a newcomer to the community, responded to an advertisement for the opening.

Questions

1. What are the advantages of hiring Ruth? of hiring Roy?
2. What impact, if any, would hiring Roy have on the prospect of future employee referrals? What could you do to mitigate against any negative effects?
3. What, if any, underlying legal issues are present in this case?

CASE 12.2
Ready to Work

Jacqueline Armstrong has been an employee of the Hartford School District for 23 years and currently is director of computing services. While driving back from a computing conference last spring, Jackie was injured in an accident that has left her permanently confined to a wheelchair. After many months of recovery, she is ready to return to work. Her office is on the second floor of the district administration office where all the computer equipment is located. The district office was formerly a high school, built in 1933, and it does not have an elevator or any wheelchair access. Architectural estimates of the cost to make the necessary renovations to the building to provide Jackie access total $163,000. The district is what would be considered a "poor" district and cannot make the renovations without either asking voters for a special assessment or making serious cuts in personnel and programs.

Questions

1. What legal obligations does the district have to Jackie? What moral obligations?
2. If you were the human resources director or superintendent and had the opportunity to talk to Jackie about the situation, what would you say?
3. What are the alternative solutions for the district? Which would you choose?

CASE 12.3
Harried Hank

Hank Sloane has been a bus driver for Hopeville School District No. 1 for 8 years. His on-time and safety record has consistently been one of the best in the district. Beginning in early February his supervisor, Mike Thompson, began to receive complaints that Hank was being verbally abusive to students on his bus. After a third parent complaint, Mike met with Hank to see what was going on. During the meeting Hank denied making the alleged statements to students, but did admit that he was having marital problems and wasn't sleeping well.

Within the next 10 days two more parents called. One complained about Hank's abusive language. Another reported that Hank had pulled away from the bus stop without her son even though he had to have seen the boy, who was half a block away and yelling for the bus to stop. The boy had to walk back home a half mile in the snow, and his mother had to cancel an important business meeting to drive him to school.

Again, Mike called Hank in and, again, Hank basically denied the charges. In the case of the first complaint, Hank said that the child in question was being disruptive on the bus and needed some sharp language to settle him down. As for the second situation, Hank claimed he did not see the child.

When asked how things were going with his wife, Hank broke down and tearfully admitted that she had left him, taking his three-year-old daughter. Mike warned Hank that his behavior must change and suggested he seek counseling through the employee assistance program. Hank seemed reluctant to do this, saying he could handle it by himself.

Questions

1. Should Mike have required Hank to seek assistance rather than just suggest it? Should Hank be moved from driving the bus to some other position in the transportation department where he is not in contact with students, even if some retraining might be involved?

2. To what extent should the district involve itself in the emotional problems of its employees? What is Hank's responsibility to the district to solve his personal problems?

REFERENCES

Brademas, D. J. (1982). Employee selection. *Journal of Physical Education, Recreation, and Dance, 53*(4), 59–63.

Candoli, I. C., Hack, W. G., & Ray, J. R. (1992). *School business administration: A planning approach* (4th ed.). Boston: Allyn & Bacon.

Cascio, W. F. (1987). *Applied psychology in personnel management* (3rd ed.). Englewood Cliffs, NJ: Prentice-Hall.

Denis, J., & Austin, B. (1992). A base(ic) course in job analysis. *Training and Development, 46*(7), 67–70.

Falcone, P. (1992). Select the best employment agency: It's a buyer's market. *H R Focus, 69*(8), 8.

Flippo, E. B. (1980). *Personnel management* (5th ed.). New York: McGraw-Hill.

Greenberg, S., & Bello, R. (1992). Rewrite job descriptions: Focus on functions. *H R Focus, 69*(7), 6.

Horwitz, H. A. (1992). New guidelines for medical examinations. *H R Focus, 69*(7), 7.

Industry report 1992. *Training, 29*(10), 25–28.

Jordan, K. F., McKeown, M. P., Salmon, R. G, & Webb, L. D. (1985). *School business administration*. Beverly Hills, CA: Sage.

Levine, H. Z. (1984). Consensus. *Personnel, 1*, 4–10.

McCormick, E. J., Jeanneret, P. R., & Mecham, R. C. (1972). A study of job characteristics and job dimensions as based on the Position Analysis Questionnaire (PAQ). *Journal of Applied Psychology, 56*, 347–368.

National School Boards Association. (1987). *The school personnel management system*. Washington, DC: Author.

Patrick, J. (1992). *Training: Research and practice*. New York: Academic Press.

Pecora, P. J., & Austin, M. J. (1987). *Managing human services personnel*. Beverly Hills, CA: Sage.

Rebore R. W. (1991). *Personnel administration in education: A management approach* (3rd ed.). Englewood Cliffs, NJ: Prentice-Hall.

Reynolds, A. S. (1990). Computers and HRD. In L. Nadler & Z. Nadler (Eds.), *The handbook of human resource development* (2nd ed., pp. 11.1–11.42). New York: Academic Press.

Rowland, K., & Ferris, G. (Eds.). (1982). *Personnel management: New perspectives*. Boston: Allyn & Bacon.

Sherman, A. W., Jr., Bohlander, G. W., & Chruden, H. J. (1988). *Managing human resources* (8th ed.). Cincinnati, OH: South-Western.

Sibon, R. E. (1992). *Strategic planning for human resources management*. New York: American Management Association.

Storey, J. (1992). *Developments in the management of human resources: An analytical review*. Oxford, UK: Blackwell.

Swan, W. W., Holmes, C. T., Brown, C. L., Short, M. L., & DeWeese, L. (1988). A generic performance appraisal system for classified employees. *Journal of Personnel Evaluation in Education, 1,* 293–310.

U.S. Department of Education, National Center for Education Statistics. (1992). *The condition of education.* Washington, DC: GPO.

U.S. Department of Labor. (1991). *The revised handbook for analyzing jobs.* Washington, DC: GPO.

13

Technology and Its Utilization in Human Resources Administration

As the information age approaches its third decade, both public and private organizations are being transformed into knowledge-intense enterprises that employ sophisticated technologies in acquiring, processing, and storing vast amounts of data. These data are used to produce information for a better understanding of the conditions facing these organizations so that they can make reliable preparations for the future.

Technological advancements, the miniaturization of electronic data processing components, and low production costs have put the great processing and storage capacities of computer systems within reach of all school districts. Human resources administrators now have the equipment available to establish information systems that can add substantial reliability to administrative decision making. School personnel can now use computer simulation models to analyze the outcomes of alternative responses to situations or problems. In addition, improved forecasting of personnel needs is possible through the rapid processing of large quantities of historical data. Moreover, computerized reports can now be routinely produced that reflect the integration of data from several data bases (e.g., payroll, human resources, and finance).

This chapter will first discuss the emergence of technology in education and describe the basic components of a computer system. This will be followed by a brief explanation of computer equipment (hardware) and the types of programs (software) used in computer systems. The development of microcomputers and the recent addition of local area networks (LAN) will also be introduced. Particular attention will be focused on software for human resources administration and the use of appropriate data in decision making. Another facet of technology that will be discussed in this chapter is the evolution of the electronic data base information system into today's management information system (MIS). The use of an MIS is explored with particular attention given to strategic, tactical, and operational decisions. Finally, a basic conceptual model of an MIS and a human resources information system (HRIS) will be presented to provide general familiarity with such systems. The focus of this chapter is the importance of using technology to improve decision-making processes. More advanced and technically oriented readers can extend their study of information systems by referring to any of the excellent books and materials available at bookstores and from professional associations.

EMERGENCE OF TECHNOLOGY IN EDUCATION

Using technology in managing human resources is a relatively recent development. The early 1970s witnessed the beginning of computerized personnel record keeping. Despite nearly three decades of technological developments, many school systems are still maintaining personnel records by employing cumbersome card files, personnel folders, and other manual procedures. Some large school systems process 10–30 thousand teacher application files annually, and the number of current and previous employee records can be several times as large. This attests to the volume of human resources records that is handled in many school districts.

As federal agencies and state governments demand more periodic reports on employment practices, school districts have found it nearly impossible to provide accurate and timely reports without the use of electronic data processing (EDP). Many use mainframe computers for financial affairs and have now expanded their EDP capabilities to accommodate human resources. Today most large school districts maintain a computerized data base for storing personnel records. Although most school systems use physical files and other manual forms of storing data, only the largest school districts have been able to augment this capability with computer systems. Until recently, computer systems large enough to accommodate personnel records have been too costly for most small districts. These districts maintained personnel records in manual files and were not using computers for data analysis to support decision making.

Now the microcomputer and the recently developed local area network (LAN) have made electronic data processing available to the smallest school districts at an affordable price. The fast-paced development of microcomputer *hardware* (equipment) provides computerized processing of human resources data at a fraction of the large mainframe cost. Some of the newest microcomputers have capacities that rival the mainframe computers of a decade ago.

The recent explosion of educational applications of the microcomputer has been monitored by the National Association of Secondary School Principals (1987). The NASSP found that the microcomputer is being used for the following administrative functions:

- Athletics
- Attendance accounting
- Budgeting
- Financial accounting
- Food service
- Grade analysis and reporting
- Guidance
- Information from databanks

- ☐   Instructional management
- ☐   Inventory and property records
- ☐   Media center
- ☐   Planning
- ☐   Scheduling
- ☐   Staff/personnel records
- ☐   Student records
- ☐   Student transportation (p. 2)

Currently there are many software packages available for performing these functions.

COMPONENTS OF A COMPUTER SYSTEM

A computer system is formed by several components working together. Each system permits the addition of new data and the alteration of existing data (input) in its permanent storage area. Moreover, specific data can be read and processed (processing) to produce information in a printed report (output). All of these functions use different components of the system, which are presented in Figure 13.1.

Computer Hardware

When several pieces of hardware are used to link the three functions depicted in Figure 13.1, a computer system is formed. It is beyond the scope of this text to review the many input, process, and output devices currently available; however, a short discussion of several is included to familiarize the reader with the more common types of hardware. For an expanded discussion of computer hardware, the reader with a limited computer background can refer to a basic text on computer literacy by Davis (1989). Readers desiring an overview of basic systems design that includes a discussion of the types of hardware and software available for an HRIS should refer to an Association of School Business Officials' publication on microcomputer systems by Kazlanskas and Picus (1990). For those interested in basic computer systems with a discussion of several popular applications programs, refer to Shelly, Cashman, Gurgel, Quasney, and Pratt (1990).

Entering new data or updating existing data is regarded as an input function. Many hardware devices are used for this purpose. Some of the most widely used include data terminals that consist of a cathode ray tube (CRT) and a typewriter-like keyboard; optical scanners that input data marked on paper forms such as tests, questionnaires, and unique paper forms designed for data entry (e.g., student attendance and demographic data); and optical scanners that read a bar code on items (e.g., those found in a grocery store). Each of these devices is designed to input (add) data into the central processing unit of the computer system.

FIGURE 13.1
Components of a
Computer System

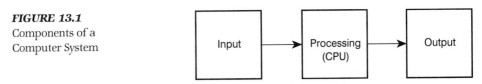

Information processing is done by the system's central processing unit (CPU). The CPU contains electronic circuitry that supports the arithmetic and logical processes. It houses internal storage capabilities, and it provides control functions for the computer system.

Output devices are many. They include the CRT of the data terminal where output information is viewed on the video screen. Another output device is the printer, which produces reports on **hard copy** (printed on paper). The plotter, a sophisticated printer, prints hard copy of graphs and figures.

Computer Software

The input, processing, and output functions are guided by a set of directions. These directions are a sequence of commands that are regarded as a computer program. When computer programs are used together or are interrelated for some purpose and accompanied by written documentation, a **software** package is formed. The programs are written in a computer language (e.g., FORTRAN, COBAL, C, and Pascal). A program can (1) tell the computer system to read data from a storage device, (2) direct the CPU to analyze the data it has read, (3) instruct the system to print a report of the analysis on a printer, and, finally, (4) direct the system to electronically store the new data that were produced in the analysis. Generally, a software package is a set of programs that "tells the computer what steps to take, which data to work on, and what to do with the results" (Cascio & Awad, 1981, p. 52). A complete software package will also include written documentation in the form of user and technical manuals.

A successful human resources information system is largely dependent upon the quality and appropriateness of the computer programs, which may be one of three distinct types: *canned*, or ready-made programs; custom designed programs, and customized canned programs (Ceriello, 1984). Each type has advantages and disadvantages that will be mentioned later.

A canned program package costs substantially less than the others because it is developed to accommodate the many possible needs of many users, and thus has broad applicability. Often vendors of canned programs allow potential users to test the programs before they are purchased. The programs usually have been extensively field tested so that nearly all of the *bugs* have been identified and modifications have been made to correct any problems. They typically run faster than other programs and possess optional procedures or routines for the user to incorporate into the human resources information system. Unfortunately, a software package that has been developed for general application by many users often will not completely meet the school system's human resources needs. It may contain programs that partly meet these needs, lack routines needed for other requirements, and possess programs that are of no value. Thus it is extremely important that a systematic process be developed to evaluate canned software and sufficient time be allotted to conduct such an evaluation before monies are committed to purchasing software packages (Ceriello, 1984).

As school systems continue to place greater emphasis on site-based management, both building-level and system-level administrators must be informed purchasers of canned software packages. Many general questions about a software package along with specific questions about software documentation, input, processing, and output must be answered before a decision can be made. These elements are more important than price alone. Crawford (1985) points out some general questions that should be investigated:

1. Will the software do what it claims to do?
2. Does the software provide more advantages than manual methods?
3. Can the dissatisfied purchaser obtain a refund or other satisfaction?
4. Does the company make adequate provision for backup copies?
5. If the software is to be used in more than one school, will the company sell multiple copies at a discount?
6. Are installation procedures reasonable?
7. Is user training provided as a part of the purchase price?
8. Is support available from the supplier through a toll-free phone number?
9. Does the software provide for some form of protection against loss of data?
10. Does the software provide for some form of security, especially for financial and confidential student data?
11. Is the software capable of being integrated with other software?
12. Is the software flexible enough to meet your school's needs and yet not so complex as to be confusing?
13. Is the software reliable? (pp. 95–96)

Crawford (1985) continues the list with questions related to software documentation:

14. Is the documentation provided with the software complete, clear, understandable, consistently written, and well organized?
15. Does the documentation have a thorough index and table of contents for quick reference, a help section, illustrations of input screen displays and output report formats, descriptions of file capacities, and an overview of the system?
16. Does the documentation provide an understandable way for the user to determine the amount of disk storage that will be needed for specific applications?
17. Does the company provide periodic updates to the documentation and the software at little or no extra costs?
18. Are the examples given relevant to the use you are making of the software? (pp. 96–97)

Several **input** function questions that should be asked are the following (Crawford, 1985):

19. Are fields for entering data well defined and self-prompting?
20. Are potential errors at the time of input well diagnosed and described in an understandable way?
21. Are data fields designed to accommodate the size and formats of data that are in common use in schools?
22. Can user-defined data fields be created? (p. 97)

Crawford (1985) poses the following ***processing*** questions that should be addressed:

23. Is the software menu-driven?
24. When the software is running does it give the user feedback about what part of the processing is taking place and about any malfunctions that might occur?
25. Does the software provide for easy restart and recovery in case problems occur?
26. Does the software run at an acceptable speed? (pp. 97–98)

Finally, Crawford (1985) sets forth the following ***output*** questions:

27. If the need exists to recall a specific item of data, can it be accessed by searching any field for its specific contents?
28. Does the design and format of information produced by the software meet district, state, and/or federal requirements so that this information will not have to be entered onto other forms by hand?
29. Does the user have the option to have output printed on paper or displayed on the screen?
30. Are reports formatted in an easy-to-read manner using appropriate abbreviations, spacing, and print size? (p. 98)

Lederer (1984) indicated that purchasing a canned software package is a conservative, low-risk approach that has a high probability of working properly. Unfortunately, when problems occur or questions arise, the user is largely dependent upon the vendor or the software developer's technical support staff.

Customized programs can be developed to the user's specifications by the district's systems analyst and programmers, or a contract can be negotiated with a commercial firm that develops customized software. The major disadvantage of customizing is cost. Development of software for a human resources information system (HRIS) requires the services of expensive systems analysts and programmers, and the development of such systems can take a long time, perhaps a year or more. Once developed, a ***parallel,*** or on-site, test of the new HRIS must be conducted, in which both the old and the new systems are maintained and operated independently. This permits a comparison of the two systems to determine the accuracy of their outputs (Lederer, 1984). The cost of simultaneously operating and maintaining two systems can be substantial, particularly if the new system contains many problems, which can be time-consuming to solve and further test.

In those school districts that have their own programmers, programs can be debugged, modified, and changed readily. Districts without their own information systems personnel should make modification contracts with the original program developer; it is more expensive if a different software development firm makes modifications.

Customized canned programs are software packages that meet most HRIS needs, but with some customization for specific demands of the school district's information system. The purpose of customizing previously developed software is to tailor it to specific human resources information system requirements at a cost lower than that of a customized system. The customization of canned programs is often impractical because modification of such systems is extremely difficult or nearly impossible due to the nature of certain programming languages. It is conceivable that such efforts could cost more than a completely customized software package. Ceriello (1980) suggested that all customizing be done by the original developer of the software package. The developer will know if requested modifications can be made in a functional manner. Ceriello further indicated that it is probably not cost effective to modify more than one-third of the original canned software package.

Like many large school districts, the Orange County Public Schools of Orlando, Florida, purchased a canned software package that was customized for its special needs. The software purchased for the district's IBM 3081 mainframe computer was the Total Education Resources Management System (TERMS). This computer system processes personnel data for all the district's employees, and it fulfills financial management requirements. The system now automates employment, recruitment, certification, position control, personnel reports, and payroll. TERM allows 30 staff members to process personnel records for 12,148 employees. This is a ratio of 1 staff member to 400 employees as contrasted with an average of 1 to 100 for most comparably sized districts (Knauth, 1989).

LOCAL AREA NETWORKS

The emergence of the microcomputer has brought great capacity to the management of human resources data, and the more recent developments that allow the linking of many microcomputers and other hardware devices have provided a potential for sharing data and information. It is now possible to **network** computers through a **local area network (LAN)** that will make it practical and cost-effective to transfer data to human resources data bases, share ancillary devices such as high-resolution printers, and communicate with other computers. Moreover, a LAN allows the sharing of software programs such as data base applications and spreadsheets.

> A local area network (sometimes referred to as a "local data network" or "intrafacility network" or simply . . . "local network") is a communication system installed in a relatively confined area, such as a single office or factory building or a small group of buildings (called a "campus" in LAN jargon). Its purpose is to interconnect a variety of computers, peripherals, workstations, terminals, and specialized digital devices, and in some cases to provide a transmission highway for video teleconferencing, security services, etc. A LAN is usually interfaced with longer-distance conventional telephone and data networks for purposes of access to remote computers and data bases and other remotely-located local area networks. (Townsend, 1987, Sec. 6.00, p. 1)

A graphical representation of local area networks is presented in Figure 13.2. In this illustration, different devices are depicted in each network and together represent interconnected networks. Figure 13.2 shows several types of microcomputers, printers, a minicomputer, and a mainframe computer linked into one network system.

Sharing information in networks does create some problems. Richards (1992) stated that the benefits of using a network system are immense and "the only question to be answered is how to realize this potential and still maintain a security system" (p. 18). Fortunately, network developers have been able to use mainframe technology to adopt a system of user passwords. Today all networks are able to control access by using this password methodology.

There are many developers and vendors of networks. Novell has developed NetWare, which enjoys about 70% of the network market (Kindley, 1992). Others that have been widely used by schools and school systems include AppleShare by Apple Computer, 3Com's 3+ network, Banyon's Vines network, Artisoft's LANtastic,

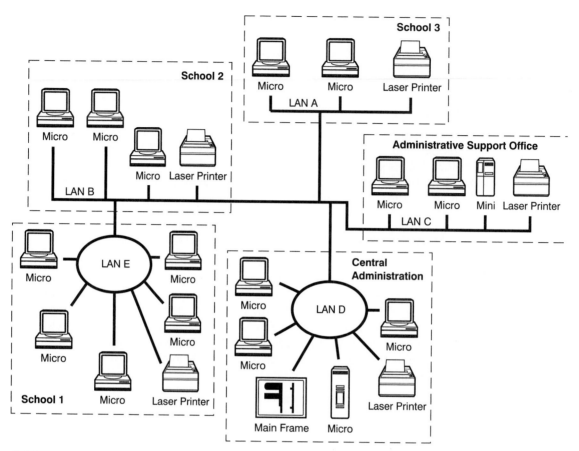

FIGURE 13.2
Interconnected Local Area Networks

and IBM's PC LAN. Each has advantages and disadvantages and is developed to operate in different computer environments. It is beyond the scope of this short discussion to present a comprehensive review of computer networks; however, it is important for students of human resource administration to have some familiarity with computer network technology. Students interested in a detailed explanation of LANs should refer to Townsend's (1987) *Data Communications Sourcebook*.

Figure 13.2 provides a simplified illustration of ways that different networks in several facilities of a school system can be linked to share data and application programs. One should readily see the important advantages of a LAN. Student and employee data can be stored on a mainframe computer in the central administrative office and accessed from remote locations that are linked by LANs. A LAN will also support the processing of these data by including human resources information software packages in the system. Although there have been many software packages developed for schools, several have been enjoying widespread adoption by schools and school systems.

The states of South Carolina and Georgia have adopted the Osiris system for their schools. Osiris is a comprehensive administrative system that provides access to vital student information. The system permits student information generated at the local school level to be **uploaded** to a computer in the central administrative offices of the school district. Subsequently, the data from all the school districts then can be uploaded to the state's department of education. Such capabilities permit analysis and reporting at all three levels of administration.

The developer of Osiris, Columbia Computing Services, a company of CTB Macmillan/McGraw Hill, has also produced a system for analyzing Osiris-generated data. The CTB District Planner allows the district administrator to access and analyze student records throughout the district, including fixed, extended, and current demographics as well as health, immunization, and enrollment information.

Olympia Computing Company and Chancery Software Ltd. have developed similar systems. Like Osiris, Olympia's Schoolmaster and Chancery's Mac School also incorporate many modules such as scheduling, report cards, and transcripts. The following functions can be performed by many of the current software packages, such as those just mentioned:

☐ Database management, including demographics
☐ Database reports
☐ Student scheduling and reports
☐ Class rosters
☐ Attendance
☐ Grade reporting
☐ Report cards
☐ Grade analysis and honor roll
☐ Transcripts
☐ School calendar
☐ Security system
☐ Discipline
☐ Guidance
☐ Health and immunization
☐ Teacher gradebook
☐ Library cataloging and circulation

For a list of available HRIS software for all classes of personnel, the reader should refer to the annual "HRIS Software Buyer's Guide" of the *Personnel Journal* (May, 1992). Also, McGregor and Daly (1989) have developed a summary of available software for human resources administration. Their report includes vendors, equipment requirements, cost, and functional area applications. Finally, students of human resources administration will find the Association of School Business Officials' *101 Templates for School Business Administration* (Graczyk & Faux, 1991) useful for applying an electronic spreadsheet to the analysis of human resources information. These templates cover a broad spectrum of analyses and reports that are made by human resources administrators.

THE EVOLUTION OF ELECTRONIC
DATA PROCESSING IN AN HRIS

Gibson and Nolan (1974) discovered four distinct developmental stages of EDP by investigating changes in program budgets. Generally they found that expenditure growth takes the form of an S-shaped curve, where very little money is budgeted in the initial stage of development. During the second stage, more money is spent for more specialized EDP personnel and hardware enhancements. Although the budget continues to grow in the third stage, there is some leveling off at the end of this period, and the fourth stage is characterized by little budgetary growth (see Figure 13.3).

The ***initial stage*** is usually staffed by operators, programmers, and some analysts. Their inaugural focus centers on EDP accounting applications to cut costs. This often includes payroll, accounts receivable, and accounts payable. These initial efforts were seen in the 1950s when the General Electric Corporation used the computer to manage payroll, the first business application of a computer (Lederer, 1984).

In the ***expansion stage,*** more specialized personnel are added to accommodate the expanding demand for new EDP applications, thus increasing the operational costs substantially. These specialists usually include specific applications programmers as well as systems analysts. During this evolutionary stage, many new EDP applications are initiated by the organization in other functional areas. Examples of such applications include capital budgeting, forecasting, personnel inventory, ordering materials and equipment, and inventory control.

The third stage is a period of ***formalization.*** The perceived out-of-control budgets for EDP generate increasing concerns for top management. They, in turn, install strict policies and procedures to control all EDP operations. Aware of the importance of EDP in the decision-making process, top management becomes more directly involved in setting strategic directions and implementing controls for all EDP operations.

The last phase was labeled by Gibson and Nolan (1974) as the ***maturity stage.*** During this period, data base applications proliferate. It is characterized by the development and application of simulation models, financial planning models, and online personnel queries.

In the early years of applying EDP to personnel record keeping, school systems were only able to maintain basic records on employees. This capability added speed and accuracy to a process previously conducted by hand. However, these incipient efforts did not provide involved data analysis procedures, such as simulations and forecast models, to support administrative decision making. It was only possibly to store and retrieve information; no data manipulation procedures could be incorpo-

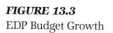

FIGURE 13.3
EDP Budget Growth

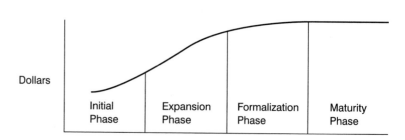

rated to produce the interpreted data needed by decision makers. In addition, the data included in personnel files could not be combined with data from other sources (i.e., financial, payroll, etc.) to produce the interpreted data needed for strategic planning. Each data file was independent, and no capability allowed drawing data from several sources to conduct a comprehensive analysis across organizational functions. Needed analyses were done by hand and, for the most part, were simple measures of central tendency.

During the mid-1970s, the information systems concept emerged. This permitted the analysis of stored data to produce interpreted data that administrators could use to ameliorate decisions in a more effective, timely manner. Generally, these information systems were developed for single functional areas such as finance, pupil personnel, payroll, and so on. Like the previous applications for EDP, each system did not have the relational capability of accessing data from one or more of the other functional area data bases. Each information system operated independently of the others, which resulted in duplicated data. Moreover, by not being an integrated or relational *database*, the interpreted data produced by the system only had limited potential for strategic decision making (see Figure 13.4).

When several information systems are implemented (e.g., human resources information system, payroll information system, pupil personnel information system, finance information system, etc.), they most often use a single mainframe computer. Each information system is developed for specifically stated purposes, and its operations are guided by written policy statements. These policies outline the kinds of information and reports that the system will produce, the authorized use of information, security requirements and specifications, and procedural guidelines for making document requests. Each system also includes the required software for managing

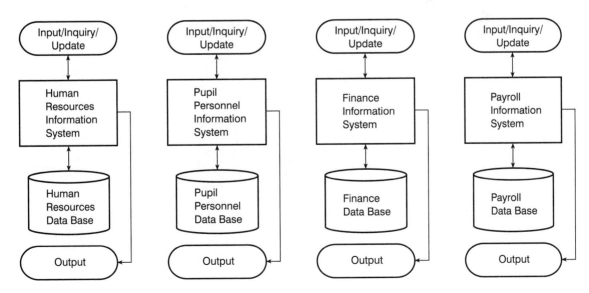

FIGURE 13.4
Independent Information Systems

and manipulating data in the data base as well as producing the specific reports required for various types of decisions. Finally, policy statements are established that identify the person responsible for maintaining and operating the information system. This is mandatory to control the integrity of the data base by preventing unauthorized entry.

Figure 13.4 represents several independent information systems. Each has a separate data base for storing data relative to its function. In such a configuration, the human resources information system might maintain data on personnel relative to job classification, assignment, salary level, background data, benefits options, leaves of absence, and perhaps evaluation and staff development. Unfortunately, many redundancies are found because some of the same data are maintained in other data bases. A case in point is the employee's name and social security number. Not only are both required in the human resources data base, they must be available to the payroll information system. Duplicate data in two or more data bases are quite difficult to maintain, storage space is wasted, and critical problems can result. Changing or updating data in several data bases is costly and increases the probability of error. One information system may be designed to update the data base as the data are received, whereas a second system permits data entry or updates periodically. Potentially this can cause discrepancies when two or more information systems produce reports that are to be used concurrently in decision deliberations.

Each information system is developed to accommodate preferred methods of entering new data, including entry via data terminals, magnetic tapes, optical scanners, or some combination of these devices. These data input methods were discussed earlier. The reader should be familiar with the optical scanner. It can be used to enter student standardized achievement test scores into the student personnel information system's data base. By contrast, the updating of annual teacher salary increments can be programmed to change by calling up a computer routine that automatically updates stored salary data in the HRIS without the actual entry of each teacher's new salary. As a third example, the background data, position classification, and so on, of a new employee may be entered via the data terminal.

As illustrated in Figure 13.4, each system provides procedures for the inquiry and retrieval of data. This permits both data updating and error correction.

Information output can take the form of routine and special reports. Routine reports are usually scheduled to accommodate periodic decision periods (e.g., a report of needed personnel by category so that recruitment and employment programs can be directed toward filling anticipated vacancies).

Generally four types of reports are used for decision making. The **scheduled reports** are produced on a regular basis (i.e., daily, weekly, monthly, etc.). As the use of data terminals increases, the production of scheduled reports will probably be reduced because the information is readily available on terminals. The **demand report** fills unanticipated needs and is generated upon request. The **exceptions report** is produced to identify those situations that need immediate attention. One example is a report of all teachers who must renew or update their state teaching certificate prior to the beginning of the next contract year or, more critically, a report identifying teachers who did not fulfill such requirements and whose certificates are out-of-date. The fourth type of report used for decision making is the **predictive report,** which addresses "what-if" questions and is used in planning processes. This type of report often employs strict statistical procedures, such as regression analysis and simulations (Hicks, 1993).

The evolution of large computer systems, the emergence of information technology, and the need for relating data from the data bases of several information systems cultivated the development of the management information concept. As information systems were developed for finance, payroll, and several other functional areas of organizations, the need to analyze data across data bases supported the development of the management information system that uses the integrated or relational *database* concept.

Within a short period of 15 years, school systems progressed from personnel records mostly processed by hand to electronic data storage and retrieval of personnel records to the development of personnel information systems. It is believed that this has improved the quality of decisions at all levels of decision making. Strategic, tactical, and operational decisions are now frequently based upon enhanced documentation produced by sophisticated data analyses.

DATA AND DECISION MAKING

Hicks (1993) identified three levels of decision making: strategic, tactical, and operational. **Strategic decisions** relate to the future. These decisions give direction to the organization and take the form of specific objectives with plans to meet the objectives. Strategic decisions may include major curriculum changes, opening new schools, closing low-enrollment schools, or setting an achievement level for a particular group of students to meet.

Tactical decisions center on implementing the objectives set at the strategic level. An example of such a decision would include the selection of a particular program to implement a strategic decision. More specifically, the introduction of sex education to the curriculum may be a decision at the strategic level. The selection of a specific program of sex education would follow as a tactical decision.

Operational decisions are concerned with the execution of specific tasks in carrying out tactical decisions. Although numerous operational decisions are made each day, the assignment of job responsibilities, the development of schedules, and the ordering of materials would be examples of operational decisions to implement the sex education program.

Each level of decision making requires different types and qualities of information to support effective decisions. Hicks (1993) identified several characteristics of information for the three levels of decisions, as set forth in Table 13.1.

Although most of the information characteristics are self-explanatory, we will discuss several for the purpose of illustration. Notice that the use of **realtime** information is very high at the operational level. In this instance any changes to the data base will be made immediately rather than at a later time, when all changes might be handled in a **batch mode.** Consider the operational decisions made in many large school systems during the first week of school. Enrollments may exceed or fall far

TABLE 13.1

Characteristics of Information Required at Each Level of Decision Making

Information Characteristic	Level of Decision Making		
	Operational	Tactical	Strategic
Depends on Computer-Based Information Systems	High	Moderate	Low to Moderate
Depends on Internal Information	Very high	High	Moderate
Depends on External Information	Low	Moderate	Very high
Degree of Information Summarization	Very low	Moderate	High
Need for On-line Information	Very high	High	Moderate
Need for Computer Graphics	Low	Moderate	High
Use of Real-time Information	Very high	High	Moderate
Use of Predictive Information	Low	High	Very high
Use of Historical Information	High	Moderate	Low
Use of What-If Information	Low	High	Very high
Use of Information Stated in Dollars	Low	Moderate	High

Source: Reprinted by permission from page 51 of *Management Information Systems* (3rd ed.) by James O. Hicks, Jr. Copyright © 1993 by West Publishing Company. All rights reserved.

short of projections. This would create an immediate need for teachers with specific skills or expertise or, conversely, create a teacher surplus. In such instances the data base can be queried to produce reports that support required changes while optimizing the mix of personnel assignments. Such reports can provide human resources administrators with several alternative personnel changes to accommodate the difficult decisions associated with enrollment shifts.

Another example that is easy for a student of human resources to understand is class registrations. A realtime capability would certainly accommodate students trying to register for classes by immediately identifying those that are open and closed. Any student who has ever waited in a long registration line only to find the desired class closed will appreciate this realtime capability.

Consider the strategic level of decision making. Decisions must be sensitive to the school system's environment; therefore, they depend on external data. To plan for the future, decision makers need summarized, interpreted data so that they can see the "big picture." This often requires the use of graphics. Decisions affecting the future frequently require enrollment or revenue projections, and cost information is critical in estimating the required resources to implement new strategies. These kinds of information, and certainly many others, must be available to allow strategic planning in school districts.

Decisions made at any of the three levels—strategic, tactical, or operational—can require data analysis from many information sources. An operational decision to fund a special program may require a specific analysis using data from the financial data base, salary levels by category from the human resources data base, and student achievement levels from the student personnel data base. The several information systems, therefore, must be integrated so that analyses can be conducted using data from any system. This capability is called a **database system.** The simplified model shown in Figure 13.5 illustrates the concept of a single management information system where a database is established for storing all district data.

MANAGEMENT INFORMATION SYSTEM (MIS)

The management of information to support administrative decisions is not new. Prior to electronic data processing, management information was processed by hand. The computer simply added speed, accuracy, and increased volume to allow for more alternatives in the decision-making process (Murdick, Ross, & Claggett, 1984).

The definition of a management information system (MIS) will be explored by addressing each part of the concept singly. First, **management** can be described in many ways. For the purposes of this discussion we will use the seven management processes described by Gulick and Urwick (1937/1978): planning, organizing, staffing, directing, coordinating, reporting, and budgeting.

Planning consists of scanning the educational environment, developing the organization's mission and strategic objectives consistent with the environment, and identifying the best strategies to achieve these objectives. **Organizing** is the process of identifying the tasks necessary to implement the strategies and assign responsibilities. **Staffing** is placing the most competent persons in positions to maximize the achievement of organizational objectives while producing an optimum professional staff mix. **Directing** is the development and implementation of administrative regulations or specifications in harmony with the culture of the organization and focused on the strategic objectives. **Coordinating** activities engage the administration in facilitating the efforts of the many functional areas of the organization. **Reporting** is communicating information related to progress made in achieving strategic objectives. **Budgeting** requires the allocation of financial resources to organizational activities and functions in the most optimum manner for achieving objectives. Each of these administrative activities requires reliable, valid information to support high-quality human resources decisions.

Information must be differentiated from data. Data are usually considered representations, observations, or characters from which an interpretation or meaning may be determined. Data are the facts and figures stored for future combination and analysis.

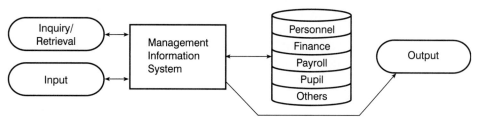

FIGURE 13.5
MIS Database Linkage

Information is the interpretation of data in regard to some purpose as well as the description of the relationship between facts and figures that bear upon some organizational goal or direction (Bassett & Weatherbee, 1971). Murdick et al. (1984) stated that "information consists of data which have been retrieved, processed, or otherwise used for informative or inference purposes, argument, or as a basis for forecasting or decision making" (p. 6). One example of information is the use of termination and separation data to forecast personnel needs. Specifically, sets of historical data about termination and reasons for separation can be analyzed to predict future personnel requirements. These interpreted data can then be used to support various recruitment and employment decisions.

School administrators must have quality information to make appropriate and timely decisions. Beatty, Montagno, and Montgomery (1985) related the importance of getting the right information to the right people by contrasting levels of detail and comprehensiveness of information. Figure 13.6 illustrates an adaptation of this distinction. It shows that top-level administrators who have responsibilities for strategic decisions must have access to considerable amounts of comprehensive information and only limited amounts of detailed information. By contrast, first-level administrators need great amounts of detailed information and reduced quantities of comprehensive information. Relationships such as these are an important consideration in developing an effective information system.

In a general sense, Silvern (1975) described a *system* as "the structure or organization of an orderly whole, clearly showing the interrelation of the parts to each other and to the whole itself" (p. 1). Within this context and specific to an organization such as a school district, a system can be described as an organized collection of parts or elements, such as departments, curriculum units, schools, divisions, and so on. They are united by policies and rules in the pursuit of a mission and specific objectives (Charp, Bozeman, Altschuler, D'Orazio, & Spuck, 1982; Murdick et al., 1984). Although the organization of a school district conforms to the definition of a system, the application of system principles have only recently been used in this context. For example, complex analysis of human resources data is now an important ingredient in planning school closings. Such analyses are particularly helpful as the district's planners attempt to maintain an optimum professional staff mix throughout all units of the school system and mitigate the impact of reduction in force procedures for the affected schools.

The systems concept of managing information optimizes the accomplishments of each unit relative to organizational objectives through a medium of information exchange (Murdick et al., 1984). Such an exchange is enhanced through a management information system.

Figure 13.5 illustrates a simple MIS linked to a database that represents the integration of several databases like those illustrated in Figure 13.4. Many of the more recent developments incorporate functional area applications into one MIS with a single database. This design came out of a need to integrate data files more effectively and efficiently. As in the previously described information system, the MIS is developed to produce reports that provide a rationale for decisions focused upon the achievement of the organization's strategic objectives. It includes policies that give direction to its use, general operations, routine analyses and reports, specific requests

FIGURE 13.6

Levels of Administration and
Types of Information Required
Source: From *The Human Resource
Information Systems Sourcebook*
(p. 144) by Richard Beatty, Ray
Montagno, and Daniel Montgomery,
1985, Amherst, MA: Human
Resource Development Press.
Copyright © 1985 by HRD Press,
Inc., 22 Amherst Rd., Amherst,
MA 01002, 1-800-822-2801 (U.S.
and Canada) or (413)253-3488.
Adapted by permission.

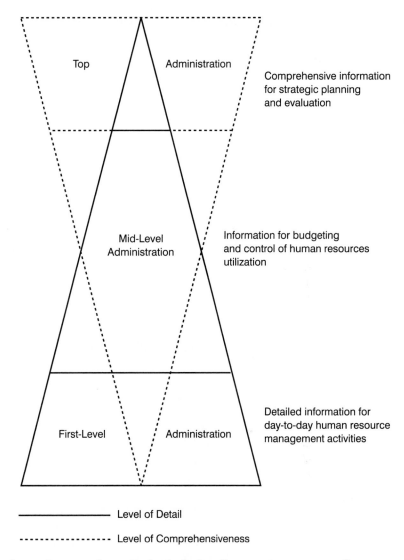

Top   Administration

Comprehensive information
for strategic planning
and evaluation

Mid-Level
Administration

Information for budgeting
and control of human resources
utilization

First-Level   Administration

Detailed information for
day-to-day human resource
management activities

——————— Level of Detail

------------------ Level of Comprehensiveness

for reports, and security procedures. It also includes all computer programs for operating the system. Moreover, the database consists of many data files that can be manipulated by the database manager of the MIS. The database manager is a specific program package designed for this exclusive purpose. The MIS possesses the quality of using data from the several files of the database to produce many types of analyses and reports (e.g., forecasts, financial simulation models, etc.).

The implementation of an integrated MIS is important for improving decision making in school districts. The growing complexity of administrative decision making mandates that administrators have the best information that technology can provide. In the past software development lagged behind hardware technology, and now it appears that inexpensive HRIS software is available to school districts. The following discussion will give specific attention to the HRIS.

HUMAN RESOURCES INFORMATION SYSTEM (HRIS)

Anthony (1977) indicated that a human resources information system is a "management information system designed for one particular function of an organization's operations—its human resources management function" (p. 179). More specifically, Whitman and Hyde (1985) related that an "HRIS is a management information system designed to provide an ongoing assessment of the use of human resources in pursuit of management objectives" (p. 105). As a part of an integrated MIS, the HRIS is designed to provide immediate information to authorized personnel of the school system. The HRIS should be integrated with all personnel records and other appropriate files of the MIS. To a large extent, HRISs should be "on-line systems, information centers, and end user reporting tools" (Knapp, 1990, p. 58). This will permit processing of data in a timely manner for improved effectiveness in administrative decision making.

Advantages and Disadvantages of an HRIS

The advantages of an HRIS include its potential for accuracy and timeliness in most operating, controlling, and planning activities. Specifically, the ability to produce timely reports is one of the most important advantages of an HRIS. Periodic state and federal reports cannot be produced manually in some school systems without an HRIS because the staff time required to do so is prohibitive. Other benefits include a single source for data, improved data accuracy, limited redundant data, readily available data, integrated data, and a single database (Knapp, 1990).

Many examples of the need for accuracy and timeliness can be identified. One is the writing of annual contracts in a school district. With over 5,000 professional employees, the DeKalb County School District of Decatur, Georgia, uses its HRIS to produce annual employee contracts. Previously this was done manually and required hundreds of hours of professional and clerical time. The present system can produce all contracts in several hours and ensure complete accuracy. The HRIS identifies all persons on an annual contract, calculates the new salary for the contract year, and prints appropriate identification and salary information in correct locations on a blank contract form. The unique feature of this district's HRIS is the inclusion of specific statements on the contract advising the employee of special conditions of employment (e.g., the need to acquire a specific number of credits toward a master's degree or an expiring professional certificate). Grant (1984) provides a complete list of information incorporated into the professional employee contracts:

School or department code (for distribution)

Social security number (for positive employee identification)

Salary code (for reference if questions arise)

Employee name (party to the contract)

Date contract prepared

Deadline date for signing and returning contract

Annual salary (advanced to the subsequent year's placement for the spring contract)

Special paragraphs for the following conditions, if applicable:

1. quarter hours toward a master's degree, necessary for renewal of contract
2. provisional certificate provisions
3. out-of-field certification provisions
4. expiring certificate provisions
5. conditions relating to supplementary activities such as athletics, instructional, and literary assignments

In a critique of this contract writing capability, Grant (1984) stated that

> manual preparation of 5000 contracts represented another exercise in supreme boredom. Thus, staff morale in the Department of Personnel was boosted with the implementation of the new service. Staff time can be redirected to other needed tasks due to the elimination of manually advancing salaries, typing contracts, proofing contracts, and troubleshooting activities. (p. 6)

Other important uses of an HRIS relate to the controlling function of a human resources department. A multiplicity of lists can be easily drawn from the database of an HRIS. Such lists permit the identification of employees eligible for certain benefit options, retirement, seniority listing, overtime, supplemental compensation, training experiences, personal leave, and sick days. In fact, any data from employees' records can be sorted and listed with the data from any other field or combination of fields in the database. The employee data fields included in such lists can be selected on the basis of specified criteria. For example, a list of all employees who have used up their personal leave time can be printed, or a list of employees who are eligible for new benefit enrollments can be produced. Some HRISs have word processing capabilities that can automatically print memoranda to these employees, apprising them of such eligibility and open enrollment periods.

The planning function is supported by reports that address the what-if questions through simulation and forecast models. Simulations can produce reports that reflect the outcomes of different scenarios (e.g., changes in state supplements for professional personnel), and forecasting models can project enrollments based on changing demographics. Both capabilities allow the human resources administrator to plan contingency strategies.

Lederer (1984) indicated that the primary disadvantages of an HRIS are the cost and the personnel required for development and installation. He believed that the financial requirements for planning, designing, and implementing are often underestimated. Despite the cost, Knapp (1990) in mentioning the benefits of an information system said, "The benefits of an integrated approach will almost always justify the additional cost" (p. 61). The final decision to install a new system should not be made until a comprehensive study is conducted to determine the cost of implementing an HRIS relative to its benefits.

Cost-Benefit Study of Instituting an HRIS

Any cost-benefit study conducted pursuant to a decision to install an HRIS should outline the problems with the existing system and show how they can be solved by the new system. It should identify emerging information needs that can be filled by an HRIS. The report should not only address the financial savings expected from implementing the new system but also the anticipated benefits of increased staff morale, as suggested by Grant (1984). Other intangible benefits can include improved federal and state reports to demonstrate compliance with equal employment opportunities and affirmative action.

Once the decision is made to develop a new system, several important question must be answered during the planning process. Questions relate to system requirements, types of administrative decisions to be made, database design, and specifications of reports. Software must be thoughtfully debated and carefully responded to by those most directly affected by the system. Finally, the system must be evaluated periodically to determine the need for possible alterations stemming from organizational changes and needs for new information resulting from policy changes.

FUTURE TECHNOLOGICAL DEVELOPMENTS FOR HUMAN RESOURCES ADMINISTRATORS

One of the most challenging aspects of developing a chapter on technology for human resources administration is dealing with the continuous and extremely rapid change in technology. The authors have attempted to do so at the risk of being out-of-date within a period of just a few years. Seemingly one breakthrough unleashes an explosion of new developments. One has only to look at the surge of very sophisticated software packages that were created once the internal storage capacity (random access memory) of the microcomputer was increased through new storage chip technology combined with more sophisticated operating systems. This permitted the development of application software that was regarded impossible just a couple of years earlier. We believe that there are several developments that will, within a short time, have important implications for human resources administrators.

The capability of microcomputers for accessing huge data files stored on CD-ROM disks and the ability to process great amounts of data will bring about new developments for improving human resources administration. Such capability will allow the integration of video images on the computer screen combined with audio sounds to support extremely sophisticated simulation and testing opportunities. For example, human resources administrators will be able to screen administrative candidates by employing an interactive system that will allow the candidate to be tested in a realistic administrative simulation. Much like the *in-basket* simulation exercise, the candidate will be placed in an administrative context with the challenge of responding to decision-making situations including written communications, telephone calls, conferences, and even unexpected interruptions. The computer will provide the capability of responding to each decision of the candidate with different consequences, producing even new sets of decisions to be made. Certainly developments such as these will unleash the imaginations of many in the creation of even better and more sophisticated developments both for administration and staff development. It is anticipated that these new applications of technology will improve the effectiveness of many aspects of the human resources administrator's responsibility.

SUMMARY

Although the use of technology in managing human resources in education is a recent development, it is becoming more common because of the great complexities of the decision-making process. Administrators are becoming increasingly aware of the need for valid, reliable information to support improved strategic, tactical, and operational decisions in school districts. In addition, enrollment counts for funding, the requirements of equal employment opportunity, and affirmative action plans necessitate error-free state and federal reports.

Computer technology and the emergence of information systems in education point to greater objectivity in decision making. Many school systems are developing human resources information systems to produce information that supports improved decisions. The HRIS is a management information system designed for the human resources function. Some school districts have developed data base systems that permit the integration of data from other functional areas. This enhances the potential for building scenarios to test the what-if questions in decision making. Such capability also supports important forecasting models.

DISCUSSION QUESTIONS

1. Divide the class into small task groups. Each group should contact a different school district and arrange an interview with the person in charge of electronic data processing. The interview should focus on the use of computers in the school system and their specific application to the management of human resources information. After the interview, the information received should be analyzed to determine which of the four stages of EDP the school system is currently experiencing. Prepare a presentation or report that emphasizes the developmental stage, uses of EDP, software, equipment, personnel, and future plans.
2. List and discuss reports that are typically produced in the elementary, middle, junior, and senior high schools of your area. Include those that can be classified as scheduled, demand, exceptions, and predictive reports.
3. Discuss the future uses of EDP in schools and school systems specific to the management of human resources. What difficulties can be anticipated in the implementation of each application? What are the implications for school systems using site-based management?

CASE 13.1
The Next Step

Terry Sanchez was very excited to learn that the school board approved the superintendent's recommendation to implement Terry's site-based management model in the several high schools of the district. Terry had worked with the other principals for over a year developing the model. The model was based on a pilot project that he implemented in his school. The two-year project was regarded as the best innovation that had been tried in years.

Unfortunately, the approval did not include that part of the recommendation calling for a networked HRIS. The proposed computer network included all high schools, the central office, and the instructional and materials resources center of the district. The board felt that the network was not satisfactorily justified for the cost involved.

Terry was disappointed that the network system was excluded from the approval. He thought that its importance was obvious in the committee's report and couldn't understand the board's action. He decided to get the committee together for a discussion of possible steps to be taken.

After all the principals were seated in Terry's conference room he said, "I thought we made it quite clear in our recommendation that the information system was required to fully implement our site-based management model. At this point, I'm not sure what we should do."

Questions

1. What action should the committee take?
2. Should other persons be added to the committee? Why?
3. What are the factors that should be included in building a stronger rationale to support the information system?
4. Are there alternatives to an information system?

CASE 13.2
Computerphobia?

Cheryl Platt is very upset that only 3 of her 36 teachers have signed up for the special technology class. The class is being offered by the district's curriculum and instructional technology departments as a first step in integrating computers into the curriculum.

Teachers have shown great resistance to using computers in the classroom, often claiming that they have too much paperwork and nonteaching responsibilities to handle without learning about computers. Moreover, the change is controversial because the development of the new curriculum units did not involve

teachers. The units were formulated by a consultant from the local university and several district coordinators.

Cheryl supports the new directions, but she is puzzled by her teacher's response to the class. She knows that a mandate by her to attend the class potentially will undermine the teachers' commitment to the change. Also, without a strong commitment by her staff, the school could lose the network system promised by the superintendent.

It is nearly time for the weekly meeting with the school's leadership team of seven teachers. Cheryl knows that she will have to say something about the class, particularly since only one member of the leadership team has enrolled in the class.

Questions

1. Does Cheryl know enough about the situation to determine the underlying problem(s)? If not, what else does she need to know?
2. If she has enough information, what is the underlying problem that Cheryl faces?
3. What plan of action should she consider at this point?

CASE 13.3
Tracy's Dilemma

As Tracy Moore read the minutes of last week's board of education meeting, he reflected with pride on the board's approval of the proposal to implement an HRIS for his human resources department. Despite the fact that the proposal was put together in a hurry at the superintendent's request, Tracy was surprised that the plan was adopted with very little discussion by members of the board.

As he was finishing the minutes, the phone rang. "Tracy, this is Jane Mahoney. What will be the procedures for making a bid on the new HRIS for your department? This is important to me, and I want to get DataNet's bid in early. My father-in-law told me that he and other board members would push hard to move on this one quickly."

Tracy was caught by surprise because he had not talked to the superintendent since the board meeting. One of his greatest concerns was that of doing a needs study before the development of bidding procedures. He was hoping to discuss this with the superintendent.

Questions

1. What is the underlying problem that Tracy faces?
2. What are some symptoms of the problem?
3. What are all the possible actions that Tracy can take to solve the problem?
4. What are the possible consequences of such actions?
5. What is the best action for Tracy to take?

REFERENCES

Anthony, W. P. (1977). Get to know your employees—The human resource information system. *Personnel Journal, 56*, 179–203.

Bassett, G. A., & Weatherbee, H. Y. (1971). *Personnel systems and data management*. New York: American Management Association.

Beatty, R., Montagno, R., & Montgomery, D. (Eds.). (1985). *The human resource information systems sourcebook*. Amherst, MA: Human Resource Development Press.

Cascio, W. F., & Awad, E. M. (1981). *Human resources management: An information systems approach*. Reston, VA: Reston.

Ceriello, V. R. (1980). Human resources management: Toy or tool? *Journal of Systems Management, 31*(5), 36–38.

Ceriello, V. R. (1984). Computerizing the personnel department: How do you pick the right software? *Personnel Journal, 63*, 53–58.

Charp, S., Bozeman, W. C., Altschuler, H., D'Orazio, R., & Spuck, D. W. (1982). *Layman's guide to the use of computers in education*. Washington, DC: The Association for Educational Data Systems.

Crawford, C. W. (May, 1985). Administrative uses of microcomputers, part III: Evaluation and selection. *Bulletin*, pp. 95–98.

Davis, W. S. (1989). *Computing fundamentals concepts* (2nd ed.). Reading, MA: Addison-Wesley.

Gibson, C. F., & Nolan, R. L. (1974). Managing the four stages of EDP growth. *Harvard Business Review, 52*(1), 76–88.

Graczyk, S., & Faux, J. (1991). *101 templates for school business administration*. Reston, VA: American Association of School Business Officials.

Grant, F.D. (1984). *Personnel applications for electronic data processing*. Unpublished manuscript, DeKalb County Public Schools, Decatur, GA.

Gulick, L., & Urwick, L. (1978). Papers on the science of administration. In J. M. Shafritz & P. H. Whitbeck (Eds.), *Classics of organizational theory* (pp. 52–61). Oak Park, IL: Moore. (Original work published 1937)

Hicks, J. O., Jr. (1984). *Management information systems: A user's perspective*. St. Paul, MN: West.

Hicks, J. O., Jr. (1993). *Management information systems* (3rd ed.). St. Paul, MN: West.

HRIS software buyer's guide. (1992). *Personnel Journal, 71*, 121–138.

Kazlanskas, E. J., & Picus, L. O. (1990). *Administrative uses of microcomputers in schools: A systems analysis approach to selecting, designing, and implementing automated systems*. Reston, VA: Association of School Business Officials International.

Kindley, M. (1992). Reaching beyond LAN. *VARBusiness, 8*(13), 75–87.

Knapp, J. (1990, April). Trends in HR management systems. *Personnel, 67*(4), 56–61.

Knauth, K. (1989, September). Automating the human perspective. *Electronic Learning, 9*(Suppl.), 18–25.

Lederer, A. L. (1984). Information technology: 1. Planning and developing a human resources information system. *Personnel, 61*(3), 14–27.

McGregor, E. B., Jr., & Daly, J. (1989). The strategic implications of automation in public sector human resource management. *Review of Public Personnel Administration, 10*(1), 29–47.

Murdick, R. G., Ross, J. E., & Claggett, J. R. (1984). *Information systems for modern management*. Englewood Cliffs, NJ: Prentice-Hall.

National Association of Secondary School Principals. (1987). Administrative uses of microcomputers. *The Practitioner*, *13*(3), 1–12.

Richards, C. (1992, January). Loading security on to a system. *Personnel Management*, pp. 18–19.

Shelly, G., Cashman, T., Gurgel, R., Quasney, J., & Pratt, P. (1990). *Learning to use WordPerfect 5.0/5.1, Lotus 1-2-3, and Dbase III plus*. Boston: Boyd and Frasher.

Silvern, L. C. (1975). *Systems engineering of education I: The evolution of systems thinking in education*. Los Angeles: Education and Training Consultants.

Townsend, M. J. (1987). *The data communications sourcebook* (vol. 1). Santa Monica, CA: Merritt.

Whitman, T. S. & Hyde, A. C. (1985). HRIS: Systematically matching the right person to the right position. In R. Beatty, R. Montagno, & D. Montgomery (Eds.), *The human resource information systems sourcebook* (pp. 105–111). Amherst, MA: Human Resource Development Press.

14

Future Trends in Human Resources Administration

People have been interested in prophesying the future for thousands of years. Some rulers used oracles such as the oracle of Apollo at Delphi to guide important decisions that affected the life and death of empires. Because her utterances were believed to be the words of Apollo, she greatly influenced Greek religion, economics, and politics. Today interest in prognosticating future events is the domain of many, including mystics, fortune-tellers, economists, and demographers. Academicians assist institutions and businesses by predicting future trends in economics, demography, politics, and society. The World Future Society, with 30,000 members, promotes the research and study of methodologies for forecasting and builds models of future societal scenarios. Students of business and economics study business trends and major economic cycles, historical trends in employment, and cycles of interest rates and commodity prices. Demographers investigate trends to determine future population changes, and historians study the past to provide a basis for anticipating prospective occurrences.

Historically people have investigated the past with the hope of identifying recurring patterns of events and behaviors to predict the future. Newland (1984) very aptly stated that "despite some discontinuities in society, the classic maxim largely holds—the past is prologue" (p. 16). Newland felt that the reason for projecting future scenarios is not simply to forecast and wait for some ultimate fate but to increase the capacity for influencing outcomes. This is critically important to strategic human resource planning for school districts, and many in business and government are so strongly committed to such action that they seek the advice of prominent future-oriented individuals to guide their strategic plans.

In this chapter we will use an external environmental scan of selected areas of investigation to build some future scenarios that are believed to support emerging issues in the administration of human resources. Having read Chapter 4, the student should realize the importance of the many external forces and influences on resources. Thus the first sections of the chapter will explore some of the emerging changes in the areas of demography, economics, politics, and society. Each area will be discussed in ways that have implications for human resources administration. Unfortunately, most of these trends project changes into the near future and provide only limited insight for those interested in a long-term perspective. Therefore, Kondratieff's (Kondratieff & Oparin, 1928/1984) long wave theory will be discussed briefly so that the reader can gain some insight into a perspective that will have a longer effect on the management of human resources. Such a view should help to anticipate possible concerns for human resources. The next section will elaborate on important implications for human resources administration that will draw from all previous sections of the chapter. But, first, let us turn to some important general trends.

GENERAL TRENDS

In John Naisbitt's (1982) book *Megatrends*, he identified 10 trends that he believed would transform our lives during the remaining years of the twentieth century. Later, Naisbitt and Aburdene (1990) published *Megatrends 2000*, which includes a second set of trends that they believe will impact America in the twenty-first century. They introduce this set of trends by first referring to trend shifts postulated in Naisbitt's 1982 book. "These shifts continue pretty much on schedule. But they are now only part of the picture as we enter the 1990's and a new set of forces come into play" (p. xvii). Each set of trends is discussed briefly to provide a general context for the remainder of the chapter.

In *Megatrends* (1982) Naisbett identified the first trend as the transformation from an industrial society to an informational society. Naisbitt and Aburdene (1990) now aptly remind us of Naisbitt's earlier observation that "we are drowning in information and starved of knowledge" (p. xviii).

A second trend is related to the change from forced technology to the "evolution of a highly personal values system to compensate for the impersonal nature of technology" (Naisbitt, 1982, p. 40). The perceived insensitivity of technology toward human needs will bring about what Naisbitt called the "high tech/high touch phenomenon."

The third is a change from a national economy to a world economy. Today this world concept of economics is characterized by interdependent nations competing in the marketplace and rekindles memories of Barbara Ward's (1966) *Spaceship Earth*. Indications of this trend are many, not the least of which is the merchandise traded among the United States, Western European countries, Canada, Mexico, and other South American countries and the concomitant impact each country's economy has on the others. For example, a recession in Great Britain could cause a decline in its imports from the other countries, thus precipitating economic declines or even recessions in the exporting countries. Also, products manufactured in one country can include parts or components from several foreign countries, not only those already mentioned but from the Pacific Rim as well.

Another trend identified is the orientation of American managers toward a long-term perspective as contrasted with short-term, quick-gain objectives. Managers have been placing greater value on multiyear planning and deferred gain with the hope of a subsequent increase in corporate profits and organizational effectiveness. This trend is also evident in education as many school districts begin to plan strategically.

The fifth major trend is a change in many public and private institutions from highly centralized organizations to more decentralized formations. This has permitted organizations to become more responsive to the needs of their clients and constituencies. Evidence of this trend is found in education with the implementation of site-based management in many school districts. On the other hand, corporations are eliminating many middle-management jobs and placing greater responsibility for decisions on the shoulders of workers (Haddad, 1992).

The sixth is the emergence of self-reliance through the rejection of many forms of institutional help, for example, health, education, and specialized services. Through technology and improved information sources, many health problems can be diagnosed and simple legal services handled by home computers, and specialized training for improved lifestyles and new careers can be achieved through a combination of new technologies such as satellite networks and computer linkages for "distance learning."

A seventh trend is the move toward participatory democracy as a replacement for representative democracy. This has evolved as those affected by decisions have demanded involvement in the decision-making processes. Much of the recent interest in teacher empowerment has related to programs that include teachers in school governance activities.

The eighth trend is the transformation of the traditional hierarchical organization to one that uses valued clusters of people with expertise or like-mindedness to collaborate in decision making. Such clusters have used networking with other clusters to solve important problems of mutual concern.

The ninth trend is the geographic shift in population from the North and East to the South and West. "The 1990 Census results have confirmed the continual shift of population to states in the West and South" (Allan, 1991, p. 10).

Finally, Naisbitt mentioned a tenth trend as the growing multiplicity of choices available to most Americans (i.e., in consumption, life-style, work, and the arts) as contrasted with the limited options individuals have had in the past. This is indicative of the growing diversity of individual interests and the emergence of a heterogeneous multicultural society.

These 10 trends have made an impact on human resources practices and policies. As they continue to unfold during the 1990s, they along with emerging trends will produce new implications for the human resources administrator.

For the beginning of the twenty-first century, Naisbitt and Aburdene (1990) identify what they call the "millennial trends." A list of these follows, along with the important reasons for each trend.

1. *The Booming Global Economy of the 1990s.* In addition to the fact that nations are becoming more concerned with economic rather than political considerations, there are several other forces that influence this change: worldwide free trade, telecommunications, plentiful natural resources, lower taxes, downsizing of economic output, low inflation and interest rates, an Asian boom in consumption, spread of democracy and free enterprise, limited risk of war, and environmental awareness.
2. *A Renaissance in the Arts.* The renewed interest in the arts will be driven by the new affluence.

3. *The Emergence of Free-Market Socialism.*   Free-market economics has become a goal of those countries that are rising from the corpus of the dismembered Soviet Union.

4. *Global Lifestyles and Cultural Nationalism.*   Renewed interest in cultural nationalism is emerging in many parts of the world (e.g., Quebec's threat to secede from Canada and the assertive independence of the previous republics of the USSR).

5. *The Privatization of the Welfare State.*   The inefficiencies of socialism have been strengthening efforts to privatize welfare programs both in the United States and other countries of the world.

6. *The Rise of the Pacific Rim.*   The Pacific Rim nations that are economically driven are experiencing great prosperity due to an economic growth rate that is five times the rate of growth during the Industrial Revolution.

7. *The Decade of Women in Leadership.*   Women are increasingly filling leadership positions. "For the last two decades U.S. women have taken two thirds of the millions of new jobs created in the information era and will continue to do so well into the millennium. . . . To be a leader in business today, it is no longer an advantage to have been socialized as a male" (p. 229).

8. *The Age of Biology.*   The nation is poised on the threshold of a great biotechnology. "We are shifting from the models and metaphors of physics to the models and metaphors of biology to help us understand today's dilemmas and opportunities" (p. 257). This is being brought on by a great interest in health care, improved crops and healthier farm animals, and the elimination of hunger in the world.

9. *The Religious Revival of the New Millennium.*   As the world approaches the millennium, religious beliefs intensify. This happened 1,000 years ago when "the Christians of Europe's Dark Ages believed the end of the world was at hand" (p. 291).

10. *The Triumph of the Individual.*   The demise of collectives in many countries is bringing about an empowered individual with the entrepreneurial spirit to explore opportunities in any part of the world.

The following sections identify additional trends that parallel those included in *Megatrends* and *Megatrends 2000*.

DEMOGRAPHIC TRENDS

Several important demographic changes are taking place that will have a profound effect on human resources administration during the remainder of the 1990s and on into the twenty-first century. One such change is referred to as the graying of America, which relates to the precipitant increase in the number of elderly citizens. During the remainder of this century the U.S. population of persons 65 years old and over will increase from 30.984 million in 1989 to 34.882 million in 2000 (U.S. Bureau of the Census, 1991). Table 14.1 presents the distribution of the U.S. population by age, showing the percentage in each age category for 1990 through 2080.

TABLE 14.1

Percentage Distribution of the Population by Age, 1990 to 2080

	Age (years)								
Year	Under 5	5–13	14–17	18–24	25–34	35–44	45–64	65 & Over	85 & Over
1990	7.2	13.0	5.3	10.4	17.5	15.2	18.8	12.7	1.3
1995	6.4	13.0	5.6	9.3	15.7	16.4	20.5	13.1	1.5
2000	5.7	12.1	5.8	9.5	13.9	16.6	23.3	13.1	1.7
2005	5.4	10.9	5.6	10.0	13.2	15.0	26.7	13.2	1.8
2010	5.2	10.1	5.0	9.7	13.7	13.4	28.9	14.1	2.0
2020	4.9	9.8	4.4	8.1	13.5	13.4	27.8	18.2	2.0
2030	4.4	9.0	4.4	7.9	11.9	13.6	26.9	22.9	2.4
2040	4.3	8.5	4.1	7.7	11.9	12.3	27.3	23.9	3.7
2050	4.2	8.4	4.0	7.3	11.7	12.5	26.9	24.9	4.7
2080	4.1	8.1	3.9	7.2	11.3	12.3	26.3	26.8	5.3

Source: From *Projections of the Population of the United States, by Age, Sex, and Race: 1988–2080* by U.S. Bureau of the Census (G. Spencer), 1989, Washington, DC: GPO.

It is first interesting to note that the number of children under the age of 5 in 1990 will decrease from 7.2% of the U.S. population to 4.1% by 2080. The U.S. Bureau of the Census found that 18.4 million were in this category in 1990 and estimated that only 17.6 million will be there in 2000, amounting to a 4.3% decrease in just 10 years. It is also interesting to note that the 1980 fertility rate was 1.84 and was considerably below the replacement rate of 2.1 births for every woman. This decrease will produce an important drop in the 18–24 age category by 2000. Moreover, the fertility rate declined from a 1960 rate of 3.449 to a low of 1.738 in 1976. Since then, it has tended upward at a very slow rate and was 1.932 in 1988 (U.S. Bureau of the Census, 1991).

The aging of the American population can be better understood by considering the 45–64 age group and the 65 and over category. The former category is estimated to increase from 18.8% of the population in 1990 to 23.3% in the year 2000, and the latter to increase from 12.7% to 13.1%. In addition to the decreasing number of youth in our society, life expectancy continues to increase and will add significantly to the older age categories. By 2080 it is projected that the elderly, age 65 and above, will constitute 26.8% of the population (U.S. Department of the Census, 1989).

The distribution of the population by race is another important change. The Bureau of the Census reported that blacks, Asians, Hispanics, and other racial minorities constituted 16.8% of the U.S. population in 1970 and 18.7% in 1980. A recent estimate showed that these minorities constituted 26% of the 1992 population (Zinn, Power, Jones, Cuneo, & Ross, 1992). Allan (1991) provides some additional statistics:

> The United States population grew by almost 10 percent between 1980 and 1990, increasing to 248.7 million people. The racial composition of the population underwent some notable changes. . . . The largest population group—accounting for 80 percent of the

total—continued to be whites [199.69 million], followed by blacks at 12 percent [29.99 million]. Asian or Pacific Islanders [7.27 million] were the fastest growing group between 1980 and 1990, however, at 108 percent, with Hispanics [22.35 million] experiencing a 53 percent growth rate. Whites represented the slowest growing population group at 6 percent. (p. 7)

These demographic trends are moving the nation toward a multicultural, multiethnic society that will necessitate more flexible human resources policies for both public and private institutions.

Another change that the future human resources administrator will have to consider is the structure of the family unit. The nuclear family of two children and two biological parents is no longer the predominant family unit in America. In 1955, 60% of all families were considered nuclear families. The 1985 figures show a momentous decrease to 7% (Hodgkinson, 1985). The growth of the single parent household during the 1970s and 1980s has resulted in great numbers of the nation's children going through childhood with only one parent. Specifically, in 1970 and 1988 the percentage of children living with two parents decreased from 85.2% to 73.1 (U.S. Bureau of the Census, 1991). Hodgkinson (1985) projected that in 2001, 59% of all persons 18 years of age will have lived with only one parent. Moreover, he projected that of every 100 children born in 1985,

12 will be born out of wedlock

40 will be born to parents who divorce before the child is 18

5 will be born to parents who separate

2 will be born to parents of whom one will die before the child reaches 18

41 will reach 18 [with both biological parents] (p. 3)

These data suggest that many children will be living with only one parent at some point in their early lives, and there is substantial data to show that single parent families, particularly during economic retrenchment, are the ones most likely to experience serious financial difficulties or poverty.

Berardo (1990) concluded in his review of research on family life "that changing economic conditions are intimately connected to the state of family health and welfare" (p. 817). And, in many instances, strained family economics have forced a continuous stream of wives and mothers into the work force. This has produced the conditions that directly impact the need for school administrators and boards of education to rethink employee concerns.

> These changing employment patterns have prompted challenges to traditional sex and gender role definitions, triggered a strong and persistent wave of renegotiations within the family regarding the division of labor and other matters, and accelerated demands of other institutions [school districts] to accommodate the realities and requirements of the changing role of women. . . . It is imperative in the decade ahead that scholars and practitioners alike use their expertise to sensitize the public and the policy makers to family needs. Applying updated research knowledge to the development, implementation, and refinement of human resources policies designed to meet those needs should be the overarching objective of the future. (Berardo, 1990, p. 817)

These demographic changes will bring about the conditions in which school administrators will have to consider many new ways of conducting the functions of human resources administration. The many implications for such changes will bring about increased pressures for new policies.

ECONOMIC TRENDS

A second factor that greatly affects the administration of human resources is the economy. When the national economy is expanding, business profits are generally up, tax revenues increase, and communities are more willing to invest in better education. Under such economic conditions, boards of education are more prone to consider seriously significant increases in salaries and benefits to attract and hold scarce human resources that might otherwise be lured away by the financial enticements of business and industry.

On the other hand, when economic conditions are poor, the pool of available human resources available for education expands in number and improves in quality. This creates a totally different set of factors that the human resources administrator must confront. The administrator who can foresee such challenges is certain to be better prepared to influence the direction of critical personnel policies, administrative regulations, and the effectiveness of all human resources planning.

The future-oriented administrator must stay abreast of changing economic conditions that affect the functions of human resources administration and communicate their impact to other top administrative team members. Although the administrator may not be able to make the expert interpretation of a professional economist, certainly an awareness of changing trends and their development and effects on the management of human resources will add greater reliability to the organization's external environmental scan. Let us now look to the future by examining selected economic trends, so that a possible view of emerging issues can be gained for further analysis. To gain a perspective on current economic trends, we must view change over a long period of time, perhaps decades or more.

In the 1960s the national economy was experiencing great economic expansion. The gross domestic product, or GDP (i.e., the dollar value of all goods and services produced in the United States), nearly doubled from $513.4 billion in 1960 to $959.5 billion in 1969. In the decade of the 1970s the GDP was $1010.7 billion in 1970 and $2488.6 in 1979. (See Table 14.2 for a display of GDP in actual and in 1987 dollars.)

Even though the growth was much greater in the 1970s, inflation contributed greatly to its increase. The consumer price index (CPI), using 1982–1984 as base years, was 29.6 in 1960 and 36.7 in 1969, for a 24% increase in consumer goods during the 10-year period. By contrast the CPI was 38.8 in 1970 and 72.6 in 1979, for an 87% increase. Though the nation was still experiencing great prosperity in the 1970s, people started to lose confidence as their dollars bought less and less. The rate of increase in the CPI peaked in 1980 with an inflation rate of 13.5% (*Economic Report of the President*, 1992).

TABLE 14.2

Gross Domestic Product (GDP),
Consumer Price Index (CPI),
and Annual Changes in CPI

Source: From *Economic Report of
the President*, 1992, Washington, DC:
GPO and *America's Economic
Diet Begins to Show Results* by
D. Ratajczak, 1992, Atlanta: Georgia
State University, Economic
Forecasting Center.

	Year	GDP in Actual $ (billion)	GDP in 1987 $ (billion)	CPI	Change in CPI %
	1960	513.4	1973.2	29.6	1.7
	1961	531.8	2025.6	29.9	1.0
	1962	571.6	2129.8	30.2	1.0
	1963	603.1	2218.0	30.6	1.3
	1964	648.0	2343.3	31.0	1.3
	1965	702.7	2473.5	31.5	1.6
	1966	769.8	2622.3	32.4	2.9
	1967	814.3	2690.3	33.4	3.1
	1968	889.3	2801.0	34.8	4.2
	1969	959.5	2877.1	36.7	5.5
	1970	1010.7	2875.8	38.8	5.7
	1971	1097.2	2965.1	40.5	4.4
	1972	1207.0	3107.1	41.8	3.2
	1973	1349.6	3268.6	44.4	6.2
	1974	1458.6	3248.1	49.3	11.0
	1975	1585.9	3221.7	53.8	9.1
	1976	1768.4	3380.8	56.9	5.8
	1977	1974.1	3533.2	60.6	6.5
	1978	2232.7	3703.5	65.2	7.6
	1979	2488.6	3796.8	72.6	11.3
	1980	2708.0	3776.3	82.4	13.5
	1981	3030.6	3843.1	90.9	10.3
	1982	3149.6	3760.3	96.5	6.2
	1983	3405.0	3906.6	99.6	3.2
	1984	3777.2	4148.5	103.9	4.3
	1985	4038.7	4279.8	107.6	3.6
	1986	4268.6	4404.5	109.6	1.9
	1987	4539.9	4540.0	113.6	3.6
	1988	4900.4	4718.6	118.3	4.1
	1989	5244.0	4836.9	124.0	4.8
	1990	5513.8	4884.9	130.7	5.4
	1991	5671.8	4848.4	136.2	4.2
Projection	1992	5743.5	4909.7	140.4	3.0
Projection	1993	5891.3	5036.0	144.7	3.0
Projection	1994	6062.4	5182.3	149.9	3.6

Ratajczak projected in 1992 that the GDP (in 1987 dollars) would be $4909.7 billion in 1992, $5036 billion in 1993, and $5182.3 billion in 1994 with inflation rates of 3%, 3%, and 3.6%, respectively. Projected trends for the remainder of the 1990s suggest that prices will continue to remain relatively stable and growth will be slow to moderate.

A number of other economic trends are projecting important changes in the economic condition of the nation. An extremely strong U.S. currency through 1985 made imports cheap to Americans and U.S. products expensive to potential foreign purchasers. This fact, along with increased competition from foreign manufacturers, caused the United States to build up record deficits in the balance of trade that peaked in 1987. Moreover, the competition placed a strain on many of our nation's industries. Numerous industries, hard hit by foreign competition, employed strong lobbyists in Washington to pressure the administration and Congress to enact import tariffs to protect domestic markets for the goods of American industry (Davidson & Rees-Mogg, 1991). Industries that experienced the greatest amount of foreign competition included manufacturing, mining, and agriculture. Since 1985 the dollar has declined in value against most other currencies, and the trade imbalance, although still high, has moderated since peaking in 1987.

The recent savings and loan debacle that is projected to cost the U.S. taxpayers nearly $500 billion has produced a ripple effect on public confidence in the country's financial system. This concern for the system's safety has been exacerbated by a rising trend in commercial bank failures and the fear of future failures. According to Nielsen and Sindt (1992),

> bad loans in the agricultural, real estate, and oil sectors, venture capital loans to finance the Third World and to fund the merger mania of major US corporations during the 1980s, and leveraged buy-outs combined with bank fraud, poor loan practices, outdated banking regulations, depressed regional economies, and weakened real estate markets have resulted in an explosion of commercial bank failures across the nation. The weakening of the commercial banking industry is continuing as the credit-quality problems, which previously had affected primarily states in the Southwest and Midwest, have spread to the Northeast. (p. 92)

From 1946 to 1981 an average of just over six banks closed each year in the United States (Forrestal, 1985). In 1982 alone 42 banks failed, and for the following seven years, more U.S. banks failed each year, reaching a peak of 206 in 1989. During 1990 and 1991 the number of failures decreased to 168 and 124, respectively (Nielsen & Sindt, 1992).

In part, inefficient management, fraud, and poor judgment have been blamed for the bank failures. However, Nielsen and Sindt (1992) also identified the following probable causes of a disproportionately high rate of state bank failures.

- ☐ A US regional banking structure that ties bank performance to regional economic performance.
- ☐ Weakening real estate markets.
- ☐ Volatile interest rates that affected the values of bank real estate assets.
- ☐ The safety nets—the Federal Reserve discount window borrowing opportunities and the deposit insurance system—that created perverse economic incentives for excessive bank risk-taking in making commercial real estate loans.
- ☐ Rising competition from nonbanking institutions that reduced bank incentives to act prudently.
- ☐ A 1980s reduction of regulatory agency supervision levels, followed by a 1990s overcorrection toward excessive regulations. (p. 92)

In addition to the 1,081 "problem banks" that the Federal Deposit Insurance Corporation identified in 1991 (Nielsen & Sindt, 1992), the massive Federal Farm Credit System has experienced staggering losses due to uncollectible loans. This situation required a federal bailout in 1987. Norton (1990) reflected,

Remember the bailout of the federal Farm Credit System (FCS) in 1987? You're forgiven if you don't. It was quickly eclipsed by the colossal losses of the savings and loans, and the cost to taxpayers was initially estimated to be relatively small—$1 billion or less.

Make that $100 billion. A new study . . . concludes that too-easy credit from the FCS was largely to blame for the speculative bubble in land prices that helped trigger the 1980s farm recession. . . . federal relief programs have already paid $75 billion to farmers as a result of that boom and bust—and the cost will mount at least $18 billion higher. (p. 20)

In addition to problem banks, the number of business failures in 1986 was 61,616, or 120 for every 10,000 enterprises. Although the number of failures in 1991 increased to 87,592, the rate of failures decreased to 98 for every 10,000 enterprises. Despite the improvement, the failure rate in 1991 was still greater than that for any year since the Great Depression (*Economic Report of the President*, 1992).

Even though the civilian labor force has increased from 106.9 million in 1980 to nearly 125.3 million in 1991, the annual unemployment rate remained locked-in above 7% during those 12 years with the exception of the 5 years from 1987 through 1991. In 1989 the rate dropped to 5.3%. The annual rates for the 12-year period 1980–1991 were 7.1, 7.6, 9.7, 9.6, 7.5, 7.2, 7.0, 6.2, 5.5, 5.3, 5.5, and 6.7, respectively (*Economic Report of the President*, 1992). Unemployment rates for 1992–1994 are projected to be 7.45, 7.2%, and 6.9% (Ratajczak, 1992).

Jobs were of such great concern to the American people in the 1992 presidential election that President George Bush was defeated by Democratic candidate Bill Clinton, who ran on a platform promising to create jobs for Americans and to fix the broken economy. President Bush's defeat came after he had enjoyed a record high popularity for an extended period of time. His popularity peaked during the war with Iraq and declined as the nation's economy slid into a recession.

Despite the concerns being raised by the current economic trends suggesting troubled waters ahead, present fears are not unlike those of the past. During the last 50 years, the recessionary periods were followed by periods of growth. Each economic downturn spawned new economic expansion and, generally, a higher standard of living for most Americans. As each economic cycle passed, new opportunities and challenges emerged. Each produced better working conditions, benefits, and salaries, and greater participation in those decisions affecting the management of human resources.

SOCIAL TRENDS

Making choices about social justice and other public policies in a declining economic environment creates problems of great proportions. During periods of prosperity and economic expansion, decisions about equalizing opportunities for Americans in areas such as education, employment, and health are made easier by the flexibility that accrues from greater tax revenues and a public propensity to share the nation's wealth. The decade of the 1960s witnessed an attitude and expectation that we could win the war in Vietnam, eliminate poverty, and put a man on the moon (Newland, 1984). The turn of events in the next decade reshaped public opinion with a mood that was decidedly different. By the late 1970s, social issues were not given the high priority by the majority of Americans that they received a decade earlier. A pessimism had grown in the public's mind. Newland (1984) reported that a 1979 Gallup poll found 84% of those surveyed displeased with the direction the nation was headed. Public spirit surrounding social issues in the 1960s was replaced in the 1970s by "a division over Vietnam, a declining economy, and acceptance of limits to growth" (p. 22).

Due to deteriorating economic conditions in the late 1970s, concerns for social issues declined. A presidential commission (President's Commission for a National Agenda for the Eighties, 1980) investigating priorities for the 1980s stated that "adverse economic circumstances, however, must never become an excuse for abandoning our pursuit of social justice" (p. 57). Despite these concerns, such issues did come under close scrutiny for possible elimination as the nation experienced a severe recession in 1981 and 1982. Growing and seemingly uncontrolled federal budget deficits of $212.3 billion in 1985 and $221.2 billion in 1986 precipitated numerous cutbacks in social programs. To a large extent, many of the program needs were shifted to the states. Now many state legislatures are facing financial crises due to state deficits. Although the federal deficits declined slightly from 1987 through 1989, they subsequently increased to all-time highs in 1990 and 1991. Unfortunately, the deficits for those two years of $220.5 billion and $268.7 billion are expected to be surpassed by 1992's deficit of $365.2 billion. This projected deficit represents over 25% of the government's total receipts of $1,441 billion and adds significantly to the nation's debt, which exceeds $4 trillion (*Economic Report of the President*, 1992).

The emerging mood of Americans during the 1970s and 1980s spawned a set of values that were generally characterized by self-interest. The cause-conscious youth of the 1960s became more interested in the business of their careers and families. Moreover, their emerging values were consistent with those that were prevalent during their childhood. Rogan (1985) stated that as this group of "baby boomers" confronted middle age, they were "wistful about their lost youth" (p. 31). This group showed a nostalgic interest in their early years. Evidence of such interest has been found in the popularity of television programs from their childhood that embody traditional values. The group abandoned a previous interest in the fast-paced activities associated with the sexual revolution, social and political protests, and drugs. In 1985 Rogan noted that their television interests were characterized by entertainment that was "bland" and "soothing." Several television shows that best characterized this interest in traditional values were "Love That Bob," "Ben Casey," and even "Leave It to Beaver."

The baby boomers will be in the age range of 36–54 by the year 2000. They were raised by parents who were influenced by the hard times of the Great Depression and were generally committed to providing most of what their children needed. Many have grown to believe in the entitlement ethic and a risk-free life. Koehn (1983) felt that the "baby boom individuals believe that they are entitled to the affluence of society and the happiness society can offer them. They believe that these things should be acquired without taking financial or emotional risks" (p. 245). The baby boomers prospered during the 1980s, and many accumulated wealth through professional careers and favorable investment opportunities, many of which were quite speculative. As the speculative investment binge of the 1980s increased, public and private debt continued to build. This is debt that the children of the baby boomers now feel will be passed on to them.

The 18- to 29-year-old children of the baby boomers, the "baby busters," are forming the next important generation of 46 million Americans who will have to confront the new set of social and economic challenges. And as Zinn et al. (1992) point out, they are "having a tough time":

> Busters are the first generation of latchkey children, products of dual-career households, or, in some 50% of cases, of divorced or separated parents. They have been entering the work force at a time of prolonged downsizing and downturn, so they're likelier than the previous generation to be unemployed, underemployed, and living at home with Mom and Dad. They're alienated by a culture that has been dominated by boomers for as long as they can remember. They're angry as they look down a career path that's crowded with thirty- and fortysomethings who are in no hurry to clear the way. (p. 74)

This generation of youth feels that the nation generally and their parents specifically have mortgaged their future by creating a mountain of public and private debt. The baby busters believe that the burden of this debt places very narrow limits on their future standard of living.

By contrast, Ben Wattenberg (1991) does not share a concern for their future well-being. In his book, *The First Universal Nation*, he documents many areas of progress and promise for America. He points to a high school drop-out rate that is at an all-time low, poverty on the decline and incomes on the rise, the great increase in the number of black college graduates since 1950, and the positive socioeconomic progress of Hispanics. He also builds a strong case for increasing immigration quotas by pointing to the advantage of having immigrants who are usually younger workers who initially take jobs many Americans deem undesirable. Eventually, like previous generations of immigrants, they become entrepreneurs. Wattenberg did not ignore the social problems of drugs, crime, and broken families. Despite the seriousness of each, he pointed to data that suggested a possible change in trends toward improvements in all three areas. In each he identified areas of progress and signs of hope.

POLITICAL TRENDS

The political tone of America appears to have made some important shifts. From the decades of the 1960s and 1970s, when the federal government was expected to solve most problems, public sentiment during the 1980s moved to a desire for less government. During the late 1970s and early 1980s, many Americans felt that the government was helpless in its efforts to solve important problems, and many were experiencing a growing disenchantment with government (Wattenberg, 1984). The Reagan administration couched its campaign for the 1980 presidential election in "getting the government off people's backs" and "turning the government back to the people." In 1988 the Bush campaign promoted a continuation of the Reagan administration's policies. As a result of the Reagan and Bush administrations, greater responsibility for many social-welfare programs was transferred to the states with less involvement of the federal government in local affairs. The elimination of numerous federally funded social programs placed a greater burden on states and private social-welfare agencies.

As one looks at the political tone of the nation and changes in government, it becomes apparent that the government's role in the nation's affairs was being reduced from what it had been in the past. The deregulation of numerous federally controlled industries had a profound impact on the transportation and banking industries. Due to growing budget deficits in the mid-1980s, the U.S. Congress struggled with tax reform out of a need to increase revenues, close loopholes, and minimize the difficulty in filing a tax return. After much debate and compromise, the tax reforms were passed by the Congress. The Tax Reform Act of 1986 also included a reduction in taxes for many Americans.

Another interesting political trend was observed by Orren (1982). He indicated that during the decades of the 1960s and 1970s, American governmental and political institutions became fragmented, atomized, and ungovernable. Subsequently political party politics declined and personalistic and limited-issue politics emerged. A widely heralded decline in partisan politics (Sundquist, 1982; Wattenberg, 1984) and political apathy (Burnham, 1982) were evidenced by the 40 million Americans whom Burnham classifies as being "outside the voting universe" (p. 52) and the emergence of special interest politics. Newland (1984) mentioned that politics in the 1980s appeared to be focused on ideology: "Coalitions are formed of the extremes of single interest politics rather than center coalitions for community inclusiveness" (p. 24).

Although special interest politics have been a part of the political arena for years, during the current economic recession "they do not stand much of a chance when the political decisions involve retrenchment rather than expansion" (Peterson, 1990–91, p. 555). It now appears that special interest politics may be less important as the nation encounters a lengthy economic retrenchment.

In 1985 Ladd (1985) described the what-have-you-done-for-us-lately mood of the electorate as indicative of a separation from party line politics. Even though the Reagan administration was given the mandate to reduce inflation, increase economic growth, and improve the U.S. position in world affairs, it was not an endorsement of a partisan ideology or indicative of party loyalty. The electorate was performance oriented, and the economy was an important part of their concern. Now the American people are again very concerned about their economic well-being. It will be a real challenge to the Clinton administration to refocus Americans' concerns to what his secretary of labor, Robert B. Reich (1991), called "a positive economic nationalism"

> in which each nation's citizens take primary responsibility for enhancing the capacities of their countrymen for full and productive lives, but who also work with other nations to ensure that these improvements not come at others' expense.... It seeks to encourage new learning within the nation, to smooth the transition of the labor force from older industries, to educate and train the nation's workers, to improve the nation's infrastructure, and to create international rules of fair play for accomplishing all these things. (p. 207)

This focus might suggest a more liberal posture for the Clinton presidency than the political orientation that was chronicled during the 1992 campaign. In the early 1980s, Scammon and Wattenberg (1980) postulated that the liberal political era had ended:

> We . . . believe that the philosophy in question—American liberalism—has rendered healthy, vigorous and constructive service to the republic: that its impact will continue to be felt, and that there will be no going back to yesteryear—but, still, it is over. The center of the political spectrum is moving; politicians will gain or keep power only insofar as they can appeal to that moving center. (p. 2)

Scammon and Wattenberg also felt that this did not reflect a change in party, only a change in opinion and direction. Some would say that this did not represent a fundamental shift, only a swing of the pendulum toward a lower propensity for social change.

Similarly, Smith (1990) argued that America has been a politically liberal nation. His rationale is based upon "two long-term forces [that] have moved America in a liberal direction: modernization and liberal idealism. Modernization promoted liberalism through the growth of rationalization, innovation, centralization, statism, and prosperity" (p. 500). He pointed out that America's history, traditions, and governmental roots reflect a liberal nation.

Historians Arthur M. Schlesinger, Sr., and Arthur M. Schlesinger, Jr., have related a broader perspective by identifying alternating periods or cycles of liberal reform and conservative retrenchment (Smith, 1990):

> While neither the Schlesingers nor any other proponents of the cycle of reform model have been able to convincingly establish their view of American historical development, they have described a pattern that both matches the shape of the liberal-conservative trend . . . (a liberal rise followed by a plateau) and which roughly predicted the timing of both the New Frontier/Great Society and the "Reagan Revolution." Using the observed length of reform cycles through 1931, Schlesinger, Sr. in 1939 predicted a conservative phase starting in 1947 or 1948 and then in 1949 forecasted: "We may expect the recession from liberalism which began in 1947 to last till 1962, with a possible margin of a year or two in one direction or another. The next conservative epoch will then be due around 1978." (p. 502)

In a somewhat similar manner and consistent with Schlesinger's cycle theory, Conlan (1990) identified changes in the political activities of the two parties and the emergence of states' influences on federal policy-making. He stated that "whether one considers the economic megatrends favoring decentralization, the renaissance of state policy activism, or the structural constraints of federal finances, continued federal policy leadership appears to be increasingly inconsistent with underlying social, economic, and fiscal developments" (p. 136). Conlan observed that it took 40 years for political party structures to reflect the centralization of governmental power, and he believes that this trend has reversed toward a more nationalized and less mediated political system, that is, party power is less centralized and dispersed among the states.

These political trends combined with the other trends previously discussed should provide an important backdrop for the application of the long wave theory. The trends appear to form a mosaic pattern of economic, social, and political behavior consistent with the declining phase of the theory.

LONG WAVE THEORY

The **long wave** is an economic phenomenon that was first hypothesized in 1922 by Nikolai Dmitrityevich Kondratyev in a Russian article entitled "The World Economy and Its Condition During and After the War." He found that the economic expansion and contraction of Western economies were characterized by a regular and predictable periodicity. His work first appeared in the West in a 1926 German article titled "Archiv fur Sozialwissenschaft und Sozialpolitik." An English translation was published in 1935, perhaps too late to affect Western economic thinking at the time (Stokes, 1980).

A Russian agricultural economist born in 1892, Kondratyev is usually referred to as Kondratieff in the economics literature. Although he is credited with discovering the long wave cycles, it is often argued in the Netherlands that two Marxist Dutchmen—Van Gelderen, who wrote under the pseudonym J. Fedder, and De Wolff—should be credited with the discovery. However, Parvus, a Russian Marxist, wrote an outline of the long wave in 1901 (van Duijn, 1983).

Kondratieff's discovery of the long wave resulted from his study of the economies of France, Germany, Britain, and the United States. The discovery was based upon data from the nineteenth century related to interest rates, wages, foreign trade, bank deposits, and several other minor data sets. His findings were so contrary to the prevailing Marxist views in Soviet Russia that attempts were made to discredit him. Although Kondratieff was arrested and sent to Siberia for being the head of an illegal party in 1930, his economic predictions about the survival of Western economies may have been an important factor in his deportation. Van Duijn (1983) surmised that

> the downswing of the long wave which, according to Kondratieff, had started around 1914–20, would eventually be followed by a new upswing, implying that the final disintegration of the capitalist system for which the Soviet leaders were waiting, would not occur. Kondratieff's views therefore ran counter to the official Marxist view. (pp. 64–65)

Kondratieff established an empirical case in finding 2.5 economic cycles using the limited data available. He found economic troughs in the years 1790, 1844–1851, and 1890–1896. Periods of expansion peaked around 1810–1817, 1870–1875, and 1914–1920 (Rostow, 1975). Although there has been considerable disagreement as to the peak of the third Kondratieff wave, van Duijn (1983) identified 1929 as the upper limit. Depression followed between 1929–1937 and the recovery started in 1937. The peak in prosperity of our current cycle is believed to be 1980.

Generally the Kondratieff wave of economic expansion and decline has a cycle mean of 54 years with a range of 45–60 years (Erickson, 1985; Forrester, 1985; van Duijn, 1983). Some believe that the long wave exists simultaneously with other widely used economic and business cycles. The noted economist Schumpeter felt that the Kondratieff wave was composed of three Kuznet construction cycles of 15–25 years, six Juglar investment cycles of 7–11 years, and 12 Kitchin inventory cycles of 3–5 years. Despite this early belief, researchers have not been able to verify this relationship (van Duijn, 1983). For years many researchers in Europe, especially in the Netherlands, have attempted to explain the long wave phenomenon. Since the mid-1970s, economists in the United States have also tried to verify it (Delbeke, 1981).

In a review of the theories developed to explain the long wave, Delbeke (1981) listed and summarized the best known: Mensch's theory related the long wave cycles to clusters of innovations; Mandel associated the cycles with the successive acceleration and deceleration of capital accumulation; Freeman identified new technologies, investment, and the subsequent demand for labor; Rostow related his theory to the scarcity and abundance of foodstuffs and raw materials; van Duijn (1981) was mentioned as one who used an eclectic approach by integrating several theories; and, finally, Forrester and his associates at the Alfred P. Sloan School of Management at MIT developed a theory using new methods of analyzing the growth dynamics of capital goods. Sterman (1985), an associate of Forrester, indicated that their simulation model, derived from an integrated theory, relates capital investment; employment, wages, and work force participation; inflation and interest rates; aggregate demand; monetary and fiscal policy; innovation and productivity; and political values.

The MIT simulation model has been recognized by researchers as an important contribution to proving the long wave theory. Emery (1982) stated that doubts about the scientific status of Kondratieff's hypothesis were put to rest by Forrester: "The MIT computer simulation of a national economy has resolved this last problem in Kondratieff's favor" (p. 1,096). Tinbergen (1981) of the University of Rotterdam identified Jay Forrester at MIT as using "the most modern methods of research" (p. 262) in developing a theory of the long wave. Thus this theory is frequently referred to in the professional literature as Kondratieff's long wave theory.

There has been much research to establish Mensch's theory related to the buildup of innovations into clusters during the down cycle. The downturn of the long wave has been a period of technological innovation (Sterman, 1990), and "the periods of rapid growth are typically characterized by the diffusion of major technologies developed in earlier periods" (Ayres, 1990, p. 128). There is a growing body of research supporting the belief that major innovations are developed during periods of depression (Sterman, 1990; Ayres, 1990). "As seen during the depression stage, firms attempt to reduce costs through restructuring and research in new technologies, the latter resulting in new inventions. Innovations, i.e., the application of inventions and new products, occurs later as favorable economic conditions develop" (Tarascio, 1988, p. 8).

Under the direction of Forrester, the System Dynamics Group (SDG) at MIT, with the sponsorship of 40 corporations, uses its computer-based simulation model to predict changes in economic conditions consistent with the Kondratieff long wave theory. Despite some early criticism of the model (Delbeke, 1981) and a later critique by Freeman (1984), a number of companies have used the group's projections to modify their investment and operating plans to reflect the economic downturn of the 1990s.

A growing body of research findings substantiates the existence of the long wave. As Forrester has done, Schumpeter, Mensch, Mandel, Freeman, van Duijn, and Rostow also have developed theories to prove its existence. In addition, a number of researchers in sociology, politics, and psychology have attempted to correlate patterns of behavior and societal changes to the long wave theory. Shuman and Rosenau (1972) have drawn parallels from the upswings and downswings of the long wave with politics, economics, psychology, and societal values. Beckman (1983) related the long wave to types of investments. Weber (1981) conducted an interesting study involving a computer-based content analysis of the British Speeches from the Throne, 1795–1972, to find a 52-year cycle of changing thematic concerns or issues. The cycles replicated the party platforms of American presidential elections during the period, and both sets of thematic concerns were found to correlate with the Kondratieff cycle. The results of this study reflect the recurring crises in capitalist society from economic peaks to depressions.

Generally the long wave is represented by approximately 20 years of prosperity, 10 years of limited growth or stagnation, and 20 years of economic decline. Many authors have observed important wars around the peaks of the upswings (Beckman, 1983; Craig & Watt, 1985; Shuman & Rosenau, 1972; Thompson & Zuk, 1982). Weber (1981) found that the political speeches of the peak years placed greater emphasis on international affairs. Thompson and Zuk (1982) related that Kondratieff never developed a theory to explain the relationship of the upswing and the incidence of war. However, in a review of his work, they did find that "the only clue he [Kondratieff] advanced was to suggest that the rising phases of the long wave tended to be characterized by high levels of interstate economic tension over markets and raw materials" (p. 623). Shuman and Rosenau (1972) believed that during times of prosperity, social tension increases as greater economic prosperity brings about increased concern for social issues. This tension is dissipated through the peak wars, and the following 10 years are usually a period in which people are glad to be freed of the tensions brought on by domestic reform movements and war. The wars in 1812, 1862, 1917, and 1973 were all at the peak of an extended period of prosperity. These wars were hotly debated and precipitated immense domestic social tension. One has only to recall the war protests of the 1960s to gain an understanding of the degree of tension.

The declining years are usually characterized by people trying to "hold on." Loss of jobs, business and bank failures, and personal bankruptcies contribute to a growing sense of fear. During this time people are more concerned about their personal welfare and are not usually interested in taking on new social causes (Shuman & Rosenau, 1972). Luxuries are replaced with necessities, and there is a general move back to the basics of economic and social life.

Some believe that the current downswing will not be as severe as the depression experienced by our parents and grandparents in the 1930s. Hamil (1979) stated that "the Great Depression was greatly exacerbated by incredible mismanagement by the Hoover Administration and the Federal Reserve System" (p. 384). Forrester (1985) also faulted the Federal Reserve in the 1930s; however, he felt that we have learned from our research. "Through the use of the System Dynamics National Model, we have for the first time a cohesive, integrated theory of how the economic long wave can be generated" (p. 20). It appears that we are now able to use what we have learned to fashion monetary and fiscal policies that will mitigate the hardships of the downturn.

One might ask then, Where are we relative to the long wave? Forrester (1990) stated,

> If we search for times in the past that exhibit conditions similar to those of the present, they are found during and after the peaks of the economic long wave—the late 1920s and early 1930s and the period around 1890. (p. 7)

Sterman (1990) concurred by stating that "the economy has been in the downturn of the long wave for about a decade" (p. 47). He further related that we are experiencing a "rolling depression rather than a single, cataclysmic collapse as in the Great Depression" (p. 45). First, rust-belt manufacturing was hard hit in the 1970s; this was followed by the oil industry, farm land, and real estate crises in the Midwest; and the real estate problems have recently spread to both the East and West coasts. Now the collapse is beginning to spread to junk bonds, retailing, the financial services industry, and equities. Sterman (1990) believes that the rolling depression is occurring because of governmental intervention by absorbing responsibilities for bad debts that have been flooding the financial markets, for example, the savings and loan bailout, Continental Illinois Bank bailout, and Farm Credit bailout. In each instance the costs of the bailouts have been shifted to the taxpayers.

In response to the question of where we are relative to the long wave, evidence suggests that the peak occurred in 1980. The plateau that follows the long wave peak was probably completed during the period 1987–1991. In 1992 we entered the steep decline of the down cycle that may not bottom out until 2000–2010.

IMPLICATIONS FOR HUMAN RESOURCES ADMINISTRATION

In the previous sections, a review of current demographic, economic, social, and political conditions and trends was outlined to establish a basis for making predictions about changes in human resources administration. Additionally, the long wave theory was presented as an important vehicle to guide the projections. Although each area was briefly reviewed, students interested in pursuing a more in-depth study of any one area should see the references at the end of this chapter.

The direction of the national economy will play a major role in influencing several areas of human resources administration. The current economic downturn with a disinflationary trend will improve the relative position of salaries for educators in the marketplace over an intermediate term of approximately 10–15 years. Although base salaries will probably not decline during this period, annual increases will be minimal or at a considerably lower rate than those of the past decade. Disinflation should also strengthen the net purchasing power of the educator's salary. These relative salary improvements have already emerged and are beginning to enhance the image of teaching. Education is gaining recognition as a profession in which one can enjoy a relatively good standard of living in a job-secure environment. This appeal has produced a great number of applicants for teaching positions.

Just a few years ago, teacher associations were predicting a severe shortage of teachers in the 1990s. Contrary to these projections, the worsening economy has caused the pool of available teacher applicants to increase greatly. Employment opportunities outside education have become more limited, and as many segments of business and industry experience reduced growth and decline, they are laying off or terminating many employees. Displaced personnel from the noneducation sector have sought opportunities in teaching careers, which has reversed the trend of declining teacher qualifications to one of stronger academic backgrounds among teaching candidates. This trend will continue throughout this decade and into the next.

Additionally, important changes have concurrently affected the size of the teacher pool: the changing values associated with work, the family, and lifestyles.

Evidence suggests that the many baby boomers and their children, the baby busters, will be less interested in experiencing potential life conflicts, risks, and personal trade-offs associated with climbing the corporate ladder and will pursue careers in education. As the limits to growth become more widely experienced and businesses wane, fewer persons will be willing to take entrepreneurial risks. Interest in personal security will manifest itself by the hold-on-to-what-we-have attitude. More traditional values characteristic of those associated with the family unit and the freedom of a new, disentangled life-style being sought by many will tend to support an increase in teaching careers. Teaching will have wide appeal to many because of the time and freedom that it offers during break and vacation periods for developing family relationships and pursuing individual interests. This decrease in material expectations combined with Naisbitt's (1982) emerging high tech/high touch phenomenon of a high personal value system also supports the appeal of teaching as a career.

Reduced revenues from lower tax receipts and the possibility of budget deficits will dampen efforts to increase benefits packages for educators. In fact, the current trend toward greater employee contributions will continue and probably increase as the economy continues to decline. It is assumed that changes in the mean age of school personnel will parallel that of the larger national population. Employee benefits packages will have to be modified to meet the unique needs of this older group of school employees. This modification will require more flexible employee benefits due to changes in individual life-styles characterized by an increase in unmarried individuals and single parents whose needs will differ from the increasing number of senior employees. The addition of more benefits options to meet a more diverse employee population will also support a cost rationale for making flexible benefits plans more self-contributory.

During the current period of economic retrenchment, educators must maintain a vigil over their pension funds. Budget deficits can cause creative politicians to look for ways to tap the large state teacher pension funds to help ease the constituent pressures and financial strains of promised services or programs.

The future will witness some job restructuring. Changing life-styles and the expansion of the labor force brought on by the increased number of women who will be working will offer important challenges for human resources administrators. Many in this group will be interested in working less than full time. Such interest will permit numerous opportunities for administrators to employ part-time teachers or structure job-sharing teaching positions. Such restructuring will require greater flexibility in working hours and more creative scheduling on the part of the administrator.

The net effect of such a change will be an improvement in teacher effectiveness. It is a case of the sum being greater than the numerical aggregate of its parts. It is believed that two part-time teachers will have greater energy to produce increased time-on-task behaviors and, ultimately, student learning. Such increases will also be supported by an improvement in the ratio of time spent teaching to teacher planning.

From the previous political analysis of a move toward participatory governance combined with the emerging mood of self-interest, it appears new governance structures in education will be characterized by participatory decision making (e.g., site-based management). Clusters of expertise will be sought wherever they exist. Individuals and clusters of persons will be called upon to deliberate possible solutions to important problems, and such groups will include those most directly affected by the eventual decisions. Participatory leadership skills will become an important crite-rion for screening the educational administrator. Moreover, the concept will receive great attention by human resources administrators not only as they screen candidates for leadership positions, but also as they attempt to provide training for incumbent administrators.

Consistent with the trend toward participatory management, superintendents and other top administrators will involve the human resources administrator in all strategic planning activities. These individuals will provide expertise in human resources forecasting and data base decision making, and they will emerge as key resource persons in nearly all strategic decisions of the school system.

The involvement of the human resources administrator in high-level decisions will require this person to have an in-depth knowledge of all functional areas of the school system as well as personnel management and the laws affecting personnel. In addition to an understanding of areas such as curriculum and finance, the adminis-trator must have expertise in the organization and administration of school-level operations. The requirement for an administrator with a broader understanding of systemwide operations should bring about important changes in the training of human resources administrators. The trend is toward requiring internships and practicums as integral components of both graduate degree programs and adminis-trator state certification.

A need for currency and expertise in the total educational enterprise places greater institutional value on persons with such competency. This value will be main-tained for personnel in all positions of a school system. The importance of retaining professional expertise in a school system combined with a greater attention to the "worth of work" will give a new emphasis to the development of human capital.

An appreciation of human capital as the most important resource of the school system will produce several results. Improvements in strategic human resources planning will place greater emphasis on planning for staff development at the school level of administration. It is anticipated that individual school budgets will include substantial sums for human capital development. School personnel will be able to identify, from a strategic perspective, the most important development priorities each year; that is, specific training targets will be established to help the school meet strategic objectives. Not only will the staff development office of the system be involved in such training, but individual schools will work more directly with personnel from other agencies for such services (e.g., universities, state depart-ments of education, intermediate units, businesses, and other schools and school sys-tems).

Additionally, the development of human resources will include a much greater concern for the physical and mental health of all personnel. It is expected that greater numbers of diagnostic and preventative health care programs will be offered on a regular basis. Programs in stress management, nutrition, and exercise will be some of the most popular. Certainly, as benefits options become more self-contributory, health programs will increase in popularity.

The emerging conservative political posture characteristic of the downward move of the long wave combined with the makeup and orientation of federal court judges suggest that the equal employment opportunity, affirmative action, and equity agendas will continue to be "back burner" issues for a number of years to come. It is believed that Congress will not approve any new and sweeping initiatives, and the judiciary will not make any significant decisions until the new upwave is well underway. Although some may feel that comparable worth and family leave are the next issues to bring about great gains in equity, the political and judicial agenda for the downwave will only chronicle them as worthy issues at the wrong time in the historical calendar of equity issues. This implies that only limited progress on social and equity issues will be made during the next 10–15 years.

A FINAL WORD

In the foregoing sections of this chapter, the authors chose to include a discussion of Naisbitt and Aburdene's *Megatrends 2000* and Wattenberg's *The First Universal Nation* to provide a glimpse of the proverbial light at the end of the tunnel. As the economic script for the long wave down cycle is played out during the next 10–15 years, one must realize that the processes of decline help to purge the excesses of the previous decades to prepare for the next cycle of growth and prosperity.

Naisbitt, Aburdene, and Wattenberg may have been a little early in their predictions of an economic boom in the 1990s. However, we believe that their analyses, visions of emerging trends, and future predictions are compelling. Each will evolve as technological innovations are developed. These technological developments will be driven by the inventions of the previous two decades and will sustain the first cycle of prosperity of the third millennium.

We speculate that the **Information Age** may become better known as the **Learning Age.** The new technologies that are being developed today represent the first real breakthrough to support learning. Powerful hardware that uses multimedia technologies will provide learning experiences for students that we can now begin to imagine as we witness demonstrations of virtual reality, interactive films, and interactive videos. These developments in combination with extremely powerful computers that have very large data storage capabilities and in conjunction with developments in telecommunications will open up a world of excitement to the learner that will stun our pedagogical fantasies.

The emerging technologies must be placed in perspective to fully appreciate what is to come. The current and past technological approaches to learning were supported by such hardware as pencils, pens, and paper; the printing press; chalk and the chalkboard; the mimeograph machines and spirit duplicators; the slide, overhead, opaque, film, and movie projectors; tape recorders, television, VCR's, and so on. The microprocessor, which is responsible for the previously mentioned developments, will render all of these devices and others obsolete.

Education is about knowledge and learning that is acquired through the processing of data and information. Now educators have devices for retrieving, storing, and processing great amounts of data. This capability offers educators the opportunity to produce learning situations that will stimulate their imaginations for even more creative developments.

We predict that these developments will move education to a place of prominence in America and that educators will enjoy a status and prestige that will be the envy of other professions. Learning will be propelled by the new technologies, and the technology-learning era will be the driving force in the next up cycle of the long wave.

SUMMARY

Demographic, economic, social, and political trends were briefly reviewed to establish a basis for projecting possible changes in human resources administration. These trends were interpreted in light of the Kondratieff long wave theory to suggest that the United States is experiencing the pains of the downswing of the Kondratieff long wave. The theory suggests that the United States will experience a decline in economic growth and deflation during the first decade of the twenty-first century. Little concern will be expressed for new social initiatives. People will be more interested in holding on to what they have and will not be willing to take risks.

In view of some of these projections, the pool of teacher applicants will continue to increase in number and quality. Changes in the family structure and individual life-styles will require more flexible personnel benefits packages and a restructuring of some professional positions. Finally, the emergence of human resources administration as an important ingredient of strategic planning will create a need for the human resources administrator to maintain an expanded expertise in all areas of the educational enterprise (e.g., curriculum, transportation, finance, etc.).

The period ahead is viewed as an opportunity for the managers of human resources to emerge as important contributors to the strategic decision-making process. Their roles will be enlarged and responsibilities increased. Expertise and professional knowledge combined with access to current human resources data will make them valuable contributors to decisions that will shape the future of educational programs.

DISCUSSION QUESTIONS

1. Using the demographic, social, economic, and political information presented in this chapter, discuss implications for human resources administration in the school systems of your state.
2. Textbooks are usually written several years prior to their publication. You may find that there have been important economic, demographic, social, and political changes since the writing of this text. Identify possible changes. Have these changes influenced the trends identified in the chapter? How will these trend changes affect human resources administration? If no changes in trends were identified, are there additional implications for human resources administration?
3. Based on the outline of the position analysis in Chapter 6, develop a position analysis for the human resources administrator in your school district that will be appropriate for the year 2000. Compare and contrast the different position analyses developed by class members.

CASE 14.1
Proactive Futuring: A Dilemma

Sanderville School District is a growing suburban system adjacent to a large metropolitan area. The community has a history of supporting the construction of new facilities. Although the current facilities are adequate, Superintendent Anna Chelsey knows that within 7 years the district will need two new elementary schools and one middle school.

Recently the area has been experiencing a serious economic downturn that is not expected to improve for at least 6 months or 1 year. Construction costs have dropped considerably, and there are many idle contractors in need of projects to put their employees back to work.

The board did not plan to go to the people with a referendum for new construction for at least 3 to 4 more years. Superintendent Chelsey believes that in 3 to 4 years construction costs and interest rates will undoubtedly increase.

Questions

1. Should the superintendent attempt to move ahead with a referendum to support the new facilities?
2. What problems should Superintendent Chelsey anticipate with members of the board?
3. What approaches could she use with the board to explore the idea of a referendum when so many people in the community are out of work?

CASE 14.2
Planning for Decline

Dr. Cheri Thomas, the superintendent of Sandy Plains School System, is convinced that the state's economy will be in difficulty for an extended period of time. State revenues are falling, and Dr. Thomas anticipates cuts in state allotments within the next 2 to 3 years. She is concerned that the district might have to terminate some teachers and support staff.

She expressed her concern to Melvin Cleaver, the associate superintendent for human resources, and asked him to develop two or three plausible scenarios that will reflect possible conditions in 2 to 3 years and alternative plans of action on personnel matters for the district.

Questions

1. What should be considered in the development of the scenarios?
2. What data sources should Mr. Cleaver consider using?
3. What format should the report of the scenarios follow?
4. Who should be involved in developing the scenarios?

CASE 14.3
A Rare Opportunity

Samuel Skinner, the human resources director of Willow Mill School District Number 9, was troubled by the prospects of an extended economic retrenchment that he read about in a report of the state university's economic forecasting agency. One positive aspect of the report was the anticipated increase of persons looking for jobs, particularly in teaching fields. As he reflected on the report, he quickly realized that this condition may offer an opportunity to upgrade his instructional staff in the district.

Questions

1. In what ways can Mr. Skinner improve the instructional staff?
2. What problems can he anticipate in implementing such plans? Is it likely that he will need the board's involvement?
3. What resources can he use or might be available?

REFERENCES

Allan, I. J. (1991, June). Final census figures confirm continuing population trends. *Government Financial Review, 7*(3), 7–11.

Ayres, R. U. (1990). Technological transformations and long waves. Part II. *Technological Forecasting and Social Change, 36*, 111–137.

Beckman, R. C. (1983). *The downwave: Surviving the second great depression.* New York: Dutton.

Berardo, F. M. (1990, November). Trends and directions in family research in the 1980s. *Journal of Marriage and the Family, 52*, 809–816.

Burnham, W. D. (1982). *The current crisis in American politics.* Oxford, UK: Oxford University Press.

Conlan, T. J. (1990, May). Politics and governance: Conflicting trends in the 1990s? *Annals of the American Academy of Political and Social Science, 509*, 128–138.

Craig, P. P., & Watt, K. E. F. (1985). The Kondratieff cycle and war: How close is the connection? *The Futurist, 19*(2), 25–27.

Davidson, J. D., & Rees-Mogg, W. (1991). *The great reckoning.* New York: Summit Books.

Delbeke, J. (1981). Recent long-wave theories. *Futures, 13*, 246–257.

Economic Report of the President. (1992, February). Washington, DC: GPO.

Emery, F. (1982). New perspectives on the world of work: Sociotechnical foundations for a new social order? *Human Relations, 35*, 1095–1122.

Erickson, S. W. (1985). The transition between eras. *The Futurist, 19*(4), 40–44.

Forrestal, R. P. (1985). Bank safety: Risks and responsibilities. *Economic Review, 70*(7), 4–12.

Forrester, J. W. (1985). Economic conditions ahead: Understanding the Kondratieff wave. *The Futurist, 19*(3), 16–20.

Forrester, J. W. (1990, March 20). *The national economy in the 1990s—The processes of change.* Paper presented as the Lewis E. Harris Lecture, University of Nebraska, Lincoln.

Freeman, C. (1984). Prometheus unbound. *Futures, 16*, 494–507.

Haddad, C. (1992, December 13). Life harsh in white-collar world. *The Atlanta Journal-Constitution,* p. R1.

Hamil, R. (1979). Is the wave of the future Kondratieff? *The Futurist, 13*, 381–384.

Hodgkinson, H. L. (1985). *All one system: Demographics of education, kindergarten through graduate school.* Washington, DC: Institute for Educational Leadership.

Koehn, H. (1983). The post-industrial worker. *Public Personnel Management Journal, 12*, 244–248.

Kondratieff, N. D., & Oparin D. I. (1984). *The long wave cycle* (G. Daniels, Trans.). New York: Richardson & Snyder. (Original work published 1928)

Ladd, E. C. (1985). As the realignment turns: A drama in many acts. *Public Opinion, 7*(6), 2–7.

Naisbitt, J. (1982). *Megatrends.* New York: Warner Books.

Naisbitt, J., & Aburdene, P. (1990). *Megatrends 2000.* New York: Avon Books.

Newland, C. A. (1984). Crucial issues for public personnel professionals. *Public Personnel Management Journal, 13*, 15–46.

Nielsen, D. A., & Sindt, R. P. (1992, Fall). Real estate, regional banking, and bank failures. *Real Estate Review, 22*(3), 91–96.

Norton, R. E. (1990, December). U.S. loses another $100 billion. *Fortune,* p. 20.

Orren, G. R. (1982). The changing styles of American party politics. In J. L. Fleishman (Ed.), *The future of American political parties: The challenge of governance* (pp. 4–41). Englewood Cliffs, NJ: Prentice-Hall.

Peterson, P. E. (1990–91). The rise and fall of special interest politics. *Political Science Quarterly, 105*, 539–556.

President's Commission for a National Agenda for the Eighties. (1980). *A national agenda for the eighties.* Washington, DC: GPO.

Ratajczak, D. (1992, November). *America's economic diet beginning to show results.* Atlanta: Georgia State University, College of Business Administration, Economic Forecasting Project.

Reich, R. B. (1991). What is a nation? *Political Science Quarterly, 106*, 193–209.

Rogan, H. (1985, August 20). TV reviving and revamping old shows in a pitch to nostalgic baby boomers. *The Wall Street Journal,* p. 31.

Rostow, W. W. (1975). Kondratieff, Schumpeter and Kuznets: Trend periods revisited. *Journal of Economic History*, *35*, 719–753.

Scammon, R. M., & Wattenberg, B. J. (1980). Is it the end of an era? *Public Opinion*, *3*(5), 2–12.

Shuman, J. B., & Rosenau, D. (1972). *The Kondratieff wave.: The future of America until 1984 and beyond*. New York: Dell.

Smith, T. W. (1990). Liberal and conservative trends in the United States since World War II. *Public Opinion Quarterly*, *54*, 479–507.

Sterman, J. D. (1985). An integrated theory of the economic long wave. *Futures*, *17*, 104–131.

Sterman, J. D. (1990, July). A long wave perspective on the economy in the 1990s. *The Bank Credit Analyst: Investment and Business Forecast*, *42*(1), 28–47.

Stokes, C. J. (1980). A long range view based on the Kondratieff cycle. *Business Economics*, *15*(1), 20–23.

Sundquist, J. L. (1982). Party decay and the capacity to govern. In J. L. Fleishman (Ed.), *The future of American political parties: The challenge of governance* (pp. 42–69). Englewood Cliffs, NJ: Prentice-Hall.

Tarascio, V. J. (1988, December). Kondratieff's theory of long cycles. *Atlantic Economic Journal*, *16*(4), 1–10.

Thompson, W. R., & Zuk, L. G. (1982). War, inflation, and the Kondratieff long wave. *Journal of Conflict Resolution*, *26*, 621–644.

Tinbergen, J. (1981). Kondratiev cycles and so-called long waves. *Futures*, *13*, 258–263.

U.S. Department of the Census. (1989, January). *Projections of the population of the United States, by age, sex, and race: 1988 to 2080* by G. Spencer (*Current Population Reports*, Series P-25, No. 1018). Washington, DC: GPO.

U.S. Bureau of the Census. (1991). *Statistical abstract of the United States: 1991*. Washington, DC: GPO.

van Duijn, J. J. (1981). Fluctuations in innovations over time. *Futures*, *13*, 264–276.

van Duijn, J. J. (1983). *The long wave in economic life*. London: Allen & Unwin.

Ward, B. (1966). *Spaceship Earth*. New York: Columbia University Press.

Wattenberg, M. P. (1984). *The decline of American political parties: 1952–1980*. Cambridge, MA: Harvard University Press.

Wattenberg, B. J. (1991). *The first universal nation*. New York: Free Press.

Weber, R. P. (1981). Society and economy in the Western world system. *Society & Economy*, *59*, 1130–1147.

Zinn, L., Power, C., Jones, D., Cuneo, A., & Ross, D. (1992, December). Move over, boomers: The busters are here—And they're hungry. *Business Week*, pp. 74–82.

Author Index

Aburdene, P., 404–406, 423
Adkison, J., 316
Alderfer, C. P., 217
Alexander, K., 263, 268, 313
Alexander, M. D., 263, 268
Allan, I. J., 405, 407–408
Alpander, G., 82, 84
Altschuler, H., 394
Anthony, P., 86
Anthony, W. P., 396
Argyris, Chris, 15
Armacost, R. L., 89
Austin, B., 352
Austin, M. J., 368
Awad, E. M., 382
Ayres, R. U., 418

Baird, L., 81, 83, 85
Barnard, Chester I., 14–16
Barnard, Henry B., 3
Bartholomew, D. J., 98
Bassett, G. A., 394
Bates, R. J., 59
Beatty, Richard, 394–395
Beckham, J., 208, 252, 259
Beckman, R. C., 418–419
Beebe, R. J., 316–317
Bell, D. J., 98
Bell, Terrel, 325
Bello, R., 356
Benson, J., 288–289, 302–303
Berardo, F. M., 408
Berry, B., 190, 193–195, 201, 205, 207–208, 319
Bible, J. D., 152, 175
Black, H. C., 258, 261

Blakey, G., 364
Bloss, J. M., 3, 32–33, 136, 139
Bobbitt, J. F., 7
Bohlander, G. W., 163, 314, 317, 334, 353, 360–361, 369
Bolton, D. L., 153
Boudreau, J. W., 89
Bozeman, W. C., 132, 394
Brademas, D. J., 355
Bradley, A., 31, 37, 40
Brayfield, A. H., 218
Bredeson, P. L., 153
Bria, R., 229–231
Brickell, H. M., 115–125, 132, 140
Brown, C. L., 370–373
Brown, M., 240
Burnham, W. D., 415
Bush, George, 318, 412, 414

Callahan, R. E., 7
Cambron-McCabe, N. H., 38, 252, 254, 258, 260, 262–263, 266, 270
Canady, R. L., 129
Candoli, I. C., 356
Carlson, R. V., 89
Carlton, P. W., 283
Carnoy, M., 62–63
Cascio, W. F., 152, 251, 353, 355, 382
Cashman, T., 381
Castetter, W. B., 50–51, 57, 313–314, 332
Cavanaugh, M. E., 227
Ceriello, V. R., 382, 384–385
Cetron, Marvin J., 28, 39, 44
Chalk, Vincent, 255
Charalambides, L. C., 89
Charp, S., 394

Chemers, Martin M., 20–21
Childs, R. A., 255
Chruden, H. J., 163, 314, 317, 334, 353, 360–361, 369
Claggett, J. R., 393–394
Cleland, D. I., 92
Clemmer, Elwin F., 113–114, 129, 140
Clinton, Bill, 318, 412, 415
Cohn, M. M., 323
Coil, A., 225–226
Collins, A., 201, 203–204
Colon, R. J., 305
Compton-Forbes, P., 277
Conlan, T. J., 416
Craig, P. P., 419
Crawford, C. W., 383–384
Cresap, 326
Creswell, A. M., 294
Crim, Alonzo, 154
Crockett, W. H., 218
Cubberly, Elwood P., 2
Cuneo, A., 407, 414
Cunningham, L. L., 277
Currence, C., 32

Daly, J., 387
Darling-Hammond, L., 39–40, 319
Davey, B., 205–206
Davidson, J. D., 411
Davies, D. R., 115–125, 132, 140, 148
Davis, D. D., 42
Davis, E., 35
Davis, W. S., 381
Decker, R. H., 136
DeGive, G., 81, 83, 85
Delbeke, J., 417–418
Delon, F. G., 252, 267–268
Denis, J., 352
Devanna, M. A., 83–84
DeWeese, L., 370–373
Dickson, William J., 13
Diegmueller, K., 31, 284
D'Orazio, R., 394
Douglass, Harl, 228–229, 231
Downey, C., 208
Draper, J. M., 157
Drew, C. J., 187, 189, 207
Dror, Y., 82
Drucker, P. E., 226
Duke, D. L., 129, 193, 195–196, 198, 207

Dunwell, R. R., 323
Duston, R. L., 152
Dyer, L., 81–82, 84, 97

Elam, S. M., 29, 32–34
Ellett, C. D., 188
Emery, F., 418
Engelhardt, N. L., 100
Erickson, S. W., 417
Ernest, Robert C., 89–90
Estabrook, R., 190, 206
Evans, M. W., 3–4, 126, 277, 284
Evertson, C. M., 196–197

Falcone, P., 360
Farrar, R. D., 67, 285
Faux, J., 387
Fayol, Henri, 8, 64
Fear, R. A., 165
Fedder, J., 417
Fellenz, R. A., 244
Fenner, M. S., 2
Ferris, G., 361
Feuer, M. J., 98
Fiedler, Fred E., 20–22
Findley, D., 190, 206
Fiorito, J., 84
Fischer, L., 263, 268
Flippo, E. B., 338, 367
Follett, Mary Parker, 11–13, 15
Fombrun, C., 83–84
Forbes, A. F., 98
Forrestal, R. P., 411
Forrester, J. W., 417–419
Forsyth, P. B., 39
Foster, C. W., 314
Foulkes, F. K., 314, 334
Frase, L. E., 208, 325
Freeman, C., 418
Friesen, D., 17
Futrell, M. H., 325

Gallup, A. M., 29, 32–34
Galosy, J. R., 96
Gantt, Henry L., 6
Gayle, Margaret E., 28, 39, 44
Gee, E. G., 259
Getzels, Jacob W., 15, 215–216, 235
Gibson, C. F., 388

Gibson, R. O., 14, 32, 65–66
Gilbreth, Frank, 6
Gilbreth, Lillian, 6
Ginsberg, R., 190, 193–195, 201, 205, 207–208
Gips, C. J., 3–4, 126, 277, 284
Glass, T. E., 30, 33, 36, 38
Glueck, W. F., 102
Goodstein, L. D., 82, 92–93
Goodwin, H. I., 283
Graczyk, S., 387
Grant, F. D., 396–398
Green, J. L., 196–197
Greenberg, S., 356
Greene, J. E., 258–259, 319, 326, 328, 336–337, 339, 341
Greer, C. R., 84
Grier, T. B., 139
Griffin, R. W., 6
Griffiths, D. E., 39
Grover, B. W., 205–206
Guba, E. G., 215–216, 235
Gulick, L., 8–9, 50, 393
Gurgel, R., 381
Gursky, D., 320, 325

Hack, W. G., 356
Haddad, C., 405
Haggart, B., 37
Haimann, T., 19
Halpin, Andrew, 15
Hamil, R., 419
Hammond, D., 364
Hanson, E. M., 10, 18
Harris, B. M., 58, 104
Harris, D. L., 89
Harris, P. R., 89
Harrison, R., 88
Harvey, L. J., 95–96
Hellriegel, D., 1, 20
Henderson, A. M., 9
Henderson, R. I., 316, 334–335, 340, 342, 344
Hentges, J. T., 277
Hernandez, D. E., 132
Herzberg, F., 15–18, 216
Heyer, N. O., 84
Hicks, James O., Jr., 391–392
Hodgkinson, H. L., 408
Holaday, E. A., 17
Holley, F. M., 196

Holmes, C. T., 370–373
Holoviak, S. B., 57
Holoviak, S. J., 57
Holzer, H. J., 104
Hoover, Herbert, 419
Horwitz, H. A., 365–366
Hoy, W. K., 10, 12–13, 15
Hunt, H. C., 14, 32
Hyde, A. C., 396

Jackson, D. L., 84
Jeanneret, P. R., 353
Jenkins, R. C., 3
Johns, R. L., 313
Johnson, B., 325
Johnson, R., 344–345
Jones, C., 407
Jones, D., 414
Jordan, K. F., 163, 356, 359, 361, 367
Jung, C. W., 228

Kazanas, H. C., 98
Kazlanskas, E. J., 381
Kelly, C., 263, 268
Kennedy, G., 288–289, 302–303
Kennedy, John, 282
Kindley, M., 385
King, R. A., 65–66, 316
King, W. R., 92
Kitchen, W. E., 316
Knapp, J., 40, 396–397
Knauth, K., 385
Koehler, M., 198
Koehn, H., 413
Kohl, J. P., 104
Kondratieff, N. D., 404, 417–419
Kottkamp, R. B., 323
Kovach, K. A., 35
Koys, R. L., 89
Kydd, C. T., 86

Laabs, J. J., 104
Ladd, E. C., 415
Lazerson, M., 31
Lederer, A. L., 384, 388, 397
Leggett, S., 100
Levine, H. Z., 359
Lewin, Kurt, 13
Lewis, D., 155

Lieberman, M., 278, 295, 297
Likert, Rensis, 15
Lindquist, Victor R., 34
Linn, H. E., 100
Lippitt, Ronald, 13
Littleton, V. C., 104
Livernash, E. R., 314, 334
Long, B. G., 301–302
Long, D. F., 104
Lopez, F. M., 174
Lucio, W. H., 1, 2
Lunenburg, F. C., 22, 29–30
Luthans, F., 35

Mackey, B. C., 337
Manser, B., 16
March, James, 15
Martini, G. R., Jr., 342
Maslow, Abraham H., 15, 217
Mausner, B., 216
Mayo, Elton, 12–13, 15
McCarthy, M. M., 38, 252, 254, 258, 260, 263, 270
McCarthy, S. J., 198
McCollum, J. K., 306
McConaughy, James L., 7
McCormick, 326
McCormick, E. J., 353
McCoy, M. W., 3–4, 126, 277, 284
McGregor, D., 15–16, 18–19, 216
McGregor, E. B., Jr., 387
McIntyre, K. E., 104
McJilton, J. N., 2
McKenzie, C. M., 316
McKeown, M. P., 163, 356, 359, 361, 367
McMahan, G. C., 84
McMillan, J., 288–289, 302–303
McNeil, O., 1–2
McWhirter, D. A., 152, 175
Mecham, R. C., 353
Medley, D. M., 195
Meshoulam, I., 81, 83, 85
Metcalf, H. C., 11, 50, 139
Mickler, M. L., 323
Miles, R. E., 83
Milkovich, G. T., 89
Mintzberg, Henry, 15
Miskel, C. G., 10, 12–13, 15
Mitchell, D. E., 323
Monahan, W. G., 12
Montagno, Ray, 394–395

Montgomery, Daniel, 394–395
Moore, H. E., 4
Morphet, E. L., 313
Moskow, Michael H., 278, 295
Murdick, R. G., 393–394
Murphy, J., 195–196, 201
Murphy, M. J., 294

Nadler, N., 58
Naisbitt, John, 404–406, 421, 423
Neill, S. B., 100
Nelson, F. H., 317
Newland, C. A., 403, 412–413, 415
Newsom, N. W., 2
Niehaus, R. J., 98
Nielsen, D. A., 411
Nixon, Richard, 282
Nkomo, S. M., 82–83
Nolan, R. L., 388
Nolan, T. M., 82, 92–93
Norris, D. R., 306
Norton, A. N., 86
Norton, M. S., 31–33, 36–38, 53, 57, 61, 67–68, 126, 139, 229–233, 277, 284–285
Norton, R. E., 411–412

Oparin, D. I., 404
Oppenheim, L., 86
Ornstein, A. C., 22, 29–30
Orren, G. R., 415
Ouchi, W., 218–219
Owen, P. E., 226

Page, R. N., 90–91
Paget, 326
Parkinson, J., 186, 190, 208
Parsons, Talcott, 9
Patrick, J., 370
Pearce, J. A., III, 35
Pecora, P. J., 368
Perry, C. R., 300
Peters, M. J., 323
Peterson, K. D., 198
Peterson, L. J., 283
Peterson, P. E., 415
Pfeiffer, J. W., 82, 92–93
Picus, L. O., 381
Popham, W. J., 187
Poston, W. K., 325
Pounder, D. G., 187, 189, 207

Power, C., 407, 414
Pratt, P., 381
Provenzo, E. F., Jr., 323

Quasney, J., 381

Raia, A. P., 218
Ratajczak, D., 410, 412
Ray, J. R., 356
Reagan, Ronald, 318, 414–416
Rebore, R. W., 50, 164, 277, 296, 308, 334, 336, 367
Reck, R. R., 301–302
Redeker, J. R., 151–152, 178–179
Rees-Mogg, W., 411
Reich, Robert B., 415
Reichrath, M. R., 89
Reller, T. L., 2
Reynolds, A. S., 369
Rice, A. W., 17
Richards, C., 385
Richardson, J. A., 315
Rieger, S. R., 325
Roethlisberger, Fritz J., 12–13
Rogan, H., 413
Rogers, J. J., 132
Rojot, J., 288
Roosevelt, Franklin D., 8
Rose, L. C., 29, 32–34
Rosenau, D., 418–419
Ross, D., 407, 414
Ross, J. E., 393–394
Rossmiller, R. A., 283
Rossow, L. F., 186, 190, 208
Rostow, W. W., 417–418
Rothwell, W. J., 98
Rowland, K., 361
Rudner, L. M., 255
Ruhl, M., 325
Rumsey, M. J., 232–233
Russell, F., 237
Russell, K. S., 152

St. John, W., 139
Salmon, R. G., 163, 356, 359, 361, 367
Saxe, R. W., 19
Scammon, R. M., 415–416
Schimmel, D., 263, 268
Schlesinger, Arthur M., Jr., 416
Schlesinger, Arthur M., Sr., 416
Schmidt, P., 40

Schoonmaker, A. N., 279, 301
Schultz, R. R., 100
Scott, W. G., 19
Seaman, D. F., 244
Seidler, E. H., 163–164
Sergiovanni, T. J., 17
Shanker, Albert, 32
Shaw, R. C., 100
Shelly, G., 381
Shepard, I. M., 152
Sheridan, J. A., 98
Sherman, A. W., Jr., 163, 314, 317, 334, 353, 360–361, 369
Short, M. L., 370–373
Shuman, J. B., 418–419
Sibon, R. E., 357
Sibson, R. E., 82
Silvern, L. C., 394
Simon, Herbert, 15
Sindt, R. P., 411
Skinner, B. F., 219
Slocum, J. W., 1, 20
Smith, E. C., 94
Smith, T. W., 416
Snow, C. C., 83
Snyderman, B., 16, 216
Sokoloff, H. J., 31
Sperry, D. J., 187, 189, 207, 259
Spuck, D. W., 394
Stahl, O. G., 50
Standohar, P. D., 293
Steele, J., 325
Stephens, D. B., 104
Sterman, J. D., 418, 420
Stiggens, R. J., 193, 195–196, 198, 206–207
Stokes, C. J., 417
Storey, J., 363
Stout, R. T., 39
Strahan, R. D., 295–296
Streitman, H. W., 157
Strevell, W. H., 100
Strong, W. B., 100
Stronge, J. H., 185–186, 207–208
Strouse, J. H., 131–132
Sundquist, J. L., 415
Swan, W. W., 370–373

Tarascio, V. J., 418
Taylor, Frederick W., 4–7, 12, 15, 18
Tead, O., 11, 50, 139

Thompson, S. R., 237
Thompson, W. R., 419
Tichy, N., 83–84
Tinbergen, J., 418
Toch, T., 59
Towne, Henry R., 1
Townsend, M. J., 385–386
Tozer, J. E., 300
Turner, M. J., 139
Tyler, R. W., 58

Uerling, D. F., 241
Uhler, S. F., 337
Urwick, L., 8–9, 393

Valente, W. D., 269–270
Valentine, Jerry W., 190, 194
van Duijn, J. J., 417–418
Van Fleet, D. D., 279
Van Zwoll, J. A., 50
Volz, M. M., 283
Vroom, V. H., 218

Walter, R. L., 283, 295
Ward, Barbara, 404
Warner, G. C., 3
Warren, L., 83–84
Wary, C., 288

Watt, H., 148
Watt, K. E. F., 419
Wattenberg, Ben J., 414–416, 423
Wattenberg, M. P., 414–415
Ways, M., 277
Weatherbee, H. Y., 394
Webb, L. D., 163, 356, 359, 361, 367
Weber, Max, 8–10
Weber, R. P., 418–419
Wendel, F. C., 241
Wesley, E. B., 279
White, Ralph, 13
Whitman, T. S., 396
Wickstrom, R. A., 17
Wildman, A. W., 300
Williams, J. T., 315
Wise, A. E., 39–40
Wittrock, M. C., 197
Wolf, K., 201, 203
Woods, F. H., 237
Wright, P. M., 84

Zimpher, N. L., 325
Zinn, L., 407, 414
Zirkel, P. A., 270
Zubay, A. H., 157
Zuk, L. G., 419

Subject Index

AASA (American Association of School Administrators), 278, 293

AASPA (American Association of School Personnel Administrators), 4, 14, 61, 72–75, 293

Academic freedom, 268
  case study, 147–148
  policy example, 132, 135

Acanfora v. Board of Education, 267

Accountability, 37

Acquired immune deficiency syndrome. *See* AIDS

Across-the-board raises, 322

Additive approach to salary determination, 330–331

Administrative management, 7

Administrative regulation, 112, 114

Administrators. *See also* Human resources director
  performance appraisal, 332
  salaries, 328–335
  supply and demand, 39–40

Adult learners, 243–244

Advanced preparation, 58

Adverse employment decisions, 265–271
  demotions, 269
  dismissals, 253, 266–268
  involuntary transfers, 269
  reassignments, 269
  reduction in force, 54, 270–271
  suspensions, 268–269

Advertisement of position openings, 162, 360

Advisory arbitration, 292, 306

Affirmative action, 104, 271, 423

AFL-CIO, 281

AFT. *See* American Federation of Teachers

Age Discrimination in Employment Act (ADEA), 261, 264, 318

Age distribution of population, 406–407

AIDS (acquired immune deficiency syndrome), 254–255
  policy example, 131–134

Albemarles Paper Company v. Moody, 256

Alfred P. Sloan School of Management, 418

Alternative certification, 39–41

Ambach v. Norwick, 253, 267

American Association of Examiners and Administrators of Educational Personnel, 14

American Association of School Administrators (AASA), 278, 293

American Association of School Personnel Administrators (AASPA), 4, 14, 61, 72–75, 293

American Federation of Labor (AFL), 280

American Federation of Labor-Congress of Industrial Organizations (AFL-CIO), 281

American Federation of Teachers (AFT), 32
  collective negotiations, 277, 279, 281, 283, 296
  membership, 283

American Hospital Supply, 84

American Management Association, 6

American Normal School Association, 2

American Psychological Association, 205

American Society of Mechanical Engineers, 6

Americans with Disabilities Act, 255, 264, 353, 356, 365

Annuity plans, 339

Apple Computer, 40, 385

AppleShare network, 385

Applicant pool, 162

Application procedure, 116–117, 362

Apprenticeship programs, 361

Arbitration

  advisory, 292, 306

  compulsory, 292

  last-best-offer, 292–293

  voluntary binding, 292, 306

Arline v. School Board of Nassau County, 254

Artisoft software company, 385

Arts renaissance, 405

Asians, in U.S. population, 408

Assessment centers

  for performance appraisal, 205–206

  for staff development, 240–241

Assignment, principle of, 9

Assignment of personnel. *See* Staff assignment

Assistant superintendent for personnel, 61

Association of School Business Officials, 387

Athletic coaching, tenure and, 260–261

Atlanta Public School System, 154–155

AT&T, 40, 205

Attribute criteria, 190

Attrition, 98

Authoritarian leadership style, 13–14

Authority, organizational, 10

Automation, 40–43. *See also* Computers; Technology

Baby boomers, 413, 421

Baby busters, 414, 421

Background checks, 163–164, 363–365

Bank failures, 411

Banyon software, 385

Bargaining. *See also* Collective negotiations

  creative, 301–302

  distributive, 278

  integrative, 278, 300–302

  lose-lose, 278, 302

  quasi-integrative, 300

  win-lose, 278

  win-win, 56, 278, 300–302

Bargaining agent, 295–296

Bargaining unit, 294–296

Batch mode, 391

Behavioral interview, 165–179

  conducting, 173–179

  developing, 166–172

  planning form, 167–171

Behavioral science movement, 14–19

  contemporary views, 19–22

Behaviorism, 217

Behavior modification, 217–219

Behavior of Organisms, The (Skinner), 219

Benchmark position, 358

Benefits. *See* Compensation; Indirect compensation

Biotechnology, 406

Blacks

  competency testing, 256

  in U.S. population, 408

Blueouts, 294

Board of Education of County of Gilmer v. Chaddock, 274–275

Board of Trustees of Hamilton Heights School Corporation v. Landry, 268

Body language, 174

Breach of contract, 253

Budgeting, defined, 393

Bureaucracy, 9–10

Business failures, 412

Bylaws, 112, 114

Cafeteria benefits plans, 344–345

Calhoun v. Cassady, 269

Campus Incentive Program, 324

Capacity of equilibrium, 15

Career development planning, 242

Career ladders, 325–326

Carnegie Forum on Education and the Economy, 319

Cathode ray tube (CRT), 381

CD-ROM disks, 398

Central human resources administrator. *See* Human resources director

Central human resources unit, 60–64

  collective negotiations and, 284–285

  organization of, 61–62

  site-based management and, 62–64

Central processing unit (CPU), 382

Certification, 38

  alternative, 39–41

  legal aspects, 252–253

  nonrenewal, 252–253

  recertification, 252–253

  revocation of, 252

  suspension of, 252

Chalk v. United States District Court, 255

Chancery Software Ltd., 387

Chance v. Board of Examiners, 256

Charismatic authority, 10

Chief executive, 7

Child care benefits, 36, 343–344

Choice, 29

Citizenship requirements, 253–254

Civic leave, 341

Civilian labor force, 412

Civil Rights Act, 255–256, 264–265, 318, 355

Civil Rights Division v. Amphitheater Unified School District, 265

Classified personnel. *See* Support personnel

Classroom observation. *See* Observation

Class size, 37, 56, 285

Clayton Act, 280

Cleveland Board of Education v. Loudermill, 263

Client survey, 201

Clinical supervision, 241–242

Coaching. *See* Athletic coaching; Mentoring

Codification systems, 118–125

Cohabitation, 267

Cohort survival forecasting method, 100–101

Collective bargaining. *See* Bargaining; Collective negotiations

Collective negotiations, 31, 55–56, 270–271, 277–278. *See also* Bargaining; Impasse procedures

    AFT and, 277, 279, 281, 283, 296

    bargaining agent, 295–296

    bargaining unit, 294–296

    central human resources unit and, 284–285

    compensation and, 316–317

    competencies for, 285

    contract agreements

      costing out, 288

      implementation, 304–306

    cost analysis, 286–288

    defined, 278

    goals and objectives, 288–289

    ground rules, 289–290

    history of, 279–284

    human resources director and, 285, 298

    information gathering, 286–288

    meeting rules, 289–290

    NEA and, 278–279, 282–283, 296

    negotiations team, 296–300

    planning, 286

    procedural considerations, 289

    process of, 286

    proposals and counterproposals, 302–304

    scope of, 290–291

    strikes, 31, 277, 284, 293–294

    table strategies, 300–304

Columbia Computing Services, 387

Columbia University, 4

Commonwealth v. Hunt, 280

Communicable diseases, 254–255

    policy example, 131–134

Communication principle, 15

Community of interest, 295

Compensation, 33–36, 56–57, 313. *See also* Direct compensation; Indirect compensation

    collective negotiations and, 316–317

    competency and, 319

    determinants of, 314–318

      ability to pay, 316

      collective negotiations, 317

      cost of living, 316–317

      government regulations, 318

      prevailing wage rate, 317

      supply and demand, 314–316

    discrimination in, 318

    for extracurricular activities, 326–331

    legislation on, 319

    policy development, 313–314

    unemployment compensation, 336

    workers' compensation, 336

Competency, 64–67

    for collective negotiations, 285

    compensation and, 319

    defined, 64–65

    indicators of, 65

Competency testing

    blacks, 256

    legal aspects, 255–257

    minorities, 255–256

    of practicing educators, 257

Competition, 410–411

Compulsory arbitration, 292

Computer-based training, 369

Computer-generated contracts, 396–397

Computer-generated reports, 390–391, 396–397

Computer hardware, 380–382

Computer keyboard, 381

Computers, 40–43. *See also* Technology

    applicant pool creation, 162

    components of, 381–385

      hardware, 380–382

      software, 382–385

    data, 391–394

    database system, 389–391, 393–395

    data entry methods, 381, 390

    educational applications, 380–381

Computers, *continued*
  electronic data processing, 380, 388–391
  forecasting models, 397
  human resources information system, 379,
    388–391, 396–398
  input, 383
  local area network, 385–387
  networks, 385–387
  output, 384
  processing, 383–384
Computer simulation, 397–398, 418
Computer software, 382–385
Conference of Teacher Examiners, 61
Confidentiality, 152, 163, 267
Connecticut v. Teal, 256
Conservatism, 416
Consultants, 14
Consumer price index (CPI), 317, 409–410
Continental Illinois Bank, 420
Contingency approaches, 19
Contingency model of leadership, 20–22
Contingency variables, 20
Continuing education. *See* Staff development
Continuing status. *See* Tenure
Contract agreements
  costing out, 288
  implementation, 304–306
Contract language, 304–305
Contract law, 257–259
Contracts, computer-generated, 396–397
Contract violation, 252–253
Convention expenses, 343
Cooperation, 15, 30–31
Coordinating, defined, 393
Coordinators, 14
Corning Glass Works, 84
Cost of benefits (COB), 33–36, 334
Cost-of-living (COL) clause, 317
Cost-of-living index, 316–317
Council of Professors of Instructional Supervision, 237
Counseling programs, 232–234
County Institute, 3
County superintendent, 2–3
CPU (central processing unit), 382
Creative bargaining, 301–302
Creative Experience (Follett), 11
Credentials checks, 164
Credit unions, 342
Criminal background checks, 164
Criterion-referenced evaluation, 187

CRT (cathode ray tube), 381
CTB District Planner, 387
Cultural nationalism, 406
Cultural types, 90–91
Cyberphobia, 42

Data
  decision making and, 391–393
  versus information, 393–394
Database manager, 395
Database system, 389–391, 393–395
Data Communications Sourcebook (Townsend),
  386
Data entry, 381, 390
Daury v. Smith, 254
Davies-Brickell System (DBS), 115, 118–125
Debt and deficit, U.S., 314
Decentralization, 405
Decision making, 405
  data and, 391–393
  strategic, 391–392
DeKalb County School District (Georgia), 396
Demand. *See* Supply and demand
Demand report, 390
Democratic administration, 14
Democratic leadership style, 13–14
Democratic personnel practices, 14
Democratic supervision, 14
Democratic teaching, 14
Demographic trends, 406–409
Demotions, 269
Deregulation, 415
De Shon v. Bettendorf Community School District,
  261
Diary analysis, 353
Differentiated staffing concept, 324–325
Direct compensation, 318–319, 420. *See also*
  Compensation; Incentive pay plans; Indirect
  compensation
  across-the-board raises, 322
  additive approach, 330–331
  administrator salaries, 328–335
  entry-level salaries, 34
  for extracurricular activities, 326–331
  independent approaches, 331–332
  index approach, 329
  market sensitive salaries, 326
  minimum salaries, 318–319
  point-factor method, 332–334
  salary studies, 357–358

single salary schedule, 10, 319–322
support personnel salaries, 357–359
teacher salaries, 10, 33–34, 284, 319–322
test-based salaries, 256
Directing, defined, 393
Director of human resources. *See* Human resources
director
Disability insurance, 339
Discrimination, 264–265
in compensation, 318
in employment, 254–255
handicapped, 254–255
sex, 261, 265
Discriminatory treatment, 264
Dismissals, 253, 266–268
policy example, 136, 139–145
Disparate impact, 264–265
Distributive bargaining, 278
Distributive strategy, 300
Division of labor, 8, 10
Domination, taxonomy of, 10
Douglass teacher load formula, 228–229
Drive-reinforcement theory, 217
Due process, 208–209, 261–264, 266
procedural, 209, 261–263
substantive, 208–209, 261, 263–264

Early retirement programs, 337
Economic trends, 404–405, 409–412
long wave theory, 417–420
Ecotran Systems, Inc., 100
Education, demand for, 314–315
Educational Data Systems, 101
Educational engineering, 7
Educational institutions, recruitment from, 360–361
Educational Policies Commission, 281
Educational Policy System of the National School
Boards Association (EPS/NSBA), 115, 118, 125
Educational policy systems, 115–118
Educational productivity plans, 324
Educational reform, 27–28, 185, 319
Educational Testing Service, 256
Education Amendments of 1972, 264
Education Logistics, Inc., 101
EDULOG, 101
EEOC (Equal Employment Opportunity
Commission), 104, 136, 264, 359, 362–363, 365
Effectiveness, defined, 15
Efficiency, 6–7, 15
Elderly population, 406–407

Electronic bulletin boards, 105, 162
Electronic data processing (EDP), 380, 388–391.
See also Computers
stages of, 388
Eligibility lists, 366
Emergency leave, 340
Employee assistance program (EAP), 57, 136,
232–234, 342
Employee benefits. *See* Indirect compensation
Employee diaries, 353
Employee introduction. *See* Orientation
Employee referrals, 361
Employee relations, 278
Employee services. *See* Indirect compensation
Employees' handbook, 367
Employee training. *See* Staff development; Training
Employment. *See also* Adverse employment decisions
discrimination and, 254–255
legal aspects, 251–252
certification, 252–253
citizenship and residency requirements, 253–254
competency testing, 255–257
contracts, 257–259
health requirements, 254–255
mandatory retirement, 261
physical requirements, 254–255
tenure, 259–261
Employment agencies, 360
Employment application, 116–117, 362
Employment interviews, 164–179, 365
behavioral interview, 165–179
impermissible inquiries, 362
interview questions, 175–178
preliminary interview, 165, 362–363
Employment tests, 363
Empowerment, 28–29
Encyclopedia of Educational Research, 188
End-of-year clause, 317
Enrollment projection, 100–101, 397
Ensley Branch, NAACP v. Seibels, 256
Entitlement, 413
Entrepreneurial culture, 90
Entry-level salaries, 34
Environmental inputs, 19
Environmental scanning, 86, 88–91
Equal Employment Opportunity Act of 1972, 318
Equal Employment Opportunity Commission
(EEOC), 104, 136, 264, 359, 362–363, 365
Equal Pay Act, 264, 318
Equal protection clause, 255–256, 264

Equilibrium
  capacity of, 15
  defined, 216
Escalator clause, 317
Ethics, 72–75
Evaluation. *See also* Performance appraisal
  criterion-referenced, 187
  formative, 187
  norm-referenced, 187
  of staff development, 237
  summative, 187
  of training, 370
  types, 187–189
Exceptions report, 390–391
Exclusive representation, 295–296
Exemplar standard, 266–267
Expansion stage of electronic data processing, 388
Expectancy theory of motivation, 218
External mandates, 38–39
External scanning, 88–89
Extinction, 219
Extracurricular activities, compensation for, 326–331

Fact finding, 292
Fair Labor Standards Act (FLSA), 318, 338
Family leave, 36
Family unit, changes in, 408
Farm Credit System, 411–412, 420
Far West Laboratory, 243
Federal deficit, 413
Federal Deposit Insurance Corporation, 411
Federal Farm Credit System, 411–412, 420
Federal Labor Relations Council, 282
Federal Reserve System, 419
Federal Service Impasse Panel, 282
Feedback, 19
Fertility rate, 407
Ficus v. Board of School Trustees of Central School District, 266
Fields v. Hallsville Independent School District, 257
First preference, 304–305
First Universal Nation, The (Wattenberg), 414
Flexible benefits plans, 344–345, 421
Flextime work schedules, 36, 42
Floyd County Board of Education v. Slone, 253
Food service, subsidized, 343
Forecasting, 97–101, 403
  cohort survival method, 100–101
  computer models, 397
  personnel needs, 98–99
  student enrollments, 100–101, 397

  teacher demand, 315–316
Foreign competition, 410–411
Formalization stage of electronic data processing, 388
Formal observation, 195–196
Formative evaluation, 187
Fourteenth Amendment, 255–256, 261, 264
Fragmentation, 295
Free-market socialism, 406
Fringe benefits. *See* Indirect compensation
Function Job Analysis (FJA), 355
Functions of the Executive, The (Barnard), 14

Gallup Poll, 29, 32, 413
Gantt charts, 6
Gantt Medal, 6
Gap analysis, 91, 93
Gaylord v. Tacoma School District No. 10, 267
General Electric Corporation, 205, 388
Generic Performance Appraisal System for Classified Employees (GPASCE), 370–371
Georgia Association of Educators v. Nix, 256
Global economy, 404–405
Global lifestyles, 406
Goals, 111–112
  collective negotiations, 288–289
  staff development, 237
Governing board policies, 112
Government regulations, compensation and, 318
Grand Prairie Independent School District v. Vaughn, 253
Graying of America, 406–407
Great Depression, 419
Green v. Board of Education, 270
Grievance procedure, 305–307
Griggs v. Duke Power Company, 256, 265
Gross domestic product (GDP), 409–410
Group life insurance, 338–339

Halo effect, 178, 195
Handbook of Research on Teaching, 196
Handicapped, discrimination against, 254–255
Hard copy, 382
Hardware, 380–382
Hawthorne effect, 12
Hawthorne studies, 12–13
Health care costs, 35–36
Health care programs, 338, 343, 422
Health insurance, 337
Health Maintenance Organization (HMO) Act of 1973, 318
Health maintenance organizations (HMOs), 338

Health policy, 131–134

Health requirements, legal aspects of, 254–255

Hispanics, in U.S. population, 408

HIV (human immunodeficiency virus), 131

Homosexuality, 267

Hospitalization insurance, 337

HRIS (human resources information system), 379, 388–391, 396–398

HRIS Software Buyer's Guide, 387

Human capital, 422

Human immunodeficiency virus (HIV), 131

Human relationships, 30–31

Human relations movement, 11–14

Human resources administration, 27–28. *See also* Strategic human resources planning

   alternative certification and, 39–41

   behavioral science movement and, 14–19

     contemporary views, 19–22

   compensation issues, 33–36

   cooperation and, 15, 30–31

   defined, 50–51

   demands on professional personnel, 36–37

   demographic trends, 406–409

   economic trends, 404–405, 409–412

   external mandates, 38–39

   future trends, 403–404, 420–424

   general trends, 404–406

   history, 1–4

   human relationships and, 30–31

   human relations movement and, 11–14

   legal impacts, 38–39

   long wave theory and, 417–420

   political trends, 414–416

   problems of, 68–72

   quality and, 32–33

   school governance and, 28–30

   scientific management and, 4–11

   social trends, 412–414

   supply and demand issues, 39–40

   technology and, 40–43

Human resources development, 51, 58–59. *See also* Staff development

Human resources director, 61

   collective negotiations and, 285, 298

   on negotiations team, 298

   position analysis for, 68

   position description for, 68–70

Human resources environment, 51, 59–60

Human resources information system (HRIS), 379, 388–391, 396–398

Human resources operational plan, 86, 94–96

Human resources process, 51–60

   development, 51, 58–59

   environment, 51, 59–60

   utilization, 51–57

Human resources utilization, 51–57

Human Side of Enterprise, The (McGregor), 18

Hygienes, 16

IBM, 84, 205, 386

Idiographic dimension, 216

Immorality, 252, 266–267

Impasse procedures, 282, 291–294

   advisory arbitration, 292, 306

   compulsory arbitration, 292

   fact finding, 292

   last-best-offer arbitration, 292–293

   mediation, 291

   strikes, 31, 277, 284, 293–294

   voluntary binding arbitration, 292, 306

Impermissible inquiries, 362

Imports, 410–411

In-basket exercise, 398

Incentive pay plans, 5, 33–34, 56, 322–326

   career ladders, 325–326

   educational productivity plans, 324

   market sensitive salaries, 326

   master teacher plans, 324–325

   merit pay, 10, 33–34, 323–324

Incompetency, 252, 267–268

Independent approaches to salary determination, 331–332

Index approach to salary determination, 329

Index of load, 228–229

Indirect compensation, 57, 334–335. *See also* Compensation; Direct compensation

   availability in 1990, 338

   cafeteria plans, 344–345

   cost of, 33–36, 334

   flexible benefits plans, 344–345, 421

   income equivalent payments, 341–344

     child care, 36, 343–344

     credit unions, 342

     employee assistance programs, 57, 136, 232–234, 342

     meeting and convention expenses, 343

     organization dues, 343

     subsidized food service, 343

     transportation allowance, 343

     tuition reimbursement, 36, 342

     wellness programs, 343

   legally required benefits, 335–336

Indirect compensation, *continued*
   as maintainer, 334
   as motivator, 334
   NEA policy, 35
   pay for time not worked, 340–341
     civic leave, 341
     emergency leave, 340
     jury duty leave, 341
     military leave, 341
     personal leave, 340
     professional leave, 341
     religious leave, 341
     sabbatical leave, 340–341
     sick leave, 340
     vacation leave, 340
   private welfare and security programs, 337–340
     group life insurance, 338–339
     health and hospitalization insurance, 337
     health maintenance organizations, 318, 338
     long-term disability insurance, 339
     professional liability insurance, 339–340
     severance pay, 339
     tax-sheltered annuity plans, 339
   state retirement plans, 336–337
Individualism, 406
Induction. *See* Orientation
Inflation, 409
Informal observation, 195
Information
   for collective negotiations, 286–288
   versus data, 393–394
   defined, 394
   realtime, 391–392
Information Age, 423
Informational society, 404
Information handbook, 223–224
Information management systems concept, 379, 391, 393–395
Information systems, 389–391
Initial stage of electronic data processing, 388
In-kind payments. *See* Indirect compensation
Input (computers), 383
In-service training, 3, 58. *See also* Staff development
Instrumentality, 218
Insubordination, 268
Insurance
   disability, 339
   health, 337
   hospitalization, 337
   liability, 339–340

   life, 338–339
Integrated culture, 90
Integrated database, 389–391
Integrative bargaining, 278, 300–302
Intentions, defined, 130
Interactive culture, 90
Internal Revenue Service, 345
Internal scanning, 89–91
International Congress on the Assessment Center, 205–206
International Foundation of Employee Benefits Plans, 36
Interstate commerce, 280
Interviews. *See* Employment interviews
Introduction of employees. *See* Orientation
Invasion of privacy, 152, 163, 267
Involuntary transfers, 269

Job analysis. *See* Position analysis
Job classification, support personnel, 355
Job descriptions. *See also* Position descriptions
   support personnel, 356
   union influence, 356
Job restructuring, 421
Job rotation, 242–243
Job satisfaction, 16
Job stress, 36, 42, 232
Joint Committee on Standards for Educational Evaluation, 208
Joint problem solving (JPS), 301–302
Jones v. Alabama State Tenure Commission, 259
Jury duty leave, 341
Just cause, 263

Keefe v. Geanakos et al., 147–148
Keyboard, 381
King v. Board of Trustees, 261

Labor agreement discussion. *See* Collective negotiations
Labor force, 412
   women in, 408, 421
Labor Management Relations Act, 281
Labor Management Reporting and Disclosure Act, 281
Lagos v. Modesto City School District, 260
Laissez-faire leadership style, 13–14
LAN (local area network), 385–387
Landrum-Griffin Act, 281
Language
   of contracts, 304–305
   of policies, 130
LANtastic network, 385

Last-best-offer arbitration, 292–293
Law, defined, 112
Leader-member relations, 21
Leader position power, 21
Leadership
  contingency model, 20–22
  peer-assisted, 243
  styles, 13–14
  women in, 406
Lead teacher, 324–325
Learning Age, 423
Legal authority, 10
Legal issues, 38–39, 251. *See also under* Employment
  adverse employment decisions, 265–271
  contract law, 257–259
  discrimination, 254–255, 261, 264–265, 318
  due process, 208–209, 261–264, 266
  performance appraisal standards, 208–209
  required benefits, 335–336
Letters of reference, 163
Liability insurance, 339–340
Liberalism, 416
Liberty interest, 262
Liberty rights, 60
Licensure requirement, 252–253
Life insurance, 338–339
Line administrator, 62
Listening skills, 174–175, 303
Load index, 228–229
Local area network (LAN), 385–387
Long-term disability insurance, 339
Long-term management objectives, 404
Long wave theory, 417–420
Lose-lose bargaining, 278, 302

Mac School, 387
Management
  defined, 393
  long-term objectives, 404
  by objectives, 218
Management and the Worker (Roethlisberger and Dickson), 13
Management by objectives (MBO), 218
Management information system (MIS), 379, 391, 393–395
Managing by Objectives (Raia), 218
Mandates, 38–39
Mandatory retirement, legal aspects of, 261
MAPNET system, 100–101
Market sensitive salaries, 326

Markovian analysis, 98–99
Marxism, 417
Maslow's hierarchy of basic needs, 217
Massachusetts Institute of Technology (MIT), 418
Master teacher plans, 324–325
Mathews v. Eldridge, 262
Maturity stage of electronic data processing, 388
McClelland v. Paris Public Schools, 254
Mediation, 291
Medical examination, 343, 365–366
Medicare, 336
Meet and confer, 278, 284. *See also* Collective negotiations
Meeting expenses, 343
Meeting rules, for collective negotiations, 289–290
Megatrends (Naisbitt), 404–406, 423
Megatrends 2000 (Naisbitt and Aburdene), 404–406, 423
Mentoring, 222–223, 225, 238, 241, 325
Mentor teacher, 325
Merck, 84
Merit pay, 10, 33–34, 323–324
  NEA policy, 34
Methods of Scheduling Salaries for Teachers, 320
Microcomputers. *See* Computers
Midvale Steel Works, 6
Military leave, 341
Millennial trends, 405–406
Millennium, religious revival and, 406
Miller v. Independent School District, 262
Minimum salaries, 318–319
Minorities
  competency testing, 255–256
  percentage of U.S. population, 407–408
  representation among personnel, 28
Mission statement, 91–93, 154
Modernization, 416
Motivation, 215
  expectancy theory, 218
  needs theory, 217
  path-goal theory, 218
  theories of, 216–219
  two-factor theory of, 15–18
Motivation to Work, The (Herzberg), 16
Motivators, 16
MPSMS dimension (materials, products, subject matter, services), 353
Multimedia, 398, 423
Multiple representation, 295–296
Multiyear planning format, 84

National Association of Personnel Consultants, 360

National Association of School Administrators, 240

National Association of School Superintendents, 2, 279

National Association of Secondary School Principals (NASSP), 205, 380

National Association of State Directors of Teacher Education and Certification, 164

National Board for Professional Teacher Standards, 203

National Center for Education Statistics, 39

National Commission on Excellence in Education, 319, 326

National Commission on Excellence in Education Administration, 39

National debt, 413

National Development Council, 237

National Education Association (NEA), 2, 280
  collective negotiations and, 278–279, 282–283, 296
  employee benefits policy, 35
  membership, 283
  merit pay policy, 34
  single salary schedule policy, 10
  strike policy, 293

National Institute of Education, 59

National Labor Relations Act, 280

National School Boards Association (NSBA)
  Educational Policy System, 115, 118, 125
  performance appraisal policy, 188
  strike policy, 293

National School Improvement Project, 237

National Society for the Study of Education, 7

National Teachers Association (NTA), 2, 279–280

National Teachers Exam (NTE), 255–256

NEA. *See* National Education Association

Need analysis, 103

Needs theory of motivation, 217

Negativism, 97

Neglect of duty, 252

Negotiation. *See* Collective negotiations

Negotiations team, 296–300
  human resources director and, 298

NetWare network, 385

Networks, 385–387

Newman v. Crews, 256

Nixon v. Board of Cooperative Educational Services, 260

Nomothetic dimension, 216

Noncertificated personnel. *See* Support personnel

Nonrenewal of certification, 252–253

Nonverbal behaviors, 174

Normal School Association, 279

Norm-referenced evaluation, 187

Norris-LaGuardia Act, 280

Norton/Bria teacher load formula, 229–231

Norwalk Teachers Association v. Board of Education, 283

Note taking, 175

Novell software company, 385

NSBA. *See* National School Boards Association

NTA (National Teachers Association), 2, 279–280

NTE (National Teachers Exam), 255–256

Nuclear family, 408

Objectives
  collective negotiations, 288–289
  management, 218, 404
  staff development, 237
  strategic, 91, 93, 154–155

Observation
  formal, 195–196
  informal, 195
  for performance appraisal, 195–196
  for position analysis, 353–355

Observer, 298–299

Off-the-job training, 369

Oklahoma City Public Schools, 324

Old-Age, Survivors, Disability and Health Insurance System, 335–336

Olympia Computing Company, 387

101 Templates for School Business Administration, 387

ONPASS planning system, 101

On-the-job training, 368–369. *See also* Staff development

Operant conditioning, 217

Operational decisions, 391–392

Operational planning, 86, 94–96

Opportunities, 89

Optical scanner, 381, 390

Orange County Public Schools (Florida), 385

Organizational authority, 10

Organizational climate, 59–60

Organizational culture, 59–60

Organization dues, 343

Organization effectiveness, principle of, 9

Organizing, defined, 393

Orientation, 54–55
  for beginning teachers, 224–225
  for new teaching personnel, 224–225
  operational procedures, 220–224
  postemployment, 222–224

preemployment, 221–222
  for support personnel, 367–368
Osiris system, 387
Output (computers), 384
Outputs, 19

Pacific Rim, 406, 408
Palmer v. Board of Trustees, 270
Palmer v. Ticcione, 261
Papers on the Science of Administration (Urwick), 9
Parallel testing, 384
Parental choice of school attendance, 29
Parochialism, 97
Passwords, 385
Path-goal theory of motivation, 218
PC LAN network, 386
Peer-assisted leadership (PAL), 243
Peer review, 198, 201
Pension funds, 421
Performance appraisal, 58–59, 242, 271. *See also*
    Evaluation
  for administrators, 332
  criteria for, 190–193
  data collection procedures, 194–195
    assessment centers, 205–206
    observation, 195–196
    peer review, 198, 201
    portfolios, 201–205
    rating scales, 195
    self-evaluation, 196–200
    student performance data, 206–207
    survey of clients, 201
  as district priority, 185–186
  legal standards for, 208–209
  NSBA policy, 188
  policy for, 130–131
  program appraisal and review, 207
  purposes of, 186–189
  reliability of, 208
  sample form, 211
  standards for, 193–194
  for support personnel, 370–373
  technical standards for, 207–208
  utility of, 208
  validity of, 207–208
Performance-based criteria, 190–193
Performance pay schedules. *See* Merit pay
Personal growth activities, 367
Personal leave, 340
Personal problems, 232–234

Personnel
  demands on, 36–37
  mix of, 85–86
  protection of, 60
  welfare of, 56–57
Personnel administration. *See* Human resources
    administration
Personnel Administration (Tead and Metcalf), 11, 50
Personnel administrative assistant, 61
Personnel director. *See* Human resources director
Personnel evaluation. *See* Performance appraisal
Personnel information handbook, 223–224
Personnel Journal, 387
Personnel needs, forecasting, 98–99
Personnel policies. *See* Policies
Personnel recruitment. *See* Recruitment
Personnel services, stability of, 57
Personnel specialist, 61
Philadelphia Cordwainers Case, 280
Physical requirements, legal aspects of, 254–255
Pittsburgh Federation of Teachers v. Aaron, 253
Planning, defined, 81–82, 393
Point-factor salary determination method, 332–334
Policies, 111–112
  adoption of, 128
  benefits of, 112–114
  codification of, 118–125
  for compensation, 313–314
  criteria for, 114–115
  development model, 127–128
  development of, 115–118, 125–128
  effectiveness of, 129–131
  examples, 131–140
    academic freedom, 132, 135
    AIDS, 131–134
    communicable diseases, 131–134
    dismissal, 136, 139–145
    sexual harassment, 136–138
  for health, 131–134
  language of, 130
  for performance appraisal, 130–131
  planning, 114
  for safety, 131–134
  for staff development, 236–237
  strategic planning and, 101–102
  topical headings for, 115–118
Policy, defined, 114
Policy and regulation manual, 223
Policy systems, 115–118
Political trends, 414–416

Population
  age distribution, 406–407
  Asians, 408
  blacks, 408
  elderly, 406–407
  geographic shift in, 405
  Hispanics, 408
  minorities, 407–408
  race distribution, 407–408
Portfolios, 201–205
POSDCoRB paradigm, 8, 50
Position analysis, 152–157
  example, 158–161
  for human resources director, 68
  job analysis for support personnel, 352–355
  observation for, 353–355
Position Analysis Questionnaire (PAQ), 353
Position application procedure, 116–117, 362
Position descriptions, 157, 162
  for human resources director, 68–70
  job description for support personnel, 356
Position openings, advertisement of, 162, 360
Position profile, 226–227
Positive reinforcement, 219
Possessiveness, 97
Postemployment orientation, 222–224
PRAM model for win-win bargaining, 301–302
Predictive report, 391
Preemployment medical examination, 343, 365–366
Preemployment orientation, 221–222
Preemployment testing, 152
Pregnancy Discrimination Act of 1978, 318
Preliminary interview, 165, 362–363
Pre-Professional Skills Test (PPST), 255
Preservice programs. *See* Orientation
President's Commission for a National Agenda for the Eighties, 413
Privacy rights, 152, 163, 267
Privatization, 406
Probationary teachers, 259–260
Problem solving, 301–302
Procedural due process, 209, 261–263
Procedure, defined, 112
Processing (computers), 383–384
Productivity plans, 324
Professional growth, 58. *See also* Staff development
Professional leave, 341
Professional liability insurance, 339–340
Professional negotiations. *See* Collective negotiations
Professional organizations, recruitment from, 361

Professional relations, 278
Property interest, 262
Property rights, 60
Psychiatric examination, 254
Psychic income, 56
Psychometric tests, 363
Pullman-Standard v. Swint, 264

Quality circles, 238–239
Quality issues, 32–33
Quasi-distributive strategy, 300
Quasi-integrative bargaining, 300

Racial distribution of population, 407–408
Racine Unified School District v. LIRC, 254
Railroad Labor Act, 280
Rand Corporation, 59
Rating scales, 195
Realtime information, 391–392
Reassignments, 269
Recertification, 252–253
Recorder, 299
Recruitment, 53–54
  sources for, 360–361
  for strategic planning, 102–105
  for support personnel, 359–361
Recurrent education. *See* Staff development
Reduction in force (RIF), 54
  tenure and, 270–271
Reference checks, 163
Reference letters, 163
Reform movement, 27–28, 185, 319
Regulation, defined, 112
Regulation development. *See* Policies
Regulation manual, 223
Rehabilitation Act of 1973, 254, 264
Relational database, 389–391
Relationships, 30–31
Religious leave, 341
Religious revival, 406
Renewal. *See* Staff development
Reopener clause, 317
Reporting, defined, 393
Reports, computer-generated, 390–391, 396–397
Residency requirements, 253–254
Resources planning, 53
Resource teacher, 14
Restructuring, 28–30, 62–64
Results criteria, 190
Resume Software, 40

Retirement
    early, 337
    mandatory, 261
    state-run plans, 336–337
Revocation of certification, 252
Richardson v. Lamar County Board of Education,
    253, 256
RIF. *See* Reduction in force
RPTIM model for staff development, 237
Rule, defined, 112

Sabbatical leave, 340–341
Safety policy, 131–134
Salaries. *See* Direct compensation
Salary studies, 357–358
Savings and loan failure, 411, 420
Scalar chain, 8
Scheduled reports, 390
School, as social system, 215–216
School board agreements, 278
School board attorney, 298–299
School boards, 297
    conflicts with, 30–31
School choice, 29
School governance, 28–30
School Improvement Project (SIP), 237
School law, 38–39
Schoolmaster system, 387
School organization, evolutionary stage of, 85
School restructuring, 28–30, 62–64
Scientific education, 7
Scientific management, 4–11
Scientific Management (Taylor), 5
Screening and selection process, 53–54, 151–152.
        See also Position analysis; Position descriptions
    advertisement of positions, 162, 360
    applicant pool, 162
    background checks, 163–164, 363–365
    interviewing, 164–179, 365
        behavioral, 165–179
        preliminary, 165, 362–363
    notification of unsuccessful candidates, 179
    offer of position, 179
    paper screening, 162
    preemployment testing, 152
    support personnel, 362–366
Sears, 205
Section 504 (Rehabilitation Act), 254, 264
Security programs. *See* Indirect compensation
Select committees, 1–2

Selection process. *See* Screening and selection process
Selectmen, 1–2
Self-evaluation, 196–200
Self-interest, 413
Self-reliance, 405
Self-renewal, 58
Seniority, 270–271
Severance pay, 339
Sex discrimination, 261, 265
Sexual harassment policy, 136–138
Sexual misconduct, 266–267
Shadow groups, 242
Shaping, 219
Sherburne v. School Board of Swannee County, 267
Sherman Antitrust Act, 280
Sherman v. School Committee of Whitman, 270
Shortage of teachers, 27, 39–40, 53, 326, 420
Sick leave, 340
Signaling techniques, 304
Significant risk, 255
Simonds Rolling Machine Company, 5
Simulations, 397–398, 418
Single parent families, 408
Single salary schedule, 319–322
    NEA policy, 10
Singleton v. Jackson Municipal Separate School
        District, 269
Site-based management, 28–29, 421
    central human resources unit and, 62–64
Social Security Act of 1935, 318, 335–336
Social systems model, 215–216, 235
Social trends, 412–414
Sociotechnology, 42
Software, 382–385
Sorenson v. School District No. 28, 253
Spaceship Earth (Ward), 404
Special education mandates, 38
Special interest politics, 415
Specialization concept, 8–10
Spokesperson, 298
Staff administrator, 62
Staff assignment, 55, 225–231
    involuntary transfers, 269
    job rotation, 242–243
    reassignment, 269
    support personnel, 366
    work load and, 227–231
Staff development, 58, 234–243. *See also* Orientation;
        Performance appraisal
    evaluation of, 237

Staff development, *continued*
  goals and objectives, 237
  methods and strategies, 238–243
    assessment centers, 240–241
    career development planning, 242
    clinical supervision, 241–242
    job rotation, 242–243
    mentoring, 222–223, 225, 238, 241, 325
    peer-assisted leadership, 243
    quality circles, 238–239
    shadow groups, 242
    task force groups, 242
    teacher center, 239–240
  operational procedures, 235–237
  policy for, 236–237
  program planning, 237
  purposes of, 235
  RPTIM model, 237
  for support personnel, 366–370
Staffing, defined, 393
Staff orientation. *See* Orientation
Standfield v. Turnbow, 257
State of Texas v. Project Principle, 257
State retirement plans, 336–337
Strategic business planning, 83–84
Strategic decisions, 391–392
Strategic human resources planning
  characteristics, 84–85
  correlation with system plan, 96–97
  defined, 81–84
  evolutionary stage of school organization, 85
  forecasting, 97–101
    personnel needs, 98–99
    student enrollment, 100–101, 397
  model, 86–96
  personnel recruitment, 102–105
  policy development and, 101–102
  professional staff mix, 85–86
Strategic objectives, 91, 93, 154–155
Strategic plan, 86, 91–96
Strategy, defined, 81
Strategy development, 91, 93–94
Strengths, 89
Stress, 36, 42, 232
Strikes, 31, 277, 284, 293–294
  NEA policy, 293
  NSBA policy, 293
Structured task, 21
Student enrollment, forecasting, 100–101, 397
Student performance data, 206–207
Substantive due process, 208–209, 261, 263–264

Summative evaluation, 187
Superintendents, 30–31, 297–298
Supervisor, 14
Supervisor of personnel. *See* Human resources
    director
Supplementary service positions, tenure and, 260–261
Supply and demand, 39–40
  administrators, 39–40
  compensation and, 314–316
  demand for education, 314–315
  studies of, 103
  teachers, 39–40, 315–316
Support personnel, 351–352
  assignment of, 366
  classification system, 352–357
  job analysis, 352–355
  job classification, 355
  job descriptions, 356
  orientation, 367–368
  performance appraisal, 370–373
  recruitment, 359–361
  responsibility for, 351–352
  salary determination, 357–359
  selection process, 362–366
  staff development, 366–370
  training, 368–370
Survey of clients, 201
Suspension of certification, 252
Suspensions, 268–269
Swanson v. Houston Independent School District, 257
Syntality, 59–60
System, defined, 394
Systematized culture, 90
System Dynamics Group (SDG), 418
System Dynamics National Model, 419
System operational plans, 95–96
Systems theory, 19–20

Table strategies for negotiation, 300–304
Tactical decisions, 391–392
Taft-Hartley Act, 281
Task force groups, 242
Tasks, 21, 64
Task system, 5–6
Taxonomy of domination, 10
Tax Reform Act of 1986, 415
Tax-sheltered annuity plans, 339
Teacher Assessment Project, 203
Teacher center, 239–240
Teacher certification. *See* Certification
Teacher empowerment, 28–29

Teacher evaluation. *See* Performance appraisal
Teacher Identification Clearinghouse (TIC), 164
Teacher pool, size of, 420–421
Teachers
  projected demand for, 315–316
  supply and demand, 39–40, 315–316
  turnover rate, 37, 315
Teacher salaries. *See* Direct compensation
Teacher shortage, 27, 39–40, 53, 326, 420
Teacher testing. *See* Competency testing
Teacher work load. *See* Work load
Teaching career, 421
Technology, 40–43, 379–380. *See also* Computers
  future of, 398, 423–424
  insensitivity of, 404
Teleconferencing, 40
Tenure
  athletic coaching and, 260–261
  legal aspects, 259–261
  reduction in force and, 270–271
  supplementary service positions, 260–261
Term life insurance, 339
Test-based salaries, 256
Testing. *See also* Competency testing
  employment, 363
  parallel, 384
  preemployment, 152
  psychometric, 363
Theory X, 18
Theory Y, 18–19, 218
Theory Z, 218–219
Threats, 89
3Com software company, 385
Time-off-with-pay provisions, 340–341
Title VII, Civil Rights Act, 255–256, 264–265, 318, 355
Topical headings for policies, 115–118
Total Education Resources Management System
  (TERMS), 385
Trade deficit, 411
Traditional power, 10
Training. *See also* Staff development
  computer-based, 369
  costs, 366
  evaluation of, 370
  in-service, 3, 58
  off-the-job, 369
  on-the-job, 368–369
  for support personnel, 368–370
Trait criteria, 190
Transfers, 366
  involuntary, 269

Transformation process, 19
Transportation allowance, 343
Troubled staff member, 232–234
Tuition reimbursement, 36, 342
Turnover rate, teachers, 37, 315
Two-factor theory of motivation, 15–18

Unemployment compensation, 336
Unemployment rate, 412
Unions. *See also* Collective negotiations
  job descriptions and, 356
  as recruitment source, 361
United States v. North Carolina, 256
United States v. South Carolina, 256
Unity of command, 8, 10
Unity of direction, 8
Unstructured task, 21
Uploaded data, 387
Utility in personnel evaluation, 208

Vacation leave, 340
Valence, 218
Validity of personnel evaluation, 207–208
Vines network, 385
Voluntary binding arbitration, 292, 306

Wage mix, 314–318
Wages, 317. *See also* Direct compensation
Wagner Act, 280
Walkouts, 294
*Walston v. County School Board of Nansemond
  County*, 256
Wards Cove Packing Co. v. Atonio, 265
Washington Education Association, 31
Washington v. Davis, 264
Weaknesses, 89
Welfare of personnel, 56–57
Welfare programs. *See* Indirect compensation
Welfare state, privatization of, 406
Wellness programs, 343
Western Electric Company, 12
What-if analysis, 397
Whites, in U.S. population, 408
Win-lose bargaining, 278
Win-win bargaining, 56, 278, 300–302
Win-Win Negotiator, The (Reck and Long), 301
Women
  in leadership, 406
  in work force, 408, 421
Work and Motivation (Vroom), 218
Worker characteristics, 353

Worker functions, 353, 355
Workers' compensation, 336
Work fields, 353
Work load, 37, 55–56
   Douglass teacher load formula, 228–229
   Norton/Bria teacher load formula, 229–231
   staff assignment and, 227–231
Work satisfaction theory, 15–16
World Future Society, 403

Wygant v. Jackson Board of Education, 271

Yanzick v. School District No. 23, 267
"You get what you write," 304

ZEBRA (zero balance reimbursement account),
   345
Zipper clause, 305

ISBN 0-02-424973-4

9 780024 249739

90000>